Advanced Amiga BASIC

Tom R. Halfhill and Charles Brannon

COMPUTE! Publications,Inc. abc

Part of ABC Consumer Magazines, Inc.
One of the ABC Publishing Companies

Greensboro, North Carolina

Dedication

To our parents

Printed in the United States of America

10 9 8 7 6 5 4 3 2

ISBN 0-87455-045-9

The authors and publisher have made every effort in the preparation of this book to insure the accuracy of the programs and information. However, the information and programs in this book are sold without warranty, either express or implied. Neither the authors nor COMPUTE! Publications, Inc., will be liable for any damages caused or alleged to be caused directly, indirectly, incidentally, or consequentially by the programs or information in this book.

The opinions expressed in this book are solely those of the authors and are not necessarily those of COMPUTE! Publications, Inc.

COMPUTE! Publications, Inc., Post Office Box 5406, Greensboro, NC 27403, (919) 275-9809, is part of ABC Consumer Magazines, Inc., one of the ABC Publishing Companies, and is not associated with any manufacturer of personal computers. Amiga is a trademark of Commodore-Amiga, Inc.

Contents

Foreword

The Amiga is the first personal computer that comes with speech capability as a standard feature. This, along with its powerful graphics chips, gives you the opportunity to create programs of a sophistication never before possible on a home computer. *Advanced Amiga BASIC* will help you take advantage of it and all the other special capabilities that your Amiga offers.

Written by two expert programmers, *Advanced Amiga BASIC* guides you logically with numerous step-by-step examples, utilities, and stand-alone programs. After an overview of BASIC, you'll move rapidly along, learning how to incorporate sound and graphics into your own programs. Then, after extensive treatment of such topics as file handling, subprograms, library calls, and programming peripherals, the last chapter presents a fully developed graphics program, "MouseSketch," complete with detailed comments so that you can see exactly how it all fits together.

There's a lot to learn, but you'll find that with *Advanced Amiga BASIC* at your side, you'll have all you need to move into the ranks of advanced programmers. Before you know it, you'll be writing programs that truly make the most of your Amiga.

> All the programs in *Advanced Amiga BASIC* are ready to type in and run. If you prefer not to type in the programs, however, you can order a disk which includes all the programs in the book. Call toll-free 1-800-346-6767 (in New York, call 212-887-8525), or use the coupon in the back of this book.

Introduction

Advanced Amiga BASIC is a book for intermediate Amiga BASIC programmers who want to become advanced programmers. Perhaps the more descriptive title *Amiga BASIC for Intermediate BASIC Programmers Who Wish to Become Advanced BASIC Programers* would have been better. But such a long title would have required a two-foot-wide cover.

Nevertheless, that title sums up our admittedly ambitious goal for *Advanced Amiga BASIC*. We've written the book to reach three different types of readers:

- Those for whom the Amiga is their first personal computer, and who have now progressed beyond beginning BASIC programming and want to make the leap toward advanced programming.
- Those who have already acquired BASIC programming experience on another personal computer, and who now want to learn the unique features of Amiga BASIC.
- Those who have a fairly firm grasp of BASIC commands, but who'd like to sharpen their skills and learn how to put all those commands together to build practical, powerful applications.

Thus, *Advanced Amiga BASIC* spans the range from intermediate to advanced programming—and is intended to help *you* cover that range, too. For instance, the first two chapters, "Overview of Amiga BASIC" and "Introduction to Amiga Graphics," lay the groundwork for deeper topics to follow: "Programming Graphics" presents a sketchpad program in embryonic form, and "Object Animation" gives an in-depth look at Amiga BASIC's provisions for animated graphics. Other chapters take a similar approach toward sound, speech synthesis, file handling, and peripherals.

Chapter 7, "Designing a User Interface," goes beyond the nuts and bolts of programming to discuss the philosophy behind the Amiga's visual link with the user and how that philosophy may affect the way you design your own programs.

Chapter 9, "Library Calls," is the most advanced chapter in the book. By explaining how to directly access routines within the Amiga's operating system, it shows that you're not limited to the commands which were provided in Amiga BASIC. Furthermore, this chapter can be a springboard toward even more advanced programming in C and machine language.

Chapter 10, "Putting It All Together," takes the sketchpad program introduced in Chapter 3, incorporates many of the techniques covered throughout the book, and expands it into a full-fledged application. Numerous comments inserted in the listing explain in great detail how the program works on a line-by-line basis.

Finally, the appendices cover additional topics of value to the upwardly mobile Amiga BASIC programmer: ISO printer codes, memory management, and subprograms. And there's a complete BASIC reference section plus tables of characters and error codes.

But the strongest point of *Advanced Amiga BASIC*, we feel, lies in its program listings. In addition to demonstrating the numerous techniques covered in the chapters, many of the programs are useful utilities that will help you write your own Amiga BASIC applications in the years to come. And if the task of typing in the listings seems too daunting, there's a disk available from COMPUTE! Books which contains all of the major programs found between these covers (ordering information for the disk is at the end of the book).

There's a lot to learn in Amiga BASIC—over 200 commands, statements, and functions. But when your first major application emerges from the video screen, we think you'll agree that it was worth the effort.

A Note on Typing In Programs

You'll notice that each complete program line has a return mark (◂) at the end. You cannot type this character—there's no left arrow character on the Amiga keyboard. It simply marks the end of a logical line and indicates that you should press the RETURN key. Do not press RETURN at the end of a line unless you see the return mark. Only a few program lines break across the right margin, but when they do, the remainder of the line is indented to the same level of indention. This is just for the sake of readability—you would type the line continuously, of course. A return mark alone on a line means to press the RETURN key to insert a blank line—handy for separating program segments.

Note: This edition of *Advanced Amiga BASIC* was prepared using version 1.0 of Amiga BASIC and versions 1.1 of Kickstart and the Workbench. Some of the information in this book may not apply to subsequent revisions of the system software. Occasionally, we have noted where future revisions may fix existing bugs or enhance certain features. Also, the majority of the programs in *Advanced Amiga BASIC* are designed for an Amiga computer with one or more disk drives and at least 512K of RAM. Optional but recommended accessories include a printer and a modem.

1 Overview of Amiga BASIC

1 Overview of Amiga BASIC

Amiga BASIC is the most powerful BASIC language included with any personal computer on the market today.

That's a bold statement, but at this writing (1986), it's true. Amiga BASIC represents the state of the art in personal computer BASIC interpreters. Designed by Microsoft, Amiga BASIC is the newest member in a family of BASICs that dates its ancestry back to one of the very first BASIC interpreters ever written for a personal computer—the original BASIC created in 1974 by Microsoft founders Bill Gates and Paul Allen for the kit-built 4K RAM Altair. Today's Amiga BASIC—which consists of more than 90K of machine language object code—combines in a single language nearly every feature found in its two nearest predecessors, IBM Advanced BASIC (BASICA) and Microsoft BASIC for the Macintosh.

Amiga BASIC bears such a strong family resemblance to these two BASICs that many programs written for the IBM PC family and Macintosh can be made to work in Amiga BASIC with relatively little translation. More than a few of the example programs in the Macintosh BASIC manual will run on the Amiga with no modification at all. (In fact, some of them are reprinted verbatim in the Amiga BASIC manual.) This makes it possible to expand your Amiga software library dramatically by taking advantage of the hundreds of public domain BASIC programs already written for the IBM PC and Macintosh. By equipping your Amiga with a modem and appropriate terminal software, you can download these programs from IBM- and Macintosh-oriented bulletin board systems (BBSs) or commercial information services and then convert them to Amiga BASIC. In addition to accumulating a lot of programs, you'll also gain a lot of knowledge about advanced BASIC programming on the Amiga.

Special Features

But when you're translating programs written for other computers—or when writing your own original programs—you'll want to make the most of the

Amiga's special features. Amiga BASIC's massive instruction set of more than 200 commands, statements, and functions gives you access to almost every special feature available on the Amiga. And that's saying a lot, because in terms of overall versatility and sheer computing force, the Amiga is one of the most powerful personal computers on the market today. No machine can match its unique combination of processing speed, high-resolution color graphics, high-fidelity sound, speech synthesis, built-in peripheral ports, multitasking operating system, and graphics-oriented user interface. Amiga BASIC supports all of these features and more. True, like all languages, it has its shortcomings—particularly in the areas of sound and high-speed animation. Still, it's possible to write programs completely in BASIC which can pass for commercial-quality software, even by Amiga standards.

Best of all, Amiga BASIC is intelligently integrated with the Amiga's multitasking operating system and is easy to use. It can run as just another tool in a window on the Amiga's Workbench screen, letting you switch between other applications running at the same time. Or it can run as a custom screen behind the Workbench screen, which can be pulled down or flipped out of the way. Using Amiga BASIC's List window, you can enter or edit programs much as you would manipulate a document with a word processor. Amiga BASIC offers true full-screen editing with vertical and horizontal scrolling, mouse and cursor-key controls, pull-down menus with alternative keyboard commands, and a cut-and-paste buffer.

To help you write programs which are more readable and logically organized, Amiga BASIC lets you call subroutines by labels instead of line numbers, invent meaningful variable names up to 40 characters long, create independent subprograms (see Appendix D), and use such advanced structures as WHILE–WEND loops and IF-THEN-ELSE-ELSEIF-ENDIF blocks. With event-trapping statements such as ON ERROR, ON MENU, ON MOUSE, and ON TIMER, the main loops of your programs can even consist of do-nothing loops which depend on BASIC interrupts to accomplish all of the work.

As we'll show in this book, Amiga BASIC is truly a powerful complement to a powerful personal computer.

IF-THEN Blocks

In this chapter we'll cover a few of the more unusual or advanced features of Amiga BASIC that you may never have seen before in other BASICs, even if you've been programming on personal computers for years. Much of Amiga BASIC will be familiar to you—it contains all the commands now considered more or less standard in BASIC, a core of about 50 statements and functions. But Amiga BASIC also embodies some new concepts borrowed from other languages. Even a few of the old, familiar commands have interesting new twists.

A prime example is the IF-THEN statement. IF-THEN is a kingpin in BASIC programming because it allows your programs to make decisions as they run, performing different operations depending on the outcome of different conditions.

In its simplest form, IF-THEN forces you to construct sequences like this when a condition can lead to two different actions:

```
100 IF A$="Y" THEN PRINT "Yes.":GOTO 120
110 PRINT "Not yes."
120 REM Program continues here...
```

Most modern BASICs have an ELSE option so that you can abbreviate this sequence:

```
100 IF A$="Y" THEN PRINT "Yes." ELSE PRINT "Not yes."
```

But even with ELSE, things start getting complicated if the outcome of each condition requires the program to execute a number of statements. Either you have to try to squeeze the statements on the same line with the IF-THEN, or you resort to jumping around certain lines with GOTOs. Now, there's nothing wrong with GOTO—although some structured programming adherents preach against its use—sometimes a well-placed GOTO is the handiest solution to a problem. Even so, lots of GOTOs grouped around IF-THEN statements can make your programs harder to understand and debug.

Amiga BASIC provides an alternative by improving on the traditional IF-THEN. You can still write IF-THEN and IF-THEN-ELSE statements as you're accustomed to doing. But for the first time, you can also list a whole series of statements to be executed depending on the outcome of a condition—without cramming them into multiple-statement lines. With a *block IF-THEN*, structures like this become possible:

```
IF A$="Y" THEN
  PRINT "Yes."
  PRINT "Anything else"
  PRINT "that needs to be done"
  PRINT "can be inserted here..."
ELSE
  PRINT "Not yes."
  PRINT "Alternative statements"
  PRINT "that need to be done"
  PRINT "can be inserted here..."
END IF
```

Not only does this lead to more readable programs, but it also makes it easier to organize nested IF-THENs:

```
IF A$="Y" THEN
  PRINT "Yes."
  IF X=7 THEN
   PRINT "Seven is a lucky number."
  ELSE
```

```
   PRINT "Better luck next time."
  END IF
ELSE
 PRINT "Not yes."
 IF X=11 THEN
  PRINT "Eleven is also lucky."
 END IF
END IF
```

And as if that weren't enough, there's also an optional ELSEIF statement:

```
IF A$="Y" THEN
   PRINT "Yes."
ELSEIF A$="N" THEN
   PRINT "No."
END IF
```

Doesn't look much like traditional BASIC, does it? Although block IF-THENs may appear confusing at first, they're crystal-clear when compared to the hodgepodge of IF-THENs and GOTOs that would be required to do the same thing in older BASICs. Actually, the *logical* construction is perfectly ordinary—only the *physical* construction and Amiga BASIC's flexible indenting make these blocks look different. (Indenting is optional in Amiga BASIC, but it offers a visual clue as to which series of statements are nested within or related to other statements. We use it liberally throughout this book.)

Consider the nested-block example. If A$ equals the letter Y, the program prints "Yes"; then, if the variable X equals 7, the message "Seven is a lucky number" is also printed. If X doesn't equal 7, the message which follows Yes is "Better luck next time." Alternatively, if A$ doesn't equal the letter Y, the first message printed is "Not yes." Then, if the variable X equals 11, the next message is "Eleven is also lucky."

A Few Tips

There are a few things to keep in mind when using IF-THEN blocks. First, although ELSE and ELSEIF are optional, the END IF is not. Every IF-THEN block *must* terminate with an END IF. Otherwise you'll get an error when you try to run the program—often, even before the lines are executed. (Amiga BASIC prescans a program before running it, catching most syntax-type errors immediately.)

More importantly, it can make a big difference where the END IF statement is placed. An END IF closes the nearest preceding IF-THEN block and also defines where the program should jump to if the IF-THEN test fails (or where execution should continue after statements within the block are finished). If your program isn't behaving the way you expected, check any IF-THEN blocks inhabiting the buggy section; occasionally, you'll find that a mislocated END IF is at the root of the problem. Nested IF-THEN blocks are primary suspects.

Here's another tip: If you want to follow a block IF-THEN with a RE-Mark (which is the only thing that can accompany a block IF-THEN on the same line), don't separate the comment statement from the IF-THEN with a co-lon. And don't use REM—use its abbreviation, the apostrophe ('). Otherwise, Amiga BASIC interprets the REMark as a new statement and responds with an error. And the error message is often misleading, because it doesn't necessarily identify the true cause of the problem. Look at this example:

```
IF A$="Y" THEN :REM Test key response
    PRINT "Yes."
ELSEIF A$="N" THEN
    PRINT "No."
END IF
```

Amiga BASIC responds by circling the ELSEIF statement in orange to in-dicate an error and then prints this message: "ELSE/ELSEIF/END IF without IF." This can seem baffling, since there's obviously a matching IF for the ELSEIF and END IF. But Amiga BASIC doesn't see it that way. The :REM fol-lowing the IF-THEN makes BASIC interpret that line as a *conventional* IF-THEN statement, not a *block* IF-THEN. Therefore, when it encounters the following ELSEIF and END IF, it figures that there's a missing IF-THEN somewhere.

Exactly the same thing happens if you try to fix the line by removing the colon:

```
IF A$="Y" THEN REM Test key response
    PRINT "Yes."
ELSEIF A$="N" THEN
    PRINT "No."
END IF
```

Amiga BASIC still sees the REM as an additional statement and inter-prets that line as a conventional IF-THEN. The solution is to replace REM with an apostrophe:

```
IF A$="Y" THEN 'Test key response
    PRINT "Yes."
ELSEIF A$="N" THEN
    PRINT "No."
END IF
```

Note, however, that putting a colon before the apostrophe would still re-sult in an error. Every language has its little quirks and peculiarities, and Amiga BASIC is no exception.

Finally, here's one more tip: To optimize execution speed when using block IF-THENs—especially nested blocks—estimate which condition you're

7

testing for is more likely to be true. Then rearrange the statements so that condition is tested first. The less likely conditions will be skipped most of the time.

WHILE–WEND Loops

Another Amiga BASIC structure which might be alien to veterans of BASICs on other computers is the WHILE–WEND loop. WHILE–WEND provides an interesting alternative to the traditional FOR-NEXT loop, a BASIC workhorse.

WHILE–WEND is particularly valuable because Amiga BASIC doesn't like it when a FOR statement has more than one NEXT. Some BASICs have no problem with this, but Amiga BASIC gets confused when it encounters the second NEXT and screams Foul! (well, actually, it beeps "NEXT without FOR"). Amiga BASIC is so fussy in this regard that it won't even let you *load* such a program without signaling an error, much less run the program. We discovered this when trying to load and translate a program written in MetaComCo ABasiC (the version of BASIC that was shipped with early Amigas before Amiga BASIC became available). In fact, Amiga BASIC flags the "NEXT without FOR" error before anything else—even though from its point of view, the ABasiC program contains at least a hundred syntax errors. This is evidence that Amiga BASIC performs a rather sophisticated prescan before attempting to run a program.

Here's a simple example of what we're talking about:

```
FOR n=1 TO 10
  IF n=5 THEN Jump
NEXT n
END
Jump:
  NEXT n
```

Amiga BASIC responds by circling the second NEXT n statement and printing "NEXT without FOR."

Why would you want to construct such a loop in the first place? Possibly when you aren't sure how many iterations the FOR-NEXT loop will repeat during the execution of your program. Maybe you're checking for a certain variable to change while the loop is executing; when the variable changes, your program temporarily jumps to another short routine before finishing the loop. This is permitted in some other BASICs, but not in Amiga BASIC. Perhaps it's just as well, since these kinds of loops often result in jumbled programs.

Amiga BASIC's answer to this problem is WHILE–WEND. The chief difference between WHILE–WEND and FOR-NEXT is that WHILE–WEND doesn't care when you exit the loop. *It waits indefinitely for a specified condition to change* rather than looping for a specified number of iterations as FOR-NEXT does. Therefore, you should continue to use FOR-NEXT when you're sure how many iterations are required, and WHILE–WEND when you're not so sure.

Here's a good example of WHILE–WEND in action:

WHILE MOUSE(0)=0:WEND
WHILE MOUSE(0)<>0:WEND

These two little loops wait indefinitely for someone to press and release the left mouse button. FOR-NEXT loops aren't appropriate here because you don't know how long the program will have to wait. Maybe ten seconds, maybe two hours. Without WHILE–WEND, the alternative would be a less efficient pair of loops patched together with (implied) GOTOs:

Loop1:
IF MOUSE(0)=0 THEN Loop1
Loop2:
IF MOUSE(0)<>0 THEN Loop2

Indeed, sometimes you'll run into a situation that defies solution if you stick to FOR-NEXT; WHILE–WEND becomes the only workable answer. A good example is the following fragment, part of a routine from a program called "Personal Address Book" found in Chapter 8. The routine takes a list of names previously stored in a two-dimensional string array, book$, and alphabetizes them (by first letter only) while printing them on a printer. This routine is practically impossible to write with FOR-NEXT alone because of the resulting "NEXT without FOR" errors:

```
alpha=65 'ASCII value of A.
rec=1 'First record in address book.
alphabetizer:
   WHILE ALPHA<=90 'ASCII value of Z.
    WHILE rec<currpage 'Current size of address book.
     IF LEFT$(book$(rec,1),1)=CHR$(alpha) THEN
       FOR j=1 TO recsize 'Loop to print record.
         PRINT#1,book$(rec,j)
       NEXT j:PRINT#1," "
     END IF
     rec=rec+1 'Increment record pointer.
    WEND
   alpha=alpha+1:rec=1 'Increment alphabet.
   WEND
```

We've got three nested loops here, and you'll notice the mixed usage of FOR-NEXT and WHILE–WEND. There is purpose to this madness. The innermost loop (FOR j=1 TO recsize) can be constructed with FOR-NEXT because the program knows exactly how many iterations are required: the difference between 1 and the value of the variable recsize, which is the maximum number of fields (address lines) in each record. In other words, if recsize has been set to 5 elsewhere in the program, the FOR-NEXT loop will pass through exactly five iterations, sending one address line at a time to the printer.

9

The other two loops are a different story. The program isn't sure how many times they have to be repeated, so WHILE–WEND is called for. Consider the outermost loop, for instance. It steps through the alphabet by using the ASCII codes for *A* to *Z* (65–90). You could try replacing it with FOR alpha=65 TO 90, but you'd run into trouble. The address book might not happen to contain names beginning with all 26 letters of the alphabet, so you'd have to test for this possibility and jump out of the loop somewhere if necessary. But jumping out of a FOR-NEXT loop is a sure-fire way to provoke a "NEXT without FOR" error in Amiga BASIC.

One answer (in a language as flexible as Amiga BASIC, there are certainly others), as shown above, is to loop with WHILE–WEND. The loop variable, alpha, begins at 65 (the ASCII value of *A*). The statement WHILE alpha<=90 means keep looping while the counter variable alpha is less than or equal to 90 (the ASCII value of *Z*). This is the logical equivalent of FOR alpha=65 TO 90 except that Amiga BASIC doesn't get upset if a program jumps out of a WHILE–WEND loop.

Some other BASICs aren't quite so picky about FOR-NEXT. If you've developed different programming habits on other computers, just remember this bottom line: When confronted by mysterious "NEXT without FOR" errors, try WHILE–WEND. It works like a charm.

Event Trapping

One of the most unusual (and potentially confusing) advanced features of Amiga BASIC is *event trapping*. Greatly expanded over the event trapping built into IBM BASIC, Amiga BASIC's event trapping is almost identical to that found in Microsoft BASIC for the Macintosh. Event trapping is a feature that takes some getting used to, however, particularly if you're accustomed to thinking of BASIC as a *linear* language—that is, a language in which instructions are always executed in a predetermined sequence. Line 10 is followed by line 20, which is followed by line 30, which may branch to a subroutine at line 1000, and so on. You can mentally trace the flow of a linear program by looking at its listing. Almost all BASICs are linear, including Amiga BASIC—except when event trapping is activated. Then, without warning, your program can branch to a subroutine *even if the lines that are executing contain no GOTO, GOSUB, or CALL statement.*

How is this possible? If you have any background in machine language, you may already know the answer—an *interrupt*. In effect, event trapping is an interrupt in BASIC. If you're not familiar with interrupts, here's how event trapping works.

Somewhere in your program, usually in the initialization section, you insert a statement which tells Amiga BASIC that you want to check for a certain event. For instance, one event-trapping statement is ON MOUSE—it checks to see whether the left mouse button has been pressed. The full statement would be ON MOUSE GOSUB *LineLabel*, where *LineLabel* is a valid line label or line number referencing a subroutine elsewhere in your program. ON MOUSE GOSUB is then followed by a companion statement, MOUSE ON.

Unlike conventional BASIC statements, however, these instructions don't make your program branch to the subroutine immediately. Instead, they *activate trapping* for that event. From that point on, whenever the user presses the left mouse button, your program branches to the specified subroutine *no matter what else the program was doing when the button was pressed*. That's why event trapping is called an interrupt—it handles the event you're checking for after interrupting your regularly scheduled program.

This can be a great advantage for programmers, because you don't have to construct loops which constantly check for events like button presses. You can simply activate trapping with ON MOUSE GOSUB and MOUSE ON, and let BASIC do the dirty work.

Of course, you still have to write your own routine to handle the event. This can be just a normal BASIC subroutine that ends with RETURN. After the RETURN is executed, your program continues running with the statement *following* the statement that was last executed when the event was trapped. In other words, the program picks up where it left off when it was interrupted.

Here's a simple example of an event trap in Amiga BASIC:

```
TheEarthIsRound=−1 'Any variable will do.
ON MOUSE GOSUB MouseClick
MOUSE ON
PRINT "Click left mouse button."
WHILE TheEarthIsRound:WEND 'Endless loop.

MouseClick:
   PRINT "Button click detected."
RETURN
```

This program loops endlessly until the left mouse button is pressed (note that the mouse pointer must be inside the current BASIC Output window). Then it jumps to the MouseClick routine, prints the short message, and RETURNs to the loop (where the main part of your program might be).

From this example, it should be clear that an event-trapping statement is just like a normal GOSUB except that it works by delayed reaction. Once an event-trapping statement is executed, it waits in the background for the event to happen—rather than forcing you to write loops that wait for the event to happen.

Since event trapping can interrupt whatever's going on, you might be wondering what happens if an event interrupts *itself*. For instance, suppose a routine which is handling a mouse click is suddenly interrupted by another mouse click. Does the routine start over from scratch to handle the second click, then resume execution in the middle of itself to handle the first click?

What if the user keeps clicking the button because he or she's impatient (or ornery)? This could lead to all kinds of recursion problems.

Fortunately, when an event trap occurs, Amiga BASIC automatically stops checking for that event. When the event-handling subroutine RETURNs, Amiga BASIC resumes its checking—again, automatically.

Statements for Event Trapping

Amiga BASIC has a good collection of event-trapping statements:

ON MOUSE GOSUB *LineLabel* specifies where the program should jump if the left mouse button is pressed (Amiga BASIC does not permit trapping of the right button, which is reserved by the system for selecting pull-down menus from the menu bar at the top of the screen). As with all the event-trapping statements, ON MOUSE GOSUB merely specifies the target line label. Event trapping for the mouse button is not actually turned on until a MOUSE ON statement is executed. At any point in your program following MOUSE ON, execution jumps to *LineLabel* on a button press.

You can turn off event trapping at any time with MOUSE OFF; your program will ignore the left button until it sees another MOUSE ON statement. Still another option is MOUSE STOP—your program continues to check for and remember a button press, but won't carry out the ON MOUSE GOSUB until another MOUSE ON is executed. And, finally, the instruction ON MOUSE GOSUB 0 disables the ON MOUSE GOSUB *LineLabel* statement entirely. This lets you define a different line label as a target for a new ON MOUSE GOSUB. (The *event* OFF, *event* STOP, and ON *event* GOSUB 0 variations are common to nearly all the event-trapping statements in Amiga BASIC.)

ON BREAK GOSUB *LineLabel* checks to see whether the user has attempted to stop your program in any of the four ways permitted by Amiga BASIC: by selecting Stop from Amiga BASIC's Run menu; or by pressing the right Amiga key and the period key together, CTRL-C, or CTRL-F3. If for any reason you want to prevent people from stopping your programs, you can use ON BREAK to branch to a subroutine that automatically bounces them back to the point where they attempted the break. Alternatively, you can route them to a subroutine which asks them to confirm their action. Since the right Amiga and period keys are so close together, it's possible to hit them inadvertently, especially in programs that require keyboard input.

Just as ON MOUSE GOSUB requires a MOUSE ON statement to activate event trapping, ON BREAK GOSUB requires BREAK ON. Likewise, BREAK OFF disables break trapping until another BREAK ON is encountered. BREAK STOP keeps the ON BREAK GOSUB from executing until a following BREAK ON, and ON BREAK GOSUB 0 turns off trapping so that you can define another line target if you wish.

ON COLLISION GOSUB *LineLabel* branches to your specified subroutine whenever a collision (overlap) is detected between a sprite, blitter object (bob), or screen border (see Chapter 4 for a discussion of bobs). COLLISION ON activates collision trapping; COLLISION OFF halts the trapping until the next COLLISION ON; COLLISION STOP keeps the ON COLLISION GOSUB statement from executing until the following COLLISION ON; and ON COLLISION GOSUB 0 disables collision trapping.

This event-trapping statement is a little different from the others, because there's an instruction (OBJECT.HIT) that lets you define which objects will register collisions with certain other objects. We'll cover collision trapping in depth in Chapter 4, "Object Animation."

ON MENU GOSUB *LineLabel* lets your programs handle selections from custom pull-down menus created with the MENU statement. Since pull-down menus are manipulated with the right mouse button, ON MENU GOSUB in a way *does* let Amiga BASIC trap the right mouse button—although it's reserved solely for this purpose. MENU ON activates menu trapping; MENU OFF halts trapping until the next MENU ON; MENU STOP forces ON MENU GOSUB to wait until the following MENU ON; and ON MENU GOSUB 0 disables menu trapping. Pull-down menus are covered in detail in Chapter 7, "Designing a User Interface."

ON TIMER*(secs)* **GOSUB** *LineLabel* is particularly interesting—the event it traps is the passage of time. By specifying a number of seconds for *secs*, you can make your program jump to the specified subroutine whenever that interval of time has passed. Possible applications: an educational drill program that waits a reasonable amount of time for a response to a question, then provides a hint or the correct answer if the student is stumped; a game that introduces some new element into play at certain intervals; a business program with an alarm clock feature; a terminal program that notifies users every 15 minutes or so how long they've been online; and so forth. The number you specify for *secs* in the ON TIMER statement must be in the range 0–86400 (the number of seconds in 24 hours) because Amiga BASIC's TIMER function always returns the current number of seconds past midnight. Keep this fact in mind when writing an alarm clock or elapsed-time routine, because you'll have to compensate when TIMER rolls over from 86400 to 0 at the witching hour.

Like the other event-trapping statements, ON TIMER GOSUB *LineLabel* doesn't become active until its associated TIMER ON statement is executed. Use TIMER OFF to deactivate TIMER trapping; use TIMER STOP to suspend execution of the ON TIMER GOSUB statement until the next TIMER ON; and use ON TIMER GOSUB 0 to disable the TIMER trap altogether so that you can define another target label if you wish.

ON ERROR GOTO *LineLabel* is a more familiar event-trap found in various forms on many other computers, including BASICs for eight-bit machines such as Applesoft and Atari BASIC. It may be the most useful event-trapping statement of all because it lets your programs recover gracefully from runtime errors. You don't expect a piece of commercial software to crash if you type a wrong filename when you're trying to load a data file, and people won't expect your Amiga BASIC programs to crash over such easy mistakes either—especially since the solution is so simple. After ON ERROR GOTO *LineLabel* is executed, your program automatically jumps to the specified routine whenever a BASIC error occurs. Your routine can then inform the user of the error and ask for a RETRY or CANCEL, just as the Amiga's own error messages do. This capability lets you add a sheen of professionalism to your programs and protects users against possibly losing some important data that they just spent hours creating.

Special Notes on Error Traps

Note that ON ERROR differs from its event-trapping cousins in two important ways: First, there are no ERROR ON, ERROR OFF, or ERROR STOP statements, and, second, ON ERROR jumps to the specified label via a GOTO, not a GOSUB.

To compensate for the first difference, use ON ERROR GOTO 0 to disable error trapping instead of the nonexistent ERROR OFF or ERROR STOP. To reactivate error trapping, use another ON ERROR GOTO *LineLabel* statement.

The second difference means that your error-handling routines can't end with a RETURN since they aren't called by a GOSUB. Instead, ON ERROR has its own special type of RETURN statement: RESUME. There are four variations of RESUME in Amiga BASIC. RESUME (and its synonym, RESUME 0) jumps back to *the statement where the error occurred*, executing it again. RESUME NEXT jumps back to *the statement following the one in which the error occurred*. And RESUME *LineLabel* jumps to any specified label or line number. Thus, ON ERROR allows more flexibility than most Amiga BASIC event-trapping statements since the others always jump back to the statement immediately following the last one that was executed when the event was trapped.

Although error trapping is extremely valuable, it should be implemented carefully. For one thing, it's advisable to make it one of the final features you add to your program. If there are any nasty bugs lurking around, you want to fix them rather than just cover them up. Also, if you activate ON ERROR before the program is fully debugged, you might get confused when it jumps to your error-handling routine due to a simple programming error. Remember that ON ERROR is intended for trapping *runtime* errors that occur when somebody is actually using your program, not run-of-the-mill mistakes that you make when writing the program.

If you want, you can place a catchall ON ERROR statement near the top of your program to trap any error that could possibly happen. Some programmers prefer to activate error trapping only within certain routines that are likely to encounter an error—usually input/output routines. Then they disable error trapping after the file is closed or the routine is finished. One advantage of the latter approach is that you can tailor your error-handling routines to fit different situations—disk I/O, keyboard input, printer output, and so forth.

Here's an example of a simple error-handling routine:

```
LoadFile:
  PRINT "Enter filename below:"
  LINE INPUT ">> ";filename$
  ON ERROR GOTO ErrorTrap
  OPEN filename$ FOR INPUT AS #1
  '(Input routine goes here)
  CLOSE #1
  ON ERROR GOTO 0

ErrorTrap:
  IF ERR=53 THEN PRINT "File Not Found!"
  RESUME LoadFile
```

Of course, this example handles only one type of error and always returns the user to the same spot. For more practical use, we've written a general-purpose error-handler routine that you can save on disk in ASCII format and merge with any of your own programs (see Chapter 7, "Designing a User Interface"). It works in tandem with the Requester window subprogram (also found in Chapter 7) to recover with grace from most types of I/O errors.

To Trap or Not to Trap

Although event trapping is a marvelous feature, it has some disadvantages, too. To begin with, it inevitably slows down a program. Why? Because Amiga BASIC checks for the events you specify between each and every statement it executes. The Amiga is fast, but it's not instant. A split-second delay per statement may not seem like much, but it adds up if you're running a long program and are checking for many different events. Sometimes the slowdown is barely noticeable; with other programs it's significant. Mouse trapping and menu trapping seem to be particular culprits. For instance, "TinySketch," the graphics-drawing program first introduced in Chapter 3 and listed in complete form in Chapter 10 doesn't use mouse trapping for this reason.

If you're writing a program that must run as fast as possible, avoid event trapping unless the alternative approach (old-fashioned polling loops) would be even slower. Sometimes you'll have to write a program both ways to see the difference. If speed isn't particularly important, or if your program isn't very long, you might as well take advantage of the shortcuts that event trapping has to offer.

It's possible, though not always practical, to write a program that is completely event-driven. In other words, the main loop is a do-nothing loop that circles endlessly until an interrupt event occurs. Such programs usually rely entirely on mouse input—either button clicks or menu selections. In these cases, you may not notice any significant loss of speed since the program isn't doing anything between its event-handling subroutines anyway. (And to make sure the program isn't interrupted *during* these subroutines, you can turn off all additional event trapping with the various *event* OFF or *event* STOP statements.)

An example of a completely event-driven program is the Object Editor that comes on the Extras disk with Amiga BASIC. It's the icon labeled ObjEdit in the BasicDemos drawer. Here's what its main loop looks like:

```
Unfinished = -1
WHILE Unfinished
   SLEEP
WEND
```

The SLEEP statement in Amiga BASIC puts your program to bed until an event is trapped. The WHILE–WEND loop in the MouseClick example shown above under the subheading "Event Trapping" does more or less the same thing.

There's a second disadvantage to event trapping which may be even more significant than loss of execution speed: Interruptions aren't always polite, and your program may get confused when it tries to pick up where it left off after it was so rudely interrupted. Here's an example.

Suppose you've got a home budget program that's currently working on balancing your checkbook. While this routine is running, you pull down a menu and pick a selection called *Enter Deposit.* Because of an active ON MENU statement, Amiga BASIC responds to this event by interrupting the checkbook-balancing routine in midstream and immediately jumping to the routine which lets you record bank deposits. Now, let's say you enter a $300 deposit into your checking account. After this is dutifully recorded and added to your bank balance, a RETURN ends the deposit routine and passes control back to the checkbook-balancing routine. The program picks up where it left off, just as if nothing had happened.

But not quite. Suddenly, the variable which keeps track of your checking account balance contains a value which is 300 greater than it was when the balancing routine started. Depending on where the routine was interrupted, it may or may not be aware of this. If the routine had already started subtracting withdrawals, maybe it will mistakenly inform you that you've overdrawn your account. Or it might report the opposite—that you've got more money on deposit than you really do. Either way, the result is going to be some confusion which could prove disastrous.

To keep this sort of thing from happening, you've got two alternatives: Avoid event-driven programming, or insert numerous safeguards in the form of *event* OFF statements. In many of the example programs in this book, you'll notice that we've avoided event trapping. Either we considered the safeguards that would be required an unnecessary complication, or we've striven for optimum execution speed.

Event trapping definitely has its place. But depending on the nature of your program, you may find yourself placing *event* OFF statements at the entry points of most of your subroutines to protect them against unruly interrupts. Trapping will remain active only in a few restricted zones of your program. In this situation, event trapping becomes almost irrelevant. You might as well discard it and restructure the program so that it checks for mouse clicks or menu selections only within certain loops, using conventional techniques. You'll no longer have to worry about what happens if a routine is interrupted at a critical point, and your program will probably run faster, too.

Souped-Up Programming

Every version of BASIC has its own set of unwritten rules that govern how efficiently it performs. Amiga BASIC is no exception. You can often increase a program's performance merely by changing a few minor details. For instance, we've already mentioned how event trapping can slow down a program. There are several other things that affect execution speed, too. To pinpoint them, we ran a series of simple benchmark tests.

First, though, it should be noted that benchmark tests on the Amiga often cannot be replicated with exact results. The Amiga is a multitasking computer, so BASIC's performance depends partly on what other operations are running simultaneously. The AmigaDOS CLI (Command Line Interface), Clock, Notepad, Calculator, and other tools are all programs that eat up memory and processing time. Even the Workbench is really an application program—it's a layer over AmigaDOS and Intuition, the underlying operating system. Still, a few tests can reveal a general pattern of performance. For these tests, we booted Amiga BASIC from a Workbench disk on a single-drive 512K Amiga with no other tasks running in the background. While a benchmark was running, we did not move the mouse pointer or manipulate any windows.

Let's start with this example:

```
elapsedtime=TIMER
FOR n=1 TO 30000
NEXT n
elapsedtime=TIMER-elapsedtime
PRINT elapsedtime
```

One sample time we obtained by running this program was 12.16016 seconds. Simply by eliminating the counter variable n in the NEXT statement, the elapsed time decreased to 11.04297 seconds—a 9 percent improvement.

Next we restored the variable n and moved the NEXT statement onto the same line as the FOR statement:

```
elapsedtime=TIMER
FOR n=1 TO 30000:NEXT n
elapsedtime=TIMER-elapsedtime
PRINT elapsedtime
```

17

A typical result, 11.94141 seconds, is about a 1.8 percent improvement over the original example. Then we again eliminated the counter variable from the NEXT statement. A typical result, 10.82031 seconds, is an improvement of 11 percent over the original example and a 2 percent improvement over a bare NEXT on a separate line.

Conclusion. Multistatement lines and NEXT statements without counter variables execute faster in Amiga BASIC, but removing counter variables is more significant. Here's one more test, this time using nested loops, that verifies this conclusion:

```
elapsedtime=TIMER
FOR n=1 TO 10
   FOR nn=1 TO 100
      FOR nnn=1 TO 100
      NEXT nnn
   NEXT nn
NEXT n
elapsedtime=TIMER-elapsedtime
PRINT elapsedtime
```

Typical result: 42.37891 seconds.

```
elapsedtime=TIMER
FOR n=1 TO 10:FOR nn=1 TO 100:FOR nnn=1 TO 100:NEXT:NEXT:NEXT
elapsedtime=TIMER-elapsedtime
PRINT elapsedtime
```

Typical result: 38.59766 seconds, an improvement of 8.9 percent.

Integer Lightning

You can reap even more dramatic benefits by using integer variables in your programs. An integer variable relieves the computer of the considerable task of dealing with floating-point numbers, and the improvement can be startling. For a demonstration, try this variation of the first benchmark program:

```
DEFINT n
elapsedtime=TIMER
FOR n=1 TO 30000
NEXT n
elapsedtime=TIMER-elapsedtime
PRINT elapsedtime
```

The DEFINT statement in the first line specifies that all variables beginning with the letter *n* should be integer variables, and the result of this minor modification is an elapsed time of 5.78125 seconds—a major 52 percent improvement. Integer variables are so fast that many programmers routinely place a statement such as DEFINT a–z at the top of their programs. This declares that all variables will be integer by default, unless specified otherwise.

Watch out, though, that you don't turn some variables into integers that *must* store floating-point values or numbers greater than 32,767. For instance, a financial program has to work with the floating-point values of dollars and cents, and the variable that stores the TIMER value above must sometimes deal with numbers as great as 86,400. You'll get an overflow error if you try to store a number greater than 32,767 into an ordinary integer variable.

To handle larger integers, use a DEFLNG statement or append an ampersand (&) to the variable name to define a *long integer*. Long integers don't execute quite as snappily as short integers, but they're still much quicker than floating-point variables. Changing DEFINT n to DEFLNG n in the example above nets an elapsed time of 5.98 seconds.

By the way, the do-nothing FOR-NEXT loops we've been using in these benchmarks are for testing purposes only; you should avoid using FOR-NEXT if you merely want a program to pause for a certain number of seconds. Although the use of FOR-NEXT delay loops is a common practice on other computers, you should be aware that future versions of Amiga BASIC and the Amiga itself may run significantly faster than today's versions. A FOR-NEXT loop that takes 30 seconds to execute on your Amiga today might be accelerated to 15 seconds or better if the computer's 68000 CPU chip is someday replaced by a 68010 or 68020—full 32-bit chips that are upwardly compatible with the 68000. Another possibility is that the Amiga's CPU clock speed may be tweaked (enhanced) up beyond its current rate of 7.16 megahertz. Or maybe Microsoft will release a faster version of Amiga BASIC or an Amiga BASIC compiler.

To be reasonably certain that your programs will perform consistently in the future, use Amiga BASIC's TIMER function whenever possible to set the duration of delay loops. TIMER derives its value directly from the Amiga's realtime clock and always returns the number of seconds past midnight. Here's a compact method of setting up a 30-second pause:

pause&=TIMER:WHILE TIMER<pause&+30:WEND

(Notice how the ampersand appended to the variable name assures that no overflow errors will be generated if the program starts with DEFINT a–z.)

You can make this loop pause for any period, of course, by changing the 30 to any number of seconds you like. Operations that normally slow down your BASIC program—such as moving the mouse pointer, manipulating screen windows, and multitasking other programs—have no effect on this delay loop.

The Truth About REM

Another issue that concerns many programmers is the effect of REMark statements on execution speed. You'll recall from the tests above that this program runs in about 12.16016 seconds:

```
elapsedtime=TIMER
FOR n=1 TO 30000
NEXT n
elapsedtime=TIMER-elapsedtime
PRINT elapsedtime
```

We inserted ten single-line REM statements within the loop:

```
elapsedtime=TIMER
FOR n=1 TO 30000
REM
REM
REM
REM
REM
REM
REM
REM
REM
REM
NEXT n
elapsedtime=TIMER-elapsedtime
PRINT elapsedtime
```

The shocking result: Elapsed time jumped to 53.03906 seconds, a whopping 400 percent deterioration in execution speed. No BASIC truly ignores REM statements, but Amiga BASIC apparently spends undue time paying attention to them until it figures out that they have nothing worthwhile to say.

Just for the heck of it, we repeated the benchmark by replacing the REMs with their abbreviations, apostrophes. Elapsed time: 86.28125 seconds, a deterioration of more than 700 percent over the original test. Frankly, we're at a loss to explain this odd result.

Next we wondered whether adding a REM to a line with an executable statement makes as much difference. For a control sample, we started with this program:

```
elapsedtime=TIMER
FOR n=1 TO 500
PRINT "Hello."
NEXT n
elapsedtime=TIMER-elapsedtime
PRINT elapsedtime
```

Result: 48.0625 seconds. Then we modified the line with the PRINT statement:

PRINT "Hello.":REM This is a test.

Result: 48.4375 seconds, an encouraging difference of less than 1 percent. Next we substituted an apostrophe for the REM and observed no significant variation. Finally, we deleted the colon separating the apostrophe from the PRINT statement and again recorded no significant change.

Conclusion. If you want to document your programs with REMs, *don't* place them on lines by themselves within loops or time-critical routines—tack them onto existing lines. It can make a big difference.

Incidentally, you'll notice that many of the programs in this book deviate from this advice. The listings have numerous REMs, single-statement lines, and NEXT statements that include counter variables. This was done to maximize clarity, and you may prefer to change these details as you type the listings.

2 Introduction to Amiga Graphics

2 Introduction to Amiga Graphics

Ever since the Amiga was first introduced to the world, at a gala media event in New York during the summer of 1985, one of its hottest selling points has been its superb graphics. Indeed, the Amiga's graphics have tended to overshadow many of its other powerful features. Yet, it's really no wonder: No other computer in its price range can match the full range of its capabilities. The Amiga can produce detailed pictures with up to 128,000 dots; each dot can be one of 32 onscreen colors. Each color can be assigned one of 4096 possible colors. You can choose from various screen resolutions and color palettes, balancing memory usage against detail and numbers of simultaneous colors.

Built-in Amiga BASIC commands let you quickly and easily draw lines, boxes, and circles. It's just as easy to fill any of these figures with solid colors or patterns, and you can design your own patterns as well. Other commands let you create custom screens and windows, pick up and manipulate pieces of the screen, and move animated shapes in any direction in many different speeds.

Graphics commands comprise the largest subset of statements and functions in Amiga BASIC, and in sheer volume alone they can seem overwhelming. Over the next three chapters, we'll help you make the most of these commands in practical ways—whether you're a computer artist, a game designer, an applications programmer, or just an enthusiast who's having fun. We'll introduce a graphics-design program as an example of a practical application and show how the graphics commands can be put to work for different purposes. We'll cover two methods for achieving animation on the Amiga and suggest which method is best for certain situations. In addition, you'll find several utility programs that can aid your understanding, increase your productivity, and expand the flexibility and power of graphics programming in Amiga BASIC.

The Screens in the Machine

The Amiga can display two different horizontal screen resolutions and two vertical resolutions for a total of four unique screen modes. Your choices are 320 × 200 pixels with up to 32 simultaneous colors; 320 × 400 with up to 32 colors; 640 × 200 with up to 16 colors; and 640 × 400 with up to 16 colors. Of course, any of these colors can be selected from the Amiga's full palette of 4096 possible colors. (A special screen mode called *hold and modify* allows all 4096 colors to be displayed at once, but this mode is much less flexible than the others and is not easily accessible from BASIC.) Depending on the size of the characters, you can fit 30 to 40 characters on a 320-pixel screen, and 60 to 80 characters on a 640-pixel screen.

Screen modes on the Amiga are usually 200 lines tall. That is, the electron beam which scans the video tube inside the monitor makes 200 horizontal sweeps during its journey from the upper left corner of the screen to the lower right corner. This journey takes only 1/60 second, which means a 200-line screen is redrawn, or *refreshed*, 60 times per second. This is known as a *noninterlaced* screen.

The Amiga can optionally weave an additional 200 lines in between the normal 200 lines to display a screen with a total of 400 lines of vertical resolution. This is called an *interlaced* screen mode.

Figure 2-1. Video Interlacing

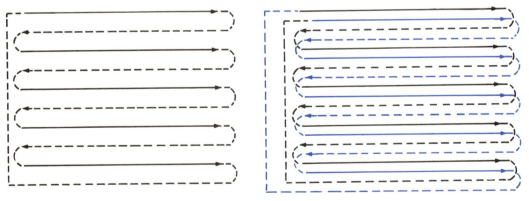

Noninterlaced screen modes, left, consist of 200 horizontal scan lines (abbreviated in this figure for clarity). Interlaced screen modes, right, weave an additional 200 scan lines in between the first 200 lines.

There's a problem with interlaced screens, though. It takes the monitor another 1/60 second to scan the extra 200 lines, which means the entire screen is refreshed only half as often—30 times per second. This usually isn't enough for most monitors. By the time an entire screen is scanned, the phosphor glow

26

of the existing image has already started to fade. As a result, interlaced screens jitter uncomfortably. This jittering is less noticeable when screen contrast is low and thin horizontal lines are avoided. (Thick horizontal lines are more stable because they are made up of two or more video scan lines.) Three other personal computers which offer vertical resolutions greater than 200 lines—the IBM PC with monochrome adapter, Apple Macintosh, and Atari ST—solve the jitter problem by requiring special monitors for those screen modes. The monitors are refreshed faster than 60 times per second, so the video image has less time to fade between scanning cycles. However, all three computers deliver these high-resolution modes in monochrome only.

There are some monitors with special long-persistence phosphors designed to stablize this type of jitter, but they are very expensive. (In the future, we can expect monitors that can support 1024 × 1024 resolution.) For most purposes, you'll probably want to stick with noninterlaced screens on the Amiga, either 320 × 200 or 640 × 200. If you want to experiment with interlaced modes, we'll suggest some color palettes which minimize the jitter while retaining good readability.

The Plane Truth

If you've had experience with other personal computers (and even if you haven't), you might find the Amiga's method of handling screen memory a bit confusing. It's easy enough to perceive computer screens as two-dimensional surfaces with breadth and height. But Amiga screens have a third dimension: depth.

The depth of an Amiga screen determines how many colors can be displayed simultaneously. It also determines how much memory is required for the screen. The more colors, the more memory.

A monochrome mode—which can actually consist of any background and foreground color, not just black and white—uses just one bit per pixel, packing eight pixels per byte. Therefore, a 320 × 200 screen uses 320*200/8, or 8000 bytes. A 640 × 200 screen uses 16,000 bytes. The 400-line interlaced modes require twice as much memory as the normal 200-line modes, since the additional 200 lines of vertical resolution require another screenful of graphics information.

To get more colors, more chunks of memory are needed. If you use two 8000-byte blocks of memory for a 320 × 200 screen, you double the number of simultaneous colors available. Each pixel has up to four color possibilities. If we represent the first bit of the first 8000-byte block as P1 and the first bit of the second 8K block as P2, there are four possibilities:

P1 = 0,   P2 = 0
P1 = 0,   P2 = 1
P1 = 1,   P2 = 0
P1 = 1,   P2 = 1

This corresponds to a binary sequence of 00, 01, 10, and 11, or a number from 0 to 3.

The more of these 8000-byte chunks—called *bit-planes*—you use, the more color combinations there are for any pixel. It's as if the bit-planes are layers of memory stacked atop each other. A pixel's color is determined by the ones and zeros in its position in each bit-plane. Each time you add one more bit-plane, you double the number of colors that can be displayed simultaneously. Bit-planes are not transparent, stacked screens; they're a memory model for storing graphics compactly.

For high-resolution 640-width screens, each bit-plane takes 16,000 bytes. In this mode, the Amiga lets you stack these bit-planes up to four deep. This yields the maximum of 16 simultaneous colors in the 640-pixel screen modes. In the 320-width modes, you can stack the bit-planes to a depth of five, for up to 32 simultaneous screen colors.

Table 2-1 shows how memory is used for various screen resolutions and bit-plane depths, and Figure 2-2 shows one way of envisioning bit-planes as towers of bits.

Table 2-1. Colors and Memory

Bit-Planes	Screen Resolution (in pixels)				Colors
	320 × 200	320 × 400	640 × 200	640 × 400	
1	8000	16000	16000	32000	2
2	16000	32000	32000	64000	4
3	24000	48000	48000	96000*	8
4	32000	64000	64000	128000*	16
5	40000	96000*	N/A	N/A	32

* Mode cannot be used in BASIC without more than 512K RAM.

One important point to note here is that all of the Amiga's screen modes are *bitmapped graphics modes*—there is no such thing as a *text mode* in the same sense as those on most other personal computers. In other words, text on the Amiga is plotted on the screen pixel by pixel just like any other type of graphics (lines, circles, and so forth). Until the Apple Macintosh appeared in 1984, all personal computers had separate text modes in which a single byte in screen memory represented a single character displayed on the screen. The Macintosh introduced to personal computing the concept of a bitmapped graphics mode simulating a text mode for all applications. This concept has since been adopted by the Atari ST and the Amiga.

When all other things are equal (though they rarely are), a true text mode is much faster than a bitmapped graphics mode simulating a text mode.

Figure 2-2. Bit-Planes

0000	0001	0010	0011

0000	0000	0000	0000	0000	0000	0000	0000	0000	000
0000	0000	0000	0000	0000	0011	0011	0010	0000	000
0000	0000	0000	0000	0011	0011	0011	0010	0000	000
0000	0000	0000	0011	0011	0000	0011	0010	0000	000
0000	0000	0011	0011	0000	0000	0011	0010	0000	00
0000	0011	0011	0001	0001	0001	0011	0010	0000	0
0011	0011	0000	0000	0000	0000	0011	0010	0000	
0011	0000	0000	0000	0000	0000	0011	0010	0000	

This shows how screen memory is mapped serially. Every pixel is represented by a four-bit binary number. We can pack two pixels per eight-bit byte. This scheme is not efficient for packing pixel sizes of three, five, or seven bits.

Below, the pixels are represented as "binary towers." The planes on the right show the three-dimensional figure separated into two-dimensional bit-planes.

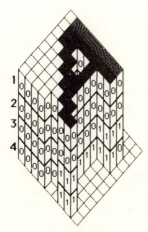

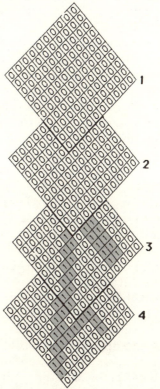

A more flexible and efficient way of representing multiple-bit objects (pixels) is to layer the bits "vertically." Each bit-plane is equivalent to one high-resolution screen. A pixel is represented by a single bit position, hence eight pixels per byte. To permit a pixel to represent more than just on or off, additional bit fields are layered. All bits in a corresponding bit position together define a four-bit value.

Why? Because it requires much less memory—therefore, much less processing time—to display, update, and scroll a true text mode screen. The simple task of merely displaying a screenful of text demands much of the extra power built into today's 68000-based bitmapped computers. Text modes, however, are not as flexible as bitmapped modes. With a bitmapped mode, it's much easier to mix graphics and text on the screen at the same time, to offer many different type fonts, and to display multiple windows on a single screen.

To speed up the bitmapped display, the Amiga contains a custom graphics chip with a component known as the *blitter*. The blitter (a compression of *bit-block transferrer*) is optimized for high-speed memory moves. Some people think the blitter was included in the Amiga just to jazz up the graphics and animation. The blitter certainly assists in these tasks, but it also makes the bitmapped text displays work more smoothly and quickly than would otherwise be possible.

Color Indirection

Although the colors available at any one time in an Amiga screen mode are numbered from 0 to 31, one of the computer's best features is that the color number does not directly encode a color. In other words, there is no unchangeable color 2 or color 30 as found on machines like the Commodore 64 or Apple II. Instead, the color number merely points to a memory location called a *color register* that contains the actual value which determines the color. If you change the value in a color register, all pixels on the screen whose color number points to that register instantly change to the new color. This system will be more familiar to those who've used an eight-bit Atari 400/800, XL, or XE computer; these machines use color registers in exactly the same way. (This is no surprise, since the Amiga is a direct descendant of the Atari 800.)

The Amiga has 32 color registers, and each register is a 12-bit cell that can hold a number from 0 to 4095. This number is made of four red bits, four green bits, and four blue bits. Red, green, and blue are the primary colors for video screens, from which the term *RGB monitor* is derived. Four bits permit 16 levels of brightness. You can combine 16 levels of brightness for each color element: 16 shades of red, 16 shades of blue, and 16 shades of green. As you can see, this works out to $16 \times 16 \times 16$, or 4096 different colors.

Amiga BASIC scales each color range of red, blue, and green as numbers ranging from 0 to 1. For example, 0.5 is half-brightness, with 0 for the darkest shade and 1 for the brightest shade. The actual increments are 1/16's, or 0.063. By combining the three primary colors with different levels of brightness, you create the actual color. If you were to use 0.5 for red, 0 for blue, and 0.5 for green, you would get a medium yellow.

You can change the picture's colors and achieve a simple form of animation by drawing different parts of a picture with different colors, then changing the color registers used to draw the picture. For example, a line drawn of ten sequentially numbered colors would appear to be flowing to the left if you rotated the color registers to the left. (Color 0 gets color 1's color, color 1 gets color 2's color, and so on.) If this is done rapidly and continuously, the motion is quite smooth. Unfortunately, there is no simple way for BASIC to read the existing values of the color registers. However, you can always access the operating system directly. See Chapter 9 for more information.

Graphics Coordinates

Amiga BASIC graphics commands all use a system of screen coordinates which is related to the resolutions of the four possible screen modes. These coordinates specify the column and row of a pixel (screen dot) and are expressed as (x,y), where x is the column (horizontal) coordinate and y is the row (vertical) coordinate. This nomenclature comes from algebra and geometry, where the Cartesian coordinate system conventionally assigns the variable x to represent the horizontal position and the variable y to represent the vertical position.

There are two important differences between Cartesian coordinates and Amiga screen coordinates, however. First, Amiga coordinates do not extend over an infinite range, as do Cartesian coordinates. The numbering system for screen coordinates starts at 0 and is never greater than 639. Therefore, the range 0–399 covers 400 rows (the maximum vertical resolution in the interlaced modes), just as 0, 1, 2, 3 are four numbers, not three.

Second, the (0,0) position of (x,y) is *not* located at the lower left corner of the screen as Cartesian coordinates would indicate. Instead, (0,0) refers to the *upper left corner* of the screen. Therefore, horizontal screen coordinates can range from 0 to 319 (from left to right) for the 320 × 200 and 320 × 400 modes, and 0 to 639 for the 640 × 200 and 640 × 400 modes. Vertical screen coordinates can range from 0 to 199 for the 320 × 200 and 640 × 200 modes, and 0 to 399 for the 320 × 400 and 640 × 400 modes.

If you're not cozy with math, the (x,y) coordinate system may seem confusing, but it's no different from speaking in terms of columns and rows. After a while, you naturally tend to think of x as horizontal and y as vertical. The position of a pixel is denoted by its (x,y) location. Remember that x, the column, always comes before y, the row, when specifying a coordinate position. The use of x and y becomes so familiar that we'll frequently use it in our programs as a convenient shorthand for variable names.

Another thing to keep in mind about Amiga screen coordinates is that they almost always refer to the current *Output window*, not the entire screen. That is, since the Amiga can display multiple windows which can be as large as the entire screen or any smaller size, the coordinates are relative to the window which you've designated as the current window for receiving graphics commands. This distinction will become clearer after we cover the SCREEN and WINDOW commands.

Custom Screens

When you first run Amiga BASIC, it defaults to the same screen mode as the Workbench: 640 × 200 with a depth of two bit-planes, which implies a maximum of four simultaneous screen colors. (In fact, it's using the same screen as the Workbench, which becomes obvious when all the windows are smaller than full-size.) For many BASIC programs, this default screen may be sufficient. But if you want a different resolution and/or more or fewer screen colors, you'll have to set up a custom screen. This is very easy with the SCREEN command. Here is the format:

SCREEN *screen-ID,width,height,depth,mode*

Screen-ID is a number from 1 to 4 (the maximum number of custom screens allowed by Amiga BASIC). You'll use this number in other graphics commands that refer to the screen. For instance, as we'll see below, a WINDOW statement uses this number to identify which screen it should appear on.

Width specifies the horizontal (*x*) resolution: either 320 or 640. *Height* specifies the vertical (*y*) resolution: either 200 or 400 (other numbers may give unpredictable results). Remember that 400-line resolution is not as stable as the noninterlaced 200-line mode.

Depth is a number from 1 to 5 which specifies the number of bit-planes; therefore, as explained above, this parameter determines the maximum number of colors which can be displayed on the screen at once:

SCREEN Depth	Simultaneous Colors
1	2
2	4
3	8
4	16
5	32

Remember that the 640 × 200 and 640 × 400 screen modes can have a maximum of only four bit-planes, so they're limited to 16 simultaneous colors.

Mode is a number from 1 to 4 which specifies the screen mode:

Mode Number	Screen Mode
1	320 × 200 noninterlaced
2	640 × 200 noninterlaced
3	320 × 400 interlaced
4	640 × 400 interlaced

Mode seems somewhat redundant, since the *width* and *height* parameters already specify the screen mode, but it can be varied when you want to create unusual screen dimensions with nonstandard values for *width* and *height*. Be careful, though; sometimes these unusual screens can lead to unusual results—including system crashes.

When you set up a custom screen with the SCREEN command, it does not replace the Workbench or CLI screen. Instead, the custom screen appears *behind* the existing default screen. Think of the custom screen as a completely separate video display, not unlike a terminal on a multiuser computer system. Only on the Amiga, this additional terminal is layered behind the main screen on the same video monitor. From Amiga BASIC's point of view, the Workbench or CLI screen has a *screen-ID* of 0, and extra custom screens are numbered from 1 to 4. The screens are like a deck of cards piled atop one another.

There are three ways to shuffle through this deck and switch between the screens. Sometimes you can click the mouse on the back gadget in the upper right corner of a screen to push it downward one layer. Or you can click on the screen's menu bar and drag it downward, gradually revealing the other screen beneath it. Finally, you can press the left Amiga–M and left Amiga–N key combinations to flip instantly between a custom screen and the Workbench screen.

When your program ends, it should close down the custom screen to release the memory it consumes. For this purpose, use the SCREEN CLOSE command followed by the *screen-ID* of the custom screen. For example, SCREEN CLOSE 1 shuts down custom screen 1 and restores the memory it was using. If you fail to close your screen, then exit BASIC, the memory is never freed up, and you have to reboot the machine in order to reclaim the lost memory fragment.

Screen Memory Management

This brings up an important consideration in setting up custom screens: Some modes require more memory than is normally available with a 512K machine.

When Amiga BASIC is first started on a 512K Amiga, it reserves only 25,000 bytes for your program. Luckily, though, the memory required for a screen's bit-planes is not taken away from BASIC's memory space (see Appendix C, "Memory Management"). There's only 512K of memory for everyone to share (unless you've expanded the memory, of course). About 128K is reserved for the operating system and the Workbench. Another 128K or so is allocated for BASIC, leaving virtually no extra memory on a 256K system.

Apparently, the operating system won't let you use up too much memory. As Table 2-1 shows, some screen modes require as much as 96,000 or even 128,000 bytes. These modes don't leave enough memory for BASIC, your program, and the operating system.

Custom Windows

The following program shows how to set up a typical custom screen:

```
'Screen 1 is medium resolution,◄
'non-interlaced, and has 5◄
```

```
'bit planes, permitting 32 colors◄
'◄
SCREEN 1,320,200,5,1◄
WINDOW 1,"New Output Window",,31,1◄
PRINT "We're Here!"◄
WHILE MOUSE(0)=0 AND INKEY$=""◄
LINE (319*RND,199*RND)-(319*RND,199*RND),31*RND,bf◄
WEND◄
WINDOW CLOSE 1◄
SCREEN CLOSE 1◄
END◄
```

As you can see from this example, it's also necessary to create a new window when you open a custom screen. Graphics and text can appear only in a window, not on a bare screen. The WINDOW statement in the example is shown in one of its simplest forms: It specifies only the window number, a title, and the custom screen on which it should appear. Strictly speaking, only the first parameter (the window number) is required, though most of the time you'll want to specify other parameters as well. Here is the complete format:

WINDOW *window-ID,title,(x1,y1)–(x2,y2),type,screen-ID*

The *window-ID* identifies the number of the window, similar to what *screen-ID* does for custom screens. It can range from 1 to almost any number, depending on how many windows you need and how much memory you have. In practice, of course, things get very cluttered if more than a few windows are open at once. Amiga BASIC's default window is WINDOW 1, so you may prefer to number additional windows in your program as WINDOW 2 or higher. It does no great harm to use WINDOW 1, but sometimes it causes problems if your program exits to BASIC. Your program's WINDOW 1 then becomes Amiga BASIC's Output window. If your program omitted the sizing gadget from the window (see below), there may be no way to shrink the window so that you can access icons which are resting on the Workbench surface.

Title is a string which puts text on the window's title bar. It usually denotes the name of the program.

The coordinates *(x1,y1)–(x2,y2)* define the window using the *(x,y)* coordinate system. The coordinates for the upper left corner are *(x1,y1)*, and the coordinates for the lower right corner are *(x2,y2)*. This defines a rectangle which determines both the size, shape, and screen position of the new window. You can make the window as large as the entire screen or almost any smaller size. Smaller windows can be positioned anywhere on the screen with these coordinates. The allowable range for the coordinates depends, of course, on the custom screen on which the window appears. The minimum numbers for *x1* and *y1* are zeros, which would place the upper left corner of the window at the upper left corner of the screen. Larger numbers for *x1* and *y1* position the window somewhere in the middle of the screen.

If you omit the *(x1,y1)–(x2,y2)* parameter, the window opens up to the current default size. In other words, if you've used the mouse to resize the Amiga BASIC Output window manually (default WINDOW 1), a subsequent WINDOW 1 statement in your program would reopen the window to that same size. Normally, the Amiga BASIC Output window is already full-screen size. But if you want to guarantee that a new window will open up to full-screen size, you must specify the maximum values allowed in *(x2,y2)*. Because room must be left for the window borders and title bar, these maximums are somewhat less than implied by the full-screen coordinates of 320 or 640 by 200 or 400. These restrictions really apply only to the WINDOW statement, though, because all graphics are automatically *clipped* at the window boundaries. If you draw outside the window area, it won't give you an error message. The pixel is just plotted in the unseen area of the window, ready to be revealed as if you could resize the window large enough. Here are the maximum numbers allowed for *(x2,y2)*:

Screen Mode	Maximum Window Size
320 × 200	311 × 185
320 × 400	311 × 385
640 × 200	617 × 185
640 × 400	617 × 385

The *type* parameter in the WINDOW statement determines what kind of window is opened—in particular, which gadgets the window will be equipped with. *Type* can range from 0 to 31. To figure out which number you need for *type*, you must add up the values representing the following attributes:

Value	Attribute
1	The window has a sizing gadget.
2	The window is movable with the title bar.
4	The window has front and back gadgets.
8	The window has a close gadget.
16	The window's contents are restored after it has been temporarily covered by another window.

For instance, if you want the window to have front and back gadgets, and to restore its contents after it is moved behind another window and then back to the top, you would specify a *type* of 20 (4+16). If you want to add a sizing gadget to this window, you'd specify a *type* of 21 (1+4+16), and so on. (As the *Amiga BASIC* manual cautions, specifying the values 1 and 16 makes BASIC reserve enough memory to restore a full-screen window, so keep this in mind if memory is at a premium.) The value you'll want for *type* depends largely on the design of your program. If, for example, your program requires a full screen to display its information and isn't designed to rescale itself automatically when the window is resized, you'll probably want to prevent people from resizing the window by omitting value 1 from your *type*. This makes sure the window has no sizing gadget.

Finally, the *screen-ID* parameter in the WINDOW command determines on which screen the window should appear. A *screen-ID* of 1 puts the window on custom SCREEN 1; a *screen-ID* of 2 puts the window on custom SCREEN 2; and so on. To force a window to appear on the Workbench screen, use −1 for the *screen-ID*. The Workbench screen is a special screen always reserved by the operating system as a background for menus and windows. Even if you don't use the Workbench, this screen is still usually referred to as the Workbench screen.

Other WINDOW Commands

When you first open a new window, it becomes the *current Output window*—all PRINT and graphics commands take effect in that window. If you have a program that opens multiple windows, you'll probably need to change this from time to time so that you can print text and display graphics in other windows as well. The WINDOW OUTPUT command lets you make any opened window the current Output window. Example: WINDOW OUTPUT 2 directs all subsequent text and graphics commands to WINDOW 2. Note that the WINDOW OUTPUT command does not bring the window to the front of the screen; that must be done manually by clicking the mouse on the window's front gadget, or in your program by reopening the window.

When your program is finished with a window, it can be closed with the WINDOW CLOSE command. Just specify the appropriate *window-ID*, for example, WINDOW CLOSE 3 for WINDOW 3. If your program closes the current Output window, the window that was most recently the current Output window and hasn't yet been closed becomes the new current Output window. The SCREEN CLOSE statement closes all windows used by the custom screen.

Sometimes your program needs to know certain information about a window: its current width, height, and so forth. Although you determine these values when opening the window with the WINDOW command, the user may have resized the window manually if you provided a sizing gadget. Fortunately, Amiga BASIC has a WINDOW( ) function which returns vital information about any window on the screen. The format is

value=WINDOW(*n*)

where *n* is a number from 0 to 8 that specifies what information you want. Table 2-2 is a list of what you can find out.

WINDOW(7) and WINDOW(8) are not of great value to the BASIC programmer; they're mainly of interest to those who are interfacing BASIC programs with machine language subroutines. See Chapter 9 for more information on structures.

WINDOW(2) and WINDOW(3) make it possible for your programs to rescale themselves automatically if the user resizes the window with the sizing gadget. You can discover when this happens by continually monitoring WIN-

DOW(2) and WINDOW(3) in your main loop. If these values change, you know the window has been resized. Then you can jump to a refresh routine that restores the display in that window. Of course, this means that all references to screen coordinates in your graphics commands must be contained in variables that are recalculated whenever WINDOW(2) and WINDOW(3) change. You may also want to scale your graphics for the new window size by using a *multiplier* with all graphics commands. The multiplier translates between absolute coordinates (like 0–639) to the actual current screen coordinates. For example, if the window is 200 pixels wide, you would scale all your graphics commands that assume 640 width by dividing by 32, the ratio of 640/200.

Table 2-2. WINDOW Functions

Function	Information
WINDOW(0)	*Window-ID* of the selected Output window.
WINDOW(1)	*Window-ID* of the current Output window.
WINDOW(2)	*Width* of the current Output window.
WINDOW(3)	*Height* of the current Output window.
WINDOW(4)	Horizontal coordinate in the current Output window where the next character will be printed.
WINDOW(5)	Vertical coordinate in the current Output window where the next character will be printed.
WINDOW(6)	Maximum color number allowed for the screen on which the current Output window is placed.
WINDOW(7)	A pointer to the *window structure* for the current Output window as maintained by the operating system.
WINDOW(8)	A pointer to the *rastport structure* for the current Output window as maintained by the operating system.

WINDOW(6) lets you write programs or subroutines that adjust themselves according to the bit-plane depth of whatever custom screen they're sitting on. For instance, if you write a routine that displays eight colors in a window, it will crash embarrassingly if it's added to a program that has a screen with only two bit-planes (for a maximum of four colors). The number returned by WINDOW(6) is not the depth in bit-planes, but rather the maximum color number allowed for that depth. Color numbers range from 0 to 31, and the maximum color number for any screen is the largest binary number that can be made with the number of bit-planes:

WINDOW(6)	Bit-Plane Depth	Maximum Colors
1	1	2
3	2	4
7	3	8
15	4	16
31	5	32

The "Palette Panel" subprogram presented in Chapter 7 is an example of a routine which adjusts itself to different screen depths with help from the WINDOW(6) function.

Plotting Pixels

Once you've opened up a custom screen and window (or decided to stick with the default screen and BASIC Output window), you can get down to the real business of drawing graphics. Amiga BASIC puts a versatile repertoire of commands at your disposal for plotting points, drawing lines, and creating boxes and circles, either hollow or filled with colors or patterns. To see how one of the simplest of these commands works, try this short program:

```
Dots:◄
  PSET (639*RND,199*RND)◄
  GOTO Dots◄
```

This program is the BASIC equivalent of the "Dotty" demo that comes on the Amiga Workbench disk; it continually plots points in Amiga BASIC's default Output window. The default Output window uses the Workbench/CLI screen as its background, so you get the resolution and color choices of the Workbench—640 × 200 pixels, four colors (depth of two bit-planes). The formulas 639*RND and 199*RND yield values from 0 to 639 and 0 to 199, respectively. You may prefer to use 616*RND and 184*RND, since the actual drawing area within the border of a window on a 640 × 200 screen is only from (0,0) to (617,185). This ensures that all the points are plotted within the visible window (assuming you haven't resized it with the mouse to less than full-screen size before running the program). Pixels plotted outside the visible range of the window don't cause an error message, but attempting to use more than 200 lines (a value over 199) can cause a system crash, since these out-of-range pixels corrupt memory outside your screen.

The reserved variable RND, incidentally, is the same as the RND(1) function; it gives an effectively random value from 0 to almost 1. Multiplying this fraction gives you a range from 0 to almost the number you're multiplying by. Since values in the range used by the PSET command are considered whole numbers (integers), values are automatically rounded to the next whole integer.

PSET. As you can see, PSET (Pixel SET) takes two numbers as parameters, the x and y position of the pixel you want to set, or turn on. Therefore, the range of numbers allowed for these parameters depends on the current screen and window sizes. Our range of numbers matches the resolution of the 640 × 200 Workbench screen. If you're using a custom graphics screen, PSET may have different limits.

What happens if the Output window is not full-size? Where do the pixels go that aren't displayed? Even though a window may only be 100 × 100 pixels, you can still execute statements that refer to a full screen's width. Any graphics command that tries to draw outside the boundaries of the current Output window automatically clips the graphics to display only the visible portion. The pixels not visible in the current window are affected, but these parts of the image are not visible unless you resize the window to reveal them. You don't have to worry about graphics straying outside your window. But if you have a problem seeing what's in a window, your program may be displaying something outside the window's visible range.

This brings up another important point about the coordinates used in graphics commands. They differ from the coordinates used in the WINDOW command in one significant way: *The x and y coordinates in graphics commands are always relative to the current Output window, not to the entire screen.* In other words, the home position (0,0) always refers to the upper left corner of the current Output window, no matter where on the screen that upper left corner may be. This is a vital distinction. Take a look at this program:

```
WINDOW 2,,(100,100)-(300,150),20◄
WHILE MOUSE(0)=0◄
  PSET (RND*199,RND*49)◄
WEND◄
WINDOW CLOSE 2◄
```

The WINDOW statement here opens up a new window whose upper left corner is at *screen position* (100,100), and whose lower right corner is at *screen position* (300,150). Thus, the window appears near the middle of the screen. From PSET's point of view, however, the upper left corner of this window is *not* (100,100), but rather (0,0). And the lower right corner is not (300,150); it is (199,49). It doesn't matter where the current Output window is. Drawing is always relative to the upper left corner of the window.

If you position the window at the upper left corner of the screen and expand it to full-screen size:

WINDOW 2,,(0,0)–(617,185),20

then the coordinates used by PSET and other graphics commands *do* coincide with the ones used by WINDOW. To display full-screen resolution, then, locate the window at (0,0) on the background screen and specify the maximum allowable values for *(x2,y2)* in the WINDOW statement.

Unfortunately, things get messy when you have more than one window on the screen, unless all windows have their upper left corner at screen position (0,0). When mapping the pointer cursor against actual screen coordinates, you need to translate the absolute screen position returned by the MOUSE function to those used by your window. No matter where your window is, MOUSE(0) returns absolute screen coordinates, so you need to add the values of your top left window coordinates to the *x* and *y* values returned by MOUSE(1) and MOUSE(2). With more than one window, though, translating between mouse values and window coordinates can be almost impossible.

    PRESET. The complement of PSET is PRESET (Pixel RESET). Where PSET turns on a dot (by default, drawing with the foreground color), PRESET(x,y) turns off a dot—it resets the dot to the background color, thus erasing it. With these two commands, you can turn pixels on and off, but you're limited to the background and foreground colors—monochrome, more or less. And although you could theoretically draw all graphics with PSET and PRESET, Amiga BASIC allows a lot more. One of the first things to master is color control with the PALETTE statement.

Your Color Palette

The Amiga BASIC default palette may suit your needs, but it's no fun limiting yourself to a maximum of just 32 color choices. Each color available in any screen mode can be selected from the Amiga's complete palette of 4096 colors. As explained earlier, this huge number is derived from the 16 possible shades of red, the 16 possible shades of green, and the 16 possible shades of blue. With 16 possibilities each, this yields 16 x 16 x 16, or 4096, combinations.

    To change any of the currently available colors to a new color, use the PALETTE statement:

PALETTE *color number,red,green,blue*

    Color number refers to the color register and can range from 0 to 31, depending on the screen mode (depth of bit-planes) currently in use:

Bit-Plane Depth	Colors	Color Numbers
1	2	0–1
2	4	0–3
3	8	0–7
4	16	0–15
5	32	0–31

    By default, color 0 is the background color, normally blue; color 1 is the foreground text color, normally white; color 2 is normally black; and color 3 is normally orange. Of course, these colors will be different if you've changed them with the Preferences tool.

    The *red*, *green*, and *blue* parameters in the PALETTE statement select from the 16 possible shades of each RGB component. These numbers are fractions that can range from 0 to 1. Lower fractions select darker shades and higher fractions select brighter shades. Although there are only 16 possible shades for each component, Amiga BASIC generalizes and pretends there's an infinitely smooth range of shades. The value for each color component can be any fraction from 0 to 1, even though increments of 1/16 (0.0625) are the only ones significant. A value of 0 reduces the component to black, a value of 1 raises the component to white, and a value of 0.5 corresponds to half-intensity.

The broad range of the RGB components in the PALETTE statement allows for compatibility between computers with varying color ranges.

For example, PALETTE 3,.5,.5,.5 changes color 3 from (default) orange to gray at half-brightness. PALETTE 3,1,0,0 selects the brightest shade of pure red. You can either estimate the RGB values or use multiples of 1/16.

With 4096 possible colors, however, it's extremely difficult to figure out which PALETTE numbers will create a certain color you want to display. We've therefore written a short utility program, "Pick-A-Palette" (Program 2-1 at the end of this chapter), that lets you control the red, green, and blue values of the PALETTE statement with onscreen slide controls. To design a color, click the mouse on one of the four color boxes at the top of the screen. Then, using the mouse, manipulate the color with the sliders. The RGB values are constantly displayed, so you can jot down the numbers and include them in a PALETTE statement in your own program. The four color boxes let you design up to four different colors. (The Palette Panel program in Chapter 7, which we mentioned above, is an extended version of this utility. It is designed as a subprogram to be attached to a larger program, and it lets you manipulate up to 32 different colors.)

When using the PALETTE statement in your programs, be careful not to set colors 0 and 1 with too little contrast, or you may have trouble reading the screen. Remember, these registers control the screen background and text foreground colors. The mouse pointer takes its colors from color registers 16, 17, 18, and 19, so unless you want custom pointer colors, you may want to avoid changing these registers. Menu highlighting is done with the last two colors usable by the current screen. Screen gadgets are also affected when you change certain registers with PALETTE.

For a readable interlaced screen in the 320 × 400 or 640 × 400 mode with two bit-planes, try these screen colors for minimum jitter with decent contrast:

```
PALETTE 0,.31,.31,.31    'gray
PALETTE 1,0,0,0          'black
PALETTE 2,.5,.15,.15     'red
PALETTE 3,.91,.48,.15    'orange
```

Of course, there are many other color combinations that will work, too.

The COLOR Statement

Parameters used with Amiga BASIC's graphics commands refer to the default foreground and background colors. The background color is used with PRESET and CLS to erase pixels. The foreground color determines which color a drawing command will use by default. You can assign any currently available colors as the new foreground and background colors with this command:

COLOR *foreground color number, background color number*

Both *color number* parameters correspond to the *color number* in the PAL-ETTE statement. The default setting is COLOR 1,0. For example, to make color 3 (normally orange) the new foreground color and color 2 (normally black) the new background color, you'd use this statement:

COLOR 3,2

Amiga BASIC's graphics commands also let you override the COLOR settings for a single statement. This saves you the trouble of using a COLOR statement each time you want to draw some graphics in a different color. With PSET, for instance, you can override the COLOR settings by adding a third parameter:

PSET (10,10),3

This draws a dot using color register 3. Of course, this is the same number used with a PALETTE statement if you want to redefine the color itself.

Drawing Lines and Boxes

It would be tedious to draw everything with individual points using PSET. Fortunately, Amiga BASIC lets you draw a line between any two points, draw a rectangle given two opposite corners, and even form a solid rectangle—all with a single command. Thanks to the special graphics chips inside the Amiga, this command executes extremely quickly. Here's the format:

LINE *(x1,y1)–(x2,y2),color number,box/fill*

When you're drawing straight lines, *(x1,y1)–(x2,y2)* are the horizontal/vertical coordinate pairs that specify the beginning and ending points of the line. For instance, LINE (0,0)–(617,185) would draw a diagonal line from the upper left corner of the default BASIC screen to the lower right corner. When the optional *box/fill* parameter is specified (see below), *(x1,y1)–(x2,y2)* specify the upper left and lower right corners of the hollow or filled box.

Color number determines which color is used to draw the line or box. It corresponds to the color numbers used by PALETTE and COLOR. Its range, therefore, depends on the current screen mode. If *color number* is omitted from a LINE statement, the default foreground color (normally white, color 1) is used.

Box/fill is an optional parameter that makes the LINE command draw a hollow box or filled box instead of a line. To draw a hollow box, append the letter *B* to the statement. To draw a filled box, add *BF* to the statement. The horizontal/vertical coordinate pairs then refer to the upper left and lower right corners of the box. For instance,

LINE (10,10)–(100,100),,B

draws a hollow box in the default foreground color between points (10,10) and (100,100), and

LINE (10,10)–(100,100),2,BF

draws a filled box at those points using color 2.

There's yet another option available with this versatile command: *relative pixel positioning*. This lets you draw lines or boxes at positions which are relative to the last graphics image that was drawn rather than at *absolute* pixel positions specified by *(x1,y1)–(x2,y2)*. When you set a pixel with any of Amiga BASIC's graphics commands, the invisible pixel cursor is moved to a new position. The pixel cursor ends up at the endpoint of the last graphics command executed. This is analogous to how a text cursor moves after a PRINT statement.

Most graphics commands move the pixel cursor to a new position, but some commands are relative to the previous pixel cursor position. If you want to draw a line from the current pixel cursor position (the endpoint of the last graphics command) to a new position, use

LINE –(x2,y2)

where *(x2,y2)* indicates the endpoint of the new line. The starting point of the line is the endpoint of the previous pixel position. You can use a series of LINE –(x2,y2) commands to draw a figure made of connected lines.

As if this weren't enough, you can also precede either coordinate pair in the LINE statement with the keyword STEP to specify that these coordinates are *relative offsets* from the current pixel position. A horizontal offset of −1 is to the left of the pixel cursor position, and a vertical offset of 1 is below the pixel cursor position. The STEP option lets you draw relative to an area without worrying about the absolute coordinates.

This program, a two-dimensional version of "Dots," randomly draws lines all over the screen:

```
Lines:◄
  LINE (639*RND,199*RND)-(639*RND,199*RND)◄
  GOTO Lines◄
```

For connected lines and a demonstration of relative positioning, change the second line of the program to

```
LINE -(639*RND,199*RND)◄
```

Again, these programs are intended for use with the standard Output window. To change colors, use something like this:

```
LINE -(639*RND,199*RND),3*RND◄
```

43

Line drawing lends itself well to interesting effects, such as kinetic string art. This program draws various unusual figures, based on simple trigonometry:

```
SnowFlakes:◄
CLS◄
RANDOMIZE TIMER◄
cx=320:cy=100:pi=3.14159265#◄
xs=cx/4+cx*RND/2:ys=cy/4+cy*RND/2◄
COLOR INT(3*RND+1)◄
FOR i=0 TO 500 STEP 4*pi*RND+1◄
x=cx+xs*COS(i):y=cy+ys*SIN(i)◄
IF i=0 THEN PSET (x,y) ELSE LINE -(x,y)◄
NEXT◄
GOTO SnowFlakes◄
```

To demonstrate the great speed of line and rectangle drawing, try this program:

```
boxes:◄
  IF MOUSE(0)=0 THEN◄
    LINE (639*RND,199*RND)-(639*RND,199*RND),3*RND,b◄
  ELSE◄
    LINE (639*RND,199*RND)-(639*RND,199*RND),3*RND,bf◄
  END IF◄
  GOTO boxes◄
```

It's similar to the other programs, but lets you switch between drawing hollow and filled boxes. Hold down the left mouse button to draw filled boxes. The MOUSE(0) command returns a 0 as long as no mouse buttons are pressed or have been pressed. MOUSE(0) returns −1 if the left button is being held down. This suggests an easy way to implement a simple sketching program. It takes advantage of MOUSE(1) and MOUSE(2), which return the current pointer position relative to the current window. If you were to PSET this position, it would appear that a bit of paint was plotted at that point. Try this program:

```
DotPlot:◄
  IF MOUSE(0)<>0 THEN PSET(MOUSE(1),MOUSE(2))◄
  GOTO DotPlot◄
```

Use this program to draw continuously:

```
Sketch:◄
  IF MOUSE(0)<>0 THEN LINE -(MOUSE(1),MOUSE(2))◄
  GOTO Sketch◄
```

For even more fun, try drawing with large squares:

```
Boxanne:◄
  x=MOUSE(1):y=MOUSE(2)◄
  IF MOUSE(Ø) THEN LINE (x,y)-(x+2Ø,y+2Ø),,bf◄
  GOTO Boxanne◄
```

It's easy to get carried away, once you realize how easy these commands are. In the next chapter, you'll see how we can build upon these commands to write a real drawing program, called "TinySketch." It's surprisingly simple and fast.

Drawing Circles

The CIRCLE command is pretty easy, too, but it has so many options that it can be a stumbling block. In its simplest form, you just give the center point and the radius of the circle:

CIRCLE *(x,y),radius*

where *(x,y)* are the by-now familiar horizontal and vertical coordinates which define the center point, and *radius* is the distance from this point to the circle's perimeter as measured in pixels.

The following one-liner draws a series of concentric circles. The center point is static, and the radius increases by four with each step through the loop:

FOR I=1 TO 100 STEP 4:CIRCLE (320,100),I:NEXT

Normally, circles are drawn in the default foreground color, or whatever new foreground color you've chosen with COLOR. But you can add another parameter to the CIRCLE command to override this and set a different drawing color:

CIRCLE *(x,y),radius,color number*

Color number is the same color register number as used by PALETTE, COLOR, and LINE.

The following program duplicates the example above, but then erases the circles in reverse order by redrawing them in the background color:

```
FOR i=1 TO 1Ø1 STEP 4:CIRCLE (32Ø,1ØØ),i:NEXT◄
FOR i=1Ø1 TO 1 STEP-4:CIRCLE (32Ø,1ØØ),i,Ø:NEXT◄
```

The next two parameters of the CIRCLE command let you set the beginning and ending points of an arc of a circle:

CIRCLE *(x,y),radius,color number,start-arc,end-arc*

Imagine that the circle sweeps around clockwise. You may want to draw only the portion of the circle between two o'clock and six o'clock. Mathematically, though, the circle's range is from 0 to 2*pi, not from twelve to twelve o'clock. (For those who haven't studied algebra, pi (π) is a special constant, about 3.14159265, based on the ratio between the radius and the circumference of a circle.) If the arc point is negative, a line is drawn from the center of the circle to the endpoint of the arc. This makes it easy to draw wedges, as in pie charts. When using these parameters, use a variable set to the value of pi. Since 2*pi is a full circle, just multiply this by the fraction of the circle you'd like to display. If pi = 3.14159265, then

CIRCLE (100,100),50,,0,pi

draws half a circle. Use pi/2 for a quarter, pi/6 for a third, and so on.

The last parameter of CIRCLE lets you control the *aspect ratio*, letting you draw either truly round circles or squashed ovals:

CIRCLE *(x,y),radius,color number,start-arc,end-arc,aspect ratio*

This setting is also straightforward. It just represents the vertical radius of the oval divided by the horizontal radius. A short and squat oval could be represented by a ratio of 2 or 2/1. Remember that you can simplify fractions: A figure that is 15 wide and 20 high is 15/20, or 3/4 (0.75). For program readability, there's no reason why you can't put in a fraction like 3/4 directly; the division is performed during runtime. The default aspect ratio is 0.44, which produces perfect circles on a 640 × 200 screen.

AREA and AREAFILL

The AREA/AREAFILL commands let you quickly draw polygons (closed figures made up of three or more sides) and instantly fill them with colors or patterns. AREA and AREAFILL can be more efficient than drawing a large polygon with connected LINE commands. Here's the format:

AREA *[STEP] (x,y)*

where *(x,y)* is the point of a vertex (corner) of the polygon, and *STEP* is an option that indicates *(x,y)* is a relative offset from the previous position of the pixel cursor.

AREA's companion command is AREAFILL:

AREAFILL *mode*

Mode is either 0 or 1 to define the type of fill, as we'll explain in a moment.

For instance, this sequence draws a filled triangle:

```
AREA (10,10)◄
AREA (0,20)◄
AREA (20,20)◄
AREAFILL 1◄
```

To use AREA and AREAFILL, just execute enough AREA statements to define a closed figure (the last endpoint is automatically connected to the first). Then execute an AREAFILL. If the AREAFILL *mode* is 0 (the default), the polygon is filled with the pattern defined by the PATTERN statement (see below). If *mode* is 1, the current color inside the polygon is *inverted*. To figure out the inverted color, subtract the current color number from the maximum color number allowed in the current screen mode. For example, if the screen mode has two bit-planes, there are four possible colors, numbered 0–3. So, if color 0 is inverted, the result is color 3 ($3-0=3$); if color 1 is inverted, the result is color 2 ($3-1=2$); if color 2 is inverted, the result is color 1 ($3-2=1$); and if color 3 is inverted, the result is color 0 ($3-3=0$).

PAINTing the Screen

When drawing filled boxes with LINE, you probably noticed that the boxes are always filled with the same color as the box's border. What if you want to fill the box with a different color? You can't do it with LINE.

Fortunately, you can do it with PAINT. Furthermore, PAINT is a general-purpose command that lets you fill almost any completely enclosed area with color. The format is

PAINT *(x,y),fill color number,boundary color number*

where *(x,y)* is any point within the area to be filled, *fill color number* is the number of the color you want to fill with, and *boundary color number* is the number of the boundary color.

Be sure the area you're filling is completely enclosed, lest paint escape and spill out. We've found that some seemingly enclosed figures still permit paint to escape. This apparent bug is not Amiga BASIC's fault; it seems to be at the operating system level and afflicts most programs that use flood fills.

If you leave out the paint color and boundary color, these default to the current foreground color (set by the COLOR statement). The fill stops only when it hits the boundary color. Even if you think an area may be enclosed, make sure it is completely enclosed with the boundary color. A limitation of PAINT is that it can't fill areas enclosed by more than one boundary color.

The following short program lets you experiment with PAINT. It works similarly to the sketch program above. Hold down the left mouse button to draw at the mouse pointer position. To fill an enclosed area, move the mouse within the area and double-click the left button.

```
CLS◄
COLOR 1◄
MainLoop:◄
WHILE MOUSE(0)=0:WEND 'wait for first click◄
button=MOUSE(0)◄
IF button=-1 THEN PSET(MOUSE(1),MOUSE(2))◄
```

```
IF ABS(button)=2 THEN PAINT (MOUSE(1),MOUSE(2))◂
WHILE button=-1◂
button=MOUSE(0)◂
LINE -(MOUSE(1),MOUSE(2))◂
WEND◂
GOTO MainLoop◂
```

Line and Paint Patterns

Normally, Amiga BASIC draws solid lines and fills with solid color. However, you can assign a new pattern to draw dotted lines or areafill with a checkered pattern. This is done with the PATTERN command:

PATTERN *line pattern,area pattern*

where *line pattern* is an integer that defines a 16-bit binary mask to be used for drawing lines, and *area pattern* is the variable name of an integer array that contains the pattern. Since this is probably as clear as mud, bear with us for an explanation.

PATTERN *line pattern* sets the current pattern to the binary shape of the integer specified. For example, the 16-bit binary number 1010101010101010, which has every other bit turned on and off, can be represented in hexadecimal as &HAAAA, or decimal 43,690. So PATTERN &HAAAA or PATTERN 43690 gives dotted-line drawing—every other pixel turned on or off. Just convert the binary pattern you'd like to use (1's for on bits, 0's for off) into a decimal or hexadecimal constant. Be sure to reset the line pattern with PATTERN &HFFFF when you're finished with your custom pattern so that subsequent drawing commands will work normally.

Optionally, you can follow the line pattern with *area pattern*, the name of an integer array containing an area pattern for use with AREAFILL (but not with PAINT). This gives texture to a filled polygon.

The integer array contains 16-bit pattern masks. The size to which you DIMension the array determines the height of the pattern shape. Sketch out your pattern on graph paper (see Figure 2-3). Convert your figure into a sequence of binary numbers, then convert from binary to hexadecimal or decimal. Assign these values to an integer array. You can then use the statement PATTERN ,*arrayname%* to customize the pattern. Note that you can omit the *line pattern* parameter by inserting a comma (PATTERN ,*arrayname%*).

Amiga BASIC doesn't include any simple way to reset these patterns. You must fill another array with all one-bits (&HFFFF) and use that array name to reset the area pattern.

To illustrate this explanation, the following program fills a triangle using the AREA statements and the pattern diagrammed in Figure 2-3.

```
DIM image%(7),default%(7)◂
FOR i=0 TO 7◂
  READ image%(i)◂
```

```
      default%(i)=&HFFFF◄
NEXT◄
DATA 0,&hFFFF,&hf00f,&hf00f,&hf00f,&hf00f,&hffff,0◄
PATTERN ,image%◄
COLOR 2,3 'set foreground and background for image◄
AREA (320,0)◄
AREA STEP (-200,100)◄
AREA STEP (400,0)◄
AREAFILL◄
PATTERN ,default%◄
```

Figure 2-3. Areafill Pattern

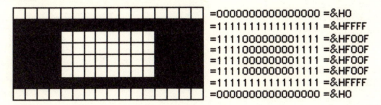

```
=0000000000000000 =&H0
=1111111111111111 =&HFFFF
=1111000000001111 =&HF00F
=1111000000001111 =&HF00F
=1111000000001111 =&HF00F
=1111000000001111 =&HF00F
=1111111111111111 =&HFFFF
=0000000000000000 =&H0
```

Putting Graphics to Work

Now that we've covered the fundamental graphics commands in Amiga BASIC, we'll show in the next chapter how these commands (and others) can be assembled into a practical application. We'll also show how you can pick up and move portions of the screen around for animation and other effects. Then, Chapter 4, "Object Animation," will cover Amiga BASIC's OBJECT commands for creating, moving, and manipulating special kinds of shapes called sprites and bobs.

Program 2-1. Pick-A-Palette

```
' *** PICK-A-PALETTE ***◄
◄
' Default Preferences=60 columns.◄
' If Preferences=80 columns,◄
' change LOCATE statements◄
' in SliderOne,SliderTwo,SliderThree◄
' subroutines as indicated below.◄
◄
Initialize:◄
  SCREEN 1,320,200,3,1◄
  WINDOW 2,"Pick-A-Palette",,20,1◄
  COLOR 1,2:CLS◄
  DIM boxcolor(4,3)◄
  ' Assign initial random colors:◄
  RANDOMIZE TIMER◄
  FOR n=1 TO 4◄
```

49

```
  FOR nn=1 TO 3◄
    boxcolor(n,nn)=RND◄
  NEXT nn◄
 NEXT n◄
 PALETTE 4,boxcolor(1,1),boxcolor(1,2),boxcolor(1,3)◄
 PALETTE 5,boxcolor(2,1),boxcolor(2,2),boxcolor(2,3)◄
 PALETTE 6,boxcolor(3,1),boxcolor(3,2),boxcolor(3,3)◄
 PALETTE 7,boxcolor(4,1),boxcolor(4,2),boxcolor(4,3)◄
 LOCATE 2,2◄
 PRINT "Click on box or RGB control:"◄
 LINE (Ø,2)-(311,25),1,b◄
 ' Draw slide controls:◄
 LINE (Ø,108)-(311,118),1,b◄
 LINE (Ø,135)-(311,145),1,b◄
 LINE (Ø,162)-(311,172),1,b◄
 slider1=303*boxcolor(1,1)+4◄
 slider2=303*boxcolor(1,2)+4◄
 slider3=303*boxcolor(1,3)+4◄
 ' Draw color display boxes:◄
 LINE (24,40)-(72,80),1,b◄
 PAINT (30,45),4,1◄
 LINE (96,40)-(144,80),1,b◄
 PAINT (100,45),5,1◄
 LINE (168,40)-(216,80),1,b◄
 PAINT (175,45),6,1◄
 LINE (240,40)-(288,80),1,b◄
 PAINT (245,45),7,1◄
 box=1:GOSUB PickBox◄
 GOTO MainLoop◄
 ◄
MainLoop:◄
 WHILE MOUSE(Ø)=Ø:WEND:' Wait for click.◄
 mx=MOUSE(1):my=MOUSE(2):' Get X,Y coords.◄
 IF mx>24 AND mx<72 AND my>40 AND my<80 THEN◄
  box=1:GOSUB PickBox:GOTO MainLoop◄
 END IF◄
 IF mx>96 AND mx<144 AND my>40 AND my<80 THEN◄
  box=2:GOSUB PickBox:GOTO MainLoop◄
 END IF◄
 IF mx>168 AND mx<216 AND my>40 AND my<80 THEN◄
  box=3:GOSUB PickBox:GOTO MainLoop◄
 END IF◄
 IF mx>240 AND mx<288 AND my>40 AND my<80 THEN◄
  box=4:GOSUB PickBox:GOTO MainLoop◄
 END IF◄
 IF mx>3 AND mx<308 AND my>108 AND my<118 THEN◄
  boxcolor(box,1)=(mx-4)/303:' Calculate new RED value.◄
  GOSUB SliderOne:' Update slider.◄
 END IF◄
 IF mx>3 AND mx<308 AND my>135 AND my<145 THEN◄
  boxcolor(box,2)=(mx-4)/303:' Calculate new GREEN value.◄
  GOSUB SliderTwo:' Update slider.◄
 END IF◄
```

```
  IF mx>3 AND mx<308 AND my>162 AND my<172 THEN
    boxcolor(box,3)=(mx-4)/303:' Calculate new BLUE value.
    GOSUB SliderThree:' Update slider.
  END IF
' Change box color on screen:
PALETTE box+3,boxcolor(box,1),boxcolor(box,2),boxcolor(box,3)
GOTO MainLoop

PickBox:
  ' Indicates which color box is selected.
  ' Erase old box:
  LINE (20,36)-(76,84),2,b
  LINE (92,36)-(148,84),2,b
  LINE (164,36)-(220,84),2,b
  LINE (236,36)-(292,84),2,b
  ' Draw new box:
  ON box GOSUB Box1,Box2,Box3,Box4
  GOSUB SliderOne
  GOSUB SliderTwo
  GOSUB SliderThree
RETURN
  Box1:
    LINE (20,36)-(76,84),1,b:RETURN
  Box2:
    LINE (92,36)-(148,84),1,b:RETURN
  Box3:
    LINE (164,36)-(220,84),1,b:RETURN
  Box4:
    LINE (236,36)-(292,84),1,b:RETURN

SliderOne:
  ' Updates RED slider.
  LINE (slider1-3,109)-(slider1+3,117),2,bf
  slider1=303*boxcolor(box,1)+4
  LINE (slider1-3,109)-(slider1+3,117),1,bf
  ' Change LOCATE to 13,1 if Preferences=80 columns:
  LOCATE 12,1:red=INT(boxcolor(box,1)*100+.5)/100
  PRINT "RED:";red;SPACE$(12)
RETURN

SliderTwo:
  ' Updates GREEN slider.
  LINE (slider2-3,136)-(slider2+3,144),2,bf
  slider2=303*boxcolor(box,2)+4
  LINE (slider2-3,136)-(slider2+3,144),1,bf
  ' Change LOCATE to 16,1 if Preferences=80 columns:
  LOCATE 15,1:green=INT(boxcolor(box,2)*100+.5)/100
  PRINT "GREEN:";green;SPACE$(12)
RETURN

SliderThree:
  ' Updates BLUE slider.
  LINE (slider3-3,163)-(slider3+3,171),2,bf
```

```
slider3=303*boxcolor(box,3)+4◄
LINE (slider3-3,163)-(slider3+3,171),1,bf◄
' Change LOCATE to 20,1 if Preferences=80 columns:◄
LOCATE 18,1:blue=INT(boxcolor(box,3)*100+.5)/100◄
PRINT "BLUE:";blue;SPACE$(12)◄
RETURN◄
```

3 Programming Graphics

3 Programming Graphics

A logical, practical application for Amiga BASIC's assortment of graphics commands is a general-purpose graphics-design program. Although you certainly can't write a *DeluxePaint*, you'll be surprised to see what a powerful drawing program *is* possible in Amiga BASIC. You can quite easily write a program that would be considered commercial-quality on almost any other computer, and which even compares favorably to Amiga's own *Graphicraft*. In this chapter, we'll introduce such a program in its embryonic state: The full listing of "TinySketch," Program 3-2, is at the end of the chapter. In Chapter 10, you'll find the complete, full-featured version, called "MouseSketch." What follows here is a stripped-down version that will help you understand the flow of the program without wading through too much clutter. It's peppered with remarks. Delete these if you want for slightly faster program execution.

Using TinySketch

TinySketch is a drawing program for the 320 × 200, 32-color mode. It allows you to sketch freehand, draw lines and circles, and erase the screen. TinySketch makes full use of BASIC's MENU commands to group commands logically. You'll notice that some menu items are ghosted out (dimmed). These are features found in the full version of the program in Chapter 10.

> The statement LIBRARY "graphics.library" used in TinySketch allows BASIC to get information about the location of the system graphics routines from a file called "Graphics.bmap", which is included on the Amiga BASIC disk in the BasicDemos directory. *This file must be present in the current disk directory when TinySketch is run.*

After running TinySketch, just select the desired drawing tool (Sketch, Line, or Oval) from the Tools menu. To use the current tool, hold down the left mouse button while dragging the mouse. With Line and Oval, you get a preview of the line or oval as long as you hold down the button. This feature, known for obvious reasons as rubber banding, makes it easy to control the size of the figure. You preview the final figure before you actually stamp it down.

However, the kind of rubber banding required for a good drawing program isn't really possible with the graphics commands built into Amiga BASIC. While rubber banding, the program has to draw a line, check to see whether the line should be moved, erase the previous line, then draw another line in the new position. But this process erases the drawing area as the line sweeps around.

Happily, Amiga BASIC doesn't limit you to its built-in commands. You can also call routines in the Amiga's operating system to perform specialized tasks. A part of this operating system is known as the *ROM Kernel* (though, ironically, the current Amiga configuration holds the operating system in the Writable Control Store, RAM simulating ROM). One Kernel call in particular is the key to achieving a professional rubber-banding effect. This call is named SetDrMd (Set Drawing Mode). More information on accessing the ROM Kernel and other operating system calls can be found in Chapter 9.

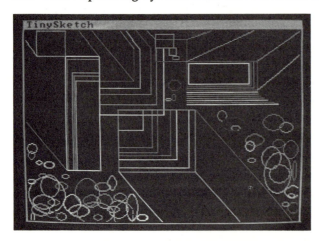

"TinySketch" is a stripped-down version of a full-featured graphics-design program written entirely in Amiga BASIC.

TinySketch uses two subprograms to toggle between two drawing states: Inverse and Normal. In Inverse mode, all graphics commands lay down a *complement* (opposite) of the drawing color and the existing color by using a mathematical process known as *exclusive OR*. The attractive feature of Inverse mode is that once an image is drawn in this mode, it can be removed simply be redrawing the image on top of itself. The pixels already on the screen are magically (well, mathematically) restored after the second drawing. (This is something like using the unary minus sign to toggle the sign of a number, as in A = −A.) The Normal subprogram just resets the drawing mode back to the replace mode. All subsequent graphics commands replace the former color of a pixel.

What this means is that the program can draw a rectangle in Inverse mode, redraw it to remove it, and allow the user to change the rectangle's size while all this is going on. The user, then, can expand an image of the final rectangle without obliterating the existing contents of the screen. When the mouse button is released, the actual rectangle is laid down in Normal mode.

Cut and Paste

Two of the most fascinating graphics commands in Amiga BASIC are screen GET and screen PUT. These are special variations of the normal GET and PUT commands which are intended for writing records to random access files (discussed in Chapter 8). With screen GET and screen PUT, you can pick up pieces of the screen and paste them back down again in various ways. When this process is repeated rapidly, you can even achieve a satisfying form of animation. Indeed, in some situations, GET and PUT are better choices for animating graphics than Amiga BASIC's own OBJECT commands. There are even tricks you can pull to minimize the flickering usually associated with this type of movement. And aside from animation, GET and PUT are invaluable for creating other interesting effects as well.

It's really quite simple. GET is used to pick up a rectangular area of the screen, storing it in an integer array. (You can use other kinds of arrays, but integers work best and conserve memory.) The image is actually copied into the array. The image on the screen is unaffected by GET.

You can then PUT the shape anywhere you want. There are several variations you can use with PUT which affect how the shape is combined with background graphics. By dragging the shape around the screen with PUT and a few mouse commands, any shape that you can draw can be used like a paintbrush. In fact, MouseSketch in Chapter 10 makes extensive use of GET and PUT for saving and restoring areas of the screen, including an Undo feature that replaces the entire picture.

Here's the basic syntax of GET:

GET *(x1,y1)–(x2,y2),array%*

where *(x1,y1)–(x2,y2)* specify opposite corners of the rectangle to be picked up, and *array%* is the integer array where the image is stored. This area is copied into the integer array. You don't have to use an integer array, but it simplifies some calculations and permits you actually to examine the array elements to analyze the image. For example, the first two array elements, *array%(0)* and *array%(1)*, contain the width and height of the object in pixels.

Before you can GET a shape, you must know how big to DIMension the integer shape array. You can guesstimate the value within a reasonable approximation, but guesswork can be bug-prone, so let's get an exact formula. It takes advantage of the definable function capability of Amiga BASIC. Just pass it the height, the width, and the number of bit-planes (depth) of the screen you're GETting the shape from:

DEF FNL(H,W,P)=INT(3+2*(H+1)*INT((W+16)/16)*P/2)

The variables *H*, *W*, and *P* are dummy variables, placeholders for the values you're passing. For instance, this line figures out the number of array elements needed to hold a 60 × 50 shape with two bit-planes:

PRINT FNL(60,50,2)

One improvement in Amiga BASIC over previous Microsoft BASICs is that you can also use a multidimensional array with PUT and GET. This is most useful when you'd like to store a number of shapes in a single array, then rapidly PUT a shape down by indexing into the array. Otherwise, you'd have to use a separate array for each object, requiring cumbersome IF-THEN statements to sort things out.

If you use a two-dimensional array, you just specify the exact array position of the shape. Instead of GET (0,0)–(10,10),shape%, you could use something like GET (0,0)–(10,10),shape%(0,0). The next shape might be stored at (1,0), and so on. The PUT statement can use the same syntax to selectively retrieve one of a multitude of shapes.

Another variation is to use a one-dimensional array to hold every shape, then keep track of where in the array each object begins. You might use GET (0,0)–(10,10),shape%(0) for the first shape, and GET (0,0)–(10,10),shape%(50) for the second. Just be sure you use a high enough subscript number to skip over the data for the first shape.

Once you've grabbed the shape into an array, you can slap it back down again anywhere on the screen as if using a rubber stamp. Here's the basic format of the PUT statement:

PUT *(x,y),array%,putmode*

where *(x,y)* is the new screen position of the upper left corner of the rectangular shape, and *array%* is the integer array in which the shape is stored (again, you can use the array name by itself or specify a position within a single- or multiple-dimensional array). *Putmode* is the way the shape will be merged with the existing background. Options available for *putmode* are PSET, PRESET, AND, OR, and XOR. The default *putmode* is XOR.

All of these *putmodes* involve binary bit manipulations between the pixels of the shape and the pixels being replaced on the screen. PSET stamps the image down, erasing the background image within the rectangle of the shape. PRESET stamps down a reversed negative image of the shape. Each color is reversed, or inverted, by subtracting its number from the maximum color number for that screen mode. If the maximum color number is 15 (a four-bit-plane mode), then color 3 would be reversed to a complement of color 12 (15−3=12). If the maximum color number is 3 (a two-bit-plane mode), then color 3 would be reversed to color 0 (3−3=0). You'll recall from Chapter 2 that this is the same formula by which colors are inverted for the AREAFILL command. AND only displays those parts of the shape that coincide with background pixels; it's relatively useless. OR merges the shape with the background. As with the other modes, there will be color distortion, since the math is performed in binary. If you use OR to combine color 2 with color 4, you get a combined pixel value of 6 (2 OR 4=6).

GETting into Shape

Now we'll try picking up objects from the screen. The following program randomly draws lines all over the screen, then randomly selects a square section and moves the object around. This also demonstrates one of the variations of PUT—the default option. Observe the strange interaction between the PUT shape and the background. This is because the shape is being *exclusive-OR*ed against the background.

```
DIM shape%(100) 'approximate
CLS:LINE (0,0)-(20,20),,bf
GET (0,0)-(20,20),shape%
xd=8:yd=-9 'velocity
x=0:y=0 'initial position
'Run for 10 seconds
t#=TIMER+10
WHILE TIMER<t#
'erase previous shape
  PUT (x,y),shape%
'update position
  x=x+xd:y=y+yd
'check for rebound
  IF x<0 OR x>WINDOW(2) THEN xd=-xd
  IF y<0 OR y>WINDOW(3) THEN yd=-yd
'draw new shape
  PUT (x,y),shape%
WEND
END
```

Exclusive OR (specified in BASIC with XOR) is a binary operation used to flip certain bits on or off. Two *one* values, when XORed, turn into a result of zero. Any other bit values combined will behave just like OR, another binary operation. This is the truth table for XOR:

Operation	Result
0 XOR 0	0
0 XOR 1	1
1 XOR 0	1
1 XOR 1	0

As we saw in the previous chapter, color numbers in Amiga BASIC can range from 0 to 31. These happen to be the numbers which can be constructed from five bits (as in five bit-planes), with values (from bit 0 to bit 4) of 1, 2, 4, 8, and 16. When using the PUT statement with the XOR option, this bit pattern is XORed against the same color value in the background. And that's what creates the unusual effect seen in the previous program.

Admittedly, if you're not familiar with binary math, this explanation is a bit hard to follow. In lay terms, XOR works something like addition and subtraction. On a screen that has a depth of five bit-planes, the maximum color is 31 ($2^5 - 1$). Exclusive OR adds the complement of the first color value (the pixel being pasted down by PUT) to the second color value (the existing screen pixel which is being replaced). The complement is the maximum color minus the second color value. So add together the value of the pixel in the shape with the difference between the maximum number of colors and the value of the pixel in the background. It looks better as a formula:

new.value = shape.color + (max.color − background.color)

This could also be expressed as

new.value = shape.color XOR background.color

When you PUT a shape against the background with the XOR option, you get a mishmash of colors. But if you repeat the PUT on the same spot, something wonderful happens—the previous PUT reverses itself, removing the shape and restoring the original background.

Using PUT for animation is tricky. Since each PUT reverses the previous one, you have to keep track of which PUT does what. You usually draw the shape at some position, erase it, then redraw it at a new position. If you get unsynchronized, by forgetting to erase an object, say, the whole program runs backward, restoring the shape when it means to erase it, and erasing the shape when it means to draw it.

Notice how the above program keeps track of the horizontal and vertical positions of the bouncing object. First, the shape is drawn with the current value of x and y, erasing the previous image. [The first time through the loop, the previous image had already been drawn at (0,0), and x and y are set to zero as well so that the first PUT erases the object, letting the second PUT draw the object.] The velocity (direction) is added to the positions to advance the row and column to the next position of the shape. If the x or y position is outside the window border, the direction is reversed, making the object rebound the next time the position is adjusted. This new position is then plotted with PUT. Next time around, the shape will be erased. The cycle continues, and you have the illusion of smooth movement.

All this trouble would be for naught if you couldn't move the shape over a background of graphics without disturbing anything. To see this, add the following line to the program after the line containing the GET:

FOR I=1 TO 100:LINE –(WINDOW(3)*RND,WINDOW(4)*RND),3*RND:NEXT

Designing Complex Shapes

One of the drawbacks of GET is that it's not always easy to construct your shape by using the built-in graphics commands. Many shapes can be assembled from circles, lines, and boxes, but it's hard to sculpt a mackerel. It would be much easier to create the shape with some sort of drawing program, then turn it into DATA statements that could be added to any BASIC program.

That's where "ShapeIt" comes into play. ShapeIt, Program 3-3, is a fast, flexible utility for developing shapes. You can draw shapes in various screen resolutions and depths, change colors, pick up the shape, save it to disk, load it back later, and write a "smart" subroutine to disk that you can merge with your own programs.

ShapeIt is fun to use, even if you're not programming shapes. It starts up with a 320 × 200 screen with two bit-planes, allowing four simultaneous colors. The full-screen grid is an eight-power zoom window onto the actual size window, which is visible at the upper left corner. You start in Draw mode, which allows you to draw in the current color anywhere on the grid. Meanwhile, the large pixels are shown in actual size in the other window. To change the current color, click on the color boxes at the bottom of the screen.

ShapeIt Menus

There are three pull-down menus: Shape (similar to the standard Project menu), Tools, and Screen. Tools lets you select either Draw, Hollow Box, or Solid Box drawing mode. In the box modes, you drag a rubber-band box over the grid, which is then filled in with the hollow or solid box when you release the button. The Actual window reflects the changes.

The Screen menu selects either the Workbench screen or lets you fill in the blanks to specify a custom screen. This program makes liberal use of the Intuit routines discussed in Chapter 7. When you select Custom, you get a requester containing the options 320, 640, 200, 400, Depth, Ok, and Cancel. You can select a horizontal resolution of either 320 or 640, a vertical resolution of either 200 or 400, and advance (with rollover) the screen depth from 1 to 5. The program won't let you pick screen modes that aren't allowed by the Amiga, such as horizontal resolutions of 640 pixels with five bit-planes. It also traps modes that are not possible in BASIC on a 512K Amiga. To escape from the Screen requester and go back to what you were doing, click on Cancel. Otherwise, click on Ok to make the change.

The Shape menu lets you *pick up* a shape. After selecting Pick Up, move the mouse pointer to the upper left corner of the shape, click and hold the mouse button, and drag to the lower right corner. You'll see a rubber-band box that shows what you're defining. When you release the mouse button, the shape appears in the Actual window and moves as you move the mouse. As long as you see the shape, it is selected and you can Redraw or Save it. (If you select empty space, though, don't expect to see anything.)

Redraw clears the screen and redraws the grid, centering the object. It's handy when you're running out of screen space and need to reposition the shape you're working on. Be sure to first pick up the shape you want to redraw.

The Discard option in the Shape menu throws out the current shape, freeing it from the Actual window. Use this when you've finished saving an object and want it out of the way.

The options New, Open, Save, and Quit work as might be expected. New clears the screen. Open lets you load a previously saved shape. You can load only shapes saved with the Binary option (see next paragraph), not BASIC DATA statements. Just click in the box, type the name, and click on Ok. Press Cancel to abort.

Use Save to save the shape as a binary file (reloadable by Open) or as DATA statements. Click in the box (containing the default filename from the previous Open), edit the filename, click on either Binary or DATA Statements, then click on Ok. Press Cancel to abort. Since you can't reload DATA statements back into the program, you'll want to save your shape as a Binary image for future editing.

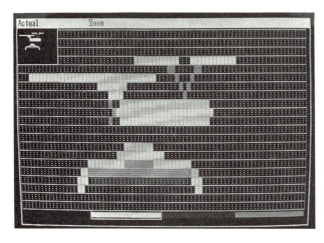

With "ShapeIt," you can create a variety of detailed shapes which can be displayed on the screen and animated with Amiga BASIC's GET and PUT commands.

ShapeIt was used to design the shapes in the demo programs which follow in this chapter. The DATA statements include the subroutine that reads them into an integer array. You can change the array name to stand for the name of the shape. Here is an example of DATA statements created by ShapeIt. The remark reminds you what screen was used to create the shape:

```
'xsize= 320 ysize= 200 depth= 3
L= 46 :DIM SHAPE%(L)
FOR I=0 TO L:READ SHAPE%(I):NEXT
RETURN
DATA &HF,&H5,&H3,&H7C0,&H1FF0,&H0,&HFFFE,&H0
DATA &H0,&H1FF0,&H2AA8,&H0,&H1FF0,&H1,&H0,&H3FF8
DATA &HFFFE,&H0,&H0,&H0,&H0,&H0,&H0,&H0
DATA &H80,&H0,&H80,&H7FC,&H80,&HAAA,&H440,&H0
DATA &H0,&H7FC,&H0,&H0,&H0,&H0,&H0,&H0
DATA &H0,&H0,&H0,&H0,&H0,&H0,&H0,&HFFE
```

The Quit option exits ShapeIt to BASIC. You may want to change this routine so that it quits back to the Workbench or CLI (just change END to SYSTEM).

PUTting Shapes into Action

This next example program lets you try out a ShapeIt shape. In some ways, it's easier to figure out than the previous example.

GOSUB InitShape sets up the shape automatically; you don't even need to know how much to DIM. The loop runs from positions (1,1) to (100,100), first erasing the previous shape—PUT (i−1,i−1),SHAPE%—then drawing the new shape—PUT (i,i),SHAPE%. The shape is initially displayed at (0,0) so the first erasure has something to erase. Otherwise, the toggle has nothing to work on, and it places a shape instead of erasing the shape.

After designing a shape with ShapeIt, use this program to test your shape in action. Just insert your subroutine after the label InitShape by typing MERGE *"filename"* to bring in your shape. Be sure to use ShapeIt's DATA Statements option when you save your shape on disk.

```
'PutDemo#2◄
CLS:GOSUB InitShape:PUT (0,0),shape%◄
FOR i=1 TO 100◄
PUT (i-1,i-1),shape%◄
PUT (i,i),shape%◄
NEXT◄
END◄
◄
InitShape:◄
```

Flickerfree Animation

The XOR option of PUT works well for most uses, but the flickering is distracting. On some computers, page flipping is used to hide flicker. First, the shape is drawn on one screen, then, while it is being erased, the program flips to another screen with the shape in its new position. After this, the shape is erased invisibly on the alternate screen while you're looking at the next frame, and so on. Although this is theoretically possible on the Amiga, Amiga BASIC just isn't fast enough to make it practical.

But if you don't care whether a shape erases the background as it moves, there's a trick for flickerfree animation. Design each shape with "white space," or areas of background color, surrounding it. Then use the PSET option of PUT to stamp down the image as is, slapping it onto the background, overwriting whatever was there before. As the shape moves, its surrounding blank space erases what it overlaps.

As long as the shape moves only in straight lines, sequentially in increments no greater than the width of its padding, it erases itself with its own wake. It's easier to demonstrate than to explain. Take a look at Program 3-1.

Program 3-1. Flickerfree

```
'Flicker-free movement◄
GOSUB InitShape◄
WINDOW 1,"Crazy Shapes",(0,0)-(320,100),31◄
n=4:DIM x(10),y(10),xd(10),yd(10)◄
velocity=3◄
FOR i=1 TO n◄
   xd(i)=velocity-2*velocity*RND◄
   yd(i)=velocity-2*velocity*RND◄
NEXT◄
◄
'Initialize x() and y() if you want◄
FOR i=1 TO n◄
   x(i)=WINDOW(3)*RND◄
   y(i)=WINDOW(4)*RND◄
NEXT◄
◄
'Wait for an event (60 secs, mouse click, keypress)◄
t#=TIMER+60:i=0◄
WHILE MOUSE(0)=0 AND INKEY$="" AND TIMER<t#◄
   i=i+1:IF i>n THEN i=1◄
'remove the apostrophe for a surprise!◄
'   LINE -(WINDOW(3)*RND,WINDOW(4)*RND)◄
   PUT (x(i),y(i)),shape%,PSET◄
   x(i)=x(i)+xd(i):y(i)=y(i)+yd(i)◄
   IF x(i)<0 OR x(i)>WINDOW(2) THEN xd(i)=-xd(i)◄
   IF y(i)<0 OR y(i)>WINDOW(3) THEN yd(i)=-yd(i)◄
WEND◄
'"Catastrophic" shape explosion◄
t#=TIMER+5 'for five seconds◄
WHILE TIMER<t#◄
   PUT (WINDOW(2)*RND,WINDOW(3)*RND),shape%◄
WEND◄
CLS◄
END◄
◄
InitShape:◄
'Put your padded object here...◄
```

```
l= 99 :DIM shape%(1)◄
FOR i=0 TO l:READ shape%(i):NEXT◄
RETURN◄
DATA &h29,&h10,&h2,&h0,&h0,&h7F,&h0,&h0◄
DATA &h0,&h0,&h0,&h7F,&h1,&hFE00,&h0,&hF◄
DATA &hFFC0,&h3,&h1C,&hFCE0,&h0,&h3C,&hFCF0,&h7F◄
DATA &h3F,&hFFF0,&h0,&h3B,&hFF70,&h7F,&h31,&hFE30◄
DATA &h0,&h1E,&h1E0,&h7F,&hF,&hFFC0,&h0,&h1◄
DATA &hFE00,&h78,&h0,&h0,&h0,&h0,&h0,&h0◄
DATA &h0,&h0,&h0,&h0,&h0,&h0,&h0,&h0◄
DATA &h0,&h0,&h0,&h0,&h1,&hFE00,&h0,&hF◄
DATA &hFFC0,&h0,&h1F,&hFFE0,&h0,&h3F,&hFFF0,&h0◄
DATA &h3F,&hFFF0,&h0,&h3F,&hFFF0,&h0,&h3F,&hFFF0◄
DATA &h0,&h1F,&hFFE0,&h0,&hF,&hFFC0,&h0,&h1◄
DATA &hFE00,&h0,&h0,&h0,&h0,&h0,&h0,&h0◄
DATA &h0,&h0,&h0,&h0,&h0◄
```

If you're moving multiple shapes, there is a drawback, however. Each shape is like a tugboat with a distorting wake. As the shapes pass over each other, you can see the edges of the otherwise invisible padding. And, of course, any background graphics are erased as the shapes move over them. Furthermore, to get really good speed, you need a small shape with lots of padding to permit a wide increment of movement. A large shape moves sluggishly.

PUT and GET work fastest with the 320 × 200 screen with a minimal number of bit-planes.

Despite these limitations, with careful programming the movement can still be fairly fast. (I wrote a similar program in Forth, a high-speed, medium-level language, and it ran only a little faster.) To make the most of GET and PUT, you can contrive games to take advantage of the various animation techniques. If you need to preserve the background while moving shapes over it, the XOR option works well, at the cost of some color distortion. If you're using only one moving shape, you could repeatedly GET and PUT to save and restore the background while it moves.

Of course, there are other applications for PUT and GET besides animation. The special binary effects of PSET, PRESET, AND, and OR can be combined in various ways for special effects. For example, you can turn a solid object into a hollow object by using PUT with XOR to stamp the shape on top of itself, but shifted over by one pixel. Only the edges remain, since the bulk of the object coincides with itself, canceling itself out.

PUT with PRESET is very useful for flashing screen objects. For example, you could GET a rectangle containing an icon, PUT it back down in the same place with the PRESET option (reversing the image), then—after a short delay—PUT the object back down with PSET, restoring it. If you only need an array temporarily for this kind of thing, you can always ERASE the array after you're through to conserve memory.

The SCROLL Statement

Another way to move shapes on the screen is with the SCROLL statement. SCROLL lets you define a rectangular screen area and scroll it in any direction. The format is

SCROLL *(x1,y1)–(x2,y2),scroll-x,scroll-y*

where *(x1,y1)–(x2,y2)* are the pixel coordinates which define the rectangular area, *scroll-x* is the number of pixels to scroll horizontally, and *scroll-y* is the number of pixels to scroll vertically. Positive values for *scroll-x* scroll to the right, and negative values scroll to the left. Positive values for *scroll-y* scroll downward, and negative values scroll upward. For diagonal scrolling, combine positive or negative values for *scroll-x* and *scroll-y*.

Each time a SCROLL statement is executed, everything within the rectangular screen area is moved the distance and direction you specified. To achieve continuous scrolling, you have to put SCROLL within a loop. Here's a short example program that shows how SCROLL works:

```
x1=10:y1=10:x2=30:y2=20
depth=1
DIM shape%(6+((y2-y1+1)*2*INT((x2-x1+16)/16)*depth)/2)
SCREEN 1,320,200,depth,1
WINDOW 1,"Scroll Test",(0,0)-(311,185),20,1
LINE (x1,y1)-(x2,y2),1,bf
GET (x1,y1)-(x2,y2),shape%
PUT (x1,y1),shape%
LOCATE 4,6:PRINT "Click mouse to stop."
LINE (0,100)-(311,150),1,b
WHILE MOUSE(0)=0
  PUT (1,110),shape%
  FOR x=1 TO 20
   SCROLL (1,101)-(310,149),5,0
  NEXT x
WEND
SCREEN CLOSE 1:END
```

Note that SCROLL isn't intended for scrolling the entire screen or window—only for scrolling a smaller section within the window. Indeed, if you try to scroll large areas of screen, SCROLL slows down considerably. SCROLL works best with lower-resolution screens that have fewer bit-planes.

Although these constraints limit the usefulness of SCROLL, you may find some applications for it nevertheless. One example might be a moving billboard text display. Or it could become the basis for an action game. SCROLL is an unusual command to find in a BASIC, and apparently it was included in Amiga BASIC because there's an underlying operating system routine which made it fairly easy to implement.

In Amiga BASIC 1.0, SCROLL seems to be afflicted by one small bug. If you look at the example program closely, you'll notice that the rectangular frame drawn around the scrolling area has a small hole at the lower left corner. The hole appears when SCROLL first executes. The size of the hole is related to the number of pixels skipped by the *scroll-x* parameter. We're not sure why this hole appears, but it seems to be unavoidable. Be aware of this if your program must display important information near the scrolling area.

Program 3-2. TinySketch

"Graphics.bmap", included on the Amiga BASIC disk in the BasicDemos directory must be present in the current disk directory when TinySketch is run.

```
'Tinysketch◄
'◄
'Integer variables are faster◄
DEFINT A-z◄
◄
'Initialize custom screen◄
GOSUB Init.Screen◄
PRINT "I'll be with you in a moment..."◄
◄
'Initialize custom menus◄
GOSUB Define.Menus◄
◄
'Borrow SetDrMd from ROM Kernel◄
'* "graphics.bmap" must be in same◄
'folder as this program◄
◄
LIBRARY "graphics.library"◄
◄
'Default drawing color◄
CurrColor=1◄
◄
'Convenient constants◄
TRUE=-1◄
FALSE=0◄
◄
'ROM Kernel SetDrMd can be◄
'used for special graphics◄
'effects not supported by BASIC◄
'Inverse uses the Complement◄
'drawing mode, handy for◄
'"rubber-banding."◄
◄
SUB Inverse STATIC◄
   CALL SetDrMd&(WINDOW(8),3)◄
END SUB◄
◄
'Subprogram to reset drawing mode◄
'to REPLACE, the normal setting◄
◄
SUB Normal STATIC◄
   CALL SetDrMd&(WINDOW(8),1)◄
```

```
  END SUB◄
◄
  CLS:BEEP 'The beep shows we're ready!◄
◄
  'Endless loop to check for mouse◄
  'button and menu status◄
◄
  MainLoop:◄
  WHILE TRUE 'i.e. forever◄
  MenuId=0◄
     WHILE MOUSE(0)=0 AND MenuId=0◄
        MenuId=MENU(0)◄
     WEND◄
     IF MenuId<>0 THEN GOSUB MenuHandler:GOTO MainLoop◄
     sx=MOUSE(1):sy=MOUSE(2)◄
     GOSUB MouseHandler◄
  WEND◄
◄
  'The left mouse button has been◄
  'pressed.  Execute appropriate◄
  'tool.◄
◄
  MouseHandler:◄
  '◄
  'Since we don't have any way to◄
  'change colors, we'll just use◄
  'random colors◄
◄
  CurrColor=INT(31*RND+1)◄
  '◄
  'Toolnum goes from 1-4◄
     ON ToolNum GOSUB Sketch,DrwLine,Rectangle,Oval◄
     RETURN◄
◄
  'Freehand drawing mode◄
     ◄
     Sketch:◄
  'Set initial point◄
     PSET(sx,sy),CurrColor◄
◄
  'if and while the button is◄
  'still held down, connect the◄
  'successive positions of the mouse◄
◄
     WHILE MOUSE(0)<>0◄
        LINE -(MOUSE(1),MOUSE(2)),CurrColor◄
     WEND◄
     RETURN◄
◄
  'Preview line until mouse button◄
  'is released, then set down◄
  'the line.◄
◄
```

```
    DrwLine:
'First point is actually the "ending point"
'point of the line
     ex=sx:ey=sy
'As long as the mouse button is held down...
     WHILE MOUSE(0)<>0
'Draw ghost line
     Inverse
        LINE (sx,sy)-(ex,ey)
        'we save this position
        cx=MOUSE(1):cy=MOUSE(2)
        'and erase the ghost line
        LINE (sx,sy)-(cx,cy)
        'set up for next ghost line
        ex=cx:ey=cy
     WEND
'Back to normal drawing mode
     Normal
'Set down the line at the last
'position ghosted
     LINE (sx,sy)-(ex,ey),CurrColor
    RETURN

'Structurally, think of Oval
'as a substitution of a
'"Circloid" command for the
'LINE command in the DrwLine
'routine above
'Circloid computes the shape
'of the oval, simplifying
'this loop considerably

   Oval:
     ex=sx:ey=sy
     WHILE MOUSE(0)<>0
     Inverse
     CALL Circloid(ex,ey)
     cx=MOUSE(1):cy=MOUSE(2)
     CALL Circloid(cx,cy)
     ex=cx:ey=cy
   WEND
     Normal
     CALL Circloid(ex,ey)
   RETURN

SUB Circloid(x,y) STATIC
   SHARED sx,sy,CurrColor,xr,yr
   xr=ABS(sx-x)+1:yr=ABS(sy-y)+1:ratio#=xr/yr
   IF xr>yr THEN radius=xr ELSE radius=yr:ratio#=yr/xr
   CIRCLE (sx+xr/2,sy+yr/2),radius,CurrColor,,,ratio#*.44
END SUB

'A general-purpose rectangle
```

```
'previewing routine.
'As long as the mouse is held down,
'it previews a "rubber rectangle"
'and when the button is released,
'it exits with the coordinates
'(sx,sy)-(ex,ey)

   RubberBox:
     ex=sx:ey=sy
     WHILE MOUSE(Ø)<>Ø
       Inverse
       LINE (sx,sy)-(ex,ey),,b
       cx=MOUSE(1):cy=MOUSE(2)
       LINE (sx,sy)-(cx,cy),,b
       ex=cx:ey=cy
     WEND
     LINE (sx,sy)-(ex,ey),,b
     Normal
   RETURN

 'See how easy this is?
 'This small routine implements
 'the rectangle command:

   Rectangle:
     GOSUB RubberBox
     LINE (sx,sy)-(ex,ey),CurrColor,b
   RETURN

 'Process the selected menu item
 'MenuId holds which menu was
 'selected, and MenuItem holds
 'the selection within the menu.
 '
MenuHandler:
   MenuItem=MENU(1)
'Branch to appropriate menu routine
   ON MenuId GOSUB Project,Tools
   RETURN

 'The Project Menu handler
 'Depending on MenuItem (1 or 2)
 'we'll branch to New Picture or Quit

   Project:
   ON MenuItem GOSUB NewPict,Quit
   RETURN

 'Pretty simple, eh?
   NewPict:
     CLS
   RETURN
```

```
'Restore BASIC's menus (a necessity, not a feature),◄
'close the screen (ditto),◄
'and exit to the listing◄
    Quit:◄
        MENU RESET◄
        SCREEN CLOSE 1◄
        CLS◄
'Change LIST to SYSTEM to exit◄
'directly to the Workbench◄
◄
        LIST◄
        END◄
◄
'The Tools menu is handled differently◄
'than Edit's.  We just select◄
'the tool number directly from◄
'the menu item, checkmark the tool,◄
'and deselect all the other tools.◄
◄
    Tools:◄
        ToolNum=MenuItem◄
        FOR i=1 TO NumTools:MENU 2,i,1:NEXT◄
        MENU 2,ToolNum,2◄
        RETURN◄
◄
Init.Screen:◄
'Initialize custom screen and◄
'window, a 32-color 320x200◄
'screen.◄
    xsize=320:ysize=200◄
    SCREEN 1,xsize,ysize,5,1◄
    WINDOW 1,"TinySketch",,16,1◄
'Set background color to◄
'zero, menu colors to dark cyan◄
'on cyan◄
    PALETTE 0,0,0,0◄
    PALETTE 30,0,.5,.5◄
    PALETTE 31,.5,1,1◄
    CLS◄
RETURN◄
◄
'It's pretty easy to declare your◄
'menus.◄
◄
Define.Menus:◄
    MENU 1,0,1,"Picture"◄
        MENU 1,1,1,"New     "◄
        MENU 1,2,1,"Quit    "◄
    MENU 2,0,1,"Tools"◄
        MENU 2,1,2," Sketch   "◄
        MENU 2,2,1," Line     "◄
        MENU 2,3,1," Rectangle"◄
        MENU 2,4,1," Oval     "◄
```

```
    ToolNum=1:NumTools=4
   'Disable unused menus
    MENU 3,0,0,"":MENU 4,0,0,""
RETURN
```

Program 3-3. ShapeIt

```
'ShapeIt
DEFINT a-Z
DEF FN1(h,w,p)=INT(3+2*(h+1)*INT((w+16)/16)*p/2)
DIM Shape%(2000),work%(400) 'required for Intuits
DIM x1(20),y1(20),x2(20),y2(20)
TRUE=-1:SideBorder=9:BotBorder=19
filename$="untitled"
maxlen=25 'length of text fields
GOSUB InitMenu
SCREEN 1,320,200,2,1:depth=2
xsize=320:ysize=200
ScrId=1 'Workbench screen=-1, else custom
Drawmode=TRUE
id=WINDOW(1):wx=311:wy=200-16 'adjust these
GOSUB DoWin
GOSUB DoDraw
ACTIVE=TRUE
'
Main:
WHILE ACTIVE
WINDOW 3
  MenuId=0:Button=0:x=-1
  WHILE Button=0 AND MenuId=0
  Button=MOUSE(0)
  IF Got AND (x<>MOUSE(1) OR y<>MOUSE(2)) THEN
    WINDOW OUTPUT 3
    IF x>=0 THEN PUT(x/8,y/8),Shape%
    x=MOUSE(1):y=MOUSE(2)
    PUT(x/8,y/8),Shape%
  END IF
    MenuId=MENU(0)
  WEND
  IF Got THEN PUT (x/8,y/8),Shape%
  WINDOW OUTPUT 1
  IF MenuId THEN GOSUB MenuHandler:GOTO Main
  sx=MOUSE(1):sy=MOUSE(2):GOSUB MouseHandler
WEND
'
MouseHandler:
WINDOW OUTPUT 1:PATTERN &HFFFF
IF sy>=cy THEN
  LINE (Currcolor*cw,cy)-(Currcolor*cw+cw,wy),0,b
  Currcolor=INT(sx/cw):IF Currcolor>maxcolor THEN Currcolor=maxcol
  or
  LINE (Currcolor*cw,cy)-(Currcolor*cw+cw,wy),1,b
  PATTERN &HAAAA
  LINE (0,cy)-(wx,cy),1
```

```
   PATTERN &HFFFF◄
   RETURN◄
END IF◄
xl=INT(sx/8):yl=INT(sy/8)◄
mxl=xl*8:myl=yl*8◄
◄
 IF GetMode=TRUE AND MOUSE(Ø)=-1 THEN◄
   GOSUB RubberBox◄
   WINDOW OUTPUT 3◄
   GET (xl,yl)-(x2,y2),Shape%:Got=TRUE◄
   swidth=ABS(x2-xl):sheight=ABS(y2-yl)◄
   MENU 1,2,1:MENU 1,3,1:MENU 1,6,1◄
   GetMode=Ø◄
END IF◄
ON Tool GOSUB Draw,Solid,Hollow◄
RETURN◄
◄
 Draw:◄
   LINE (mxl+1,myl+1)-(mxl+7,myl+7),Currcolor,bf◄
   PATTERN &HAAAA◄
   LINE (mxl,myl)-(mxl+8,myl+8),1,b◄
   PATTERN &HFFFF◄
   WINDOW OUTPUT 3◄
   PSET (xl,yl),Currcolor◄
RETURN◄
◄
 Solid:◄
IF MOUSE(Ø)<Ø THEN◄
   GOSUB RubberBox◄
   WINDOW OUTPUT 1◄
   LINE (mxl,myl)-(mx2+8,my2+8),Currcolor,bf◄
   PATTERN &HAAAA◄
   FOR x=mxl TO mx2+8 STEP 8◄
     LINE (x,myl)-(x,my2+8),1◄
   NEXT◄
   FOR y=myl TO my2+8 STEP 8◄
     LINE (mxl,y)-(mx2+8,y),1◄
   NEXT◄
   PATTERN &HFFFF◄
   WINDOW OUTPUT 3◄
   LINE (xl,yl)-(x2,y2),Currcolor,bf◄
END IF◄
RETURN◄
◄
 Hollow:◄
IF MOUSE(Ø)<Ø THEN◄
   GOSUB RubberBox◄
   WINDOW OUTPUT 1◄
   FOR x=mxl TO mx2 STEP 8◄
     PATTERN &HFFFF◄
     LINE (x,myl)-(x+8,myl+8),Currcolor,bf◄
     LINE (x,my2)-(x+8,my2+8),Currcolor,bf◄
     PATTERN &HAAAA◄
     LINE (x,myl)-(x+8,myl+8),1,b◄
     LINE (x,my2)-(x+8,my2+8),1,b◄
   NEXT x◄
```

```
    FOR y=myl TO my2 STEP 8◄
      PATTERN &HFFFF◄
      LINE (mx2,y)-(mx2+8,y+8),Currcolor,bf◄
      LINE (mxl,y)-(mxl+8,y+8),Currcolor,bf◄
      PATTERN &HAAAA◄
      LINE (mxl,y)-(mxl+8,y+8),1,b◄
      LINE (mx2,y)-(mx2+8,y+8),1,b◄
    NEXT y◄
    PATTERN &HFFFF◄
    WINDOW OUTPUT 3◄
    LINE (x1,y1)-(x2,y2),Currcolor,b◄
  END IF◄
  RETURN◄
◄
  RubberBox:◄
  linepat=&HAAAA◄
  x2=xl:y2=yl:mx2=x2*8:my2=y2*8◄
  WHILE MOUSE(0)<>0◄
    ex=MOUSE(1):ey=MOUSE(2)◄
    IF ey>cy-8 THEN ey=cy-8◄
    tx=INT(ex/8):ty=INT(ey/8)◄
    IF tx>=xl THEN x2=tx◄
    IF ty>=yl THEN y2=ty◄
    mx2=x2*8:my2=y2*8◄
    PATTERN NOT linepat◄
    LINE (mxl,myl)-(mx2+8,my2+8),Currcolor,b◄
    PATTERN linepat◄
    LINE (mxl,myl)-(mx2+8,my2+8),1,b◄
  WEND◄
  IF mxl>mx2 THEN SWAP mxl,mx2:SWAP xl,x2◄
  IF myl>my2 THEN SWAP myl,my2:SWAP yl,y2◄
  RETURN◄
◄
  MenuHandler:◄
  MenuItem=MENU(1)◄
  ON MenuId GOSUB Shape,Tools,CScreen◄
  RETURN◄
◄
  Shape:◄
  ON MenuItem GOSUB Pick,Discard,ReDraw,SNew,SOpen,SSave,SQuit◄
  RETURN◄
◄
  Pick:◄
  GOSUB Discard:GetMode=TRUE:RETURN◄
◄
  Discard:◄
  Got=0◄
  MENU 1,2,0:MENU 1,3,0:MENU 1,6,0◄
  RETURN◄
◄
  ReDraw:◄
  CLS:GOSUB DoDraw:GOSUB Refresh◄
  RETURN◄
◄
  SNew:◄
  GOSUB Discard◄
  CLS:GOSUB DoDraw◄
```

```
RETURN◄
◄
SOpen:◄
CALL OpenRequest(filename$)◄
IF filename$="untitled" THEN OpenExit◄
ON ERROR GOTO OpenErr◄
OPEN filename$ FOR INPUT AS #1◄
INPUT #1,1:INPUT#1,swidth:INPUT#1,sheight◄
INPUT#1,xsize:INPUT#1,ysize:INPUT#1,depth◄
INPUT#1,ScrId◄
FOR i=0 TO 1◄
   INPUT#1,Shape%(i)◄
NEXT◄
CLOSE #1◄
GOSUB Delay◄
SCREEN CLOSE 1◄
wx=xsize-SideBorder:wy=ysize-BotBorder:ScrId=1◄
type=-(xsize<=640)-(xsize=640)-2*(ysize=400)◄
SCREEN 1,xsize,ysize,depth,type◄
MENU 3,1,2:MENU 3,2,1◄
IF ScrId=1 THEN MENU 3,1,1:MENU 3,2,2◄
GOSUB DoWin:GOSUB DoDraw:GOSUB Refresh◄
MENU 1,2,1:MENU 1,3,1:MENU 1,6,1◄
Got=TRUE◄
OpenExit:◄
CLOSE#1◄
ON ERROR GOTO 0◄
RETURN◄
◄
OpenErr:◄
CALL Alert("Error #"+STR$(ERR),"on open.",which)◄
IF which=1 THEN RESUME ELSE RESUME OpenExit◄
STOP◄
◄
SSave:◄
BoxIndex=1:height=PEEKW(WINDOW(8)+58)◄
winwidth=maxlen*(8-2*(height=9))+40◄
WINDOW 2,"Save As",(0,0)-(winwidth,100),0,ScrId◄
PRINT "Save object as:":PRINT◄
CALL TxBox(filename$+SPACE$(16-LEN(filename$)))◄
Xpos=1:Ypos=CSRLIN 'for GetString◄
PRINT :PRINT:CALL TxBox(""):PRINT "Binary"◄
PRINT:CALL TxBox(""):PRINT "DATA statements."◄
PRINT:CALL TxBox("Save")◄
PRINT TAB(11);:CALL TxBox("Cancel")◄
CALL CheckBox(2,1)◄
which=0:binflag=1◄
WHILE which<BoxIndex-2◄
   CALL WaitBox(which)◄
   IF which=1 THEN◄
     maxlen=15◄
     CALL GetString(Xpos,Ypos,filename$)◄
   ELSEIF which=2 THEN◄
     binflag=1◄
     CALL CheckBox(3,0)◄
     CALL CheckBox(2,1)◄
   ELSEIF which=3 THEN◄
```

```
      binflag=0◂
      CALL CheckBox(2,0)◂
      CALL CheckBox(3,1)◂
   END IF◂
WEND◂
CALL FlashRelease(which)◂
IF which=BoxIndex-1 OR filename$="untitled" THEN WINDOW CLOSE 2:
RETURN◂
'do save.  binflag=0 for binary◂
'binflag=1 for data statements◂
'do binary save◂
ON binflag+1 GOSUB SaveData,SaveBin◂
WINDOW CLOSE 2◂
RETURN◂
◂
SaveBin:◂
ON ERROR GOTO ExitSave◂
OPEN filename$ FOR OUTPUT AS #1◂
l=FN1(sheight,swidth,depth)◂
PRINT#1,l:PRINT#1,swidth:PRINT#1,sheight◂
PRINT#1,xsize:PRINT#1,ysize:PRINT#1,depth◂
PRINT#1,ScrId◂
FOR i=0 TO l◂
   PRINT#1,Shape%(i)◂
NEXT◂
CLOSE #1◂
ON ERROR GOTO 0◂
GOSUB Delay◂
RETURN◂
◂
SaveData:◂
ON ERROR GOTO ExitSave◂
l=FN1(sheight,swidth,depth)◂
OPEN filename$ FOR OUTPUT AS #1◂
PRINT#1,"'xsize=";xsize;"ysize=";ysize;"depth=";depth◂
PRINT#1,"l=";l;":dim shape%(l)"◂
PRINT#1,"FOR i=0 TO l:READ shape%(i):NEXT"◂
PRINT#1,"return"◂
FOR i=0 TO l STEP 8◂
   PRINT#1,"DATA ";◂
   FOR j=0 TO 7◂
     PRINT#1,"&h";HEX$(Shape%(i+j));◂
     IF i+j<=l THEN◂
       IF j<7 THEN PRINT#1,",";◂
     ELSE◂
       i=l:j=7◂
     END IF◂
   NEXT j:PRINT#1,""◂
NEXT i◂
SaveOut:◂
CLOSE #1◂
GOSUB Delay◂
ON ERROR GOTO 0◂
RETURN◂
◂
ExitSave:◂
CALL Alert("Error #"+STR$(ERR),"on save.",which)◂
```

```
IF which=1 THEN RESUME ELSE RESUME SaveOut◄
STOP◄
◄
SQuit:◄
MENU RESET◄
WINDOW CLOSE 3◄
WINDOW CLOSE 2◄
SCREEN CLOSE 1◄
LIST◄
END◄
◄
Delay:◄
t#=TIMER+2◄
WHILE TIMER<t#:WEND◄
RETURN◄
◄
Tools:◄
GOSUB Exclude◄
Tool=MenuItem◄
MENU 2,Tool,2◄
RETURN◄
◄
Exclude:◄
Tool=0◄
FOR i=1 TO NumTools:MENU 2,i,1:NEXT◄
RETURN◄
◄
CScreen:◄
IF MenuItem=1 THEN◄
   ScrId=-1◄
   SCREEN CLOSE 1◄
   xsize=640:ysize=200◄
   wx=xsize-9:wy=ysize-14◄
   MENU 3,1,2:MENU 3,2,1◄
   GOSUB DoWin:GOSUB DoDraw◄
   RETURN◄
END IF◄
'Get Custom screen parameters:◄
WINDOW 2,"Custom Screen",(0,0)-(160,120),0,ScrId◄
depth=INT(LOG(WINDOW(6))/LOG(2)+1)◄
BoxIndex=1:PRINT◄
CALL TxBox(""):PRINT "320 columns":PRINT◄
CALL TxBox(""):PRINT "640 columns":PRINT◄
CALL TxBox(""):PRINT "200 rows":PRINT◄
CALL TxBox(""):PRINT "400 rows":PRINT◄
Ypos=CSRLIN◄
CALL TxBox(CHR$(48+depth)):PRINT "Depth":PRINT◄
CALL TxBox("OK")◄
PRINT TAB(8);:CALL TxBox("Cancel")◄
CALL CheckBox(1-(xsize=640),1)◄
CALL CheckBox(3-(ysize=400),1)◄
which=0◄
WHILE which<BoxIndex-2◄
   CALL WaitBox(which)◄
   ON which GOSUB c320,c640,r200,r400,Planes◄
WEND◄
CALL FlashRelease(which)◄
```

```
   IF which=BoxIndex-1 THEN WINDOW CLOSE 2:RETURN◄
   wx=xsize-SideBorder:wy=ysize-BotBorder:ScrId=1◄
   type=-(xsize<=640)-(xsize=640)-2*(ysize=400)◄
   memory&=INT(depth*xsize*ysize/8)◄
   IF memory&>=64000& THEN◄
      CLS◄
      PRINT "Not enough":PRINT◄
      PRINT "memory for":PRINT◄
      PRINT "this mode.":PRINT :PRINT◄
      PRINT " *Click* "◄
      WHILE MOUSE(0)=0:WEND◄
      WHILE MOUSE(0)<>0:WEND◄
      WINDOW CLOSE 2◄
      RETURN◄
   END IF◄
   SCREEN CLOSE 1◄
   SCREEN 1,xsize,ysize,depth,type◄
   MENU 3,1,1:MENU 3,2,2◄
   GOSUB DoWin:GOSUB DoDraw◄
   RETURN◄
◄
   c320:◄
   CALL CheckBox(2,0):CALL CheckBox(which,1)◄
   xsize=320:RETURN◄
   c640:◄
   CALL CheckBox(1,0):CALL CheckBox(which,1)◄
   xsize=640:IF depth=5 THEN depth=3:GOSUB Planes◄
   r200:◄
   CALL CheckBox(4,0):CALL CheckBox(3,1)◄
   ysize=200:RETURN◄
   r400:◄
   CALL CheckBox(3,0):CALL CheckBox(4,1)◄
   ysize=400:RETURN◄
◄
   Planes:◄
   depth=depth+1◄
   IF depth>=(5-(xsize=320)) THEN depth=1◄
   LOCATE Ypos,2:PRINT CHR$(48+depth);◄
   WHILE MOUSE(0)<>0:WEND◄
   RETURN◄
◄
   Refresh:◄
   WINDOW OUTPUT 3:CLS◄
   ox=INT((wx-swidth*8)/16)◄
   oy=INT((wy-sheight*8)/16-.5)◄
   PUT (ox,oy),Shape%,PSET◄
   FOR y=oy TO oy+sheight◄
     FOR x=ox TO ox+swidth◄
        WINDOW OUTPUT 3◄
          c=POINT(x,y)◄
        WINDOW OUTPUT 1◄
        PATTERN &HFFFF◄
        LINE (x*8,y*8)-(x*8+8,y*8+8),c,bf◄
        PATTERN &HAAAA◄
        LINE (x*8,y*8)-(x*8+8,y*8+8),1,b◄
     NEXT x◄
   NEXT y◄
```

```
PATTERN &HFFFF◄
RETURN◄
◄
InitMenu:◄
MENU 1,0,1,"Shape"◄
MENU 1,1,1,"Pick Up"◄
MENU 1,2,0,"Discard"◄
MENU 1,3,0,"Redraw "◄
MENU 1,4,1,"New    "◄
MENU 1,5,1,"Open.. "◄
MENU 1,6,0,"Save.. "◄
MENU 1,7,1,"Quit   "◄
MENU 2,0,1,"Tools"◄
MENU 2,1,2,"  Draw      "◄
MENU 2,2,1,"  Solid Box "◄
MENU 2,3,1,"  Hollow Box"◄
Tool=1:NumTools=3◄
MENU 3,0,1,"Screen"◄
MENU 3,1,1,"  WBScreen"◄
MENU 3,2,2,"  Custom.."◄
MENU 4,0,0,""◄
RETURN◄
◄
DoWin:◄
WINDOW 1,SPACE$(20)+"Zoom",(0,0)-(wx,wy),16,ScrId◄
maxcolor=WINDOW(6)◄
resx=INT(wx/8):resy=INT(wy/8)◄
wx=resx*8:wy=resy*8◄
RETURN◄
     ◄
DoDraw:◄
WINDOW OUTPUT 1:CLS◄
PATTERN &HAAAA◄
FOR y=0 TO wy-8 STEP 8:LINE (0,y)-(wx,y):NEXT◄
FOR x=0 TO wx STEP 8:LINE (x,0)-(x,wy-8):NEXT◄
cw=INT(wx/(maxcolor+1)):cy=wy-8◄
PATTERN &HFFFF◄
FOR i=0 TO maxcolor◄
  LINE(i*cw+2,cy+2)-(i*cw+cw-2,wy-2),i,bf◄
NEXT i◄
Currcolor=maxcolor◄
WINDOW 3,"Actual",(0,0)-(8+resx,resy+8),16,ScrId◄
WINDOW OUTPUT 1◄
LINE (Currcolor*cw,cy)-(Currcolor*cw+cw,wy),1,b◄
PATTERN &HAAAA◄
LINE (Currcolor*cw,cy)-(Currcolor*cw+cw,cy),1,b◄
PATTERN &HFFFF◄
RETURN◄
◄
'**** Intuits: ****◄
◄
SUB OpenRequest(filename$) STATIC◄
CALL StringRequest("Open Request","Open filename:","Open","Cance
l",filename$)◄
END SUB◄
◄
SUB SaveRequest(filename$) STATIC◄
```

```
    CALL StringRequest("Save Request","Save as:","Save","Cancel",fil
    ename$)◄
    END SUB◄
◄
    SUB StringRequest(title$,msg$,b1$,b2$,default$) STATIC◄
    SHARED maxlen,ScrId,which,BoxIndex◄
    BoxIndex=1:height=PEEKW(WINDOW(8)+58)◄
    winwidth=maxlen*(8-2*(height=9))+40◄
    WINDOW 2,title$,(0,0)-(winwidth,80),0,ScrId◄
    PRINT:PRINT " ";msg$:PRINT◄
    PRINT " ";:CALL TxBox(default$+SPACE$(1+maxlen-LEN(default$))) '
    reserve space◄
    Xpos=2:Ypos=CSRLIN 'for GetString◄
    PRINT :PRINT :LOCATE ,2:CALL TxBox(b1$)◄
    PRINT TAB(maxlen+3-LEN(b2$));:CALL TxBox(b2$)◄
    which=0◄
    WHILE which<=1◄
       CALL WaitBox(which) 'Get box #◄
       IF which=1 THEN 'if GetString◄
          CALL GetString(Xpos,Ypos,default$)◄
       END IF◄
    WEND 'must be Open or Cancel◄
    CALL FlashRelease(which) 'Flash the box◄
    WINDOW CLOSE 2◄
    IF which=BoxIndex-1 THEN filename$=""◄
    END SUB◄
◄
    SUB Alert(msg1$,msg2$,which) STATIC◄
    CALL Request(msg1$,msg2$,"Retry","Cancel",which)◄
    END SUB◄
◄
    SUB Request(msg1$,msg2$,b1$,b2$,which) STATIC◄
    SHARED BoxIndex,ScrId◄
    SHARED x1(),y1(),x2(),y2()◄
    BoxIndex=1:height=PEEKW(WINDOW(8)+58)◄
    winwidth=20*(8-2*(height=9))+30◄
    WINDOW 2,"System Request",(0,0)-(winwidth,50),0,ScrId◄
    PRINT :PRINT TAB(11-LEN(msg1$)/2);msg1$◄
    PRINT TAB(11-LEN(msg2$)/2);msg2$:PRINT◄
    LOCATE ,2:TxBox b1$◄
    PRINT TAB(20-LEN(b2$));:TxBox b2$:which=0◄
    CALL WaitBox(which)◄
    CALL FlashRelease(which)◄
    WINDOW CLOSE 2◄
    END SUB◄
◄
    SUB FlashRelease(which) STATIC◄
    SHARED x1(),y1(),x2(),y2(),work%()◄
    SHARED RelVerify◄
    'These two lines flash the box◄
    GET (x1(which),y1(which))-(x2(which),y2(which)),work%◄
    PUT (x1(which),y1(which)),work%,PRESET◄
    ix=MOUSE(1):iy=MOUSE(2):RelVerify=-1◄
    WHILE MOUSE(0)<>0◄
    IF MOUSE(1)<>ix OR MOUSE(2)<>iy THEN RelVerify=0◄
    WEND◄
    'This line restores the box◄
```

```
    PUT (xl(which),yl(which)),work%,PSET
    END SUB

 SUB TxBox(msg$) STATIC
 SHARED xl(),yl(),x2(),y2()
 SHARED BoxIndex
 xl=WINDOW(4):yl=WINDOW(5)-10
 PRINT " ";msg$;" ";
 x2=WINDOW(4):y2=yl+14
 CALL Box(BoxIndex,xl,yl,x2,y2)
 BoxIndex=BoxIndex+1
 PRINT SPC(1);
 END SUB

 SUB Box(i,xl,yl,x2,y2) STATIC
 SHARED xl(),yl(),x2(),y2()
 IF x2<xl THEN SWAP xl,x2
 LINE (xl,yl)-(x2,y2),1-(WINDOW(6)>1),b
 LINE (xl,yl)-(x2-1,y2-1),1,b
 xl(i)=xl:yl(i)=yl:x2(i)=x2:y2(i)=y2
 END SUB

 SUB CheckBox(i,flag) STATIC
 SHARED xl(),yl(),x2(),y2()
 xl=xl(i)+2:yl=yl(i)+2
 x2=x2(i)-2:y2=y2(i)-2
 LINE (xl+3,yl+3)-(x2-3,y2-3),WINDOW(6)*-(flag<>0),bf
 END SUB

 SUB WaitBox(which) STATIC
 which=0
 WHILE which=0
    CALL WhichBox(which)
 WEND
 EXIT SUB
 RETURN
 END SUB

 SUB WhichBox(which) STATIC
 SHARED xl(),yl(),x2(),y2(),BoxIndex
 IF MOUSE(0)=0 THEN EXIT SUB
 x=MOUSE(1):y=MOUSE(2):i=1
 WHILE i<BoxIndex AND NOT (x>xl(i) AND x<x2(i) AND y>yl(i) AND y<
 y2(i))
    i=i+1
 WEND
 which=i:IF i=BoxIndex THEN which=0
 END SUB

 SUB GetString(Xpos,Ypos,default$) STATIC
 SHARED maxlen,which
 answer$=default$
 IF maxlen=0 THEN maxlen=40
 'Cursor appears at end of default string
 csr=LEN(default$)+1
 k$=""
 WHILE k$<>CHR$(13)
```

81

```
   LOCATE Ypos,Xpos+1:PRINT default$;" ";◄
   LOCATE Ypos,Xpos+csr◄
   COLOR Ø,WINDOW(6) 'cursor is max color◄
   PRINT MID$(default$+" ",csr,1)◄
   COLOR 1,Ø:k$=""◄
 WHILE k$="":k$=INKEY$◄
   CALL WhichBox(i)◄
   IF i>1 AND i<>which THEN which=i:k$=CHR$(13)◄
 WEND◄
 LOCATE Ypos,Xpos+1:PRINT default$;" ";◄
 k=ASC(k$)◄
 IF k>=32 AND k<127 THEN◄
   default$=LEFT$(default$,csr-1)+k$+MID$(default$,csr)◄
   default$=LEFT$(default$,maxlen)◄
   csr=csr-(csr<maxlen)◄
 END IF◄
 IF k=31 OR k=8 THEN csr=csr+(csr>1)◄
 IF k=127 OR k=8 THEN◄
   default$=LEFT$(default$,csr-1)+MID$(default$,csr+1)◄
 END IF◄
 IF k=3Ø THEN csr=csr-(csr<maxlen)◄
WEND◄
END SUB◄
◄
```

4 Object Animation

4 Object Animation

By far the largest group of advanced graphics commands in Amiga BASIC are the OBJECT commands. Not counting minor variations, there are no less than 16 OBJECT commands exclusively devoted to creating, moving, and managing animated screen objects. These commands let you create objects of almost any size, shape, and color; place those objects anywhere on the display, in any window or custom screen; move the objects in any direction at any speed and at any rate of acceleration; declare display priorities that define how the objects should overlap as they pass through each other; and determine which objects should register collisions when they hit other objects.

That's the good news.

The bad news is that the OBJECT commands suffer from some maddening limitations—at least with the version of Amiga BASIC (1.0) and the operating system (1.1) that we used when writing this book.

First, if you put more than a couple of objects on the screen at once, they have a tendency to flicker, even when they're sitting still. This flickering is unpredictable—some objects flicker and some don't. And sometimes they flicker only when moving through certain areas of the screen. Sometimes they don't flicker at all, and sometimes the flickering comes and goes.

Second, it's very difficult to achieve fast, smooth animation with the OBJECT commands. Although you can specify any rate of acceleration and speed, the faster values make the objects jump as they move across the screen. Smooth movement is possible, but not at very fast speeds. Fast movement is possible, but not very smoothly.

Third, and perhaps worst of all for game programmers, the collision checking suffers from some flaws. Sometimes, when two objects collide, BASIC simply doesn't see the collision or report it. At other times, collisions can be reported *too* fast for your BASIC program to keep up. Either way, your program is prevented from properly responding to the collision—by zapping the spaceship, bouncing the ball off a wall, or whatever.

These limitations are especially frustrating given the graphics and animation capabilities that hum beneath the Amiga's hood. Thanks to its custom chips, the Amiga packs more graphics power than any other personal computer now on the market. Yet, one of the most fascinating applications of this power—arcade-quality animation—is extremely difficult to achieve in Amiga BASIC.

85

Why Use the OBJECT Commands?

Does all this mean that the OBJECT commands in Amiga BASIC are useless and not worth learning? No—not quite. Although you'll encounter numerous roadblocks if you attempt to write a high-speed action game to rival those in the arcades, there are still many types of games and graphics programs that can benefit from object animation. For instance, one software developer we know is bringing out a chess game that is written largely in Amiga BASIC. Of course, the intelligence routines are coded in 68000 machine language for maximum speed and efficiency, but the screen display is created entirely with BASIC. This saves precious development time, and the results are practically as good as could be achieved with machine language anyway. Fast onscreen action is not a requirement in a chess game; the OBJECT commands are ideally suited for picking up a piece, moving it smoothly across the board to a new square, and putting it down again. Even this simple task would entail a lot of work in some other languages that don't have Amiga BASIC's range of animation commands.

Another good reason not to ignore the OBJECT commands is that Amiga BASIC—and the Amiga itself—is constantly evolving and improving. The first major revision of the operating system (Kickstart and Workbench 1.1) was released less than three months after the Amiga first hit the market. As any early Amiga owner can attest, 1.1 fixed a great many bugs in version 1.0. More revisions are on the way, and it's likely that the animation problems will be addressed in a future version of the operating system or Amiga BASIC. Indeed, a major revision may have already been issued by the time you're reading this.

Finally, if you're working on a program that absolutely *must* move screen objects at high speed—and you can't get the OBJECT commands to cooperate—there is a workable alternative. As discussed in the previous chapter, Amiga BASIC lets you pick up a piece of the screen and paste it down elsewhere. Not only can this be made to happen very fast, but it's also possible to move the piece of the screen over other screen images smoothly and nondestructively.

There are some disadvantages to this method, of course. Your program has to control the animation manually—you can't just specify a direction and speed for a shape and then cut it loose, as you can with the OBJECT commands—and there is no built-in collision checking. But for many applications, this method succeeds where the OBJECT commands fail. At any rate, you'll have two choices, depending on the demands of your particular program.

Sprites

We've been using the word *objects* rather loosely to describe animated screen objects, but actually the Amiga is capable of displaying two distinct types of objects: *sprites* and *bobs*.

Sprites should be familiar to those with experience on such popular home computers as the Commodore 64, Commodore 128, Atari

400/800/XL/XE, and Texas Instruments TI-99/4A. All of these computers can display some type of sprites. (On Atari computers they're usually called *player/missiles*.) Sprites evolved as a hardware solution to a software problem: What's the best way to move a screen object over other parts of the screen nondestructively—that is, without erasing or disturbing the rest of the screen? Programmers faced this problem very early in the history of videogames. The very first videogame—*Pong*, designed by Atari founder Nolan Bushnell—simulates a game of tennis in which two players knock a ball back and forth over a net. Naturally, you wouldn't want the ball to erase parts of the net as it travels to and fro. Eventually, the net would appear severely moth-eaten or would disappear altogether.

One approach to this problem is to save the portion of the background that is covered by the moving object, then restore it as the object moves on. But this requires valuable processing time and makes it difficult to move the object very fast—especially if there are several objects, and if the objects are large.

So, sprites were invented. Sprites are completely independent of the screen background. In effect, two video images—the normal screen and the sprite—are displayed on the same screen at the same time. Computers aren't the only devices that can do this. If you've seen one of the newer videocassette recorders or TV sets (such as the Sony KV-1311CR, a popular monitor for Amiga computers) that momentarily superimpose channel numbers and other information on the screen, you've got a good idea of how sprites work. Sprites don't disturb the screen background in any way because they aren't part of the screen background. It's almost as if you cut a shape out of tinted, clear plastic and taped it on the screen. Except, of course, a sprite can appear, move, change its shape and color, and disappear under program control.

Development of Amiga Sprites

A very primitive form of sprites first appeared in 1977 on the Atari VCS 2600, a home videogame machine that accepts plug-in cartridges. (As late as 1986, it was still popular and selling by the truckload.) The special graphics chip in the 2600 was designed by a young engineer named Jay Miner. Miner's next big project was to design the custom graphics chips inside the Atari 400 and 800— machines which defined the state of the art in personal computer graphics for several years after they were introduced in 1979. The Atari computers improved on the 2600 by allowing more colors (up to 256) and more sprites (up to eight—four large ones called *players* and four small ones called *missiles*). Moreover, the sprites were more easily controlled and could be as tall as the entire screen.

Miner didn't stop there. He left Atari and joined a small company in California's Silicon Valley that primarily manufactured joysticks. At this company, he played a major role in designing the custom chips for a new personal computer that can display up to 4096 colors and even better sprites—the Amiga.

The Amiga contains eight *sprite processors*, which means it has the equipment to display eight independent sprite objects on the screen simultaneously. Actually, because these sprite processors can be reused before the video beam finishes painting one frame of the screen, the Amiga isn't limited to displaying only eight sprites. However, every pair of sprites share the same set of color registers. If the sprites are separated vertically, many more than eight can be displayed simultaneously, and each sprite can contain three different colors. There are also ways to obtain more colors by combining two or more sprites.

Amiga sprites can be up to 16 pixels wide and as tall as the screen window. The pixels are the same size as those which make up the default 640 × 200 Workbench/CLI screen. Since sprites are independent of the screen background, their pixels remain at a constant size even when you set up custom screens with 320 horizontal pixels.

Although sprites are most often used in action games, don't be misled into thinking that's all they're good for. Sprites are useful any time you need to move an object on the screen without messing up the background. Even in a business program, such as a spreadsheet, a sprite might be the easiest way to implement a cursor. As a matter of fact, the Amiga's mouse pointer is a sprite.

Hi, Bob

Despite their flexibility and popularity on other computers, sprites have been downplayed on the Amiga—even by the Amiga's own designers. Why? Because the Amiga incorporates another type of movable screen object that is even more flexible than a sprite.

Known as *bobs*, short for *blitter objects*, these shapes derive their name from a component of the custom chip which controls them. The chip, dubbed Agnes by Jay Miner, contains two major components: the *copper* (coprocessor, or controller) and the *blitter*. (Another of Miner's custom chips, Daphne, controls the sprites.) The blitter derives its name from the term *bit-block transferrer*. In other words, the blitter is optimized for moving blocks of memory at very high speeds. Since the Amiga employs a bitmapped screen display, the blitter is especially useful for manipulating screen graphics. The blitter is responsible for the Amiga's line drawing, area fills, and bob animation.

Just how fast is the blitter? According to Amiga, it can plot an amazing *one million pixels per second*. Even in a high-level interpreted language like Amiga BASIC, line drawing and area fills seem to happen almost instantaneously, thanks to the blitter.

Bobs differ from sprites in several important ways. First, they aren't as independent of the screen background as sprites; in fact, they're actually *part* of the screen background—although usually they behave transparently like sprites. Bobs can move across the screen nondestructively, exhibit different display priorities, and trigger collisions with each other, just like sprites. But these functions are not handled by a sprite processor that's displaying the object as an independent, superimposed image. When a bob moves, the blitter repeatedly preserves and restores the portions of the screen over which it travels, so the bob appears to move independently.

As mentioned before, this kind of animation eats up valuable processing time, which is exactly why the Amiga is endowed with a blitter. Without a blitter, bobs would quickly bog down the 68000 CPU and seriously impair other operations that might be taking place at the same time. Even with a blitter, bobs tax the Amiga's power. That's why bobs are inherently slower than sprites, although the difference in speed is often considered a fair tradeoff for their other advantages.

One of those advantages is that bobs aren't limited to a width of 16 pixels as are sprites. Bobs can be virtually any size, even as large as the entire screen, if there's enough memory available. Because of the way they move, the amount of memory required for a bob is whatever it takes to define its shape, size, color, and other attributes, *plus* the memory which must be set aside to preserve and restore the screen background when it moves. Hence, big bobs equal mucho memory.

Another advantage of bobs over sprites is that they aren't limited to only three colors; they can display the full range of colors permitted by the screen mode currently in use. So if you set up a 320 × 200 or 320 × 400 custom screen with the maximum depth of five bit-planes, you can display bobs with up to 32 simultaneous colors.

Because of these advantages, most commercial software for the Amiga uses bobs, not sprites, for animation. If you've ever seen the graphics demo called "Robo City" at your Amiga dealer, or the famous Amiga bouncing ball demo, you may be surprised to learn that it's all done with the blitter—no sprites. Although the bouncing ball demo has been successfully imitated on some other personal computers, these imitations miss the point. Thanks to help from the blitter, the Amiga's 68000 CPU can display that bouncing, spinning, checkered ball in 3-D while working at only 8 percent capacity. You can pull down the demo screen to reveal another screen behind it—and run a completely separate program, if you wish.

Creating Objects in BASIC

Despite the differences between bobs and sprites, Amiga BASIC attempts to treat them as more or less synonymous objects. For instance, there are no separate groups of commands in Amiga BASIC for manipulating bobs and sprites; the OBJECT statements are general-purpose commands that work interchangeably with both. Indeed, Amiga BASIC makes so few distinctions between bobs and sprites that it's more practical to think of them as generic *objects*.

To create these objects, you use a utility program included in the BasicDemos drawer on the Amiga BASIC Extras disk. Known as the "Object Editor," this utility lets you draw either sprites or bobs and save them on disk as data files. (A good description of how to use the Object Editor can be found in Chapter 7 of the *Amiga BASIC* manual that comes with the computer.) When you run the Object Editor, it asks whether you want to design a sprite or a bob. Your answer should depend on the requirements of your program; remember that sprites can be only 16 pixels wide and can display only three simultaneous colors. Also, if your program needs to display more than four objects on the screen at once, remember that only four sprites can appear on the same horizontal scan line. Due to these limitations, you'll probably arrive at the same conclusion that the commercial software developers have—it's usually more convenient to use bobs for objects instead of sprites.

When you design an object with the Object Editor, keep in mind that its final size is defined by the entire area of the resizable drawing canvas. If you draw a small object surrounded by lots of empty space within this canvas, the final object appears onscreen with this empty space around it. Therefore, you should resize the canvas with the mouse before designing your shape and make sure the shape fills the canvas as completely as possible. (You can't resize the canvas after you start drawing.)

OBJECT.SHAPE

Once you've created and saved an object with the Object Editor, the next step is to include it in your program with the OBJECT.SHAPE statement. OBJECT.SHAPE allocates memory for the shape data and assigns the object a unique number. This number is the ID tag that you use whenever referring to that object with any of the other OBJECT commands.

There are three ways to use OBJECT.SHAPE. The procedure described by the *Amiga BASIC* manual is to open the disk file containing the shape data that was created with the Object Editor, read the shape data into the OBJECT.SHAPE statement, and then close the disk file. Here's the format for this routine:

OPEN *"filename"* **FOR INPUT AS #1**
OBJECT.SHAPE *object-ID*,**INPUT$(LOF(1),1)**
CLOSE #1

Filename is the name of the disk file created with the Object Editor, and *object-ID* is the unique identification number for the object (any number from 1 to *n*, where *n* is limited only by the amount of memory available).

For instance, if you created an alien spaceship with the Object Editor and saved the shape on disk with the filename Alien, and if this is the first object you're defining in your program, the routine would look like this:

```
OPEN "Alien" FOR INPUT AS #1
OBJECT.SHAPE 1,INPUT$(LOF(1),1)
CLOSE #1
```

It's that simple.

There are two small problems with this method, however. First, the disk file containing the object's shape data must be in the current disk directory. For instance, if you run your program from a drawer named "BasicProgs" and the object file is in another drawer called "BasicDemos," or perhaps on another disk, your program crashes with a *File not found* error. You either have to move the object file to the current directory, or point the OPEN statement to the proper directory. If you know when writing your program that the object file will be in a drawer named "Objects" on a disk volume named "BASIC2", you could modify the OPEN statement to read

OPEN "BASIC2:Objects/Alien" FOR INPUT AS #1

Unfortunately, if you're writing programs that will be used by other people, you can't always know ahead of time that their disks, drawers, and object files will be organized this way.

The second problem with object files is that they prevent you from publishing your program listing in a book, magazine, or newsletter. People can type in your program, but how will they get your disk file containing the object's shape data?

Both of these problems could be solved if there were some way to include the shape data as part of your program. As a bonus, your program would initialize faster, too, since it wouldn't have to load the shapes from disk.

The Object Datamaker

Our solution is Program 4-4, "Object Datamaker," listed at the end of this chapter. It's a short utility for converting data files created with the Object Editor into DATA statements that can be merged with your own programs. The DATA statements contain the numbers which describe the object's shape, size, colors, and other attributes. Follow these steps to convert any object file:

1. Run the Object Datamaker. It opens up as a small window on the Workbench/CLI screen and asks you for the filename of the object file. Be sure to specify the proper volume name and drawer if the object file is not in the current directory.
2. Next, the Datamaker prompts you for the output filename; this is for the ASCII file of DATA statements that you'll later merge into your own program. Since you'll probably discard this file after it has been merged, you may want to create it on the RAM disk (specify RAM:*filename* when prompted for the output filename).

3. Depending on the size of your object, it takes about 10 or 20 seconds for the Datamaker to do its job. When it's done, it asks if you want to convert another object file or quit. If you're converting more than one object file, remember to give them different output filenames.
4. Now you're ready to merge the newly created DATA statements into your program. Load your program into memory, then switch to Amiga BASIC's Output window. Type MERGE *"filename"* and press RETURN (*filename* is the output filename you created with the Datamaker).
5. Switch to Amiga BASIC's List window and press the ALT–cursor down keys to scroll to the end of your program. You should see the DATA statements that have just been merged. Scroll upward until you reach the top of the DATA statements. The Object Datamaker automatically adds a REMark statement here which includes the output filename (so you can tell which shape the DATA statements represent) and the number of DATA elements. *This number is important, because you'll need it to read the DATA elements into a string with a FOR-NEXT loop.*
6. Insert a label or line number at the top of the DATA statements. A descriptive label like AlienShapeData: helps make your program self-documenting.
7. In the initialization section of your program—the part where you'd normally read the object file from disk—insert a short routine built around this format:

DIM *shape$(elements)*
RESTORE *LineLabel*
FOR n=1 TO *elements*
  READ a
  shape$=shape$+**CHR$(a)**
NEXT n
OBJECT.SHAPE *object-ID,shape$*

where *shape$* is a string variable you assign for that particular object, *elements* is the number of DATA elements as noted by the REMark statement created by the Object Datamaker, *LineLabel* is the line number or label you've inserted at the top of the DATA statements, and *object-ID* is the identification number you've assigned to that particular object.

  For example, let's assume you've created an alien spaceship with the Object Editor, converted the disk file with the Object Datamaker, merged the DATA statements into your program, and learned from the REMark statement that the shape data happens to consist of 114 numbers. Here's how your routine might look:

DIM alien$(114)
RESTORE AlienShapeData
FOR n=1 TO 114
  READ a
  alien$=alien$+CHR$(a)
NEXT n
OBJECT.SHAPE 1,alien$

In effect, this method of defining objects binds or links the shape data to your program, making it a self-contained unit. There's no need to worry about disk files in separate directories and *File not found* errors. Also, you can print out or publish your program with the shape data included.

Sharing Shapes

If your program needs more than one object, you can define additional objects the same way. But for the sake of convenience and memory conservation, Amiga BASIC provides another form of OBJECT.SHAPE. If you plan to assign the same shape to two or more objects, you can create the additional objects by copying from an existing one:

OBJECT.SHAPE *object-ID1,object-ID2*

where *object-ID1* is the new object you're creating, and *object-ID2* is an object whose shape has already been defined.

For example, if you're writing a game that needs four alien spaceships, and all of them are the same shape, only object 1 has to be defined with the DATA statements or disk file methods shown above. The others can be defined like this:

OBJECT.SHAPE 2,1
OBJECT.SHAPE 3,1
OBJECT.SHAPE 4,1

Copying shapes with OBJECT.SHAPE is recommended whenever possible because the objects defined this way share significant amounts of memory. Yet, they're still independent objects. As we'll see in a moment, you can assign them completely different screen positions, speeds, display priorities, and collision masks.

Positioning Objects

Once objects have been defined with OBJECT.SHAPE, positioning and moving them on the screen is fairly easy.

To place an object anywhere on the screen, you specify its horizontal and vertical coordinates with OBJECT.X and OBJECT.Y, respectively:

OBJECT.X *object-ID,horizontal coordinate*
OBJECT.Y *object-ID,vertical coordinate*

where *object-ID* is the object's identification number, *horizontal coordinate* is the horizontal pixel position, and *vertical coordinate* is the vertical pixel position. These *(x,y)* coordinates are the same ones used by other graphics statements—such as PSET, PRESET, POINT, PAINT, and LINE—and depend on the screen mode of the current Output window (up to 320 or 640 pixels horizontally and 200 or 400 pixels vertically).

Note that the *(x,y)* coordinates refer to the *upper left corner* of the object's rectangle—the rectangle defined by the canvas on which the object was created with the Object Editor. If you left a generous amount of empty space around the shape when drawing the object, the *(x,y)* coordinates referred to by OBJECT.X and OBJECT.Y will be offset from the visible shape by a like amount.

This example of OBJECT.X and OBJECT.Y would place object 1 at pixel position (10,20) near the upper left corner of the current Output window:

OBJECT.X 1,10
OBJECT.Y 1,20

The object won't actually appear onscreen, however, until the program executes an OBJECT.ON command. Follow OBJECT.ON with one or more object-ID numbers: OBJECT.ON 1 and OBJECT.ON 1,2,3,4 are both valid statements (assuming, of course, that the objects referred to have already been defined with OBJECT.SHAPE). If you execute OBJECT.ON without any object-IDs, all objects previously defined with OBJECT.SHAPE are turned on within the current Output window.

The opposite of OBJECT.ON is OBJECT.OFF. As you might expect, it turns off any objects in the current Output window whose object-IDs are specified. OBJECT.OFF by itself turns off all objects displayed in the current Output window.

OBJECT.X and OBJECT.Y have other forms, too. They can serve as functions which *return* the pixel positions of an object. For instance, if you execute the following statements after the previous example, the variables *x* and *y* would return the values 10 and 20, respectively.

x=OBJECT.X(1)
y=OBJECT.Y(1)

You can determine the current screen position of any object in this manner by substituting its object-ID number within the function.

Motion Commotion

Once you've defined an object and positioned it on the screen, setting it into motion is pretty straightforward. Amiga BASIC provides a pair of OBJECT statements for specifying an object's horizontal and vertical velocities, another pair of OBJECT statements for specifying the acceleration, and two more commands that start and stop the object.

To set the horizontal velocity, use OBJECT.VX; to set the vertical velocity, use OBJECT.VY. Here's the general form:

OBJECT.VX *object-ID,velocity*
OBJECT.VY *object-ID,velocity*

where *object-ID* is the object's ID number, and *velocity* is a number representing the object's speed in pixels per second.

    If you want the object to move only in a straight horizontal or vertical direction, you don't have to use both of these statements. For instance,

OBJECT.VX 1,20

moves object 1 from left to right across the screen at a speed of 20 pixels per second. You don't have to specify a value for OBJECT.VY because Amiga BASIC automatically sets it to zero when the object is created. Similarly,

OBJECT.VY 1,10

moves object 1 straight down the screen from top to bottom at a speed of ten pixels per second. If you haven't previously executed an OBJECT.VX command for that object, the horizontal speed is already set to zero.

Controlling Movement

When you specify nonzero numbers for a shape's OBJECT.VX *and* OBJECT.VY values, diagonal movement results. The angle of the diagonal depends on the relative horizontal and vertical speeds. A slightly tilted diagonal path would require a higher OBJECT.VX value and lower OBJECT.VY value; a steeper path would call for the opposite. You might think that assigning equal values to OBJECT.VX and OBJECT.VY would move the object at an exact 45-degree angle, but remember that the screen dimensions are not the same horizontally and vertically. For instance, if you assigned equal speeds of ten pixels per second for OBJECT.VX and OBJECT.VY in the 640 × 200 mode, the object would actually travel in a very steep diagonal. Assuming it started at the upper left corner, it would reach the bottom of the screen before it got a third of the way across horizontally. In the 320 x 400 mode, though, equal OBJECT.VX and OBJECT.VY speeds *would* result in a diagonal angle that's very close to 45 degrees.

    To move an object from right to left horizontally or from bottom to top vertically, you have to specify negative numbers in the OBJECT.VX and OBJECT.VY statements. For example, these commands move object 3 across the screen diagonally from the lower right toward the upper left:

OBJECT.VX 3,−30
OBJECT.VY 3,−20

    Note that OBJECT.VX and OBJECT.VY *don't actually take effect until your program executes an OBJECT.START statement.* OBJECT.START followed by no additional parameters starts all objects in motion in the current Output window—at least, all objects whose speeds have been defined with OBJECT.VX and OBJECT.VY. If you follow OBJECT.START with an object-ID number, only that particular object is set into motion. OBJECT.START comes in handy when you want several objects to begin moving at once; you can predefine their speeds with OBJECT.VX and OBJECT.VY statements, then cut them all loose at once with a single OBJECT.START. Or you can start them individually by specifying their object-IDs.

To stop an object that's moving, you can specify zero values in OBJECT.VX and OBJECT.VY. Or you can use OBJECT.STOP. Again, as you might expect, OBJECT.STOP is the exact opposite of OBJECT.START. Used by itself, it stops all moving objects in the current Output window. When followed by an object-ID, it stops only that particular object.

As you experiment with OBJECT.VX and OBJECT.VY, you'll soon discover that the animation is not very smooth, particularly at fast speeds. As we mentioned at the beginning of the chapter, this is a general problem with Amiga BASIC's OBJECT commands. The reason is that the OBJECT commands work in a similar way as the event-trapping commands covered in Chapter 1— they are updated by interrupts that occur only *between* BASIC statements, not continuously. When you specify a speed in pixels per second with OBJECT.VX or OBJECT.VY, Amiga BASIC checks the object's position between each statement that is executed in your program. If BASIC decides that the object should have moved a certain number of pixels since the last time it checked the object's position, it goes ahead and moves the object that number of pixels. Unfortunately, if there are several other objects to be moved, and if your program is busy doing many other things as well—handling collisions and so forth— BASIC falls behind. To deliver the pixels-per-second speed you asked for, it has to move the object in rapid jumps. This makes the animation look coarse and jerky.

Until something is changed, the only solution is to limit the number of objects you try to move at once and also limit their speeds.

Reading the Speedometer

As with OBJECT.X and OBJECT.Y, the OBJECT.VX and OBJECT.VY statements also have a second format: They can act as functions to *return* the current horizontal and vertical velocities of an object.

For instance, these lines would return values of 20 in the variable x and −10 in the variable y for object 2:

OBJECT.VX 2,20
OBJECT.VY 2,−10
x=OBJECT.VX(2)
y=OBJECT.VY(2)

You might be wondering why you'd need to check on numbers that you've already assigned and therefore should know perfectly well. One answer is that your program may not be assigning velocities with constants; if the object's speed needs to change while the program runs, you'll be using variables in the OBJECT.VX and OBJECT.VY statements. Should the program need to determine the current speed of an object for some reason, these functions will do the trick. In effect, they read the object's speedometer.

Another use for these functions is to deduce an object's current *direction* of movement. If OBJECT.VX( ) returns a positive number, you know the object is moving in a general left-to-right path; the opposite is true if the number is negative. Likewise, a positive or negative number reported by OBJECT.VY( ) tells you whether the object is moving upward or downward on the screen. This information might be important to your program.

Gas and Brake Pedals

Amiga BASIC's final two commands for controlling movement are OBJECT.AX and OBJECT.AY. They govern acceleration in the horizontal and vertical directions, respectively. The format is almost identical to that of the velocity commands:

OBJECT.AX *object-ID,rate*
OBJECT.AY *object-ID,rate*

where *object-ID* is the familiar object ID number, and *rate* is a value that represents acceleration in pixels per second per second.

For example, let's say you've got an object designed to look like the space shuttle. You want it slowly to lift off a launchpad at the bottom of the screen and gather speed as it rockets toward the top of the screen. You could use this statement:

OBJECT.AY 1,−5

The negative value doesn't indicate *deceleration*; instead, it specifies *upward acceleration* at the rate of five pixels per second per second. (Recall that the OBJECT.VX and OBJECT.VY statements also demand negative numbers for right-to-left or upward motion.) To make this object accelerate *down* the screen at the same rate, you could use a line like this:

OBJECT.AY 1,5

This command accelerates the object from left to right:

OBJECT.AX 1,10

And this one, from right to left:

OBJECT.AX 1,−10

What if you want to make an object decelerate—that is, step on the brakes? Simple. Just execute another OBJECT.AX or OBJECT.AY command that counteracts the previous one by specifying acceleration in the opposite direction.

Program 4-1 demonstrates this technique. It uses DATA statements generated with the Object Datamaker utility to create a simple alien spaceship. When you run the example, it starts off by accelerating the alien down the screen at the rate of ten pixels per second per second. When the alien's speed hits 100 pixels per second (as measured by the OBJECT.VY( ) speedometer), the program abruptly *reverses* the acceleration (OBJECT.AY 1, -10) to make the alien slow to a stop and begin moving *up* the screen. When the alien hits a speed of -100 pixels per second, the sequence repeats. In effect, we've turned the alien into a yo-yo.

Program 4-1. Yo-Yo

```
WINDOW 1,"Yo-Yo",(0,0)-(631,184),20◄
DIM alien$(114)◄
RESTORE AlienShapeData◄
FOR n=1 TO 114◄
  READ a:alien$=alien$+CHR$(a)◄
NEXT◄
OBJECT.SHAPE 1,alien$◄
OBJECT.X 1,300:OBJECT.Y 1,10◄
OBJECT.ON:OBJECT.START◄
WHILE MOUSE(0)=0◄
  OBJECT.AY 1,10◄
  WHILE OBJECT.VY(1)<100:WEND◄
  OBJECT.AY 1,-10◄
  WHILE OBJECT.VY(1)>-100:WEND◄
WEND◄
OBJECT.STOP:OBJECT.CLOSE◄
AlienShapeData:◄
DATA    0,   0,   0,   0,   0,   0,   0,   0◄
DATA    0,   0,   0,   2,   0,   0,   0,  26◄
DATA    0,   0,   0,  11,   0,  24,   0,   3◄
DATA    0,   0,   0,127,128,   0,   1,255◄
DATA  224,   0,   7,255,248,   0,  31,255◄
DATA  254,   0,248,225,199,192,248,225◄
DATA  199,192,255,255,255,192,  12,127◄
DATA  140,   0,  12,127,140,   0,252,   0◄
DATA   15,192,252,   0,  15,192,   0,   0◄
DATA    0,   0,   0,   0,   0,   0,   0,   0◄
DATA    0,   0,   0,   0,   0,   0,   7,  30◄
DATA   56,   0,   7,  30,  56,   0,   0,   0◄
DATA    0,   0,   0,127,128,   0,   0,127◄
DATA  128,   0,   0,   0,   0,   0,   0,   0◄
DATA    0,   0◄
```

(To stop the program, press and hold the left mouse button.)

OBJECT.AX and OBJECT.AY can be useful, but Program 4-1 also reveals their flaws. Like the other object animation commands, they produce jerky movement when you try to push the object too fast. You'll notice that the acceleration is so irregular that it doesn't correspond very closely to the pixels-per-second-per-second value you specify. For smoother motion, you'll have to restrict the objects to slower rates of acceleration.

Controlling Object Colors

Amiga BASIC provides three more OBJECT commands for defining additional attributes of objects once they are created with OBJECT.SHAPE. These commands are OBJECT.PLANES, which lets you change an object's colors; OBJECT.PRIORITY, which lets you define how two or more objects should overlap onscreen; and OBJECT.HIT, which determines which objects should collide with each other. We'll start with OBJECT.PLANES.

Using OBJECT.PLANES

OBJECT.PLANES is a difficult command to grasp, especially since it's barely mentioned in the *Amiga BASIC* manual (and the skimpy information that *is* included is in error). It doesn't work as you might expect it to—you can't just specify an object-ID and the same red-green-blue values used with PALETTE. Instead, the colors assigned to an object by OBJECT.PLANES are determined not only by PALETTE's color register values and the number of bit-planes in the current SCREEN mode, but also by a complicated combination of three binary bit patterns: the image-shadow of the object itself plus two more optional bit masks which you specify in OBJECT.PLANES.

Sound confusing? It is. But we've worked out a solution that makes it easy to manipulate the colors of any object, in any SCREEN mode.

First, here's the basic format for OBJECT.PLANES:

OBJECT.PLANES *object-ID,plane-pick,plane-on-off*

where *object-ID* is the usual object ID number, *plane-pick* is a number that sets up a binary bit mask, and *plane-on-off* is an optional number that sets up another binary bit mask. The *Amiga BASIC* manual says that *plane-pick* and *plane-on-off* can range from 0 to 255, but we've found that this advice leads to error messages. Actually, the range of values allowed for these parameters depends on the *bit-plane depth* of the current screen mode.

How's that again? Let's back up for a moment. The number of simultaneous colors allowed in an object is determined by three factors: (1) whether the object is a sprite or a bob, (2) the way you designed the object with the Object Editor, and (3) the bit-plane depth of your program's screen mode.

- Sprites, you'll recall, are always limited to only three simultaneous colors. Therefore, the following discussion applies only to bobs.
- The Object Editor supplied on the Amiga BASIC Extras disk lets you design bobs with only four colors. To design bobs with more than four colors, you'll have to modify the Object Editor. There are comments embedded in the program listing to help you do this.
- The maximum number of simultaneous screen colors—for either bobs or background graphics—always depends on the bit-plane depth of the screen mode. You'll recall from Chapter 2 that *depth* is the fourth parameter of the SCREEN statement (after *screen-ID*, *width*, and *height)* and can range from 1

to 5. The maximum number of simultaneous colors is the largest binary number that can be made from the number of bit-planes, as this table shows:

SCREEN Depth and Simultaneous Colors

Bit-Plane Depth	Maximum Colors
1	2
2	4
3	8
4	16
5	32

Of course, these colors can be freely selected from any of the Amiga's 4096 different hues—only the number of colors that can be displayed *simultaneously* is restricted.

Unmasking OBJECT.PLANES

Now, with this in hand, it's easier to understand the relationship between the screen mode and OBJECT.PLANES. The bit-plane depth you specify in your program's SCREEN statement determines the maximum number of simultaneous bob colors *and* the maximum values allowed for the plane-pick and plane-on-off parameters in OBJECT.PLANES. (Incidentally, if your program doesn't have a SCREEN statement, it defaults to the Workbench or CLI screen mode—640 × 200 with two bit-planes, or the equivalent of SCREEN −1,640,200,2,2.)

This table shows the relationship between screen depth, plane-pick, and plane-on-off:

SCREEN Depth and Plane-Pick/Plane-On-Off Values

SCREEN Depth	Maximum Plane-Pick/ Plane-On-Off
1	1
2	3
3	7
4	15
5	31

Notice how this differs just slightly from the previous table: the numbers in the right-hand column here are each *one less* than the number of maximum colors in the other table. (The reason is that computer designers have a peculiar habit of counting from zero instead of from one like the rest of us.) Therefore, if your screen mode has a bit-plane depth of 3, the values allowed for the plane-pick and plane-on-off parameters in OBJECT.PLANES can range from 0 to 7. And the maximum number of simulaneous colors would be 8. With a screen depth of 5, plane-pick and plane-on-off could range from 0 to 31, and the maximum number of simultaneous colors would be 32. If you try to exceed these ranges, you'll get an error message.

Another way of expressing this is that the maximum values allowed for plane-pick and plane-on-off correspond to the maximum color number for the current screen mode.

Okay so far. Now we know what numbers are legal for plane-pick and plane-on-off. But what are plane-pick and plane-on-off anyway, and how do they determine a bob's color? That's the tricky part.

Plane-pick is a binary value that tells the computer which bit-planes the bob should be drawn on. When a bit is set by plane-pick, the computer draws the bob on the corresponding bit-plane. For this purpose, bit-planes at the system level are numbered from zero rather than from one as in the BASIC SCREEN statement. Therefore, a plane-pick value of zero draws the bob on SCREEN bit-plane 1; a plane-pick value of one draws the bob on SCREEN bit-plane 2; and a plane-pick value of three draws the bob on *both* SCREEN bit-plane 1 *and* bit-plane 2, because the binary pattern of the decimal number 3 switches on the binary bits 1 and 2.

We warned you it was confusing. But hold on—it gets still worse.

Plane-on-off tells the computer what to do with the bit-planes that are *not picked* by plane-pick. Like plane-pick, plane-on-off is a binary bit pattern that corresponds to the bit-planes. But the bits in plane-on-off do something different. They fill the bit-planes not picked by plane-pick in every pixel occupied by the bob's *image-shadow*. The image-shadow, in turn, is the bob's shape when all of its bit-planes are combined.

If you don't quite follow this explanation, don't worry. The bottom line is that you don't have to understand fully how plane-pick and plane-on-off work in order to manipulate bob colors. In fact, even if you have a good working knowledge of how they function at the system level, you can still go crazy trying to figure out how a bob's colors will appear onscreen just by looking at the plane-pick, plane-on-off, and bit-plane values. The ideal way to design the colors would be to display the bob on the screen, experiment with various values, and observe the effects. And that's exactly what you can do with "PlanePick," a utility we've written expressly for this purpose.

Using PlanePick

You'll find PlanePick, Program 4-5, at the end of this chapter. Fully mouse-controlled, it lets you load any bob designed with the Object Editor and interactively manipulate the bob's colors. It works in all of the 320 × 200 screen modes, one to five bit-planes. You can alter the screen depth at any time from within the program and also change the entire color palette which corresponds to that depth. The plane-pick and plane-on-off values are constantly displayed, so you can jot them down to plug into your own programs when you find a color combination you like.

Here's how it works. When you run PlanePick, it asks for a bob file to load. Specify the folder and filename of a bob created with the Object Editor. (Be careful to type the correct filename—keep this utility as short as possible; there's no trapping for disk errors.) PlanePick then loads the bob file and sets up a custom 320 × 200 screen with five bit-planes—32 colors. At the top of the screen is the bob. At the bottom of the screen are two rows of buttons, one row for changing the plane-pick value and another row for changing the plane-on-off value. Each button represents a color register in the current color palette. Therefore, the number of buttons in each row depends on the current screen depth.

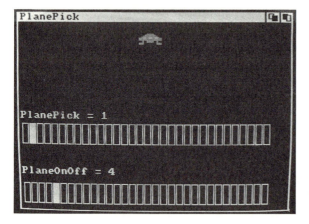

"PlanePick" is a utility program that lets you design object colors on the screen.

For instance, since the depth is five bit-planes when you first run PlanePick, each row contains 32 buttons—one button for each of the 32 colors in the palette. If you switch to a screen depth of four bit-planes, the PlanePick program readjusts itself to display two rows of 16 buttons. A screen depth of three would display two rows of eight buttons, and so on. The minimum screen depth of only a single bit-plane results in only two buttons for each row since this mode is limited to just two colors (background and foreground).

To change screen depths, simply pull down the Project menu and select the desired mode. PlanePick automatically readjusts.

To manipulate the bob's colors, point to a button in either row and click the mouse. You'll see the colors change, and the plane-pick and plane-on-off values shown on the screen will change, too. These are the values you would use in your own program to obtain the same color combination.

Try some experiments. If you want to see what a bob's image-shadow looks like, set plane-pick to zero by clicking on its leftmost button, then select any button for plane-on-off. The result will be an image-shadow of the same color as the corresponding color register (as determined by the PALETTE statement). The image-shadow disappears when you set plane-pick to any nonzero value.

If you want to redesign the color palette, select Change Palette from the Project menu. This brings up a screen which shows all the colors for the current SCREEN mode (2–32). To change a particular color to any of the Amiga's 4096 possible hues, simply click on the appropriate color box and readjust the slide controls at the bottom of the screen. These sliders control the red, green, and blue values used by the PALETTE statement. When you're satisfied with the new palette, click on the OK box; you'll return to the main PlanePick screen with the new palette in effect. If you don't like your new colors, click on the CANCEL box; you'll return to the main screen with the old colors intact. (This palette screen is an independent subprogram which can be added to any of your own programs; it's fully explained in Chapter 7.)

Incidentally, when PlanePick is set for a 32-color SCREEN mode, you'll notice that the Amiga's mouse pointer changes color. This is normal. The 32-color modes share color registers with the sprites—and as mentioned before, the mouse pointer is actually a sprite.

You can load a new bob into PlanePick any time you want by selecting Open Bob from the Project menu.

Getting Your Priorities Straight

Another object attribute under your control is the *display priority*. If there's a chance in your program that two or more objects might overlap on the screen, you can determine ahead of time which object will be displayed in front of the others. In fact, every object can have its own priority relative to all other objects, a sort of video pecking order.

There are numerous applications for this, particularly in games. Suppose you want an airplane to fly behind some clouds. You can design the airplane and clouds as objects, then assign a higher priority to the plane. Or you could design an object-cursor that moves over object-icons.

Such effects are easy to achieve with the OBJECT.PRIORITY statement. Here's the format:

OBJECT.PRIORITY *object-ID,rank*

Object-ID is the usual object ID number, and *rank* is a value from −32768 to 32767. The higher the rank, the higher the priority.

For instance, let's say you've got a program with four objects. You want object 1 to have the highest priority, object 2 to have the lowest priority, and objects 3 and 4 to share the same priority, which is lower than object 1, but higher than object 2. These statements would do the trick:

OBJECT.PRIORITY 1,3
OBJECT.PRIORITY 2,1
OBJECT.PRIORITY 3,2
OBJECT.PRIORITY 4,2

According to this scheme, object 1 always moves to the front when it passes through any other object. Object 2 is always covered when it meets another object. Objects 3 and 4 always pass beneath object 1, but over object 2. When objects 3 and 4 overlap, the computer randomly decides which one should get priority.

Note that all of these objects must be bobs; sprites are not affected by OBJECT.PRIORITY. Sprites always have display priority over bobs, as demonstrated when you move the Amiga's mouse pointer over a bob.

Program 4-2 is a short demo that you can run to experiment with OBJECT.PRIORITY. It defines objects 1–5 as alien spaceships, then draws them on the screen in a diagonal row and lets you move one of them with the mouse. Wherever you move the mouse pointer, the alien defined as object 1 follows. Since object 1 has higher rank than objects 2 and 3, it appears to pass in front of these ships. Object 4 has the same priority as object 1, so the mobile ship may pass either in front of or behind this ship. And object 5, the ship in the lower right corner, has a higher priority than object 1, so the mobile ship will always appear to pass behind that ship. Click the left mouse button to exit the program to BASIC:

Program 4-2. Object Priority Demo

```
SCREEN 1,320,200,3,1◄
WINDOW 2,"Object Priority Demo",(0,0)-(311,185),20,1◄
PALETTE 0,0,.45,0:PALETTE 1,.9,.9,.9◄
PALETTE 2,0,0,0:PALETTE 3,.9,.48,.15◄
ON BREAK GOSUB Quit:BREAK ON◄
DIM alien$(114):RESTORE AlienShapeData◄
FOR n=1 TO 114◄
  READ a:alien$=alien$+CHR$(a)◄
NEXT n◄
OBJECT.SHAPE 1,alien$◄
OBJECT.SHAPE 2,1:OBJECT.SHAPE 3,1◄
OBJECT.SHAPE 4,1:OBJECT.SHAPE 5,1◄
OBJECT.PLANES 2,5:OBJECT.PLANES 3,6◄
OBJECT.PLANES 4,7:OBJECT.PLANES 5,6,1◄
OBJECT.PRIORITY 1,3:OBJECT.PRIORITY 2,1◄
OBJECT.PRIORITY 3,2:OBJECT.PRIORITY 4,3◄
OBJECT.PRIORITY 5,4 'Highest priority.◄
FOR n=2 TO 5◄
OBJECT.X n,n*50-40:OBJECT.Y n,n*12+20◄
NEXT n◄
OBJECT.ON:LOCATE 18,5◄
PRINT "<<Click mouse to exit>>"◄
WHILE MOUSE(0)=0◄
  OBJECT.X 1,MOUSE(1)-12:OBJECT.Y 1,MOUSE(2)-12◄
WEND◄
WHILE MOUSE(0)<>0:WEND◄
Quit:◄
  OBJECT.CLOSE:WINDOW CLOSE 2:SCREEN CLOSE 1:END◄
AlienShapeData:◄
DATA   0,   0,   0,   0,   0,   0,   0,   0◄
```

```
DATA    0,   0,   0,   2,   0,   0,   0,  26
DATA    0,   0,   0,  11,   0,  24,   0,   3
DATA    0,   0,   0,127,128,   0,   1,255
DATA  224,   0,   7,255,248,   0,  31,255
DATA  254,   0,248,225,199,192,248,225
DATA  199,192,255,255,255,192,  12,127
DATA  140,   0,  12,127,140,   0,252,   0
DATA   15,192,252,   0,  15,192,   0,   0
DATA    0,   0,   0,   0,   0,   0,   0,   0
DATA    0,   0,   0,   0,   0,   0,   7,  30
DATA   56,   0,   7,  30,  56,   0,   0,   0
DATA    0,   0,   0,127,128,   0,   0,127
DATA  128,   0,   0,   0,   0,   0,   0,   0
DATA    0,   0
```

Collision Detection

Most programs that animate objects on the screen also need to check for and respond to collisions between the objects. Whether your objects are alien invaders and missiles or cursors and icons, it's useful to know when two of them have overlapped so that you can destroy the alien or select the icon. You can do it the hard way—keep track of each object's screen coordinates and respond when two of them enter each other's predefined zones. Or you can depend on the computer's built-in collision-detection system, if it has one. Collision detection is a common feature on personal computers with sprite graphics, such as the Commodore 64 and 128, Atari 400/800/XL/XE, and TI-99/4A.

The Amiga, too, has built-in collision detection as a hardware feature. However, as versions 1.0 and 1.1 of the *Amiga ROM Kernel Manual* point out, this feature is not currently implemented. Instead, collision detection is handled in software by the Amiga's operating system. Whether a future version of the Amiga or its operating system will implement the true collision detection is a matter of conjecture. At this point, the software substitute is what we have to work with.

Unfortunately, the ersatz collision detection suffers from some serious problems. It does work, but just barely. There's a proverb which holds that it's better to light a candle than to curse the darkness, so we'll show you some ways to program around these problems. But if you're offended by inelegant programming, you might prefer to avert your eyes and handle collision detection the hard way—or wait for the inevitable revision. Looking at the bright side, collision detection is usually a feature that's left out of high-level languages and supported only at the system level, so perhaps we should be grateful for what we've got, even if it's imperfect.

Amiga BASIC's support for collision detection is fairly complete. It consists of the OBJECT.HIT statement, which lets you define which objects should be sensitive to collisions with other objects; COLLISION ON, COLLISION OFF, and COLLISION STOP, event-trapping statements that automatically watch for collisions and let you turn the trapping on or off; and the COLLI-

SION( ) function, which returns values that allow you to determine what type of collision has occurred. The only major omission is that there's no way to detect collisions between objects and other graphics images on the background screen.

We'll tackle these statements one by one, then show how they can be used in a simple arcade-style game.

More Bit Masks

After you've created your objects with OBJECT.SHAPE, chosen their colors with OBJECT.PLANES, and established their priorities with OBJECT.PRIORITY, the next step is to set up their collision definitions with OBJECT.HIT. This is the general format:

OBJECT.HIT *object-ID,me-mask,hit-mask*

Object-ID is the familiar object ID number, *me-mask* is a 16-bit binary mask that describes the collision class to which the object belongs, and *hit-mask* is another 16-bit binary mask that defines what other classes of objects this particular object should collide with.

Here we go with those bit masks again. If you thought OBJECT.PLANES was a headache, you'll probably regard OBJECT.HIT with equal enthusiasm. Fortunately, as before, we've come up with a solution. But first, let's attempt an explanation for those who are comfortable with binary arithmetic.

When two objects make contact on the screen, Amiga BASIC compares their me-masks and hit-masks. BASIC takes the me-mask of the leftmost or uppermost object, logically ANDs it with the hit-mask of the rightmost or lowermost object, and examines the result. If the result is nonzero, a collision is triggered. BASIC then reports that the first object has been hit by the second object. But if the result of the logical AND is zero, no collision is triggered. The two objects pass through each other as if they weren't there.

In order for a logical AND to yield a nonzero result, the same bit must be set in the first object's me-mask and the second object's hit-mask. Therefore, your job is to assign values for these masks that evaluate to the desired results for all possible collisions you want to detect. Simple, isn't it?

Class Warfare

In practice, it's not quite as difficult as it sounds. The first step is to decide how many different *collision classes* of objects your program needs. Note that we said *classes* of objects, not *numbers* of objects. Your program might have 50 objects, but only two classes. Or it might have 12 objects and 12 classes. It all depends on what you want.

For instance, let's say you're writing an *Asteroids*-type game. You need an object for the player-controlled spaceship, another object for the missile that can be fired by the spaceship, and numerous other objects for the asteroids that drift around and threaten to crush the spaceship. Suppose that adds up to a total of ten objects (the spaceship, the missile, and eight asteroids).

According to the rules you've designed for the game, the spaceship can fire a missile at an asteroid to destroy it. Therefore, you need to check for missile/asteroid collisions. The asteroids can crush the ship on contact, so you need to check for asteroid/ship collisions. You don't need to check for collisions between the missile and the ship, because the ship can't fire missiles at itself. Nor are you interested in collisions between asteroids; you'll just let them pass through each other.

If an asteroid hits a screen border, you want it to bounce off. Therefore, you need to check for asteroid/border collisions. If the ship hits the border, it's supposed to bounce off, too, so you need to check for ship/border collisions. And finally, if the missile hits the border, you don't care—it can just fly off. So you don't need to check for missile/border collisions.

What all this boils down to is three collision classes of objects. In other words, there are three *unique types of objects* that can collide with each other in some combination of ways: the spaceship, the missile, and the asteroids. It doesn't matter if you have more or fewer asteroids, or more missiles. As long as you've set up the rules this way, there are only three basic classes.

Once this has been determined, the next step is to assign each class of object its own, unique me-mask. You do this by specifying a number that works out to a binary value representing one *on* bit in the me-mask. Because the least-significant bit is reserved for border collisions, me-mask numbers always fall into the pattern 2, 4, 8, 16, 32, 64, 128, and so on. The order in which you assign these numbers to objects doesn't really matter as long as it's consistent within that program. For this example, let's assign the spaceship a me-mask of 2, the missile a me-mask of 4, and the asteroids a me-mask of 8. If this game had a fourth class of object, you'd assign it a me-mask of 16. The fifth class would get a me-mask of 32, and so on.

Bit by Bit

Now for the hit-masks. For any two classes of objects that are supposed to collide, you have to assign values for the hit-masks that have *on* bits in the same bit positions as the *on* bits in the objects' me-masks.

Table 4-1 may make this explanation a little easier to understand. (For clarity, only 8-bit masks are shown, since we don't have enough classes of objects to require 16-bit masks anyway.)

Table 4-1. Me-Masks and Hit-Masks

	Me-Masks									
Bit Values =	128	64	32	16	8	4	2	1		
Spaceship	0	0	0	0	0	0	1	0	=	2
Missile	0	0	0	0	0	1	0	0	=	4
Asteroids	0	0	0	0	1	0	0	0	=	8
	Hit-Masks									
Bit Values =	128	64	32	16	8	4	2	1		
Spaceship	0	0	0	0	1	0	0	1	=	9
Missile	0	0	0	0	1	0	0	0	=	8
Asteroids	0	0	0	0	0	1	1	1	=	7

Therefore, if we use OBJECT.SHAPE to define the spaceship as object-ID 1, the missile as object 2, and the asteroids as objects 3 through 10, the proper OBJECT.HIT statements would be

OBJECT.HIT 1,2,9
OBJECT.HIT 2,4,8
OBJECT.HIT 3,8,7
OBJECT.HIT 4,8,7
OBJECT.HIT 5,8,7
OBJECT.HIT 6,8,7
OBJECT.HIT 7,8,7
OBJECT.HIT 8,8,7
OBJECT.HIT 9,8,7
OBJECT.HIT 10,8,7

Here's how we arrived at these numbers. We know that each class of object gets its own unique me-mask; we assigned 2, 4, and 8 for this purpose. The hit-masks are computed by adding up the bit values for the *on* bits which match the *on* bits in a colliding object's me-mask. For example, we wish to detect collisions between the spaceship and an asteroid, and between the spaceship and the border. Referring to Table 4-1, you can see that the spaceship's hit-mask should therefore be 9. This is the sum of 8+1—8 is the value of the asteroid's me-mask, and 1 signifies border collisions. All other bits are *off*—set to zero.

In the case of the missile, which is supposed to collide only with the asteroids and not with the ship or the screen borders, the hit-mask is 8. This bit corresponds to the 8 in the asteroid's me-mask, and all other bits are set to zero.

The asteroids' hit-masks are each set to 7, the sum of 4+2+1. The four bit corresponds to the missile's me-mask, the two bit matches the spaceship's me-mask, and the one bit signifies border collisions.

From all this we can deduce several conclusions:

- Me-masks are always even numbers that start at 2 and double for each collision class of objects.
- Hit-masks are always even numbers for objects that aren't supposed to collide with the border, and odd numbers for those that are.
- Since me-masks are 16-bit masks, and since the least-significant bit is reserved for border collisions, you can define a maximum of 15 collision classes. If border collisions are counted, the system can handle up to 16 different types of collisions.

The MaskMaker Solution

Still with us? If you've followed everything so far, you'll be overjoyed to learn that there's just one small, additional detail which gums up the whole works. Thanks to a complication in binary arithmetic called *two's complement binary*, a fully utilized 16-bit mask actually shows up in decimal as a *negative* number.

Rather than get involved in another long explanation, we've come up with a better solution—"MaskMaker," a short utility program that automatically calculates me-masks and hit-masks for you. You don't have to know anything about binary to use it. MaskMaker is listed as Program 4-6 at the end of this chapter.

MaskMaker is simplicity itself. When you run the program, it asks you how many different collision classes of objects are in your program; then it asks you to enter a brief descriptive name for each class (Ship, Missile, Asteroids, and so on.)

Next, MaskMaker starts going through the list of classes, asking you one by one whether each class should collide with the screen borders. Then it asks whether certain classes should collide with certain other classes. It covers every possible combination of collisions for the number of classes you've specified. That includes mutual collision combinations: ship/asteroids, asteroids/ship, missile/asteroids, asteroids/missile, and so forth.

When MaskMaker has finished asking these questions—and there'll be a lot of them if you have lots of classes of objects—it displays sample OBJECT.HIT statements on the screen with the calculated me-masks and hit-masks. Jot the numbers down and plug them into your own program. (You can pause a long listing with the right mouse button.)

MaskMaker takes the binary drudgery out of calculating me-masks and hit-masks, and even handles two's complement binary if you define enough classes of objects to require the whole 16 bits.

Collision Trapping

Once you've set up collision masks with OBJECT.HIT, you can activate collision trapping with the ON COLLISION statement.

ON COLLISION works pretty much like the other event-trapping statements in Amiga BASIC: ON MOUSE, ON MENU, ON BREAK, and so on. It's capable of trapping object-to-object and object-to-border collisions, but not collisions between objects and other images on the background screen. You activate collision trapping like this:

ON COLLISION GOSUB *LineLabel*
COLLISION ON

where *LineLabel* is a line number or Amiga BASIC line label.

Like the other event-trapping statements, this sets up an automatic BASIC interrupt. Between the execution of each statement in your program, Amiga BASIC checks to see whether any object collisions are occurring. If it detects one, it checks to see whether the collision fits any of the definitions in your OBJECT.HIT statements. If so, it records the collision and immediately jumps to the line specified by ON COLLISION GOSUB. It also executes an OBJECT.STOP for both objects involved in the collision, effectively freezing them in place.

At this point, it's up to you to handle the collision with a subroutine. The first step is to check which object triggered the collision, then what type of collision occurred (object-to-object or object-to-border). This information is stored in a place called the *collision queue*, and you can read the queue with the COLLISION( ) function. There are three ways to use this function:

COLLISION(-1)	Reads the queue and removes the most recent number stored there. The number returned indicates the ID number of the window in which the collision happened: 1 for WINDOW 1, 2 for WINDOW 2, etc.
COLLISION(0)	Reads the queue without removing any information from the queue. The number it returns tells you which object triggered the collision. In object-to-object collisions, the object which triggers the collision is the leftmost or uppermost object. In object-to-border collisions, the number returned is the object-ID of the object.
COLLISION(*object-ID*)	*Object-ID* is a positive number representing the object-ID returned by COLLISION(0). This function reads the queue and removes the most recent number stored there. In object-to-object collisions, this number indicates the object-ID of the second object. In border collisions, this number indicates which screen border the object has collided with (-1 for the top border, -2 for the left border, -3 for the bottom border, and -4 for the right border).

Interpreting Collisions

If your program has objects moving in more than one window, you'll probably need to call COLLISION(−1) first. But usually, you'll be interested only in figuring out which object was involved in the collision, and whether it hit another object or a screen border. Here's how your subroutine might start:

Collide:
  objectID=COLLISION(0)
  collisionID=COLLISION(objectID)

The first statement tells us which object triggered the collision. Let's say it's object 1. The next statement would then reveal the type of collision. In the case of an object-to-object collision, the variable *collisionID* would return the object-ID of the second object. Otherwise, it's a negative number indicating a border collision.

Now your routine can handle the collision—blow up the asteroid, bounce the ball off the border, or whatever. Before RETURNing, a housekeeping chore may need to be performed. Since ON COLLISION automatically executes an OBJECT.STOP on the object(s) which collided, you may need to restart the objects with OBJECT.START.

You can deactivate collision trapping at any time with COLLISION OFF. All subsequent collisions are ignored until the next COLLISION ON. Another option is COLLISION STOP. Collisions are still recorded in the collision queue, but ON COLLISION GOSUB won't execute until the next COLLISION ON. At that point, you can call the COLLISION( ) function to return the most recent collision recorded in the queue.

This brings up an important point: The collision queue is not a bottomless vessel. It remembers only 16 collisions. Nor is it a stack; after the sixteenth collision is recorded, the queue ignores all subsequent collisions. This can become a problem in programs that have lots of moving objects generating lots of collisions. They can pile up in the collision queue faster than your BASIC program can possibly handle them. When the queue overflows, your program stumbles onward, often with bizarre results. Typically, objects start flying off the screen, since border collisions are among those being ignored. And once objects start escaping the screen, things can get really strange. Sometimes, apparently, the objects' images wander through memory. You'll know they've hit a sensitive area when the computer crashes.

One solution to this problem is to include a COLLISION OFF at the beginning of your collision-handling routine. This keeps new collisions from piling up while your program is still struggling to cope with the current one. However, it also means that your program will be blind to collisions which happen while your routine is executing. If you run into these kinds of problems, perhaps the best solution is to redesign your program to reduce the number of possible collisions.

Program 4-3 demonstrates collision handling. It creates five objects and lets you move one of them around the screen with the mouse. Collision values are displayed in the upper left corner of the screen. Experiment with different types of mutual collisions by moving the object onto the other objects from the top and the bottom. You'll see how a collision between object 1 and object 2, for instance, is sometimes reported as a collision between object 2 and object 1. The leftmost or uppermost object is the one which triggers the collision as reported by COLLISION(0). In your own programs, you'll often have to check for both possibilities to see if two particular objects have bumped into each other.

Program 4-3. Object Collision Demo

```
SCREEN 1,320,200,3,1◄
WINDOW 2,"Object Collision Demo",(0,0)-(311,185),20,1◄
WIDTH 40◄
PALETTE 0,0,.45,0:PALETTE 1,.9,.9,.9◄
PALETTE 2,0,0,0:PALETTE 3,.9,.48,.15◄
ON BREAK GOSUB Quit:BREAK ON◄
ON COLLISION GOSUB Collide:COLLISION ON◄
DIM alien$(114):RESTORE AlienShapeData◄
FOR n=1 TO 114◄
  READ a:alien$=alien$+CHR$(a)◄
NEXT n◄
OBJECT.SHAPE 1,alien$◄
OBJECT.SHAPE 2,1:OBJECT.SHAPE 3,1◄
OBJECT.SHAPE 4,1:OBJECT.SHAPE 5,1◄
OBJECT.PLANES 2,5:OBJECT.PLANES 3,6◄
OBJECT.PLANES 4,7:OBJECT.PLANES 5,6,1◄
OBJECT.HIT 1,2,5 'Collide with other aliens and borders.◄
OBJECT.HIT 2,4,2 'Other aliens collide with moving alien...◄
OBJECT.HIT 3,4,2◄
OBJECT.HIT 4,4,2◄
OBJECT.HIT 5,4,2◄
FOR n=2 TO 5◄
  OBJECT.X n,n*50-40:OBJECT.Y n,n*12+20◄
NEXT n◄
OBJECT.ON 1,2,3,4,5:OBJECT.START:LOCATE 19,5◄
PRINT "<<Click mouse to exit>>"◄
◄
WHILE MOUSE(0)=0 'Main loop.◄
  OBJECT.X 1,MOUSE(1)-12:OBJECT.Y 1,MOUSE(2)-11◄
WEND◄
WHILE MOUSE(0)<>0:WEND◄
◄
Quit:◄
  OBJECT.CLOSE:WINDOW CLOSE 2:SCREEN CLOSE 1:END◄
◄
Collide:◄
  objectID=COLLISION(0)◄
  collisionID=COLLISION(objectID)◄
  LOCATE 1,1:PRINT SPACE$(20):PRINT SPACE$(20)◄
  LOCATE 1,1:PRINT "Object #";objectID;"hit"◄
  IF collisionID=-1 THEN PRINT "top border."◄
  IF collisionID=-2 THEN PRINT "left border."◄
```

```
IF collisionID=-3 THEN PRINT "bottom border."◄
IF collisionID=-4 THEN PRINT "right border."◄
IF collisionID>-1 THEN PRINT "object #";collisionID◄
OBJECT.START:COLLISION ON◄
RETURN◄
◄
AlienShapeData:◄
DATA    0,   0,   0,   0,   0,   0,   0,   0◄
DATA    0,   0,   0,   2,   0,   0,   0,  26◄
DATA    0,   0,   0,  11,   0,  24,   0,   3◄
DATA    0,   0,   0,127,128,   0,   1,255◄
DATA  224,   0,   7,255,248,   0,  31,255◄
DATA  254,   0,248,225,199,192,248,225◄
DATA  199,192,255,255,255,192,  12,127◄
DATA  140,   0,  12,127,140,   0,252,   0◄
DATA   15,192,252,   0,  15,192,   0,   0◄
DATA    0,   0,   0,   0,   0,   0,   0,   0◄
DATA    0,   0,   0,   0,   0,   0,   7,  30◄
DATA   56,   0,   7,  30,  56,   0,   0,   0◄
DATA    0,   0,   0,127,128,   0,   0,127◄
DATA  128,   0,   0,   0,   0,   0,   0,   0◄
DATA    0,   0◄
```

Collision-Trapping Problems

While Program 4-3 demonstrates how Amiga BASIC's collision trapping works, it also reveals how it doesn't work. You'll notice two flaws: (1) BASIC responds rather sluggishly, not reporting collisions until the two objects are overlapping quite a bit, and (2) the same type of collision isn't detected twice in a row. In other words, if object 1 and object 2 collide, the system ignores any subsequent collisions between those two objects until another type of collision occurs. Likewise, if object 1 collides with a screen border, all following collisions with that same border are ignored until object 1 hits a different border or another object.

It's the second flaw that can present great difficulties, especially in games. If your spaceship shoots an asteroid with a missile, it can't hit the same asteroid with the same missile until it shoots a different asteroid in the meantime.

Is this a bug in BASIC? Maybe, but maybe not. It could be a deliberate attempt to protect your BASIC program from getting bogged down in multiple collisions that can't be handled fast enough. Suppose, for example, you've got several asteroids drifting around the screen and you want the rocks to bounce off each other if they meet. When two of them collide, your collision routine starts moving them in opposite directions. But when your routine ends, the asteroids are still slightly overlapped. Before they can disengage, what would happen if BASIC reported another collision? Your routine would kick in a second time, once more reversing the asteroids' directions. Now they're moving toward each other again, triggering yet another identical collision. The process would repeat endlessly, and the asteroids would seem glued together on the screen.

Apparently, to resolve this dilemma, BASIC simply doesn't report the additional collisions until a different type of collision happens in the meantime. This solves the problem of the glued-together asteroids, but makes it impossible for the spaceship to defend itself by shooting the same asteroid twice in a row.

After wrestling with this paradox in our own programs, we've come up with a partial answer that we call the *clone kludge*. (In programmer's parlance, a kludge—pronounced *klooj*—is an inelegant solution to a problem.) The clone kludge may not be pretty, but it's practical. To demonstrate how it can circumvent a typical collision-trapping problem, we've written a simple (very simple) arcade-style game. It's Program 4-7, "BattleStation," at the end of this chapter.

The Clone Switcheroo

Here's how BattleStation works. In the center of the screen is an immobile space station, your home base. It's under constant attack on four sides by alien spaceships. You've got a laser cannon you can fire at the aliens, but it's not powerful enough to destroy them—it only bumps them backward a short distance. And each time you shoot an alien ship, it comes at you faster the next time. Your only hope is to hold them off for as long as possible.

To play, plug a joystick into port 2 (not the mouse port) and run the program. The game starts when the aliens begin moving. To fire the laser cannon, simply move and release the joystick handle in the appropriate direction—it's not necessary to press the fire button. When you hit an alien—and you can't really miss—the alien jumps back to its starting position and begins moving faster. Eventually, the aliens will close in on you and blow up your space station on contact. Your final score is computed by adding up ten points for each alien you've hit plus the number of seconds that elapsed since the game started. Press the joystick button to begin another game.

"BattleStation" is a simple arcade-style game that demonstrates numerous OBJECT commands and collision-trapping techniques.

114

BattleStation isn't very sophisticated, but its main purpose is to demonstrate a typical example of collision trapping as well as the clone kludge. You'll notice that it's possible to shoot the same alien twice in a row with the laser cannon, and each time the alien registers a hit. How does this work?

The answer is that the bullet fired by the laser cannon has a clone. Although you're only aware that the game has six objects—the four aliens, the space station, and the laser bullet—there are actually two objects defined as laser bullets. The original bullet is set up as object 6. With the statement OBJECT.SHAPE 7,6 we make a copy of the bullet as object 7. Each time the bullet is fired, a flag is set to indicate that the next shot should use the other twin. So the first shot fires object 6, the second shot fires object 7, the third shot fires object 6, the fourth shot fires object 7, and so on.

The variable *clone* is the flag that determines which object is the current bullet. To flip this flag back and forth, the collision-handling routine (labeled Collide:) contains this line:

IF clone=6 THEN clone=7 ELSE clone=6

You can also study this listing for further examples of OBJECT.SHAPE, OBJECT.PLANES, and OBJECT.HIT. All of the shapes were created with the Object Editor and then converted to DATA statements with the Object Datamaker described earlier. The plane-pick and plane-on-off masks for OBJECT.PLANES were arrived at after experimenting with the PlanePick utility. And the me-masks and hit-masks for the OBJECT.HIT statements were generated with the MaskMaker.

Liberating Memory

Only two more OBJECT commands remain to be covered; one of them is OBJECT.CLOSE.

OBJECT.CLOSE frees up the memory reserved by OBJECT.SHAPE after the object is no longer needed. The logical place for this command is within a routine that lets the user quit your program to BASIC or the Workbench/CLI. If you don't liberate the memory with OBJECT.CLOSE, it remains reserved, apparently even when you exit BASIC.

The format for OBJECT.CLOSE is simple, with *object-ID* the usual object ID number:

OBJECT.CLOSE *object-ID, ...*

You can specify any number of object-IDs to close any number of objects (such as OBJECT.CLOSE 1,2,3,4). Or you can simply execute OBJECT.CLOSE with no object-IDs to close all objects.

Don't confuse OBJECT.CLOSE with OBJECT.OFF. The latter command merely erases the object from the screen while preserving it in memory for a subsequent OBJECT.ON. (However, we've noticed that sometimes an

OBJECT.OFF followed by no object-IDs also deactivates the objects in some way, causing errors or crashes if you attempt an OBJECT.ON. Avoid turning off all objects with OBJECT.OFF.)

The final OBJECT command in Amiga BASIC is OBJECT.CLIP. It's supposed to let you define rectangular zones within a screen window and keep objects from appearing anywhere outside this zone. The format is

OBJECT.CLIP *(x1,y1)–(x2,y2)*

where *(x1,y1)* specify the upper left corner of the rectangle, and *(x2,y2)* specify the lower right corner (just like the LINES statement).

Unfortunately, OBJECT.CLIP doesn't seem to be implemented in Amiga BASIC 1.0. It doesn't cause an error if you use it—but it doesn't do anything, either. Nevertheless, in case it is implemented in a future revision of Amiga BASIC, we've written a short program that demonstrates its use. "OBJECT.CLIP Demo" is listed at the end of this chapter as Program 4-8.

Program 4-4. Object Datamaker

```
' *** OBJECT DATAMAKER ***◄
◄
 WINDOW 1,"Object Datamaker",(0,100)-(400,180),22◄
 WIDTH 38◄
◄
 OpenData:◄
  'Read object data from disk...◄
  CLS:PRINT◄
  PRINT "Enter filename of BOB or SPRITE:"◄
  LINE INPUT ">> ",filename$◄
  ON ERROR GOTO ErrorTrap◄
  OPEN filename$ FOR INPUT AS 1◄
  object$=INPUT$(LOF(1),1)◄
  CLOSE 1◄
  ON ERROR GOTO 0◄
◄
 MakeData:◄
  'Create new disk file of shape data.◄
  CLS:PRINT◄
  PRINT "Enter output filename for shape data:"◄
  LINE INPUT ">> ",filename2$◄
  IF filename2$=filename$ THEN◄
   msg1$="Output filename=input name..."◄
   msg2$="Replace existing object file?"◄
   CALL Requester (msg1$,msg2$,"REPLACE","CANCEL",2,answer%)◄
   IF answer%=0 GOTO MakeData◄
  END IF◄
  ON ERROR GOTO ErrorTrap◄
  OPEN filename2$ FOR OUTPUT AS 1◄
  PRINT:PRINT "Creating ";filename2$;"..."◄
  datalines=INT(LEN(object$)/8) 'DATA lines to make.◄
  remainder=LEN(object$)-datalines*8 'Final DATA line.◄
  PRINT# 1,"' ";filename2$;" --";LEN(object$);"bytes."◄
  FOR n=1 TO datalines*8 STEP 8◄
```

```
   PRINT# 1,"DATA ";
   FOR nn=0 TO 7
    PRINT#1,USING"###";ASC(MID$(object$,nn+n,1));
    IF nn<7 THEN PRINT#1,","; ELSE PRINT#1,""
   NEXT nn
  NEXT n
  PRINT# 1,"DATA ";
  FOR n=1 TO remainder
   PRINT#1,USING"###";ASC(MID$(object$,(LEN(object$)-remainder)+1,1
   ));
   IF n<remainder THEN PRINT#1,","; ELSE PRINT#1,""
  NEXT n
  CLOSE 1
  temp&=TIMER 'Wait for drive to finish...
  WHILE TIMER<temp&+6:WEND 'Wait 6 seconds.
  PRINT:PRINT "FINIS."
  ON ERROR GOTO 0

  'Allow chance to repeat process:
  msg1$="Create another data file"
  msg2$="or quit to BASIC?"
  CALL Requester (msg1$,msg2$,"REPEAT","QUIT",0,answer%)
  IF answer%=1 GOTO OpenData
  WINDOW 1,"Basic",(0,0)-(617,185),31:END

SUB Requester (msg1$,msg2$,b1$,b2$,hilite%,answer%) STATIC
  'Requester window subprogram
  SHARED scrid 'Global variable for SCREEN ID.
  IF scrid<1 OR scrid>4 THEN scrid=-1 'Default to Workbench.
  WINDOW 3,"Program Request",(0,0)-(311,45),16,scrid
  maxwidth=INT(WINDOW(2)/8) 'Truncate prompts if too long...
  PRINT LEFT$(msg1$,maxwidth):PRINT LEFT$(msg2$,maxwidth)
  b1$=LEFT$(b1$,12):b2$=LEFT$(b2$,12) 'Truncate buttons.
  bsize1=(LEN(b1$)+2)*10:bsize2=(LEN(b2$)+2)*10 'Button size.
  x1=(312-(bsize1+bsize2))/3  'Calculate button positions...
  x2=x1+bsize1:x3=x1+x2:x4=x3+bsize2
  'Draw buttons:
  LINE (x1,20)-(x2,38),2,b:LINE (x3,20)-(x4,38),2,b
  IF hilite%=1 THEN LINE (x1+2,22)-(x2-2,36),3,b
  IF hilite%=2 THEN LINE (x3+2,22)-(x4-2,36),3,b
  LOCATE 4,1:PRINT PTAB(x1+10);b1$;
  PRINT PTAB(x3+10);b2$
  reqloop: 'Loop which acts on mouse clicks...
  WHILE MOUSE(0)=0:WEND:m1=MOUSE(1):m2=MOUSE(2)
  IF m1>x1 AND m1<x2 AND m2>20 AND m2<38 THEN
   answer%=1 'Left button was selected.
   LINE (x1,20)-(x2,38),1,bf 'Flash left button.
  ELSEIF m1>x3 AND m1<x4 AND m2>20 AND m2<38 THEN
   answer%=0 'Right button was selected.
   LINE (x3,20)-(x4,38),1,bf 'Flash right button.
  ELSE
   GOTO reqloop 'Neither button selected; repeat loop.
  END IF
  WHILE MOUSE(0)<>0:WEND:WINDOW CLOSE 3
END SUB

  ErrorTrap:
```

```
' Version 1.5.
' Traps common errors, mostly disk.
' Requires Requester window subprogram.
BEEP ' Get user's attention.
IF ERR=53 THEN
 request1$="FILE NOT FOUND."
 GOTO ExitError
END IF
IF ERR=61 THEN
 request1$="DISK FULL."
 GOTO ExitError
END IF
IF ERR=64 THEN
 request1$="BAD FILENAME."
 GOTO ExitError
END IF
IF ERR=67 THEN
 request1$="DIRECTORY FULL."
 GOTO ExitError
END IF
IF ERR=68 THEN
 request1$="DEVICE UNAVAILABLE."
 GOTO ExitError
END IF
IF ERR=70 THEN
 request1$="DISK WRITE-PROTECTED."
 GOTO ExitError
END IF
IF ERR=74 THEN
 request1$="UNKNOWN DISK VOLUME."
 GOTO ExitError
END IF
request1$="ERROR NUMBER"+STR$(ERR)
ExitError:
' Abort operation or try again.
CALL Requester (request1$,"","Retry","CANCEL",2,answer%)
IF answer%=0 THEN
 CLOSE 1
 RESUME OpenData
ELSE
 CLOSE 1
 ON ERROR GOTO ErrorTrap
 RESUME
END IF
```

Program 4-5. PlanePick

```
' *** PlanePick & PlaneOnOff Utility ***
' For designing colors of bobs.

 Initialize:
  CLS:WIDTH 80:LOCATE 2,1
  INPUT "Preferences set for 60 or 80";prefs
  IF prefs<>60 AND prefs<>80 THEN Initialize
  IF prefs=80 THEN pos1=12:pos2=19:ELSE pos1=11:pos2=17
```

```
      CLS:SCREEN 1,320,200,5,1:maxcolors=32:WIDTH prefs/2◄
      scrn=1:CALL PanelSetup(scrn)◄
      DIM status(5):FOR n=1 TO 5:status(n)=1:NEXT:status(5)=2◄
      GOSUB NewScreen:GOSUB OpenBob◄
      ON MENU GOSUB MenuHandler:MENU ON◄
      ON BREAK GOSUB Quit:BREAK ON◄
    GOTO MainLoop◄
      ◄
    NewScreen:◄
      WINDOW 2,"PlanePick",(0,0)-(311,185),20,1◄
      MENU 1,0,1,"Project"◄
      MENU 1,1,1,"Open Bob          "◄
      MENU 1,2,1,"Change Palette    "◄
      MENU 1,3,status(1),"   SCREEN Depth 1"◄
      MENU 1,4,status(2),"   SCREEN Depth 2"◄
      MENU 1,5,status(3),"   SCREEN Depth 3"◄
      MENU 1,6,status(4),"   SCREEN Depth 4"◄
      MENU 1,7,status(5),"   SCREEN Depth 5"◄
      MENU 1,8,1,"Quit to BASIC     "◄
      MENU 2,0,0,"":MENU 3,0,0,"":MENU 4,0,0,""◄
    RETURN◄
      ◄
    DrawButtons:◄
      x1=2:y1=100:x2=9:y2=120◄
      FOR n=1 TO 2◄
       FOR nn=0 TO maxcolors-1◄
         LINE (x1,y1)-(x2,y2),1,b◄
         x1=x2+2:x2=x2+9◄
       NEXT nn◄
      x1=2:y1=160:xlimit=x2-9:x2=9:y2=180◄
      NEXT n◄
    RETURN◄
      ◄
    MainLoop:◄
    LOCATE pos1,1:PRINT "PlanePick =";PlanePick◄
    LINE ((PlanePick)*9+3,101)-((PlanePick)*9+8,119),1,bf◄
    LOCATE pos2,1:PRINT "PlaneOnOff =";PlaneOnOff◄
    LINE ((PlaneOnOff)*9+3,161)-((PlaneOnOff)*9+8,179),1,bf◄
    WHILE MOUSE(0)=0:WEND 'Wait here for mouse press.◄
     mx=MOUSE(1):my=MOUSE(2)◄
     IF my>100 AND my<120 AND mx>2 AND mx<xlimit THEN◄
       LINE ((PlanePick)*9+3,101)-((PlanePick)*9+8,119),,0,bf◄
       PlanePick=INT((mx-2)/9) 'Get new PlanePick value.◄
     ELSEIF my>160 AND my<180 AND mx>2 AND mx<xlimit THEN◄
       LINE ((PlaneOnOff)*9+3,161)-((PlaneOnOff)*9+8,179),,0,bf◄
       PlaneOnOff=INT((mx-2)/9) 'Get new PlaneOnOff value.◄
     END IF◄
    WHILE MOUSE(0)<>0:WEND 'Wait here for mouse release.◄
    OBJECT.PLANES 1,PlanePick,PlaneOnOff◄
    GOTO MainLoop◄
    ◄
    MenuHandler:◄
     MENU 1,0,0:item=MENU(1)◄
     IF item=1 THEN OBJECT.CLOSE 1:GOSUB OpenBob◄
     IF item=2 THEN CALL PalettePanel(scrn,prefs)◄
     IF item>2 AND item<8 THEN GOSUB ChangeSCREEN◄
     IF item=8 THEN Quit◄
```

```
MENU 1,0,1:MENU ON:GOTO MainLoop◀
 ◀
OpenBob:◀
 'Loads bob file created with Object Editor.◀
 CLS:WIDTH prefs/2◀
 PRINT "Enter filename of bob to load:"◀
 LINE INPUT ">> ";filename$◀
 IF filename$="" THEN OpenBob◀
 OPEN filename$ FOR INPUT AS #1◀
 bob$=INPUT$(LOF(1),1)◀
 CLOSE #1◀
 CLS:GOSUB DrawButtons:GOSUB MakeShape◀
RETURN◀
 ◀
ChangeSCREEN:◀
'Changes SCREEN mode (depth of bit-planes).◀
 OBJECT.CLOSE:WINDOW CLOSE 2:SCREEN CLOSE 1◀
 SCREEN 1,320,200,item-2,1:maxcolors=2^(item-2)◀
 FOR n=1 TO 5:status(n)=1:status(item-2)=2:NEXT◀
 GOSUB NewScreen◀
 FOR n=0 TO WINDOW(6) 'Restore previous PALETTE values...◀
   PALETTE n,hue(n,0),hue(n,1),hue(n,2)◀
 NEXT n◀
 GOSUB MakeShape:GOSUB DrawButtons◀
 RETURN◀
◀
Quit:◀
 'It's polite to clean up after ourselves...◀
 OBJECT.CLOSE:WINDOW CLOSE 2◀
 SCREEN CLOSE 1:CLS:END◀
◀
MakeShape:◀
 OBJECT.SHAPE 1,bob$◀
 PlanePick=1:PlaneOnOff=0◀
 OBJECT.PLANES 1,PlanePick,PlaneOnOff◀
 OBJECT.X 1,140:OBJECT.Y 1,10:OBJECT.ON◀
RETURN◀
◀
SUB PanelSetup (screenwindow) STATIC◀
'See "Designing A User Interface" chapter for info.◀
PanelSetup:◀
 IF screenwindow<1 OR screenwindow>4 THEN screenwindow=-1◀
 WINDOW 2,,,,screenwindow◀
 DIM SHARED hue(31,2) ' Holds current PALETTE values.◀
 DIM SHARED newhue(31,2) ' Holds new PALETTE values.◀
 'Define default colors here (you can insert your own values):◀
 hue(0,0)=0:hue(0,1)=.46:hue(0,2)=0 'Color 0◀
 hue(1,0)=.9:hue(1,1)=.9:hue(1,2)=.9 'Color 1◀
 hue(2,0)=0:hue(2,1)=0:hue(2,2)=0 'Color 2◀
 hue(3,0)=.91:hue(3,1)=.48:hue(3,2)=.15 'Color 3◀
 FOR n=4 TO 31 'We'll use random colors for the rest.◀
  FOR nn=0 TO 2◀
   hue(n,nn)=RND◀
  NEXT nn◀
 NEXT n◀
 FOR n=0 TO 31 'Copy current colors into temp array.◀
```

```
   newhue(n,0)=hue(n,0)◄
   newhue(n,1)=hue(n,1):newhue(n,2)=hue(n,2)◄
  NEXT n◄
  FOR n=0 TO WINDOW(6) ' Change PALETTE values.◄
   PALETTE n,hue(n,0),hue(n,1),hue(n,2)◄
  NEXT n◄
 WINDOW CLOSE 2◄
 EXIT SUB◄
 END SUB◄
       ◄
 SUB PalettePanel (screenwindow,preferences) STATIC◄
 'See "Designing A User Interface" chapter for info.◄
 PalettePanel:◄
  IF screenwindow<1 OR screenwindow>4 THEN screenwindow=-1◄
  WINDOW 3,"Palette Panel",(0,0)-(311,185),16,screenwindow◄
  WIDTH 80◄
  colr=0 'Current PALETTE color selected on panel.◄
  r=hue(colr,0) 'RED value for current color.◄
  g=hue(colr,1) 'GREEN value for current color.◄
  b=hue(colr,2) 'BLUE value for current color.◄
  mx=0:my=0 'Clear mouse coordinates.◄
  FOR n=0 TO 3 'Draw color panel...◄
   FOR nn=0 TO 7◄
    IF n*8+nn<WINDOW(6)+1 THEN 'Fill color box on panel:◄
     LINE (nn*39+1,n*20)-(nn*39+38,n*20+20),n*8+nn,bf◄
    END IF◄
    LINE (nn*39+1,n*20)-(nn*39+38,n*20+20),1,b 'Draw frame.◄
   NEXT nn◄
  NEXT n◄
  FOR n=100 TO 140 STEP 20 'Draw color controls...◄
   LINE (1,n)-(310,n+10),2,b◄
  NEXT n◄
  'Draw exit buttons:◄
  IF preferences=80 THEN y=22 ELSE y=20◄
  LOCATE y,5:PRINT "USE";:LOCATE y,y:PRINT "CANCEL";◄
  LINE (1,160)-(156,184),1,b:LINE (156,160)-(310,184),1,b◄
 SubMainLoop:◄
  IF my>160 THEN btn=INT(mx/153):GOTO ExitPanel◄
  IF mx>2 AND mx<309 AND my>100 THEN 'Clicked on a slider.◄
   IF my<110 THEN 'Clicked on RED slider.◄
    LINE (r*300+2,101)-(r*300+9,109),0,bf 'Erase RED slider.◄
    r=(mx-2)/307 'Calculate new position of RED slider.◄
    newhue(colr,0)=r 'New RED color value.◄
   ELSEIF my>120 AND my<130 THEN 'Clicked on GREEN slider.◄
    LINE (g*300+2,121)-(g*300+9,129),0,bf 'Erase GREEN slider.◄
    g=(mx-2)/307 'Calculate new position of GREEN slider.◄
    newhue(colr,1)=g 'New GREEN color value.◄
   ELSEIF my>140 AND my<150 THEN 'Clicked on BLUE slider.◄
    LINE (b*300+2,141)-(b*300+9,149),0,bf 'Erase BLUE slider.◄
    b=(mx-2)/307 'Calculate new position of BLUE slider.◄
    newhue(colr,2)=b 'New BLUE color value.◄
   END IF◄
  END IF◄
  IF mx>0 AND mx<311 AND my<80 THEN 'Clicked on color panel.◄
   LINE (r*300+2,101)-(r*300+9,109),0,bf 'Erase RED slider.◄
   LINE (g*300+2,121)-(g*300+9,129),0,bf 'Erase GREEN slider.◄
   LINE (b*300+2,141)-(b*300+9,149),0,bf 'Erase BLUE slider.◄
```

```
    colr=8*INT(my/20)+INT(mx/39) 'Calculate chosen color box.◄
    IF colr>WINDOW(6) THEN colr=0 'Color 0 if out of range.◄
    r=newhue(colr,0):g=newhue(colr,1):b=newhue(colr,2)◄
  END IF◄
  IF preferences=80 THEN y=12 ELSE y=11◄
  LOCATE y,1:PRINT USING "R=#.##";r◄
  LINE (r*300+2,101)-(r*300+9,109),1,bf ' RED slider.◄
  LOCATE y,9:PRINT USING "G=#.##";g◄
  LINE (g*300+2,121)-(g*300+9,129),1,bf ' GREEN slider.◄
  LOCATE y,17:PRINT USING "B=#.##";b◄
  LINE (b*300+2,141)-(b*300+9,149),1,bf ' BLUE slider.◄
  LOCATE y,24:PRINT USING "Color=##";colr◄
  PALETTE colr,r,g,b 'Set new PALETTE colors.◄
  newhue(colr,0)=r:newhue(colr,1)=g:newhue(colr,2)=b◄
  WHILE MOUSE(0)=0:WEND◄
mx=MOUSE(1):my=MOUSE(2)◄
GOTO SubMainLoop◄
ExitPanel:◄
  IF btn=0 THEN◄
    LINE (1,160)-(156,184),1,bf 'Flash USE button.◄
    FOR n=0 TO 31 'Copy new values to current hue array.◄
      hue(n,0)=newhue(n,0)◄
      hue(n,1)=newhue(n,1):hue(n,2)=newhue(n,2)◄
    NEXT n◄
  ELSE◄
    LINE (156,160)-(310,184),1,bf 'Flash CANCEL button.◄
    FOR n=0 TO WINDOW(6) 'Restore previous PALETTE values...◄
      PALETTE n,hue(n,0),hue(n,1),hue(n,2)◄
    NEXT n◄
  END IF◄
  WHILE MOUSE(0)<>0:WEND◄
  WINDOW CLOSE 3◄
END SUB◄
```

Program 4-6. MaskMaker

```
' *** MaskMaker ***◄
' Makes MeMasks and HitMasks for object animation.◄
◄
Initialize:◄
  WINDOW 1,"MaskMaker",(0,0)-(631,185),20◄
  WIDTH 80◄
  DIM memask(15,15) 'MeMask array for 15 classes of objects.◄
  DIM hitmask(15,15) 'HitMask array for 15 classes of objects.◄
  DIM object$(15) 'Names array for 15 classes of objects.◄
  DIM bit(15) 'Holds bit values for 16-bit mask.◄
  bitvalue=1:FOR n=0 TO 15 'Fill array with bit values...◄
    bit(n)=bitvalue:bitvalue=bitvalue*2◄
  NEXT n◄
◄
EntryPoint:◄
  CLS:PRINT:PRINT "Enter number of CLASSES of objects"◄
  PRINT "(not actual NUMBER of objects):"◄
  INPUT ">> ",numobjects◄
```

```
IF numobjects>15 THEN◄
 BEEP:PRINT:PRINT "Sorry, system can handle"◄
 PRINT "only 15 classes of objects."◄
 GOSUB Clickmouse◄
 GOTO EntryPoint◄
END IF◄
IF numobjects<2 THEN◄
 BEEP:PRINT:PRINT "Sorry, too few classes of objects."◄
 GOSUB Clickmouse◄
 GOTO EntryPoint◄
END IF◄
CLS:PRINT◄
PRINT "Enter brief name for each class of objects."◄
PRINT "(Example: Aliens, Ship, Missile, Ball, etc.):"◄
FOR n=0 TO numobjects-1◄
 Getnames:◄
 PRINT "Object class number";n+1;":"◄
 LINE INPUT ">> ";object$(n)◄
 IF object$(n)="" THEN Getnames◄
 memask(n,n+1)=1◄
NEXT n◄
◄
MakeMask:◄
 FOR n=0 TO numobjects-1◄
 Askborders:◄
 CLS:PRINT:PRINT "Should OBJECT CLASS: ";object$(n)◄
 INPUT "collide with the screen borders (Y/N)";a$◄
 IF a$="" THEN Askborders◄
 IF UCASE$(a$)="Y" THEN hitmask(n,0)=1◄
 NEXT n◄
 FOR n=0 TO numobjects-1◄
 FOR nn=0 TO numobjects-1◄
  Askobjects:◄
  CLS:PRINT◄
  IF n<>nn THEN◄
   PRINT "Should OBJECT CLASS: ";object$(n)◄
   PRINT "collide with OBJECT CLASS: ";object$(nn)◄
   INPUT "Y/N";a$◄
   IF a$="" THEN Askobjects◄
   IF UCASE$(a$)="Y" THEN hitmask(n,nn+1)=1◄
  END IF◄
 NEXT nn◄
NEXT n◄
 ◄
DisplayMask:◄
 CLS:PRINT "Here is the MeMask and Hitmask data:":PRINT◄
 FOR n=0 TO numobjects-1◄
  mask1=0:mask2=0◄
  PRINT "OBJECT.HIT ";object$(n);◄
  FOR nn=0 TO 15◄
   IF memask(n,nn)=1 THEN mask1=mask1+bit(nn)◄
  NEXT nn◄
  mask1=mask1-65536&*(mask1>32767)◄
  PRINT mask1;",";◄
  FOR nn=0 TO 15◄
   IF hitmask(n,nn)=1 THEN mask2=mask2+bit(nn)◄
  NEXT nn◄
```

```
    mask2=mask2-65536&*(mask2>32767)◄
    PRINT mask2:PRINT "MeMask:   ";◄
    FOR nn=15 TO 0 STEP -1:PRINT USING "#";memask(n,nn);:NEXT◄
    PRINT:PRINT "HitMask: ";◄
    FOR nn=15 TO 0 STEP -1:PRINT USING "#";hitmask(n,nn);:NEXT◄
    PRINT:PRINT◄
  NEXT n◄
  END◄
          ◄
Clickmouse:◄
  PRINT:PRINT "<< CLICK MOUSE IN THIS WINDOW TO CONTINUE >>"◄
  WHILE MOUSE(0)=0:WEND◄
  WHILE MOUSE(0)<>0:WEND◄
  RETURN◄
```

Program 4-7. BattleStation

```
  ' *** BATTLESTATION ***◄
◄
 Initialize:◄
  DEFINT a-z◄
  SCREEN 1,320,200,3,1◄
  WINDOW 1,"BattleStation",(0,0)-(311,185),20,1◄
  WIDTH 40◄
  PRINT "One moment, please..."◄
  DIM alien(4,4) 'Array to hold alien positions and speeds.◄
  RESTORE AlienShapeData◄
  FOR n=1 TO 114 'Read data for alien shapes.◄
    READ a:alien$=alien$+CHR$(a)◄
  NEXT n◄
  OBJECT.SHAPE 1,alien$◄
  OBJECT.SHAPE 2,1 'Right screen alien.◄
  OBJECT.PLANES 2,7 'Right alien's color.◄
  OBJECT.SHAPE 3,1 'Bottom screen alien.◄
  OBJECT.PLANES 3,5 'Bottom alien's color.◄
  OBJECT.SHAPE 4,1 'Left screen alien.◄
  OBJECT.PLANES 4,5,6 'Left alien's color.◄
  RESTORE BattlestationData◄
  FOR n=1 TO 162◄
    READ a:battle$=battle$+CHR$(a)◄
  NEXT n◄
  OBJECT.SHAPE 5,battle$◄
  RESTORE LaserData◄
  FOR n=1 TO 66◄
    READ a:laser$=laser$+CHR$(a)◄
  NEXT n◄
  OBJECT.SHAPE 6,laser$◄
  OBJECT.SHAPE 7,6:clone=6 'Clone of laser bullet.◄
  'Define collision masks:◄
  OBJECT.HIT 1,2,12 'Aliens can hit bullets, battlestation...◄
  OBJECT.HIT 2,2,12◄
  OBJECT.HIT 3,2,12◄
  OBJECT.HIT 4,2,12◄
  OBJECT.HIT 5,4,2 'Battlestation can hit aliens.◄
  OBJECT.HIT 6,8,2 'Laser bullets can hit aliens...◄
```

124

```
   OBJECT.HIT 7,8,2◄
   'Define some more colors:◄
   PALETTE 4,1,.2,0 'Fire engine red.◄
   PALETTE 5,.73,1,0 'Lime green.◄
   PALETTE 6,.8,0,.93 'Purple.◄
   PALETTE 7,1,1,.13 'Yellow.◄
Restart: 'Jump here to restart game.◄
   COLOR 1,2:CLS 'Black screen background.◄
   'Draw starfield:◄
   RANDOMIZE TIMER◄
   FOR n=1 TO 200◄
    x=INT(RND*310):y=INT(RND*190)◄
    PSET (x,y),1◄
   NEXT n◄
   OBJECT.ON 1,2,3,4,5◄
   'Place battlestation on screen:◄
   OBJECT.X 5,142:OBJECT.Y 5,82◄
   'Define initial positions and speeds of aliens...◄
   'Second-dimension array elements = X,Y,VX,VY:◄
   RESTORE AlienData◄
   FOR n=1 TO 4◄
    FOR nn=1 TO 4◄
     READ a:alien(n,nn)=a◄
    NEXT nn◄
   NEXT n◄
   AlienData: 'Define starting alien positions and speeds.◄
   DATA 142,1,0,2,285,85,-4,0,142,175,0,-3,1,85,4,0◄
   'Place alien ships on screen:◄
   FOR n=1 TO 4◄
    OBJECT.X n,alien(n,1):OBJECT.Y n,alien(n,2)◄
   NEXT n◄
   'Define directions and speeds:◄
   FOR n=1 TO 4◄
    OBJECT.VX n,alien(n,3):OBJECT.VY n,alien(n,4)◄
   NEXT n◄
   score&=0:timestart&=TIMER◄
   OBJECT.START 1,2,3,4◄
   ON COLLISION GOSUB Collide:COLLISION ON◄
GOTO MainLoop◄
   ◄
MainLoop:◄
   WHILE STICK(2)=0 AND STICK(3)=0:WEND◄
   GOSUB Joystick◄
GOTO MainLoop◄
   ◄
Joystick:◄
   IF STICK(3)=-1 THEN 'Fire bullet upward.◄
    OBJECT.X clone,150:OBJECT.Y clone,80:OBJECT.ON clone◄
    OBJECT.VY clone,-90:OBJECT.VX clone,0◄
    OBJECT.START clone:RETURN◄
   END IF◄
   IF STICK(3)=1 THEN 'Fire bullet downward.◄
    OBJECT.X clone,150:OBJECT.Y clone,100:OBJECT.ON clone◄
    OBJECT.VY clone,90:OBJECT.VX clone,0◄
    OBJECT.START clone:RETURN◄
   END IF◄
   IF STICK(2)=-1 THEN 'Fire bullet leftward.◄
```

```
    OBJECT.X clone,135:OBJECT.Y clone,85:OBJECT.ON clone◄
    OBJECT.VX clone,-90:OBJECT.VY clone,0◄
    OBJECT.START clone:RETURN◄
  END IF◄
  IF STICK(2)=1 THEN 'Fire bullet rightward.◄
    OBJECT.X clone,170:OBJECT.Y clone,85:OBJECT.ON clone◄
    OBJECT.VX clone,90:OBJECT.VY clone,0◄
    OBJECT.START clone:RETURN◄
  END IF◄
RETURN◄
  ◄
Collide:◄
  OBJECT.OFF clone 'Turn off laser bullet.◄
  object=COLLISION(0) 'Which object had a collision?◄
  collID=COLLISION(object) 'Which object hit the object?◄
  IF collID<1 THEN RETURN 'Ignore spurious border collisions.◄
  IF object=5 OR collID=5 GOTO BattlestationExplosion◄
  IF object=clone THEN object=collID 'Missile hit by alien.◄
  IF clone=6 THEN clone=7 ELSE clone=6 'Swap bullet clones.◄
  GOSUB BopAlien◄
  score&=score&+10:LOCATE 2,1:PRINT "SCORE =";score&◄
  ON object GOSUB Alien1,Alien2,Alien3,Alien4◄
  OBJECT.VX object,alien(object,3)◄
  OBJECT.VY object,alien(object,4)◄
  OBJECT.START object◄
  COLLISION ON◄
RETURN◄
  ◄
Alien1:◄
  alien(1,4)=alien(1,4)+1◄
RETURN◄
  ◄
Alien2:◄
  alien(2,3)=alien(2,3)-1◄
RETURN◄
  ◄
Alien3:◄
  alien(3,4)=alien(3,4)-1◄
RETURN◄
  ◄
Alien4:◄
  alien(4,3)=alien(4,3)+1◄
RETURN◄
  ◄
BopAlien:◄
  OBJECT.OFF object◄
  OBJECT.X object,alien(object,1)◄
  OBJECT.Y object,alien(object,2)◄
  OBJECT.ON object◄
RETURN◄
  ◄
BattlestationExplosion:◄
  OBJECT.STOP:OBJECT.OFF 5:OBJECT.OFF object◄
  FOR n=1 TO 100◄
    temp1=102+RND*100◄
    temp2=42+RND*100◄
    LINE (152,92)-(temp1,temp2),1◄
```

```
     NEXT n◄
     LOCATE 2,1:PRINT "SCORE =";INT(score&+(TIMER-timestart&))◄
     LOCATE 19,1:PRINT "PRESS FIRE BUTTON TO PLAY AGAIN"◄
     WHILE STRIG(3)=Ø:WEND◄
   GOTO Restart◄
   ◄
   AlienShapeData:◄
     DATA    Ø,    Ø,    Ø,    Ø,    Ø,    Ø,    Ø,    Ø◄
     DATA    Ø,    Ø,    Ø,    2,    Ø,    Ø,    Ø,   26◄
     DATA    Ø,    Ø,    Ø,   11,    Ø,   24,    Ø,    3◄
     DATA    Ø,    Ø,    Ø,127,128,    Ø,    1,255◄
     DATA  224,    Ø,    7,255,248,    Ø,   31,255◄
     DATA  254,    Ø,248,225,199,192,248,225◄
     DATA  199,192,255,255,255,192,  12,127◄
     DATA  140,    Ø,   12,127,140,    Ø,252,    Ø◄
     DATA   15,192,252,    Ø,   15,192,    Ø,    Ø◄
     DATA    Ø,    Ø,    Ø,    Ø,    Ø,    Ø,    Ø,    Ø◄
     DATA    Ø,    Ø,    Ø,    Ø,    Ø,    Ø,    7,   3Ø◄
     DATA   56,    Ø,    7,   3Ø,   56,    Ø,    Ø,    Ø◄
     DATA    Ø,    Ø,    Ø,127,128,    Ø,    Ø,127◄
     DATA  128,    Ø,    Ø,    Ø,    Ø,    Ø,    Ø,    Ø◄
     DATA    Ø,    Ø◄
   ◄
   BattlestationData:◄
     DATA    Ø,    Ø,    Ø,    Ø,    Ø,    Ø,    Ø,    Ø◄
     DATA    Ø,    Ø,    Ø,    2,    Ø,    Ø,    Ø,   29◄
     DATA    Ø,    Ø,    Ø,   17,    Ø,   24,    Ø,    3◄
     DATA    Ø,    Ø,    Ø,127,224,    Ø,    Ø,127◄
     DATA  224,    Ø,    Ø,127,224,    Ø,    1,255◄
     DATA  252,    Ø,227,134,  14,  56,254,  15◄
     DATA    7,248,252,  31,131,248,255,249◄
     DATA  255,248,255,249,255,248,252,  31◄
     DATA  131,248,254,  15,    7,248,227,134◄
     DATA   14,  56,    1,255,252,    Ø,    Ø,   63◄
     DATA  192,    Ø,    Ø,  63,192,    Ø,    Ø,   63◄
     DATA  192,    Ø,    Ø,  63,192,    Ø,    Ø,   31◄
     DATA  128,    Ø,    Ø,  31,128,    Ø,    Ø,    6◄
     DATA    Ø,    Ø,    Ø,    6,    Ø,    Ø,    Ø,127◄
     DATA  240,    Ø,    1,239,248,    Ø,227,223◄
     DATA  252,  56,255,255,255,248,255,255◄
     DATA  255,248,227,223,252,  56,    1,239◄
     DATA  248,    Ø,    Ø,127,240,    Ø,    Ø,    6◄
     DATA    Ø,    Ø,    Ø,    6,    Ø,    Ø,    Ø,    6◄
     DATA    Ø,    Ø,    Ø,  31,128,    Ø,    Ø,   31◄
     DATA  128,128◄
   ◄
   LaserData:◄
     DATA    Ø,    Ø,    Ø,    Ø,    Ø,    Ø,    Ø,    Ø◄
     DATA    Ø,    Ø,    Ø,    2,    Ø,    Ø,    Ø,   12◄
     DATA    Ø,    Ø,    Ø,  1Ø,    Ø,  24,    Ø,    3◄
     DATA    Ø,    Ø,  15,    Ø,  31,128,  63,192◄
     DATA  127,224,255,240,255,240,127,224◄
     DATA   63,192,  31,128,  15,    Ø,  15,    Ø◄
     DATA   31,128,  63,192,127,224,255,240◄
     DATA  255,240,127,224,  63,192,  31,128◄
     DATA   15,  15◄
```

127

Program 4-8. OBJECT.CLIP Demo

```
SCREEN 1,320,200,2,1◄
WINDOW 2,"Object Clip Demo",(0,0)-(311,185),20,1◄
PALETTE 0,0,.45,0:PALETTE 1,.9,.9,.9◄
PALETTE 2,0,0,0:PALETTE 3,.9,.48,.15◄
ON BREAK GOSUB Quit:BREAK ON◄
DIM alien$(114):RESTORE AlienShapeData◄
FOR n=1 TO 114◄
 READ a:alien$=alien$+CHR$(a)◄
NEXT n◄
OBJECT.SHAPE 1,alien$◄
LINE (81,50)-(231,136),2,b◄
OBJECT.CLIP (81,50)-(231,136)◄
OBJECT.ON:LOCATE 19,5◄
PRINT "<<Click mouse to exit>>"◄
WHILE MOUSE(0)=0◄
 OBJECT.X 1,MOUSE(1)-12:OBJECT.Y 1,MOUSE(2)-12◄
WEND◄
WHILE MOUSE(0)<>0:WEND◄
Quit:◄
 OBJECT.CLOSE:WINDOW CLOSE 2:SCREEN CLOSE 1:END◄
AlienShapeData:◄
DATA     0,   0,   0,   0,   0,   0,   0,   0◄
DATA     0,   0,   0,   2,   0,   0,   0,  26◄
DATA     0,   0,   0,  11,   0,  24,   0,   3◄
DATA     0,   0,   0,127,128,   0,   1,255◄
DATA   224,   0,   7,255,248,   0,  31,255◄
DATA   254,   0,248,225,199,192,248,225◄
DATA   199,192,255,255,255,192,  12,127◄
DATA   140,   0,  12,127,140,   0,252,   0◄
DATA    15,192,252,   0,  15,192,   0,   0◄
DATA     0,   0,   0,   0,   0,   0,   0,   0◄
DATA     0,   0,   0,   0,   0,   0,   7,  30◄
DATA    56,   0,   7,  30,  56,   0,   0,   0◄
DATA     0,   0,   0,127,128,   0,   0,127◄
DATA   128,   0,   0,   0,   0,   0,   0,   0◄
DATA     0,   0◄
```

5 Sound and Music

5 Sound and Music

Of the three ready-to-run computers which launched the personal computing age in 1977—the Commodore PET, the TRS-80 Model I, and the Apple II—only the Apple had any kind of sound capability. To be sure, it was primitive—just a tiny speaker that could be clicked on and off under program control. Yet even though it remains essentially unchanged to this day, it's capable of generating simple tones, melodies, and sound effects.

The computers which followed the Apple gradually improved upon this system. In 1979, the Atari 400 and 800 were introduced with four tone generators (also called *voices*) capable of producing a fairly wide range of sound effects and musical notes in four-part harmony. The Commodore VIC-20 came out in 1981 with a similar system employing three tone generators. And in 1982, the Commodore 64 became the first personal computer to incorporate a true "synthesizer on a chip"—SID, the Sound Interface Device. The SID chip, with its programmable sound envelopes and selectable waveforms, defined the state of the art in personal computer sound for almost three years.

That all changed when the Amiga made its debut in mid-1985. At first glance, the Amiga's sound capabilities look only moderately impressive: four voices connected to a pair of stereo outputs. Yet, the Amiga's sound system is radically different from those found on other personal computers. It's a logical extension of the sound capabilities developed in personal computers over the past decade and is the most advanced sound system currently available as a standard feature on any personal computer.

Waveform-Oriented Sound

Unlike its predecessors, the Amiga has a sound system that is completely *waveform oriented*. That means you're not limited to one or a few waveforms chosen for you by the sound chip or computer manufacturer. You're free to design or sample your own waveforms, so in theory you can write a program to produce virtually *any* kind of sound perceptible to the human ear. This is what makes it possible for the Amiga to closely simulate nearly any musical instrument, to play multiple-note chords with a single voice, and to synthesize humanlike speech.

131

In practice, however, Amiga BASIC imposes certain limitations that make it difficult (if not impossible) to produce certain types of sounds. Also, having full waveform control at your fingertips means that your programming task is more difficult—just as it is harder to operate a complicated view camera than it is to snap pictures with a simple Instamatic. In particular, the Amiga's waveform-oriented sound system makes it necessary to understand something about the basic physical nature of sound before you can take full advantage of what the computer has to offer.

Still, by the conclusion of this chapter, we think you'll agree that the results are worth the effort.

Pumping Air

Aside from the speech synthesis commands (which are covered in full detail in Chapter 6), there are only three sound statements in Amiga BASIC: BEEP, SOUND, and WAVE. (Two additional statements, SOUND WAIT and SOUND RESUME, are associated with SOUND.) The simplest one by far is BEEP. It does exactly what it sounds like and requires no arguments or parameters. Example:

BEEP

What could be easier, right? BEEP is useful when your program needs to generate a simple tone to grab the user's attention or to signal that some sort of operation is beginning or ending. For instance, Amiga BASIC itself uses a beep to alert you that you've made a programming error, and the general error-trapping routine we'll present in Chapter 7 uses BEEP for a similar purpose. There's not much else to know about BEEP.

The SOUND and WAVE statements require considerably more explanation, however. Both let you tinker with elements that make up the fundamental physical structure of a sound.

As you probably learned in school, all sounds are composed of *sound waves* that travel through the air from the sound source to our ears. The source can be anything from a tree falling in a (presumably inhabited) forest to a loudspeaker that translates electrical signals into vibrations of a speaker cone. When some physical event generates a sound wave, it pumps air—although really the air itself scarcely moves; the sound wave merely travels through it. Sound waves spread out through the air much like the ripples created by tossing a pebble into a puddle of water, except they spread out in three dimensions. The nature of this wave determines the kind of sound that we hear.

Surf's Up

Sound waves have many properties, and the study of acoustics is a science in itself. But to keep things relatively simple, three properties of sound waves are the most important as far as our ears and Amiga BASIC programs are concerned: *frequency, amplitude,* and *waveform.* More everyday terms for these properties are *pitch, volume,* and *tone,* respectively.

The pitch of a sound—that is, whether we perceive it as high or low—depends on the number of waves that ripple through the air in a given period of time. For instance, let's assume that Figure 5-1 is a diagram of a sound wave over one second of time.

Figure 5-1. Sound Wave—One Second

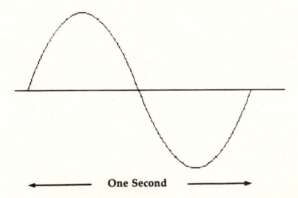

Notice that this is a complete wave; if it's placed end to end with another wave just like it, the wave repeats (Figure 5-2).

Figure 5-2. Repeating Wave

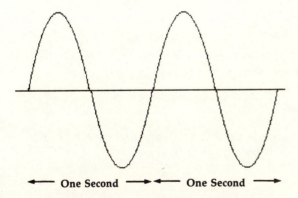

And so on. Since this sound wave makes one complete *cycle* each second, its frequency is described as *1 cps* (one cycle per second). Figure 5-3 is what a 2-cps sound wave looks like.

Figure 5-3. Two Cycles per Second

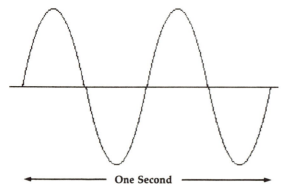

One Second

If you could actually hear this sound (you can't—it's much too low for the human ear), its pitch would seem *twice as high* as the 1-cps sound wave. And in turn, a 4-cps sound wave (Figure 5-4) would sound twice as high in pitch as the 2-cps sound wave.

Figure 5-4. Four Cycles per Second

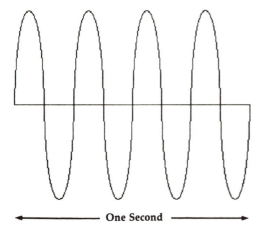

One Second

Each time the frequency of a sound wave is doubled, it sounds twice as high. Or, in musical terms, it increases in pitch by one octave.

Jackhammer Damage

Normal human hearing in a young person ranges from a low of about 20 cps to a high of about 20,000 cps. Those two numbers might look familiar if you've ever shopped around for a stereo. The specifications of high-fidelity sound equipment often state that the receiver, speaker, or whatever has a frequency response of 20 to 20,000 *hertz*. Hertz, often abbreviated Hz, means the same thing as cycles per second (hertz is the preferred modern term). A frequency response of 20 to 20,000 Hz means that the audio equipment is capable of reproducing the full range of sounds audible to the human ear. (The difference between a good stereo and a poor stereo, of course, is how faithfully it reproduces this spectrum of sound.)

Now, not everyone can actually *hear* sounds over the full 20 to 20,000 hertz range. Even under ideal conditions—say, with a young person in a quiet room—sounds at the extreme limits of this range will be very hard to pick up. Furthermore, hearing begins to deteriorate after our mid-twenties. Sensitivity to higher frequencies is affected most. The rate of hearing loss depends on many factors, including gender (the decline is faster in men than in women), heredity, and environment. If you're an army veteran of an artillery battery, live in a street-level apartment in Manhattan, operate a jackhammer eight hours a day, attend a rock concert every weekend, and go jogging with a cranked-up Walkman plugged into your ears, you're obviously headed for trouble. But even if you avoid loud noise, by the time you're 30 years old, your hearing rolls off to about 18,000 Hz. In an elderly person, hearing might deteriorate to 12,000 Hz or even much less.

Fortunately, very few sounds soar that high. The highest note on a piano, for instance, is less than 4000 Hz. Human voices—even those of trained concert singers—range from only about 80 to 1400 Hz. A bass tuba ranges from about 50 to 300 Hz, and a piccolo from about 500 Hz to slightly higher than a piano.

The Amiga is capable of producing sounds from 20 to 15,000 Hz—close to the range of hearing in the average adult. Coupled with the stereo outputs, this broad frequency response qualifies the Amiga as a high-fidelity component. FM radio and most cassette decks have a similar ceiling. Indeed, unless your Amiga is plugged into a good stereo system, you won't be hearing anything near this range. The tiny speakers in most TVs and monitors are definitely lo-fi, limited to a range of about 200 to 4000 Hz or less.

The Shape of Waves to Come

Another important characteristic of sound is amplitude, or volume. The apparent loudness of a sound depends on the *size* of its wave. Figure 5-5 is a diagram of what a quiet sound might look like.

A louder sound wave (Figure 5-6) has greater distances between the peaks and valleys of its ripples.

Naturally, the bigger the wave, the louder the sound, because it exerts more pressure on our eardrums.

Figure 5-5. Quiet Sound

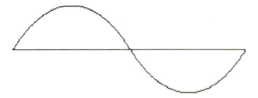

Figure 5-6. Louder Sound

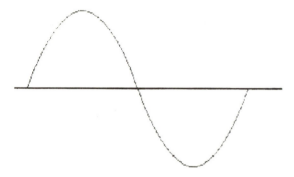

Frequency and amplitude are important components of sound waves, familiar to anyone who has twiddled with the tone and volume knobs on a stereo. But the third main characteristic of sound is even more important: waveform. The middle C note played on a piano sounds quite different from the middle C played on a guitar or french horn, even though each note may have nearly identical frequency and volume. The reason is that their sound waves have different shapes.

A middle C note is measured at 261.63 Hz, no matter what instrument it's played on. But the 261.63 Hz frequency is merely the *fundamental tone*—the main tone which makes up the note. Most sounds actually contain many additional frequencies called *overtones*, or *harmonics*. The overtones are mathematically related to the fundamental tone. For instance, the strongest overtones produced by musical instruments are exact multiples of the fundamental tone. If the fundamental tone is 1000 Hz, there will be extra overtones of 2000 Hz, 4000 Hz, 8000 Hz, and so on. You can't hear these harmonics as distinct tones, but they're there. When they interact with each other and with the fundamental tone, the result is a sound wave with a unique shape. And that shape determines the quality of the sound. Unpleasant sounds that we dismiss as noise are mixtures of many different frequencies and overtones that aren't harmonically related.

The SOUND Statement

Until now, the sound systems on personal computers have provided only a limited selection of predefined waveforms. Most computers, in fact, contain tone generators capable of producing nothing but square waves. The SID chip in the Commodore 64 lets programmers select from four different waveforms— square, sawtooth, triangle, and noise (Figure 5-7).

Figure 5-7. Four Waveforms

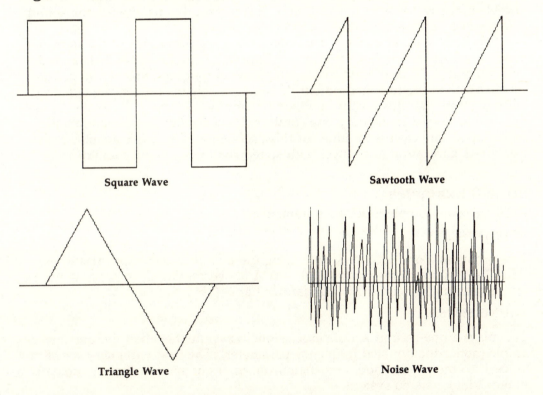

Square Wave

Sawtooth Wave

Triangle Wave

Noise Wave

But the Amiga lets you design nearly infinite variations of your own waveforms with the WAVE statement. You can even mix two or more waveforms together to get the effect of multiple-note chords from a single voice. To

play those waveforms aloud, you use the SOUND statement. SOUND allows four parameters, although the last two are optional:

SOUND *frequency,duration,volume,voice*

Frequency, a required parameter, can range from 20 to 15000 (Hz). This determines the sound's pitch as described above.

Duration is another required parameter that specifies the length of time the sound will be played. The allowable range is 0 to 77, where 18.2 equals a duration of one second. Therefore, the maximum value of 77 would be 4.25 seconds. What if you want to play a longer sound? Simple: Just chain two SOUND statements together. If there's nothing between them to cause a delay, you won't hear an interruption.

Volume, an optional parameter, specifies the sound's loudness. The allowable range is 0 (silent) to 255 (loud). If you omit this parameter, the sound defaults to a volume of 127.

Voice is another optional parameter that specifies which of the four independent voices will produce the sound. This value can be either 0, 1, 2, or 3. Voices 0 and 3 are connected to the left stereo output, and voices 1 and 2 are connected to the right stereo output. If you omit this parameter, the default is voice 0. (Note that this means you won't hear any sounds at all if your Amiga's right stereo output is the only one connected to your monitor's monophonic audio input. The easiest solution for this problem is to buy a Y adapter at an electronics parts store to connect both stereo channels to your monitor.)

SOUND Examples

Here are some sample SOUND statements:

SOUND 440,18.2

This produces a one-second A note using the default voice 0 and default volume. The A note corresponds to the first A above middle C on a piano, which by international agreement is standardized at 440 Hz.

SOUND 880,18.2,,1

This plays a one-second A note exactly one octave higher than the previous example (notice the doubled frequency parameter). The next parameter specifies voice 1, so the sound should emanate from the right speaker if your Amiga is plugged into a stereo system.

SOUND 1760,36.4,255,3

This plays a two-second A note exactly one octave higher than the previous tone and two octaves higher than our first A note. Also, the note should emanate from the left speaker (voice 3) and sound twice as loud as the previous tones (volume 255).

One fortunate feature of the SOUND statement is that it releases BASIC for other tasks while it goes about its work. Try this:

```
SOUND 440,77◄
FOR n=1 TO 100◄
 PRINT "Hello"◄
NEXT◄
```

As you'll see, the computer keeps printing *Hello* while it's playing the sound. On some other computers, an example like this would completely freeze up the machine until the sound stopped. On the Amiga, this feature means that with clever programming you can have music playing in the background while the rest of the program continues. Exceptions are statements which compete for the same voice channel—another SOUND statement that uses the same voice, or a BEEP or a SAY that attempts to use the same channel for speech synthesis. You can get around this problem by being careful to specify different voices for SOUND and SAY statements if you anticipate any conflicts. Otherwise, the second SOUND or SAY won't begin executing until the first one is finished.

As a matter of fact, quite a number of SOUND statements can become stacked up like this, because Amiga BASIC maintains a *queue*, or list, of every SOUND it encounters. Eventually, it gets around to playing them all, but if the SOUND statements pile up *too* fast, there'll be a noticeable delay while BASIC sets up the queue. Here's an illustration:

```
a=103.83◄
semitone=1.059463094#◄
FOR n=1 TO 48◄
 a=a*semitone◄
 SOUND a,4,255,0◄
NEXT◄
PRINT "Hello"◄
```

This example loads the SOUND queue with four octaves of notes starting with the second A below middle C. You'll notice a lengthy delay before the *Hello* message is printed because it takes time for BASIC to load the queue. Nevertheless, the SOUND statements continue executing—in the sequence they were encountered—after the message is printed.

For still more flexibility, Amiga BASIC provides two special sound statements that give you even greater control over SOUND timing: SOUND WAIT and SOUND RESUME. After a SOUND WAIT is executed, all subsequent SOUND statements are held in a state of suspended animation, so to speak, until the next SOUND RESUME. Then they're played in the order they were encountered in your program. This makes it easy to synchronize sounds with other events in your program, including graphics.

Here's an example of SOUND WAIT and SOUND RESUME:

```
SOUND WAIT◄
PRINT "Waiting..."◄
SOUND 261.63,20,255,0◄
SOUND 329.63,20,255,1◄
SOUND 392,20,255,2◄
SOUND 523.25,20,255,3◄
delay&=TIMER◄
WHILE TIMER<delay&+5:WEND◄
PRINT "This is a C major chord:"◄
SOUND RESUME◄
```

This program suspends four SOUND statements in the sound queue, waits exactly five seconds, prints the message, and finally empties the queue to play the C chord.

The WAVE Statement

Until now, all of the SOUND examples we've shown have used Amiga BASIC's default waveform. This waveform, called a *sine wave*, produces a pleasant, full tone. Figure 5-8 is a cross section of the default sine wave.

Figure 5-8. Default Sine Wave

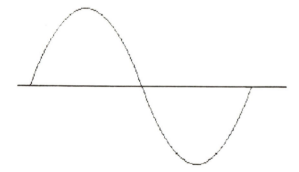

Notice that this wave is only one cycle long. You'll recall that a one-cycle-per-second (1 Hz) sound wave is far below the lower range of human hearing (20 Hz). How is it possible, then, that we can hear this sound?

The answer is that the Amiga repeats this wave many times per second—enough times to bring it within range of our eardrums. As a matter of fact, when you specify the frequency parameter in the SOUND statement, in effect you're telling the Amiga how many times to repeat this wave cycle each second (20 to 15,000 times).

The real power behind the Amiga's waveform-oriented sound system is that you can change this waveform for any voice with the WAVE statement. The syntax is straightforward:

WAVE *voice, array*

140

where *voice* is 0, 1, 2, or 3, and *array* is an array of at least 256 integers in the range of −128 to 127. Numbers outside this range trigger an *Illegal function call* error. Arrays longer than 256 elements are allowed but ignored. (Unfortunately, multidimensional arrays aren't allowed for this parameter. This makes it impossible to fill a two-dimensional array with several waveforms and then re-define a voice by changing the array pointer. Instead, you must use separate arrays for each waveform definition.)

The numbers between −128 and 127 in the array are what determine the shape of the new waveform. These integers are translated into amplitude values that define the shape of the wave's curve. Since the data can range from −128 to 127, a value of 0 represents zero amplitude—silence.

Try this experiment:

```
DIM waveform%(255)
FOR n=0 TO 255
 waveform%(n)=0
NEXT
WAVE 0,waveform%
SOUND 440,20,255,0
```

Even though the SOUND statement is set to maximum volume (255), you won't hear a whisper when you run this program. The reason is that we've defined a dead flat waveform with no amplitude at all (Figure 5-9).

Figure 5-9. Flat Waveform

This example isn't very practical, but it clearly demonstrates how the shape of a custom waveform implemented with WAVE can drastically alter the output of the SOUND statement.

Defining Custom Waveforms

Now let's try some more practical examples by imitating the waveforms built into the SID chip on the Commodore 64. Remember that the waveforms we're defining in the following arrays are single cycles that, when placed end to end, reveal the continuing shape of the wave.

141

Here's a square waveform:

```
DIM waveform%(255)
FOR n=0 TO 127
  waveform%(n)=127
NEXT
FOR n=128 TO 255
  waveform%(n)=-128
NEXT
WAVE 0,waveform%
SOUND 440,20,255,0
```

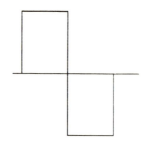

Here's a triangle waveform:

```
DIM waveform%(255)
wavedata=-128
FOR n=0 TO 127
  waveform%(n)=wavedata
  wavedata=wavedata+2
NEXT
wavedata=127
FOR n=128 TO 255
  waveform%(n)=wavedata-2
NEXT
WAVE 0,waveform%
SOUND 440,20,255,0
```

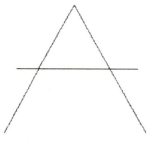

Here's a sawtooth waveform:

```
DIM waveform%(255)
wavedata=-128
FOR n=0 TO 255
  waveform%(n)=wavedata
  wavedata=wavedata+1
NEXT
WAVE 0,waveform%
SOUND 440,20,255,0
```

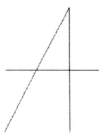

And finally, here's a noise waveform:

```
DIM waveform%(255)
RANDOMIZE TIMER
FOR n=0 TO 255
  waveform%(n)=INT(RND(1)*255-128)
NEXT
WAVE 0,waveform%
SOUND 440,20,255,0
```

When you run these examples, you'll notice marked differences between the sounds produced by the square, triangle, and sawtooth waveforms. But the noise wave is another story—it's a pure tone, more like the sawtooth wave than true white noise. This reveals a glaring weakness in Amiga BASIC: A 256-element array is sufficient for producing musical tones, but isn't long enough to generate a real white noise sound. As a result, it's much easier to play music in Amiga BASIC than it is to create unusual sound effects. Let's hope a future version of Amiga BASIC will remove this limitation by permitting waveform arrays of up to 32,768 elements or more.

For a clear demonstration of how a waveform's frequency affects the pitch we hear, add these lines to the sawtooth example above:

```
wavedata=-128
FOR n=0 TO 255
   waveform%(n)=wavedata
   wavedata=wavedata+2
   IF wavedata>127 THEN wavedata=-128
NEXT
WAVE 0,waveform%
SOUND 440,20,255,0
```

This defines a sawtooth wave with two teeth per cycle, and the result is a tone that sounds twice as high as the single-toothed wave.

Figure 5-10. Double-Toothed Wave

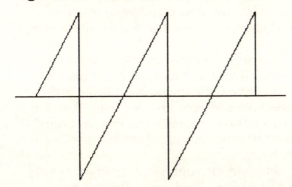

To restore the default waveform, incidentally, you can use this simple statement:

WAVE 0,SIN

which is the equivalent of this sine wave formula:

DIM waveform%(255)
FOR n=0 to 255
  waveform%(n)=127*SIN(n*3.1416/128)
NEXT

143

Just because the Amiga has only four voices doesn't mean you're limited to four-part harmonies. One of the most interesting and powerful advantages of a waveform-oriented sound system is that you can combine two or more waveforms in a single definition to produce the effect of multiple tones using only a single voice. The following example mixes two different sine waves:

```
DIM waveform%(255)◄
k=2*3.1416/256◄
FOR n=0 TO 255◄
 waveform%(n)=65*(SIN(n*k)+SIN(n*7*k))◄
NEXT◄
WAVE 0,waveform%◄
SOUND 440,20,255,0◄
```

If you listen closely, the result is a multifrequency sound that seems to be two voices chiming in unison—even though only one voice is clearly in play.

SoundBoard: A Sound Editor

To make your own experiments with Amiga sound easier, we've written a sound editor program. Program 5-1, "SoundBoard," at the end of this chapter, gives you full control over all the parameters for each voice, a selection of predefined waveforms, the ability to assign different waveforms to each voice for mixed sounds, a screen which graphically plots waveforms in a window, the ability to design custom waveforms with the mouse and save the data to disk, and an option to create DATA statements of a custom waveform to merge as a subroutine into your own programs.

Set Preferences to 60 columns, then run SoundBoard. After a pause while the numerous waveform arrays initialize, a C major chord announces that the program is ready. You'll need to have both speakers on to hear chords.

The first screen you'll see shows three slide controls for voice 0 and a large button. Whenever you point to this button and click the mouse, SoundBoard plays whatever voices are currently turned on, using the parameters and waveforms currently selected for each voice.

To change voice 0's frequency, duration, or volume parameters, simply point to the appropriate slide control and click or hold down the left mouse button. Indicators show the changing values as would be reflected in the corresponding SOUND statement.

To choose which voice's slide controls are displayed on the screen, press the right mouse button, pull down the Voices menu, and select from the first four options: Set Voice 0, Set Voice 1, Set Voice 2, or Set Voice 3. The slide controls for each voice retain their values as you switch from voice to voice.

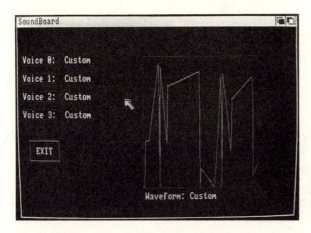

This "SoundBoard" screen lets you assign predefined waveforms to any voice or design your own custom waveforms.

The other four options on the Voices menu let you independently switch each voice on or off. A checkmark indicates that a voice is currently turned on. (SoundBoard defaults to all four voices on.)

Although Amiga BASIC permits a frequency range of 20 to 15,000 Hz, the frequency sliders in SoundBoard default to a range of 200 to 4000 Hz. This is the most usable range, and the small speakers typically found in computer monitors can't reproduce tones outside this range anyway. But you can change the scale of the frequency sliders by selecting the Frequency Range option under the Special menu. Type in any values you wish for the lower and upper limits—even a range as narrow as 440 to 441 is valid (although the program rejects any values outside the 20-to-15,000 limits of the SOUND statement). All four slide controls are rescaled to the new range, and the frequency for each voice readjusts itself to the middle of this range.

Custom Waves

The Waveforms menu in SoundBoard presents six predefined waveforms—sine (the Amiga's default), square, triangle, sawtooth1, sawtooth2, and a multiple waveform consisting of four summed sine waves. There's also a Custom waveform option. When SoundBoard first runs, it defines the custom waveform with random data.

To view any of these waveforms, pick the matching menu selection. A screen pops up with a window that graphically plots the waveform. To the left are buttons for all four voices, plus indicators which show the waveform currently assigned to each voice. To change a voice's waveform to the wave displayed in the graphics window, simply click on that voice's button. To return to the screen with the slide controls, click on the EXIT button. In this way, you can independently assign different waveforms to any of the voices for special effects.

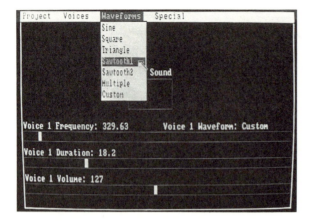

"SoundBoard" lets you manipulate Amiga BASIC SOUND parameters with slide controls for each of the four voices.

To design your own custom waveform, select Custom from the Waveforms menu. Move the pointer inside the waveform window and hold down the mouse button. The old custom waveform disappears, and the mouse pointer displays a rubber-band line as you move it within the window. Start from the left side of the window and draw your waveform toward the right, being careful not to leave any gaps (they'll be interpreted as −128 data elements). You can draw multiple lines by releasing and repressing the mouse button. If you draw a line you don't like, simply move the pointer outside the waveform window and release the mouse button to make it disappear. When the custom wave is finished, click on the EXIT button. Expect a long pause while the program reads the waveform off the screen pixel by pixel to create the WAVE array. A countdown timer shows the progress.

The next time you select the Custom option under Waveforms, your new wave is displayed. If you don't like it, you can design another. Or you can click on the adjacent buttons to assign the new wave to the desired voices, then exit to the main screen to play the waveform.

If you design a waveform you really like, you can save it on disk by selecting Save Waveform under the Project menu. You can reload it later by selecting Open Waveform.

Another option under this menu, *Waveform > BASIC*, lets you convert the custom wave data into BASIC DATA statements and save them on disk. Since the DATA statements are written out as an ASCII file, you can merge them with your own programs to reproduce the waveform later. All that's required is a loop to read the data into a waveform array:

DIM waveform%(255):FOR n=0 to 255:READ waveform%(n):NEXT

And don't forget to execute a WAVE statement to assign the custom waveform to the desired voice.

Making Music

Amiga BASIC's SOUND statement is easy enough to use, but it has some deficiencies if you're trying to play music. For one thing, you have to specify the pitch in hertz, which is not as convenient as simply specifying the desired note. A brief table in the *Amiga BASIC* manual lists the frequency equivalents for a few octaves of notes around middle C. For a more complete list, see Figure 5-11. It shows the frequencies for every note on a standard piano keyboard.

Figure 5-11. Piano Note Frequencies

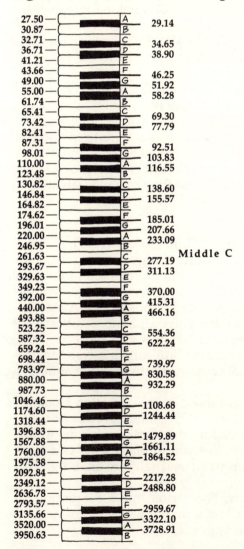

Interestingly, all of these frequency values were computed with a single formula. We've already mentioned how octaves are related to frequencies: a step of one octave represents a doubling of the frequency value. It's not surprising, therefore, that all of the notes within an octave are mathematically related, too. The modern musical scale—called the *even-tempered*, or *equal-tempered*, scale—consists of 12 half-steps called *semitones*. On a piano, for instance, each white key or black key is a semitone. On a guitar, each fret is a semitone.

All semitones are spaced equally apart in terms of pitch, so the frequency in hertz of the next higher semitone can be calculated by multiplying the first semitone by the twelfth root of 2 (1.059463094). Looking at Figure 5-11, you can see that a standard A note is 440 Hz. The next higher semitone, A-sharp, is 466.16 Hz; the next semitone, B, is 493.88 Hz; the following semitone, C, is 523.25 Hz; and so on. You can use this method to calculate the frequency value of any note in any octave.

The mathematical relationship between note *durations* is even simpler. A *whole note* is a note of the longest duration; a *half note* is half the duration of a whole note; a *quarter note* is one-fourth the duration of a whole note; and so on. Note durations are expressed in relative rather than absolute terms, so the relationships among notes are maintained no matter how fast or slowly the music is played. The *Amiga BASIC* manual has a table under the SOUND heading that relates musical tempos to *duration* values for the SOUND statement.

ToneDialer

The final demonstration program in this chapter, ''ToneDialer'' (Program 5-2), shows how SOUND statements can be used for other things besides music. The standard frequencies for the Touch-Tone dialing system are defined in an array, so you can dial any digit on the keypad, including the special * and # symbols. (It would be more efficient to place the frequency definitions in DATA statements, but we've done it this way for clarity.) Just enter a phone number at the input prompt, hold the mouthpiece of a telephone handset very close to your monitor speaker, and press RETURN. If your phone line supports true tone dialing and your monitor has a fairly good quality speaker, the number should be dialed for you.

ToneDialer ignores any hyphens, parentheses, spaces, or other characters in the phone number you enter. One exception is the comma: This causes ToneDialer to pause for two seconds before dialing the numbers following the comma. If you're on a phone system that requires you to dial a digit and wait for a dial tone to get an outside line, you can use ToneDialer by entering something like 9,555–1212.

An interesting project would be to turn ToneDialer into a subroutine for an address book program, or perhaps add it to a terminal program designed for use with acoustic modems that lack autodial features.

Program 5-1. SoundBoard

```
' *** SOUNDBOARD ***
'
' Set Preferences to 60 columns.
'
Initialize:
  CLEAR ,32000 'Grab extra memory for all the arrays.
  WINDOW 1,"SoundBoard",(0,0)-(631,185),20
  PALETTE 0,0,.45,0:PALETTE 1,.9,.9,.9
  PALETTE 2,0,0,0:PALETTE 3,.9,.48,.15:CLS:WIDTH 60
  LOCATE 2,1:PRINT "(Set Preferences to 60 columns.)"
  PRINT:PRINT "Just a moment, please..."
  DIM voice(3) 'Switches for Voice menu:
  FOR n=0 TO 3:voice(n)=2:NEXT
  voice=0 'Voice # sliders currently displayed.
  customflag=0 'Indicates if custom waveform redesigned.
  saveflag=1 'Indicates if new custom waveform is saved.
  DIM waveform$(7) 'Available waveforms.
  FOR n=1 TO 7:READ waveform$(n):NEXT
  DATA Sine,Square,Triangle,Sawtooth1
  DATA Sawtooth2,Multiple,Custom
  DIM wform(3) 'Indicates each voice's waveform.
  FOR n=0 TO 3:wform(n)=1:NEXT 'Default waveform: Sine.
  'Arrays for waveforms:
  DIM waveform%(7,255) 'Holds all wave data for plotting only.
  DIM sineform%(255) 'Holds sine waveform data.
  'Define sine waveform:
  FOR n=0 TO 255
    sineform%(n)=127*SIN(n*3.1416/128)
    waveform%(1,n)=sineform%(n)
  NEXT
  DIM squareform%(255) 'Holds square waveform data.
  'Define square waveform:
  FOR n=0 TO 127
    squareform%(n)=127:waveform%(2,n)=127
  NEXT
  FOR n=128 TO 255
    squareform%(n)=-128:waveform%(2,n)=-128
  NEXT
  DIM triform%(255) 'Holds triangle waveform data.
  'Define triangle waveform:
  temp=-128
  FOR n=0 TO 127
    triform%(n)=temp:waveform%(3,n)=temp
    temp=temp+2
  NEXT
  temp=127
  FOR n=128 TO 255
    triform%(n)=temp:waveform%(3,n)=temp
    temp=temp-2
  NEXT
  DIM sawform1%(255) 'Holds sawtooth1 waveform data.
  'Define sawtooth1 waveform:
  temp=-128
  FOR n=0 TO 255
```

```
  sawform1%(n)=temp:waveform%(4,n)=temp◄
  temp=temp+1◄
NEXT◄
DIM sawform2%(255) 'Holds sawtooth2 waveform data.◄
'Define sawtooth2 waveform:◄
temp=-128◄
FOR n=0 TO 255◄
  sawform2%(n)=temp:waveform%(5,n)=temp◄
  temp=temp+2◄
  IF temp>127 THEN temp=-128◄
NEXT◄
DIM multiform%(255) 'Holds sawtooth3 waveform data.◄
'Define multiple-sine waveform:◄
FOR n=0 TO 255◄
  p#=2*3.1416/256◄
  multiform%(n)=31*(SIN(n*p#)+SIN(n*2*p#)+SIN(n*3*p#)+SIN(n*4*p#))
  ◄
  waveform%(6,n)=multiform%(n)◄
NEXT◄
DIM customform%(255) 'Holds custom-designed waveform data.◄
'Define custom waveform at random for default:◄
RANDOMIZE TIMER◄
FOR n=0 TO 255◄
  customform%(n)=INT(RND(1)*255-128)◄
  waveform%(7,n)=customform%(n)◄
NEXT◄
'Set default waveforms (sine wave):◄
FOR n=0 TO 3:WAVE n,SIN:NEXT◄
'Set initial values and slide controls:◄
lofreq=100 'Lower limit of Frequency sliders.◄
hifreq=4000 'Upper limit of Frequency sliders.◄
DIM frequency(3) 'Stores voice frequencies.◄
DIM duration(3) 'Stores voice durations.◄
DIM volume(3) 'Stores voice volumes.◄
'Set default voice parameters (a 1-second C major chord):◄
frequency(0)=261.63:frequency(1)=329.63◄
frequency(2)=392:frequency(3)=523.25◄
FOR n=0 TO 3:duration(n)=18.2:NEXT◄
FOR n=0 TO 3:volume(n)=127:NEXT◄
DIM slider(3,3) 'Stores slider values for all voices.◄
freqfactor=(hifreq-lofreq)/621 'Frequency slider factor.◄
'Calculate slider values:◄
FOR n=0 TO 3◄
  slider(1,n)=(frequency(n)-lofreq)/freqfactor+4◄
  slider(2,n)=duration(n)*8.06+4◄
  slider(3,n)=INT(volume(n)*2.43)+4◄
NEXT◄
GOSUB MenuSetup◄
GOSUB ScreenSetup◄
ON MENU GOSUB MenuHandler◄
MENU ON:SOUND WAIT◄
FOR n=0 TO 3◄
  SOUND frequency(n),duration(n),volume(n),n◄
NEXT◄
SOUND RESUME◄
GOTO MainLoop◄
  ◄
```

```
MenuSetup:
 'Design custom menu bar:
 MENU 1,0,1,"Project"
 MENU 1,1,1,"Open Waveform"+SPACE$(3)
 MENU 1,2,1,"Save Waveform"+SPACE$(3)
 MENU 1,3,1,"Waveform > BASIC"
 MENU 1,4,1,"Quit"+SPACE$(12)
 MENU 2,0,1,"Voices"
 MENU 2,1,1,SPACE$(3)+"Set Voice 0"+SPACE$(3)
 MENU 2,2,1,SPACE$(3)+"Set Voice 1"+SPACE$(3)
 MENU 2,3,1,SPACE$(3)+"Set Voice 2"+SPACE$(3)
 MENU 2,4,1,SPACE$(3)+"Set Voice 3"+SPACE$(3)
 MENU 2,5,voice(0),SPACE$(3)+"Voice 0 On/Off"
 MENU 2,6,voice(1),SPACE$(3)+"Voice 1 On/Off"
 MENU 2,7,voice(2),SPACE$(3)+"Voice 2 On/Off"
 MENU 2,8,voice(3),SPACE$(3)+"Voice 3 On/Off"
 MENU 3,0,1,"Waveforms"
 MENU 3,1,1,waveform$(1)+SPACE$(5)
 MENU 3,2,1,waveform$(2)+SPACE$(3)
 MENU 3,3,1,waveform$(3)+SPACE$(1)
 MENU 3,4,1,waveform$(4)
 MENU 3,5,1,waveform$(5)
 MENU 3,6,1,waveform$(6)
 MENU 3,7,1,waveform$(7)+SPACE$(3)
 MENU 4,0,1,"Special"
 MENU 4,1,1,"Frequency Range"
RETURN

ScreenSetup:
 'Draw slide controls:
 CLS:LOCATE 12,1
 PRINT "Voice";voice;"Frequency:";frequency(voice)
 LINE (0,108)-(629,118),2,b
 LINE (slider(1,voice)-3,109)-(slider(1,voice)+3,117),1,bf
 LOCATE 15,1
 PRINT "Voice";voice;"Duration:";duration(voice)
 LINE (0,135)-(629,145),2,b
 LINE (slider(2,voice)-3,136)-(slider(2,voice)+3,144),1,bf
 LOCATE 18,1
 PRINT "Voice";voice;"Volume:";volume(voice)
 LINE (0,162)-(629,172),2,b
 LINE (slider(3,voice)-3,163)-(slider(3,voice)+3,171),1,bf
 LOCATE 12,34 'Show waveform for current voice.
 PRINT "Voice";voice;"Waveform: ";waveform$(wform(voice));
 'Draw Play button:
 LOCATE 6,26:PRINT "Play Sound"
 LINE (250,55)-(350,85),2,b
RETURN

MainLoop:
 WHILE MOUSE(0)=0:WEND:mx=MOUSE(1):my=MOUSE(2)
 IF mx>3 AND mx<626 AND my>108 AND my<118 THEN
  LINE (slider(1,voice)-3,109)-(slider(1,voice)+3,117),0,bf 'Erase
   old slider.
  frequency(voice)=(mx-4)*freqfactor+lofreq 'Calculate new frequen
  cy.
```

```
  slider(1,voice)=mx 'Draw new slider...◄
  LINE (slider(1,voice)-3,109)-(slider(1,voice)+3,117),1,bf◄
  LOCATE 12,1◄
  PRINT "Voice";voice;"Frequency:";frequency(voice);SPACE$(5)◄
ELSEIF mx>3 AND mx<626 AND my>135 AND my<145 THEN◄
  LINE (slider(2,voice)-3,136)-(slider(2,voice)+3,144),0,bf 'Erase
   old slider.◄
  duration(voice)=(mx-4)/8.06 ' Calculate new duration.◄
  slider(2,voice)=mx 'Draw new slider...◄
  LINE (slider(2,voice)-3,136)-(slider(2,voice)+3,144),1,bf◄
  LOCATE 15,1◄
  PRINT "Voice";voice;"Duration:";duration(voice);SPACE$(6)◄
ELSEIF mx>3 AND mx<626 AND my>162 AND my<172 THEN◄
  LINE (slider(3,voice)-3,163)-(slider(3,voice)+3,171),0,bf 'Erase
   old slider.◄
  volume(voice)=INT((mx-4)/2.43) 'Calculate new volume.◄
  slider(3,voice)=mx 'Draw new slider...◄
  LINE (slider(3,voice)-3,163)-(slider(3,voice)+3,171),1,bf◄
  LOCATE 18,1◄
  PRINT "Voice";voice;"Volume:";volume(voice);SPACE$(5)◄
ELSEIF mx>250 AND mx<350 AND my>55 AND my<85 THEN◄
  LINE (251,56)-(349,84),1,bf 'Flash button.◄
  WHILE MOUSE(0)<>0:WEND ' Wait for mouse button release.◄
  GOSUB PlaySound◄
  LINE (251,56)-(349,84),0,bf 'Restore button.◄
  END IF◄
GOTO MainLoop◄
◄
MenuHandler:◄
 'Determines which menu item was selected.◄
 MenuID=MENU(0)◄
 menuitem=MENU(1)◄
 ON MenuID GOTO ProjectMenu,VoicesMenu,WaveMenu,SpecialMenu◄
  ◄
ProjectMenu:◄
 'Handles selection from Project menu.◄
 ON menuitem GOTO OpenWave,SaveWave,BASICwave,Quit◄
◄
 VoicesMenu:◄
 'Handles selection from Voices menu.◄
 IF menuitem>4 THEN VoiceChoice 'Voice On/Off selection.◄
 voice=menuitem-1 'Set Voice selection.◄
 GOSUB ScreenSetup◄
 RETURN◄
◄
 WaveMenu:◄
 'Handles selection from Waveforms menu.◄
 GOTO PickWave◄
◄
 SpecialMenu:◄
 'Handles selection from Special menu.◄
 ON menuitem GOTO FreqRange◄
  ◄
 OpenWave:◄
 'Loads custom waveform data from disk.◄
 MENU OFF:MENU 1,0,0:MENU 2,0,0◄
 MENU 3,0,0:MENU 4,0,0◄
```

```
CLS:LOCATE 5,10
PRINT "* Press RETURN to exit *"
LOCATE 6,10:PRINT STRING$(24,"-")
IF saveflag=0 THEN
 LOCATE 7,10
 PRINT "NOTE: New custom waveform is NOT saved."
END IF
LOCATE 8,10:PRINT "Enter filename to open:"
LOCATE 9,10:LINE INPUT ">> ";filename$
IF filename$="" THEN GOTO ExitOpen 'Abort routine.
ON ERROR GOTO ErrorTrap
OPEN filename$ FOR INPUT AS #1
LOCATE 11,10:PRINT "Opening filename"
LOCATE 12,10:PRINT CHR$(34);filename$;CHR$(34);"..."
FOR n=0 TO 255 'Input custom waveform array values...
 INPUT #1,customform%(n)
 waveform%(7,n)=customform%(n)
NEXT
CLOSE #1:ON ERROR GOTO 0
saveflag=1 'Set saved flag.
ExitOpen:
FOR v=0 TO 3 'Update new waveform assignments to voices...
 ON wform(v) GOSUB Sine,Square,Triangle,Sawtooth1,Sawtooth2,Multi
 ple,Custom
NEXT
MENU ON:MENU 1,0,1:MENU 2,0,1
MENU 3,0,1:MENU 4,0,1
GOSUB ScreenSetup
RETURN

SaveWave:
'Saves custom waveform data to disk.
MENU OFF:MENU 1,0,0:MENU 2,0,0
MENU 3,0,0:MENU 4,0,0
CLS:LOCATE 5,10
PRINT "* Press RETURN to exit *"
LOCATE 6,10:PRINT STRING$(24,"-")
LOCATE 8,10:PRINT "Enter filename to save:"
LOCATE 9,10:LINE INPUT ">> ";filename$
IF filename$="" THEN GOTO ExitSave ' Abort routine.
ON ERROR GOTO ErrorTrap
OPEN filename$ FOR OUTPUT AS #1
LOCATE 11,10:PRINT "Saving under filename"
LOCATE 12,10:PRINT CHR$(34);filename$;CHR$(34);"..."
FOR n=0 TO 255 'Output custom waveform array values...
 WRITE #1,customform%(n)
NEXT
CLOSE #1:ON ERROR GOTO 0
pause&=TIMER 'Wait for disk drive to finish...
WHILE TIMER<pause&+6:WEND
saveflag=1 'Current custom waveform now saved.
ExitSave:
MENU ON:MENU 1,0,1:MENU 2,0,1
MENU 3,0,1:MENU 4,0,1
GOSUB ScreenSetup
RETURN
```

```
BASICwave:
 'Converts custom waveform to BASIC subroutine.
 MENU OFF:MENU 1,0,0:MENU 2,0,0
 MENU 3,0,0:MENU 4,0,0
 CLS:LOCATE 5,15
 PRINT "* Press RETURN to exit *"
 LOCATE 6,15:PRINT STRING$(24,"-"):PRINT
 PRINT "Enter output filename to create custom waveform routine:"
 LINE INPUT ">> ";filename$
 IF filename$="" THEN GOTO ExitBASICwave 'Abort routine.
 ON ERROR GOTO ErrorTrap
 OPEN filename$ FOR OUTPUT AS #1
 PRINT "Creating ";CHR$(34);filename$;CHR$(34);"..."
 PRINT #1," ' ";filename$
 FOR n=0 TO 255 STEP 8
  PRINT #1,"DATA ";
  FOR nn=0 TO 7
   PRINT #1,USING "+###";waveform%(7,n+nn);
   IF nn<7 THEN PRINT #1,","; ELSE PRINT #1,""
  NEXT nn
 NEXT n
 CLOSE #1:ON ERROR GOTO 0
 pause&=TIMER 'Wait for disk drive to finish...
 WHILE TIMER<pause&+6:WEND
 PRINT:PRINT "FINIS."
 pause&=TIMER:WHILE TIMER<pause&+2:WEND
 ExitBASICwave:
 MENU ON:MENU 1,0,1:MENU 2,0,1
 MENU 3,0,1:MENU 4,0,1
 GOSUB ScreenSetup
RETURN

Quit:
 'Exits program to Amiga BASIC.
 MENU OFF:MENU 1,0,0:MENU 2,0,0
 MENU 3,0,0:MENU 4,0,0
 msg1$="Quit program to BASIC?"
 IF saveflag=0 THEN
  msg2$="(Custom waveform is NOT saved.)"
 ELSE
  msg2$=""
 END IF
 CALL Requester (msg1$,msg2$,"QUIT","CANCEL",2,answer%)
 IF answer%=0 THEN 'CANCEL was selected.
  MENU ON:MENU 1,0,1:MENU 2,0,1
  MENU 3,0,1:MENU 4,0,1
  RETURN
 END IF
 CLS:END

VoiceChoice:
 IF voice(menuitem-5)=1 THEN
  voice(menuitem-5)=2
 ELSE
  voice(menuitem-5)=1
 END IF
```

```
   MENU 2,5,voice(0):MENU 2,6,voice(1)◂
   MENU 2,7,voice(2):MENU 2,8,voice(3)◂
 RETURN◂
      ◂
 PickWave:◂
  ' Picks waveforms for voices.◂
  GOSUB WavescreenSetup◂
 WaveLoop:◂
  WHILE MOUSE(0)=0:WEND:mx=MOUSE(1):my=MOUSE(2)◂
  IF mx>21 AND mx<99 AND my>108 AND my<132 THEN◂
   LINE (23,109)-(98,131),1,bf 'Flash exit button.◂
   WHILE MOUSE(0)<>0:WEND 'Wait for mouse button release.◂
   GOTO ExitWave◂
  ELSEIF mx>8 AND mx<90 AND my>25 AND my<35 THEN◂
   WHILE MOUSE(0)<>0:WEND 'Wait for mouse button release.◂
   v=0:wform(0)=menuitem 'Set choice of new waveform.◂
   ON menuitem GOSUB Sine,Square,Triangle,Sawtooth1,Sawtooth2,Multi
   ple,Custom◂
   LOCATE 4,12:PRINT waveform$(menuitem);SPACE$(5)◂
  ELSEIF mx>8 AND mx<90 AND my>43 AND my<53 THEN◂
   WHILE MOUSE(0)<>0:WEND 'Wait for mouse button release.◂
   v=1:wform(1)=menuitem 'Set choice of new waveform.◂
   ON menuitem GOSUB Sine,Square,Triangle,Sawtooth1,Sawtooth2,Multi
   ple,Custom◂
   LOCATE 6,12:PRINT waveform$(menuitem);SPACE$(5)◂
  ELSEIF mx>8 AND mx<90 AND my>61 AND my<71 THEN◂
   WHILE MOUSE(0)<>0:WEND 'Wait for mouse button release.◂
   v=2:wform(2)=menuitem 'Set choice of new waveform.◂
   ON menuitem GOSUB Sine,Square,Triangle,Sawtooth1,Sawtooth2,Multi
   ple,Custom◂
   LOCATE 8,12:PRINT waveform$(menuitem);SPACE$(5)◂
  ELSEIF mx>8 AND mx<90 AND my>79 AND my<89 THEN◂
   WHILE MOUSE(0)<>0:WEND 'Wait for mouse button release.◂
   v=3:wform(3)=menuitem 'Set choice of new waveform.◂
   ON menuitem GOSUB Sine,Square,Triangle,Sawtooth1,Sawtooth2,Multi
   ple,Custom◂
   LOCATE 10,12:PRINT waveform$(menuitem);SPACE$(5)◂
  END IF◂
  IF menuitem=7 THEN GOSUB DesignWave 'Design custom wave.◂
  GOTO WaveLoop◂
 ExitWave:◂
  IF customflag=1 THEN GOSUB MakeWave 'Calculate custom wave.◂
  customflag=0◂
  GOSUB ScreenSetup◂
  MENU 1,0,1:MENU 2,0,1:MENU 3,0,1:MENU 4,0,1◂
  RETURN◂
◂
 DesignWave:◂
  'Allows design of custom waveforms.◂
  IF mx>286 AND mx<544 AND my>27 AND my<157 THEN 'Wave box.◂
   IF customflag=0 THEN LINE (287,28)-(543,156),0,bf 'Erase.◂
   customflag=1 'Signals new custom waveform.◂
   saveflag=0 'Signals that new waveform is not yet saved.◂
   WHILE MOUSE(0)<>0◂
    mx2=MOUSE(1):my2=MOUSE(2) 'Get new mouse coordinates.◂
    IF mx2>286 AND mx2<544 AND my2>27 AND my2<157 THEN◂
```

```
       LINE (mx,my)-(mx2,my2),3 'Draw rubber band line...◄
       LINE (mx,my)-(mx2,my2),0◄
      END IF◄
    WEND◄
    IF mx2>286 AND mx2<544 AND my2>27 AND my2<157 THEN◄
      LINE (mx,my)-(mx2,my2),3◄
    END IF◄
   END IF◄
 RETURN◄
◄
 MakeWave:◄
   'Reads custom-designed waveform off screen.◄
   FOR n=0 TO 255◄
    LOCATE 19,8◄
    PRINT "Processing waveform data. Please be patient:";◄
    PRINT -n+255;SPACE$(2)◄
    y=29 'Starting point of vertical scan.◄
    pixel=0 'Pixel values to be read off screen.◄
    WHILE pixel=0 AND y<156◄
     pixel=POINT (n+287,y):y=y+1◄
    WEND◄
    customform%(n)=-(y-92)*2 'Put value in waveform array.◄
    waveform%(7,n)=customform%(n) 'Copy to plotting array.◄
   NEXT◄
   FOR v=0 TO 3 'Update new waveform assignments to voices...◄
    ON wform(v) GOSUB Sine,Square,Triangle,Sawtooth1,Sawtooth2,Multi
    ple,Custom◄
   NEXT◄
 RETURN◄
◄
 Sine:◄
   'Sets selected voice to sine waveform.◄
   WAVE v,sineform%◄
 RETURN◄
◄
 Square:◄
   'Sets selected voice to square waveform.◄
   WAVE v,squareform%◄
 RETURN◄
◄
 Triangle:◄
   'Sets selected voice to triangle waveform.◄
   WAVE v,triform%◄
 RETURN◄
◄
 Sawtooth1:◄
   'Sets selected voice to sawtooth1 waveform.◄
   WAVE v,sawform1%◄
 RETURN◄
◄
 Sawtooth2:◄
   'Sets selected voice to sawtooth2 waveform.◄
   WAVE v,sawform2%◄
 RETURN◄
◄
 Multiple:◄
   'Sets selected voice to multiple-sine waveform.◄
```

```
    WAVE v,multiform%◄
  RETURN◄
◄
 Custom:◄
  'Sets selected voice to custom waveform.◄
  WAVE v,customform%◄
 RETURN◄
◄
 WavescreenSetup:◄
  'Sets up screen for waveform selections.◄
  CLS:MENU 1,0,0:MENU 2,0,0◄
  MENU 3,0,0:MENU 4,0,0◄
  LOCATE 19,30:PRINT "Waveform: "+waveform$(menuitem)◄
  LINE (286,27)-(544,157),2,b 'Draw waveform box.◄
  FOR n=1 TO 254 STEP 2 'Plot waveform on screen...◄
   x1=n-1+287:y1=-waveform%(menuitem,n-1)/2+92◄
   x2=n+1+287:y2=-waveform%(menuitem,n+1)/2+92◄
   LINE (x1,y1)-(x2,y2),3◄
  NEXT◄
  LOCATE 4,2:PRINT "Voice 0:";SPACE$(2);waveform$(wform(0))◄
  LINE (8,25)-(90,35),2,b 'Draw voice 0 button.◄
  LOCATE 6,2:PRINT "Voice 1:";SPACE$(2);waveform$(wform(1))◄
  LINE (8,43)-(90,53),2,b 'Draw voice 1 button.◄
  LOCATE 8,2:PRINT "Voice 2:";SPACE$(2);waveform$(wform(2))◄
  LINE (8,61)-(90,71),2,b 'Draw voice 2 button.◄
  LOCATE 10,2:PRINT "Voice 3:";SPACE$(2);waveform$(wform(3))◄
  LINE (8,79)-(90,89),2,b 'Draw voice 3 button.◄
  LOCATE 14,5:PRINT "EXIT"◄
  LINE (25,110)-(95,130),3,b 'Draw exit button.◄
  LINE (21,108)-(99,132),2,b◄
 RETURN◄
◄
 FreqRange:◄
  'Adjusts range of Frequency sliders.◄
  MENU OFF:MENU 1,0,0:MENU 2,0,0◄
  MENU 3,0,0:MENU 4,0,0◄
  CLS◄
  LOCATE 5,7:PRINT "This selection lets you change"◄
  LOCATE 6,7◄
  PRINT "the lower and upper limits of the Frequency sliders."◄
  LOCATE 7,7◄
  PRINT "Default settings are 100 (lower) and 4000 (upper)."◄
  LOCATE 8,7◄
  PRINT "Current settings are";lofreq;"(lower) and";hifreq;"(upper
)."◄
  LOCATE 9,7:PRINT "Allowable range is 0 to 15000."◄
  LOCATE 11,7◄
  PRINT "Press RETURN below to exit..."◄
  LOCATE 12,7:PRINT "Or enter new limits and press RETURN."◄
  LOCATE 14,7:LINE INPUT "Lower limit >> ";lotemp$◄
  IF lotemp$="" THEN Exitfreq◄
  lotemp=VAL(lotemp$)◄
  IF lotemp>14999 OR lotemp<0 THEN FreqRange◄
  LOCATE 16,7:LINE INPUT "Upper limit >> ";hitemp$◄
  IF hitemp$="" THEN Exitfreq◄
  hitemp=VAL(hitemp$)◄
  IF hitemp>15000 OR hitemp<=lotemp THEN FreqRange◄
```

```
    lofreq=lotemp:hifreq=hitemp 'Set changes.◄
    freqfactor=(hifreq-lofreq)/621 'New Frequency slider factor.◄
    'Set new default frequencies:◄
    FOR n=Ø TO 3◄
      frequency(n)=(hifreq-lofreq)/2+lofreq◄
      slider(1,n)=(frequency(n)-lofreq)/freqfactor+4◄
    NEXT◄
    Exitfreq:◄
      GOSUB ScreenSetup◄
      MENU ON:MENU 1,Ø,1:MENU 2,Ø,1◄
      MENU 3,Ø,1:MENU 4,Ø,1◄
    RETURN◄
◄
  PlaySound:◄
    'Plays selected sound.◄
    SOUND WAIT◄
    FOR n=Ø TO 3◄
      IF voice(n)=2 THEN◄
        SOUND frequency(n),duration(n),volume(n),n◄
      END IF◄
    NEXT◄
    SOUND RESUME◄
  RETURN◄
◄
  ErrorTrap:◄
    'Traps common errors, mostly disk.◄
    'Requires Requester window subprogram.◄
    BEEP 'Get user's attention.◄
    IF ERR=53 THEN◄
      msg1$="FILE NOT FOUND."◄
      GOTO ExitError◄
    END IF◄
    IF ERR=61 THEN◄
      msg1$="DISK FULL."◄
      GOTO ExitError◄
    END IF◄
    IF ERR=64 THEN◄
      msg1$="BAD FILENAME."◄
      GOTO ExitError◄
    END IF◄
    IF ERR=67 THEN◄
      msg1$="DIRECTORY FULL."◄
      GOTO ExitError◄
    END IF◄
    IF ERR=68 THEN◄
      msg1$="DEVICE UNAVAILABLE."◄
      GOTO ExitError◄
    END IF◄
    IF ERR=7Ø THEN◄
      msg1$="DISK WRITE-PROTECTED."◄
      GOTO ExitError◄
    END IF◄
    IF ERR=74 THEN◄
      msg1$="UNKNOWN DISK VOLUME."◄
      GOTO ExitError◄
    END IF◄
    msg1$="ERROR NUMBER "+STR$(ERR)◄
```

```
ExitError:◄
'Abort operation or try again.◄
msg2$=""◄
CALL Requester (msg1$,msg2$,"Retry","CANCEL",2,answer%)◄
IF answer%=0 THEN 'CANCEL was selected.◄
  CLOSE #1◄
  MENU ON:MENU 1,0,1:MENU 2,0,1◄
  MENU 3,0,1:MENU 4,0,1◄
  GOSUB ScreenSetup◄
  RESUME MainLoop◄
ELSE◄
  CLOSE #1◄
  ON ERROR GOTO ErrorTrap◄
  RESUME◄
END IF◄
◄
SUB Requester (msg1$,msg2$,b1$,b2$,hilite%,answer%) STATIC◄
  ' Requester window subprogram version 3.4.◄
  SHARED scrid 'Global variable for SCREEN ID.◄
  IF scrid<1 OR scrid>4 THEN scrid=-1 'Default to Workbench.◄
  WINDOW 3,"Program Request",(0,0)-(311,45),16,scrid◄
  maxwidth=INT(WINDOW(2)/8) 'Truncate prompts if too long...◄
  PRINT LEFT$(msg1$,maxwidth):PRINT LEFT$(msg2$,maxwidth)◄
  b1$=LEFT$(b1$,12):b2$=LEFT$(b2$,12) 'Truncate buttons.◄
  bsize1=(LEN(b1$)+2)*10:bsize2=(LEN(b2$)+2)*10 'Button size.◄
  x1=(312-(bsize1+bsize2))/3  'Calculate button positions...◄
  x2=x1+bsize1:x3=x1+x2:x4=x3+bsize2◄
  'Draw buttons:◄
  LINE (x1,20)-(x2,38),2,b:LINE (x3,20)-(x4,38),2,b◄
  IF hilite%=1 THEN LINE (x1+2,22)-(x2-2,36),3,b◄
  IF hilite%=2 THEN LINE (x3+2,22)-(x4-2,36),3,b◄
  LOCATE 4,1:PRINT PTAB(x1+10);b1$;◄
  PRINT PTAB(x3+10);b2$◄
  reqloop: 'Loop which acts on mouse clicks...◄
  WHILE MOUSE(0)=0:WEND:m1=MOUSE(1):m2=MOUSE(2)◄
  IF m1>x1 AND m1<x2 AND m2>20 AND m2<38 THEN◄
   answer%=1 'Left button was selected.◄
   LINE (x1,20)-(x2,38),1,bf 'Flash left button.◄
  ELSEIF m1>x3 AND m1<x4 AND m2>20 AND m2<38 THEN◄
   answer%=0 'Right button was selected.◄
   LINE (x3,20)-(x4,38),1,bf 'Flash right button.◄
  ELSE◄
   GOTO reqloop 'Neither button selected; repeat loop.◄
  END IF◄
  WHILE MOUSE(0)<>0:WEND:WINDOW CLOSE 3◄
END SUB◄
```

Program 5-2. ToneDialer

```
' *** TONEDIALER ***◄
◄
Initialize:◄
  DIM touchtone(11,2) ' Array for tone values.◄
  'Define tones for keys (frequencies in Hertz):◄
  'official Touch-Tone system uses two tones per digit:◄
```

```
touchtone(0,1)=941:touchtone(0,2)=1336 ' 0
touchtone(1,1)=697:touchtone(1,2)=1209 ' 1
touchtone(2,1)=697:touchtone(2,2)=1336 ' 2
touchtone(3,1)=697:touchtone(3,2)=1477 ' 3
touchtone(4,1)=770:touchtone(4,2)=1209 ' 4
touchtone(5,1)=770:touchtone(5,2)=1336 ' 5
touchtone(6,1)=770:touchtone(6,2)=1477 ' 6
touchtone(7,1)=852:touchtone(7,2)=1209 ' 7
touchtone(8,1)=852:touchtone(8,2)=1336 ' 8
touchtone(9,1)=852:touchtone(9,2)=1477 ' 9
touchtone(10,1)=941:touchtone(10,2)=1209 ' *
touchtone(11,1)=941:touchtone(11,2)=1477 ' #

GetNumber:
 WINDOW 1,"ToneDialer",(300,140)-(620,185),22
 WIDTH 30
 ReEnter:
 CLS:PRINT "Enter number to dial:"
 PRINT STRING$(21,"-")
 LINE INPUT ">> ";number$
 IF number$="" THEN ReEnter

ToneDial:
 FOR n=1 TO LEN(number$)
  'Check for * and # keys:
  IF MID$(number$,n,1)="*" THEN number=10:GOTO PlayTone
  IF MID$(number$,n,1)="#" THEN number=11:GOTO PlayTone
  'Pause two seconds for comma:
  IF MID$(number$,n,1)="," THEN
   pause&=TIMER
   WHILE TIMER<pause&+2:WEND
  END IF
  'Ignore all nondigit characters:
  IF ASC(MID$(number$,n,1))<48 THEN Nextnumber
  IF ASC(MID$(number$,n,1))>57 THEN Nextnumber
  'Convert input to proper digit:
  number=VAL(MID$(number$,n,1)) 'Digits 0 to 9
  PlayTone:
   SOUND WAIT 'Makes sure tones are synchronized...
   SOUND touchtone(number,1),5,,0 'Lo tone, left channel.
   SOUND touchtone(number,2),5,,2 'Hi tone, left channel.
   SOUND touchtone(number,1),5,,1 'Lo tone, right channel.
   SOUND touchtone(number,2),5,,3 'Hi tone, right channel.
   SOUND RESUME
   FOR delay=1 TO 200:NEXT 'Short delay between tones.
 Nextnumber:
 NEXT n
 GOTO ReEnter 'Do it again...
```

6 Speech Synthesis

6 Speech Synthesis

Even after thousands of years of biological and technological evolution, speech remains the primary form of communication among human beings. Our written languages are more efficient for many purposes, but speech still adds a dimension of immediacy and personality that's hard to capture in purely visual forms of communication. Why? Because in the hierarchy of human senses, hearing takes second place only to vision. When talkies were invented in the late 1920s, they supplanted silent films almost overnight. When telephones became widespread, phone calls rapidly replaced telegrams. Despite the fact that long-distance rates are still more expensive than postage stamps, many people nowadays prefer to pick up the phone rather than write a letter to a friend or relative who lives many miles away.

It's no surprise, therefore, that engineers have been striving for years to add the capability of speech to one of our newest inventions: the computer. Computerized speech synthesis is reaching a high level of sophistication and is more common that some people realize. An everyday example is the messages you hear after dialing a wrong number or calling long-distance information in the United States—these messages are actually digitized voices.

Voice *recognition*, on the other hand, is proving to be much more difficult. Computers have a hard time coping with the wide variations in human speech, pronunciation, and accents, not to mention the complexity of our spoken languages. It will still be some years before reliable *talk*writers replace typewriters. In the meantime, speech synthesis at least makes it possible for our computers to talk, if not listen.

Speech synthesis is one of the most revolutionary and often-overlooked features of the Amiga. The Amiga is the first personal computer that comes with speech capability as a standard feature. Even the most minimal Amiga system you can buy is capable of talking. This feature is revolutionary because it means that Amiga programmers are free to use speech in their programs without worrying about whether the user has bought a particular speech synthesizer. This isn't true with other computers. Programmers who write speech programs for other computers automatically limit their potential audience to the minority of users who have added an optional speech peripheral. Amiga pro-

163

grammers know that all Amiga owners already have a speech synthesizer and that it's standardized.

Better yet, the full capabilities of Amiga speech synthesis are available to programmers in Amiga BASIC. Your BASIC programs can make the Amiga talk in a humanlike voice or a robotized monotone, with a male voice or a female voice, as an adult or as a child, in a high, squeaky tone or in a low rumble. You can make the Amiga talk faster than the most hyperactive carnival barker or slower than a zombie. You can even make the Amiga talk out of either speaker on your stereo, argue with itself, and interrupt itself in midsentence.

Speech Applications

What are all the applications for these capabilities? Since no personal computer has ever included speech as a built-in feature before, no one knows for sure. Some applications are obvious: An added dimension to games and educational programs, *Eliza*-type programs that come even closer to simulating heart-to-heart discussions with a shrink, and, of course, aids for handicapped people. You can write programs that read aloud the text files created with word processors or programs that perform dramatic plays—complete with different voices for all the characters, who can move around the stage in stereo. Thanks to the SAY command added in version 1.1 of AmigaDOS, batch files can announce what they're doing as they execute or speak important instructions aloud. And because the Amiga's RS-232 serial port includes an audio output pin, the addition of a little extra hardware can turn the computer into an extremely sophisticated telephone answering machine, capable of speaking different responses to different callers.

As usual, however, this new freedom is accompanied by a new responsibility. Amiga programmers have to decide when speech is appropriate in their programs. Should speech always be included just because it's available? Which parts of a program should talk and which should print conventional messages on the screen? Is speech a possible source of distraction in business programs that are used in offices? If a program does include speech, should there be an option to turn it off in case the user prefers to work in silence? In educational programs for children, should the speech default to a male or a female voice?

These issues and others must be decided by individual programmers. If you're writing programs only for your own use, then you're the only one you have to please. But if you're writing programs to be used by others, you need to address these concerns. It's likely that some unwritten standards will evolve after the Amiga is around for a while and speech synthesis becomes a common feature on other personal computers.

Until then, it might help to keep one thing in mind: For several years it has been technologically and economically possible to add speech capability to a great many products, such as cars, microwave ovens, washing machines, dryers, dishwashers, coffee makers, and vending machines. Prototypes of such products have been test-marketed all over the U.S. in recent years. The fact that most appliances still lack this feature indicates that manufacturers have discovered something—the general public doesn't seem quite ready yet for talking machines. Indeed, some people react unpredictably. One manufacturer reportedly canceled plans for a talking vending machine that yelled Ouch! when it was kicked or punched; the poor machine suffered even more abuse than usual because some customers enjoyed hearing it yelp.

The Speech Commands

Amiga BASIC contains two keywords for implementing speech synthesis: SAY and TRANSLATE$. With only two keywords, there doesn't seem much to learn. However, SAY is actually the doorway to a whole sublanguage of additional commands for creating high-quality speech. Furthermore, there are a number of optional parameters which determine how the SAY statement controls the Amiga's voice.

By far the easiest way to make the Amiga talk is to couple SAY with TRANSLATE$. TRANSLATE$ is an extremely powerful function that converts ordinary English text into the special codes which the SAY statement requires to create humanlike speech. These codes are called *phonemes*. Phonemes are the basic building blocks of speech, an alphabet of spoken sounds. (The Amiga's phoneme alphabet is an expanded version of *Arpabet*, developed by the Advanced Research Products Agency specifically for computer speech synthesis.)

If the designers of Amiga BASIC had been mean or lazy, they could have omitted the TRANSLATE$ function from the language and forced you to construct all speech by linking together these phonemes. The Amiga would still be capable of all the varieties of speech that it is now; you'd just have to work harder. A lot harder.

By including TRANSLATE$, the designers have done quite a bit of this work for you. Thanks to TRANSLATE$, you can make the Amiga pronounce almost any English sentence with better than 90 percent accuracy on the first try. That's pretty amazing when you consider all the grammatical and syntactical complexities inherent in a written language, especially one as complex as English.

There are dozens of contradictory rules for spelling and pronunciation—just take a look at this sentence: "It is tough to put a cow through the ceiling." The *ough* in *tough* is pronounced *uff*, but the *ough* in *through* is pronounced *oo*. And the *c* in *cow* is a hard *k*, while the *c* in *ceiling* is a soft, sibilant *s*. Yet, the Amiga is capable of speaking this confusing sentence with a high degree of accuracy. With TRANSLATE$, it's this simple:

SAY TRANSLATE$ ("It is tough to put a cow through the ceiling.")

The syntax of this BASIC statement is pretty straightforward. Precede the English text you want the Amiga to speak with the keywords SAY TRANS-

LATE$, and then enclose the text within quotation marks inside parentheses. The TRANSLATE$ function converts the text into phonemes and then passes the phonemes along to the SAY statement. (By itself, TRANSLATE$ isn't capable of uttering a sound.)

Of course, you can also specify a string variable within the TRANS-LATE$ parentheses:

A$="It is tough to put a cow through the ceiling."
SAY TRANSLATE$ (A$)

The result is identical to the first example.

Comprehending Phonemes

The TRANSLATE$ function works by calling upon a library of predefined rules which guide it through the thickets of English syntax. Yes, it does fail occasionally, mispronouncing words with amusing results. But the more you think about all the rules and exceptions to rules in the English language, the more you'll appreciate TRANSLATE$. To gain an even better appreciation, let's take a look at how much work TRANSLATE$ is saving us. If you enter this line in direct mode:

PRINT TRANSLATE$ ("It is tough to put a cow through the ceiling.")

the result is

IHT IHZ TAH3F TUW PUHT AH KOW4 THRUW DHAX SIY4LIHNX.

Welcome to the world of phonemes. What appears to be a mess of gibberish is actually the string of phonemes required by the SAY statement to pronounce the sentence translated by TRANSLATE$. You can make the Amiga speak this sentence by entering this line:

SAY "IHT IHZ TAH3F TUW PUHT AH KOW4 THRUW DHAX SIY4LIHNX."

If it weren't for TRANSLATE$, you'd have to convert that sentence into phonemes yourself, and chances are pretty good that it would take you longer than it takes the Amiga. So maybe we can forgive the machine if it occasionally mangles the king's English.

If 100 percent proper pronunciation is important, however—and it often is, especially in educational programs for youngsters—you'll have to break down and translate the text into phonemes yourself. For background, you can read Appendix H, "Writing Phonetically for the SAY Command," in the *Amiga BASIC* reference manual that came with your computer. Then you can experiment on your own.

We've devised a method of learning about phonemes that is more fun, however. It's also a useful way to construct phoneme-based sentences for your own Amiga BASIC programs.

Speech Constructor

Take a look at Program 6-1 at the end of this chapter. "Speech Constructor" puts the entire phoneme vocabulary of the Amiga into pull-down menus and gives you a complete set of functions for building words, phrases, and sentences. You can save and load phoneme-based phrases on disk or print them out for future reference. The utility also translates English words and phrases into phonemes so that you can touch up the pronunciation of words that are just slightly off.

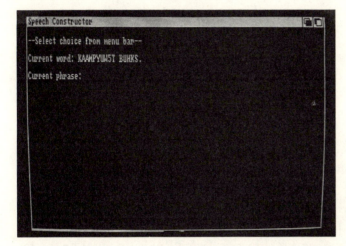

"Speech Constructor" makes it easier to put together phoneme-based words and phrases by making all valid Amiga phonemes available in pull-down menus.

When you run Speech Constructor, it asks you—aloud—to wait a few moments as it sets itself up. If you don't hear this message, make sure your Amiga is plugged into the audio input jacks of your monitor or sound system. When the program is ready, you should see this display on the screen:

—Select choice from menu bar—

Current word:
Current phrase:

Holding down the right mouse button reveals Speech Constructor's menu bar: Project, Speech, Vowels, Diphthongs, Cons1, Cons2, and Special. By pulling down these menus, you'll see that there are quite a few selections at your disposal. As usual, the selections are lit up or ghosted out as appropriate for your particular point in the program. Let's examine what these menus and selections do.

The Project menu contains these selections: *Make Phrase, Erase Word, Erase Phrase, Open Phrase, Save Phrase, Print Phrase, Type Word, Translate,* and *Quit.* When you first start the program, the only selections lit up are Open Phrase, Type Word, Translate, and Quit.

Open Phrase lets you load a previously saved phrase from disk. If you're running Speech Constructor for the first time, obviously there aren't any phrases to load yet.

The Quit selection is pretty standard; it lets you stop the program and exit to BASIC. A requester window pops up when you select Quit so you can confirm or cancel this function.

The Type Word selection in the Project menu lets you enter a word in phonemes from the keyboard. Simply type any string of valid Amiga phonemes and press RETURN. (Pressing RETURN without entering any other input cancels and exits this function—something which is true of all menu selections in Speech Constructor which ask for keyboard response.) You can enter one word or several words with the Type Word function. When you enter some phonemes and press RETURN, the main screen displays your entry as the current word.

The Phoneme Menus

To help you become fluent in the sublanguage of phonemes, Speech Constructor provides an alternative to typing in phonemes on the keyboard. If you want, you can simply pick the phonemes one at a time from the pull-down menus.

The menus entitled Vowels, Diphthongs, Cons1, Cons2, and Special contain the complete set of valid Amiga phonemes, stress marks, and punctuation marks (with the minor exception of the parentheses). This saves you the trouble of constantly referring to Appendix H in the *Amiga BASIC* manual or the tables accompanying this chapter. It also makes it easier to enter valid Amiga phonemes, since invalid ones aren't available for selection.

Table 6-1 lists the phonemes found in Speech Constructor's Vowels menu. Like most Amiga phonemes, they pair two letters to represent each sound. This is necessary because there are more vowel sounds in the English language than there are vowels.

Table 6-1. Vowel Phonemes

Phoneme	Example	Phoneme	Example
IY	beet	IH	bit
EH	bet	AE	bat
AA	hot	AH	under
AO	talk	UH	look
ER	bird	OH	border
AX	about	IX	solid

Table 6-2 lists the Amiga phonemes found in Speech Constructor's Diphthongs menu. If you've never heard of diphthongs, they're vowel sounds that change while they are pronounced. A good example is the word *boil*—you start by pronouncing the letter *o* as a long vowel, then end by pronouncing the letter *i* as a short vowel. The Amiga phoneme for this diphthong is OY. You could construct diphthongs by linking together two vowel phonemes—as some speech synthesizers force you to do—but the Amiga makes it easier by providing the common diphthongs as separate phonemes.

Table 6-2. Diphthong Phonemes

Phoneme	Example
EY	made
OY	boil
OW	low
AY	hide
AW	power
UW	crew

Table 6-3 gives the Amiga's consonant phonemes. There are too many consonants to fit on a single pull-down menu, so Speech Constructor divides them into two menus: Cons1 and Cons2. You'll notice that not all of the consonants found in our written alphabet are on the phoneme list. That's because some consonants, such as the letter *c*, are unnecessary for the purposes of speech synthesis. The phoneme S takes the place of a soft, sibilant *c*, and the phoneme K serves as a hard *c*.

Table 6-3. Consonant Phonemes

Phoneme	Example	Phoneme	Example
R	red	L	yellow
W	away	Y	yellow
M	men	N	men
NX	sing	SH	rush
S	sail	TH	thi
F	fed	ZH	pleasure
Z	has	DH	then
V	very	J	judge
CH	check	/C	loch
/H	hole	P	put
B	but	T	toy
D	dog	G	guest
K	Commodore		

Finally, Table 6-4 lists the phonemes, stress marks, and punctuation marks available under the Special menu. These are special sounds which sometimes can't be exactly duplicated with the other phonemes or which combine a pair of phonemes as a shortcut.

For instance, the special phoneme IL combines the sounds of the vowel phoneme IX (as in *solid*) and the consonant phoneme L *(yellow)*. The special phoneme DX imitates a *tongue flap*, the sound of a tongue flapping against the roof of a mouth *(pity)*. Since the Amiga has neither a mouth nor a tongue, DX serves as a silicon substitute. You'll find hints for using these special phonemes in Appendix H of the *Amiga BASIC* manual, but there are so many possible combinations and situations that the only real way to master phonemes is to experiment.

Table 6-4. Special Phonemes

Phoneme	Example
DX (tongue flap)	pity
QX (silent vowel)	pause
Q (glottal stop)	kitt-en
RX	car
LX	call
UL	AXL
UM	AXM
UN	AXN
IL	IXL
IM	IXM
IN	IXN
Numbers 1–9 (stress)	
. (period)	
? (question mark)	
, (comma)	
— (dash)	
( ) (parentheses)	

Speech Constructor's Special menu also lets you choose the punctuation marks included in the Amiga's phoneme library and assign stress marks as well. The punctuation marks are the period (.), question mark (?), dash (—), and comma (,). Terminating a sentence with a period causes a slight drop in pitch, while ending a sentence with a question mark causes a slight rise in pitch. Both of these also allow the Amiga to finish the sentence's final word cleanly. Without them, sentences often end as if chopped off in midword. The comma inserts a pause, and a pair of dashes acts as a *phrase delimiter*. This causes the speech to drop slightly in pitch for the duration of the phrase within the dashes.

Stress

To add stress to a phoneme, select Stress from the Special menu and type a key from 1 to 9. A stress mark affects the phoneme it follows, and stress marks are allowed only after vowel phonemes (with the exceptions of AX and IX). If you try to stress other types of phonemes, the result is an *Illegal function call* error. You'll also get an error if a SAY statement ends with a stress mark that isn't followed by a punctuation mark or space. (Speech Constructor traps all these errors, however, alerting you with a requester window.)

The Space selection under the Special menu lets you add a space character at the end of words.

Stress marks can make all the difference in the world when you're trying to make certain words sound right. Any number following a syllable places *stress*—elongation and emphasis—on the syllable. The value of the number determines the *intonation* of the syllable, which in turn determines how that word stands out in relation to other words in the same sentence. The *Amiga BASIC* manual recommends stress values of 9 for exclamations, 7 for adverbs and quantifiers, 5 for nouns and adjectives, 4 for verbs, 3 for pronouns, 2 or 1 for secondary stress in polysyllabic words, and no stress for articles, prepositions, and conjunctions. In practice, stress and intonation can vary according to the intended meaning of a sentence. Consider this example:

SAY TRANSLATE$ ("Please pet the cat.")

The TRANSLATE$ function converts this text into these phonemes:

PLIY4Z PEH4T DHAX KAE4T.

The word *the* (DHAX), an article, is the only word in the sentence which isn't stressed. The other three words are assigned equal stress, a value of 4. By changing these relative stress values, the sentence can convey slightly different meanings:

PLIY9Z PEH4T DHAX KAE4T.

Raising the stress value from 4 to 9 in PLIY9Z says, *"Please* pet the cat," emphasizing the strength of the request.

PLIY4Z PEH9T DHAX KAE4T.

By restoring normal stress to PLIY4Z and increasing the stress in PEH9T, the sentence now says, "Please *pet* the cat," placing emphasis on the type of action you're requesting.

PLIY2Z PEH2T DHAX KAE9T.

This version says, "Please pet the *cat*," emphasizing that the cat (instead of, perhaps, the dog) should be the object of affection. Notice that it reduces the stress values in PLIY2Z and PEH2T in addition to increasing the stress value in KAE9T. That's because the normal drop in pitch caused by the period following KAE9T requires corresponding drops in PLIY2Z and PEH2T to compensate.

This brings up an interesting point: Changing a stress number often has no audible effect when the word is pronounced by itself. But when the word is joined together with other words of varying stress into a sentence, the Amiga recognizes the relative stress values in context and pronounces the sentence accordingly. This helps simulate the normal contour of human speech. So even when you're assembling words manually with phonemes instead of using TRANSLATE$, the Amiga does some work for you.

Constructing Words

With this background on phonemes, you're all set to start building words and sentences with Speech Constructor. To make a word, either type the phonemes on the keyboard by selecting the Type Word function in the Projects menu, or pick the appropriate phonemes from the Vowels, Diphthongs, Cons1, Cons2, and Special menus.

When you select a phoneme from a menu, three things happen. First, Speech Constructor displays both the phoneme and an example word from the tables accompanying this chapter (which were derived from Appendix H in the *Amiga BASIC* manual). Second, Speech Constructor temporarily appends the phoneme to the current word and attempts to speak the resulting combination. (If there is no current word, the program may not be able to speak the phoneme until it is linked with another phoneme.) Third, a requester window asks if you want to add the phoneme to the current word. If you click on the OK box, the new current word becomes the existing word plus the new phoneme. If you click on the CANCEL box, the new phoneme isn't added, and you're bounced back to the main screen. In this fashion, you can assemble words a phoneme at a time until they're exactly right.

For an example, let's build the word *computer*. The first phoneme we need is a hard *c*, represented by the consonant phoneme K. Run Speech Constructor and wait until the screen reads:

—Select choice from menu bar—

Current word:
Current phrase:

Pull down the Cons1 menu. K is the last selection on the list. When you pick it, the screen reads:

Phoneme: K
Example: commodore
Current word + phoneme: K

In addition, a requester window asks:

Add phoneme to current word?
[OK]   **[CANCEL]**

Click on the OK box. The requester window disappears and the main screen returns, with one slight difference:

—Select choice from menu bar—

Current word: K
Current phrase:

To complete the first syllable in *computer*, we need the sounds for a short *o* and the consonant *m*. We could combine the vowel phoneme AX and the consonant phoneme M, but there's a shortcut. The phoneme we need is UM, found under the Special menu. Selecting it brings up this display:

Phoneme: UM
Example: =AXM
Current word + phoneme: KUM

The computer pronounces the syllable that will result if we add UM to K. It sounds right, so click on the OK box to add UM to the current word. The main screen now looks like this:

—Select choice from menu bar—

Current word: KUM
Current phrase:

Continue in this manner by adding the phonemes P and Y under the Cons2 menu, and the phoneme UW under the Diphthongs menu. The current word should then be KUMPYUW.

At this point, it's time to think about stress. As any dictionary shows, the word *computer* is accented on the second syllable. Remember that stress values affect the phonemes they follow, and that they must follow a vowel phoneme. Since *computer* is a noun, let's add the recommended stress value of 5 to the syllable represented by the phonemes PYUW. When you select Stress under the Special menu, you'll see this display:

Press key 1 to 9 to add stress to current word
Press RETURN to exit

When you press the 5 key, the main screen confirms that the current word is now KUMPYUW5. (If you ever select the Stress item by accident, don't forget that you can cancel the function by pressing RETURN instead.)

Now we're ready for the final syllable in *computer*. Select the phonemes T and ER from the Cons2 and Vowel menus, respectively. The current word becomes KUMPYUW5TER. You can confirm proper pronunciation by pulling down the Speech menu and selecting the first item, Say Word.

Constructing Sentences

Although it can become tedious to assemble long words by picking phonemes from the menus in this way, at least you don't have to worry about *Illegal function call* errors caused by invalid phonemes or misplaced stress marks. As you become more familiar with the Amiga's phoneme vocabulary, you may prefer to enter words directly on the keyboard with the Type Word item under Project. If so, you'll notice that Speech Constructor's phoneme menus remain lit during this function for reference purposes. (Selecting a phoneme while Type Word is waiting for keyboard input has no effect.)

If KUMPYUW5TER is to be the only word in your sentence, terminate it by selecting the period or question mark from the Special menu.

If you want to combine KUMPYUW5TER with other words to construct a longer sentence, follow it with a space character available under the same menu. Then pick Make Phrase, the first item under Project. You'll see this display:

Current word: KUMPYUW5TER
Current phrase:

A requester window asks:

Add current word to phrase?
[OK]   [CANCEL]

After you click on the OK box, the main screen looks like this:

—Select choice from menu bar—

Current word: KUMPYUW5TER
Current phrase: KUMPYUW5TER

Now a number of additional items in the menus become available. Under the Speech menu, you can select Say Phrase; under Project, you can pick Erase Phrase (erase the current phrase in memory), Save Phrase (save the current phrase on disk in the directory and file you specify), and Print Phrase (dump the current phrase on a printer). Among other things, these functions make it easy to preserve finished phrases for later reference or for inclusion in your own programs. To add a phoneme-based phrase to a BASIC program, simply precede it with the SAY statement as demonstrated before:

SAY "KUMPYUW5TER."

Note: Although some examples in the *Amiga BASIC* manual show otherwise, all phonemes used with the SAY statement must be in uppercase letters. Otherwise you'll get an error. Lowercase letters are okay if you're using TRANSLATE$ with SAY, because TRANSLATE$ automatically converts the phonemes to uppercase.

If you want to continue building a sentence with Speech Constructor, select Erase Word under Project to clear out the current word, KUMPYUW5TER.

The current phrase, which at this point also happens to be KUMPYUW5TER, remains intact. Now you can start on a new word by selecting phonemes from the menus as before, or by using the Type Word option. Add each new word to the current phrase by selecting Make Phrase. (Remember to end each word with a space, or they'll run together.) When you're done with the phrase, make it a complete sentence by terminating it with a period or question mark. If you want to start from scratch, select Erase Phrase.

Before going to all the trouble of assembling a word from phonemes, you may want to use another feature in Speech Constructor: the Translate option under Project. It lets you type in a word or phrase in ordinary English text, then it displays the equivalent phonemes generated by TRANSLATE$. Since the Amiga's text-to-speech translation is so accurate, you might as well take advantage of it whenever possible. When you're putting together a sentence, try the *Translate* option first to see how many words the computer speaks correctly. You can copy those phonemes verbatim or modify them slightly to polish the pronunciation. Resort to assembling phonemes yourself only for those few words which the Amiga has difficulty handling.

Voice Manipulation

There's one more option available in Speech Constructor that offers as much flexibility as the phonemes: the Alter Voice item in the Speech menu.

This function lets you experiment with the Amiga's rich variety of vocal characteristics. You can make the computer talk quickly or slowly, with a male or female voice, with a high pitch or low pitch, with expressiveness or in a monotone. You can change the volume of the voice and even make the speech emanate from different speakers in a stereo system. All of these effects and more are available in Amiga BASIC by appending an optional array of parameters to the SAY statement.

To manipulate these features in your own programs, three steps are required:

1. When your program starts, it should DIMension a one-dimensional *integer* array of nine elements.
2. Fill the array with the default speech values or your own modified values.
3. Following any SAY or SAY TRANSLATE$ statement that you want to manipulate, append the variable name of the array.

For an example, glance at the Initialize routine at the beginning of Speech Constructor (Program 6-1). Near the bottom of this routine you'll find the following lines:

```
DIM voice%(8) 'Array for voice parameters
FOR x=0 TO 8
  READ voice%(x)
NEXT x
DATA 110,0,150,0,22200,64,10,0,0
```

Voice% is the nine-element integer array (remember that arrays begin with element 0 unless you specify OPTION BASE 1). The FOR-NEXT loop simply reads the nine numbers in the DATA statement and puts them into the array. In this case, the numbers are the default voice values recognized by the SAY statement. By changing one or more of these numbers—either during this initialization step or at any point in your program—you can subtly or radically change the way the Amiga speaks.

Vocal Parameters

Table 6-5 shows the speech characteristics under your control. Be careful not to stray outside the allowable range for a parameter, or an error will result. A blow-by-blow explanation of these values follows.

Table 6-5. Amiga Voice Characteristics

Array Element	Control	Range	Default
0	Pitch	65–320	110
1	Inflection	0–1	0
2	Speed	40–400	150
3	Gender	0–1	0
4	Tuning	5000–28000	22200
5	Volume	0–64	64
6	Channel	0–11	10
7	Synch mode	0–1	0
8	Asynch mode	0–2	0

Pitch. This value corresponds to the frequency in hertz (Hz), or cycles per second. A higher number creates a high-pitched voice, and a lower number creates a low-pitched voice. The default, 110, results in a male voice. Higher numbers are useful for simulating the voices of women and children.

Inflection. There are only two choices here, 0 and 1. The default, 0, results in a voice that speaks expressively, adding stress to various syllables and words to imitate human speech more closely. If you change this value to 1, the Amiga speaks in a stiff monotone. This is useful for simulating the voices of robots and computers as they are usually depicted in TV shows and movies.

Speed. Have you ever heard a tape recorder with dying batteries? You can make the Amiga seem to speak even slower by plugging a low value into this slot. The default, 150, is a normal rate of speed for everyday conversation. For some real fun, try changing this value to the maximum of 400—the Amiga totally blows away that guy in the Federal Express commercials.

Gender. As you might expect, there are only two choices here: 0 for a male voice (the default) and 1 for a female voice. Frankly, the female voice sounds more like a male imitating a female, but you can improve it somewhat by tinkering with the pitch and tuning parameters.

Tuning. This controls the *sampling frequency*, or the number of samples per second on which the speech synthesis is based. Stick fairly close to the default value of 22200 for realism. If you experiment with the very lowest values, you're guaranteed to hear some extremely weird sounds.

Volume. This is pretty straightforward: 0 is silent and 64 is loud (or actually normal, since 64 is the default). Incidentally, this is an easy way to make speech optional in your programs. Simply include a menu function that lets a user set the volume throughout this entire range. By setting the volume to 0, all speech output is effectively shut off. If your program already prints every spoken message on the screen (a good practice to ensure maximum intelligibility), you don't have to write your program to skip certain speech routines depending on how a "switch" is set. This can save you a lot of work, and it also keeps your programs from alienating people who don't like talking computers.

Channel. If your Amiga is plugged into a stereo sound system, you can have fun with this parameter. The Amiga has four sound channels—numbered 0, 1, 2, and 3—which are split between the left and right audio outputs on the back of the computer. Channels 0 and 3 are routed to the left audio output, and channels 1 and 2 are routed to the right audio output. You can make the Amiga's voice come from either speaker by changing the default value of 10, which assigns the voice to any available left/right pair of channels. For instance, changing the value to 0 or 3 redirects the voice to the left speaker, and a value of 1 or 2 redirects the voice to the right speaker. (If you get opposite results, make sure your left/right speaker cables are plugged into the corresponding outputs.) Table 6-6 gives all the possibilities.

Table 6-6. Audio Channel Parameters

Element 6 Value	Audio Channel
0	0 (left)
1	1 (right)
2	2 (right)
3	3 (left)
4	0 and 1 (left and right)
5	0 and 2 (left and right)
6	3 and 1 (left and right)
7	3 and 2 (left and right)
8	Either available left channel
9	Either available right channel
10	Either available left/right pair
11	Any available single channel

Synch mode. A value of 0 (the default) sets up *synchronous speech mode*. That means the Amiga finishes what the SAY statement told it to say before executing any further statements. If you change this value to 1, *asynchronous speech mode*, the Amiga continues executing subsequent lines while it's speaking. If your program calls for the voice to echo whatever is being printed on the screen, you'll want to retain the default value. Otherwise, the voice will get left behind—unless you've accelerated its speed to some incredible (and probably incomprehensible) rate. On the other hand, if for some reason your program can't wait for the voice to finish, you'll need to switch to asynchronous mode. This could result in a problem if another SAY statement is encountered before a previous one is finished, so the next parameter lets you decide how the Amiga will handle such conflicts. (If the synch mode parameter is left at its default setting, the next parameter is irrelevant.)

Asynch mode. When synch mode is set to 1, you have three choices for asynchronous speech. The default value, 0, tells the Amiga to finish the current SAY statement before beginning the next one. This ensures that no speech is lost. A value of 1 stops the speech and cancels the previous SAY statement. A value of 2 makes subsequent SAY statements interrupt any currently executing SAY statement. This override mode has some interesting possibilities. For instance, you could make the Amiga seem to debate itself by sending different voices out the left and right speakers, interrupting each other in midsentence. It's also useful for making sure your programs don't fall behind themselves by getting bogged down in a long list of SAY statements.

Changing Voice Parameters

Modifying any of these voice parameters in your BASIC programs is simply a matter of plugging the desired value into the appropriate element of the array. This assumes, of course, that the array has been initialized as shown above in the example from Speech Constructor.

For instance, to change the volume from the default 64 to 50, use a line such as

voice%(4)=50

since volume is the fifth element in the array. (Remember that arrays normally begin with element 0.) To change the gender from a male to a female voice, try

voice%(3)=1

and so on.

The new settings aren't used unless you tack the array variable onto the SAY statement:

SAY "KUMPYUW5TER.",voice%

or

SAY TRANSLATE$ ("Computer."),voice%

178

If you omit the array variable, the voice retains its default characteristics.

To get a feel for the Amiga's range of speech capabilities, experiment with the Alter Voice option under Speech Constructor's Speech menu. It lets you manipulate everything but the synch modes, and it won't let you enter illegal values. Also, the default values are displayed for reference in case things get out of hand.

When you choose Speech Constructor's Save Phrase option under Project, the voice parameters are saved on disk along with the current phrase. When you later select Open Phrase to load a sentence from disk, the voice is automatically adjusted to the settings in effect when the phrase was saved.

Another easy way to experiment with voice settings is to run the "Speech" program found in the BasicDemos drawer on the Amiga BASIC disk. This program lets you change most of the speech parameters by clicking the mouse on a series of simulated slide controls. You'll quickly discover all the amusing and practical possibilities of the Amiga's electronic mouth.

A Sample Application

For an example of how a program can be improved with the addition of speech, run "Spelling Quizzer," Program 6-2, at the end of this chapter. You've probably seen spelling-practice programs before, but they usually must resort to such tricks as briefly flashing each word on the screen before requesting the youngster to spell it. Spelling Quizzer pronounces each word, and even spells a word letter by letter if the child misspells it more than twice.

Spelling Quizzer Menus

Most of the menu options are fairly self-explanatory, but here's a quick rundown.

Project
New Words	Erases a spelling list that's currently in memory.
Open Words	Lets you load a previously saved spelling list from disk.
Save Words	Saves a list on disk under the filename "Quizwords".
Save As...	Lets you specify a directory and/or filename of your own when saving a word list.
Print Words	Makes a hardcopy of the list currently in memory.
Quit	Exits the program to BASIC.

Tools
Start Quiz	Begins a spelling quiz.
Enter Words	Lets an adult type in a word list ranging from 2 to 50 words.
Study Words	Prints the word list currently in memory on the screen.

Voice
Male and *Female*	Let you change the voice's gender.
Volume	Brings up a slide control for adjusting the loudness.

Because proper pronunciation is critical if youngsters are to figure out the word they're supposed to be spelling, the Enter Words selection asks you to enter each word more than once. The first entry is the word as it's supposed to be spelled; the second entry is for the program's use only, as a guide for pronunciation. When the program asks

Enter phonetic spelling or RETURN >>

it doesn't want phonemes; it's asking you to (mis)spell the word as it sounds.

"Spelling Quizzer" is an example of an application program that takes advantage of speech synthesis.

For instance, suppose the spelling word is *radio*. Enter it as it should be spelled at the first prompt, then listen to the computer's pronunciation. If it sounds okay, you could simply press RETURN at the phonetic spelling prompt to continue on to the next spelling word. Usually, however, the pronunciation can be improved by adding a period or spelling the word somewhat differently. In this case, the computer mispronounces *radio*. At the phonetic spelling prompt, try entering it as *radeeo.*—including the period. When you press RETURN, the computer speaks it using this spelling. This sounds better, so press RETURN again without any further input to continue. Otherwise, keep trying other phonetic spellings until you find one that's just right.

A Few Hints

You'll find some programming techniques in Spelling Quizzer which you may want to adopt in your own speech programs.

For one thing, notice how some SAY statements use phonemes, while others use TRANSLATE$ to convert English text. There's a reason for this inconsistency—it saves work to try a spoken message with TRANSLATE$ first, turning to phonemes only if you can't get a certain word or sentence to sound quite as it should. (The phoneme-based phrases in Spelling Quizzer, inciden-

180

tally, were assembled with Speech Constructor.) An alternative to phonemes is to spell words phonetically in SAY TRANSLATE$ statements, as done when Spelling Quizzer asks you to enter phonetic spellings for each word.

For another programming tip, look at Spelling Quizzer's Initialize routine. Notice the order of these statements:

SAY TRANSLATE$ ("Just a moment please.")
scrid=1 'Set screen-ID for Requester subprogram.
SCREEN 1,320,200,2,1
WINDOW 1,label$(0),(0,0)–(311,185),20,1

In all Amiga programs that use speech, it's a good idea to place a SAY statement *before* the first statement that sets up your custom screen and window. Here's why.

The Amiga's speech synthesizer is not really a hardware feature—it's implemented in software. To be specific, the speech synthesizer consists of a 23,000-byte file named "narrator.device" found in the *devs* directory on the Workbench disk. The narrator device isn't normally resident in memory; when Amiga BASIC encounters the first SAY statement in a program, it must load this file from disk. If the proper disk isn't currently mounted in a drive, the Amiga opens up a requester window which asks you to insert it.

A problem arises, however, if your BASIC program has executed a SCREEN statement prior to the first SAY. The system requester opens up on the *primary* (Workbench/CLI) screen, invisible to a user who is looking at your newly created secondary screen. So the computer patiently waits for the user to insert a different disk, while the user not so patiently waits for the program to start. Result: A classic breakdown in communication.

Of course, the user could simultaneously press the left Amiga key and N to flip the primary screen and requester window into view, but you can't be sure everyone will think of that. Lots of people might assume the computer has mysteriously crashed or gone comatose.

The solution is to place your first SAY before the SCREEN and WINDOW statements. The spoken message can be something innocuous, such as, "Just a moment, please," or even a null string (" "). The object is to force the system requester window to appear—if it's necessary—before your secondary screen displaces the primary screen. Spelling Quizzer and Speech Constructor both use this technique.

Finally, the VolumeVoice and GenderVoice routines in Spelling Quizzer are modular enough to be easily adapted to your own speech programs. To prevent possible conflicts with existing program variables, you might even convert these routines into subprograms if you think you'll use them often.

Program 6-1. Speech Constructor

```
' *** Speech Constructor ***

Initialize:
 DEFINT a-z
 DIM label$(10) 'For often-used messages.
 label$(0)="Speech Constructor"
 label$(1)="*Press RETURN to exit*"
 label$(2)="*Click in this window*"
 label$(3)="    *to continue*"
 label$(4)="Just a moment, please..."
 label$(5)="Press RETURN to keep current value."
 SAY TRANSLATE$ ("Just a moment please.")
 WINDOW 1,"Speech Constructor",(0,0)-(631,185),20
 PRINT label$(4)
 DIM vowels$(12,2) 'Array for vowels.
 FOR x=1 TO 12
  READ vowels$(x,1) 'Actual phonemes.
  READ vowels$(x,2) 'Example words.
 NEXT x
 DATA IY,beet,EH,bet,AA,hot,AO,talk,ER,bird,AX,about
 DATA IH,bit,AE,bat,AH,under,UH,look,OH,border,IX,solid
 DIM diphthongs$(6,2):' Array for diphthongs.
 FOR x=1 TO 6
  READ diphthongs$(x,1) 'Actual phonemes.
  READ diphthongs$(x,2) 'Example words.
 NEXT x
 DATA EY,made,OY,boil,OW,low,AY,hide,AW,power,UW,crew
 DIM consonants1$(13,2):' Array for 1st consonants.
 FOR x=1 TO 13
  READ consonants1$(x,1) 'Actual phonemes.
  READ consonants1$(x,2) 'Example words.
 NEXT x
 DATA R,red,W,away,M,men,NX,sing,S,sail,F,fed,Z,has
 DATA V,very,CH,check,/H,hole,B,but,D,dog,K,commodore
 DIM consonants2$(12,2) 'Array for 2nd consonants.
 FOR x=1 TO 12
  READ consonants2$(x,1) 'Actual phonemes.
  READ consonants2$(x,2) 'Example words.
 NEXT x
 DATA L,yellow,Y,yellow,N,men,SH,rush,TH,thin,ZH,pleasure
 DATA DH,then,J,judge,/C,loch,P,put,T,toy,G,guest
 DIM special$(16,2):' Array for special phonemes.
 FOR x=1 TO 16
  READ special$(x,1) ' Actual phonemes.
  READ special$(x,2) ' Examples & equivalents.
 NEXT x
 DATA DX,pity,QX,pause,RX,car,UL,=AXL,UM,=AXM,UN,=AXN
 DATA Q,kitt-en,LX,call,IL,=IXL,IM,=IXM,IN,=IXN
 DATA " ",(space),".",period,"?",question mark
 DATA "-",dash,",",comma
 DIM voice%(8) 'Array for voice parameters.
 FOR x=0 TO 8
  READ voice%(x)
 NEXT x
```

182

```
    DATA 110,0,150,0,22200,64,10,0,0↵
    GOSUB MenuSetup↵
GOTO MainMenu↵
    ↵
MenuSetup:↵
    'Design custom menu bar:↵
    MENU 1,0,0,"Project"↵
    MENU 1,1,0,"Make Phrase "↵
    MENU 1,2,0,"Erase Word   "↵
    MENU 1,3,0,"Erase Phrase"↵
    MENU 1,4,0,"Open Phrase "↵
    MENU 1,5,0,"Save Phrase "↵
    MENU 1,6,0,"Print Phrase"↵
    MENU 1,7,0,"Type Word   "↵
    MENU 1,8,0,"Translate   "↵
    MENU 1,9,0,"Quit        "↵
    MENU 2,0,0,"Speech"↵
    MENU 2,1,0,"Say Word    "↵
    MENU 2,2,0,"Say Phrase "↵
    MENU 2,3,0,"Alter Voice"↵
    MENU 3,0,0,"Vowels"↵
    MENU 3,1,1,"IY      "↵
    MENU 3,2,1,"EH      "↵
    MENU 3,3,1,"AA      "↵
    MENU 3,4,1,"AO      "↵
    MENU 3,5,1,"ER      "↵
    MENU 3,6,1,"AX      "↵
    MENU 3,7,1,"IH      "↵
    MENU 3,8,1,"AE      "↵
    MENU 3,9,1,"AH      "↵
    MENU 3,10,1,"UH     "↵
    MENU 3,11,1,"OH     "↵
    MENU 3,12,1,"IX     "↵
    MENU 4,0,0,"Diphthongs"↵
    MENU 4,1,1,"EY      "↵
    MENU 4,2,1,"OY      "↵
    MENU 4,3,1,"OW      "↵
    MENU 4,4,1,"AY      "↵
    MENU 4,5,1,"AW      "↵
    MENU 4,6,1,"UW      "↵
    MENU 5,0,0,"Consl"↵
    MENU 5,1,1,"R       "↵
    MENU 5,2,1,"W       "↵
    MENU 5,3,1,"M       "↵
    MENU 5,4,1,"NX      "↵
    MENU 5,5,1,"S       "↵
    MENU 5,6,1,"F       "↵
    MENU 5,7,1,"Z       "↵
    MENU 5,8,1,"V       "↵
    MENU 5,9,1,"CH      "↵
    MENU 5,10,1,"/H     "↵
    MENU 5,11,1,"B      "↵
    MENU 5,12,1,"D      "↵
    MENU 5,13,1,"K      "↵
    MENU 6,0,0,"Cons2"↵
    MENU 6,1,1,"L       "↵
    MENU 6,2,1,"Y       "↵
```

```
    MENU 6,3,1,"N     "◄
    MENU 6,4,1,"SH    "◄
    MENU 6,5,1,"TH    "◄
    MENU 6,6,1,"ZH    "◄
    MENU 6,7,1,"DH    "◄
    MENU 6,8,1,"J     "◄
    MENU 6,9,1,"/C    "◄
    MENU 6,10,1,"P    "◄
    MENU 6,11,1,"T    "◄
    MENU 6,12,1,"G    "◄
    MENU 7,0,0,"Special"◄
    MENU 7,1,1,"DX    "◄
    MENU 7,2,1,"QX    "◄
    MENU 7,3,1,"RX    "◄
    MENU 7,4,1,"UL    "◄
    MENU 7,5,1,"UM    "◄
    MENU 7,6,1,"UN    "◄
    MENU 7,7,1,"Q     "◄
    MENU 7,8,1,"LX    "◄
    MENU 7,9,1,"IL    "◄
    MENU 7,10,1,"IM   "◄
    MENU 7,11,1,"IN   "◄
    MENU 7,12,1,"Space "◄
    MENU 7,13,1,"Period"◄
    MENU 7,14,1,"? mark"◄
    MENU 7,15,1,"- dash"◄
    MENU 7,16,1,",comma"◄
    MENU 7,17,1,"Stress"◄
RETURN◄
 ◄
MainMenu:◄
 ON ERROR GOTO 0◄
 CLS◄
 'Define status of menu selections◄
 'for Main Menu bar.◄
 'Following items always on:◄
 MENU 1,0,1:MENU 1,8,1:MENU 1,9,1◄
 MENU 2,0,1:MENU 2,3,1:MENU 3,0,1:MENU 4,0,1◄
 MENU 5,0,1:MENU 6,0,1:MENU 7,0,1◄
 'Following items on or off◄
 'depending on whether a word◄
 'or phrase is currently in memory:◄
 IF LEN(phrase$)=0 THEN◄
   MENU 1,3,0:MENU 1,4,1:MENU 1,5,0:MENU 1,6,0:MENU 2,2,0◄
 ELSE◄
   MENU 1,3,1:MENU 1,4,0:MENU 1,5,1:MENU 1,6,1:MENU 2,2,1◄
 END IF◄
 IF LEN(word$)=0 THEN◄
   MENU 1,1,0:MENU 1,7,1:MENU 1,2,0:MENU 2,1,0◄
 ELSE◄
   MENU 1,1,1:MENU 1,2,1:MENU 1,7,0:MENU 2,1,1◄
 END IF◄
 WIDTH 80◄
 PRINT:PRINT "--Select choice from menu bar--"◄
 PRINT:PRINT "Current word: ";word$◄
 PRINT:PRINT "Current phrase: ";phrase$◄
 Checkmenloop:◄
```

```
   MenuID=MENU(0)◄
    IF MenuID=0 THEN Checkmenloop◄
   MenuItem=MENU(1)◄
   ON MenuID GOTO ProjectMenu,SpeechMenu,VowMenu,DipMenu,Cons1Menu,
   Cons2Menu,SpecMenu◄
   GOTO Checkmenloop◄
        ◄
ProjectMenu:◄
   'Handles selections from Project menu.◄
   ON MenuItem GOTO MakePhrase,NewWord,NewPhrase,OpenPhrase,SavePhr
   ase,PrintPhrase,TypeWord,Translate,Quit◄
◄
SpeechMenu:◄
   'Handles selections from Speech menu.◄
   ON MenuItem GOTO SayWord,SayPhrase,AlterVoice◄
◄
VowMenu:◄
   'Handles selections from Vowels menu.◄
   MENU 1,0,0:MENU 2,0,0:MENU 3,0,0◄
   MENU 4,0,0:MENU 5,0,0:MENU 6,0,0◄
   MENU 7,0,0:CLS◄
   phoneme$=vowels$(MenuItem,1)◄
   WIDTH 80:LOCATE 8,1:PRINT "Phoneme: ";phoneme$◄
   PRINT:PRINT "Example: ";vowels$(MenuItem,2)◄
   PRINT:PRINT "Current word + phoneme: ";word$+phoneme$◄
   ON ERROR GOTO ErrorTrap◄
   SAY word$+phoneme$,voice%◄
   ON ERROR GOTO 0◄
   msg1$="Add phoneme to current word?"◄
   CALL Requester (msg1$,"","ADD","CANCEL",0,answer%)◄
   IF answer%=0 GOTO MainMenu 'CANCEL was selected.◄
   word$=word$+phoneme$ 'ADD was selected.◄
GOTO MainMenu◄
   ◄
DipMenu:◄
   'Handles selections from Diphthongs menu.◄
   MENU 1,0,0:MENU 2,0,0:MENU 3,0,0◄
   MENU 4,0,0:MENU 5,0,0:MENU 6,0,0◄
   MENU 7,0,0:CLS◄
   phoneme$=diphthongs$(MenuItem,1)◄
   WIDTH 80:LOCATE 8,1◄
   PRINT "Phoneme: ";phoneme$◄
   PRINT:PRINT "Example: ";diphthongs$(MenuItem,2)◄
   PRINT:PRINT "Current word + phoneme: ";word$+phoneme$◄
   ON ERROR GOTO ErrorTrap◄
   SAY word$+phoneme$,voice%◄
   ON ERROR GOTO 0◄
   msg1$="Add phoneme to current word?"◄
   CALL Requester (msg1$,"","ADD","CANCEL",0,answer%)◄
   IF answer%=0 GOTO MainMenu 'CANCEL was selected.◄
   word$=word$+phoneme$ 'ADD was selected.◄
GOTO MainMenu◄
   ◄
Cons1Menu:◄
   'Handles selections from Cons1 menu.◄
   MENU 1,0,0:MENU 2,0,0:MENU 3,0,0◄
   MENU 4,0,0:MENU 5,0,0:MENU 6,0,0◄
```

```
     MENU 7,0,0:CLS◄
     phoneme$=consonants1$(MenuItem,1)◄
     WIDTH 80:LOCATE 8,1:PRINT "Phoneme: ";phoneme$◄
     PRINT:PRINT "Example: ";consonants1$(MenuItem,2)◄
     PRINT:PRINT "Current word + phoneme: ";word$+phoneme$◄
     ON ERROR GOTO ErrorTrap◄
     SAY word$+phoneme$,voice%◄
     ON ERROR GOTO 0◄
     msg1$="Add phoneme to current word?"◄
     CALL Requester (msg1$,"","ADD","CANCEL",0,answer%)◄
     IF answer=0 GOTO MainMenu 'CANCEL was selected.◄
     word$=word$+phoneme$ 'ADD was selected.◄
   GOTO MainMenu◄
 ◄
   Cons2Menu:◄
     'Handles selections from Cons2 menu.◄
     MENU 1,0,0:MENU 2,0,0:MENU 3,0,0◄
     MENU 4,0,0:MENU 5,0,0:MENU 6,0,0◄
     MENU 7,0,0:CLS◄
     phoneme$=consonants2$(MenuItem,1)◄
     WIDTH 80:LOCATE 8,1:PRINT "Phoneme: ";phoneme$◄
     PRINT:PRINT "Example: ";consonants2$(MenuItem,2)◄
     PRINT:PRINT "Current word + phoneme: ";word$+phoneme$◄
     ON ERROR GOTO ErrorTrap◄
     SAY word$+phoneme$,voice%◄
     ON ERROR GOTO 0◄
     msg1$="Add phoneme to current word?"◄
     CALL Requester (msg1$,"","ADD","CANCEL",0,answer%)◄
     IF answer%=0 GOTO MainMenu 'CANCEL was selected.◄
     word$=word$+phoneme$ 'ADD was selected.◄
   GOTO MainMenu◄
     ◄
   SpecMenu:◄
     'Handles selections from Special menu.◄
     MENU 1,0,0:MENU 2,0,0:MENU 3,0,0◄
     MENU 4,0,0:MENU 5,0,0:MENU 6,0,0◄
     MENU 7,0,0:CLS◄
     'Next line skips to Stress selection:◄
     IF MenuItem=17 GOTO AddStress◄
     phoneme$=special$(MenuItem,1)◄
     WIDTH 80:LOCATE 8,1:PRINT "Phoneme: ";phoneme$◄
     PRINT:PRINT "Example: ";special$(MenuItem,2)◄
     PRINT:PRINT "Current word + phoneme: ";word$+phoneme$◄
     ON ERROR GOTO ErrorTrap◄
     SAY word$+phoneme$,voice%◄
     ON ERROR GOTO 0◄
     msg1$="Add phoneme to current word?"◄
     CALL Requester (msg1$,"","ADD","CANCEL",0,answer%)◄
     IF answer%=0 GOTO MainMenu 'CANCEL was selected.◄
     word$=word$+phoneme$ 'ADD was selected.◄
   GOTO MainMenu◄
 ◄
   AddStress:◄
     CLS:WIDTH 80:LOCATE 10,1◄
     PRINT "Press key 1 to 9 to add stress to current word."◄
     PRINT:PRINT label$(1)◄
```

```
Stressloop:
 temp$=INKEY$
 IF temp$="" GOTO Stressloop
IF temp$=CHR$(13) GOTO MainMenu 'Abort routine.
IF ASC(temp$)>48 AND ASC(temp$)<58 THEN
 'Key 1-9 was pressed.
 word$=word$+temp$
 GOTO MainMenu
ELSE
 'Keypress was out of range.
 GOTO AddStress
END IF

MakePhrase:
 'Adds current word to phrase.
 MENU 1,0,0:MENU 2,0,0:MENU 3,0,0
 MENU 4,0,0:MENU 5,0,0:MENU 6,0,0
 MENU 7,0,0:CLS
 WIDTH 80:LOCATE 8,1:PRINT "Current word: ";word$
 PRINT:PRINT "Current phrase: ";phrase$
 ON ERROR GOTO ErrorTrap
 SAY phrase$+word$,voice%
 ON ERROR GOTO 0
 msg1$="Add current word to phrase?"
 CALL Requester (msg1$,"","ADD","CANCEL",0,answer%)
 IF answer%=0 GOTO MainMenu 'CANCEL was selected.
 phrase$=phrase$+word$ 'ADD was selected.
GOTO MainMenu

NewWord:
 'Erases current word.
 MENU 1,0,0:MENU 2,0,0:MENU 3,0,0
 MENU 4,0,0:MENU 5,0,0:MENU 6,0,0
 MENU 7,0,0:CLS:LOCATE 10,1
 PRINT "Current word: ";word$
 msg1$="Erase current word?"
 CALL Requester (msg1$,"","ERASE","CANCEL",2,answer%)
 IF answer%=0 GOTO MainMenu 'CANCEL was selected.
 word$="" 'ERASE was selected.
GOTO MainMenu

NewPhrase:
 'Erases current phrase.
 MENU 1,0,0:MENU 2,0,0:MENU 3,0,0
 MENU 4,0,0:MENU 5,0,0:MENU 6,0,0
 MENU 7,0,0:CLS:LOCATE 10,1
 PRINT "Current phrase: ";phrase$
 msg1$="Erase current phrase?"
 CALL Requester (msg1$,"","ERASE","CANCEL",2,answer%)
 IF answer%=0 GOTO MainMenu 'CANCEL was selected.
 phrase$="" 'ERASE was selected.
GOTO MainMenu

OpenPhrase:
 'Loads previously stored phrase
 'and voice parameters from disk.
 MENU 1,0,0:MENU 2,0,0:MENU 3,0,0
```

```
MENU 4,0,0:MENU 5,0,0:MENU 6,0,0
MENU 7,0,0:CLS:WIDTH 80:LOCATE 8,1:PRINT label$(1)
PRINT:PRINT "Enter filename of phrase to load:"
LINE INPUT ">> ";filename$
IF filename$="" GOTO MainMenu 'Abort routine.
ON ERROR GOTO ErrorTrap
OPEN filename$ FOR INPUT AS #1
 PRINT:PRINT "Loading ";filename$;"..."
 FOR x=0 TO 8 'Get voice parameters.
  INPUT# 1,voice%(x)
 NEXT x
 INPUT# 1,phrase$ 'Get phrase.
CLOSE #1
ON ERROR GOTO 0
GOTO MainMenu

SavePhrase:
 'Saves current phrase
 'and voice parameters on disk.
 MENU 1,0,0:MENU 2,0,0:MENU 3,0,0
 MENU 4,0,0:MENU 5,0,0:MENU 6,0,0
 MENU 7,0,0:CLS:WIDTH 80:LOCATE 8,1
 PRINT label$(1):PRINT:PRINT "Enter filename to save:"
 LINE INPUT ">> ";filename$
 IF filename$="" GOTO MainMenu 'Abort routine.
 ON ERROR GOTO ErrorTrap
 OPEN filename$ FOR OUTPUT AS #1
  PRINT:PRINT "Saving under filename ";filename$;"..."
  FOR x=0 TO 8 'Save voice parameters.
   WRITE# 1,voice%(x)
  NEXT x
  WRITE# 1,phrase$ 'Save phrase.
 CLOSE #1
 ON ERROR GOTO 0
 temp&=TIMER 'Wait for drive to finish...
 WHILE TIMER<temp&+6:WEND
GOTO MainMenu

PrintPhrase:
 'Prints current phrase on printer.
 MENU 1,0,0:MENU 2,0,0:MENU 3,0,0
 MENU 4,0,0:MENU 5,0,0:MENU 6,0,0
 MENU 7,0,0:CLS
 msg1$="Click PRINT when ready."
 msg2$="(Be sure printer is online.)"
 CALL Requester (msg1$,msg2$,"PRINT","CANCEL",0,answer%)
 IF answer%=0 GOTO MainMenu 'CANCEL was selected.
 'PRINT was selected:
 ON ERROR GOTO ErrorTrap
 OPEN "prt:" FOR OUTPUT AS #1
 PRINT# 1,"":PRINT# 1,""
 PRINT# 1,phrase$
 PRINT# 1,"":PRINT# 1,""
 CLOSE #1
 ON ERROR GOTO 0
GOTO MainMenu
```

```
TypeWord:◄
 'Allows keyboard entry of phonemes.◄
 MENU 1,0,0:MENU 2,0,0:CLS:PRINT label$(1):PRINT◄
 PRINT "This allows direct keyboard entry"◄
 PRINT "of a word or series of words in phonemes."◄
 PRINT "Phoneme menus are available for reference only."◄
 PRINT:PRINT "Enter valid phonemes and press RETURN:"◄
 PRINT:LINE INPUT ">> ",word$◄
 word$=UCASE$(word$) 'Convert to uppercase.◄
 Clearmenu:◄
  MenuID=MENU(0)◄
  IF MenuID=0 GOTO MainMenu◄
  MenuItem=MENU(1)◄
 GOTO Clearmenu◄
◄
Translate:◄
 'Translates English text to phonemes.◄
 'Accepts input from keyboard.◄
 MENU 1,0,0:MENU 2,0,0:MENU 3,0,0◄
 MENU 4,0,0:MENU 5,0,0:MENU 6,0,0◄
 MENU 7,0,0:CLS:PRINT label$(1):PRINT◄
 PRINT "Enter English text to translate"◄
 PRINT "into phonemes and press RETURN:"◄
 PRINT:LINE INPUT ">> ",temp$◄
 IF temp$="" GOTO MainMenu 'Abort routine.◄
 PRINT:PRINT TRANSLATE$ (temp$)◄
 ON ERROR GOTO ErrorTrap◄
 SAY TRANSLATE$ (temp$),voice%◄
 ON ERROR GOTO 0◄
 PRINT:PRINT:GOSUB Clickmouse◄
GOTO MainMenu◄
◄
Quit:◄
 'Exits program to BASIC.◄
 MENU 1,0,0:MENU 2,0,0:MENU 3,0,0◄
 MENU 4,0,0:MENU 5,0,0:MENU 6,0,0:MENU 7,0,0:CLS◄
 'Different warning if phrase in memory:◄
 msg1$="Quit program to BASIC?"◄
 IF LEN(phrase$)=0 THEN◄
  msg2$=""◄
 ELSE◄
  msg2$="Current phrase will be erased."◄
 END IF◄
 CALL Requester (msg1$,msg2$,"QUIT","CANCEL",2,answer%)◄
 IF answer%=0 GOTO MainMenu 'CANCEL was selected.◄
CLS:END 'QUIT was selected.◄
  ◄
SayWord:◄
 'Speaks current word.◄
 MENU 1,0,0:MENU 2,0,0:MENU 3,0,0◄
 MENU 4,0,0:MENU 5,0,0:MENU 6,0,0◄
 MENU 7,0,0:CLS:LOCATE 10,1◄
 PRINT "Current word: ";word$◄
 ON ERROR GOTO ErrorTrap◄
 SAY word$,voice%◄
 ON ERROR GOTO 0◄
GOTO MainMenu◄
```

```
 ◄
  SayPhrase:◄
   'Speaks current phrase.◄
   MENU 1,0,0:MENU 2,0,0:MENU 3,0,0◄
   MENU 4,0,0:MENU 5,0,0:MENU 6,0,0◄
   MENU 7,0,0:CLS:LOCATE 10,1◄
   PRINT "Current phrase: ";phrase$◄
   ON ERROR GOTO ErrorTrap◄
   SAY phrase$,voice%◄
   ON ERROR GOTO 0◄
  GOTO MainMenu◄
 ◄
  AlterVoice:◄
   'Alters voice parameters.◄
   MENU 1,0,0:MENU 2,0,0:MENU 3,0,0◄
   MENU 4,0,0:MENU 5,0,0:MENU 6,0,0:MENU 7,0,0◄
   parameter$="PITCH:"◄
   parnum=0 'Parameter number of voice% array.◄
   default=110 'Default value of parameter.◄
   loval=65:hival=320 'Legal lo & hi values.◄
   GOSUB NewVoice◄
   parameter$="INFLECTION:"◄
   parnum=1:default=0:loval=0:hival=1◄
   GOSUB NewVoice◄
   parameter$="SPEAKING RATE:"◄
   parnum=2:default=150:loval=40:hival=400◄
   GOSUB NewVoice◄
   parameter$="GENDER:"◄
   parnum=3:default=0:loval=0:hival=1◄
   GOSUB NewVoice◄
   parameter$="SAMPLING FREQUENCY:"◄
   parnum=4:default=22200:loval=5000:hival=28000◄
   GOSUB NewVoice◄
   parameter$="VOLUME:"◄
   parnum=5:default=64:loval=0:hival=64◄
   GOSUB NewVoice◄
   parameter$="CHANNEL:"◄
   parnum=6:default=10:loval=0:hival=11◄
   GOSUB NewVoice◄
  GOTO MainMenu◄
 ◄
  NewVoice:◄
   CLS:PRINT label$(5):PRINT◄
   PRINT "Alter ";parameter$◄
   PRINT "Default value = ";default◄
   PRINT "Current value = ";voice%(parnum)◄
   PRINT "Enter value from";loval;"to";hival;"> ";◄
   INPUT "",temp$◄
   IF temp$="" THEN RETURN:' Keep current value.◄
   temp=INT(VAL(temp$)) 'Convert string to value.◄
   IF temp<loval OR temp>hival GOTO NewVoice◄
   voice%(parnum)=temp◄
  RETURN◄
     ◄
  Clickmouse:◄
   'Patiently waits for mouse click & release.◄
   PRINT label$(2):PRINT label$(3)◄
```

```
 WHILE MOUSE(0)=0:WEND:WHILE MOUSE(0)<>0:WEND
RETURN

SUB Requester (msg1$,msg2$,b1$,b2$,hilite%,answer%) STATIC
 ' Requester window subprogram version 3.4.
 SHARED scrid 'Global variable for SCREEN ID.
 IF scrid<1 OR scrid>4 THEN scrid=-1 'Default to Workbench.
 WINDOW 3,"Program Request",(0,0)-(311,45),16,scrid
 maxwidth=INT(WINDOW(2)/8) 'Truncate prompts if too long...
 PRINT LEFT$(msg1$,maxwidth):PRINT LEFT$(msg2$,maxwidth)
 b1$=LEFT$(b1$,12):b2$=LEFT$(b2$,12) 'Truncate buttons.
 bsize1=(LEN(b1$)+2)*10:bsize2=(LEN(b2$)+2)*10 'Button size.
 x1=(312-(bsize1+bsize2))/3  'Calculate button positions...
 x2=x1+bsize1:x3=x1+x2:x4=x3+bsize2
 'Draw buttons:
 LINE (x1,20)-(x2,38),2,B:LINE (x3,20)-(x4,38),2,B
 IF hilite%=1 THEN LINE (x1+2,22)-(x2-2,36),3,B
 IF hilite%=2 THEN LINE (x3+2,22)-(x4-2,36),3,B
 LOCATE 4,1:PRINT PTAB(x1+10);b1$;
 PRINT PTAB(x3+10);b2$
 reqloop: 'Loop which acts on mouse clicks...
 WHILE MOUSE(0)=0:WEND:m1=MOUSE(1):m2=MOUSE(2)
 IF m1>x1 AND m1<x2 AND m2>20 AND m2<38 THEN
  answer%=1 'Left button was selected.
  LINE (x1,20)-(x2,38),1,bf 'Flash left button.
 ELSEIF m1>x3 AND m1<x4 AND m2>20 AND m2<38 THEN
  answer%=0 'Right button was selected.
  LINE (x3,20)-(x4,38),1,bf 'Flash right button.
 ELSE
  GOTO reqloop 'Neither button selected; repeat loop.
 END IF
 WHILE MOUSE(0)<>0:WEND:WINDOW CLOSE 3
END SUB

ErrorTrap:
 'Version 1.5
 BEEP 'Get user's attention.
 IF ERR=5 THEN
  request1$="Speech error. Check stress."
  GOTO ExitError
 END IF
 IF ERR=53 THEN
  request1$="FILE NOT FOUND."
  GOTO ExitError
 END IF
 IF ERR=61 THEN
  request1$="DISK FULL."
  GOTO ExitError
 END IF
 IF ERR=64 THEN
  request1$="BAD FILENAME."
  GOTO ExitError
 END IF
 IF ERR=67 THEN
  request1$="DIRECTORY FULL."
  GOTO ExitError
 END IF
```

191

```
IF ERR=68 THEN◄
 request1$="DEVICE UNAVAILABLE."◄
 GOTO ExitError◄
END IF◄
IF ERR=70 THEN◄
 request1$="DISK WRITE-PROTECTED."◄
 GOTO ExitError◄
END IF◄
IF ERR=74 THEN◄
 request1$="UNKNOWN DISK VOLUME."◄
 GOTO ExitError◄
END IF◄
request1$="ERROR NUMBER"+STR$(ERR)◄
ExitError:◄
' Abort operation or try again.◄
CALL Requester (request1$,"","Retry","CANCEL",2,answer%)◄
IF answer%=0 THEN◄
 CLOSE #1◄
 RESUME MainMenu◄
ELSE◄
 CLOSE #1◄
 ON ERROR GOTO ErrorTrap◄
 RESUME◄
END IF◄
```

Program 6-2. Spelling Quizzer

```
'   *** Spelling Quizzer ***◄
◄
 Initialize:◄
  DEFINT a-z 'Integer variables for speed◄
  DIM label$(10) 'For often-used messages...◄
  label$(0)="Spelling Quizzer"◄
  label$(1)="*Press RETURN to exit*"◄
  label$(2)="*Click in this window*"◄
  label$(3)="    *to continue*"◄
  label$(4)="Just a moment, please..."◄
  label$(5)=" Click OK to retry."◄
  maxwords=50 'Maximum words allowed in list.◄
  DIM wordlist$(maxwords,2) 'Stores word list.◄
  FOR j=0 TO 8 'Set voice characteristics.◄
    READ voice%(j)◄
  NEXT j◄
  'Next line contains voice parameters.◄
  DATA 110,0,150,0,22200,55,10,0,0◄
  male=2:female=1 'Gender flags for menu.◄
  SAY TRANSLATE$ ("Just a moment please.")◄
  scrid=1 'Set screen-ID for Requester subprogram.◄
  SCREEN 1,320,200,2,1◄
  WINDOW 1,label$(0),(0,0)-(311,185),20,1◄
  PRINT label$(4)◄
  GOSUB MenuSetup◄
  GOTO MainMenu◄
  ◄
```

```
MenuSetup:◄
 'Design custom menu bar.◄
 MENU 1,0,0,"Project"◄
 MENU 1,1,0,"New"+SPACE$(8)◄
 MENU 1,2,0,"Open Words"+SPACE$(1)◄
 MENU 1,3,0,"Save Words"+SPACE$(1)◄
 MENU 1,4,0,"Save As"+SPACE$(4)◄
 MENU 1,5,0,"Print Words"◄
 MENU 1,6,0,"Quit"+SPACE$(7)◄
 MENU 2,0,0,"Tools"◄
 MENU 2,1,0,"Start Quiz"+SPACE$(1)◄
 MENU 2,2,0,"Enter Words"◄
 MENU 2,3,0,"Study Words"◄
 MENU 3,0,0,"Voice"◄
 MENU 3,1,0,SPACE$(2)+"Male"+SPACE$(2)◄
 MENU 3,2,0,SPACE$(2)+"Female"◄
 MENU 3,3,0,SPACE$(2)+"Volume"◄
 MENU 4,0,0,""◄
RETURN◄
 ◄
MainMenu:◄
 ON ERROR GOTO 0◄
 CLS:WIDTH 30◄
 'Define status of menu selections◄
 'for Main Menu bar.◄
 'Following menu items always on:◄
 MENU 1,0,1:MENU 2,0,1:MENU 3,0,1◄
 MENU 1,6,1:MENU 3,3,1◄
 MENU 3,1,male:MENU 3,2,female 'Gender status.◄
 'Following menu items on or off◄
 'if no word list in memory.◄
 IF wordlist$(1,1)="" THEN◄
  MENU 1,1,0:MENU 1,2,1◄
  MENU 1,3,0:MENU 1,4,0◄
  MENU 1,5,0:MENU 2,1,0◄
  MENU 2,2,1:MENU 2,3,0◄
 'Following menu items on or off◄
 'if word list in memory:◄
 ELSE◄
  MENU 1,1,1:MENU 1,2,0◄
  MENU 1,3,1:MENU 1,4,1◄
  MENU 1,5,1:MENU 2,1,1◄
  MENU 2,2,0:MENU 2,3,1◄
 END IF◄
 PRINT:PRINT "-Select choice from menu bar-"◄
 Checkmenloop:◄
  MenuID=MENU(0)◄
  IF MenuID=0 THEN Checkmenloop◄
 MenuItem=MENU(1)◄
 ON MenuID GOTO ProjectMenu,ToolsMenu,VoiceMenu◄
 GOTO Checkmenloop◄
  ◄
ProjectMenu:◄
 'Handles selection from Project menu.◄
 ON MenuItem GOTO NewWords,OpenWords,SaveWords,SaveAsWords,PrintW
ords,Quit◄
◄
```

```
ToolsMenu:
  'Handles selection from Tools menu.
  ON MenuItem GOTO StartQuiz,EnterWords,StudyWords

VoiceMenu:
  'Handles selection from Voice menu.
  ON MenuItem GOTO GenderVoice,GenderVoice,VolumeVoice

NewWords:
  'Erases current spelling word list.
  MENU 1,0,0:MENU 2,0,0:MENU 3,0,0:CLS
  msg1$="Erase current word list?"
  CALL Requester (msg1$,"","ERASE","CANCEL",2,answer%)
  IF answer%=0 GOTO MainMenu 'CANCEL was selected.
  ERASE wordlist$:DIM wordlist$(maxwords,2)
GOTO MainMenu

OpenWords:
  'Loads spelling word list from disk.
  MENU 1,0,0:MENU 2,0,0:MENU 3,0,0
  CLS:LOCATE 2,4:PRINT label$(1)
  PRINT:PRINT "Enter filename of word list"
  PRINT "to open [QuizWords]:"
  LINE INPUT ">> ";filename$
  IF filename$="" GOTO MainMenu 'Abort routine.
  ON ERROR GOTO ErrorTrap
  OPEN filename$ FOR INPUT AS 1
  INPUT#1,listlen 'Get length of word list.
  FOR j=1 TO listlen 'Get words and phonetics.
    INPUT#1,wordlist$(j,1),wordlist$(j,2)
  NEXT j
  CLOSE #1
  ON ERROR GOTO 0
GOTO MainMenu

SaveWords:
  'Saves spelling word list on disk
  'with default filename "QuizWords".
  'Shares code with SaveAsWords routine.
  MENU 1,0,0:MENU 2,0,0:MENU 3,0,0:CLS
  msg1$="Save with filename:"
  msg2$=CHR$(34)+"QuizWords"+CHR$(34)+"?"
  CALL Requester (msg1$,msg2$,"SAVE","CANCEL",0,answer%)
  IF answer%=0 GOTO MainMenu 'CANCEL was selected.
  filename$="QuizWords" 'SAVE was selected.
  GOTO SaveIt 'Jump to shared code.
SaveAsWords:
  'Saves spelling word list on disk
  'under filename chosen by user.
  'Shares code with SaveWords routine.
  MENU 1,0,0:MENU 2,0,0:MENU 3,0,0
  CLS:LOCATE 1,4:PRINT label$(1):PRINT
  PRINT "Enter filename"
  PRINT "to save [QuizWords]"
  LINE INPUT ">> ";filename$
  IF filename$="" GOTO MainMenu 'Abort routine.
  SaveIt:
```

```
    WIDTH 31
    ON ERROR GOTO ErrorTrap
    OPEN filename$ FOR OUTPUT AS 1
    WRITE# 1,listlen 'Save # of words in list.
    FOR j=1 TO listlen
      'Save spelling word and phonetic spelling.
      WRITE# 1,wordlist$(j,1),wordlist$(j,2)
    NEXT j
    CLOSE #1
    ON ERROR GOTO 0
    temp&=TIMER 'Wait for disk drive to finish...
    WHILE TIMER<temp&+6:WEND
GOTO MainMenu

PrintWords:
 'Prints spelling word list on printer.
 MENU 1,0,0:MENU 2,0,0:MENU 3,0,0
 CLS:LOCATE 2,4:PRINT label$(1)
 PRINT:PRINT "Enter title for word list:"
 LINE INPUT ">> ";temp$
 IF temp$="" GOTO MainMenu 'Abort routine.
 ON ERROR GOTO ErrorTrap
 OPEN "prt:" FOR OUTPUT AS 1
 PRINT# 1,"":PRINT# 1,""
 PRINT# 1,temp$:PRINT# 1,"":PRINT# 1,""
 FOR j=1 TO listlen
   PRINT# 1,wordlist$(j,1)
 NEXT j
 CLOSE #1
 ON ERROR GOTO 0
GOTO MainMenu

Quit:
 'Quits program to BASIC.
 MENU 1,0,0:MENU 2,0,0:MENU 3,0,0:CLS
 'Check if word list is in memory:
 IF wordlist$(1,1)="" THEN
  msg1$="Quit program to Workbench?"
  msg2$=""
 ELSE
  msg1$="Quit program (erase words)"
  msg2$="and exit to Workbench?"
 END IF
 CALL Requester (msg1$,msg2$,"QUIT","CANCEL",2,answer%)
 IF answer%=0 GOTO MainMenu 'CANCEL was selected.
 WINDOW CLOSE 1:SCREEN CLOSE 1:SYSTEM

StartQuiz:
 'Begins spelling word quiz.
 MENU 1,0,0:MENU 2,0,0:MENU 3,0,0
 CLS:LOCATE 2,4
 IF kidname$="" THEN
  PRINT label$(1)
  PRINT:PRINT "What is your name?"
  SAY TRANSLATE$ ("What is your name?"),voice%
  LINE INPUT ">> ";kidname$
  IF kidname$="" GOTO MainMenu 'Abort routine.
```

```
END IF◄
CLS:PRINT:PRINT "Hello, ";UCASE$(kidname$)◄
SAY TRANSLATE$ ("Hello "+kidname$+"."),voice%◄
PRINT:PRINT "I am going"◄
PRINT " to test your spelling."◄
SAY TRANSLATE$ ("I am going to test your spelling."),voice%◄
PRINT:PRINT "Type each word"◄
PRINT " and press RETURN."◄
SAY "TAY4P IY4CH WER4D AEND PREH4S RIYTER4N.",voice%◄
mistakes=0 'Current number of spelling mistakes.◄
correct=0 'Current number of words spelled correctly.◄
FOR j=1 TO listlen◄
 try=1 'Current number of tries to spell word.◄
 Quizloop:◄
  PRINT:PRINT "Word #";j;":"◄
  SAY TRANSLATE$ ("The word is."),voice%◄
  SAY TRANSLATE$ (wordlist$(j,2)),voice%◄
  LINE INPUT ">> ";temp$◄
  IF UCASE$(temp$)<>UCASE$(wordlist$(j,1)) THEN◄
   mistakes=mistakes+1 'Keep track of score.◄
   try=try+1◄
   IF try>3 THEN◄
    'Spell the word aloud after three mistakes...◄
    PRINT:PRINT "The word"◄
    PRINT "is spelled: ";UCASE$(wordlist$(j,1))◄
    SAY TRANSLATE$ ("The word "+wordlist$(j,2)+" is spelled."),voice
    %◄
    FOR k=1 TO LEN(wordlist$(j,1))◄
     SAY TRANSLATE$ (MID$(wordlist$(j,1),k,1)+"."),voice%◄
    NEXT k◄
   ELSE◄
    PRINT:PRINT "Sorry. Try again."◄
    SAY TRANSLATE$ ("Sorry. Try again."),voice%◄
    GOTO Quizloop◄
   END IF◄
  ELSE◄
   PRINT:PRINT "You spelled it right!"◄
   SAY "YUW SPEHLD IHT RAY9T.",voice%◄
   IF try=1 THEN correct=correct+1 'Spelled right 1st try.◄
  END IF◄
 CLS:NEXT j◄
CLS◄
PRINT:PRINT "You spelled";correct;"words"◄
PRINT " right on the first try."◄
SAY TRANSLATE$ ("You spelled "+STR$(correct)+" words right on th
e first try."),voice%◄
PRINT:PRINT "You made";mistakes;"mistakes."◄
SAY TRANSLATE$ ("You made "+STR$(mistakes)+"mistakes."),voice%◄
grade=100-((100/listlen)*mistakes)◄
IF grade>89 THEN◄
 PRINT:PRINT "You did very well."◄
 SAY "YUW DIHD VEH1RIY WEHL",voice%◄
ELSE◄
 PRINT:PRINT "You can do better."◄
 SAY TRANSLATE$ ("You can do better."),voice%◄
 PRINT:PRINT "Study the words and try again."◄
 SAY "STAH4DIY DHAX WER4DZ AEND TRAY4 AX1GEH3N.",voice%◄
```

```
      END IF
      PRINT:GOSUB Clickmouse
GOTO MainMenu

EnterWords:
  'Lets user enter spelling word list.
  MENU 1,0,0:MENU 2,0,0:MENU 3,0,0
  CLS:LOCATE 2,4:PRINT label$(1):PRINT
  Inloop1:
    PRINT "Number of words"
    INPUT "in spelling list";listlen
    IF listlen=0 GOTO MainMenu 'Abort routine.
    IF listlen<2 OR listlen>maxwords THEN
      BEEP:PRINT:PRINT "List must have"
      PRINT "between 2 and";maxwords;"words."
      PRINT:GOTO Inloop1
    END IF
  CLS
  FOR j=1 TO listlen
    Inloop2:
      PRINT "Spelling word #";j;"?"
      LINE INPUT ">> ";word$
      IF word$="" GOTO Inloop2
    wordlist$(j,1)=word$
    SAY TRANSLATE$ (word$),voice%
    phonetic$=word$
    Inloop3:
      PRINT:PRINT "Enter phonetic spelling"
      LINE INPUT "or RETURN>> ";temp$
      IF temp$="" THEN
        wordlist$(j,2)=phonetic$
      ELSE
        phonetic$=temp$
        SAY TRANSLATE$ (phonetic$),voice%
        GOTO Inloop3
      END IF
    CLS
  NEXT j
GOTO MainMenu

StudyWords:
  'Displays spelling word list on screen.
  MENU 1,0,0:MENU 2,0,0:MENU 3,0,0:CLS:PRINT
  j=1:k=1 'Counters for loops.
  WHILE j<=listlen
    WHILE k<11
      PRINT SPACE$(5);j;wordlist$(j,1)
      j=j+1:k=k+1
    WEND
    k=1:PRINT:PRINT
    GOSUB Clickmouse
    CLS:PRINT
  WEND
GOTO MainMenu

GenderVoice:
  'Lets user choose male or female voice.
```

```
  MENU 1,0,0:MENU 2,0,0:MENU 3,0,0:CLS
  IF MenuItem=1 THEN
   male=2:female=1 'Select MALE on menu.
   voice%(0)=110 'Set pitch for male.
   voice%(3)=0 'Set gender to male.
  ELSE
   male=1:female=2 'Select FEMALE on menu.
   voice%(0)=220 'Set pitch for female.
   voice%(3)=1 'Set gender to female.
  END IF
  SAY TRANSLATE$ ("This is my new voice."),voice%
  GOTO MainMenu

VolumeVoice:
  'Lets user adjust volume of voice.
  MENU 1,0,0:MENU 2,0,0:MENU 3,0,0:CLS
  setting=voice%(5)*4+28 'Current volume setting.
  LINE (23,100)-(289,110),1,b 'Draw slider box.
  LINE (setting-3,101)-(setting+3,109),1,bf 'Draw slider.
  LINE (123,150)-(183,180),1,b 'Draw OK box.
  LOCATE 19,1:PRINT PTAB(140);"OK"
  LOCATE 4,2:PRINT "Click in box to change volume"
  LOCATE 10,4:PRINT "< Softer"
  LOCATE 10,21:PRINT "Louder >"
  Volumeloop:
   WHILE MOUSE(0)=0:WEND 'Wait for button press.
   mx=MOUSE(1):my=MOUSE(2)
   WHILE MOUSE(0)<>0:WEND 'Wait for button release.
   IF mx>26 AND mx<286 AND my>100 AND my<110 THEN
    LINE (setting-3,101)-(setting+3,109),0,bf 'Erase slider.
    setting=mx 'New volume setting.
    LINE (setting-3,101)-(setting+3,109),1,bf 'Draw new slider.
    voice%(5)=INT((setting-28)/4)
    SAY "IHZ THIHS OH1KEY?",voice%
   ELSE
    IF mx>123 AND mx<183 AND my>150 AND my<180 THEN
     GOTO MainMenu
    END IF
   END IF
  GOTO Volumeloop

Clickmouse:
  'Patiently waits for mouse click & release.
  PRINT label$(2):PRINT label$(3)
  WHILE MOUSE(0)=0:WEND
  WHILE MOUSE(0)<>0:WEND
  RETURN

  SUB Requester (msg1$,msg2$,b1$,b2$,hilite%,answer%) STATIC
  ' Requester window subprogram version 3.4.
  SHARED scrid 'Global variable for SCREEN ID.
  IF scrid<1 OR scrid>4 THEN scrid=-1 'Default to Workbench.
  WINDOW 3,"Program Request",(0,0)-(311,45),16,scrid
  maxwidth=INT(WINDOW(2)/8) 'Truncate prompts if too long...
  PRINT LEFT$(msg1$,maxwidth):PRINT LEFT$(msg2$,maxwidth)
  b1$=LEFT$(b1$,12):b2$=LEFT$(b2$,12) 'Truncate buttons.
```

```
bsizel=(LEN(bl$)+2)*1Ø:bsize2=(LEN(b2$)+2)*1Ø 'Button size.◄
x1=(312-(bsizel+bsize2))/3  'Calculate button positions...◄
x2=x1+bsizel:x3=x1+x2:x4=x3+bsize2◄
'Draw buttons:◄
LINE (x1,2Ø)-(x2,38),2,b:LINE (x3,2Ø)-(x4,38),2,b◄
IF hilite%=1 THEN LINE (x1+2,22)-(x2-2,36),3,b◄
IF hilite%=2 THEN LINE (x3+2,22)-(x4-2,36),3,b◄
LOCATE 4,1:PRINT PTAB(x1+1Ø);bl$;◄
PRINT PTAB(x3+1Ø);b2$◄
reqloop: 'Loop which acts on mouse clicks...◄
WHILE MOUSE(Ø)=Ø:WEND:ml=MOUSE(1):m2=MOUSE(2)◄
IF ml>x1 AND ml<x2 AND m2>2Ø AND m2<38 THEN◄
 answer%=1 'Left button was selected.◄
 LINE (x1,2Ø)-(x2,38),1,bf 'Flash left button.◄
ELSEIF ml>x3 AND ml<x4 AND m2>2Ø AND m2<38 THEN◄
 answer%=Ø 'Right button was selected.◄
 LINE (x3,2Ø)-(x4,38),1,bf 'Flash right button.◄
ELSE◄
 GOTO reqloop 'Neither button selected; repeat loop.◄
END IF◄
WHILE MOUSE(Ø)<>Ø:WEND:WINDOW CLOSE 3◄
END SUB◄
◄
ErrorTrap:◄
 'Version 1.5.◄
 BEEP 'Get user's attention.◄
 IF ERR=53 THEN◄
  requestl$="FILE NOT FOUND."◄
  GOTO ExitError◄
 END IF◄
 IF ERR=61 THEN◄
  requestl$="DISK FULL."◄
  GOTO ExitError◄
 END IF◄
 IF ERR=64 THEN◄
  requestl$="BAD FILENAME."◄
  GOTO ExitError◄
 END IF◄
 IF ERR=67 THEN◄
  requestl$="DIRECTORY FULL."◄
  GOTO ExitError◄
 END IF◄
 IF ERR=68 THEN◄
  requestl$="DEVICE UNAVAILABLE."◄
  GOTO ExitError◄
 END IF◄
 IF ERR=7Ø THEN◄
  requestl$="DISK WRITE-PROTECTED."◄
  GOTO ExitError◄
 END IF◄
 IF ERR=74 THEN◄
  requestl$="UNKNOWN DISK VOLUME."◄
  GOTO ExitError◄
 END IF◄
 requestl$="ERROR NUMBER"+STR$(ERR)◄
ExitError:◄
```

```
' Abort operation or try again.◄
CALL Requester (request1$,"","Retry","CANCEL",2,answer%)◄
IF answer%=0 THEN◄
 CLOSE 1◄
 RESUME MainMenu◄
ELSE◄
 CLOSE 1◄
 ON ERROR GOTO ErrorTrap◄
 RESUME◄
END IF◄
◄
```

7 Designing a User Interface

7 Designing a User Interface

Ever since ENIAC roared to life in 1945 as the first electronic thinking machine, computers have always boasted the ability to solve extremely complex problems with ease. Unfortunately, it hasn't always been as easy for people to tap that vast power.

The most powerful users of computers are programmers, people who can write their own custom-tailored programs. They have nearly full access to the features of the machine because they can speak its language.

The typical user of prepackaged software, however, cannot be expected to share the same skills laboriously acquired by programmers. In an attempt to bridge the gap between easy-to-use programs and advanced, though cryptic, programmable applications, software designers have invented a visual approach which tries to make computing concepts more intuitive—more analogous to everyday tasks.

This approach to computing attempts to give people a strong sense of flow with the machine. Ideally, they should never be left wondering what to do next, or puzzling over what key activates which command, or struggling with syntax errors. Instead, commands and program concepts are represented symbolically and visually. By rolling a mouse controller, the operator of a program can point to various screen icons that represent commands or objects, such as files and toggle switches.

The Amiga user interface evolved from original research into these problems at the Xerox Palo Alto Research Center (PARC). Most visual features of the Macintosh, Atari ST, and Amiga operating systems echo the original concepts developed at PARC as far back as the 1960s. These include features similar to our familiar windows, menus, requesters (dialog boxes), and icons. All these interface elements allow the user to interact directly with the screen using the mouse and keyboard.

The Screen as a Desktop

None of these devices by itself provides a facile interaction between the user and the program. Instead, it helps to think of windows, gadgets, and so forth, as valuable gimmicks that strip away the mystique of computing, making complex programs seem no more tricky than the slider controls on a stereo equalizer. People still have to know how to solve their problems with the program, just as you must understand how to use an equalizer to get the best sound from a stereo. But the process of using the program is simplified when it simulates tasks or actions with which users are already familiar.

The Macintosh Finder, Atari ST GEM, and Amiga Workbench are all *desktop metaphors*. That is, they simulate, in video, a desktop. Windows are a convenient and vital part of this flexible screen display—they can be compared to papers arranged on a desk. Where computers formerly displayed just one screen at a time, windowing systems permit many simultaneous displays on the same screen. While a program can still hog the whole screen if it needs the space, the Amiga operating system cleverly provides facilities to switch between different windows and background screens.

Since the Amiga is a multitasking computer, support for multiple windows and screens, even multiple graphics modes, is a must. Each program must have seemingly complete access to the resources of the machine. Amiga windows and screens are like tiny, independent video monitors, much like the separate terminals hooked up to a multiuser computer system.

To manage these multiple windows, the Amiga Workbench provides various *gadgets*. Since windows can overlap, front and back gadgets let you select the priority of window displays. The front gadget pulls the window to the top of the heap. The back gadget buries the window underneath all others. By manipulating the front and back gadgets, you can set up an integrated, uncluttered work area. Other gadgets let you resize the window, change its position on the screen, and close the window (remove it from the screen). For specialized applications, custom gadgets can be created. And screens, too, can be rearranged on top of each other, either with front/back gadgets, the mouse, or the left Amiga–N and left Amiga–M key combinations.

It's Supported in BASIC

Following through on this philosophy, Amiga BASIC is designed to let you take full advantage of the desktop metaphor when writing your own programs. There are enough built-in commands to let you convincingly reproduce most of the user interface features found in commercial software for the Amiga. Actions such as window resizing, closing, and repositioning are handled for you automatically. When setting up the initial conditions of the window, you decide what gadgets it should have.

Amiga BASIC also contains complete support for pull-down menus. When the right mouse button is pressed, the menu bar at the top of the screen highlights the available menu titles. When the mouse is pointed at a title, the menu drops down, displaying its contents. By pointing at an item on the menu and releasing the right mouse button, the option is selected. If the mouse is moved away from the menu before it's released, no menu action is performed.

All of this is also handled automatically in Amiga BASIC, thanks to the MENU and ON MENU GOSUB commands. You just set up a list of menus, indexed by menu number and menu item, containing the titles and menu entries. When the user selects the menu, a function tells your program which menu was selected and which item was picked. If the menu attempt is aborted, nothing happens. Using BASIC interrupts, you can redirect the flow of BASIC execution to your own menu-handling subroutines. Alternatively, you can control program execution yourself by polling the menu title and menu item functions, MENU(0) and MENU(1). (We'll discuss polling later in this chapter.)

Requesters and alerts are also effective input/output techniques. A requester is a small window that can display text or graphics. Gadgets such as text boxes, edit fields, and on/off switches let the user graphically view or change text, affirm an operation, escape from a command, or toggle a flag. You've already seen the familiar OK/CANCEL requesters that ask whether you're sure you want to quit or write over a file. They display a message, then wait for you to click on little boxes containing OK and CANCEL. A more complex, super-requester is the Preferences tool.

An alert is like an error requester, displaying a caution message and asking if you want to RETRY or CANCEL. RETRY gives you a chance to fix the mistake; CANCEL aborts the operation. You've seen an alert when you *Discard* a file on the Workbench. And, of course, we've all seen the most attention-grabbing alert of all, the dreaded Guru Meditation message when the machine grinds to a halt due to a program crash.

All these gadgets and gimmicks work together to present a cohesive, intuitive, consistent working environment. Once you get the hang of using menus and windows, you feel at home in any program that uses the standard menuing and windowing techniques.

Software Design Philosphy

Perhaps the first goal a program must strive for is an interface that is user-friendly—a term that is much overworked, but with good reason. This simply means that the way a person interacts with the program should be straightforward, consistent, and intuitive, no matter what type of interface the program uses.

If all the programs in a system behave in similar ways, you have greatly simplified the task of learning new programs. Once you've learned one program, you can expect other programs to be consistently similar. If you've been working with the Amiga very long, you're familiar with how to use menus, windows, requesters, and gadgets, even if you don't know the names for these objects. All Intuition-based programs use these techniques.

One of the latest design philosophies is to avoid modality. In other words, some programs have an insert mode, a delete mode, a file mode, a cursor mode, and so forth. You can't enter text in the delete mode, cursor mode, or file mode, and you can't save your document unless you're in the file mode. You can move the cursor only when you're in cursor mode. You get the idea. A program that requires constant switching from mode to mode quickly becomes tedious.

Even if you can't avoid modes, pull-down menus let you quickly and easily show what state the program is in. Menu items can be dimmed (ghosted), displayed normally, or checked. Simply by scanning the pull-down menu, a user can easily tell what commands are appropriate.

It's a little more difficult to define what makes a program intuitive. There are several paths to this goal. One way is to simulate real-world objects. By manipulating pictures of familiar objects such as scissors, a pencil, trash can, or desk, you actually perform the underlying computer commands. Instead of typing something as cryptic as

COPY SYS:BASICDEMOS/MUSIC TO DF1:BPROGS/MUSIC

the user simply uses the mouse to drag the picture of a program representing the file MUSIC into the window of an open disk. This approach works to the extent that you can represent underlying computer commands symbolically. Of course, some operations aren't quite so easy to symbolize.

The mouse is an essential part of this type of user interface. Although other pointing devices can work as well, it is the pointing method that matters. Menus spring to life at a click. Files and commands become almost tangible objects which you can pick up and move with your hand, via the mouse. A single click anywhere on the screen relocates the cursor—an advantage over using cursor keys that must be pressed repeatedly to move around. Instead of laboriously typing text-formatting commands, you can move the cursor anywhere on the screen with the mouse, selecting text that appears in the same font and style as it will on paper. By dragging the mouse across the text, it's selected. You can change margin settings just by sliding small sliders along a ruler.

Of course, some people never feel comfortable with the mouse and prefer to use the keyboard as much as possible. To be courteous, you may want to build special keyboard provisions into your programs.

User Interface Standards

Programs are consistent only if they adhere to certain standards. There's no law preventing people from writing whatever kind of program they like. A program doesn't have to use pull-down menus or the mouse. You can always use commands or function keys to drive a program. But most programs written for the Amiga are consistent with Intuition standards because of the advantages that standardization brings. Even within these standards, there is endless room for flexibility.

The following suggestions come from *Intuition: the Amiga User Interface*, a software developer's manual on the operating system which controls the windows, menus, icons, and gadgets. They're also derived from an observation of popular application and system software for the Macintosh, Atari ST, and Amiga.

A major advantage of standardization is that some actions are common to many programs: saving and loading data files, deleting or inserting text or graphics, making hardcopy on a printer, and so on. If the actions are similar, why not make the commands which invoke them similar, too? For example, programs that can read or write a file can use the standard Amiga menu entries Open, Save, and Save As. The Intuition manual recommends that a program contain a Project menu containing the familiar New, Open, Save, Save As, Print, Print As, and Quit. Of course, your program may not use the printer, and you could combine the functions of Save/Save As, and Print/Print As. Save As lets the user type in the filename for the save, whereas Save uses the current or default filename. If there is no current filename, Save often works like Save As. Print is used to start printing, while Print As lets the user change various print settings.

Many programs can also benefit from a standard Edit menu supporting Cut and Paste operations. Although it would be desirable to use the system clipboard, which allows information to be transferred between applications, there is no good way to do this with the current version of Amiga BASIC. However, programs that allow users to move data around within the program can still use familiar names for these actions. An Edit menu usually contains the entries Undo, Cut, Copy, Paste, and Erase (or Clear):

Edit Menu
Undo Lets you go backward in time, usually to cancel a recent change.
Cut Removes selected text or graphics into a buffer.
Copy Moves selected text or graphics into the buffer without removing it from the screen.
Paste Inserts the contents of the buffer somewhere on the screen.
Erase Used to clear a selected area without affecting the buffer.

In a future version of Amiga BASIC, it may be possible to cut and paste directly to and from the clipboard device.

The Intuition manual also contains advice on requesters. First, every requester needs a safe exit from the operation. If you try to perform an operation that could change (and potentially harm) useful data, the program can verify the action in case it was selected by mistake. Most requesters have a CANCEL button that is used to exit a requester safely to prevent nasty surprises.

Some standards are unspoken and therefore ambiguous. For instance, on the Amiga, the Preferences tool is used to customize the display colors, mouse behavior, text width, and more. Should a program try to honor these settings, or override them for its own purposes? It's usually considered at least polite to try to maintain these preferred settings, but your program may have a superior color scheme for a particular screen, or it may simply need to have 80 columns instead of 60 for its screen display. (A good example is a terminal program.) Also, to conserve memory and processing speed for other applications which may be multitasking in the background, programs with plain-vanilla display needs can stick to the Workbench screen rather than create custom screens. A window smaller than the full screen also helps people who are trying to juggle several tasks. As memory gets cheaper and more Amigas are equipped with memory in excess of 512K, multitasking considerations will become even more important when writing BASIC programs.

To make it easier for you to write applications which look professional, this chapter provides several user interface routines ready to be merged with your own BASIC programs. They carefully follow the techniques used by commercial software and the Amiga itself. You'll find subroutines and subprograms to set up requester windows and dialog boxes with various selectable gadgets. The handy "Palette Panel" subprogram lets a user customize any program's colors. And the general-purpose "ErrorTrap" routine neatly catches most common I/O errors. For more guidance on using these elements to build complete applications, see the program in Chapter 10 as well as many of the other programs in this book.

Designing a Menu Structure

Once you've thought about how your program will be designed—what features it should have, what options should be available, and so forth—the next step is to organize the menu structure. If, for the sake of consistency, you want to follow the guidelines recommended to software developers by Commodore-Amiga, some of these decisions are already made for you.

As mentioned above, Amiga programs that allow device I/O always have the leftmost menu entitled Project. These are typical items in the Project menu:

Project Menu
New   Reinitializes the program.
Open   Loads a data file from disk.
Save   Saves a data file to disk using an existing or predetermined filename.
Save As Saves a data file to disk with a filename entered by the user.
Print   Makes a hardcopy of the data file on the printer.
Quit   Exits the program to either BASIC, the Workbench, or the CLI.

Of course, this isn't a rigid, carved-in-stone structure. Depending on the program, you may see Save and Save As combined into a single item, and various other items dropped or added as appropriate.

Likewise, most Amiga programs accompany the Project menu with a

Tools menu. Under Tools, you'll generally find options that enable you to work with whatever type of data the program is designed to manipulate. In a graphics-drawing program, items available in Tools might include Box, Circle, Line, Fill, Copy, and Undo. In a word processor, Tools might include Cut, Copy, Paste, and Search.

The Project and Tools menus are fairly standard in Amiga software, but additional menus are usually tailored to the needs of the individual program. For instance, Amiga BASIC's Windows menu lets you call forth the Output window or List window. The Workbench's Disk menu offers a couple of options when you click on a disk icon. One popular menu title on the Amiga is Special, which seems to be a euphemism for Miscellaneous.

The key point here is that you should decide at the outset exactly how many menus your program needs, what their titles should be, and which options should be listed as items under which menus. These decisions all play a major role in determining how you'll write your program. And although you're certainly free to modify this design as the program takes shape, you'll save a lot of labor, time, false starts, and aggravation if you establish the basic structure early on. Some people like to jot down a rough outline of these details on paper before they start programming, while others prefer to keep it all in their heads. These are matters of personal style, and the only thing that really counts is whether your own system is the most efficient and comfortable for you.

The MENU Command

Setting up your own custom menus is a snap with Amiga BASIC's MENU command. Not only can you define the text that should appear in the menus, but you can also indicate to the user whether certain items are currently selected or available. Here's the general format for MENU:

MENU *menu-ID,item-ID,status,text*

Menu-ID is a number from 1 to 10 that indicates the menu's position on the title bar, starting with position 1 at the far left; *item-ID* is a number from 0 to 19 that identifies either the menu's title (0) or items (1–19); *status* is a number from 0 to 2 that defines the on/off status of the entire menu or individual menu item; and *text* is an optional character string that defines the text of the menu's title or items.

Before we look at some examples, let's backtrack for a minute and review how Amiga menus indicate the status of menus and menu items. There are four possible states:

1. A menu or item that is *on*—that is, available for use at the current time—appears as regular text.
2. A menu or item that is *off*—unavailable for some reason at the current time—is ghosted, or dimmed. In other words, it's rendered in a special type font that's readable, but just barely.

209

3. A menu item that has a checkmark immediately to its left is currently switched on. It can be switched off by reselecting the item.
4. A menu item that isn't dimmed and doesn't have a checkmark—but clearly has room to its left for a checkmark—is currently switched off. It can be switched on by reselecting the item.

The checkmark option confuses some programmers. Why should some menu items indicate that they're on or off with a checkmark as opposed to being lit or dimmed? The prevailing practice seems to be that menu items which are toggles get checkmarks, while menu items that choose modes or operations indicate their status with ghosting. A *toggle* is an option that can be either on or off, but must always be one or the other. A common light switch is a good example of a toggle; it's either on or off, as indicated by its position up or down. In an Amiga program, let's say you provide speech synthesis as an option that can be turned on or off by the user. You might set up a menu entitled Speech with the item Voice On/Off. When selected, the item gets a checkmark to show that it's currently on; when selected again, the checkmark disappears to show that speech synthesis is off.

The *status* parameter in the MENU statement lets you specify whether the menu or item should be dimmed (0), lit (1), or checked (2). Only menu items can be checked—not menu titles. To switch a whole menu on or off, specify a 1 or 0 for the status parameter and a 0 for the item-ID parameter.

Controlling Menus

Here's an example of a typical menu definition:

MENU 1,0,1,"Project"
MENU 1,1,1,"New"
MENU 1,2,1,"Open"
MENU 1,3,0,"Save"
MENU 1,4,0,"Save As"
MENU 1,5,0,"Print"
MENU 1,6,1,"Quit"

Notice how all these statements share the same menu-ID of 1. That makes them all part of the same menu, which will appear at the leftmost position on the screen's title bar.

The first statement's item-ID is 0, signifying that this is the title-item of the menu. The following item-IDs are numbered sequentially starting from 1, indicating their positions in the menu.

The status numbers are set to either 1 or 0, indicating whether the item is currently lit or dimmed. Since the title-item is turned on, the menu is ready to accept some selections—but not all of the selections are available, as indicated by the following status numbers. The status arrangement seen here is fairly typical for a Project menu when a program first gets underway. Customarily, New is always available, ready to restart the program with a new blank slate. Open is lit, so you can load some sort of file that was created with the program earlier. Save, Save As, and Print are all dimmed, because you obviously can't save or print something that has yet to be created or loaded; and Quit, again by custom, is always available so that you can exit the program.

It's up to your program to monitor and change the status of these items as it runs. For instance, let's say the user selects Open and loads some kind of data file created earlier. Now that there's a file in memory, you'll probably want to dim out Open to prevent the user from loading another file and destroying the current one. At the same time, you can light up Save, Save As, and Print to show that these options have now become available. You can do all this by including the following lines before RETURNing from your OpenFile routine:

MENU 1,2,0
MENU 1,3,1
MENU 1,4,1
MENU 1,5,1

Notice that it's not necessary to define the text strings again when simply changing a menu's status. Nor is it necessary to define the status of every item on the menu. Items that should remain unchanged can be left alone.

In some programs, you may find it more convenient to create a menu refresh routine whose job it is to monitor and reset the status of all the menus. By defining variables for the status parameters, you can call the refresh routine and make it automatically reset the menus according to the current state of the program. For an example of this approach, see the program "Personal Address Book" listed at the end of Chapter 8.

Turning Off the Lights

Sometimes you'll need to dim out every single item on a particular menu. You could use a separate MENU statement for every item, but there's a shortcut. Just dim the title-item, and all of the following items will be dimmed, too. For example,

MENU 1,0,0

dims out every item in menu-ID 1.

Here's an example of a menu with toggles:

MENU 2,0,1,"Speech"
MENU 2,1,2,"   Voice On/Off"

This places a checkmark beside Voice On/Off to indicate that speech synthesis is currently turned on. To remove the checkmark and switch off speech, use the statement MENU 2,1,0.

By the way, notice the two leading spaces in the above text definition for Voice On/Off. These spaces are required to leave room for the checkmark; otherwise, the first couple of characters will be overwritten. In other menu definitions, *trailing* spaces can be handy, too. Use them to pad out the titles of short menu items to make them the same length as longer menu items. This makes it easier to select from the menu, because the mouse pointer doesn't have to be moved directly atop the item's title. To illustrate, try running both versions of the following menu.

Without trailing spaces:	With trailing spaces:
MENU 1,0,1,"Project"	MENU 1,0,1,"Project "
MENU 1,1,1,"New"	MENU 1,1,1,"New "
MENU 1,2,1,"Open"	MENU 1,2,1,"Open "
MENU 1,3,0,"Save"	MENU 1,3,0,"Save "
MENU 1,4,0,"Save As"	MENU 1,4,0,"Save As"
MENU 1,5,0,"Print"	MENU 1,5,0,"Print "
MENU 1,6,1,"Quit"	MENU 1,6,1,"Quit "

Because it's often hard to count the number of padded spaces in a published program listing, many of the listings in this book use the SPACE$ statement to add extra spaces. For example,

MENU 1,1,1,"New"+SPACE$(4)

You can simply type four trailing spaces inside the text string when you see a statement like this.

Trapping Versus Polling

Once you've got your program's pull-down menus defined, you can decide how it is going to trap the user's selections. There are two methods: event trapping and polling.

Event trapping is the automatic interrupt method as used by ON MOUSE, ON BREAK, ON COLLISION, and so forth. With ON MENU GOSUB, you can tell Amiga BASIC to activate an interrupt which checks for menu selections between the execution of every BASIC statement in your program. When a menu item is chosen, control immediately passes to the subroutine named by ON MENU GOSUB. The next RETURN then passes control back to the place where your program was interrupted.

Polling is the old-fashioned method of continuously checking for input within a loop. Why revert to polling when true menu trapping is available? As discussed in Chapter 1, there are two major reasons.

First, event trapping in some cases can noticeably slow down the execution of an Amiga BASIC program. Second, sometimes it's inconvenient to surrender control of your program to an interrupt-driven event trap. The new menu selection might force your program to suddenly jump out of a routine that's currently executing, change some critical variables, and then return control to the original routine—which is now confused because some of its variables have been altered.

The decision of whether to check for menu selections with event trapping or polling depends a great deal on the design of your individual program, so we'll cover both approaches.

Springing the Trap

ON MENU works just like the other event-trapping statements in Amiga BASIC. The following two statements, customarily executed when your program initializes, set up and activate menu trapping:

ON MENU GOSUB *LineLabel*
MENU ON

LineLabel is a line number or Amiga BASIC line label—the location of your menu-handling routine. MENU ON then activates the interrupt. To disable the interrupt, use ON MENU GOSUB 0.

Once a menu selection has been trapped, it's up to your handler routine to determine which menu was pulled down and which item was selected from that menu. This is quite easy with the MENU( ) function:

- MENU(0) returns the menu-ID number from 1 to 10.
- MENU(1) returns the item-ID number from 1 to 19.

All you have to do is call both of these functions to isolate the menu choice, then jump to the appropriate subroutine. "Skeleton1" shows how menu trapping might look in a typical program:

Program 7-1. Skeleton1

```
MenuSetup:◄
 MENU 1,0,1,"Project"◄
 MENU 1,1,1,"New    "◄
 MENU 1,2,1,"Open   "◄
 MENU 1,3,1,"Save   "◄
 MENU 1,4,1,"Print  "◄
 MENU 1,5,1,"Quit   "◄
 MENU 2,0,1,"Tools"◄
 MENU 2,1,1,"Cut  "◄
 MENU 2,2,1,"Copy"◄
 MENU 2,3,1,"Glue"◄
 MENU 3,0,0,""◄
 MENU 4,0,0,""◄
ON MENU GOSUB MenuHandler◄
MENU ON◄
PRINT "Press right mouse button to select menus."◄
PRINT "Press left mouse button to quit."◄
```

```
WHILE MOUSE(0)=0:WEND 'Your main loop goes here...
WHILE MOUSE(0)<>0:WEND:END

MenuHandler:
 menuID=MENU(0)
 itemID=MENU(1)
 CLS
 ON menuID GOSUB ProjectMenu,ToolsMenu
 PRINT "Press mouse left mouse button to continue."
 WHILE MOUSE(0)=0:WEND:WHILE MOUSE(0)<>0:WEND:CLS
 PRINT "Press right mouse button to select menus."
 PRINT "Press left mouse button to quit."
RETURN

ProjectMenu:
 ON itemID GOSUB NewFile,OpenFile,SaveFile,PrintFile,Quit
RETURN

ToolsMenu:
 ON itemID GOSUB Cut,Copy,Glue
RETURN

NewFile:
 PRINT "Routine for restarting the program."
RETURN

OpenFile:
 PRINT "Routine for loading a file from disk."
RETURN

SaveFile:
 PRINT "Routine for saving a file to disk."
RETURN

PrintFile:
 PRINT "Routine for printing a hardcopy."
RETURN

Quit:
 PRINT "Routine for exiting the program."
RETURN

Cut:
 PRINT "Routine for cutting info from file."
RETURN

Copy:
 PRINT "Routine for copying info in the file."
RETURN

Glue:
 PRINT "Routine for pasting info in the file."
RETURN
```

What we've got here is a highly organized bucket brigade of branches that pass control to the appropriate subroutines, and then eventually return control back to where the program was interrupted by the event trap. In fact, this skeleton can serve as a model; all it needs is some beef hanging on its bones to transform it into a fully working program.

Here's how the bucket brigade works. The program circles endlessly in the WHILE–WEND loop which waits for a button press to end the program. When the user pulls down a menu and selects an item, the menu trap is triggered. BASIC jumps to the label specified by ON MENU GOSUB—in this case, MenuHandler. MenuHandler immediately determines which menu and item was selected by asking the MENU( ) function. MENU(0) returns a value of 1 or 2 in the variable *menuID*, representing the choice of either the Project menu or the Tools menu. MENU(1) is then asked which item was selected, and the answer comes back in the variable *itemID*.

MenuHandler then passes the bucket to the next subroutine with an ON GOSUB. If menuID=1, the ProjectMenu routine gets the bucket. If menuID=2, the ToolsMenu routine takes over.

These routines, in turn, pass control with another ON GOSUB based on the variable *itemID*.

At last the bucket arrives at the subroutine which is supposed to carry out the actual work. When it's done, a RETURN jumps backward to either the ProjectMenu or ToolsMenu routine, then back to MenuHandler, and finally back to the point where the program was interrupted by the menu selection—in this case, the WHILE–WEND loop that waits for a button press.

Menu Hints

Like other Amiga BASIC event-trapping statements, ON MENU can be turned off and on in various ways. MENU OFF disables trapping, ignoring any menu selections until the next MENU ON. MENU STOP suspends trapping until the next MENU ON, then executes any menu selection that might have occurred in the meantime.

When an event trap is triggered, BASIC automatically stops checking for that event until the handler routine RETURNs. Therefore, you don't have to turn menu trapping on and off yourself.

You may, however, wish to dim the menus to signal to the user that additional selections are temporarily unavailable. As mentioned before, you can dim out an entire menu merely by turning off its title-item: MENU 1,0,0 or MENU 2,0,0, for instance.

If your program sets up fewer than four custom menus—as seen in Program 7-1—you can keep BASIC's menus from appearing in those slots by defining null strings for titles: MENU 3,0,0," " or MENU 4,0,0," ".

To restore BASIC's default menus, use MENU RESET. This can be executed either in direct mode or, preferably, by a Quit routine in your program.

Keep in mind that menu trapping, like all event trapping in Amiga BASIC, occurs only *between* the execution of each statement in your program, not *during* execution (see Chapter 1). Therefore, if your program encounters a statement such as INPUT which temporarily freezes execution until a key is pressed, menu trapping is disabled. Even though your menus are still lit and can be pulled down, nothing will happen when a selection is made. To keep from confusing the user in these instances, you may want to dim out all your menus before the INPUT and reinstate them afterward.

Taking a Poll

If you discover that menu trapping is seriously slowing down your program, or if various routines are conflicting with each other as interrupts jump back and forth between them, you may want to consider the polling alternative.

With this method, you set up your menus and subroutines exactly as shown above. But instead of relying upon ON MENU to detect menu selections, you check for them yourself by continuously calling MENU(0) within a loop. Here's an example:

```
MainLoop:
  menuID=MENU(0)
  IF menuID=0 THEN MainLoop
  itemID=MENU(1)
  ON menuID GOSUB ProjectMenu,ToolsMenu
GOTO MainLoop
```

You can also construct a similar loop with WHILE–WEND.

This loop ends up returning the same values in the variables *menuID* and *itemID*, so the rest of your program can be identical to one that uses true event trapping.

Optional Keyboard Commands

A polling loop also makes it possible to check simultaneously for keyboard input. Amiga BASIC is clearly oriented toward the menu-style user interface, as evidenced by its lack of an ON KEY event trap. However, you may want to include keyboard commands as a supplement to your pull-down menus or as an alternative for those who favor this style. If so, a polling loop is a good way. The loop might look like Program 7-2.

Program 7-2. Skeleton2

```
MenuSetup:◄
  MENU 1,0,1,"Project"◄
  MENU 1,1,1,"New (N)   "◄
  MENU 1,2,1,"Open (O)  "◄
  MENU 1,3,1,"Save (S)  "◄
  MENU 1,4,1,"Print (P)"◄
```

```
    MENU 1,5,1,"Quit (Q) "◄
    MENU 2,0,1,"Tools"◄
    MENU 2,1,1,"Cut (X) "◄
    MENU 2,2,1,"Copy (C)"◄
    MENU 2,3,1,"Glue (G)"◄
    MENU 3,0,0,""◄
    MENU 4,0,0,""◄
    keycommands$(1)="NOSPQ"◄
    keycommands$(2)="XCG"◄
    PRINT "Press right mouse button to select menus."◄
     ◄
  MainLoop:◄
    menuID=MENU(0)◄
    key$=INKEY$◄
    IF menuID=0 AND key$="" GOTO MainLoop◄
    itemID=MENU(1)◄
    IF key$<>"" THEN◄
     n=1:WHILE n<3◄
      s=INSTR(keycommands$(n),UCASE$(key$))◄
      IF s=0 THEN n=n+1 ELSE itemID=s:menuID=n:n=3◄
     WEND◄
    END IF◄
    ON menuID GOSUB ProjectMenu,ToolsMenu◄
  GOTO MainLoop◄
    ◄
  ProjectMenu:◄
    ON itemID GOSUB NewFile,OpenFile,SaveFile,PrintFile,Quit◄
  RETURN◄
    ◄
  ToolsMenu:◄
    ON itemID GOSUB Cut,Copy,Glue◄
  RETURN◄
    ◄
  NewFile:◄
    PRINT "Routine for restarting the program."◄
  RETURN◄
    ◄
  OpenFile:◄
    PRINT "Routine for loading a file from disk."◄
  RETURN◄
    ◄
  SaveFile:◄
    PRINT "Routine for saving a file to disk."◄
  RETURN◄
    ◄
  PrintFile:◄
    PRINT "Routine for printing a hardcopy."◄
  RETURN◄
    ◄
  Quit:◄
    PRINT "Routine for exiting the program."◄
  RETURN◄
    ◄
  Cut:◄
    PRINT "Routine for cutting info from file."◄
  RETURN◄
    ◄
```

```
Copy:◄
  PRINT "Routine for copying info in the file."◄
RETURN◄
◄
  Glue:◄
  PRINT "Routine for pasting info in the file."◄
RETURN◄
```

To use this loop in your own programs, only three steps are required:

1. Put the keystrokes you're polling for in a string array called *keycommands$* during the initialization stage of your program. Each array holds the keystrokes for a single menu. In this example,

   keycommands$(1)="NOSPQ"
   keycommands$(2)="XCG"

   "NOSPQ" are the keystrokes for menu 1 (New, Open, Save, Print, and Quit), and "XCG" are the keystrokes for menu 2 (Cut, Copy, and Glue). If your program has more than two menus, add additional arrays and keystrokes in *keycommands$(3)*, *keycommands$(4)*, and so on. (Be careful not to use the same key for two different functions.)

2. Change the WHILE statement to loop for the number of menus in your program. As in Program 7-2, the loop is set up for a program with two menus—WHILE n<3. If your program has three menus, change this statement to WHILE n<4. If your program has four menus, use WHILE n<5. (The WHILE–WEND loop searches through all the *keycommands$* arrays, seeking a match between the keypress and the predefined command keys.)

3. Make a similar change to the final statement in the IF-THEN-ELSE line within the loop. If your program has three menus, n=4. If your program has four menus, n=5. (This statement terminates the WHILE–WEND loop when the INSTR search is successful.)

As a final touch, you can add the key commands to the text definitions of your pull-down menus:

MENU 1,1,1,"New (N)"
MENU 1,2,1,"Open (O)"
MENU 1,3,1,"Save (S)"

And so on. This method gives the user the option of either menu or keyboard input, yet still adheres to recognized Amiga standards—as demonstrated by Amiga BASIC's own menus.

Custom Building Blocks

Although Amiga BASIC includes strong support for menus and mouse trapping, it lacks any commands for requester windows, alert boxes, and other types of dialog boxes with buttons (such as the ones which the system pops up to prompt you to insert a different disk or to flag an error). Instead, you have to build these features into your programs manually, combining BASIC's atoms of windows, rectangle-drawing commands, mouse traps, and calculations to create analogs of the system requesters.

The simplest requester might just display a short message and the buttons OK and CANCEL. The message might be a prompt such as ERASE DISK?, so you're giving the user a chance to back out of a potentially dangerous operation. When the mouse is clicked on either button, the requester routine could return a value to your program indicating the choice, and your program could proceed accordingly. This simple kind of requester would be sufficient for many programs, because they can rely primarily on menus for command control.

Still, your programs look more professional (and conform more closely to Amiga software standards) if they can pop up requesters that mimic the system's own requesters. That's why we've written a package of routines to add these features to any Amiga BASIC program. You'll notice that nearly all of the full-length programs in this book take advantage of at least one of these routines. Before describing them in detail, here's a quick preview of what they have to offer.

Requester is a self-contained subprogram that lets you open a small Program Request window in any screen mode. You can define up to two prompt lines and two custom buttons, and optionally highlight a button to indicate the preferred or safest choice. Requester then returns a value to your program indicating which button was clicked.

ErrorTrap is a general-purpose error-trapping routine that catches most input/output errors, especially those involving disk access (which is when most errors happen). It interprets the error, calls the Requester routine to display the appropriate error message, and offers two buttons—Retry and CANCEL—just like the system's own error alerts.

Palette Panel is a specialized version of the "Pick-A-Palette" program in Chapter 2. Whenever you write a program that should allow users to change the color palette—such as a drawing program—you can simply attach Palette Panel as a subprogram. When CALLed, it opens up a window that lets users click on a color box to select a palette color, then manipulate three slide controls for the RGB values. It automatically adjusts itself for any screen mode, presenting anywhere from 2 to 32 color boxes as required. Two buttons, USE and CANCEL, let users keep their color changes or exit Palette Panel with the original colors intact.

Intuits is a collection of building blocks for constructing nearly any type of custom requester. You can build very attractive requesters for saving and loading disk files and accepting string input. Although Intuits is a little more difficult to set up than the plug-in Requester subprogram mentioned above, it is more flexible and powerful.

The Requester Subprogram

Requester, Program 7-3, is listed in complete form with liberal REMark statements at the end of this chapter. (The REMarks help make the subprogram self-documenting when you save it on your programming disks.) It is designed to be a nearly foolproof, plug-in module that can be attached to any Amiga BASIC program with a minimum of fuss. Like most of the other tools included in this chapter, it's written as a subprogram to avoid variable conflicts with your main program. In fact, it's so easy to use that in effect you'll be adding a new command to BASIC. (See Appendix D for more information on using subprograms for this purpose.)

After typing in Requester, save it on your work disk in ASCII format:

SAVE "Requester",a

This lets you add it to any of your BASIC programs with this command:

MERGE "Requester"

Only two steps are required before CALLing Requester:

• Set the integer variable *scrid%* to the ID number of the screen on which you want the requester window to appear. If you don't set a value for *scrid%*, it defaults to −1 for the Workbench screen. If your program uses a custom screen numbered 1–4, set *scrid%* to that ID. You have to do this only once if you always want the requester to appear on the same screen. (The variable *scrid%* is a global variable SHARED by Requester and your main program.)

• Using string variables, define the text for the prompts you want to appear inside the requester. You can display one or two lines of text. If Preferences is set for 60 columns, each line can be up to 31 characters long; if Preferences is set for 80 columns, each line can be up to 39 characters long. The Requester subprogram automatically truncates the prompts if they exceed these limits.

Now you're ready to CALL Requester. Here's the format:

CALL Requester (*msg1$*,*msg2$*,"*Left Button*","*Right Button*",*hilite%*,*answer%*)

where *msg1$* and *msg2$* are the two lines of text you previously defined for the prompts (any string variable names will do, of course); "*Left Button*" and "*Right Button*" are the labels for the two buttons which appear inside the requester (limit 12 characters each); *hilite%* is an integer variable or a constant that indicates which button should be highlighted (1=left button, 2=right button, 0=neither button); and *answer%* is the integer variable which returns the value indicating which button was clicked (1=left button, 0=right button).

Here's an example:

msg1$="Quit program to BASIC?"
msg2$="(Click on OK or CANCEL)"
CALL Requester (msg1$,msg2$,"OK","CANCEL",2,answer%)

When you CALL Requester, the subprogram opens up a small window titled Program Request in the upper left corner of the screen. (In the 320-width modes, the requester spans the entire width of the screen.) Like a system requester, it has no close or sizing gadgets, but does have a front/back gadget. This particular CALL would pop open a requester that looks like this:

Quit program to BASIC?
(Click on OK or CANCEL)
    OK   CANCEL

In addition, since the fifth parameter in the CALL statement is the constant 2, the right-hand button (CANCEL) is highlighted with an extra box drawn around it in a contrasting color. This imitates the button highlighting sometimes seen in system requesters. Usually, the button which is emphasized is the preferred choice, or the one which can cause the least potential harm (as in this case, when CANCEL prevents the user from stopping the program and possibly losing some data).

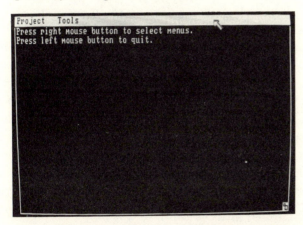

Using the mouse to quit.

All mouse clicks outside the buttons are ignored. As soon as the user clicks on either button, the requester disappears and control returns to the main program. The result is returned in the variable *answer%*. In this case, OK returns 1 and CANCEL returns 0. (Again, like most system requesters, the left button generally indicates the positive response and the right button indicates the negative response.)

When the subprogram returns control to the main program, you can test the value in *answer%* and proceed accordingly. Here's an example of a simple Quit routine:

Quit:
  msg1$="Exit program to BASIC?"
  CALL Requester (msg1$,"","QUIT","CANCEL",2,answer%)
  IF answer%=1 THEN
    MENU RESET:END

```
ELSE
    RETURN
END IF
```

If the user clicks on QUIT, the routine restores BASIC's menus and then ENDs the program. If the user clicks on CANCEL (which is highlighted), control returns to the main program which called the Quit routine.

Notice in this example how we define only one prompt for the requester in *msg1$*. If you don't need two lines of text, blank out the second line by setting that parameter to a null string ("").

To make Requester seem even more like a built-in BASIC command, you can call the subprogram by using this alternative syntax:

Requester msg1$,msg2$,"OK","CANCEL",2,answer%

When the keyword CALL and the parentheses around the parameters are omitted, Amiga BASIC knows that CALL is implied and control immediately jumps to the specified subprogram as usual. (Again, refer to Appendix D.)

Note: Requester opens and closes WINDOW 3. If your main program already uses WINDOW 3 for something else, simply change the WINDOW statement in the Requester subprogram to a higher number.

Trapping Errors

In Chapter 1 we described how you can use Amiga BASIC's ON ERROR GOTO statement to automatically trap runtime errors and pass control to an error-handling routine. Although different programs may require different error handlers, we've found that most programs can get by with a general-purpose routine to trap disk I/O errors. Disk errors are the most common: *File not found, Disk full, Disk write-protected,* and so on.

"ErrorTrap," Program 7-4, at the end of this chapter, is such a general-purpose routine. It's easy to add to almost any program, and it helps protect your programming reputation from the embarrassment of unanticipated crashes. When an error happens, ErrorTrap opens up a requester window, displays the appropriate error message, and offers two buttons, Retry and CANCEL. If the user clicks on Retry, ErrorTrap returns control to the line which triggered the error, thereby repeating the operation. So, for instance, if the error was *Disk write-protected,* the user can unprotect the disk, reinsert it, and click on Retry to continue. If another error results, ErrorTrap traps that one, too.

If the user clicks on CANCEL, ErrorTrap returns control to any point in your main program that you specify.

Type in and save ErrorTrap on your work disk in ASCII format so that you can MERGE it with your own programs. To set it up, follow these instructions:

• ErrorTrap CALLs the Requester subprogram to display the error message, so make sure your program includes Requester, too.

• Change one line in ErrorTrap to indicate where control should return within your main program if the user clicks on CANCEL. This line can be found near the end of ErrorTrap:

```
ExitError:◄
' Abort operation or try again.◄
' Define global variable scrid (SCREEN ID) if required:◄
scrid=-1 'Error Requester will appear on Workbench screen.◄
CALL Requester (request1$,"","Retry","CANCEL",2,answer%)◄
IF answer%=0 THEN◄
  CLOSE 1◄
  RESUME MainMenu ' Substitute your reentry point here.◄
ELSE◄
  CLOSE 1◄
  ON ERROR GOTO ErrorTrap◄
  RESUME◄
END IF◄
```

Instead of RESUME MainMenu, plug in any line label or line number destination in your main program. You could repeat the routine which led to the error, or move the user back to a point before he or she attempted the operation which caused the error. It's up to you.

Note the CLOSE 1 statement above. This is executed if the user clicks on Retry. Since most disk errors are triggered by an OPEN, the CLOSE statement makes it possible to Retry the operation without causing a *File already open* error. If your main program's OPEN uses a file number other than 1, change the CLOSE statement here to the same number. (For more information on file handling, see Chapter 8.)

ErrorTrap displays the following error messages: *File not found, Disk full, Bad filename, Directory full, Device unavailable, Disk write–protected,* and *Unknown disk volume.* These are all disk errors, although *Device unavailable* can pop up if you try to print something when the printer is offline. If another error besides these is triggered, ErrorTrap displays the error number in the requester.

It's easy to add more error messages to ErrorTrap if you like. Just insert additional checks into the top section of ErrorTrap. Use this format:

IF ERR=*errnum* **THEN**
  request1$=*"Error message."*
  GOTO ExitError
END IF

where *errnum* is an Amiga BASIC or AmigaDOS error number (see the *Amiga BASIC* manual), and *Error message* is the first line of text you want ErrorTrap to display in the requester window. If Preferences is set for 60 columns, the error message can be up to 31 characters long; if Preferences is set for 80 columns, the error message can be up to 39 characters long. You can also display a second prompt line if you wish by defining the string variable *request2$* just before CALLing Requester.

Customizing Colors with Palette Panel

In many graphics-oriented programs, it would be nice if the user could change the color palette from within the program using a Preferences-style tool. It would also be nice if this color-customizing tool could work in all of the Amiga's screen modes, from 2 to 32 colors, offering the full Amiga palette of 4096 hues to choose from.

That's exactly what you get with "Palette Panel," Program 7-5 at the end of this chapter. It's an independent subprogram that can be added to any Amiga BASIC program that needs flexible color control. You may want to add it to "ShapeIt," the GET and PUT shape editor found in Chapter 3.

Palette Panel is actually two subprograms: PanelSetup and PalettePanel. The first is for initialization purposes only—it predefines the palette to any colors you desire and makes sure Palette Panel is properly adjusted for the current screen mode. You have to CALL PanelSetup only once, at the beginning of your main program. With this done, the PalettePanel subprogram is ready for use whenever your main program beckons. You can simply include it as an option in your pull-down menus, then CALL it as required.

First, type in the Palette Panel listing and save it on your work disk in ASCII format so that you can MERGE it with your own programs. If you want, you can try running it—the listing also includes a short demo that shows how it works. (Delete the demo before using Palette Panel in a program of your own.)

Using Palette Panel

To use Palette Panel, follow these steps:

1. If you wish, define your preferred default colors within the PanelSetup subprogram. This is simply a matter of assigning RGB values to the hue( ) array in PanelSetup which stores the colors; these are the same values you'd use in a PALETTE statement. For example, as listed at the end of this chapter, PanelSetup already predefines the first four colors to green, white, black, and orange:

'Define default colors here (you can insert your own values):
hue(0,0)=0:hue(0,1)=.46:hue(0,2)=0 'Color 0
hue(1,0)=.9:hue(1,1)=.9:hue(1,2)=.9 'Color 1
hue(2,0)=0:hue(2,1)=0:hue(2,2)=0 'Color 2
hue(3,0)=.91:hue(3,1)=.48:hue(3,2)=.15 'Color 3

You can just plug in your own RGB values here.

hue(0,0)	Red value for color 0
hue(0,1)	Green value for color 0
hue(0,2)	Blue value for color 0
hue(1,0)	Red value for color 1
hue(1,1)	Green value for color 1
hue(1,2)	Blue value for color 1

And so on.

To figure out the RGB values you want, you can use the "Pick-A-Palette" utility in Chapter 2 or even Palette Panel itself once it's running. An alternative is simply to assign random colors. As listed in this chapter, PanelSetup defines all colors beyond the first four to random values:

```
FOR n=4 TO 31 'We'll use random colors for the rest.
  FOR nn=0 TO 2
    hue(n,nn)=RND
  NEXT nn
NEXT n
```

2. Then, after setting up a custom screen during the initialization phase of your main program, CALL the PanelSetup subprogram. Here is the format:

CALL PanelSetup(*screen-ID*)

where *screen-ID* is the SCREEN number of your custom screen (1–4). If your program doesn't use a custom screen, set *screen-ID* to −1 for the default Workbench screen. Here's an example of how you might CALL PanelSetup if there is a custom screen:

SCREEN 1,320,200,5,1
CALL PanelSetup(1)

3. After steps 1 and 2, the PalettePanel subprogram itself is ready to be CALLed at any time. No more CALLs to PanelSetup are required unless your program switches to a different screen mode. To CALL PalettePanel, use this format:

CALL PalettePanel (*screen-ID,prefs-columns*)

where *screen-ID* is the number of your main program's screen (−1 for the default Workbench screen or 1–4 for a custom screen), and *prefs-columns* is the number of columns which has been set with the Preferences tool (either 60 or 80). For example, if your program is using a screen mode such as SCREEN 1,320,200,5,1, and Preferences is set for 80 columns, here's the proper CALL:

CALL PalettePanel (1,80)

Of course, you can also use the alternative implied syntax for the CALL statement:

PalettePanel 1,80

What you'll see when Palette Panel opens is a window with 32 color boxes, three slide controls, two buttons, an indicator which shows the currently selected color number, and readouts for the RGB values of the currently selected color (see photograph).

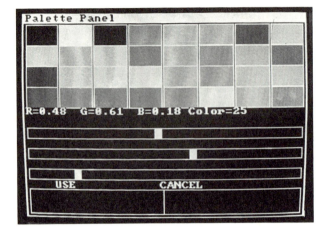

"Palette Panel" works in any Amiga screen mode; this is the 32-color screen.

Changing Colors

To select which color you want to change, click on the desired color box. (If the current screen mode allows fewer than 32 colors, the unused color boxes default to color 0.) Instantly, the color number indicator changes, the slide controls readjust themselves to reflect the RGB values for that color, and the indicators for the actual RGB values change also.

To modify a color, position the mouse pointer on the R, G, or B slide control and press the left button. The slider jumps to the new position and the color box changes. You can also hold down the mouse button and move the slider for fine adjustments.

When you're satisfied with the new color, select another color box if you wish. When you're done modifying colors, click on the USE button to exit Palette Panel and return to the main program. The new colors will be in effect. If you don't like the new colors you've designed, click on the CANCEL button instead. The entire color palette instantly restores itself to the values that were in effect when Palette Panel was CALLed.

Two final notes: When Palette Panel is used with a 32-color mode, you'll notice that the mouse pointer's colors are changed. This is normal. Since the mouse pointer takes its colors from color registers 16, 17, 18, and 19, any changes to those registers affect the pointer, too.

And finally, the PanelSetup subprogram briefly opens and closes WINDOW 2, and the PalettePanel subprogram opens and closes WINDOW 3. If your program already uses these windows for some other purpose, change the WINDOW statements to higher numbers to avoid possible conflicts.

The Intuits: Specialized Tools

The Requester subprogram described above is good enough for most cases, but if you'd like your programs to incorporate some really fancy requesters and buttons, we've provided a collection of routines that let you construct your own special tools. Since these routines echo those found in Intuition, we've named them Intuits.

Each Intuit subprogram is a primitive command, like a single command in BASIC, providing you the ultimate in flexibility. Like a construction set, these tools can be combined in myriad ways to build exquisite control panels and consoles. For convenience, we have also provided high-level subroutines for common operations such as opening/saving files, displaying error messages, putting messages in boxes, and requesting a line of editable input from the user (without the hassles of the generic INPUT and LINE INPUT statements). As long as you're using this package, we also supply much shorter versions of the Requester subroutine built upon these commands. So you don't need to use the Requester subprogram above if you're using the Intuits.

Program 7-6 at the end of this chapter is an example program that combines all the Intuit functions, along with the complete source listing of all Intuit routines. We'll also list the routines individually as we cover them below.

Intuit-troduction

An elegant approach to solving the problem of missing requester commands in Amiga BASIC would be to write a machine language library of subprograms. However, this would require that the library file always be on the same disk, and it would have to be loaded at runtime. Instead, we've found that Amiga BASIC is easily fast enough to simulate requesters, gadgets, and edit fields. It may seem a bit clumsy at times, but the final effect can be stunning.

All routines that simulate requesters and buttons revolve around scanning for rectangular areas of the screen. A requester window marked with OK and CANCEL buttons has two selectable rectangles. Each rectangle consists of an upper left corner's row and column (x1,y1) and the lower right corner's row and column (x2,y2). Determining which button has been clicked involves examining MOUSE(1) and MOUSE(2) to get the current pixel position pointed to by the mouse pointer. If this (x,y) position is greater than the box's upper left corner and less than the box's lower right corner, then the arrow is within the box. If the mouse has been clicked, the routine knows which button was selected.

This is simplified by not even checking for the mouse position unless the button is clicked. The user, then, can quickly move the mouse around while the program waits for a click. When the left mouse button is pressed, the routine examines the current mouse position and compares it to the coordinates of the rectangular buttons to see if it falls within the buttons' ranges.

The Requester subprogram does these checks manually. Since it has only two buttons to check (OK and CANCEL, or whatever you define), it can afford to use IF-THEN statements to check for each rectangle. The Palette Panel sub-program also checks manually for clicks on the USE or CANCEL buttons, but uses a different technique to check for clicks on the color boxes. This is necessary because there can be up to 32 color boxes, and 32 sets of IF-THENs would not only execute very sluggishly, but would also take up a lot of memory. Since the color boxes in Palette Panel fall into evenly divisible squares, a single formula translates the mouse position into a color number. The program loops until it finds out which box was clicked.

Although you can figure out your own formulas and IF-THEN constructions to design requesters and buttons (and we encourage you to), it helps to have plug-in routines that automate some of this. The Intuits let you define any rectangular areas as objects, add them to an object list, then poll the mouse to see which object was selected.

The WhichBox SUB

The Intuits use some global variables and arrays, most obviously the corner position arrays x1( ), y1( ), x2( ), and y2( ). These hold the vertices of an object. Any object you want to use must be enclosed in this container. For a sliding knob, the entire height or width of the knob's range can be the container, wherein you check for the position of the knob.

You could fill up these arrays yourself, and then loop through them looking for a match. If you knew the position of the mouse, you could compare it against each rectangle in the list of rectangles. In fact, this is the loop performed by the WhichBox SUB:

```
SUB WhichBox(which) STATIC◄
SHARED x1(),y1(),x2(),y2(),BoxIndex◄
IF MOUSE(0)=0 THEN EXIT SUB◄
x=MOUSE(1):y=MOUSE(2):i=1◄
WHILE i<BoxIndex AND NOT (x>x1(i) AND x<x2(i) AND y>y1(i) AND y<
y2(i))◄
  i=i+1◄
WEND◄
which=i:IF i=BoxIndex THEN which=0◄
END SUB◄
```

The SHARED statements make the global arrays and variables available to the subprogram. The WHILE–WEND loop continues as long as all the boxes haven't been checked yet, *and* none of the boxes has been selected. If the mouse button isn't even held down, the routine immediately exits, returning a zero. You have to poll WhichBox continually to see *which box*, if any, has been selected. We'll come back to this in a moment.

You should include these array DIMensions and global variable declarations in the initialization section of your program, then add all the SUBs in the Intuits package. Remember to save the Intuits on your work disk in ASCII format so that you can use MERGE.

Here are the global arrays and variables your main program should initialize:

```
DEFINT a-z
'Global arrays and variables
DIM work%(400)
'more than 20 gadgets is impractical
DIM x1(20),y1(20),x2(20),y2(20)
ScrId=-1 'Screen for windows
which=0 'which box is selected
BoxIndex=1 'How many gadgets
maxlen=15 'length of text fields
```

The array work% will be explained later; it's used to flash a box when it is selected. The corner arrays are only DIMensioned to 20, since it becomes impractical to scan for more than about 20 objects without losing too much speed. Set the variable *ScrId* to the screen-ID of the custom screen you're using. If your program doesn't use a custom screen, set this to −1 for the default Workbench screen.

When a requester appears in a window, it uses WINDOW 2. Change this if your program already uses this window. We have found that windows other than the primary window must start at the top left corner of the screen, position (0,0). In fact, the main window must also originate at (0,0) so the two windows overlap. If the windows are in other positions, mouse reports become devilishly difficult to decipher, beyond practical use. Perhaps a future version of Amiga BASIC will address this problem. In the meantime, the Intuits windows use no gadgets, so you can't close, resize, or relocate them.

An Intuit Requester

Let's see how you could construct a requester window using the Intuits routines. This will be a more generalized requester than the Requester subprogram described above:

```
SUB Request(msg1$,msg2$,b1$,b2$,which) STATIC
SHARED BoxIndex,ScrId
SHARED x1(),y1(),x2(),y2()
BoxIndex=1:height=PEEKW(WINDOW(8)+58)
winwidth=20*(8-2*(height=9))+30
WINDOW 2,"System Request",(0,0)-(winwidth,50),0,ScrId
PRINT :PRINT TAB(11-LEN(msg1$)/2);msg1$
PRINT TAB(11-LEN(msg2$)/2);msg2$:PRINT
LOCATE ,2:TxBox b1$
PRINT TAB(20-LEN(b2$));:TxBox b2$:which=0
CALL WaitBox(which)
CALL FlashRelease(which)
WINDOW CLOSE 2
END SUB
```

This subprogram is designed to accept two messages to print at the top of the requester window, two button prompts, and a variable to receive the number of the selected box. Pass the messages in *msg1$* and *msg2$*, the names of the two buttons (as in OK and CANCEL) in *b1$* and *b2$*, and expect the variable *which* to return either 1 or 2 for either button 1 or button 2. There is no provision to highlight a preferred button selection. You can use different variable names, of course, as well as direct string values. Examples:

CALL Request("Ok to explode","your Amiga?","NAH","SURE",button)

And, using the alternative subprogram CALL syntax:

Request "Save program",filename$,"SAVE","CANCEL",which

You can use your own variable names in the call, since the subprogram has its own local copies of the values. Duplication of the same variable name (as in the latter example) is no problem, either.

These previous two calls would display requesters that look like this:

Example of customized requester made with the Intuits package.

If you analyze this subroutine, you'll see that it reveals embedded calls to building-block routines like TxBox, WaitBox, and FlashRelease. The next section will describe how they work.

Adjustable Buttons

TxBox solves a common need to draw a button enclosing some text. Just pass TxBox the text it should print. TxBox pads the text with a space on each side, and uses the extra space to draw a box around the text. You must allow a blank line between areas used by TxBox, since the border uses more than one text line of screen space.

TxBox adjusts automatically to the current text font by examining WINDOW(4) and WINDOW(5), the pixel position where the next text character originates. It saves the initial value, prints the text, then uses the new value to draw the rectangle. It stores the rectangle in the x1( ), y1( ), x2( ), and y2( ) arrays, and increments the global variable BoxIndex, which points to the next available space for a new box. It therefore represents the total number of boxes plus one. Be sure to initialize BoxIndex to 1 before you begin setting up a list of boxes.

If you want to display a box without text, just call TxBox with blank spaces—(CALL TxBox(" "). This makes it easy to coordinate the size of your box with text alongside. After a call to TxBox, the cursor is still on the same printing line, but is one space past the end of the box displayed.

Even if you don't follow how TxBox works internally, it's easy simply to CALL it. Think of TxBox as a special PRINT statement.

```
SUB TxBox(msg$) STATIC◄
SHARED x1(),y1(),x2(),y2()◄
SHARED BoxIndex◄
x1=WINDOW(4):y1=WINDOW(5)-10◄
PRINT " ";msg$;" ";◄
x2=WINDOW(4):y2=y1+14◄
CALL Box(BoxIndex,x1,y1,x2,y2)◄
BoxIndex=BoxIndex+1◄
PRINT SPC(1);◄
END SUB◄
```

TxBox uses yet another Intuit building block, Box. You can also use Box to draw an unlabeled box of any size. An example call might be

CALL Box(BoxIndex,10,10,50,50)

This draws a shadowed box from (10,10) to (50,50) and stores the coordinates in the corner arrays. The two LINE statements in this SUB are used to draw a box with a drop-shadow. We use WINDOW(6) to make sure that there are enough colors for a shadow. You can invent variations on this routine for your own custom boxes. Or just draw your own graphics, store the coordinates of the rectangle containing the graphics in the corner arrays, and set BoxIndex to the number of boxes plus one.

```
SUB Box(i,x1,y1,x2,y2) STATIC◄
SHARED x1(),y1(),x2(),y2()◄
IF x2<x1 THEN SWAP x1,x2◄
LINE (x1,y1)-(x2,y2),1-(WINDOW(6)>1),b◄
LINE (x1,y1)-(x2-1,y2-1),1,b◄
x1(i)=x1:y1(i)=y1:x2(i)=x2:y2(i)=y2◄
END SUB◄
```

So now you've set up your display, with separate text, text in boxes, text alongside boxes, and blank boxes for text entry. You now need to wait for the user to pick one of the boxes, then act on the box selected.

Detecting Button Selections

It's really not much different from using menus. You can poll or wait for a menu to be selected, and the subprograms WaitBox( ) and WhichBox( ) let you see which button was clicked on. Whereas MENU(0) returns the menu number and MENU(1) returns the menu-ID, these routines return the number of the button that was clicked.

One limitation of Intuits is that you can have only one requester with a set of buttons going at a time since there's only one master index (BoxIndex) and only one set of corner arrays. With multidimensional arrays and very tricky programming, this system could be expanded, but the performance would probably suffer.

Returning to the Requester example, we can now understand what is happening. It starts out by setting BoxIndex to 1, starting the list at the beginning (elements 0 of the arrays are reserved for future use). It then prints the two messages and uses TxBox to display the OK and CANCEL buttons (or whatever text you've defined in b1$ and b2$).

WaitBox returns the number of the selected box. Since it patiently waits forever, some value (1 or 2) is inevitable. Since the mouse button may still be held down (causing weird repeating effects), we prevent the problem by calling FlashRelease, which both highlights the box area in reverse video and waits for the mouse button to be released.

The WaitBox routine just calls WhichBox until some value is returned:

```
SUB WaitBox(which) STATIC◄
which=0◄
WHILE which=0◄
  CALL WhichBox(which)◄
WEND◄
EXIT SUB◄
RETURN◄
END SUB◄
```

FlashRelease uses the GET command (see Chapter 2) to pick up the rectangle of the chosen box, and then PUT it down in reverse colors with PRESET. After the mouse button is released, the area is restored with the PSET stamping action of PUT. The work% array is big enough for a variety of small boxes, but you may need to adjust its size for some applications.

FlashRelease also sets a global variable called RelVerify. You can use this flag to see if the user moved the mouse while releasing the button. If RelVerify$= -1$, the user did not move the mouse while releasing the button; otherwise, RelVerify$=0$. You might check this flag to make sure that the user meant to select that box. If RelVerify$=0$, the user might have accidentally clicked the box while moving the mouse. However, none of our example programs use this flag.

```
SUB FlashRelease(which) STATIC◄
SHARED x1(),y1(),x2(),y2(),work%()◄
SHARED RelVerify◄
'These two lines flash the box◄
GET (x1(which),y1(which))-(x2(which),y2(which)),work%◄
PUT (x1(which),y1(which)),work%,PRESET◄
ix=MOUSE(1):iy=MOUSE(2):RelVerify=-1◄
WHILE MOUSE(Ø)<>Ø◄
IF MOUSE(1)<>ix OR MOUSE(2)<>iy THEN RelVerify=Ø◄
WEND◄
'This line restores the box◄
PUT (x1(which),y1(which)),work%,PSET◄
END SUB◄
```

For switch boxes that can toggle on and off, use the CheckBox subprogram. Pass it the number of the button to change and a value of zero or non-zero (1 or −1) for the state of the flag. A zero erases a small inner box; otherwise, the flag is displayed in the current maximum allowable color.

```
SUB CheckBox(i,flag) STATIC◄
SHARED x1(),y1(),x2(),y2()◄
x1=x1(i)+2:y1=y1(i)+2◄
x2=x2(i)-2:y2=y2(i)-2◄
LINE (x1+3,y1+3)-(x2-3,y2-3),WINDOW(6)*-(flag<>Ø),bf◄
END SUB◄
```

Foolproof Text Input

Occasionally, your programs need to request strings of keyboard input, such as filenames and the like. You can use INPUT or LINE INPUT (as do many of the programs in this book), but a more elegant approach is to simulate the system's own *edit fields*. An example of a system edit field is seen in the Amiga BASIC requester that appears when you select Save As from the Project menu.

The GetString routine lets the user edit a field of text. The cursor keys can move left and right within the field, and both the DEL and BACK SPACE keys can be used to erase. Any text that is typed is inserted automatically.

When using GetString, you pass it the column and row of the editing area *(Xpos,Ypos)* and the initial value of the string. This default value is displayed when GetString is called, and the user can edit it if desired. This lets you display a default filename, and so forth. Whatever string you use to pass the default value will be changed to the edited value after the user presses RE-TURN. If you aren't using a default, be sure to set this string to null (" ") before calling GetString. Example:

```
response$="default"◄
GetString 5,5,response$◄
PRINT response$◄
```

Note: There are two versions of GetString. The first is a stand-alone version that you can use in your programs without having to include the rest of the Intuits package. It is listed at the end of this chapter as Program 7-7.

The second version of GetString assumes the presence of the complete Intuits package (Program 7-6) and is included in Intuits. This version of GetString allows the user to terminate editing either by pressing RETURN or by clicking on another box. So, for example, the user can type in a filename and click directly on an OPEN button without pressing RETURN. After GetString exits, you can use the global variable *which* to see which other button, if any, was clicked.

For both GetString subprograms, you are responsible for drawing your own border around the editing field. The TxBox subprogram is handy for this purpose, and you can pad out a field with the SPACE$( ) function.

For all the requesters that use GetString, use the global variable *maxlen* to set the maximum width of the edit field. This can be larger than the size of the default string. It is the length, in characters of the current font, of the editing container.

Macro Intuits

It can be tedious to build your own custom requesters every time you want to use them. It's more convenient to use some canned requesters for common tasks. Following is a summary of these higher level calls, along with their listings. All depend on the other Intuits subprograms, and are also listed within Intuits, Program 7-6.

Alert   The Alert SUB is a simpler version of the Intuit Request routine. Since it's designed for flagging errors, it uses Retry and Cancel buttons. It also passes along two messages to be printed. The last parameter returns whether Retry (1) or Cancel (2) was pressed. Alert is little more than a simplified front end for Request. So the call is streamlined, as in

Alert "Error #"+str$(ERR),"on save",button

```
SUB Alert(msg1$,msg2$,which) STATIC◂
CALL Request(msg1$,msg2$,"Retry","Cancel",which)◂
END SUB◂
```

OpenRequest   This simplifies requesting a filename to open, integrating buttons with an edit field. Just give it a string in which to store the filename. You can assign a default filename to the string if you like. Here are some example fragments:

```
CALL OpenRequest(Filename$)◄
OPEN Filename$ FOR OUTPUT AS #1◄
WHILE NOT EOF(1)◄
PRINT HEX$(ASC(INPUT$(1,1)))◄
WEND:PRINT◄
CLOSE#1◄


SUB OpenRequest(Filename$) STATIC◄
CALL StringRequest("Open Request","Open filename:","Open","Cance
l",Filename$)◄
END SUB◄
```

SaveRequest   The complement of OpenRequest, SaveRequest prompts for a filename with which to save:

```
CALL SaveRequest(fsave$)◄
OPEN fsave$ FOR OUTPUT AS #1◄
FOR i=1 TO 10:PRINT#1,i:NEXT◄
CLOSE#1◄


SUB SaveRequest(Filename$) STATIC◄
CALL StringRequest("Save Request","Save as:","Save","Cancel",Fil
ename$)◄
END SUB◄
```

StringRequest   StringRequest is called by OpenRequest and SaveRequest. It edits a string field and checks for two buttons. Just pass it the title of the window, one message line, the text of both buttons, and the string to be edited. Remember to set the variable *ScrId* to the custom screen-ID or to −1 for the Workbench screen. Note how this routine saves the position of the text field in *Xpos* and *Ypos* so that GetString can be called at the position of the edit field. This avoids many of the problems in the differences between 60 and 80 columns. For this reason, all windows are wider than necessary for 80 columns, but sufficient for 60-column displays.

```
SUB StringRequest(title$,msg$,b1$,b2$,default$) STATIC◄
SHARED maxlen,ScrId,which,BoxIndex◄
BoxIndex=1:height=PEEKW(WINDOW(8)+58)◄
winwidth=maxlen*(8-2*(height=9))+40◄
WINDOW 2,title$,(0,0)-(winwidth,80),0,ScrId◄
PRINT:PRINT " ";msg$:PRINT◄
PRINT " ";:CALL TxBox(default$+SPACE$(1+maxlen-LEN(default$))) '
reserve space◄
Xpos=2:Ypos=CSRLIN 'for GetString◄
PRINT :PRINT :LOCATE ,2:CALL TxBox(b1$)◄
PRINT TAB(maxlen+3-LEN(b2$));:CALL TxBox(b2$)◄
which=0◄
WHILE which<=1◄
  CALL WaitBox(which) 'Get box #◄
  IF which=1 THEN 'if GetString◄
    CALL GetString(Xpos,Ypos,default$)◄
```

```
   END IF◄
WEND 'must be Open or Cancel◄
CALL FlashRelease(which) 'Flash the box◄
WINDOW CLOSE 2◄
IF which=BoxIndex-1 THEN Filename$=""◄
END SUB◄
```

Two More Examples

As already mentioned, Program 7-6 is the complete listing for the Intuit routines. To demonstrate them, this listing also contains example programs that show off many of the Intuit features. You don't need these lines in your own programs, but they are quite illustrative and peppered with comments. (Run it for a surprise.)

By running this demo and the other programs in this book, you'll get a good feel for the design of a consistent user interface that adheres closely to Amiga standards. A user interface is clear, uncluttered, and most elusively of all, intuitive. Simply adding error checking and mistake proofing can make a program huge, and the added complexity of user-interface tools can make the job seem even more difficult. But the programming sweat is worth it—the pay-off is a powerful, good-looking, easy-to-use application, with the look of professional software.

Program 7-3. Requester

```
SUB Requester (msg1$,msg2$,b1$,b2$,hilite%,answer%) STATIC◄
' Requester window subprogram ◄
' Prints up to 2 definable prompt lines◄
' and 2 definable buttons. Can also highlight a button.◄
' If Preferences is set for 80 columns,◄
' each prompt line can be up to 39 characters long.◄
' If Preferences is set for 60 columns,◄
' each prompt line can be up to 31 characters long.◄
' If program uses custom screen, must put SCREEN ID◄
' in global variable scrid before CALL.◄
' (scrid=1 for custom SCREEN 1, scrid=2 for SCREEN 2, etc.)◄
' Defaults to Workbench screen (scrid=-1).◄
' Example of CALL Requester statement:◄
' msg1$="This is the first prompt line."◄
' msg2$="This is the second prompt line."◄
' CALL Requester (msg1$,msg2$,"Button 1","Button 2",1,answer%)◄
' or alternate syntax:◄
' Requester msg1$,msg2$,"Button #1","Button #2",1,answer%◄
' First two arguments are prompt lines for Requester.◄
' To omit a prompt line, pass null string ("").◄
' Next two arguments are labels for buttons.◄
' (Limit 12 characters for each button.)◄
' Fifth argument allows highlighting of a button.◄
' 1 = highlight left button, 2 = highlight right button.◄
' (Any other value highlights neither button.)◄
' Last argument returns which button pressed:◄
' answer%=1 for left button (usually positive response),◄
```

```
' answer%=0 for right button (usually negative response).
' Subprogram opens and closes WINDOW 3;
' change to higher number if necessary.
SHARED scrid 'Global variable for SCREEN ID.
IF scrid<1 OR scrid>4 THEN scrid=-1 'Default to Workbench.
WINDOW 3,"Program Request",(0,0)-(311,45),16,scrid
maxwidth=INT(WINDOW(2)/8) 'Truncate prompts if too long...
PRINT LEFT$(msg1$,maxwidth):PRINT LEFT$(msg2$,maxwidth)
b1$=LEFT$(b1$,12):b2$=LEFT$(b2$,12) 'Truncate buttons.
bsize1=(LEN(b1$)+2)*10:bsize2=(LEN(b2$)+2)*10 'Button size.
x1=(312-(bsize1+bsize2))/3  'Calculate button positions...
x2=x1+bsize1:x3=x1+x2:x4=x3+bsize2
'Draw buttons:
LINE (x1,20)-(x2,38),2,b:LINE (x3,20)-(x4,38),2,b
IF hilite%=1 THEN LINE (x1+2,22)-(x2-2,36),3,b
IF hilite%=2 THEN LINE (x3+2,22)-(x4-2,36),3,b
LOCATE 4,1:PRINT PTAB(x1+10);b1$;
PRINT PTAB(x3+10);b2$
Reqloop: 'Loop which acts on mouse clicks...
WHILE MOUSE(0)=0:WEND:m1=MOUSE(1):m2=MOUSE(2)
IF m1>x1 AND m1<x2 AND m2>20 AND m2<38 THEN
 answer%=1 'Left button was selected.
 LINE (x1,20)-(x2,38),1,bf 'Flash left button.
ELSEIF m1>x3 AND m1<x4 AND m2>20 AND m2<38 THEN
 answer%=0 'Right button was selected.
 LINE (x3,20)-(x4,38),1,bf 'Flash right button.
 ELSE
  GOTO Reqloop 'Neither button selected; repeat loop.
 END IF
 WHILE MOUSE(0)<>0:WEND:WINDOW CLOSE 3
END SUB
```

Program 7-4. ErrorTrap

```
ErrorTrap:
 ' Traps common errors, mostly disk.
 ' Requires Requester window subprogram.
 BEEP ' Get user's attention.
 IF ERR=53 THEN
  request1$="FILE NOT FOUND."
  GOTO ExitError
 END IF
 IF ERR=61 THEN
  request1$="DISK FULL."
  GOTO ExitError
 END IF
 IF ERR=64 THEN
  request1$="BAD FILENAME."
  GOTO ExitError
 END IF
 IF ERR=67 THEN
  request1$="DIRECTORY FULL."
  GOTO ExitError
 END IF
 IF ERR=68 THEN
```

```
requestl$="DEVICE UNAVAILABLE."◄
 GOTO ExitError◄
END IF◄
IF ERR=70 THEN◄
 requestl$="DISK WRITE-PROTECTED."◄
 GOTO ExitError◄
END IF◄
IF ERR=74 THEN◄
 requestl$="UNKNOWN DISK VOLUME."◄
 GOTO ExitError◄
END IF◄
requestl$="ERROR NUMBER"+STR$(ERR)◄
ExitError:◄
' Abort operation or try again.◄
' Define global variable scrid (SCREEN ID) if required:◄
scrid=-1 'Error Requester will appear on Workbench screen.◄
CALL Requester (requestl$,"","Retry","CANCEL",2,answer%)◄
IF answer%=0 THEN◄
 CLOSE 1◄
 RESUME MainMenu ' Substitute your reentry point here.◄
ELSE◄
 CLOSE 1◄
 ON ERROR GOTO ErrorTrap◄
 RESUME◄
END IF◄
```

Program 7-5. Palette Panel

```
' *** PALETTE PANEL ***◄
' Following line for demo purposes only --◄
' insert similar line in your own program:◄
SCREEN 1,320,200,5,1 'Lo-res, noninterlaced, 32 colors.◄
' Before using Palette Panel for the first time in a program,◄
' you must CALL its setup subprogram (PanelSetup).◄
' Subsequent CALLs to Palette Panel don't require setup.◄
' When CALLing PanelSetup,◄
' set argument to number of custom SCREEN (usually 1);◄
' default is -1 (Workbench screen). Example:◄
CALL PanelSetup(1) 'Argument=1 for custom screen above.◄
' When CALLing Palette Panel,◄
' also set first argument to number of custom SCREEN◄
' and second parameter to 60 or 80 (Preferences columns).◄
' Example:◄
CALL PalettePanel(1,60)◄
SCREEN CLOSE 1:END 'End of demo.◄
◄
SUB PanelSetup (scrn%) STATIC◄
PanelSetup:◄
'Sets up arrays for PalettePanel subprogram.◄
'Call once during initialization.◄
'Requires SCREEN # argument passed in CALL (1 to 4).◄
'Defaults to Workbench screen (-1).◄
'Opens and closes WINDOW 2.◄
'◄
  'Display WINDOW on specified SCREEN (default=Workbench):◄
```

```
IF scrn%<1 OR scrn%>4 THEN scrn%=-1◄
WINDOW 2,,,,scrn%◄
DIM SHARED hue(31,2) ' Holds current PALETTE values.◄
DIM SHARED newhue(31,2) ' Holds new PALETTE values.◄
'Define default colors here (you can insert your own values):◄
hue(0,0)=0:hue(0,1)=.46:hue(0,2)=0 'Color 0◄
hue(1,0)=.9:hue(1,1)=.9:hue(1,2)=.9 'Color 1◄
hue(2,0)=0:hue(2,1)=0:hue(2,2)=0 'Color 2◄
hue(3,0)=.91:hue(3,1)=.48:hue(3,2)=.15 'Color 3◄
FOR n=4 TO 31 'We'll use random colors for the rest.◄
  FOR nn=0 TO 2◄
   hue(n,nn)=RND◄
  NEXT nn◄
NEXT n◄
FOR n=0 TO 31 'Copy current colors into temp array.◄
  newhue(n,0)=hue(n,0)◄
  newhue(n,1)=hue(n,1):newhue(n,2)=hue(n,2)◄
NEXT n◄
FOR n=0 TO WINDOW(6) ' Change PALETTE values.◄
  PALETTE n,hue(n,0),hue(n,1),hue(n,2)◄
NEXT n◄
WINDOW CLOSE 2◄
EXIT SUB◄
END SUB◄
◄
SUB PalettePanel (scrn%,prefs%) STATIC◄
PalettePanel:◄
'Sets PALETTE colors with slide controls.◄
'Requires SCREEN # argument passed in CALL (1 to 4);◄
'Defaults to Workbench screen (-1).◄
'Also requires Preferences columns passed in 2nd argument.◄
'Uses WINDOW 3.◄
'◄
  'Display WINDOW on specified SCREEN (default=Workbench):◄
  IF scrn%<1 OR scrn%>4 THEN scrn%=-1◄
  WINDOW 3,"Palette Panel",(0,0)-(311,185),16,scrn%◄
  WIDTH 80◄
  colr=0 'Current PALETTE color selected on panel.◄
  r=hue(colr,0) 'RED value for current color.◄
  g=hue(colr,1) 'GREEN value for current color.◄
  b=hue(colr,2) 'BLUE value for current color.◄
  mx=0:my=0 'Clear mouse coordinates.◄
  FOR n=0 TO 3 'Draw color panel...◄
    FOR nn=0 TO 7◄
      IF n*8+nn<WINDOW(6)+1 THEN 'Fill color box on panel:◄
        LINE (nn*39+1,n*20)-(nn*39+38,n*20+20),n*8+nn,bf◄
      END IF◄
      LINE (nn*39+1,n*20)-(nn*39+38,n*20+20),1,b 'Draw frame.◄
    NEXT nn◄
  NEXT n◄
  FOR n=100 TO 140 STEP 20 'Draw color controls...◄
    LINE (1,n)-(310,n+10),1,b◄
  NEXT n◄
  'Draw exit buttons:◄
  IF prefs%=80 THEN y=22 ELSE y=20◄
  LOCATE y,5:PRINT "USE";:LOCATE y,y:PRINT "CANCEL";◄
```

```
  LINE (1,160)-(156,184),1,b:LINE (156,160)-(310,184),1,b
SubMainLoop:
  IF my>160 THEN btn=INT(mx/153):GOTO ExitPanel
  IF mx>2 AND mx<309 AND my>100 THEN 'Clicked on a slider.
    IF my<110 THEN 'Clicked on RED slider.
      LINE (r*300+2,101)-(r*300+9,109),0,bf 'Erase RED slider.
      r=(mx-2)/307 'Calculate new position of RED slider.
      newhue(colr,0)=r 'New RED color value.
    ELSEIF my>120 AND my<130 THEN 'Clicked on GREEN slider.
      LINE (g*300+2,121)-(g*300+9,129),0,bf 'Erase GREEN slider.
      g=(mx-2)/307 'Calculate new position of GREEN slider.
      newhue(colr,1)=g 'New GREEN color value.
    ELSEIF my>140 AND my<150 THEN 'Clicked on BLUE slider.
      LINE (b*300+2,141)-(b*300+9,149),0,bf 'Erase BLUE slider.
      b=(mx-2)/307 'Calculate new position of BLUE slider.
      newhue(colr,2)=b 'New BLUE color value.
    END IF
  END IF
  IF mx>0 AND mx<311 AND my<80 THEN 'Clicked on color panel.
    LINE (r*300+2,101)-(r*300+9,109),0,bf 'Erase RED slider.
    LINE (g*300+2,121)-(g*300+9,129),0,bf 'Erase GREEN slider.
    LINE (b*300+2,141)-(b*300+9,149),0,bf 'Erase BLUE slider.
    colr=8*INT(my/20)+INT(mx/39) 'Calculate chosen color box.
    IF colr>WINDOW(6) THEN colr=0 'Color 0 if out of range.
    r=newhue(colr,0):g=newhue(colr,1):b=newhue(colr,2)
  END IF
  IF prefs%=80 THEN y=12 ELSE y=11
  LOCATE y,1:PRINT USING "R=#.##";r
  LINE (r*300+2,101)-(r*300+9,109),1,bf ' RED slider.
  LOCATE y,9:PRINT USING "G=#.##";g
  LINE (g*300+2,121)-(g*300+9,129),1,bf ' GREEN slider.
  LOCATE y,17:PRINT USING "B=#.##";b
  LINE (b*300+2,141)-(b*300+9,149),1,bf ' BLUE slider.
  LOCATE y,24:PRINT USING "Color=##";colr
  PALETTE colr,r,g,b 'Set new PALETTE colors.
  newhue(colr,0)=r:newhue(colr,1)=g:newhue(colr,2)=b
  WHILE MOUSE(0)=0:WEND
mx=MOUSE(1):my=MOUSE(2)
GOTO SubMainLoop
ExitPanel:
  IF btn=0 THEN
    LINE (1,160)-(156,184),1,bf 'Flash USE button.
    FOR n=0 TO 31 'Copy new values to current hue array.
      hue(n,0)=newhue(n,0)
      hue(n,1)=newhue(n,1):hue(n,2)=newhue(n,2)
    NEXT n
  ELSE
    LINE (156,160)-(310,184),1,bf 'Flash CANCEL button.
    FOR n=0 TO WINDOW(6) 'Restore previous PALETTE values...
      PALETTE n,hue(n,0),hue(n,1),hue(n,2)
    NEXT n
  END IF
  WHILE MOUSE(0)<>0:WEND
  WINDOW CLOSE 3:EXIT SUB
END SUB
```

Program 7-6. Intuits

```
'Intuits ◄
'Intuition gadgets simulator◄
'All automatic SUBs use◄
'WINDOW 2. Set global◄
'variable ScrId to current◄
'SCREEN id (-1 for Workbench screen)◄
'NOTE THAT SECONDARY WINDOWS◄
'MUST ORIGIN AT (0,0) FOR MOUSE◄
'POSITION REPORTS TO MAKE ANY SENSE◄
'◄
'**** Intuits header ****◄
◄
DEFINT a-z◄
'Global arrays and variables◄
DIM work%(400)◄
'more than 20 gadgets is impractical◄
DIM x1(20),y1(20),x2(20),y2(20)◄
ScrId=-1 'Screen for windows◄
which=0 'which box is selected◄
BoxIndex=1 'How many gadgets◄
maxlen=15 'length of text fields◄
'◄
'Recommended default for filenames◄
Filename$="untitled"◄
◄
'*********************************◄
'Following is not a part of◄
'the Intuits package.  It tests all◄
'Intuit functions◄
'*********************************◄
◄
'Read happy/sad faces◄
l= 43:DIM happy%(l)◄
'RESTORE Sad.Data◄
FOR i=0 TO l:READ happy%(i):NEXT◄
Happy.Data:◄
DATA &h12,&hA,&h2,&h7F8,&h0,&h3FFF,&h0,&h73F3◄
DATA &h8000,&hF3F3,&hC000,&hFFFF,&hC000,&hEFFD,&hC000,&hC7F8◄
DATA &hC000,&h7807,&h8000,&h3FFF,&h0,&h7F8,&h0,&h7F8◄
DATA &h0,&h3FFF,&h0,&h7FFF,&h8000,&hFFFF,&hC000,&hFFFF◄
DATA &hC000,&hFFFF,&hC000,&hFFFF,&hC000,&h7FFF,&h8000,&h3FFF◄
DATA &h0,&h7F8,&h0,&h0◄
l= 43 :DIM sad%(l)◄
'RESTORE Sad.Data◄
FOR i=0 TO l:READ sad%(i):NEXT◄
Sad.Data:◄
DATA &h12,&hA,&h2,&h7F8,&h0,&h3FFF,&h0,&h73F3◄
DATA &h8000,&hF3F3,&hC000,&hFFFF,&hC000,&hF807,&hC000,&hC7F8◄
DATA &hC000,&h6FFD,&h8000,&h3FFF,&h0,&h7F8,&h0,&h7F8◄
DATA &h0,&h3FFF,&h0,&h7FFF,&h8000,&hFFFF,&hC000,&hFFFF◄
DATA &hC000,&hFFFF,&hC000,&hFFFF,&hC000,&h7FFF,&h8000,&h3FFF◄
DATA &h0,&h7F8,&h0,&h0◄
◄
IntuiTest:◄
```

```
CALL Request("Which demo?","","Demo 1","Demo 2",whichdemo)
ON whichdemo GOSUB Demo1,Demo2
GOTO IntuiTest

Demo1:
f$=""
'Insist on input
WHILE f$="" AND which<3
  CALL OpenRequest(f$)
WEND
'unless Cancel was pressed
IF which=3 THEN Quit
'Verify entry
CALL Request("Did you really","mean "+f$+"?","Yes","No",button)
IF button=1 THEN
'If yes, pretend to save file
  CALL SaveRequest(f$)
  IF which=3 THEN Quit
ELSE
'otherwise, pretend there's an error
  CALL Alert("FILENAME ERROR","",button)
  IF button=1 THEN IntuiTest
END IF
'See if user wants to quit
Quit:
GOSUB IntuiQuit
RETURN

'A most unusual demo
Demo2:
WINDOW 2,"Hi!",(0,0)-(200,50),0,ScrId
PRINT :PRINT "How are you feeling?"
CALL Box(1,10,20,40,40):PUT (15,25),happy%
CALL Box(2,70,20,100,40):PUT (75,25),sad%
BoxIndex=3
CALL WaitBox(which)
CALL FlashRelease(which)
CLS
ON which GOSUB happy,sad
WINDOW CLOSE 2
RETURN

happy:
t&=TIMER+5:xd=10:yd=10:x=0:y=0
PUT (0,0),happy
WHILE TIMER<t&
  PUT (x,y),happy
  x=x+xd:y=y+yd
  IF x<0 OR x>200 THEN xd=-xd
  IF y<0 OR y>50 THEN yd=-yd
  PUT (x,y),happy
WEND
RETURN

sad:
FOR y=10 TO 50 STEP 12
```

```
     FOR x=1 TO 200 STEP 20
       PUT (x,y),sad%
     NEXT x
NEXT y
t&=TIMER+5
WHILE TIMER<t&
   PUT (200*RND,50*RND),happy%,PSET
WEND
RETURN


'Example of three-button requester:
IntuiQuit:
w=25*(8-2*(PEEKW(WINDOW(8)+58)=9))
WINDOW 2,"EXIT DEMO",(0,0)-(w,50),0,ScrId
PRINT "    Quit Intuit Demo?":PRINT
BoxIndex=1:PRINT TAB(11);:CALL TxBox("NO!"):PRINT :PRINT
LOCATE ,2:CALL TxBox("To System")
PRINT TAB(15);:CALL TxBox("To BASIC")
'Disable Stop during WaitBox
ON BREAK GOSUB Ignore
CALL WaitBox(which)
CALL FlashRelease(which)
ON BREAK GOSUB IntuiQuit
WINDOW CLOSE 2
IF which=1 THEN RETURN
IF which=2 THEN SYSTEM 'CAREFUL!
IF which=3 THEN LIST:END
Ignore:
RETURN

'*****************************
'           Intuits
'*****************************

'Ask for a file to open
'returns in string (Filename$)
'(Filename$) can be a default
'Set global variable maxlen to
'maximum length of filename
'Example call:
'CALL OpenRequest(which$)
'OPEN which$ FOR INPUT AS #1 'etc.
'Examine global variable which to see
'whether Open or Cancel is selected
SUB OpenRequest(Filename$) STATIC
CALL StringRequest("Open Request","Open filename:","Open","Cance
l",Filename$)
END SUB

'Ask for a file to save
'returns in (Filename$)
'You can pass a default, too.
'Global variable maxlen is maximum
'length of string
'Example call:
'Call SaveRequest(temp$)
```

```
'OPEN temp$ FOR OUTPUT AS #1 'etc.◄
'Examine global which for Save (=1)◄
'or Cancel (=2)◄
SUB SaveRequest(Filename$) STATIC◄
CALL StringRequest("Save Request","Save as:","Save","Cancel",Fil
ename$)◄
END SUB◄
                                      ◄
'Primitive for OpenRequest and SaveRequest◄
'Gets a string with button verify◄
'Pass title of window, a message, two button names,◄
'and a default in (default$)◄
'and selected button in global Which (1 or 2)◄
'Receive edited string in (default$)◄
'global variable maxlen should be◄
'set to maximum length of file◄
'Example of call:◄
'CALL StringRequest("Request","Enter name:","OK","Cancel",answer
$)◄
'                                     ◄
SUB StringRequest(title$,msg$,b1$,b2$,default$) STATIC◄
SHARED maxlen,ScrId,which,BoxIndex◄
BoxIndex=1:height=PEEKW(WINDOW(8)+58)◄
winwidth=maxlen*(8-2*(height=9))+40◄
WINDOW 2,title$,(0,0)-(winwidth,80),0,ScrId◄
PRINT:PRINT "  ";msg$:PRINT◄
PRINT " ";:CALL TxBox(default$+SPACE$(1+maxlen-LEN(default$))) '
reserve space◄
Xpos=2:Ypos=CSRLIN 'for GetString◄
PRINT :PRINT :LOCATE ,2:CALL TxBox(b1$)◄
PRINT TAB(maxlen+3-LEN(b2$));:CALL TxBox(b2$)◄
which=0◄
WHILE which<=1◄
  CALL WaitBox(which) 'Get box #◄
  IF which=1 THEN 'if GetString◄
    CALL GetString(Xpos,Ypos,default$)◄
  END IF◄
WEND 'must be Open or Cancel◄
CALL FlashRelease(which) 'Flash the box◄
WINDOW CLOSE 2◄
IF which=BoxIndex-1 THEN Filename$=""◄
END SUB◄
◄
◄
'Easy Alert.  Pass two lines of text◄
'in msg1$,msg2$.  Receive button status◄
'(1=retry, 2=cancel) in (which)◄
SUB Alert(msg1$,msg2$,which) STATIC◄
CALL Request(msg1$,msg2$,"Retry","Cancel",which)◄
END SUB◄
◄
'Generalized requester◄
'Pass two messages lines in msg1$,msg2$◄
'and two button prompts in b1$,b2$◄
'Confine text to a width of 16◄
' button (usually Cancel)◄
'No buttons are highlighted◄
```

```
SUB Request(msg1$,msg2$,b1$,b2$,which) STATIC
SHARED BoxIndex,ScrId
SHARED x1(),y1(),x2(),y2()
BoxIndex=1:height=PEEKW(WINDOW(8)+58)
winwidth=20*(8-2*(height=9))+30
WINDOW 2,"System Request",(0,0)-(winwidth,50),0,ScrId
PRINT :PRINT TAB(11-LEN(msg1$)/2);msg1$
PRINT TAB(11-LEN(msg2$)/2);msg2$:PRINT
LOCATE ,2:TxBox b1$
PRINT TAB(20-LEN(b2$));:TxBox b2$:which=0
CALL WaitBox(which)
CALL FlashRelease(which)
WINDOW CLOSE 2
END SUB

'Flashes button (which), waits for
'release of mouse button
'if mouse moved during release,
'global variable RelVerify is set to null,
'else is -1 (true).
SUB FlashRelease(which) STATIC
SHARED x1(),y1(),x2(),y2(),work%()
SHARED RelVerify
'These two lines flash the box
GET (x1(which),y1(which))-(x2(which),y2(which)),work%
PUT (x1(which),y1(which)),work%,PRESET
ix=MOUSE(1):iy=MOUSE(2):RelVerify=-1
WHILE MOUSE(0)<>0
IF MOUSE(1)<>ix OR MOUSE(2)<>iy THEN RelVerify=0
WEND
'This line restores the box
PUT (x1(which),y1(which)),work%,PSET
END SUB

'TxBox automatically draws a box
'around text in (msg$), stores box
'vertices in corner arrays
'Sub BOX automatically increments
'global index BoxIndex
SUB TxBox(msg$) STATIC
SHARED x1(),y1(),x2(),y2()
SHARED BoxIndex
x1=WINDOW(4):y1=WINDOW(5)-10
PRINT " ";msg$;" ";
x2=WINDOW(4):y2=y1+14
CALL Box(BoxIndex,x1,y1,x2,y2)
BoxIndex=BoxIndex+1
PRINT SPC(1);
END SUB

'Draw and store a box (i) whose corner
'coords are (x1,y1)-(x2,y2)
'Can be used to change a box's coords
SUB Box(i,x1,y1,x2,y2) STATIC
SHARED x1(),y1(),x2(),y2()
```

```
IF x2<x1 THEN SWAP x1,x2
LINE (x1,y1)-(x2,y2),1-(WINDOW(6)>1),b
LINE (x1,y1)-(x2-1,y2-1),1,b
x1(i)=x1:y1(i)=y1:x2(i)=x2:y2(i)=y2
END SUB

'Check a box
'Pass variable (flag)
'for on/off (-1/0)
SUB CheckBox(i,flag) STATIC
SHARED x1(),y1(),x2(),y2()
x1=x1(i)+2:y1=y1(i)+2
x2=x2(i)-2:y2=y2(i)-2
LINE (x1+3,y1+3)-(x2-3,y2-3),WINDOW(6)*-(flag<>0),bf
END SUB

'Wait for a box to be selected
'return number in (which)
SUB WaitBox(which) STATIC
which=0
WHILE which=0
  CALL WhichBox(which)
WEND
EXIT SUB
RETURN
END SUB

'See if a box is selected,
'otherwise (which)=0
'Used to poll for box selection

SUB WhichBox(which) STATIC
SHARED x1(),y1(),x2(),y2(),BoxIndex
IF MOUSE(0)=0 THEN EXIT SUB
x=MOUSE(1):y=MOUSE(2):i=1
WHILE i<BoxIndex AND NOT (x>x1(i) AND x<x2(i) AND y>y1(i) AND y<
y2(i))
  i=i+1
WEND
which=i:IF i=BoxIndex THEN which=0
END SUB

'Customized GetString integrated for
'use with other box gadgets
'Exits when RETURN is pressed or
'when another button is clicked
'(button selected is returned in
' global variable Which)
'Provide your own border.
'Pass position of field (Xpos,Ypos)
'Pass default prompt in default$,
'find return in default$
'global variable maxlen=length of edit field in characters
'(default length is 40)
SUB GetString(Xpos,Ypos,default$) STATIC
SHARED maxlen,which
answer$=default$
```

```
IF maxlen=0 THEN maxlen=40◄
'Cursor appears at end of default string◄
csr=LEN(default$)+1◄
k$=""◄
WHILE k$<>CHR$(13)◄
    LOCATE Ypos,Xpos+1:PRINT default$;" ";◄
    LOCATE Ypos,Xpos+csr◄
    COLOR 0,WINDOW(6) 'cursor is max color◄
    PRINT MID$(default$+" ",csr,1)◄
    COLOR 1,0:k$=""◄
  WHILE k$="":k$=INKEY$◄
    CALL WhichBox(i)◄
    IF i>1 AND i<>which THEN which=i:k$=CHR$(13)◄
  WEND◄
  LOCATE Ypos,Xpos+1:PRINT default$;" ";◄
  k=ASC(k$)◄
  IF k>=32 AND k<127 THEN◄
    default$=LEFT$(default$,csr-1)+k$+MID$(default$,csr)◄
    default$=LEFT$(default$,maxlen)◄
    csr=csr-(csr<maxlen)◄
  END IF◄
  IF k=31 OR k=8 THEN csr=csr+(csr>1)◄
  IF k=127 OR k=8 THEN◄
    default$=LEFT$(default$,csr-1)+MID$(default$,csr+1)◄
  END IF◄
  IF k=30 THEN csr=csr-(csr<maxlen)◄
WEND◄
END SUB◄
RETURN◄
```

Program 7-7. GetString Routine, Stand-Alone Version

```
'Stand-Alone GetString◄
'Does not require Intuits package.◄
'Exits when RETURN is pressed.◄
'Provide your own border.◄
'Pass position of field (Xpos,Ypos)◄
'Pass default prompt in default$,◄
'find return in default$◄
'global variable maxlen=length of edit field in characters◄
'(default length is 40)◄
SUB GetString(Xpos,Ypos,default$) STATIC◄
SHARED maxlen,which◄
answer$=default$◄
IF maxlen=0 THEN maxlen=40◄
'Cursor appears at end of default string◄
csr=LEN(default$)+1◄
k$=""◄
WHILE k$<>CHR$(13)◄
  LOCATE Ypos,Xpos+1:PRINT default$;" ";◄
  LOCATE Ypos,Xpos+csr◄
  PRINT MID$(default$+" ",csr,1);◄
  LOCATE Ypos,Xpos+csr◄
  k$=""◄
  WHILE k$="":k$=INPUT$(1):WEND◄
```

```
    LOCATE Ypos,Xpos+1:PRINT default$;" ";◄
◄
  k=ASC(k$)◄
  IF k>=32 AND k<127 THEN◄
    default$=LEFT$(default$,csr-1)+k$+MID$(default$,csr)◄
    default$=LEFT$(default$,maxlen)◄
    csr=csr-(csr<maxlen)◄
  END IF◄
  IF k=31 OR k=8 THEN csr=csr+(csr>1)◄
  IF k=127 OR k=8 THEN◄
    default$=LEFT$(default$,csr-1)+MID$(default$,csr+1)◄
  END IF◄
  IF k=30 THEN csr=csr-(csr<=LEN(default$))◄
WEND◄
END SUB◄
RETURN◄
```

8 Programming Peripherals

8 Programming Peripherals

Although the Amiga itself is a pretty powerful box, it needs certain peripherals to take full advantage of its power. The obviously essential peripherals are a display device (composite or RGB monitor), a keyboard, and some form of mass storage.

In the early, more expensive days of personal computing, mass storage was an exotic peripheral. Programmers of simple computers like the KIM-1 or Ohio Scientific C1P had to type in a program with a hexadecimal calculator-style keypad (or worse, flip toggle switches to change bit settings in individual memory cells) every time they wanted to run the machine. Naturally, a popular project was to adapt an ordinary audiocassette recorder for storing programs. Cassettes worked at a rate of about 30 characters per second. If you had the money and technical skill, you could add a 32-column, cash-register-tape printer. Your main display was usually a row of small LEDs, but deluxe models such as the OSI C1P could actually display text on a television set.

Very quickly, though, computers dropped in price while they gained power. The Commodore PET, at about $800, had a whopping 8K of RAM, a built-in tape drive, and built-in screen. The evolution continued with the business-series PETs, which could use expensive disk drives that managed to get 170K of data on a 5¼-inch floppy disk. The first Commodore home computer, the VIC-20, was just a keyboard unit with 5K of RAM, but it could display 16 colors with graphics on a home TV set—quite remarkable for its introductory price of $299. You could buy optional disk drives, narrow-width, spring-driven printers, and even telephone modems, although some of these peripherals cost more than the computer itself. The Commodore 64 used upgraded VIC-20 peripherals, and with 64K of RAM at an introductory price of $599 was pretty much the evolution of the old PET into a color home computer.

We now have the Amiga, the most powerful Commodore product yet (although the Amiga actually traces its lineage back to the Atari home computers). The monitor is optional, but an 880K disk drive is built in, along with 256K of RAM (512K if you count the *Writeable Control Store*, WCS, that holds the operating system). By making the display device optional, Commodore lets you choose from monitors with varying prices and capabilities. But the built-in disk drive shows the true necessity of mass storage—the Amiga requires what would have been a rare luxury ten years ago. Within a few years, built-in hard disks will probably be considered a requirement; they're already becoming indispensable in small business computers.

The Amiga can be attached to innumerable power-boosting attachments, from 1200/2400 bits-per-second telephone modems and color ink-jet printers to exotic peripherals such as frame grabbers and sound digitizers. Writing programs to take advantage of all these peripherals may seem a boggling task. But with the Amiga's powerful operating system and Amiga BASIC, it's actually quite easy.

Making the Connection

To let the Amiga talk to a peripheral, you must first open a communications channel between the computer and the peripheral. Data to be stored, retrieved, transmitted, or printed is sent in the appropriate direction along this pipeline. The communications channel is also called a *file*, not to be confused with a disk file—although quite often you do set up a communications file to access a disk file.

Accessing any peripheral requires three steps. First, you must *open* a communications file to the peripheral. Then you *read* data from the peripheral or *write* new data to it. After you're done, you *close* the file.

The Amiga lets you open and access several files at once. These files don't necessarily have to be opened to different peripherals; some peripherals, such as the disk drive, let you open several files to them simultaneously. To avoid confusion, each file is assigned a unique *file number*. This file number is like a TV channel dedicated to that file. Although you can receive (open) many channels, you can refer to only one at a time, according to the channel number.

The Amiga also assigns certain *device names* to its peripherals. When opening a channel to a peripheral, you must specify its proper device name. For instance, PRT: is the device name for a printer attached to the computer's parallel or serial port (the actual port that is accessed when you specify PRT: depends on which one has been selected with the Preferences tool). Table 8-1 gives all the device names recognized by AmigaDOS and Amiga BASIC.

You'll notice that there is more than one device name for certain devices. These devices can be accessed in different ways by addressing them with different device names, as we'll see in a few examples below.

The concept of device names is an important one. Among other things, it means that the Amiga supports *generalized device I/O* (also called *device-independent I/O* or *I/O redirection*). Merely by changing a device name, you can direct output to or receive input from any specified device. For instance, let's say you've got a program that dumps a data file on the printer. It's quite simple to generalize this routine so the user can choose to view the data on the screen instead. All Amiga BASIC commands that send output to or receive input from a device will work with *all* devices. The only exceptions, of course, are types of I/O which are inappropriate to a certain device—you obviously can't receive input from a printer or send output to the keyboard.

Table 8-1. Device Names

Device Name	Device	I/O Type
COM1:	RS-232 port	Input/Output*
SER:	RS-232 port	Input/Output
LPT1:	Printer	Output*
LPT1:BIN	Printer	Output*
PRT:	Printer	Output
PAR:	Parallel port	Output
DF0:	Internal drive	Input/Output
DF1:	External drive	Input/Output
DH0:	Hard disk	Input/Output
KYBD:	Keyboard	Input*
RAM:	RAM disk	Input/Output
RAW:	System	Input/Output
SCRN:	Screen	Output*
CON:	Console	Input/Output

*Device name recognized only by Amiga BASIC.

OPENing a Device File

To set up a communications channel in Amiga BASIC, use the OPEN statement. There are two versions of OPEN in Amiga BASIC, and both do the same thing. Here is the first syntax:

OPEN *device* **FOR** *access mode* **AS** *filenumber* **LEN**=*file buffer size*

Device is the name of a peripheral device recognized by the Amiga; *access mode* specifies whether you are retrieving, sending, or appending data; *filenumber* is the unique identification number you assign to the communications channel; and *file buffer size* is an optional parameter that specifies the size of the file buffer or the record size for use with random files (we'll discuss the different file types in a moment). The maximum limit for *file buffer size* is 32,767 bytes.

For disk files, *device* includes the AmigaDOS filename. If you leave out one of BASIC's devices, an AmigaDOS device or filename is assumed. If the filename doesn't include a drive specifier or a volume name, the current directory for BASIC is used to reference the file.

A word of explanation about *file buffer size:* The file buffer is a section of memory that holds the data which is read from or written to the file. The size of this buffer is normally 128 bytes for random files and 512 bytes for sequential files. When you access a file, BASIC always fills the file buffer to capacity, even if you don't ask it to. For instance, if you try to read only a single character from a file, BASIC goes ahead and reads enough characters to fill the current file buffer. Why? So that any subsequent reads from the same file may avoid actually accessing the device—the data can be retrieved from memory. This speeds up I/O. For random files, you should use the optional LEN parameter to set the file buffer size to the number of characters in one record of the file. For sequential files, you can make a buffer of any size, since sequential records may be of different lengths. The larger the buffer, the faster the I/O. Larger buffers also consume more BASIC memory, however.

Here are some examples of typical OPEN statements:

OPEN "LPT1:" FOR OUTPUT AS #1

This opens the device named LPT1: (a printer attached to either the parallel or serial port) for output through channel number 1. Note that opening a channel for *input* from a printer would be illogical and therefore triggers an error.

OPEN "Addresses" FOR INPUT AS #4

This opens the disk file "Addresses" on the current directory for input through channel 4.

OPEN "Addresses" FOR APPEND AS #3

This opens the disk file "Addresses" on the current directory for appending data through channel 3.

OPEN "Workbench:BasicProgs/MyFile" FOR OUTPUT AS #2

This opens the disk file "MyFile" in the subdirectory "BasicProgs" on the disk named Workbench for output through channel 2. If the disk named Workbench is not currently mounted in a drive when you try to access this file, the Amiga automatically pops up a system requester window asking you to insert Workbench.

Here is the alternative syntax of the OPEN statement:

OPEN *access mode, filenumber, device, file buffer size*

Access mode is "R" for random file input/output, "I" for sequential file input, "O" for sequential file output, or "A" for appending data to a sequential file; *filenumber* is the unique number you assign to the communications channel; *device* is the device name of a peripheral recognized by Amiga BASIC; and *file buffer size* is the optional parameter described above. The following statements are equivalent to the four previous examples:

OPEN "O",#1,"LPT1:"
OPEN "I",#4,"Addresses"

OPEN "A",#3,"Addresses"
OPEN "O",#2,"Workbench:BasicProgs/MyFile"

Here are some additional examples:

OPEN "R",#3,"CASH_RECEIPTS",150

This opens the disk file "CASH_RECEIPTS" on the current directory for random access input/output as file 3. The size of each record is 150 bytes. (We'll devote special coverage to random files later.) The other form of this statement is OPEN "Cash_Receipts" AS #3 LEN=150.

OPEN "A",#1,"CheckFile"

This opens the sequential disk file "CheckFile" on the current directory through channel 1 for adding data to the end of the file. It could also be written as OPEN "Checkfile" FOR APPEND AS #1.

It's really quite straightforward. Just combine OPEN with FOR INPUT, FOR OUTPUT, FOR APPEND, the keyword AS, and the file number. Just remember that you must use a different file number for every file you want to open simultaneously. And since this file number is reserved as long as the file is open, you must close a file before you can reuse its file number (example: CLOSE #1 or CLOSE 1). Some programmers like to precede every OPEN with a CLOSE to make sure the channel is available, avoiding a *File already open* error. However, a well-written program cleans up after itself, closing any files that are no longer needed, so this precaution shouldn't be necessary.

Input from the keyboard works much like the normal INPUT or INKEY$ statements. Likewise, output to SCRN: is the same as an ordinary PRINT or WRITE statement. Therefore, we'll concentrate on the more useful applications of programming device I/O for printers, disk files, and modems.

About the RAM Disk

The RAM disk (device name RAM:) is designed to simulate a physical disk drive in random access memory. Every function pertinent to disk programming applies to the RAM: device—just substitute RAM: for DF0:, DF1:, DH0:, or the volume name of the disk.

The first time you access the RAM disk, the Amiga has to load the RAM: device driver from your startup disk (that's why a system requester appears if your boot disk isn't currently mounted). An exception to this is when you've previously edited a BASIC program in the List window with the Cut, Copy, or Paste options in BASIC's Edit menu. Whenever you define and cut or copy something from a program, Amiga BASIC stores the defined text in the RAM disk in a file called "BasicClip". You can confirm this by entering the command

TYPE RAM:BasicClip

in a CLI window.

The RAM disk grows as you add to it. As the INFO command in AmigaDOS shows, it's always 100 percent full, yet there is no upward limit to its size (and on multi-megabyte machines it can be very big indeed). Access to the RAM: device is blindingly fast, even faster than a hard disk drive, since no actual fetching has to be performed. The data is already in memory, so it just needs to be moved.

The RAM disk is usually for temporary files, since everything in RAM: is lost when the Amiga is turned off (or when its power is temporarily diverted to another galaxy during a brownout). A CTRL-Amiga-Amiga reset also wipes out the RAM disk. Although using the RAM disk is an easy way to speed up a disk-intensive program, either the programmer or the user must take the responsibility to copy the file to physical, durable media.

Reading the Keyboard

Many people don't think of a keyboard as a peripheral, but it is. This status is a little more obvious on computers like the Amiga that have detached keyboards. In fact, the keyboard is a computer's most important input device—even more important than a mouse.

Unlike most Amiga devices, the keyboard doesn't require you explicitly to OPEN a file to fetch input. Amiga BASIC commands such as INKEY$, INPUT$, INPUT, and LINE INPUT refer to the keyboard by default.

INKEY$ is a function common to many Microsoft BASICs. When you reference it in a statement, Amiga BASIC checks the keyboard to see whether a key has recently been pressed. If so, INKEY$ returns the character. Otherwise, INKEY$ doesn't contain anything, which for strings means it is equal to the null string (""). The INPUT$ function, on the other hand, sits and waits for a keystroke before continuing. To read a single character from the keyboard, use IN-PUT$(1). You can also use INPUT$ to read more than one character from the keyboard, but since the characters typed are not echoed to the screen, you can't see what you're typing. On the other hand, this is ideal for such purposes as entering a password invisibly .

The advantage of using INKEY$ is that your program can continue working while it is waiting for a keystroke, rather than being tied up in an INPUT$ loop. This is especially important when you're using event trapping (see Chapter 1). Since Amiga BASIC traps for events only between individual statements, trapping is suspended until the INPUT$ statement is finished—until the user presses a key. Try the following short program to see what we mean. It draws dots all over the screen while it waits for a keystroke, then prints the ASCII value of the keystroke on the screen. If you substitute INPUT$(1) for INKEY$, the program seems to freeze up.

```
WHILE -1 'i.e. forever◄
  a$=INKEY$:IF a$<>"" THEN PRINT ASC(a$)◄
  PSET (639*RND,199*RND)◄
WEND◄
```

One warning about INKEY$: Referencing INKEY$ in a statement always sends it back to look at the keyboard to see whether there is a keystroke. If there isn't one, INKEY$ is reset to a null string, " ". If you use INKEY$ twice in a statement, you've lost the first value of INKEY$ in favor of the second. That's why we assign the value to A$ in the example above. Also, the ASC function crashes with an *Illegal function call* error if you try to get the ASCII value of a null string returned by INKEY$. To get around this, you can pad a suspicious string with CHR$(0) before using ASC, as in PRINT ASC(A$+CHR$(0)). Since ASC looks at the first character in a string to get the ASCII value, it works the same as always if the string contains any characters. If the string is a null, ASC will see the CHR$(0) and return a value of 0, since " "+CHR$(0) is the same as CHR$(0).

While running the above program, try pressing every key on the keyboard. As you can see, even the cursor keys and function keys return unique ASCII values. The CTRL key modifies the ASCII value of a key. For function keys, CTRL-F1 through CTRL-F10 return the same values as CTRL-A through CTRL-J. In fact, CTRL-F3 breaks out of your program, since it is the same as CTRL-C.

So even though the function keys aren't predefined to do anything in Amiga BASIC, you can still read them and act upon them in your own programs. Just check for the keys you're interested in, and act accordingly:

```
'Fkeys◄
WINDOW 1,,,31◄
PRINT "Press Fl-Fl0"◄
ReadAgain:◄
FKEY$=INPUT$(1)◄
which=ASC(FKEY$)-128 'convert from 129-138 to 1-10◄
IF which<1 OR which>10 THEN ReadAgain 'if function key is not pr
essed◄
PRINT "Function #";which◄
```

And so on.

Refer to Appendix E, "The Amiga Character Set," for a complete list of the ASCII codes for every keyboard and display character.

Amiga Printer Drivers

Similar to the keyboard input statements, Amiga BASIC also contains a shortcut for sending text output to the printer without using an OPEN statement. Just substitute LPRINT for PRINT or LPRINT USING for PRINT USING. BASIC recognizes LPRINT as a printer-specific command and opens a communication channel for you. Most of the printing techniques that work on the screen work on paper, too. You can use LPRINT TAB(10), read the printhead position with LPOS( ), and generate hardcopies of program listings with LLIST instead of LIST.

When a file is opened to the printer (either explicitly with OPEN or implicitly with LPRINT or LLIST) for the first time in a session, you'll notice that the Amiga accesses the disk drive for a few moments before starting the printout. If your boot disk is not currently mounted, a system requester asks you to insert it. This happens because the Amiga's operating system depends on disk-based *printer drivers*. A printer driver is a program that lets you use special printer features such as underline, boldface, and italics without worrying about printer compatibility. Since most printers don't share the same command codes to activate these features, printer drivers are required so that an application program can work with many different kinds of printers. But the Amiga approaches printer drivers quite differently than do other personal computers.

On other machines, it is the application programmer's job to write printer drivers. If you write a word processor for, say, a Commodore 64, you've also got to write printer drivers to ensure that your program is compatible with all the popular printers. Since printers aren't standardized, you can easily end up writing a dozen or more printer drivers to make your word processor appeal to the widest possible market. Sometimes the job of writing printer drivers is as daunting as the original task of writing the application program which they support.

To lift this burden off the shoulders of application programmers, the Amiga includes a set of printer drivers as an extension to its operating system. When you open the Preferences tool, go to the printer screen, and select a printer, what you're actually doing is telling the Amiga which printer driver to use for all output to the PRT: device—whether that output is coming from an Amiga BASIC program that you've written or a piece of commercial software.

If you can't find a printer driver to fit your particular printer, version 1.1 of the Amiga operating system contains a driver called GENERIC. If you specify GENERIC as a custom printer with Preferences, you get a plain-vanilla driver that's capable of sending text to almost any printer. However, you can't use special printer features or print graphics dumps with the GENERIC driver.

Incorporating printer drivers as part of the system software is a great advantage for application programmers. All your program has to do to access a special printer feature is send a standardized code to the PRT: device. The printer driver automatically translates this standardized code into the nonstandard code required by the printer. Every program you write can work with every printer supported by the Amiga's operating system, and you don't have to write a single printer driver yourself.

Sending Printer Driver Codes

Here's an example. Let's say you want to print some text in italics. All you do is pass the standardized printer code for italics, followed by your text:

OPEN "PRT:" FOR OUTPUT AS #1
PRINT #1,CHR$(27);"[3m";"This text appears in italics."
CLOSE #1

The result is *This text appears in italics.* If you don't get italics, there are three possible reasons: (1) your printer doesn't support italics, (2) you've selected the wrong printer driver with Preferences, or (3) the Amiga presently has no driver for your printer and you're using the GENERIC driver. (Printer driver builders are available commercially if you have the third problem.) If you get a *File already open* error, make sure the proper printer is selected with Preferences and click on SAVE, not USE, when exiting Preferences. Then reboot with this disk and try again. Sometimes, switching printers with Preferences and clicking on USE seems to confuse Amiga BASIC.

Notice the strange characters in the PRINT #1 statement above. These characters don't appear in the printout; they are the special code for switching on italics. The ASCII sequence 27 91 51 109, represented in BASIC as

CHR$(27);CHR$(91);CHR$(51);CHR$(109)

or

CHR$(27);"[3m"

is the standardized printer driver code for italics. For convenience, you may want to assign these codes to a string variable and just insert that string whenever you want to switch modes. ITAL$=CHR$(27)+"[3m" will do the trick. Then you can use a statement like

PRINT #1,ITAL$;"This is italics."

To switch off italics, you could use

PRINT #1,ITALOFF$;"This is not italics."

if you've defined

ITALOFF$=CHR$(27)+"[23m"

The printer driver codes are cumulative, so you can combine two codes to get special styles. For instance, the code for boldface type is

CHR$(27);"[1m"

If you pass this code plus the one for italics, the result is boldface italics. To get back to normal printing, you can either switch off each feature individually or issue this code:

CHR$(27);"[0m"

Note something else in the above example: We open a file to the printer via the PRT: device, not the LPT1: device. There's a very good reason for this. PRT: supports the special printer codes, but LPT1: does not. Neither does LPT1:BIN, PAR:, SER:, or LPRINT. If you want to access special printer features, you're limited to PRT:, although it isn't really a limitation. You can do everything you want with PRT:. Amiga BASIC includes LPT1: probably to make it easier to translate programs written in other versions of Microsoft BASIC, such as IBM BASIC, which use the device name LPT1:. The other printer device names,

PAR: and SER:, address the parallel and serial ports directly. For the great majority of applications, they're really not that useful.

Thanks to the Amiga's generalized device I/O, you can even use the special printer codes to change text on the monitor screen. To see for yourself, open a CLI window. At the CLI prompt, press the ESC key followed by [3m and press RETURN. None of these characters will appear on the screen, and you'll get an *Unknown command* message when you hit RETURN. But *Unknown command* appears in italics, and all subsequent characters entered at the prompt or displayed in the CLI window appear in italics, too. To get back to the normal font, press ESC; then type [0m and press RETURN.

You can do the same thing in BASIC. Although the SCRN: device doesn't support the codes, the CON: device does. CON: is the console device used by the CLI. It's really like a small terminal that you can open up as a window on the Amiga screen. It supports keyboard input and text output. For an example, run this short program:

```
OPEN "con:20/20/310/100/Type Styles" FOR APPEND AS #1 LEN=1
PRINT #1,CHR$(27);"[3m";"Italics"
PRINT #1,CHR$(27);"[4m";"Underlined italics"
PRINT #1,CHR$(27);"[1m";"Underlined boldface italics"
PRINT #1,CHR$(27);"[0m";"Back to normal."
PRINT #1,""
WHILE MOUSE(0)=0:WEND
WHILE MOUSE(0)<>0:WEND
CLOSE #1
```

To stop the program, move the mouse pointer outside the CON: window and click the left mouse button.

Incidentally, these special codes weren't just made up one day by someone at Amiga with nothing better to do. They're issued by the International Standards Organization (ISO), the same group which establishes uniform standards for everything from units of measure to film speed ratings. A complete listing of the ISO printer codes is found in Appendix B. If more computers adopt these codes, it will be much easier for programmers to write applications that work with the hundreds of different printers on the market.

Printer Input/Output

In the above examples, you've undoubtedly noticed the PRINT# statement. This works just like PRINT, except it sends the output to the file specified by the file number. PRINT# USING, in turn, works like PRINT USING. Don't confuse these statements with LPRINT and LPRINT USING. If you OPEN a file to the printer and then attempt to use LPRINT before CLOSEing the file, you'll get a *File already open* error. Although you can open two files to the disk drive simultaneously, the printer device doesn't allow this. (Remember that LPRINT implicity opens a file to the printer.)

To avoid *File already open* errors, it's a good practice to CLOSE a file once you're done with it. There's another reason for CLOSEing a file, too—it flushes the file buffer—that is, it makes sure that any data remaining in the file buffer is sent along for input or output as required. To see what we mean, switch to the Amiga BASIC Output window and type the following lines in direct mode, pressing RETURN at the end of each line:

OPEN "PRT:" FOR OUTPUT AS #1
PRINT #1,"Delayed reaction"
CLOSE #1

You might expect the message *Delayed reaction* to print out as soon as you press RETURN at the end of the second line, but it doesn't. Instead, it prints out only after you press RETURN on the third line. Here's why.

Recall that if you omit the LEN parameter from the OPEN statement, BASIC automatically assigns a file buffer size of 128 bytes for random files and 512 bytes for sequential files. When opening a file to the printer, BASIC considers it a sequential file (although the distinction is really meaningless with a printer). So, in effect, you get a 512-byte printer buffer. You can PRINT# up to 512 characters before anything is actually sent to the printer. When you PRINT# fewer than 512 characters, nothing happens until you CLOSE the file and force BASIC to empty the buffer.

Now try this, again typing each line in the BASIC Output window and pressing RETURN:

OPEN "PRT:" FOR OUTPUT AS #1 LEN=1
PRINT #1,"Instant printing"
CLOSE #1

This time when you press RETURN on the second line, the message appears on the printer immediately. We set the file buffer size to 1 (the minimum allowed), so BASIC was forced to flush the buffer each time it received a character. By manipulating the size of the file buffer, then, you can determine how the device will respond to input/output commands.

Print Formatting

The PRINT# and PRINT# USING statements are invaluable for neatly formatting text in your printouts. Virtually all of the Amiga BASIC commands that work with PRINT also function with PRINT#.

For instance, you can use PRINT# with SPACE$ to quickly send some spaces to the printer. PRINT# with STRING$(80,"–") prints a scored line and can be used to print any series of characters. As we mentioned before, it can be convenient to assign common printing sequences to strings. To center some text, use PRINT# with a statement like

TAB(40−LEN(MSG$)/2);MSG$

Of course, this assumes a column width of 80.

If linefeeds are turned off, you can return the carriage without advancing the paper, letting you overstrike to create special effects. CHR$(13) moves the printhead to column 1. You can use this to underline if your printer doesn't normally support underlining; just print the text, return the carriage, and print some underscores where appropriate:

PRINT #1,"This is underlined";CHR$(13);
PRINT #1,"   _____   "

You can overstrike a single character by sending a backspace code, CHR$(8) (note that this may not work on every printer). To create the cents sign (¢), overstrike a lowercase *c* with a vertical bar (|):

PRINT #1,"That'll be 5c";CHR$(8);"|"

This prints as

```
That'll be 5¢
```

Parsing (making sure that words aren't split at the ends of lines) is another problem that can be solved with clever printer programming. Let's say you have a text file that is completely unformatted—perhaps a *Textcraft* document that was saved with the text-only option. You might be writing your own formatter or simply trying to print the text legibly. Since the text is unformatted, words may be split in the middle as they fall off the margins.

One way to parse is just to print until you get to within ten characters of the right margin. If the word you're about to print is longer than ten characters, you know it won't fit, so you break to the next line. Without doing any word counting, you could just break the line when you find a space (every word or sentence is normally followed by a space) and you're within ten characters from the margin. This can give you a very ragged margin, though, and a word longer than ten characters would defeat the algorithm, spilling over the margin.

```
'Parser◄
OPEN "Chapter8" FOR INPUT AS #1◄
WHILE NOT EOF(1)◄
  a$=INPUT$(1,1)◄
  LPRINT a$;◄
  IF a$=" " AND LPOS(Ø)>=7Ø THEN LPRINT ""◄
WEND◄
CLOSE 1:CLOSE 2◄
```

Notice the use of three special commands for file handling: EOF, IN-PUT$, and LPOS. EOF(*filenumber*) is a function that checks for an *end-of-file* condition. If EOF returns a true value (−1), the end of the file has been reached. This lets you read data from a file of indeterminate length and end cleanly without an *Input past end* error. We're using it here in conjunction with

INPUT$, which reads characters from a file. The general format of INPUT$ is

INPUT$(*characters,filenumber*)

where *characters* is the number of characters you want to read from the file, and *filenumber* is the same number used in the matching OPEN statement. (If *filenumber* is not specified, INPUT$ reads from the keyboard.)

In this example, we've set up a loop that continually reads one character at a time from a disk file until an end-of-file condition is returned:

WHILE NOT EOF(1):A$=INPUT$(1,1)

As long as the loop is not at the end of the file, the program gets a character from the disk file, prints it, and then checks to see whether the position of the printhead is greater than or equal to 70, as reported by the LPOS(0) function (the number inside the parentheses of LPOS is a dummy parameter that has no significance). If so, the program sends a blank line to terminate the current line and returns the carriage for the next character.

It can be a fascinating and practical exercise to expand this program into a print formatter capable of adjusting to different margins, single and double spacing, even left, center, and right justification. A good model is *RUNOFF*, a popular formatting package for minicomputers such as the VAX-11/70. Or just try to emulate the formatting codes of a word processor, then expand upon them to truly enhance the power of your word processor.

Disk Files

Because of their obvious flexibility, disk files are by far the most commonly used types of files. They allow both input and output, so you can store and retrieve information for various kinds of processing. And disk files include files on the floppy drives, hard drive, and RAM disk.

You've probably already figured out from the above examples how to create a disk file: Just OPEN it, PRINT# to it (as you would with a printer), and CLOSE it. Again, thanks to the Amiga's generalized device I/O, logically there is no difference between writing to a printer or writing to a disk file. The same character sequences go out to either device. This saves you the trouble of mastering whole new sets of commands for I/O with different types of devices.

However, you'll probably want to be pickier in creating disk files. You want the data to be as compact as possible to save disk space, while storing it in a format that's convenient to read later on.

There are special considerations here: You don't want to use TABs to separate data items. You don't want the space-skipping characteristics of the comma in a PRINT statement. While you can write some numbers as the ASCII digits representing the number, you may prefer to use CHR$ to translate numbers in the range 0–255 into characters.

For example, the statement PRINT #1,−14.22 stores the number on disk like this:

```
− 1 4 . 2 2
```

followed by a carriage return—either a CHR$(13) or a CHR$(10). You can use INPUT# to read the number back. INPUT# accepts a stream of digits and can convert the stream into a number. When INPUT#1,A sees the characters

```
5 5 3 4 2 . 3 1 4
```

followed by a carriage return, it puts the number 55342.314 into the variable A.

If you want to store numbers as characters, you can use the statement PRINT#1,CHR$(A) to store a number in A from 0 to 255. Using ASC(INPUT$(1,1)) will retrieve the value.

It's important to keep your PRINT# statements matched up with the INPUT# statements you'll use to read the file. An example can clarify this:

```
'Namage◄
INPUT "What is your name";N$◄
INPUT "and your age (don't be vain)";AGE◄
OPEN "TEST" FOR OUTPUT AS #1◄
PRINT#1,N$◄
PRINT#1,AGE◄
CLOSE 1◄
OPEN "TEST" FOR INPUT AS #1◄
INPUT#1,AGE:PRINT AGE◄
INPUT#1,N$:PRINT N$◄
CLOSE 1◄
```

We've intentionally made an error here—can you find it? The order in which the name (a string) and the age (a number) are printed is name first, then age. However, when reading the file, we try to read the age first, then the name. This gives us a *Type mismatch* error. Just switch the line containing INPUT#1,AGE with the one containing INPUT#1,N$ to set things straight.

An even more likely error of this kind happens when you leave out one of the variables when reading the file:

```
PRINT#1,count 'write number of elements◄
PRINT#1,rarebits 'save valuable bit settings◄
FOR i=1 TO count:PRINT#1,array(i):NEXT 'send array out◄
INPUT#1,count 'get number of array elements◄
FOR i=1 TO count:INPUT#1,array(i):NEXT 'read array◄
```

Here, we've forgotten to read the *rarebits* value. This value ends up in the first element of ARRAY, throwing off all the array values by one. The last element is never even read. This can be a baffling bug.

Some programmers like to use constructions like this:

PRINT#1,BX%,A$(10),"Fer sure"

and

INPUT#1,BX%,TEMP$,MSG$

(Note that you don't have to use the same variable name when reading a value that was written to a file with a different variable name. The *values* are saved, not the variables themselves.) Although using commas with PRINT is legal and usually works, there's no way for INPUT to decide whether the data saved out from A$(10) should go with "Fer sure" or not. An actual comma isn't sent out, only spaces.

One solution is to use WRITE# instead of PRINT#. Multiple items sent with WRITE# are enclosed in quotation marks and separated by commas. The quotation marks protect any enclosed commas, since otherwise INPUT sees a comma as "end of this field." The commas sent out by WRITE# between each value make sure that each value is a separate entity. You can then safely use INPUT# with commas to read the data. Of course, when you want data to be stored verbatim, you'll need to use PRINT#. For more information on the differences between PRINT# and WRITE#, see the discussion below on "Personal Address Book," a full-length program that demonstrates a practical application using sequential files.

Filing Techniques

Every programmer has a bag of tricks relating to disk files. Some programmers like to store a count value at the start of the file. This count specifies how many items follow. Other programmers just depend on EOF to tell them when the file has been read, enclosing their READ statements with WHILE NOT EOF(1):WEND. The EOF( ) function uses the file number you give it to figure out whether the next INPUT# would read past the end of the file, generating an *Input past end* error. By using EOF, you can detect this condition before it generates an error message. The EOF( ) function usually returns 0, but holds −1 when the last line or character of a file has just been read.

This program scans through a file until it reaches the end, incrementing the variable NUMLINES to compute the total number of lines in the file:

```
'Numlines◄
OPEN "TestFile" FOR INPUT AS #1◄
Numlines=0◄
WHILE NOT EOF(1)◄
  Numlines=Numlines+1◄
  LINE INPUT#1,a$◄
WEND◄
PRINT Numlines;"lines in file."◄
CLOSE#1◄
```

We mentioned the trick of using characters to store information. For values from 0 to 255, use CHR$(A) to encode the value and ASC(INPUT$(1,1)) to decode it. Watch out for null values returned by INPUT$—you could use

ASC(INPUT$(1,1)+CHR$(0))

to give you a zero for nulls instead of an *Illegal quantity error.* Since ASCII looks at the first character in a string, it finds the CHR$(0) if INPUT$(1,1) returns a null value. The null value just isn't part of the string.

Another way to store numbers compactly is to take advantage of the binary coding system used by the floating-point routines. Any number, from a short number like 0, to a long number like 1423282.314159827, always uses a fixed number of bytes.

Variable Type	Symbol	Bytes	Use:
Integer	%	2	MKI$,CVI
Long integer	&	4	MKL$,CVL
Single precision	!	4	MKS$,CVS
Double precision	#	8	MKD$,CVD

For example, the MKI$ (*make integer string*) function converts integers into two-byte strings. You could multiply the ASCII value of the second character times 256 and sum this with the ASCII value of the first character, and you've got the original number back. It's easier to use the CVI function to convert a two-byte string back into an integer.

Don't confuse CVI, MKI$, and their cousins CVD, MKS$, and so on, with VAL and STR$. VAL converts a string of ASCII numerals into a number. STR$ converts a number into a string of ASCII digits. Both forms of the number are human-readable. But MKI$, MKL$, MKS$, and MKD$ strings appear meaningless until reconverted with CVI, CVL, CVS, or CVD. Try this program to see what we mean:

```
'CVI&CVS
INPUT "Give me an integer";N%
INPUT "Give me a floating-point number";N
NI$=MKI$(N%):NS$=MKS$(N)
PRINT "MKI$ looks like this:";NI$
PRINT "MKS$ looks like this:";NS$
PRINT "Converted back to integer:";CVI(NI$)
PRINT "Converted back to single precision";CVS(NS$)
```

These functions provide a more compact way of storing numbers. Use MKI$ to make an integer string (two bytes), MKL$ to make a long integer string (four bytes), MKS$ to create a single-precision string (four bytes), or MKD$ to create a double-precision string (eight bytes). Naturally, you'd use CVI, CVL, CVS, and CVD to reconvert these strings into numbers.

These functions are especially valuable with random access files, where every field has a fixed length. It would be inconvenient to have to reserve space for the longest number someone might use, from 0 (1 digit) to 134822412.23423 (15 digits). If you use MKS$ with double-precision numbers, no number uses more than or fewer than exactly eight bytes. Of course, you still have to reconstitute the number with CVS before you can display it or use it in calculations.

Adding to an Existing File

Very often, a program doesn't need to rewrite an entire file to add a small additional piece of information. It just needs to make an update. An example of this is a check register in which each check is recorded as it is written. There's no need to read the whole file into memory, add to the end, then write the new file back out. Just use the APPEND option of OPEN. The following check register takes advantage of this:

```
'Append◄
CLS◄
INPUT "Check number";CN◄
INPUT "Written on DD-MMM-YY";DAY$◄
INPUT "Payee";PAYEE$◄
INPUT "Amount";AMOUNT◄
LINE INPUT "Notes:";NOTES$◄
'Form filename using the month◄
File$="Checks-"+UCASE$(MID$(DAY$,4,3))◄
'Update the check register◄
OPEN File$ FOR APPEND AS #1◄
WRITE#1,CN,DAY$,PAYEE$,AMOUNT,NOTES$◄
CLOSE#1◄
```

The program simply gets the essential check information (check number, date of check, payee, amount of check, and a comment line). The date determines which of 12 files (one for each month) the data will be appended to. For consistency, UCASE$ enforces uppercase as part of the filename, although AmigaDOS doesn't really care.

Here's how you could read this check file:

```
'ReadChecks◄
INPUT "Search for check number";cn◄
FOR i=1 TO 12:READ month$◄
   ON ERROR GOTO ErrHandler◄
   OPEN "Checks-"+month$ FOR INPUT AS #1◄
GetRecord:◄
   INPUT#1,n,Day$,Payee$,amount,note$◄
   IF n<>cn AND NOT EOF(1) THEN GetRecord◄
   IF n=cn THEN i=12◄
SkipMonth:◄
   ON ERROR GOTO 0◄
   CLOSE 1◄
NEXT i◄
IF n<>cn THEN◄
   PRINT "Check not found."◄
ELSE◄
   PRINT "Check number";cn◄
   PRINT "Date ";UCASE$(Day$)◄
   PRINT "Payee ";Payee$◄
```

```
   PRINT  USING "Amount: $$######.##";amount◄
   PRINT note$◄
END IF◄
END◄
DATA jan,feb,mar,apr,may,jun,jul,aug,sep,oct,nov,dec◄
◄
ErrHandler:◄
RESUME SkipMonth◄
```

Given a check number, this program should be able to find it in the file. There are 12 files, and the month names are in DATA statements, so it just loops 12 times—each time opening the file and looking all the way through it to see whether the check is found. If so, the loop index is set to 12 to terminate the search.

High Speed I/O

For special applications, you can take advantage of certain features of Amiga BASIC. Since strings can be of any length, you could store an entire file in a single string. For example, this program reads the entire contents of a file into the string GIANT$:

```
OPEN "RAM:Clipboard" FOR INPUT AS #1◄
GIANT$=INPUT$(1,LOF(1))◄
CLOSE#1◄
```

The INPUT$ function uses the first two parameters, the number of characters you want to read followed by the file number (the same number used to OPEN the file). The LOF function returns the length of the file. It, too, looks for the file number within the parentheses.

You can store the string to disk simply by PRINTing or WRITEing it:

```
OPEN "RAM:Clipboard" FOR OUTPUT AS #1◄
PRINT#1,GIANT$◄
CLOSE#1◄
```

I/O Error Trapping

When you run any of these simple examples, you'll notice that they quickly crash when their safe environment evaporates due to a simple disk error. Perhaps the disk is not inserted or it's full or write-protected. Users won't infallibly enter the proper filename, so you need to check for *File not found* errors. They'll inevitably make typos, so you need to check for *Bad filename* errors. A bulletproof computer program expects humans to make human mistakes, so it is suspicious of all input, guarding against any condition that could crash the program. Although this kind of error checking can lengthen a program, it's better than shortening tempers.

In some cases, you can limit the user's ability to make errors. Rather than typing a filename, the user could move the mouse to point to a list of predefined filenames. But with free-form input, anything can happen. In the check register programs above, the user could make two fatal mistakes: entering an invalid date (the most likely kind of error) or triggering a disk error by having the wrong disk in the drive (or no disk at all, or write-protected, and so on). The user may enter nonnumeric characters when asked for a number. This nonfatal error causes BASIC to protest *Redo from start* and ask for the input again. But some errors can't be detected: an invalid check number, incorrect amount, misspelled payee, and on and on. There are limits to what a program can detect. Study this updated check-register program to see how much error trapping adds to a program, both in length and in value.

```
'BigCheck
CLS
GetCN:
INPUT "Check number";cn$
'avoids non-numbers, fractions
cn=INT(VAL(cn$))
IF cn<1 OR cn>9999 THEN GetCN 'optional range check

GetDate:
PRINT "Please enter the date in"
INPUT "the form DD-MMM-YY";day$
whichday$=LEFT$(day$,2)
month$=MID$(day$,4,3)
year$=MID$(day$,8)
'Check for hyphens
IF MID$(day$,3,1)+MID$(day$,7,1)<>"--" THEN GetDate
IF VAL(day$)<1 OR VAL(day$)>31 THEN GetDate
IF VAL(year$)<0 OR VAL(year$)>99 THEN GetDate

GetPayee:
INPUT "Payee";payee$
'No error checking is needed here, except for null entries
IF payee$="" THEN GetPayee

GetAmount:
INPUT "Amount $";amount$:amount=VAL(amount$)
IF amount<=0 OR amount>=10000 THEN GetAmount 'if $10,000 is the
check limit
LINE INPUT "Notes:";note$
IF note$="" THEN note$=" "
'Form filename using the month
file$="Checks-"+UCASE$(MID$(day$,4,3))
'Update the check register
ON ERROR GOTO ErrTrap
OPEN file$ FOR APPEND AS #1
WRITE#1,cn,day$,payee$,amount,note$
CLOSE#1
ON ERROR GOTO 0
END

ErrTrap:
```

```
CLOSE#1◄
PRINT "You made a disk error."◄
PRINT "Press R to Retry, I to ignore."◄
a$=INPUT$(1,1)◄
IF UCASE$(a$)="R" THEN RESUME ELSE RESUME NEXT◄
END◄
```

We put in a trap for an invalid check number, forcing it to be a positive integer between 1 and 9999 (an arbitrary limit). Ideally, we'd also make sure that the check number hasn't been used yet to guard against multiple checks with the same number. But as the program is currently written, this would require searching through all the files.

The date is checked for proper position of the hyphen, a legal day of the month from 1 to 31, and a reasonable year from 0 to 99. It's easy to sneak past these checks. We don't check for a legal month name (that would require comparing the month against a list of the 12 months) or for oddities like February 31. This should be all the error checking necessary to catch casual mistakes, though.

We can't make a judgment on whether the payee name is accurate—the computer doesn't understand what the string means; it just keeps track of what the string contains. We can check for a null input, though, and it's a good thing. If the string were a null, it wouldn't be written to the file (you can't write *nothing* where something is required). This would cause all following lines to be off by one, wreaking havoc with the program that fetches a check. If the Notes field is null, though, we just change it to a space, in case the user doesn't have a comment to make, thus preventing the null string problem.

We could also trap for illegal dollar amounts—checks written for negative sums are not very popular among recipients. Likewise, every financial institution has a maximum limit for checks, if only to limit embezzlement. If the amount starts with invalid characters, VAL returns a zero, which is also the kind of amount you don't see on a check.

For disk errors, the ON ERROR statement is our savior. Depending on how you use it, however, it can catch all errors indiscriminately, even errors you may have made when writing the program. That's why it's often best not to enable ON ERROR until the program is fully debugged. And limit the range of lines ON ERROR traps by placing an ON ERROR GOTO 0 after the last line you are intentionally trapping.

The error-trapping routine presented in Chapter 7, "ErrorTrap," is useful but not very smart. It just declares that there was an error, closes the file, and allows the user either to repeat the statement that caused the error (assuming that the user can correct the problem by doing something like inserting a disk), or simply to skip the statement that caused the error. It could also allow for quitting the program after an error. Ideally, a full-blown error-trapping routine would check the error number with the BASIC reserved variable ERR to see what kind of disk error happened, then act appropriately.

Personal Address Book

"Personal Address Book," Program 8-1 at the end of this chapter, demonstrates a typical application of sequential disk files. Though not elaborate, it's quite functional and handy for storing and maintaining lists of addresses and phone numbers. It pops up as a small window on the Workbench screen with its own set of custom menus. With a little reworking, it could be made into a general-purpose database filer for storing and retrieving almost any kind of information.

Here's a quick summary of the menu selections available in Personal Address Book.

Project Menu	Tools Menu	Options Menu
New	Retrieve Name	New Record Size
Open Book	Enter Name	New Book Size
Save Book	Delete Name	
Save As		
Print Book		
View Book		
Quit		

When you run Personal Address Book, the only menu items highlighted for selection are Open Book and Quit under the Project menu, Enter Name under the Tools menu, and New Record Size and New Book Size under the Options menu. The remaining menu items become available only when an address book is in memory.

Before you begin creating an address book by entering names, take a look at the Options menu. The two items under this menu let you define the maximum record and file sizes for the address book. By default, the Initialize routine in the program sets these values to maximums of five lines per record (recsize=5) and 100 records per file (booksize=100). In other words, each entry in the address book can have up to five lines (name, address, city/state/zip, phone number, etc.), and the address book can hold a total of 100 such entries. This should be sufficient for most purposes.

If you prefer to change these values, however, simply select the appropriate item under the Options menu. New Record Size accepts any value from three to ten address lines. New Book Size accepts any value from 25 to 200 entries. Personal Address Book stores its database in a string array, so memory usage is dynamic: Amiga BASIC allocates only as much memory for the array as is required by the actual number of entries. If you intend to store a large number of addresses, a CLEAR statement will probably be necessary to reserve enough extra memory for the string array. Otherwise, you'll encounter an *Out of memory* error when Personal Address Book exceeds the 25,000-byte buffer that Amiga BASIC allocates by default.

If you change the record or book sizes with the Options menu, be generous; Personal Address Book doesn't let you change these values again once an address book has been created. When you save the address book to disk, the program also saves the record- and book-size values as headers in the sequential disk file. That way, when you load the address book from disk later, the sizes you previously defined automatically override the program's defaults. (Although you could alter these header values with a text editor, you'll probably cause problems if you try to shrink the sizes rather than expand them.) Of course, you're free to create multiple address books as separate files, each with its own maximum record and book sizes.

Creating an Address Book

At any time, you can enter new names into an existing address book or begin creating a new one by selecting the Enter Name item under the Tools menu. The Personal Address Book window clears and reports how much room is left for additional entries. Then it prompts you to begin entering a name and address.

If you selected this item by mistake, just press RETURN at the prompt without typing anything else. You'll be returned to the main Personal Address Book window, which always displays the message —*Select choice from menu bar*—. Every routine in Personal Address Book which asks for keyboard input lets you escape in this manner. Other routines let you escape by clicking on a CANCEL button in a requester window, so you can always recover from accidental menu selections.

When you're entering names and addresses, Personal Address Book allows considerable flexibility. Entries can be typed last name first, first name last, in upper/lowercase, all uppercase, or all lowercase. None of these variations has any affect on searches; Personal Address Book retrieves any record that contains the search string you specify (see below). However, if you want the address book to be alphabetized by last name when printing out a hardcopy, type the entries last name first.

Press RETURN after each line in the address entry. If record size permits, you can even enter a line or two of extra information, like this:

Amiga, Carole
9999 Wyandot Avenue
Akron, OH 44305
216-555-1212
(My tax attorney.)

If you use up the maximum number of lines allowed per record, pressing RETURN on the final line automatically returns you to the main Personal Address Book screen. Otherwise, press RETURN without any other input at the next prompt.

Now that there's an address book in memory, you'll see that a number of previously ghosted menu items are available. Also, the Options menu is dimmed out. If you wish, you can continue to enter any additional names/addresses that you wish.

Creating a Sequential File

The other functions in Personal Address Book are pretty much self-explanatory and self-prompting, so here's just a quick rundown:

Project Menu

New   Erases an address book currently in memory, a prerequisite for loading another address book from disk (a requester window asks you to confirm this choice by clicking OK or CANCEL).

Open Book   Loads a previously saved address book from disk after you specify a *diskname:subdirectory/filename* (a requester window flags any disk errors that result).

Save Book   Saves the address book currently in memory under the default filename *Addresses* (no diskname or subdirectory is specified).

Save As   Saves the address book currently in memory under the *diskname:subdirectory/filename* you specify, an alternative to the more rigid *Save Book* function.

Print Book   Prints out a hardcopy of the address book currently in memory on your printer (alphabetized by the first letter only in each entry).

View Book   Resizes the Personal Address Book window to nearly full-screen height and scrolls through the book (press and hold the right mouse button to pause the display temporarily).

Quit   Exits Personal Address Book to BASIC (a requester window asks you to confirm the choice by clicking on QUIT).

Tools Menu

Retrieve Name Searches through the address book currently in memory and retrieves any record containing the target string you specify. If the string isn't found, the program informs you; if the string is found, a requester window asks if you want to continue searching for additional occurrences of the same target string. You can retrieve as many multiple occurrences as exist in the address book.

Delete Name   Retrieves the first record it finds with the target string you specify and asks if you want to delete it; if not, click on the CANCEL button. If you want to delete a name that coincides with another name in the address book, you may have to specify a fuller version of the target string to delete the record you want (for example, SMITH, ROBERTA instead of just SMITH).

To see how Personal Address Book creates its sequential disk file, take a look at the SaveBook and SaveAsBook routines. Sequential files are pretty straightforward compared to random files, so it's not too difficult to understand what's happening here. Here's a fragment from the SaveBook routine:

```
ON ERROR GOTO ErrorTrap◄
OPEN filename$ FOR OUTPUT AS #1◄
WRITE #1,booksize;recsize;currpage 'Save all sizes.◄
FOR j=1 TO currpage-1 'Save records on disk...◄
 FOR k=1 TO recsize◄
  WRITE #1,book$(j,k)◄
 NEXT k◄
NEXT j◄
 CLOSE #1:ON ERROR GOTO 0◄
saveflag=1 'Address book in memory is saved.◄
pause&=TIMER 'Wait for drive to finish.◄
WHILE TIMER<pause&+6:WEND 'Six seconds...◄
```

Now that the sequential file is opened for output, the next line writes out the header values required by Personal Address Book. Then the nested FOR-NEXT loops write the various elements of the string array containing addresses to the file.

There are two general statements for writing information to a sequential file: PRINT# (including its close cousin, PRINT# USING) and WRITE#. You'll probably use WRITE# most often. As the *Amiga BASIC* manual explains, WRITE# automatically supplies its own delimiters for numeric and string values. It inserts commas between numeric values and puts quotation marks around strings. PRINT# makes you do this work yourself. This routine could be rewritten using PRINT#, but it would be clumsier.

WRITE# Versus PRINT#

A good way to see the difference between the formats created by WRITE# and PRINT# is to save out some sample files and then examine them with the TYPE command in AmigaDOS. Consider this example:

```
OPEN "RAM:TEST" FOR OUTPUT AS 1
A=12345
B=67890
A$="Hello"
B$="there."
WRITE #1,A,B
WRITE #1,A$,B$
WRITE #1,A,B,A$,B$
PRINT #1,A,B
PRINT #1,A;B
PRINT #1,A$,B$
PRINT #1,A$;B$
PRINT #1,A;B;A$;B$
CLOSE 1
```

Here's how the resulting file looks on disk when examined in AmigaDOS with the TYPE RAM:TEST command:

12345,67890
"Hello","there"
12345,67890,"Hello","there"
12345   67890
12345   67890
Hello   there
Hellothere
12345   67890 Hellothere

Obviously, the disorganized information written out by the PRINT# statements is going to be harder to read back in. A statement such as INPUT #1,A$,B$ would interpret *Hellothere* as a single string instead of as two separate strings and would generate an *Input past end* error. But because of the quotation marks and comma inserted by the WRITE# statement, INPUT# 1,A$,B$ would work just fine.

PRINT# is handiest when teamed with its USING option. This works exactly like PRINT USING on the screen, except the image is saved in your sequential file. PRINT# USING lets you format the data with much more flexibility than individual PRINT# or WRITE# statements.

There are special cases when you'll want to choose PRINT# over WRITE#, however. A good example can be seen in the "Object Datamaker" program in Chapter 4. This utility converts bobs and sprites created by the Amiga's Object Editor into DATA statements that can be merged with another BASIC program. In this case, the sequential file created is not intended to be read later as data with INPUT# or LINE INPUT# statements; instead, the sequential file is intended to be an ASCII file like those created when the ,A option is appended to a SAVE command in BASIC. Therefore, the quotation marks that would be automatically inserted by WRITE# are undesirable. PRINT# USING is perfect for the task.

Evading the Guru

Incidentally, you may have noticed a puzzling few lines in the fragment of the SaveBook routine listed above:

pause&=TIMER 'Wait for drive to finish.
WHILE TIMER<pause&+6:WEND 'Six seconds...

What's going on here?

In short, a kludge. You may have noticed a few warnings in your Amiga manuals about removing disks while the disk drive's red busy light is on. The warnings are for real: The fastest way to trash a disk is to pop the eject button before the drive is finished. What the manuals don't mention is that certain other activities initiated before the red light is off can also result in unfortunate consequences. Sometimes the result is the dreaded "Guru Meditation" message that accompanies system crashes on the Amiga. The only recovery from this type of crash is to reboot the system, wiping out whatever unsaved program or file you were working on.

The two program lines above can help prevent an unexpected visit by the guru. The first line reads the current TIMER value (which contains the number of seconds past midnight) and stores it in the variable *pause&*. (We used a long integer variable here because Personal Address Book includes a DEFINT a–z statement in its Initialize routine, and large TIMER values can overflow short integer variables.) The second line is a short WHILE–WEND loop that waits until TIMER equals pause&+6, which is simply a way to make the computer (and more to the point, the user) do nothing for six seconds. Why six seconds? Because that's the approximate amount of time it takes for the little red light to blink off after the address file is saved out.

To play safe, you might want to include these lines in any programs of your own that create data files. You can always remove them if the problem is fixed in future versions of the Amiga operating system.

Managing Directories

You should already be familiar with how AmigaDOS stores files on disk by using a root directory and a chain of nested subdirectories. Amiga BASIC includes several commands for changing the current directory path, renaming files, and deleting files.

Use CHDIR to change the current directory. If you don't use an explicit pathname in a filename, the file is searched for in BASIC's current directory. This is not necessarily the same as the system current directory. Just follow CHDIR with the pathname (directory specification) you'd like to use, as in

CHDIR "Extras:Demos"

To delete a file from a disk, use KILL followed by an AmigaDOS filename. You must specify the exact filename here; KILL won't automatically erase a file's associated .INFO file, used to store the icon image. You might use KILL within a program to delete a scratch file or when you are replacing one file with another. For example,

KILL "NotWanted"
KILL "NotWanted.info"

Use the NAME command to rename a file:

NAME "Merrimac" AS "Virginia"

Don't try to use TO in place of AS, as in NAME ftemp$ TO "Final". You'll get a syntax error.

Both KILL and NAME can be used together when updating files. When you write a file to disk, instead of overwriting an existing file, you could pre-serve the previous file as a backup, delete the previous backup, and save the file under a new name. Instead of

OPEN filename$ FOR OUTPUT AS #1

you could use

NAME FILENAME$+".BKP" AS FILENAME$+".OLD"
NAME FILENAME$ AS FILENAME$+".BKP"
OPEN FILENAME$ FOR OUTPUT AS #1
CLOSE#1
KILL FILENAME$+".OLD"

Random Access Files

Some people regard random access files with the same fear and awe they feel when contemplating machine language programming. Both are seemingly for-bidding worlds that are actually quite manageable once you get your feet wet. Although quite different from ordinary (sequential) disk files, random files are logical and easy to program in Amiga BASIC, thanks to several statements ded-icated to making random files a snap.

Just think of random files as segmented sequential files of indeterminate length. Instead of reading serially through the file, as if it were on a tape, you can skip to any segment in the file and read from there. You can also skip to any segment and replace just that segment, overwriting it. A random file is a long chain of these segments, called *records*. Each record is like a predeter-mined slot, ready for holding data. The length of a random file expands as you add to the end of it, but has no fixed length, other than that imposed by disk space.

Opening up a communications channel for a random file is easy. Here are two examples using the alternative syntaxes of the OPEN statement:

OPEN "Random" AS #1 LEN=100

or

OPEN "R",1,"Random",100

Both statements create a random file called "Random" with a record size of 100. If you don't specify a length, it defaults to 128 bytes. The record size is the length of each data segment. In this example, the data in each record must add up to a length of exactly 100 bytes.

Within a record, data is stored in fixed-length *fields*. The record could be composed of five individual fields that are 40, 20, 25, 5, and 10 bytes long, re-spectively. Since each field is fixed in length, you can see why the number-cruncher routines like MKI$ and CVI$ are so valuable. They let you set aside just 2, 4, or 8 bytes for a numeric field, store the data in compact form, and then convert it back to a number.

The traditional random file analogy is that of a mailing list. In fact, Personal Address Book could be rewritten to use random files instead of sequential files. Random files would allow for huge mailing lists, hundreds of thousands of bytes long. Such a huge list could not easily fit in memory, but that's where random files are handy. The file is stored only on disk—only one record at a time needs to be in memory.

Organizing a Random File

Let's see how you'd tackle this problem. First, consider that each record is one address. For each record, we'll define seven fields: name, address, city, state, zip code, current balance, and an optional note. The balance field would be used for accounting purposes. Since you can't expand the size of a record once you've created the file, the note field offers some opportunity for expansion.

Next, you assign lengths to each field. The proper lengths, of course, depend on the types of information to be stored in the field. We'll set the field lengths at 20 characters for the name (most names will fit in this limit), 30 characters for the address, 20 characters for the city name, 2 characters for the state, 10 characters for the zip code (5 characters for the zip, one for the hyphen, and four for the extended zip code), 8 bytes for the balance, and 40 bytes for the notes field. This adds up to 130 characters.

The balance will be stored as a double-precision floating-point number. This allows a huge range of numbers, as well as more accurate numbers. Since every field in a random access file must be of fixed length, we'll store the number with MKD$( ), the function that converts a number into its internal representation. Double-precision numbers require eight bytes, so we allocate eight bytes for the balance record. This is much more efficient than simply leaving enough room for the length of the longest possible number and storing the number as an ASCII string of digits. When we write the number into the random buffer, we'll use a statement like this:

LSET BALANCE$=MKD$(BALANCE#)

And when we're ready to display the balance, we'll convert it back to a double-precision number with CVD( ):

BALANCE#=CVD(BALANCE$)

Our command to create the random file (and to OPEN it for access if it already exists) is

OPEN "Addresses" AS #1 LEN=130

To declare the fields we'll be using, we use the FIELD statement:

FIELD #1,20 AS NAME$,30 AS ADDR$,20 AS CITY$,2 AS STATE$,10 AS ZIP$,8 AS BALANCE$,40 AS NOTE$

Each field is given a string variable name and a length. The lengths must add up to the record length, 130. (It's helpful to those reading your program if you place the FIELD statement immediately after the OPEN.) Amiga BASIC now knows which string variables you'll be using and how they fit into the record.

When you create a record, the record contents are stored in the random file buffer. As mentioned earlier in the chapter, one way to flush this buffer and actually write its contents to disk is to CLOSE the file. But maybe you're not ready to CLOSE; you'll generally want to write out several records without OPENing and CLOSEing the file each time.

The solution is the PUT statement. It writes the contents of the file buffer to disk immediately. The format is

PUT#*filenumber,record number*

Filenumber corresponds to the file number in the OPEN statement, and *record number* is an optional parameter that specifies which record in the file should be written. If you omit *record number*, BASIC automatically uses the next higher record number after the last PUT. The allowable range for *record number* is 1 to 16,777,215. It would take a lot of mass storage to let you store over 16 million records, so this range should be sufficient. If you use a record number that already exists in the random file, that record is replaced with the new record.

The opposite of random-file PUT is GET:

GET#*filenumber,record number*

Filenumber is the usual number used in OPEN, and *record number* is the number of the record within the file. Again, *record number* can range from 1 to 16,777,215 and is optional; if it's omitted, BASIC automatically reads the next higher record number after the last GET.

When a GET is executed, the random file buffer is filled with one record and the string variables take on new values. Don't attempt to read a record that hasn't been created yet. The EOF function detects if you attempt to read a record that is past the end of the file. This lets you find out the number of the last record in a file. Once you know what the last record is, you can use this number to add to the end of a random file. Of course, there are other ways to keep track of the number of records in a file. You could use the LOF function to find the length of the file and divide this by the record size. Alternatively, you could store this information in a sequential file or in the first record of the random file.

```
OPEN "Addresses" AS #1 LEN=128
LR=1 'number of records, pointing to last record
WHILE NOT EOF(1) AND LR<16777215&
   GET#1,LR 'Read the record
WEND
PRINT "Last record is:";LR
CLOSE#1
```

The LOC function is used to read the current file pointer, which for random files is the number of the last record read or written. Note that this is not the same as the last record in the file, but the number of the record most recently referenced with a GET or PUT statement. With sequential files, LOC returns the ratio between the number of bytes read or written so far divided by the file buffer size for the file. With the default file buffer length for sequential files (512 bytes), this works out to the number of sectors read or written so far.

Using Fielded Strings

There are two important catches to keep in mind when using random access string variables, also known as *fielded strings*. They are a little different from ordinary strings. First, you *must not* use the equal sign (=) or LET statement to assign or change the values of fielded strings. Nor can you use fielded strings in an INPUT statement. Either action would make Amiga BASIC forget that the strings are associated with the random file, and BASIC would turn them into ordinary strings.

Second, fielded strings must always be padded out to the full length declared in the FIELD statement. This seems to present a paradox—since you can't reassign or change a fielded string's value, how can you add spaces to it?

Amiga BASIC's answer is the LSET and RSET statements:

LSET *string variable=string expression*

and

RSET *string variable=string expression*

String variable is the fielded string variable, and *string expression* is usually a literal string or, most likely, an ordinary (nonfielded) string variable. Since you can't INPUT directly into a fielded string, this is also how you convert the user's input into a valid field. First, you accept the user's data via INPUT in a regular string variable—say, INPUT T$. Then you transfer it to the field string variable with LSET or RSET—for instance, LSET NAME$=T$ or RSET NAME$=T$.

LSET and RSET both pad out a short field to the full length specified in the FIELD statement. The difference between them is that LSET pads the field by adding spaces at the end of the data, and RSET pads the field by inserting spaces at the beginning of the data. In other words, LSET sets the field to the left, and RSET sets the field to the right. For example, in our ten-character zip code field, let's say the user omits the hyphen and four digits of the extended code. The entry might look like this (quotation marks are added for clarity):

"27403"

LSET would pad out the unused five characters like this:

"27403   "

280

while RSET would pad out the field like this:

"   **27403**"

    If you try to assign a string too big to fit into the fielded string, Amiga BASIC just uses what will fit, throwing out the rest.

A Random File Example

Now let's add a few lines to our program to make it functional:

```
'RandFiles
OPEN "Addresses" AS #1 LEN=130
FIELD#1,20 AS Nam$,30 AS Addr$,20 AS City$,2 AS State$,10 AS Zip
$,8 AS Balance$,40 AS note$
INPUT "Read or write (r/w)";rw$
INPUT "Which record to access";rn
IF rn=0 THEN END
IF rw$="r" THEN ReadRecord

'Notice the use of T$.
'You can't directly use INPUT with fielded variables
LINE INPUT "Name:      ";t$:LSET Nam$=t$
LINE INPUT "Address:   ";t$:LSET Addr$=t$
LINE INPUT "City:      ";t$:LSET City$=t$
LINE INPUT "State:     ";t$:LSET State$=t$
LINE INPUT "Zip code: ";t$:LSET Zip$=t$
LINE INPUT "Balance:   ";t$:b#=VAL(t$):LSET Balance$=MKD$(b#)
LINE INPUT "Notes:     ";t$:LSET note$=t$
PUT#1,rn 'write this record
CLOSE#1
RUN

ReadRecord:
GET#1,rn
PRINT "Name:      ";Nam$
PRINT "Address:   ";Addr$
PRINT "City:      ";City$
PRINT "State:     ";State$
PRINT "Zip Code: ";Zip$
PRINT "Balance: ";CVD(Balance$)
PRINT "Notes:     ";note$
CLOSE#1
PRINT :LINE INPUT "Press RETURN:";t$
RUN
```

    When using the above program, you may notice that it works only if you create your records sequentially. You would first write to record 1 before writing to record 2. You can read the records in any order. If you don't do this, any attempt to read a record only gives you record 1. Some programmers like to format their random access files by writing dummy records throughout the range of records used by a program. That way, reading a nonexistent record won't give you meaningless garbage for the uninitialized fields.

Although this is a large program, it's easy to follow. The entry routine is complicated by the fact that you can't use INPUT with a fielded string. As described above, notice how we solve this by INPUTting into a temporary string, and using LSET to put the string into the fielded variable. The only way to access the file is by its record number, but this simple program can be a handy tool of its own or the start of your own program.

When working with very large or very complex files, you'll need to manage your data carefully. Many programmers find it handy to keep a sequential file on the same disk to keep track of certain facts about the random file, such as its record size.

An indexed random file technique would use an array to hold the record numbers of every record that hasn't been used yet (the *inactive* array). Another array would hold the record numbers of every record that *has* been used already (the *active* array). When you are adding to the file, you can use any of the numbers in the active array for your PUT statement, then remove the number from the active list, preventing the same record from being used again. You then add the record number of the new record to the end of the active array so that you can find it when you later use GET.

When you delete a record, the number of the deleted record is simply added to the list of inactive records and removed from the list of active records. This makes the record available for reuse by future PUT statements. It doesn't actually delete the information, but deallocates it. GET would only be interested in the records listed in the array of active records. This is similar to the way a disk directory keeps track of files scattered randomly across a disk.

Indexing a random file with a sequential file can also be very useful when you are searching or sorting a random file. Instead of actually rewriting the record as you rearrange its order, you just change the pointers to the records. The array of pointers would initially be a list of every active record. As you sort the list, you exchange the pointers, not the data on disk. You would refer to the sorted pointer array when you want to retrieve from disk in sorted order.

Programming for a Modem

From Amiga BASIC's point of view, a modem is just like any other peripheral. As an output device, it takes data and sends it to the remote computer. As an input device, it receives data from the remote computer and sends it back to you.

But forgetting the remote computer, the modem is just a box that accepts output and returns input. When there's no input for it to send, it sends nulls. If the remote computer can't keep up with the modem, too bad. The data is sent out at a fixed rate (usually, 300, 1200, or 2400 bits per second—bps for short), and if you're not ready to read the character, it's gone.

This is unlike disk or printer I/O. A printer works much slower than the computer, but the computer waits for the printer to accept and print each character. A disk drive can't keep up with the enormous speed of the Amiga, but here, too, the computer patiently waits for the disk to yield its store. Not so with modems. Anything not captured at the instant that the data is sent spills off into the bit bucket. The main lesson here is that Amiga BASIC programs must be written for speed in order to keep up with 300 or 1200 bps. Otherwise, you may lose characters.

A special protocol called XON/XOFF can help smooth the problem. Whenever the remote computer needs to catch its breath, it sends an XOFF code to say, "Hey! Hold on a minute. Don't send any more data until I send you an XON code." This way no data is lost. When the remote computer is ready to continue, it sends XON. Naturally, the roles are simply reversed when your program needs to pause transmission. An XOFF is a CTRL-S character, or CHR$(19). XON is CTRL-Q, or CHR$(17). So both computers, while sending data, can listen for the XON/XOFF codes, just in case.

A Simple Terminal Program

In Amiga BASIC, the modem is addressed as the COM1: device. This refers to the RS-232 serial port into which the modem is plugged. In the OPEN statement, COM1: requires certain parameters not used with other devices:

OPEN "COM1:*baudrate,parity,data bits,stop bits*" AS #1

Baudrate is the desired I/O speed in bps; *parity* is an optional parameter for setting a checksum value that helps detect transmission errors—either E for Even, O for Odd, or N for None (the default is E); *data bits* is an optional parameter that defines how many bits in each byte transmitted are actual data bits, not parity or stop bits (allowable values are 5, 6, 7, or 8); and *stop bits* is an optional parameter that defines the end of the transmitted byte. When *baudrate* is 110, *stop bits* defaults to 2. If *baudrate* is any other value, *stop bits* defaults to 1.

The definition of these terms is not necessary as long as you know the values used by the remote computer. Both must be in agreement. Generally, a combination of 8 data bits, 1 stop bit, and no parity works fine.

The following example program plays both the roles of receiver and transmitter, so the same program can be used on both ends of the phone connection. It looks for keyboard input from the host computer (the one the program is running on), echoes the key to the screen if DUPLEX=1, and sends the character to the remote computer. It then checks to see whether the remote computer has anything to say. If so, it prints the character to the screen. Such a tight loop is plenty fast enough to keep up with high baud rates.

```
'Terminal I
OPEN "com1:300,N,8,1" AS #1
duplex=0 '=1 for half, 0 for full
```

```
WHILE -1 'forever...◄
  key$=INKEY$:IF key$>"" THEN◄
    IF duplex THEN PRINT key$;◄
    PRINT#1,key$;◄
  END IF◄
  IF LOC(1) THEN◄
    char$=INPUT$(1,1)◄
    IF char$>"" THEN PRINT char$;◄
  END IF◄
WEND◄
```

This is the perfect kind of program to build upon. You have a simple skeleton here. Here's a variation on the above program that handles XON/XOFF:

```
'Terminal II◄
OPEN "com1:300,N,8,1" AS #1◄
duplex=1 '=1 for half, 0 for full◄
WHILE -1 'forever...◄
  key$=INKEY$:IF key$>"" THEN◄
    IF duplex THEN PRINT key$;◄
    PRINT#1,key$;◄
  END IF◄
  IF LOC(1) THEN◄
    char$=INPUT$(1,1)◄
    IF char$>"" THEN PRINT char$;◄
    IF char$=CHR$(19) THEN◄
      WaitForXon:◄
      IF INPUT$(1,1)<>CHR$(17) THEN WaitForXon◄
    END IF◄
  END IF◄
WEND◄
```

Finally, here's a version of "Terminal" that is quick enough to handle character translation. Why is character translation necessary when virtually all computers use ASCII (American Standard Code for Information Interchange)? Because unfortunately, ASCII isn't always ASCII. There's Commodore ASCII, Atari ASCII, IBM ASCII, Amiga ASCII, and so on. For example, the remote computer might be sending CHR$(20) for a backspace character, whereas the Amiga would like to see CHR$(8).

You could use a bank of IF-THENs to check for and translate every character, but the program would run too slowly. Instead, use a lookup table. The table is 256 bytes long, enough to hold the full ASCII character set. Each position in the table holds the translated value of that position. Normally, the table just echos the index. TR%(65) equals 65, so if you feed in an *A* character, you get back an *A*. But if you set up TR%(20)=8, then if you feed in and index 20, you get back 8.

For this technique to work, you need two arrays, one for translating from the other computer to yours, and one for translating from your code to that of the other's. The following program illustrates this method of high-speed trans-

284

lation. The translation tables are set up to convert Amiga carriage returns (ASCII 13) to those used by the Atari eight-bit home computer (ASCII 155). In addition, we translate between the Amiga backspace key (ASCII 8) and the Atari's (ASCII 126). By the way, if you're using a smart modem such as the Hayes SmartModem, you won't be able to send the commands to dial the phone since the carriage return used by the modem to detect the end of the command line (ASCII 13) has been changed to the Atari-style carriage return.

```
'Terminal III◄
OPEN "com1:300,N,8,1" AS #1◄
duplex=1 '=1 for half, Ø for full◄
DIM th%(255),tr%(255)◄
FOR i=0 TO 255:th%(i)=i:tr%(i)=i:NEXT◄
'Set up your translations here:◄
'TH% translates from host, TR% from remote◄
th%(8)=126:tr%(126)=8 'translate Atari backspace◄
th%(13)=155::tr%(155)=13 'translate Atari carriage return◄
WHILE -1 'forever...◄
  key$=INKEY$:IF key$>"" THEN◄
    IF duplex THEN PRINT key$;◄
    PRINT#1,CHR$(th%(ASC(key$)));◄
  END IF◄
  IF LOC(1) THEN◄
    char$=INPUT$(1,1)◄
    IF char$>"" THEN PRINT CHR$(tr%(ASC(char$)));◄
    IF char$=CHR$(19) THEN◄
      WaitForXon:◄
      IF INPUT$(1,1)<>CHR$(17) THEN WaitForXon◄
    END IF◄
  END IF◄
WEND◄
```

This program can be enhanced with upload/download capabilities, user-alterable parameters, and a mouse-driven user interface. It might be a good exercise to write such a program yourself.

Many other programs in this book work with disk and printer files, so you can study them for further insight.

Program 8-1. Personal Address Book

```
' *** PERSONAL ADDRESS BOOK ***◄
◄
Initialize:◄
 DEFINT a-z:DIM label$(10)◄
 label$(Ø)="Personal Address Book"◄
 label$(1)="*Press RETURN to exit*"◄
 label$(2)="*Click in this window*"◄
 label$(3)=SPACE$(4)+"*to continue*"◄
 booksize=100:recsize=5 'Max size book & record.◄
 DIM book$(booksize,recsize)◄
 currpage=1 'Current blank page pointer.◄
 saveflag=Ø 'Flags if latest updates saved on disk.◄
 WINDOW 1,label$(Ø),(290,100)-(600,180),22◄
```

```
WIDTH 31
PRINT "Just a moment..."
GOSUB MenuSetup
GOTO MainMenu

MenuSetup:
 'Design custom menu bar.
 MENU 1,0,0,"Project"
 MENU 1,1,0,"New"+SPACE$(7)
 MENU 1,2,0,"Open Book"+SPACE$(1)
 MENU 1,3,0,"Save Book"+SPACE$(1)
 MENU 1,4,0,"Save As"+SPACE$(3)
 MENU 1,5,0,"Print Book"
 MENU 1,6,0,"View Book"+SPACE$(1)
 MENU 1,7,0,"Quit"+SPACE$(6)
 MENU 2,0,0,"Tools"
 MENU 2,1,0,"Retrieve name"
 MENU 2,2,0,"Enter Name"+SPACE$(3)
 MENU 2,3,0,"Delete Name"+SPACE$(2)
 MENU 3,0,0,"Options"
 MENU 3,1,0,"New Record Size"
 MENU 3,2,0,"New Book Size"+SPACE$(2)
 MENU 4,0,0,""
RETURN

MainMenu:
 ON ERROR GOTO 0
 CLS
 'Define status of menu selections.
 MENU 1,0,1:MENU 2,0,1:MENU 1,7,1 'Always on.
 'Following menu items on or off
 'if no address book in memory:
 IF LEN(book$(1,1))=0 THEN
  MENU 1,1,0:MENU 1,2,1
  MENU 1,3,0:MENU 1,4,0
  MENU 1,5,0:MENU 1,6,0
  MENU 2,1,0:MENU 2,2,1
  MENU 2,3,0:MENU 3,0,1
  MENU 3,1,1:MENU 3,2,1
 'Following menu items on or off
 'if address book in memory:
 ELSE
  MENU 1,1,1:MENU 1,2,0
  MENU 1,3,1:MENU 1,4,1
  MENU 1,5,1:MENU 1,6,1
  MENU 2,1,1:MENU 2,2,1
  MENU 2,3,1:MENU 3,0,0
 END IF
 PRINT:PRINT "--Select choice from menu bar--"
 Checkmenloop:
  MenuID=MENU(0)
  IF MenuID=0 THEN Checkmenloop
 MenuItem=MENU(1)
 ON MenuID GOTO ProjectMenu,ToolsMenu,OptionsMenu
 GOTO Checkmenloop

ProjectMenu:
```

```
 'Handles selection from Project menu.◄
 ON MenuItem GOTO NewBook,OpenBook,SaveBook,SaveAsBook,PrintBook,
 ViewBook,Quit◄
◄
ToolsMenu:◄
 'Handles selection from Tools menu.◄
 ON MenuItem GOTO RetrieveName,EnterName,DeleteName◄
◄
OptionsMenu:◄
 'Handles selection from Options menu.◄
 ON MenuItem GOTO NewRecsize,NewBooksize◄
 ◄
NewBook:◄
 'Erases address book in memory.◄
 MENU 1,0,0:MENU 2,0,0:MENU 3,0,0◄
 CLS◄
 IF saveflag=0 THEN◄
  msg1$="Latest updates are NOT saved --"◄
  msg2$="really want to erase them?"◄
  hilite%=2◄
 ELSE◄
  msg1$="Erase addresses in memory?"◄
  msg2$="(Latest updates are saved.)"◄
  hilite%=1◄
 END IF◄
 CALL Requester (msg1$,msg2$,"OK","CANCEL",hilite%,answer%)◄
 IF answer%=0 GOTO MainMenu 'CANCEL was selected.◄
 'Otherwise, OK was selected:◄
 booksize=100:recsize=5:currpage=1 'Restore defaults.◄
 saveflag=0 'Reset saved flag.◄
 ERASE book$:DIM book$(booksize,recsize)◄
 GOTO MainMenu◄
 ◄
OpenBook:◄
 'Loads address book file into memory.◄
 MENU 1,0,0:MENU 2,0,0:MENU 3,0,0◄
 CLS◄
 PRINT label$(1)◄
 PRINT:PRINT "Enter filename of address book"◄
 PRINT "to open [Addresses]:"◄
 LINE INPUT ">> ";filename$◄
 IF filename$="" GOTO MainMenu 'Abort routine.◄
 ON ERROR GOTO ErrorTrap◄
 CLOSE 1:OPEN filename$ FOR INPUT AS #1◄
 INPUT #1,booksize,recsize,currpage 'Set sizes.◄
 ERASE book$:DIM book$(booksize,recsize)◄
 FOR j=1 TO currpage-1 'Read records from disk...◄
  FOR k=1 TO recsize◄
   INPUT #1,book$(j,k)◄
  NEXT k◄
 NEXT j◄
 CLOSE #1:ON ERROR GOTO 0◄
 saveflag=1 'Reset saved flag.◄
 GOTO MainMenu◄
 ◄
SaveAsBook:◄
 'Saves address book on disk◄
```

```
'under filename chosen by user.
'Shares code with SaveBook routine.
MENU 1,0,0:MENU 2,0,0:MENU 3,0,0
CLS:PRINT label$(1)
PRINT:PRINT "Enter filename to save:"
LINE INPUT ">> ";filename$
IF filename$="" GOTO MainMenu 'Abort routine.
GOTO SaveIt
SaveBook:
'Saves address book on disk.
'Default filename = "Addresses"
'Shares code with SaveAsBook routine.
MENU 1,0,0:MENU 2,0,0:MENU 3,0,0:CLS
msg1$="Save with filename:"
msg2$=CHR$(34)+"Addresses"+CHR$(34)+"?"
CALL Requester (msg1$,msg2$,"SAVE","CANCEL",0,answer%)
IF answer%=0 GOTO MainMenu 'CANCEL was selected.
filename$="Addresses" 'SAVE was selected.
SaveIt:
  PRINT:PRINT "Saving under filename"
  PRINT CHR$(34);filename$;CHR$(34);"..."
  ON ERROR GOTO ErrorTrap
  OPEN filename$ FOR OUTPUT AS #1
  WRITE #1,booksize;recsize;currpage 'Save all sizes.
  FOR j=1 TO currpage-1 'Save records on disk...
    FOR k=1 TO recsize
      WRITE #1,book$(j,k)
    NEXT k
  NEXT j
  CLOSE #1:ON ERROR GOTO 0
 saveflag=1 'Address book in memory is saved.
 pause&=TIMER 'Wait for drive to finish.
 WHILE TIMER<pause&+6:WEND 'Six seconds...
 GOTO MainMenu

PrintBook:
 'Prints address book on printer.
 'Shares code with ViewBook routine.
ViewBook:
 'Prints address book on screen.
 'Shares code with PrintBook routine.
 MENU 1,0,0:MENU 2,0,0:MENU 3,0,0
 CLS
 'Confirm choice:
 IF MenuItem=6 THEN
  msg1$="View address book on screen?"
  CALL Requester (msg1$,"","VIEW","CANCEL",1,answer%)
  IF answer%=0 GOTO MainMenu 'Abort routine.
  WINDOW 1,label$(0),(290,10)-(600,180),22:WIDTH 31
  ON ERROR GOTO ErrorTrap
  OPEN "SCRN:" FOR OUTPUT AS #1
 ELSE
  msg1$="Click PRINT when ready."
  msg2$="(Click CANCEL to abort.)"
  CALL Requester (msg1$,msg2$,"PRINT","CANCEL",1,answer%)
  IF answer%=0 GOTO MainMenu 'Abort routine.
  ON ERROR GOTO ErrorTrap
```

```
    OPEN "LPT1:" FOR OUTPUT AS #1◄
    PRINT# 1,"":PRINT# 1,""◄
    PRINT# 1,label$(Ø) 'Print title.◄
    PRINT# 1,"Updated ";DATE$◄
  END IF◄
  PRINT# 1,"":PRINT# 1,""◄
  'This section alphabetizes by 1st character:◄
  alpha=65 'ASCII value of A.◄
  rec=1 'First record in address book.◄
  alphabetizer:◄
   WHILE alpha<=9Ø 'ASCII value of Z.◄
    WHILE rec<currpage 'Current size of address book.◄
     IF LEFT$(book$(rec,1),1)=CHR$(alpha) THEN◄
      FOR j=1 TO recsize 'Loop to print record.◄
       PRINT# 1,book$(rec,j)◄
      NEXT j:PRINT# 1,""◄
     END IF◄
     rec=rec+1 'Increment record pointer.◄
    WEND◄
   alpha=alpha+1:rec=1 'Increment alphabet.◄
   WEND◄
  PRINT# 1,""◄
  CLOSE #1:ON ERROR GOTO Ø◄
  IF MenuItem=6 THEN◄
   PRINT "<End of address book>"◄
   PRINT:GOSUB Clickmouse◄
   'Restore normal window:◄
   WINDOW 1,label$(Ø),(29Ø,1ØØ)-(6ØØ,18Ø),22:WIDTH 31◄
  END IF◄
  GOTO MainMenu◄
  ◄
Quit:◄
  'Exits program to BASIC.◄
  MENU 1,Ø,Ø:MENU 2,Ø,Ø:MENU 3,Ø,Ø:CLS◄
  'Following section warns if addresses in memory:◄
  IF LEN(book$(1,1))>Ø AND saveflag=Ø THEN◄
   msg1$="Latest updates are NOT saved --"◄
   msg2$="Quit program to BASIC?"◄
   CALL Requester (msg1$,msg2$,"QUIT","CANCEL",2,answer%)◄
   IF answer%=1 GOTO Goodbye ELSE GOTO MainMenu◄
  END IF◄
  msg1$="Quit program to BASIC?"◄
  CALL Requester (msg1$,"","QUIT","CANCEL",2,answer%)◄
  IF answer%=1 GOTO Goodbye ELSE GOTO MainMenu◄
  Goodbye:◄
   WINDOW 1,"Basic",(Ø,Ø)-(617,185),31:END 'QUIT was selected.◄
   ◄
RetrieveName:◄
  'Retrieves entry from address book.◄
  MENU 1,Ø,Ø:MENU 2,Ø,Ø:MENU 3,Ø,Ø:CLS◄
  PRINT label$(1):target$=""◄
  PRINT:PRINT "Keyword for search?"◄
  LINE INPUT ">> ";target$◄
  IF target$="" GOTO MainMenu 'Abort routine.◄
  rec=1:item=1 'Start search at 1st record, field.◄
  Retriever:◄
  GOSUB Search 'Search routine.◄
```

```
  IF match=0 THEN◄
   PRINT:PRINT "Not found."◄
   GOSUB Clickmouse 'Wait for button click.◄
   GOTO MainMenu◄
  ELSE◄
   PRINT:FOR j=1 TO recsize◄
   PRINT book$(rec,j):NEXT j 'Print entry.◄
  END IF◄
  msg1$="Continue searching for next"◄
  msg2$="occurrence of same name?"◄
  CALL Requester (msg1$,msg2$,"SEARCH","CANCEL",0,answer%)◄
  IF answer%=0 GOTO MainMenu 'CANCEL was selected.◄
  'Otherwise, SEARCH was selected:◄
  rec=rec+1:item=1 'Increment record pointer.◄
  IF rec=>currpage THEN◄
   CLS:PRINT:PRINT "Not found.":PRINT◄
   GOSUB Clickmouse 'Wait for button click.◄
   GOTO MainMenu◄
  ELSE◄
   GOTO Retriever 'Repeat search...◄
  END IF◄
   ◄
EnterName:◄
  'Adds new entries to address book.◄
  MENU 1,0,0:MENU 2,0,0:MENU 3,0,0:CLS◄
  PRINT "Room for";booksize-currpage+1;"more entries."◄
  IF booksize=currpage GOTO MainMenu 'Abort if book full.◄
  PRINT:PRINT "Enter each line of address"◄
  PRINT "(up to";recsize;"lines)"◄
  PRINT "and press RETURN."◄
  PRINT:PRINT label$(1)◄
  'This section accepts new entry◄
  'and/or ends/aborts routine◄
  'when RETURN is pressed:◄
  temp=1 'Counter for loop.◄
  Entryloop:◄
   LINE INPUT ">> ";temp$◄
   IF temp$="" THEN◄
    IF temp=1 GOTO MainMenu ELSE next1◄
    next1:currpage=currpage+1:saveflag=0:GOTO MainMenu◄
   ELSE◄
    book$(currpage,temp)=temp$◄
   END IF◄
   temp=temp+1◄
   IF temp<=recsize GOTO Entryloop◄
   currpage=currpage+1 'Increment page pointer.◄
   saveflag=0 'This update is not yet saved on disk.◄
   GOTO MainMenu◄
    ◄
DeleteName:◄
  'Removes entry from address book.◄
  MENU 1,0,0:MENU 2,0,0:MENU 3,0,0◄
  CLS:PRINT label$(1)◄
  PRINT:PRINT "Name to delete?"◄
  LINE INPUT ">> ";target$◄
  IF target$="" GOTO MainMenu 'Abort routine.◄
  rec=1:item=1 'Start search at 1st record, field.◄
```

```
 GOSUB Search 'Search routine.◄
 IF match=0 THEN◄
  PRINT:PRINT "Not found."◄
  GOSUB Clickmouse 'Wait for button click.◄
  GOTO MainMenu◄
 ELSE◄
  PRINT:FOR j=1 TO recsize◄
  PRINT book$(rec,j):NEXT j 'Print entry.◄
 END IF◄
 msg1$="Delete this name?"◄
 CALL Requester (msg1$,"","DELETE","CANCEL",2,answer%)◄
 IF answer%=0 GOTO MainMenu 'CANCEL was selected.◄
 'Otherwise, DELETE was selected:◄
 FOR j=rec TO currpage 'This loop fills the gap.◄
  FOR k=1 TO recsize 'This loop replaces records.◄
   book$(j,k)=book$(j+1,k)◄
  NEXT k◄
 NEXT j◄
 currpage=currpage-1 'Decrement page pointer.◄
 saveflag=0 'This update is not yet saved on disk.◄
 GOTO MainMenu◄
 ◄
NewRecsize:◄
 'Sets new size for address book entries.◄
 'Default = 5 lines.◄
 MENU 1,0,0:MENU 2,0,0:MENU 3,0,0:CLS◄
  PRINT "Current number"◄
  PRINT "of address lines =";recsize◄
 loop1:◄
  PRINT:PRINT label$(1)◄
  PRINT:PRINT "Enter new number"◄
  PRINT "of address lines (3-10):"◄
  INPUT;">> ",temp◄
  IF temp=0 THEN GOTO MainMenu 'Abort routine.◄
  IF temp<3 OR temp>10 THEN loop1◄
 recsize=temp◄
 ERASE book$:DIM book$(booksize,recsize)◄
 GOTO MainMenu◄
 ◄
NewBooksize:◄
 'Sets new size for address book file.◄
 'Default = 100 entries.◄
 MENU 1,0,0:MENU 2,0,0:MENU 3,0,0◄
 CLS:PRINT "Current number"◄
 PRINT "of maximum entries =";booksize◄
 loop2:◄
  PRINT:PRINT label$(1)◄
  PRINT:PRINT "Enter new number"◄
  PRINT "of maximum entries (25-200):"◄
  INPUT;">> ",temp◄
  IF temp=0 THEN GOTO MainMenu 'Abort routine.◄
  IF temp<25 OR temp>200 THEN loop2◄
 booksize=temp◄
 ERASE book$:DIM book$(booksize,recsize)◄
 GOTO MainMenu◄
 ◄
Search:◄
```

```
'Finds a specified entry in address book.◄
'Requires target string in target$.◄
'Requires starting points in rec and item.◄
'Returns result in variable match.◄
'If found, match>1 (value of INSTR).◄
'If not found, match=Ø.◄
CLS:PRINT "Searching..."◄
loop4:◄
 match=INSTR(UCASE$(book$(rec,item)),UCASE$(target$))◄
 IF match=Ø AND item<recsize THEN item=item+1:GOTO loop4◄
 IF match=Ø AND rec<currpage THEN rec=rec+1:item=1:GOTO loop4◄
RETURN◄
◄
Clickmouse:◄
 'Patiently waits for mouse click and release.◄
 PRINT label$(2):PRINT label$(3)◄
 WHILE MOUSE(Ø)=Ø:WEND◄
 WHILE MOUSE(Ø)<>Ø:WEND◄
 RETURN◄
◄
SUB Requester (msg1$,msg2$,b1$,b2$,hilite%,answer%) STATIC◄
 ' Requester window subprogram version 3.4.◄
 SHARED scrid 'Global variable for SCREEN ID.◄
 IF scrid<1 OR scrid>4 THEN scrid=-1 'Default to Workbench.◄
 WINDOW 3,"Program Request",(Ø,Ø)-(311,45),16,scrid◄
 maxwidth=INT(WINDOW(2)/8) 'Truncate prompts if too long...◄
 PRINT LEFT$(msg1$,maxwidth):PRINT LEFT$(msg2$,maxwidth)◄
 b1$=LEFT$(b1$,12):b2$=LEFT$(b2$,12) 'Truncate buttons.◄
 bsize1=(LEN(b1$)+2)*1Ø:bsize2=(LEN(b2$)+2)*1Ø 'Button size.◄
 x1=(312-(bsize1+bsize2))/3  'Calculate button positions...◄
 x2=x1+bsize1:x3=x1+x2:x4=x3+bsize2◄
 'Draw buttons◄
 LINE (x1,2Ø)-(x2,38),2,b:LINE (x3,2Ø)-(x4,38),2,b◄
 IF hilite%=1 THEN LINE (x1+2,22)-(x2-2,36),3,b◄
 IF hilite%=2 THEN LINE (x3+2,22)-(x4-2,36),3,b◄
 LOCATE 4,1:PRINT PTAB(x1+1Ø);b1$;◄
 PRINT PTAB(x3+1Ø);b2$◄
 reqloop: 'Loop which acts on mouse clicks...◄
 WHILE MOUSE(Ø)=Ø:WEND:m1=MOUSE(1):m2=MOUSE(2)◄
 IF m1>x1 AND m1<x2 AND m2>2Ø AND m2<38 THEN◄
  answer%=1 'Left button was selected.◄
  LINE (x1,2Ø)-(x2,38),1,bf 'Flash left button.◄
 ELSEIF m1>x3 AND m1<x4 AND m2>2Ø AND m2<38 THEN◄
  answer%=Ø 'Right button was selected.◄
  LINE (x3,2Ø)-(x4,38),1,bf 'Flash right button.◄
 ELSE◄
  GOTO reqloop 'Neither button selected; repeat loop.◄
 END IF◄
 WHILE MOUSE(Ø)<>Ø:WEND:WINDOW CLOSE 3◄
END SUB◄
◄
ErrorTrap:◄
 BEEP ' Get user's attention.◄
 IF ERR=53 THEN◄
  request1$="FILE NOT FOUND."◄
  GOTO ExitError◄
 END IF◄
```

```
IF ERR=61 THEN◄
 request1$="DISK FULL."◄
 GOTO ExitError◄
END IF◄
IF ERR=64 THEN◄
 request1$="BAD FILENAME."◄
 GOTO ExitError◄
END IF◄
IF ERR=67 THEN◄
 request1$="DIRECTORY FULL."◄
 GOTO ExitError◄
END IF◄
IF ERR=68 THEN◄
 request1$="DEVICE UNAVAILABLE."◄
 GOTO ExitError◄
END IF◄
IF ERR=70 THEN◄
 request1$="DISK WRITE-PROTECTED."◄
 GOTO ExitError◄
END IF◄
IF ERR=74 THEN◄
 request1$="UNKNOWN DISK VOLUME."◄
 GOTO ExitError◄
END IF◄
request1$="ERROR NUMBER"+STR$(ERR)◄
ExitError:◄
' Abort operation or try again.◄
CALL Requester (request1$,"","Retry","CANCEL",2,answer%)◄
IF answer%=0 THEN◄
 CLOSE 1◄
 RESUME MainMenu◄
ELSE◄
 CLOSE 1◄
 ON ERROR GOTO ErrorTrap◄
 RESUME◄
END IF◄
```

9 Library Calls

9 Library Calls

Amiga BASIC is a huge language with hundreds of commands and functions, covering nearly every aspect of programming. In earlier days, programmers often had to resort to POKEing directly into system memory to perform tricks not possible with their BASICs alone. With Amiga BASIC, this is rarely necessary. In fact, most of the programs in this book contain no PEEKs or POKEs at all. Whether you're drawing complex color pictures, calculating your biorhythm, or storing client records on a 20-megabyte hard disk, Amiga BASIC covers all the bases.

Well, almost all.

Even though Amiga BASIC has dozens of commands for controlling the Amiga's special features, there's just no way a single language can include enough commands to take advantage of everything such a powerful computer has to offer. There are times when Amiga BASIC is missing a command you find you suddenly need. For example, although you can set the color palette with PALETTE, there is no BASIC command for reading the current palette values.

On the other hand, if you've read any of the Amiga operating system manuals, especially the *Amiga ROM Kernel Manual*, you may have found just the routine you're looking for. There are hundreds of powerful machine language subroutines in the Amiga's operating system, some permitting you to achieve amazing effects normally impossible in Amiga BASIC. All you need is a way to access these routines, a bridge to another plane of programming.

Unlocking the LIBRARY

The key to unlocking the secrets of the Kernel is Amiga BASIC's LIBRARY command. LIBRARY loads a table of pointers into memory. These pointers are numbers that stand for certain memory locations in the computer. If you transfer control of the Amiga's 68000 CPU to these new memory locations, the machine language code at these locations is executed. Once you've transferred control, you're no longer in BASIC. Your program is put on hold, so to speak, while the machine language does its thing. When the machine language program is finished, it returns control back to your BASIC program. The desired

297

action has been performed, and/or you have received information from the routine. It's almost as if you've added a new command to BASIC.

As long as you have a list of these pointers, the *addresses* of each machine language routine, you can execute them with the CALL statement. If you already know the address of a machine language routine, you only need to CALL it. Although CALL can pass information to and from the machine language routine, in its simplest form it simply transfers control of the 68000 CPU to the new address:

CALL *Addr&*

The address of a machine language program is its starting location in memory. Since the Amiga can address up to 16 megabytes of memory (ROM and RAM), you must use a long integer variable to store this address. A long integer uses four bytes of memory and can store a number from $-2,147,483,648$ to $2,147,483,647$. Of course, you could also use a single- or double-precision variable, but the long integer type is not only more appropriate, but also more efficient. We'll use the long integer type extensively in these examples.

As with subprograms (see Appendix D), you can omit the keyword CALL and leave off the outer parentheses. For example,

CALL Draw&(WINDOW(8),10,y)

and

Draw& WINDOW(8),10,y

are equivalent. As with subprograms, you can't use this abbreviated style immediately following a THEN statement, or BASIC gets confused. Whether to use CALL or not is a matter of style. The CALL makes it clear that you are accessing an external routine, but leaving off CALL lets you pretend that these library routines are extended Amiga BASIC commands. (Besides, it saves typing.)

Shifty Addresses

If you know the address of a routine, you can simply use CALL to execute it. Unfortunately, there is no single, static list of addresses for every operating system routine. For one thing, Commodore-Amiga reserves the right to change the operating system as needed to fix bugs or add new features, so these addresses may change, too. Also, since this is a multitasking system, no one program can be allowed to demand control of a particular section of memory; some other program might already be using that memory.

Instead, programs must be written so they don't need to know the actual memory addresses they're referencing. It seems impossible, but this kind of code, called *relocatable* or *position-independent* code, can move around in memory. This lets the operating system allocate memory as efficiently as possible.

The libraries don't contain the actual addresses of every routine. Instead, the entries in a library are numeric *offsets*. If you do know one address for sure, all other addresses can be specified as relative to this base address. The offsets for routines in a library are added to the effective address of the first routine in the library.

For example, one routine ends up at location 5000 in memory. The next two might be at 5100 and 6410. Instead of storing all these addresses as absolute values, they might be stored as 0, 100, and 1410, offsets relative to the base address of 5000. No matter where the routines are stored, if you can find the address of the first routine, you can use the offsets to locate the rest.

The actual format of a library is not important here. What matters is that a LIBRARY call sets a list of variables to the effective addresses of every routine in the library. For example, the statement

LIBRARY "graphics.library"

loads the Graphics library table from disk, creating variables named after the routines listed in the *Amiga ROM Kernel Manual*. It gets these names from the *libs* subdirectory on the system disk and a file called *graphics.bmap*. This file (as well as *dos.bmap*, which permits access to AmigaDOS routines) is included on the Amiga BASIC Extras disk and must be within the current directory in order for LIBRARY to find it. We'll discuss .BMAP files in more detail later.

An example of a Graphics library routine is the Draw( ) function, which draws lines on the screen. When you use CALL Draw&, Amiga BASIC initializes a variable called Draw& to the address of the Draw( ) function, computed from the library. When you CALL Draw&, control is transferred to the Draw( ) command.

If you execute PRINT Draw& after using CALL Draw&, you'd get the address of the Draw( ) routine in the ROM Kernel, a number over 16 million. Don't try to use this absolute address for any purpose—future revisions of the operating system would make absolute addresses obsolete.

Do You Need Them?

If the preceding explanation seems intimidating, you can just think of the LIBRARY command as simply making it possible for you to use extra commands which are not built into Amiga BASIC, but are supported by the operating system. These ROM routines are not part of Amiga BASIC, but you can use them as if they are. However, because you're calling the operating system directly, you take on some of the responsibilities of a machine language programmer. If your program doesn't use the operating system properly, it can fail miserably, crashing Amiga BASIC and possibly freezing up the entire machine. The routines have very little error checking, so you have to be extra careful when using them.

Before we delve into the operating system, keep in mind that you may rarely need to use these routines. If there's a way to do something with BASIC commands, why clutter a program with external references to machine language routines? There are ROM routines to set a pixel; to draw lines, boxes, and filled rectangles; and to animate objects. But you can do the same things almost as well with PSET, LINE, and the OBJECT commands. Much of the operating system is filled with routines to perform the same commands built into Amiga BASIC. In fact, Amiga BASIC calls some of these routines itself when you execute a built-in BASIC command.

A C or machine language programmer must use the Intuition library to access windows and menus, but Amiga BASIC has the easy and convenient MENU and WINDOW commands. The ROM routines aren't inherently better than the equivalent BASIC routines and usually aren't any faster when called from BASIC. If Amiga BASIC were more limited, library calls would be more valuable.

A program's speed is partly determined by how long it takes BASIC to analyze each command and decide what to do. BASIC can then execute the command directly. The command itself executes at machine language speed since it is written in machine language. The BASIC interpreter continually scans through your program, deciphering keywords and deciding which routines to call. It's the time spent interpreting each statement that makes BASIC slower than machine language.

For instance, the BF option of the LINE command, used to draw a filled box, executes nearly as fast as the ROM RectFill( ) routine and may actually use RectFill( ) to do its job. The great speed of rectangle drawing is due to the Amiga's special graphics processing power, but is not an attribute of Amiga BASIC. A FOR-NEXT routine in BASIC which repeatedly draws rectangles will still draw rectangles more slowly than a machine language program. Each individual rectangle is drawn nearly instantly, but BASIC spends much time interpreting each command.

Conflicts with BASIC

Ironically, some valuable operating system routines can't be called because they already exist in BASIC. For instance, the DOS library lets you open files, read or write a buffer of data, then close the file when you're finished. Amiga BASIC's capabilities for input/output are powerful indeed, but it would be advantageous to use the ROM Read and Write routines to transfer data directly from an area of memory at top speed. There's nothing inherently difficult about using these ROM routines, but they share the same names as BASIC keywords. The DOS Open( ), Close( ), Read( ), and Write( ) routines are simple to use, but they conflict with the BASIC keywords OPEN, CLOSE, READ, and WRITE. There seems to be no simple way to prevent Amiga BASIC from treating these words as BASIC keywords. The names in the ROM library can't be changed either, so these routines are invisible to BASIC.

Watch out for this trap when calling certain ROM routines. If the variable you're using in a ROM call becomes uppercase when you enter the line, it's a warning signal that BASIC thinks it has found a keyword. For example,

FileLock&=Lock&(SADD("testfile"+CHR$(0)),−2&)
Handle&=Open&(SADD("testfile"+CHR$(0)),1005&)
CALL Write&(VARPTR(buffer%(0)),1000&)
CALL Unlock&(FileLock&)
CALL Close&(Handle&)

becomes

FileLock&=Lock&(SADD("testfile"+CHR$(0)),−2&)
Handle&=OPEN &O0(SADD("testfile"+CHR$(0))),1005&)
CALL WRITE &O0(VARPTR(buffer%(0)),1000&)
CALL Unlock&(FileLock&)
CALL CLOSE &O0(Handle&)

Lock and Unlock (used to protect a file from other multitasking programs while it is altered) work fine, but the variables Open&, Write&, and Close& are seen as the keywords OPEN, WRITE, and CLOSE, followed by a nonsensical ampersand (&), interpreted as the octal constant of 0 (&O0).

This phenonenom could be addressed by calling a small machine language subroutine that itself calls the library Open, Read, Write, and Close routines, but the whole point of using the ROM library is to avoid having to write your own machine language extensions.

Other ROM routines aren't really appropriate for use with Amiga BASIC, such as those used to set up and maintain system interrupts, modify the copper list, or primitive routines to maintain layers, libraries, and linked lists. You can access almost any operating system routine, but there are several potential problems. First, BASIC may not be fast enough to respond to the demand of interrupt calls and message port handling. There are usually higher level, hence more useful, Kernel calls that obviate the need for the most primitive functions. It usually just isn't worth the payoff to use BASIC to dabble with the most intricate ROM routines.

Instead, we'll concentrate on the ROM routines that can really enhance your programming capabilities. Some calls permit functions that would ideally be built into BASIC, such as reading the color registers or changing fonts and type styles. Others are more specialized, such as routines to allocate and deallocate blocks of memory outside of BASIC, change window titles, redefine the mouse pointer, read the color registers, directly access the hardware sprites, and much more.

What's on the Library Shelves

The most commonly used libraries are the DOS.LIBRARY, EXEC.LIBRARY, GRAPHICS.LIBRARY, and INTUITION.LIBRARY. You can also access the lower level and less useful CLIST.LIBRARY, LAYERS.LIBRARY, ICON.LIBRARY, and DISKFONT.LIBRARY, and the libraries that duplicate BASIC's built-in capabilities, and are therefore largely unneeded: MATHFFP.LIBRARY, MATHTRANS.LIBRARY, MATHIEEEDOUB.BAS (math routines), and TRANSLATOR.LIBRARY (text-to-speech translation).

The DOS library is a hook into AmigaDOS. BASIC already contains plenty of statements for disk management, but there are some valuable techniques that revolve around the DOS library, including the ability to execute CLI commands from a BASIC program (as long as BASIC was started from an open CLI).

The Graphics library is the biggest ROM library and controls almost every graphics function of the Amiga. Included are calls to plot points, draw lines, initialize graphics modes, draw connected lines, outline and fill areas, write text, change text styles, animate sprites and bobs, and control the blitter.

Many of these routines, however, duplicate Amiga BASIC's own commands and may not be useful to you. On the other hand, the Graphics library is the key to some high-speed effects, and lets you change fonts and font styles. Lower-level graphics calls, such as accessing the blitter, are more powerful than BASIC's equivalent routines, such as PUT and GET, but are far trickier to use.

Similarly, the Exec library contains powerful low-level operating system commands, such as an Allocate command that can reserve a chunk of memory. However, these commands permit BASIC to perform some quite impressive feats of mischief if used improperly. If you use Allocate, but fail to free the memory when you're done with it, that memory is lost and inaccessible until you reboot the computer.

The Intuition library is responsible for Amiga's friendly user interface. It implements windows, pull-down menus, requesters, and gadgets. Many of these capabilities are built into BASIC or easily simulated in BASIC. (See Chapter 7.)

The Layers library manages multiple overlapping graphics areas. You really don't need to use the Layers library, since the more useful higher-level routines automatically use layer library calls. The CLIST library, used to manage character lists, has little meaning in BASIC programming. However, the Diskfont library is invaluable—it lets you access the disk-based character fonts.

Most of these routines are documented in volume 1 of the *Amiga ROM Kernel Manual* and are presented in quick-reference form in volume 2. Both volumes are hundreds of pages long, so we can't duplicate such a mammoth body of knowledge. Instead, we'll work with a cross section of the operating system, routines that work well with Amiga BASIC. The manuals are almost a necessity when working with the operating system, especially if you're trying to access these routines from Amiga BASIC.

Making .BMAP Files

The libraries themselves are found in the *libs* subdirectory of your boot disk, under the filenames DOS.LIBRARY, EXEC.LIBRARY, GRAPHICS.LIBRARY, and so on. But for BASIC to access these libraries, it needs a list of the routine names and other information. In machine language or C, this information is listed in an *include file* or *header file* which is incorporated within assembly or compilation. There are no equivalents to these header files in BASIC, other than the .BMAP files.

A .BMAP file is compiled from a list of subroutine specifications called an .FD file, for *function definition*. There are .FD files for each library. An entry in an .FD file gives the routine name and lists the parameters for the function, including notation for machine language parameters passed via registers.

The .FD files do you no good in themselves. They need to be converted into a file that is directly loadable by Amiga BASIC when it encounters a LIBRARY statement. The ConvertFd program, found on the Amiga BASIC Extras disk, is used to compile an .FD file into the .BMAP file usable by BASIC. Given GRAPHICS.FD, it would create GRAPHICS.BMAP. Two libraries have already been converted for you on the Extras disk: GRAPHICS.BMAP and DOS.BMAP. These are found in the BasicDemos drawer on Extras. Copy them to the same directory (or root directory) as your program. You may also want to copy them to the *sys:libs* directory (or simply LIBS:). This puts them in the same subdirectory as the libraries themselves.

Unfortunately, Commodore neglected to include the .BMAP files for any libraries except the Graphics library and DOS library. If you had the .FD file, such as EXEC_LIB.FD or DISKFONT_LIB.FD, you could create the .BMAP file, for example, EXEC.BMAP and DISKFONT.BMAP.

We can't list these .FD files in this book, since they are copyrighted material. The .FD files were originally listed in version 1.0 of the *Amiga ROM Kernel Manual*, but have been omitted from the two-volume version 1.1 manual. If you have access to these listings, you can type them in with any ASCII text editor, such as ED, then save them to disk. You can then process the .FD file with ConvertFd. (By the way, ConvertFd automatically puts the newly created .BMAP file in the *libs* directory.)

As a substitute, we've run the .FD files through the .FD converter and have developed programs that create .BMAP files for you. These programs, found at the end of this chapter, create .BMAP files from DATA statements. When you run one of these programs, such as "IntuitionMaker" (Program 9-20), it creates a corresponding .BMAP file (such as Intuition.bmap), storing it in a drawer called BMAPS.

If you purchased the companion disk to this book, this directory already exists on the disk. You only need to run "IntuitionMaker," "ExecMaker," and "DiskfontMaker" (found in the Chapter 9 drawer) to create these libraries.

Otherwise, you need to copy the Empty folder from your Workbench disk to your Amiga BASIC work disk, and then use the Workbench Rename command to change its name to BMAPS.

After you've typed in and saved the programs at the end of this chapter (ExecMaker, IntuitionMaker, and DiskfontMaker), run them. They first check the DATA statements to see whether you typed them correctly. Don't be surprised if a program doesn't work the first time you run it—it's not easy to type in over 1K of hexadecimal code without making some mistakes.

If the DATA statements are okay, the files Exec.bmap, Intuition.bmap, and Diskfont.bmap are created and stored in the BMAPS directory.

Finding the BMAP

We use the BMAPS directory in all our examples that call libraries. In order for LIBRARY to find a .BMAP file, the .BMAP file must be in the current directory. Normally, this would require you to copy these files to every subdirectory, quite an inconvenience. An alternative is always to store these files in the root directory.

You can't redirect the pathname with the LIBRARY command itself—that is, a statement like this won't work:

LIBRARY "Demos/graphics.library"

The filename used in the LIBRARY command is used to search for the library itself. The above statement would look for the Graphics library in the Demos subdirectory. You may have put the graphics.bmap file there, but the actual library is in the *libs* subdirectory on your system disk.

You must use the CHDIR command to change the current directory to the one containing the .BMAP file. All our example programs look for the .BMAP files in the subdirectory called :BMAPS; the colon (:) prefix means to use the root directory to find the BMAPS subdirectory. The statements look something like this to find the .BMAP file:

CHDIR ":BMAPS"
LIBRARY "graphics.library"

The only danger is that since the BMAPS directory is now the current directory, any future disk access uses the BMAPS directory. If you save the program after running it, it will go in BMAPS unless you change the current directory or override the current directory by using the : prefix at the beginning of the filename.

Amiga BASIC lets you open as many as five libraries at once. In other words, you can use the LIBRARY statement only five times in a program. When your program ends, it must execute a LIBRARY CLOSE statement to free up the library. LIBRARY CLOSE is executed automatically if you subsequently run the program or erase it with NEW, but it's better to control this yourself.

Library Functions

Some Kernel calls not only perform an action, but also return a value. These calls are referred to as *functions* and are analagous to BASIC functions. For example, the BASIC function SQR calculates the square root of a value passed to it and returns that value as a numeric expression. You can assign a variable to this value, as in A=SQR(4), so A would equal 2. Or you could simply PRINT SQR(4) to display the value of 2, or use it as part of a complex expression, as in

C=SQR(A^2+B^2)/2*3.1415927

The machine language operating system functions behave similarly. They expect that the values you send them are long integers, and they return a value as a long integer. (Remember, long integers in BASIC are denoted with the & suffix.)

A literal number in a program listing, such as 1 or 34, is actually an integer constant. It is stored internally as a short integer, two bytes. On the other hand, a value of 1.0 or 1! (BASIC automatically adds the exclamation mark) connotes a single-precision number.

So the constant 345& or 1643323& is a long integer constant, using four bytes per number. A long integer variable might be ATTR& or Handle&. You can use DEFLNG A–Z to make all variables long integer type by default. This can be handy if you use a lot of library calls and functions. Unless you use DEFLNG, you must use & at the end of a function name:

CALL SetRast&(WINDOW(8),3)

not

CALL SetRast(WINDOW(8),3)

It's important to keep track of the type of values you pass or receive from functions. Although you can use Amiga BASIC's CLNG function to convert any variable expression to a long integer value, it's easiest to stick to long integer variables or constants.

To use a machine language function, you must tell BASIC that the function name exists as a function. Otherwise, BASIC has no way to distinguish the function Lock&(s&,−2&) from an illegal array reference to a two-dimensional array called Lock&( ). You declare a function with the DECLARE FUNCTION statement, along with the keyword LIBRARY. To declare the function ReadPixel( ), used like BASIC's POINT function to read the value of an *(x,y)* coordinate on the graphics screen, you would use

DECLARE FUNCTION ReadPixel&( ) LIBRARY

You're also allowed to show the parameters of the function. Although these parameters are ignored by Amiga BASIC, it can be handy to refer to the DECLARE statement when using the function to see what the parameters are.

In the following example the parameters *rp*, *x*, and *y* are ignored, as if they were remarks, but it lets us see that this library call requires the RastPort address (WINDOW(8)) followed by the horizontal and vertical position of the desired pixel value:

DECLARE FUNCTION ReadPixel&*(rp,x,y)* LIBRARY

If you use the above statement with LIBRARY "graphics.library", you can use the ReadPixel function within your program, as in

PSET (*x,y*),ReadPixel&(WINDOW(8),*x,y*)

You could use the CLNG function to ensure that the *x* and *y* values are long integer types, but Amiga BASIC usually forces the variable to fit its expected type. New values attempt to become the type of the most recently referenced expression. The reference to WINDOW(8) is a long integer expression, so the variables *x* and *y* are converted to long integer values. To be safe, though, you may prefer always to use long integer variables and constants.

As a reminder that many of these routines are redundant, the following example does the same thing with BASIC's own POINT function:

PSET (*x,y*),POINT(*x,y*)

Let's now take a whirlwind tour of the Amiga operating system. We don't have the space to cover the ramifications of every routine we mention, but by following the examples and modifying the demo programs, you can add system power to your own Amiga BASIC programs.

The Graphics Library

We'll pass over the functions already supported by Amiga BASIC commands and discussed in previous chapters. For instance, there are ROM routines for polygon drawing and filling as well as object animation, but these routines are transparently supported by Amiga BASIC's own AREA and OBJECT commands.

The graphics commands we'll cover can be divided into three classes: drawing functions, text functions, and sprite animation functions.

Drawing Functions

Most of these functions require that you specify which *RastPort* to use. A RastPort symbolizes a particular screen area, such as the inside of a window. Specifically, a RastPort is a pointer to an instance of a RastPort structure. We'll talk about structures later, but you usually don't need to know the definition of this structure to use the functions.

The RastPort identifies which window area will be used for the rendering. Amiga BASIC's WINDOW(8) function returns the RastPort for the current window. If you're using more than one window, you can save this value in a variable immediately after declaring the window, since creating a window makes it the current window.

WINDOW 1,,,31
myRastPort& = WINDOW(8)

The ROM drawing routines are independent of Amiga BASIC, of course. The pixel cursor maintained by the PSET, LINE, and CIRCLE statements is not honored by the Graphics library, and you cannot reposition the Graphics library cursor with Amiga BASIC commands. This pixel cursor is local to the current window. It is used as the origin for line drawing and text printing.

You can move the system's pixel cursor with the Move( ) function. The syntax of Move( ) is

CALL Move&(*RastPort,x,y*)

To move the pixel cursor to position (20,30), you could use a statement like this:

CALL Move&(WINDOW(8),20,30)

The Draw( ) function draws a line between the current pixel position and a specified endpoint. For instance, to draw a line from (20,20) to (50,70) (analagous to LINE (20,20) − (50,70)), use this:

CALL Move&(WINDOW(8),20,20)
CALL Draw&(WINDOW(8),50,70)

To set a single pixel, use WritePixel( ):

CALL WritePixel&(WINDOW(8),*x,y*)

The Draw& and WritePixel& routines (and many other drawing functions) use the current foreground drawing color. The foreground color (or pen) is a number ranging from 0 to 31, depending on the screen depth, that specifies which color register is the color source. The background color is used as the background for text and as a secondary color for patterned fills. You can set these colors with the SetAPen( ) and SetBPen( ) functions:

CALL SetAPen&(WINDOW(8),*fg*)
CALL SetBPen&(WINDOW(8),*bg*)

However, Amiga BASIC's own COLOR statement works just as well, so you can just as easily use COLOR *fg,bg* to set the foreground and background colors.

Outline Mode

There's another drawing pen, too: the outline pen. Outline drawing mode is not directly supported by Amiga BASIC. This mode lets you automatically create an outline around objects you draw. When outline mode is turned on, solid figures like filled rectangles are bordered by the outline pen color. Hollow figures are not drawn in the foreground color since their edges are considered an outline that is to be drawn with the outline pen.

There are no Amiga BASIC commands to turn outline mode on or off or to set the outline pen's color. Instead, you can use the following subprograms.

```
'Simulates C-language SetOPen macro
'
SUB SetOPen(rp&,c%) STATIC
 AREAOUTLINE=8
 AolPen&=rp&+27:Flags&=rp&+32
 POKE AolPen&,c%
 POKEW Flags&,PEEKW(Flags&) OR AREAOUTLINE
END SUB

 'Turns on or off outlining mode
 'pass WINDOW(8) and mode% (1=on, 0=off)

 SUB Outline (rp&,mode%) STATIC
  AREAOUTLINE=8:Flags&=rp&+32
  POKEW Flags&,(PEEKW(Flags&) AND NOT AREAOUTLINE) OR ABS(AREAOUTL
  INE*mode%)
END SUB
```

The SetOPen subprogram lets you select an outline color. It also turns on outline mode. Without changing the outline color, you can use the Outline subprogram to turn outline mode on and off. To set the outline color and enable outline mode, use this statement:

CALL SetOPen(WINDOW(8),*pencolor*)

Again, the WINDOW(8) RastPort function lets you use separate outline colors with different windows. The last parameter, *pencolor*, is a number from 0 to 31, specifying which color register to use with outline mode.

The next call turns off outline mode. You need to disable outline mode before exiting your program, since text printing doesn't work properly in this mode:

CALL Outline(WINDOW(8),0)

If you need to turn outline mode back on, you can CALL SetOPen again. If you're using the same outline color, just CALL Outline:

CALL Outline(WINDOW(8),1)

The Graphics library RectFill function quickly fills a rectangular area of the screen, just like the BF option of LINE. The ROM equivalent of LINE $(x1,y1)-(,y2),,bf$ is

CALL RectFill&(WINDOW(8),*x1,y1,x2,y2*)

Program 9-1 demonstrates outline mode and RectFill( ):

Program 9-1. Outline Demo

```
'Outline Demo◄
'Demonstrates the use of SetOPen,◄
'Outline, SetAPen, SetRast, RectFill◄
   ◄
  DEFLNG a-Z◄
   ◄
  CHDIR ":BMAPS"◄
  LIBRARY "graphics.library"◄
◄
WINDOW 1,,,31:CLS◄
wlrp=WINDOW(8)◄
xmax=WINDOW(2):ymax=WINDOW(3)◄
CALL SetRast(wlrp,3)◄
FOR i=1 TO 200◄
 x1=xmax*RND:y1=ymax*RND◄
 x2=xmax*RND:y2=ymax*RND◄
'Same as COLOR 1◄
 CALL SetAPen(wlrp,1)◄
'Use Outline mode◄
 CALL SetOPen(wlrp,2)◄
' Used just like◄
' LINE (x1,y1)-(x2,y2),,bf◄
 IF x1>x2 THEN SWAP x1,x2◄
 IF y1>y2 THEN SWAP y1,y2◄
 CALL RectFill(wlrp,x1,y1,x2,y2)◄
NEXT◄
◄
CALL Outline(wlrp,0)◄
WINDOW CLOSE 1◄
LIBRARY CLOSE◄
END◄
◄
'Simulates C-language SetOPen macro◄
'◄
SUB SetOPen(rp&,c%) STATIC◄
 AREAOUTLINE=8◄
 AolPen&=rp&+27:Flags&=rp&+32◄
 POKE AolPen&,c%◄
 POKEW Flags&,PEEKW(Flags&) OR AREAOUTLINE◄
END SUB◄
◄
'Turns on or off outlining mode◄
'pass WINDOW(8) and mode% (1=on, 0=off)◄
◄
SUB Outline (rp&,mode%) STATIC◄
 AREAOUTLINE=8:Flags&=rp&+32◄
 POKEW Flags&,(PEEKW(Flags&) AND NOT AREAOUTLINE) OR ABS(AREAOUTL
 INE*mode%)◄
END SUB◄
```

Additional Graphics Library Functions

The Graphics library ScrollRaster( ) function scrolls a portion of the screen. Since Amiga BASIC already has a SCROLL command, we'll mention this function just to be complete:

CALL ScrollRaster(WINDOW(8),*dx,dy,x1,y1,x2,y2*)

The values *dx* and *dy* are the direction and amount of the shift. Negative values shift to the left or upward. The variables *x1*, *y1*, *x2*, and *y2* define a rectangle whose coordinates are (*x1,y1*)–(*x2,y2*). Only the screen area within this rectangle is scrolled.

Another Graphics library function is Flood( ), which more or less duplicates Amiga BASIC's PAINT command. However, Flood( ) has some distinct advantages over PAINT. Although PAINT is a quick and easy way to fill enclosed areas of the screen with color, it has some limitations. With a command like PAINT (*x,y*), the current foreground color is substituted for all pixels surrounding the origin of (*x,y*). This sweeping, flooding fill stops when it hits a border defined by the outline pen. Therefore, you can fill only those areas which are completely enclosed by a single color.

The Flood( ) function lets you use another variation of flood fill called *color mode*. In color mode, the pixel from which the flood fill originates is first examined. The color of this (*x,y*) position becomes the color that is displaced by the flood fill.

For instance, an ordinary flood fill might fill a green rectangle with blue. Anything else drawn within the green borders is erased with blue. On the other hand, a color fill only fills the "empty space."

You might never need color mode, so PAINT may be sufficient. To use color mode, though, you need to directly access the Flood( ) function.

A nasty obstacle to using Flood( ) is that special memory buffers must be initialized. Flood( ) works in this memory buffer until it's finished, then copies the fill onto the visible screen. Setting up these memory areas can be quite cumbersome if you try to emulate a C or machine language program. Fortunately, it turns out that simply using the AREA commands creates the necessary buffer. So before calling Flood( ), draw a dummy figure by executing a line like this:

AREA (10,10):AREAFILL:CLS

This should be executed before drawing anything on the screen you want to keep, since the CLS command quicky erases the dummy figure.

Now you're ready to use the Flood( ) function, as demonstrated by Program 9-2. The second parameter of Flood( ) is the mode value—0 for outline mode (the same mode used by PAINT), or 1 for color mode—followed by the *x* and *y* origin of the fill.

Program 9-2. Flood Fill

```
CHDIR ":bmaps"◄
LIBRARY "graphics.library"◄
WINDOW 1,,,31◄
AREA (10,10):AREAFILL◄
LINE (50,50)-(100,100),,B◄
CALL Flood&(WINDOW(8),1,70,70)◄
LIBRARY CLOSE◄
END◄
```

Another Graphics library function duplicated in BASIC is ReadPixel( ). This function is the same as Amiga BASIC's POINT function. Where you would normally use A=POINT(20,30) to read the color of the pixel at position (20,30), you could use this call:

A=ReadPixel&(WINDOW(8),20,30)

The Drawing Mode

You've probably never thought twice about it, but text or graphics drawn on the screen with standard Amiga BASIC commands displace existing screen images. The source image (dot, line, character) is combined with the background image (what's already on the screen at the drawing position). This normal display mode is called the *JAM2* mode, because two colors, the foreground and background colors, are jammed into the screen. Any zero bits (*off* pixels) in the source image erase the corresponding positions of the background, changing them to the current background color. The one bits in the source image also replace the pixels they overwrite. When you print text, the background of the text erases anything it overlays.

But the Amiga's operating system offers other drawing modes as well. The additional modes—not directly supported by BASIC—affect existing background pixels differently than does the JAM2 mode. With an operating system function called *SetDrMd*, you can gain access to these other drawing modes. You can call this function with a statement like

CALL SetDrMd&(WINDOW(8),*mode*)

where *mode* is

0 JAM1
1 JAM2
2 COMPLEMENT
3 INVERSID

In JAM1 mode, only the foreground color is jammed onto the screen display. Any *off* (0, or background color) pixels in the source image don't bother the previous pixels that they overlap. This is handy when you want to stamp

311

down an image without the background of the image cutting a rectangular hole in the existing background. When you print text in JAM1 mode, the background color is transparent.

COMPLEMENT mode works something like the XOR option of PUT (see Chapter 3). The *on* bits in the source image control whether the on bits in the background image are reversed. COMPLEMENT mode is like negative ink—the foreground image cuts a hole in the background image. COMPLEMENT mode is also known as the cookie-cutter mode.

The INVERSID mode replaces the destination area with a reversed image of the source area. Text drawn in the INVERSID mode comes out with the colors reversed, as if you used COLOR to reverse the foreground and background pens. You would use INVERSID along with either JAM1 or JAM2 to reverse the colors of the foreground and background pens. Since the value of INVERSID is 4, the inverted value of JAM1 would be 4 (4+0), and the inverted value of JAM2 would be 5 (4+1). You could use this inverted value as a shortcut for reverse-video text.

The COMPLEMENT mode is handy for rubber-band effects, as seen when drawing a line in "MouseSketch" (Chapter 10). MouseSketch lets you preview a line before actually drawing it on the screen by displaying a rubber-band image while you move the mouse. This keeps the line from erasing existing screen images until you decide on its final length and orientation. The line is animated as if it were an elastic band attached to a nail. When you release the mouse button, the line is actually drawn.

To achieve this rubber-band effect, the program must rapidly erase and redraw the line at whatever position is indicated by the mouse. This action is repeated continuously as the mouse is moved. Although you could do this with Amiga BASIC's LINE command—repeatedly drawing the line in the foreground color and redrawing it in the background color—the moving line would damage the background image.

A much better approach is to take advantage of the SetDrMd function to draw the line in COMPLEMENT mode. A white line drawn over a white background cuts out a black line. This is the *on* image of the rubber band. When you repeat the process, the white line again stamps a negative of the background image, creating a white line that effectively restores the background. The background controls how the foreground is drawn. Although this temporarily distorts the color of the background image, it always provides good contrast. When the rubber banding is finished, the line is drawn in JAM1 or JAM2 mode.

Miscellaneous Graphics Commands

None of the following calls is earthshaking, but they let you do things not built into Amiga BASIC, such as selectively clearing parts of the screen.

- CALL ClearEOL&(WINDOW(8)) erases the remainder of a screen line to the right of the current pixel cursor position. You may also need to call the Move( ) function to set the cursor position.
- To clear from the current pixel position to the end of the screen, use CALL ClearScreen&(WINDOW(8)).
- Finally, CALL SetRaster&(WINDOW(8),Pen) sets the entire drawing area to a single color. This is like using the COLOR statement before CLS.

Table 9-1 is a summary of the drawing functions.

Table 9-1. Drawing Functions Summary

```
ClearEOL&(WINDOW(8))
ClearScreen&(WINDOW(8))
Draw&(WINDOW(8),x,y)
Flood&(WINDOW(8),mode,x,y)
Move&(WINDOW(8),x,y)
pen=ReadPixel&(WINDOW(8),x,y)
RectFill&(WINDOW(8),xmin,ymin,xmax,ymax)
ScrollRaster&(WINDOW(8),dx,dy,xmin,ymin,xmax,ymax)
SetAPen&(WINDOW(8),pen)
SetBPen&(WINDOW(8),pen)
SetDrMd&(WINDOW(8),mode)
SetRast&(WINDOW(8),pen)
WritePixel&(WINDOW(8),x,y)
```

Text Functions

As you've noticed by using the Amiga Notepad or a word processor such as *Textcraft*, the Amiga's operating system supports fancy onscreen text in multiple styles, sizes, typefaces, and colors. None of this is directly supported by Amiga BASIC, although the CON: device does give you limited access to a few different type styles (see Chapter 8). Again, you have to dip into the operating system to take advantage of these features. The functions we're interested in are found in the Graphics library and the Diskfont library.

In the Graphics library, the Text( ) function lets you print text on the screen much faster than BASIC's own PRINT statement. Unlike PRINT, Text( ) isn't followed by a string you want to display. Instead, you pass it the address of a previously defined string followed by the length of the string. Program 9-3 displays a message using Text( ):

Program 9-3. Text Example

```
CHDIR ":BMAPS"◄
LIBRARY "graphics.library"◄
CLS:PRINT:PRINT◄
```

```
MSG$="Hello there!"◄
CALL Text&(WINDOW(8),SADD(MSG$),LEN(MSG$))◄
CALL Text&(WINDOW(8),SADD("Hi!"),3◄
LIBRARY CLOSE◄
END◄
```

If you run this example, you'll notice that the second call of the Text( ) function displays its *Hi!* message on the same line as the previous message. Text( ), unlike PRINT, does not automatically follow the string with a carriage return. Since PRINT tracks the pixel position, as updated by Text( ), you can use a dummy PRINT to advance to the next line:

CALL Text&(WINDOW(8),SADD(MSG$)):PRINT

Another interesting text function lets you change the type style of the current font. There are three special styles: underline, boldface, and italics. The SetSoftStyle( ) function sets these styles.

Each style has a mode number. By adding up the numbers of each style you want to use (they are cumulative) and passing the sum with SetSoftStyle( ), you can select a style or combination of styles. The mode numbers are

Underline 1
Boldface   2
Italics   4

Amiga BASIC's default font (Topaz) works with these three styles. But you should be aware that not all Amiga fonts are compatible with all these styles. Some fonts can be italicized but not underlined, for example. Therefore, before calling SetSoftStyle( ), you should call a function named AskSoftStyle( ) to see if the current font allows the desired style. Use a statement such as this:

Allowed%=AskSoftStyle&(WINDOW(8))

Before you can use AskSoftStyle( ), you must insert a DECLARE FUNCTION reference immediately after the LIBRARY call. This tells Amiga BASIC that AskSoftStyle( ) is a function, not an array reference:

LIBRARY "graphics.library"
DECLARE FUNCTION AskSoftStyle&( ) LIBRARY

The value returned in the variable Allowed% is an *enable flag* which indicates whether a certain font/style combination is allowed. For example, if the current font can't be underlined—but can be boldfaced or italicized—the enable flag would be 6 (style mode 2 plus style mode 4). If all three style modes are allowed, the enable flag would be 7 ($1+2+4$). The enable flag is then passed as one of the parameters in the SetSoftStyle( ) call. The format is

CALL SetSoftStyle&(WINDOW(8),*style mode,enable flag*)

where *style mode* is 1, 2, or 4 (for underline, boldface, or italics) or any combination of these numbers, and *enable flag* is the value returned by the AskSoftStyle( ) call.

 If you're using the default Topaz font, you can skip the call to SetSoftStyle. You can also specify an enable flag of 255 to set all of the flag's bits, just for the sake of convenience. For instance, to print in boldface italics, you'd use a statement like this:

CALL SetSoftStyle&(WINDOW(8),6,255)

where *style mode* is 6 (2+4, boldface + italics) and the enable flag is 255, since Topaz allows all three styles (even though we're only using two of them here). The following series of statements does the same thing, but checks AskSoftStyle( ) first just to play safe:

Allowed%=AskSoftStyle&(WINDOW(8))
CALL SetSoftStyle&(WINDOW(8),6,Allowed%)

 Try this demo to see all the possible style combinations:

Program 9-4. SetSoft Style

```
'SetSoftStyle
DEFLNG a-Z
CHDIR ":bmaps"
LIBRARY "graphics.library"
DECLARE FUNCTION AskSoftStyle() LIBRARY

'Get legal style settings
Allowed%=AskSoftStyle(WINDOW(8))

'Display them
GOSUB DoStyles

LIBRARY CLOSE
END

DoStyles:
FOR i=0 TO 7
   CALL SetSoftStyle(WINDOW(8),i,Allowed%)
   'check bits
   IF i=0 THEN CALL PrintMsg("plain ")
   IF (i AND 1) THEN CALL PrintMsg("underlined ")
   IF (i AND 2) THEN CALL PrintMsg("boldface ")
   IF (i AND 4) THEN CALL PrintMsg("italics ")
   PRINT
NEXT
'Back to normal
CALL SetSoftStyle(WINDOW(8),0,255)
RETURN

'Handy shortcut
SUB PrintMsg(msg$) STATIC
   CALL Text(WINDOW(8),SADD(msg$),LEN(msg$))
END SUB
```

Notice that this example doesn't use PRINT to display the various font styles, but instead calls the subprogram PrintMsg. PrintMsg is a shortcut for the Text( ) function. You can simply use

PrintMsg "Hi there":PRINT

instead of

CALL Text&(WINDOW(8),SADD("Hi there"),8):PRINT

It's a good idea to use Text( ) instead of PRINT when displaying special font styles. The faster speed of Text( ) is reason enough, but there's a more important reason. The styles for a font are algorithmically generated. There aren't actually separate fonts on disk for underline, boldface, and italic characters. Instead, the new style is created on the fly—by slanting the characters for italics, drawing a baseline for underlining, or superimposing the text one pixel to the right of itself for boldface.

PRINT tends to mangle these styles, especially when used with italics. Italicized characters lean into the character space of the next character. When the next character is printed, it chops off part of the previous italic character. This is because PRINT makes a separate call to the Text( ) function for each character in the line. But when you pass the entire line to Text( ), it formats the printed string to leave enough space between the italic characters. Consequently, the text is no longer monospaced, but proportional, since both italic and boldface are wider than normal characters.

The rest of the text library functions require the use of structures, those preformatted areas of memory we mentioned earlier. Rather than discussing structures as theory, we'll show you how they can be used with the graphics text functions.

What Are Structures?

When you call a subroutine, you usually need to pass values, and when the subroutine is finished, you may want to examine information returned by the subroutine. The values you send the subprogram can be part of the call, as in CALL SetDrMd&(WINDOW(8),2), where we send the RastPort and the drawing mode number. You can retrieve a single value from a function if you use DECLARE FUNCTION (see above).

Imagine a routine that needs a dozen parameters, though. Including all these values in the subroutine call would be very inconvenient. If a routine needs hundreds of values, passing all these values via a subroutine call is out of the question.

The Amiga operating system attempts to cut down the amount of information that is passed between routines. Not only does this save memory, but with less data to transfer and process, the whole system runs faster. When you print something with Text( ), you don't send the actual string to be printed. Instead, you pass the address of the string. This address is the memory location of the first character of the string.

Using pointers in this way streamlines a program. An alphabetizer program, sorting an array of strings, could simply exchange two pointers in a pointer array instead of exchanging the actual strings. The strings are displayed or referenced via the pointer array, so by switching the pointers which retrieve the string values, you've effectively changed the order of the strings.

One way to pass a lot of information is to store it in an array, then pass the address of the array. This can work well when all the values can be stored in an array, but it forces all the values to be of the same type. Obviously, an integer array can't directly store long integer or string values. Instead, we need something like an array that can store variables of many different types and sizes.

Such a memory layout is called a *structure*. A structure can hold many different variables of different types and sizes. In C, a popular language for professional software development, the concept of structures is built into the language. This isn't a book about C, but we must describe how structures work in C to adapt the the structure definitions for use with BASIC.

Structures in C

For example, the following C structure stores the various attributes of printed text (hence, TextAttr, for Text Attributes):

struct TextAttr
```
{
    STRPTR    ta_Name;    /* name of the font */
    UWORD     ta_Ysize;   /* height of the font */
    UBYTE     ta_Style;   /* font style */
    UBYTE     ta_Flags;   /* font preferences */
};
```

The keyword *struct* tells the C compiler that a structure named TextAttr follows. These are the elements of the structure (akin to individual array elements):

ta_Name A pointer to a string (STRPTR) containing the font name.
ta_Ysize A 16-bit unsigned word (UWORD) containing the height of the font in pixels.
ta_Style An unsigned byte-length quantity (UBYTE) that contains the font's default style.
ta_Flags A byte holding special font flags.

As you can see, the various fields of the structure are of different types and sizes. STRPTR is a synonym to an address pointer—it says that the element is used to hold a machine address that points to a string. This requires up to 32 bits, so STRPTR is a long integer, using four bytes of memory. UWORD means *unsigned word*; 16 bits of data, or two bytes, are used to store the value. All 16 bits of the data are used to store a positive number from 0 to 65,535. BASIC uses only signed integers (bit 15 is the sign bit) in the range −32,768 to 32,767, but negative values like −36 actually represent the unsigned value 65,500.

To convert from a negative integer to a positive integer, just add 65,536. The result is no longer a signed integer, since BASIC can't use a positive integer higher than 32,767, so you would store this value as a long integer.

For the most part, though, you can use integer quantities for UWORD values. If you need to pass an unsigned integer value higher than 32,767, you can use a negative number as an equivalent. The quantity 40,000 works out to −25,536 (40,000−65,536).

A UBYTE value represents a number from 0 to 255, as opposed to a signed byte that can only represent −128 to 127. Both signed and unsigned variable types use the same number of bits, but signed variables reserve the topmost bit as the sign bit. It's really just a matter of perspective. In binary, there is no such thing as a negative number. The format used to store negative numbers is an arbitrary convention.

The structure block above simply defines a type of structure, the TextAttr structure. It does not create a usable structure, however. This would be accomplished with a statement like

struct TextAttr myText;

This creates a TextAttr structure called *myText*. The elements of the structure are called *myText.ta_Name*, *myText.ta_Ysize*, *myText.ta_Style*, and *myText.ta_Flags*. The structure name is on the left, and the structure element (also called the structure tag) is on the right, separated by a period. In C, you would use commands such as the following to reference these variables:

myText.ta_Ysize=8; /* use topaz 8 */
myText.ta_Name="topaz.font";

(The string reference compiles to a 32-bit address that points to the actual string stored elsewhere.) These structure elements can also be initialized in the structure declaration:

struct TextAttr myText =
{
    "topaz.font",   /* name of the font */
    8, /* height of the font */
    0, /* font style */
    0 /* font preferences */
};

Structures in ML and BASIC

Machine language programs don't know about structures. There are no commands for manipulating blocks of memory containing different size fields in the
vernacular of the 68000 microprocessor. Instead, special templates called *macros*
simulate the C structure references. The machine language declaration of the
TextAttr structure looks like this:

```
STRUCTURE TextAttr,0
    APTR ta_Name
    UWORD ta_Ysize
    UBYTE ta_Style
    UBYTE ta_Flags
    LABEL ta_SIZEOF
```

The assembler maintains an address pointer, a program counter. If your
program started at the imaginary address 35000, the program counter would
start at 35000. As various instructions are compiled, this program counter is
bumped up to point to the next available memory location. Special instructions
like .DS set aside areas of memory for later storage. The STRUCTURE macros
simulate the C structures by skipping the program counter by the byte length
of each element. This leaves behind "holes" in memory which can be filled in
later. The structure names become assembler labels that hold the addresses of
each reserved memory chunk. The final label, ta_SIZEOF, stores the size of the
structure, in bytes.

To access structures in BASIC, we have to take the machine language
approach, since there are no commands in BASIC to manage structures (although the FIELD statement used with random files is analogous and might be
adapted with some trouble).

One technique is to use a string or an array to store the structure values.
We have to format our own area of memory manually. For example, the TextAttr
structure has four fields: a long integer (four bytes), an integer (two bytes), and
two one-byte fields. The total number of bytes in this structure is $4+2+1+1=8$
bytes. So we could use an eight-character string or a four-element integer array
(two bytes per element). The following code fragment is equivalent to an instance of a TextAttr structure:

```
DIM TextAttr&(1)
TextAttr&(0)=SADD("topaz.font"+CHR$(0))
TextAttr&(1)=8*65536&
```

We use a long integer array to create a memory buffer to simulate the
structure. We can use the first element to store the long integer address of the
font name and pack the remaining four bytes (two bytes for font height, one
byte each for style and flags) into the second array element. You can safely set
the style and flags settings to zero, so we just put the address of the font name

in the first element of the long integer array and multiply the font height by 65536 to shift it to the first word of the second array element.

Now that we've formatted the structure, we can use it with any operating system routine that requires a pointer to the structure. The pointer to our array structure is the address of the array, VARPTR(TextAttr&(0)).

Opening a New Font

The OpenFont( ) function opens a RAM- or ROM-resident font. In practice, only the Topaz font is resident; the others have to be loaded from disk with OpenDiskFont( ). Using OpenFont( ), you can choose one of the two Topaz fonts, Topaz 8 or Topaz 9. After you open the font, you use SetFont( ) to make this font the active one for subsequent printing. Both BASIC's PRINT statement and the Text( ) routine will use this font. When you're finished with the font, you call CloseFont( ).

Try Program 9-5 to see how this is done. Note that it declares all variables as long integers with DEFLNG, so variables and arrays with no trailing suffix are long integers by default. This also applies to the function names, so we can use CALL OpenFont( ) instead of OpenFont&( ).

Program 9-5. SysFonts

```
'SysFonts
DEFLNG a-Z
CHDIR ":bmaps"
LIBRARY "graphics.library"
DECLARE FUNCTION OpenFont() LIBRARY
DIM TextAttr(1)
TextAttr(0)=SADD("topaz.font"+CHR$(0))
TextAttr(1)=8*65536&
topaz8=OpenFont(VARPTR(TextAttr(0)))
IF topaz8=0 THEN Abort
CALL SetFont(WINDOW(8),topaz8)
PRINT :PRINT  "This is Topaz 8"
'Now change the height and open Topaz 9
TextAttr(1)=9*65536&
topaz9=OpenFont(VARPTR(TextAttr(0)))
IF topaz9=0 THEN Abort
CALL SetFont(WINDOW(8),topaz9)
PRINT :PRINT "This is Topaz 9"
CALL SetFont(WINDOW(8),topaz8)
PRINT :PRINT "Back to Topaz 8"
CALL CloseFont(WINDOW(8),topaz8)
CALL CloseFont(WINDOW(8),topaz9)
Abort:
LIBRARY CLOSE
```

We first format the TextAttr( ) array as discussed earlier, then call OpenFont( ) to open the font and get a font handle. The font handle is a unique identification number for that font. It works like the file-ID used with

320

BASIC's OPEN, PRINT#, and CLOSE statements. Just as you CLOSE #2 to close the file 2, you would

CALL CloseFont(WINDOW(8),*font.handle*)

to close a font identified by *font.handle*.

If the font handle returned by OpenFont is zero, then it was not possible to open the font. Although there is little reason to assume any problem when opening the system fonts, it's safest to check the font handle. If it is zero, the ball game is over, so you should exit the program before trying to use any functions that need this font handle.

Our font handles are TOPAZ8 and TOPAZ9. The exact value of the font handle is unimportant. You just save this value for later use. It is used with SetFont( ) to make this font the active one, and CloseFont( ) to cancel the font. You can open more than one font at time, and the font handle identifies which one to use.

Notice how the program reuses the same TextAttr( ) structure to open Topaz 9 simply by changing the text height in TextAttr(1). The next OpenFont( ) enables this font, and SetFont( ) uses this font for subsequent printing. As long as the font is open, you can switch between fonts just by using SetFont( )—you don't have to open and close the font every time you use it in a program.

The program ends by switching back to Topaz 8, Amiga BASIC's default 80-column font. However, this may not be the user's default font as selected with the Preferences tool. When you select a width of 60 with Preferences, Topaz 9 is used. To preserve the user's choice, we should find out which font was in effect before we changed it. The key is the AskFont( ) routine.

AskFont( ) fills a TextAttr structure with the settings for the current font. You can then use OpenFont( ) and SetFont( ) to switch to this font. When you're using the Topaz font anyway, and just want to change the font height, it can be doubly convenient. AskFont( ) will initialize the structure for you. You merely need to modify the settings you want.

Before our program runs, we'll save the current font height so that it can be restored later. Program 9-6 is how it would now read.

Program 9-6. AskFont

```
'AskFont
DEFLNG a-Z
CHDIR ":bmaps"
LIBRARY "graphics.library"
DECLARE FUNCTION OpenFont() LIBRARY
DIM TextAttr(1)

'Get default font settings
CALL AskFont(WINDOW(8),VARPTR(TextAttr(0)))

'Save the font height
```

```
SaveHeight=TextAttr(1)\65536&◄
TextAttr(1)=8*65536&◄
◄
'Open the font◄
topaz8=OpenFont(VARPTR(TextAttr(0)))◄
IF topaz8=0 THEN Abort◄
◄
'Use this font◄
CALL SetFont(WINDOW(8),topaz8)◄
PRINT :PRINT  "This is Topaz 8"◄
◄
'Now change the height and open Topaz 9◄
TextAttr(1)=9*65536&◄
topaz9=OpenFont(VARPTR(TextAttr(0)))◄
IF topaz9=0 THEN Abort◄
CALL SetFont(WINDOW(8),topaz9)◄
PRINT :PRINT "This is Topaz 9"◄
◄
'If default height is 8, reset◄
IF SaveHeight=8 THEN◄
   CALL SetFont(WINDOW(8),topaz8)◄
END IF◄
◄
'We're finished, so close the fonts◄
CALL CloseFont(WINDOW(8),topaz8)◄
CALL CloseFont(WINDOW(8),topaz9)◄
Abort:◄
LIBRARY CLOSE◄
END◄
```

By the way, there is a shortcut you can use to get the height of the current font. The following line PEEKs directly into the height parameter of the current window's RastPort. It would return 8 for the 80-column Topaz 8 font, or 9 for the 60-column Topaz 9 font:

height%=PEEKW(WINDOW(8)+58)

Structure Simulators

Although many times you can use arrays to simulate structures, there is one serious problem. Structures can be located anywhere in memory, but once they're initialized, they're expected to stay right where they are. Amiga BASIC can't comply; it needs to move arrays around in memory during program execution.

For more details on this, refer to Appendix C, "Memory Management." Briefly, you should know that arrays are stored in memory after all simple (nonarray) variables. BASIC doesn't know all the variables ahead of time, though; it adds them to its variable list as they're encountered in the program. When BASIC encounters a new simple variable, the arrays have to be pushed downward to make room for the new variable. If a program uses very long arrays, this can cause a noticeable delay. Program 9-7 illustrates this delay and shows how the array moves when new variables are encountered.

Program 9-7. ShowDelay

```
'Show delay
CLEAR ,25000
CLEAR ,100000&
DIM big%(30000&) '60K!
PRINT "Array is at";VARPTR(big%(0))
PRINT "Notice the delay..."
a=1:b=2:c=3:d=4:e=5
PRINT "when variables are encountered."
PRINT "Array is now at";VARPTR(big%(0))
CLEAR ,25000
END
```

If we initialize the simple variable before the DIM statement, the array doesn't have to be moved (Program 9-8).

Program 9-8. NoDelay

```
'No delay
CLEAR ,25000
CLEAR ,100000&
a=1:b=2:c=3:d=4:e=5
DIM big%(30000&) '60K!
PRINT "Array is at";VARPTR(big%(0))
PRINT "Notice there is now no delay..."
a=1:b=2:c=3:d=4:e=5
PRINT "when variables are encountered."
PRINT "Array is now at";VARPTR(big%(0))
CLEAR ,25000
END
```

To keep arrays stable, you would have to initialize every simple variable before any DIM statements. In practice, this is very difficult. Amiga BASIC, unlike many compiler languages, doesn't require you to declare simple variables, so programmers tend to invent variable names and use them when needed. You could sift through a finished program to identify and initialize every variable, but there has to be a better way.

Away with Arrays

Our solution is to discard the concept of using arrays to hold structures. When there is no problem with arrays moving around, you can use them, but the technique we'll discuss works well for a variety of structures. Instead of using arrays to store a memory block, we'll use the system's Exec library to allocate and deallocate memory.

Before using the following examples, make sure you've typed in and run ''ExecMaker'' (Program 9-21 at the end of this chapter) to create the EXEC.BMAP file.

Instead of dimensioning an array, we'll just allocate a block of memory

323

and POKE the values directly into it. This sounds messy, but it's really an efficient technique. The Exec AllocMem( ) function can reserve various-sized blocks of memory. You tell AllocMem( ) how much memory you need and what kind of memory you'd like, and it gives you the memory address of that block. If AllocMem( ) returns zero, though, it was unable to get a block of memory that size. Either the system is out of memory, or there is no single continuous chunk of memory of the size requested.

AllocMem( ) lets you choose what kind of memory you get by forming a flag value. The flag value is the sum of the bit values for the desired combination of memory types. Usually, you'll just want to get a chunk of memory and don't care what you get. For this, use a value of zero. Here is a list of the symbolic names and values used with AllocMem( ) to choose other kinds of memory:

MEMF_PUBLIC **1**   **Stable, nonrelocatable memory area**
MEMF_CHIP   **2**   **Chip memory, the lower 512K**
MEMF_FAST   **4**   **Fast memory, memory above the 512K boundary**
MEMF_CLEAR **65536** **Memory area is cleared**

Public memory (type 1) is assumed to be used by many different routines, so the system memory manager is not allowed to relocate it. During the execution of a BASIC program, this is not likely, but it's still safer to use this flag.

Chip memory is the lower 512K of system memory. The graphics chips can only access this area of memory. Memory beyond the 512K boundary doesn't exist as far as the graphics chips are concerned. Right now, few people have more than 512K, but the distinction between chip memory and expansion memory becomes important as more people upgrade their machines.

If you need a section of memory that will be directly addressed by the DMA (direct memory access) hardware, it must be chip memory. If a section of memory is being referenced by the coprocessing chips, the main processor is put on hold until the special chips are finished. If you don't want these delays, you need to use memory beyond the 512K region. If such memory exists, using the MEMF_FAST flag will get it for you.

So, to get a chunk of precleared, nonrelocatable chip memory for graphics processing, you'd use MEMF_PUBLIC plus MEMF_CHIP plus MEMF_CLEAR, or $1+2+65536=65539$. The call to allocate 500 bytes of this memory would be

myMem&=AllocMem&(500&,65539&)

You now have a pointer to your own private area of memory. This memory is outside BASIC's own memory, so it doesn't steal anything from BASIC's memory space. Hoewever, since BASIC doesn't know about this memory, it's up to you to release it when you are done with it. Otherwise, it is never freed up, and only a reboot can recover the lost fragment. To liberate the memory, use the FreeMem( ) function:

CALL FreeMem&(myMem&,500&)

Program 9-9 shows how you could use AllocMem( ) as a substitute for an array.

Program 9-9. AllocMem

```
'AllocMem◄
DEFLNG a-Z◄
◄
   CHDIR ":BMAPS"◄
   LIBRARY "graphics.library"◄
   LIBRARY "exec.library"◄
   DECLARE FUNCTION AllocMem() LIBRARY◄
   DECLARE FUNCTION OpenFont() LIBRARY◄
   ◄
TextAttr=AllocMem(8&,65539&) 'get 8 bytes◄
'Poke in the font name◄
POKEL TextAttr,SADD("topaz.font"+CHR$(0))◄
'next field is four bytes later◄
POKEW TextAttr+4,8 'font height◄
handle=OpenFont(TextAttr)◄
IF handle=0 THEN END◄
CALL SetFont(WINDOW(8),handle)◄
PRINT :PRINT  "This is Topaz 8"◄
CALL CloseFont(handle)◄
CALL FreeMem(TextAttr,8&)◄
LIBRARY CLOSE◄
END◄
```

As you can see, we have to use POKE to change this memory. The first four bytes of the TextAttr structure hold a long integer value, the address of the font name. Next come two bytes holding a word value containing the font height. We use POKEL to store a long integer value, and POKEW to store a word (integer). If you want to change a single byte, you could use POKE.

The complementary functions to read the memory are PEEKL(*address*) to get a long integer value from four bytes of memory, PEEKW(*address*) to fetch a word (integer), and PEEK(*address*) to get a byte.

It's important to note that you can use PEEKW and PEEKL only to read an even memory address. This means that all nonbyte fields must be *word-aligned*. This is for the sake of the 68000 processor, which has the same requirements. Strictly speaking, you don't have to align a long integer value on a four-byte boundary, but the memory address must be an even value. If you are creating a structure which contains an odd number of bytes followed by a word or long integer value, you must include a dummy byte value before the word or long integer to ensure that the word or long integer will be stored at an even address.

If you're just using one or two structure references, you can use arrays (if it doesn't matter if the structure moves around) or AllocMem to create your structure memory. But this can be cumbersome in a large program with lots of structures. Perhaps a future version of Amiga BASIC will include an equivalent to the structure statements in C.

The Structs Package

We couldn't wait for a revision of Amiga BASIC, so what follows is a package of subprograms that elegantly simulate C structures. They work somewhat like the machine language macros. First, type in the programs "StructsHeader" and "StructsTail," Programs 9-18 and 9-19, at the end of this chapter. You must include the statements in StructsHeader at the beginning of your program, and merge StructsTail at the end of your program. StructsHeader is a reminder to use the Exec library, and it dimensions a global array used by the Structs package:

```
'Structure Header◄
'STRUCTS.HEAD◄
'DEFLNG a-Z 'optional◄
◄
DECLARE FUNCTION AllocMem&() LIBRARY◄
◄
   CHDIR ":BMAPS"◄
   LIBRARY "exec.library"◄
◄
'This DIM is REQUIRED◄
◄
DIM StructAddr&(32),StructValue&(32),StructSize&(32)◄
```

Using the Structs package, we can define the TextAttr structure:

```
STRUCT TextAttr
   STRPTR TextAttr.Name,SADD("topaz.font"+CHR$(0))
   WORD     TextAttr.Ysize,8
   BYTE     TextAttr.Style,0
   BYTE     TextAttr.Flags,0
ENDSTRUCT TextAttr,TextAttr.SizeOf
```

This is remarkably readable and similar to the C structure declaration. The machinations of the Structs package are too complex to get into, but what it does is simple. AllocMem() opens a block of memory to store the structure. The pseudo-keywords STRUCT, STPTR, LONG, WORD, BYTE, and END-STRUCT are actually subprogram calls. More conventionally, the program fragment could also be typed like this:

```
CALL STRUCT(TextAttr)
CALL STRPTR(TextAttr.Name,SADD("topaz.font"+CHR$(0)))
CALL WORD(TextAttr.Ysize,8)
CALL BYTE(TextAttr.Style,0)
CALL BYTE(TextAttr.Flags,0)
CALL ENDSTRUCT(TextAttr,TextAttr.SizeOf)
```

Obviously, the first example shows what's happening more clearly, a good argument for leaving off the CALL keyword. Similarly, the subprogram names are entered in uppercase to make the subprogram calls look like built-in commands.

These calls end up assigning values to the variables shown. Since BASIC allows you to use a period in a variable name, these variables even look like C structure references. The variables hold the addresses of each structure element, so you must use a long integer variable for these values. These examples assume you've used DEFLNG a–z in your program.

After declaring the above structure, you could use statements like

POKEL TextAttr.Name,SADD("ruby.font"+CHR$(0))

and

POKEW TextAttr.Ysize,12

to change structure elements. To read a structure element, use PEEK, PEEKW, or PEEKL:

Height=PEEKW(TextAttr.Ysize)

You should refer to your structure declaration to see which type of POKE or PEEK to use.

You must start a structure declaration with STRUCT followed by a variable name to hold the address of the first element of the structure (hence, the address of the structure itself). You'll get an error (triggered within the subprogram with the ERROR command) if you have already defined this structure.

Next, include the pseudo-keywords LONG, STRPTR (a synonym for LONG), WORD, or BYTE to declare various-sized fields. Each declaration must include a variable name to hold the address of the field, followed by the initialization value for the field. This lets you create and fill in a structure at the same time. If you don't know what value to use for an element, it's usually safe to use zero.

Wrap up your structure declaration with ENDSTRUCT, followed by the same variable name that was used with STRUCT, and a variable used to hold the size of the structure in bytes. The latter is used with the FREESTRUCT command to deallocate the structure from memory when your program ends or no longer needs the structure.

When you're finished with a program (or when your program ends), be sure to use FREESTRUCT to release the memory used by the structure, or this memory will never be freed. Although this is not a big problem with small memory blocks, subsequent program runs will continue to allocate memory, and you'll eventually run out. Besides, in a multitasking system which may be running other applications, failing to deallocate memory is impolite, to say the least. Follow FREESTRUCT with the variable name used with the STRUCT statement, containing the address of the structure, followed by the length of the structure, as set by the ENDSTRUCT command.

When a subroutine requires the address of a structure, use the variable name you initialized in the STRUCT statement. The best teacher is a well-commented, complete program. The TextAttr demo, listed after the discussion of the Diskfont library, uses the TextAttr structure to display text in the Topaz 8, Topaz 9, and the disk-based Ruby 12 font. The TextAttr structure is passed to the OpenFont( ) routine:

topaz8 = OpenFont(TextAttr)

The DiskFont Library

Why stick with just the Topaz font when there's a whole disk of fonts to use? These fonts are located in the *fonts* directory on the system disk. AmigaDOS reserves a special device name for the fonts directory called FONTS:. To see a list of all fonts, just enter FILES "FONTS:". Each entry is a subdirectory with the same name as one of the fonts. This subdirectory, in turn, contains entries named after the height of a font. For example, Ruby 12 is stored as a file named "12" in the Ruby subdirectory. Its complete file specification would be "FONTS:Ruby/12".

The only difference in opening a disk font is substituting OpenDisk-Font( ) for OpenFont( ). OpenDiskFont( ) uses the same TextAttr structure. Similarly, you use SetFont( ) to make this the active font, AskSoftStyle( ) and SetSoftStyle( ) to change the font styles, and Text( ) to display some text in the current font and style.

OpenDiskFont( ) is not part of the Graphics library, but rather part of the Diskfont library. You'd use LIBRARY "diskfont.library" to use the function within your program. Before running the following examples, be sure you have created the DISKFONT.BMAP file by running the program "DiskfontMaker," Program 9-22, at the end of this chapter.

Program 9-10. TextAttr

```
'TextAttr.Example◀
DEFLNG a-Z◀
◀
 DECLARE FUNCTION AskSoftStyle() LIBRARY◀
 DECLARE FUNCTION OpenFont() LIBRARY◀
 DECLARE FUNCTION OpenDiskFont() LIBRARY◀
 DECLARE FUNCTION AllocMem() LIBRARY◀
◀
   CHDIR ":BMAPS" 'look for libraries◀
   LIBRARY "graphics.library"◀
   LIBRARY "diskfont.library"◀
   LIBRARY "exec.library"◀
◀
 'This DIM is REQUIRED for structs package◀
 DIM StructAddr&(32),StructValue&(32),StructSize&(32)◀
```

```
'Test the structure calls with◄
'a Text Attribute structure:◄
◄
'Creates a static string:◄
fontname$="topaz.font"+CHR$(0)◄
fontname=SADD(fontname$)◄
◄
STRUCT TextAttr◄
   STRPTR TextAttr.Name,fontname◄
   WORD    TextAttr.Ysize,9◄
   BYTE    TextAttr.Style,0◄
   BYTE    TextAttr.Flags,0◄
ENDSTRUCT TextAttr,TextAttr.SizeOf◄
◄
topaz9=OpenFont(TextAttr)◄
IF topaz9=0 THEN PRINT "Can't open Topaz 9":GOTO Quit◄
'Change a structure element◄
POKEW TextAttr.Ysize,8◄
'POKE TextAttr.Style,1 'bold?◄
topaz8=OpenFont(TextAttr)◄
IF topaz8=0 THEN PRINT "Can't open Topaz 8":GOTO Quit◄
SetFont WINDOW(8),topaz8◄
PRINT "This is Topaz 8"◄
SetFont WINDOW(8),topaz9◄
PRINT "This is Topaz 9"◄
◄
'We'll re-use the same structure and◄
'try to open a disk-based font◄
POKEL TextAttr.Name,SADD("ruby.font"+CHR$(0))◄
POKEW TextAttr.Ysize,12◄
ruby12=OpenDiskFont(TextAttr)◄
SetFont WINDOW(8),ruby12◄
PRINT :PRINT "This is the RUBY 12-point font"◄
PRINT "AaBbCcDdEeFfGgHhIiJjKkLlMmNnOoPpQqRrSsTtUuVvWwXxYyZz"◄
SetFont WINDOW(8),topaz8◄
PRINT "Back to topaz 8..."◄
CloseFont topaz8◄
CloseFont topaz9◄
CloseFont ruby10◄
◄
Quit:◄
FREESTRUCT TextAttr&,TextAttr.SizeOf&◄
PRINT "Program terminated."◄
END◄
◄
'Structure simulators:◄
◄
SUB STRUCT (addr&) STATIC◄
SHARED StructIndex%◄
   IF addr&<>0 THEN ERROR 10 'duplicate definition◄
   StructIndex%=1◄
END SUB◄
◄
'Remembers parameters passed◄
'addr&=pointer to variable (VARPTR)◄
◄
```

```
SUB STORE (addr&,value&,size%) STATIC
SHARED StructIndex%
SHARED StructAddr&(),StructValue&(),StructSize&()
   IF addr&+size%=0 THEN ERROR 5 'Illegal function call
   IF StructIndex%=32 THEN ERROR 9 'Subscript out of range
'we save the pointer to the variable
'so that it can be filled in later
'serving as the pointer to a value
'Tricky!
   StructAddr&(StructIndex%)=addr&
'Save the value and size in bytes
   StructValue&(StructIndex%)=value&
   StructSize&(StructIndex%)=CLNG(size%)
'Point to next item
   StructIndex%=StructIndex%+1
END SUB

 SUB LONG (addr&,value&) STATIC
   STORE VARPTR(addr&),value&,4
 END SUB

 SUB STRPTR (addr&,value&) STATIC
   STORE VARPTR(addr&),value&,4
 END SUB

 SUB WORD (addr&,value%) STATIC
   STORE VARPTR(addr&),CLNG(value%),2
 END SUB

 SUB BYTE (addr&,value%) STATIC
   STORE VARPTR(addr&),CLNG(value%),1
 END SUB

 SUB ENDSTRUCT (StructName&,sizeof&) STATIC
SHARED StructIndex%
SHARED StructAddr&(),StructValue&(),StructSize&()
'Only one ENDSTRUCT per customer:
IF StructName&<>0 THEN ERROR 10 'duplicate definition
sizeof&=0
FOR i=1 TO StructIndex%-1
   sizeof&=sizeof&+StructSize&(i)
NEXT i
StructName&=AllocMem&(sizeof&,65536&)
IF StructName&=0 THEN ERROR 7 'not enough memory
StructAddr&(0)=StructName&
StructSize&(0)=sizeof&
count&=0
FOR i=1 TO StructIndex%-1
   ptrvar&=StructAddr&(i) 'point to variable to be changed
'sneakily POKE right into the variable
   POKEL ptrvar&,StructName&+count&
   MOVE StructValue&(i),StructName&+count&,StructSize&(i)
   count&=count&+StructSize&(i)
NEXT i
END SUB

 SUB MOVE (value&,addr&,sizeof&) STATIC
```

```
    IF sizeof&=1 THEN
       POKE addr&,CINT(value&) AND 255
    ELSEIF sizeof&=2 THEN
       POKEW addr&,CINT(value&)
    ELSEIF sizeof&=4 THEN
       POKEL addr&,value&
    ELSE
       ERROR 5 'illegal function
    END IF
 END SUB

 'Deallocate structure memory
 'just for consistency's sake
 '
 SUB FREESTRUCT (addr&,sizeof&) STATIC
    CALL FreeMem&(addr&,sizeof&)
 END SUB

 'Move null-terminated string at sadr&
 'into string

 SUB STRCOPY(source&,build$) STATIC
 c=-1:i=0:build$=""
 WHILE c<>0
    c=PEEK(source&+i)
    build$=build$+CHR$(c)
    i=i+1
 WEND
 END SUB
```

As you can see, using disk-based fonts is really quite easy. As we discussed above, you can open many fonts at the same time and use the font handles returned by OpenFont( ) and OpenDiskFont( ) to switch fonts by calling SetFont( ).

Looking for Fonts

It would be nice if your programs could get a list of all the available fonts. Otherwise, you have to examine the "FONTS:" directory to see what fonts are available. You could store these font names and heights in DATA statements, but then the program couldn't take advantage of any new fonts which may be added to the system in the future.

You may already suspect that there's yet another operating system routine to do the job—the Amiga's operating system is really quite thorough. The AvailFonts( ) routine creates a formatted section of memory, something like an array of structures, containing the font names, heights, styles, and flags for every font in the system.

You first need to create a memory buffer to hold the list built by AvailFonts( ). Again, you can't use an array to hold this list, since as you try to examine the array, it moves in memory, unless you declare all your simple variables ahead of time. As you assign the address of the array to a variable, the new variable assignment causes the array to move. It's like using latex gloves to get a better grip on a wet fish—the very tool makes the fish even slippier, and it will probably slide away.

Instead, we can use AllocMem( ), as discussed above. The list of available fonts is loaded into arrays containing the font names, heights, styles, and flags. When the array has captured the buffer, we use FreeMem( ) to release the buffer memory.

You can use a subroutine from Program 9-11 to see what fonts are available. After GOSUB GetFonts, the arrays font$( ) and height%( ) are filled with the font names and heights of all the disk-based fonts. The variable *numfonts* reflects the total number of fonts. Since arrays start at element 0, the last entry is actually at font$(numfonts−1).

We're into the operating system pretty deeply now, and a further discussion of using AvailFonts( ) is beyond the scope of this chapter. The *Amiga ROM Kernel Manual* devotes nearly seven pages to this subject. Rather than going into excruciating detail on using AvailFonts( ) along with OpenFont( ), OpenDiskFont( ), SetFont( ), and CloseFont( ), we present a demo (Program 9-11) that loads all the fonts into memory and lets you choose a font and font style from menus. It's an excellent demonstration of how to use system fonts and library calls in your own programs.

The MenuHandler portion of the program is designed to be easily detached for your own use. You can excerpt most of this program, then alter MenuHandler to use the menu numbers you set aside for your Fonts and Style menus.

Program 9-11. FontDemo

```
'Font Demo◄
DEFLNG a-Z◄
◄
DECLARE FUNCTION AskSoftStyle() LIBRARY◄
DECLARE FUNCTION OpenFont() LIBRARY◄
DECLARE FUNCTION OpenDiskFont() LIBRARY◄
DECLARE FUNCTION AllocMem() LIBRARY◄
◄
   CHDIR ":BMAPS"◄
   LIBRARY "graphics.library"◄
   LIBRARY "diskfont.library"◄
   LIBRARY "exec.library"◄
◄
'This DIM is REQUIRED for structs package◄
◄
DIM StructAddr&(32),StructValue&(32),StructSize&(32)◄
◄
'Main program starts here:◄
'Initialize font menus◄
MENU RESET◄
MENU 1,Ø,1,"Font Menu"◄
```

```
MENU 1,1,1,"Open Fonts  "◄
MENU 1,2,1,"Quit        "◄
MENU 1,3,1,"topaz 8     "◄
MENU 1,4,1,"topaz 9     "◄
'clear font names...◄
'FOR i=2 TO 17:MENU 1,i,0,"":NEXT◄
MENU 2,0,1," Styles"◄
MENU 2,1,2,"  Plain     "◄
MENU 2,2,1,"  Underline "◄
MENU 2,3,1,"  Bold      "◄
MENU 2,4,1,"  Italics   "◄
MENU 3,0,0,""◄
MENU 4,0,0,""◄
'◄
WINDOW 1," Font Demo",(0,0)-(320,100),31◄
◄
'Current font name and height◄
Current.Font$="topaz.font"◄
height%=8◄
◄
'Holds font handles, heights, and names of all fonts◄
DIM fontid(32),height%(32),font$(32)◄
◄
'Get system fonts◄
FetchFont "topaz.font",8,fontid(0)◄
FetchFont "topaz.font",9,fontid(1)◄
◄
'Initialize arrays for default fonts◄
height%(0)=8:height%(1)=9◄
font$(0)="topaz.font":font$(1)=font$(0)◄
whichfont=0:attr=0◄
numfonts=2◄
◄
'Create the text display◄
DIM tex$(3)◄
FOR i=1 TO 3◄
  FOR j=0 TO 31◄
    tex$(i)=tex$(i)+CHR$(i*32+j)◄
  NEXT j◄
NEXT i◄
◄
'Main loop◄
WHILE -1◄
  'Use current font/style◄
  SetFont WINDOW(8),fontid(whichfont)◄
  SetSoftStyle WINDOW(8),attr,255◄
  SetRast WINDOW(8),1◄
  COLOR 0,1:LOCATE 2◄
  PrintLine "Now using "+Current.Font$+STR$(height%)◄
  LOCATE 3◄
  FOR i=0 TO 3:PrintLine tex$(i):NEXT◄
  'Poll the menus◄
  MenuId=0◄
  WHILE MenuId=0◄
    MenuId=MENU(0):MenuItem=MENU(1)◄
  PRINT INKEY$;◄
```

```
  WEND◄
  ON MenuId GOSUB FontMenu,Styles◄
WEND 'end of main loop◄
◄
'The menu handler◄
FontMenu:◄
IF MenuItem=1 THEN◄
  'Open fonts◄
  IF NOT got THEN◄
    GOSUB GetFonts◄
  'fill menu with new font names◄
    IF numfonts>2 THEN◄
      got=-1◄
      MENU 1,1,0◄
      FOR i=0 TO numfonts-1◄
        f$=font$(i)◄
        f$=LEFT$(f$,LEN(f$)-5)◄
        f$=LEFT$(f$+STR$(height%(i))+SPACE$(12),12)◄
        MENU 1,i+3,1,f$◄
      NEXT i◄
    END IF◄
  END IF◄
ELSEIF MenuItem=2 THEN◄
    GOTO Quit◄
ELSE◄
  'A font is chosen◄
  whichfont=MenuItem-3◄
  Current.Font$=font$(whichfont)◄
  height%=height%(whichfont)◄
END IF◄
RETURN◄
    ◄
'Change current style◄
Styles:◄
IF MenuItem=1 THEN◄
  attr=0:FOR i=2 TO 4:MENU 2,i,1:NEXT◄
  MENU 2,1,2◄
ELSE◄
  attr=attr OR 2^(MenuItem-2)◄
  MENU 2,1,1◄
  MENU 2,MenuItem,2◄
END IF◄
RETURN◄
◄
Quit:◄
SetFont WINDOW(8),fontid(0)◄
SetSoftStyle WINDOW(8),0,0◄
MENU RESET◄
FOR i=0 TO numfonts-1◄
  CloseFont fontid(i)◄
NEXT◄
COLOR 1,0:CLS:LIST◄
END◄
◄
'Opens a ram or disk font◄
'fh is the font handle◄
    ◄
```

334

```
SUB FetchFont(fontname$,height%,fh) STATIC
TextAttr&(0)=SADD(fontname$+CHR$(0))
TextAttr&(1)=65536&*height%
IF fontname$="topaz.font" THEN
   fh=OpenFont(VARPTR(TextAttr&(0)))
ELSE
   fh=OpenDiskFont(VARPTR(TextAttr&(0)))
END IF
END SUB


'This subroutine builds a list
'of font names, font$() and heights,
'height%().  All fonts are loaded.
'
GetFonts:
MEMF.CLEAR=2^16 'clear memory block
AF.SIZE=2000 'size of fonts block
AllFonts=AllocMem(AF.SIZE,MEMF.CLEAR)
IF AllFonts=0 THEN ERROR 7 'not enough memory
'Build list of all fonts
AvailFonts AllFonts,AF.SIZE,2
entries%=PEEKW(AllFonts)
'Transfer names and heights to list
CLS:PRINT "Loading the fonts...":PRINT
FOR i=0 TO entries%-1
   entry=AllFonts+4+i*10
   fontname=PEEKL(entry)
   height=PEEKW(entry+4)
   STRCOPY fontname,font$
   IF font$<>font$(numfonts-1) OR height<>height%(numfonts-1) THEN
      font$(numfonts)=font$
      height%(numfonts)=height
'Remove next line for quiet operation
      PRINT "Found ";font$;height%(numfonts)
      FetchFont font$,height%(numfonts),fontid(numfonts)
      numfonts=numfonts+1
   END IF
NEXT i
FreeMem AllFonts,AF.SIZE
RETURN

'Move null-terminated string at sadr&
'into string

SUB STRCOPY(source&,build$) STATIC
c=-1:i=0:build$=""
WHILE c<>0
   c=PEEK(source&+i)
   IF c>0 THEN build$=build$+CHR$(c)
   i=i+1
WEND
END SUB

SUB PrintMsg(msg$) STATIC
   Text WINDOW(8),SADD(msg$),LEN(msg$)
```

```
END SUB◄
◄
 SUB PrintLine(msg$) STATIC◄
   PrintMsg msg$:PRINT◄
 END SUB◄
```

Table 9-2 summarizes the text functions you can CALL in the operating system.

Table 9-2. Text Functions Summary

In Graphics.library

AskFont(WINDOW(8),*TextAttr*)
AskSoftStyle(WINDOW(8))
SetFont(WINDOW(8),*font.handle*)
SetSoftStyle(WINDOW(8),*style,enable*)
Text(WINDOW(8),*string address,count*)
CloseFont(WINDOW(8))
OpenFont(*TextAttr*)

In Diskfont.library:

OpenDiskFont(*TextAttr*)
Availfonts(*buffer,bufsize,type*)

Simple Sprite Animation

Although Amiga BASIC contains numerous OBJECT commands for animating sprites and bobs, they have some drawbacks (see Chapter 4). There is a way, though, to directly access the eight hardware sprites without POKEing directly into the sprite registers in the graphics coprocessor.

Before you can use a hardware sprite, you must steal the sprite from the rest of the operating system. Again keeping in mind that the Amiga is a multitasking system, more than one program may want to use the limited resources of eight hardware sprites. To prevent ugly clashes (and crashes), all other programs are denied access to a hardware sprite while you're using it.

It's cleaner to use what are called *virtual sprites*, also known as *vsprites*, since the same mechanism is used for vsprites and blitter objects (bobs). The OBJECT commands, for instance, use vsprites instead of actual hardware sprites. It can be quite a bit faster to use hardware sprites, although there is no automatic movement: Your program would have to continuously change the sprite position in order to move it.

To request an actual hardware sprite, call GetSprite( ). GetSprite( ) is a function that returns the number of the sprite. As mentioned earlier, you need to use the DECLARE FUNCTION command at the top of your program before you can use a ROM library function, for example,

LIBRARY "graphics.library"
DECLARE FUNCTION GetSprite&( ) LIBRARY

You can ask for a particular sprite, or for any sprite that is not already tied up. The statement

spritenum = GetSprite&(Sprite&,2)

attempts to get sprite number 2 (incidentally, sprites are numbered from 0 to 7). To ask for any sprite, use −1. If no sprites are available, GetSprite( ) returns −1.

What's that reference to Sprite&, though? To use a sprite, you need to use a SimpleSprite structure. Here is the format of SimpleSprite, using the Structs notation:

STRUCT Sprite&,0
  LONG Sprite.SprDat&,0
  WORD Sprite.Height&,0
  WORD Sprite.X&,0
  WORD Sprite.Y&,0
  WORD Sprite.Num&,0
ENDSTRUCT Sprite&,Sprite.Sizeof&

Of course, if you use DEFLNG a–z, you don't need to use the & suffix. And you're free to substitute your own variable names for your sprite structure—what counts is the format. You don't need to initialize this structure, so all the elements can be set to zero.

To set up the sprite image, call ChangeSprite( ), whose format is

CALL ChangeSprite&(0,*Sprite&*,*Sprdata&*)

The first parameter should be zero, unless you want to invent your own Viewport (we won't get into that). The Sprite& parameter is the address of a SimpleSprite structure, as shown above. The Sprdata& parameter is the address of a buffer containing the sprite data. This is usually an array, but as we mentioned earlier, arrays move around in memory as new variables are encountered. Just when you've displayed your sprite, the array could move, displaying sheer garbage for your sprite image.

Defining the Sprite Shape

Instead, we'll use the structure mechanism to hold the sprite data buffer. There really is no structure for this image defined by the system, but you can use the following structure and just fill in the blanks with the data for your sprite.

STRUCT SprData&
  LONG PosCtl&,0
  WORD L1P0&,&HFFFF
  WORD L1P1&,0

```
    WORD L2P0&,&HFFFF
    WORD L2P1&,0
    WORD L3P0&,&HFFFF
    WORD L3P1&,0
    WORD L4P0&,&HFFFF
    WORD L4P1&,0
    WORD FIN0&,0
    WORD FIN1&,0
ENDSTRUCT SprData&,SprData.SizeOf&
```

The PosCtl& entry is used later to hold sprite attributes and the *x* and *y* positions of the sprite. You don't need to initialize this yourself, though, so we just chunk all three values into a single LONG quantity.

The important part of this structure is the sprite data, a list of words for each line of the sprite. For each row of the sprite definition, you have two words of data. The two words are superimposed on one another to define 16 four-color pixels, just as whole bit-planes of memory are superimposed to create a screen display.

Each line, then, consists of two planes of data, hence the variables L1P0, L1P1, and so on, for *line 1/plane 0, line 1/plane 1*. With two bit-planes, you have two bits for each pixel. The total number of combinations are 00, 01, 10, and 11, corresponding to color offsets of 0, 1, 2, and 3. Each sprite can therefore display a maximum of four colors.

To create these bytes, it helps to sketch out your sprite on graph paper, noting which colors to use. You can use up to 16 columns and 200 rows (more rows are possible, but only 200 are visible on the screen). Compose the two words for each line by setting bits in the first word that correspond to the first bit of the color, and by setting bits in the second word that correspond to the first bit of the second color.

For example, a single dot in the first column of the sprite is represented by bit 15, which has a value of 32768. For color 0, both bits would be clear, so the values for plane 0 and plane 1 would both be 0. For color 1, bit 15 of plane 0 would be 0, and bit 15 of plane 1 would be 1, so the values for plane 0 and plane 1 would be 0 and 32768. Similarly, for colors 2 and 3 (binary 10 and 11), you would use (32768,0) and (32768,32768).

The structure definition shown above is for use with a four-row sprite. If you need more lines, just add them to the structure, using new variable names. End the list with two zeros, as shown above.

You specify the height of the sprite by changing the Height value in the SimpleSprite structure:

POKEW Sprite.Height&,4

for a four-line sprite.

After you've initialized the SimpleSprite and sprite data structures, you can link them together with ChangeSprite:

CALL ChangeSprite&(0,Sprite&,SprData&)

Now you're ready to use MoveSprite( ) to change the sprite's position. This command moves the sprite to screen position (50,70):

CALL MoveSprite&(0,Sprite&,50,70)

The first value is always zero for our purposes. Next comes the address of a SimpleSprite structure, as defined above, followed by the x and y positions of the sprite. Sprite coordinates correspond to 320×200 resolution, so you can specify values from 0 to 319 for x and 0 to 199 for y.

This line moves the sprite diagonally down the screen:

FOR n=1 TO 120:CALL MoveSprite&(0,Sprite&,n,n):NEXT

When you're finished with the sprite, be sure to call FreeSprite( ) to release your exclusive access to it. If you don't do this, the sprite is locked out until you reboot the computer. This line would free up the sprite we've used:

CALL FreeSprite&(spritenum)

As shown below, be sure to use FREESTRUCT also to free up the SimpleSprite and sprite data structures:

FREESTRUCT Sprite&,Sprite.Sizeof&

Program 9-12 is a simple sprite animation demonstration. It creates a checkerboard sprite image and moves it diagonally across the screen.

Program 9-12. Sprite Demo

```
DEFLNG a-z◄
◄
DECLARE FUNCTION GetSprite() LIBRARY◄
DECLARE FUNCTION AllocMem() LIBRARY◄
◄
  CHDIR ":BMAPS" 'put all .bmap files here◄
◄
  LIBRARY "graphics.library"◄
  LIBRARY "exec.library"◄
◄
'used by Structs package◄
DIM StructAddr&(32),StructValue&(32),StructSize&(32)◄
◄
WINDOW 1,,,31◄
◄
Height=4◄
◄
STRUCT SprData◄
  LONG PosCtl,0&◄
  WORD L1P0,&HFFFF◄
  WORD L1P1,&HAAAA◄
  WORD L2P0,&HFFFF◄
  WORD L2P1,&HAAAA◄
  WORD L3P0,&HFFFF◄
```

```
   WORD L3P1,&HAAAA◄
   WORD L4P0,&HFFFF◄
   WORD L4P1,&HAAAA◄
   WORD FIN0,0◄
   WORD FIN1,0◄
 ENDSTRUCT SprData,SprData.SizeOf◄
◄
 'Simulate a Sprite structure◄
◄
 STRUCT Sprite◄
   LONG Sprite.Data,SprData◄
   WORD Sprite.Height,CINT(Height)◄
   WORD Sprite.X,0◄
   WORD Sprite.Y,0◄
   WORD Sprite.Num,0◄
 ENDSTRUCT Sprite,Sprite.SizeOf◄
◄
 'Get a free sprite◄
◄
 Got=GetSprite(Sprite,-1)◄
 IF Got=-1 THEN PRINT "No sprites available.":GOTO Quit◄
 CALL ChangeSprite(0,Sprite,SprData)◄
 FOR i=1 TO 200◄
   CALL MoveSprite(0,Sprite,i,i)◄
   FOR j=1 TO 50:NEXT j◄
 NEXT◄
◄
 CALL FreeSprite(Got)◄
 Quit:◄
 FREESTRUCT Sprite,Sprite.SizeOf◄
 FREESTRUCT Shape,Shape.SizeOf◄
 LIBRARY CLOSE◄
 END◄
◄
 'Structure simulators:◄
◄
 SUB STRUCT (addr&) STATIC◄
 SHARED StructIndex%◄
   IF addr&<>0 THEN ERROR 10 'duplicate definition◄
   StructIndex%=1◄
 END SUB◄
◄
 'Remembers parameters passed◄
 'addr&=pointer to variable (VARPTR)◄
◄
 SUB STORE (addr&,value&,size%) STATIC◄
 SHARED StructIndex%◄
 SHARED StructAddr&(),StructValue&(),StructSize&()◄
   IF addr&+size%=0 THEN ERROR 5 'Illegal function call◄
   IF StructIndex%=32 THEN ERROR 9 'Subscript out of range◄
 'we save the pointer to the variable◄
 'so that it can be filled in later◄
 'serving as the pointer to a value◄
 'Tricky!◄
   StructAddr&(StructIndex%)=addr&◄
 'Save the value and size in bytes◄
   StructValue&(StructIndex%)=value&◄
```

340

```
    StructSize&(StructIndex%)=CLNG(size%)
  'Point to next item
    StructIndex%=StructIndex%+1
  END SUB

  SUB LONG (addr&,value&) STATIC
    STORE VARPTR(addr&),value&,4
  END SUB

  SUB STRPTR (addr&,value&) STATIC
    STORE VARPTR(addr&),value&,4
  END SUB

  SUB WORD (addr&,value%) STATIC
    STORE VARPTR(addr&),CLNG(value%),2
  END SUB

  SUB BYTE (addr&,value%) STATIC
    STORE VARPTR(addr&),CLNG(value%),1
  END SUB

  SUB ENDSTRUCT (StructName&,sizeof&) STATIC
  SHARED StructIndex%
  SHARED StructAddr&(),StructValue&(),StructSize&()
  'Only one ENDSTRUCT per customer:
  IF StructName&<>0 THEN ERROR 10 'duplicate definition
  sizeof&=0
  FOR i=1 TO StructIndex%-1
    sizeof&=sizeof&+StructSize&(i)
  NEXT i
  StructName&=AllocMem&(sizeof&,65539&)
  IF StructName&=0 THEN ERROR 7 'not enough memory
  StructAddr&(0)=StructName&
  StructSize&(0)=sizeof&
  count&=0
  FOR i=1 TO StructIndex%-1
    ptrvar&=StructAddr&(i) 'point to variable to be changed
  'sneakily POKE right into the variable
    POKEL ptrvar&,StructName&+count&
    MOVE StructValue&(i),StructName&+count&,StructSize&(i)
    count&=count&+StructSize&(i)
  NEXT i
  END SUB

  SUB MOVE (value&,addr&,sizeof&) STATIC
      IF sizeof&=1 THEN
        POKE addr&,CINT(value&) AND 255
      ELSEIF sizeof&=2 THEN
        POKEW addr&,CINT(value&)
      ELSEIF sizeof&=4 THEN
        POKEL addr&,value&
      ELSE
        ERROR 5 'illegal function
      END IF
  END SUB

  'Deallocate structure memory
```

```
◄
 SUB FREESTRUCT (addr&,sizeof&) STATIC◄
   CALL FreeMem&(addr&,sizeof&)◄
 END SUB◄
    ◄
 'Move null-terminated string at sadr&◄
 'into string◄
◄
 SUB MAKESTR(source&,build$) STATIC◄
 c=-1:i=0:build$=""◄
 WHILE c<>0◄
   c=PEEK(source&+i)◄
   build$=build$+CHR$(c)◄
   i=i+1◄
 WEND◄
 END SUB◄
```

Table 9-3 is a summary of the sprite routines.

Table 9-3. Sprite Commands Summary

ChangeSprite(0,*SimpleSprite*,*newdata*)
FreeSprite(*which*)
MoveSprite(0,*SimpleSprite*,*x*,*y*)
SpGot=GetSprite(*which*)

The DOS Library

As we mentioned above, the most useful commands in the DOS library can't be used, simply because their names conflict with the Amiga BASIC keywords OPEN, CLOSE, READ, and WRITE. The only useful command is Execute( ), used to send AmigaDOS commands.

In order for Execute( ) to work, the BASIC program must have been run from an open CLI, not the Workbench, since Execute( ) uses this CLI to run the commands from the C: directory. To run Amiga BASIC from a CLI, first change the current directory to that of your BASIC work disk, with a statement like

1>**CD BasicWork:**

Now you can run Amiga BASIC by entering its filename:

1>**AmigaBASIC**

If you want to run Amiga BASIC simultaneously with the CLI, which would keep the CLI active, you can use

1>**RUN AmigaBASIC**

Having to run Amiga BASIC from a CLI is a small limitation, since it opens up vast potential for BASIC. Instead of mere batch files, you have the full power of Amiga BASIC at your fingertips. You can run any DOS command, even execute other batch files. This gives BASIC the power to start other multitasking programs and load machine language modules. You can even capture the values returned by a DOS function for later processing.

The following example program uses Execute( ) to build a string array containing the entries in a directory. Amiga BASIC's FILES command can only display a directory, but this program can read and process the directory as well. The program is similar to a program on the Extras disk called Library. You can include the GetDir subprogram in your own program. Just pass it the name of an array that has been previously dimensioned and the name of a variable to receive the number of directory entries.

Program 9-13. DirDemo

```
'DirDemo
'Build a disk directory
'This routine only works if Amiga BASIC
'was started from an open CLI

DEFLNG a-Z

   CHDIR ":BMAPS"
   LIBRARY "dos.library"

DIM a$(20)
CALL GetDir(a$(),items)

FOR i=0 TO items-1
   PRINT a$(i)
NEXT i

LIBRARY CLOSE
END


'Fills a string array with the
'filenames of the current directory

SUB GetDir( ln$(),count ) STATIC
   command$="list > ram:capture quick"
   CALL Execute(SADD(command$+CHR$(0)),0,0)
   OPEN "ram:capture" FOR INPUT AS #1
   count=0
   WHILE NOT EOF(1)
      LINE INPUT#1,ln$(count)
      count=count+1
   WEND
   CLOSE#1
   count=count-1 'ignore last line
   KILL "ram:capture"
END SUB
```

If this program isn't run from an open CLI, the system crashes, locking out the keyboard and freezing BASIC (as you might expect).

The Intuition Library

Amiga BASIC's built-in MENU and WINDOW commands, along with the programs in Chapter 7, have largely obviated the need to call routines in the powerful Intuition library. The Intuition library permits C or machine language programs to access the same features already built into BASIC: multiple windows and pull-down menus. Although Amiga BASIC contains no explicit BUTTON or DIALOG command (as found in Macintosh BASIC), Chapter 7 shows how to implement requesters with subprograms.

Nevertheless, there are some interesting Intuition calls to experiment with. It's worth your while to type in "IntuitionMaker," Program 9-20, at the end of this chapter to create the necessary Intuition.bmap file.

The most glamorous Intuition trick lets you create a custom cursor pointer to replace the system's arrow cursor. Maybe you've already done this with the Preferences tool, which contains an excellent cursor editor (Change Pointer). This changes the shape of the pointer for the entire session, though.

Intuition's SetPointer( ) routine lets you create a cursor that is associated with a particular window. When the user makes that window active, the arrow cursor changes into the custom cursor. This lets a single program use many different cursors, one for each window. You can use the cursor as a context cue. A program might have a writing window for text entry, a graphics window for graphics editing, and a music window for sound manipulation. When the user is in the writing window, the cursor could become a pencil; when in the graphics window, the cursor might be a paintbrush. You could use a musical note for the cursor in the music window.

SetPointer( ) uses a sprite data structure as discussed above for the cursor shape, since the cursor is a hardware sprite. If you use the following sprite structure:

```
STRUCT SprData&
    LONG CtlPos&,0
    WORD L1P0&,&HFFFF
    WORD L1P1&,0
    WORD L2P0&,&HFFFF
    WORD L2P1&,0
    WORD L3P0&,&HFFFF
    WORD L3P1&,0
    WORD L4P0&,&HFFFF
    WORD L4P1&,0
    WORD FIN0&,0
    WORD FIN1&,0
ENDSTRUCT SprData&,SprData.SizeOf&
```

then the call to SetPointer( ) would be

```
Height=4:Width=16:Xoffset=0:Yoffset=0
CALL SetPointer&(WINDOW(7),SprData&,Height,Width,Xoffset,Yoffset)
```

The WINDOW(7) function returns a pointer to the current window's Window structure. You don't need to initialize a Window structure—the WINDOW command has already done that for you. WINDOW(7) returns the address of the Window structure. SetPointer( ) uses this value to associate the cursor with a particular window.

The Height and Width values seem obvious enough—the sprite is four lines high and 16 bits wide. But if you use a smaller image, you can use a smaller Width value to ignore the empty space to the right of your image. Height should be the same as the height of your sprite, of course.

The Xoffset and Yoffset values are trickier. They are the relative offset of the sprite image from the actual position pointed to by the cursor. The hot spot of the cursor would be the tip of the arrow or the center of a crosshair. The Xoffset and Yoffset values let you reposition the hot spot. If you use (0,0) for Xoffset and Yoffset, the hot spot of the sprite is its upper left corner.

On the other hand, a value of $(-4,-4)$ places the hot spot at position (4,4) within the sprite image. The sprite is moved four (-4) pixels upward and four (-4) pixels to the left of the hot spot position. With an 8×8 cursor shape, this would place the hot spot in the center of the cursor.

Program 9-14 demonstrates how to set up your own cursor pointer. It defines an elegant crosshair, assuming that your pointer colors are at least similar to the default colors.

Program 9-14. SetPointer

```
'SetPointer() Demo
DEFLNG a-z

DECLARE FUNCTION AllocMem&() LIBRARY

   CHDIR ":BMAPS"
   LIBRARY "graphics.library"
   LIBRARY "intuition.library"
   LIBRARY "exec.library"

WINDOW 1,,,31

'This DIM is required by Structs package
DIM StructAddr&(32),StructValue&(32),StructSize&(32)

'Crosshair image
STRUCT SprData
  LONG PosCtL,0&
  WORD L1P0,&H1000
  WORD L1P1,&H2800
  WORD L2P0,&H1000
  WORD L2P1,&H2800
  WORD L3P0,&H1000
  WORD L3P1,&H6C00
  WORD L4P0,&HEE00
  WORD L4P1,&H0
```

```
      WORD L5P0,&H1000
      WORD L5P1,&H6C00
      WORD L6P0,&H1000
      WORD L6P1,&H2800
      WORD L7P0,&H1000
      WORD L7P1,&H2800
      WORD FIN0,&H0
      WORD FIN1,&H0
ENDSTRUCT SprData,SprData.SizeOf

'Change the pointer
SprWidth=8:SprHeight=7:Xoff=-4:Yoff=-3
CALL SetPointer(WINDOW(7),SprData,SprHeight,SprWidth,Xoff,Yoff)

'Wait for click
WHILE MOUSE(0)=0:WEND
'Restore normal cursor
CALL ClearPointer(WINDOW(7))
'Wait for button release
WHILE MOUSE(0)<>0:WEND
WINDOW CLOSE 1
'Free up resources
FREESTRUCT Sprite,Sprite.SizeOf
LIBRARY CLOSE
END

'Structure simulators:

SUB STRUCT (addr&) STATIC
SHARED StructIndex%
   IF addr&<>0 THEN ERROR 10 'duplicate definition
   StructIndex%=1
END SUB

'Remembers parameters passed
'addr&=pointer to variable (VARPTR)

SUB STORE (addr&,value&,size%) STATIC
SHARED StructIndex%
SHARED StructAddr&(),StructValue&(),StructSize&()
   IF addr&+size%=0 THEN ERROR 5 'Illegal function call
   IF StructIndex%=32 THEN ERROR 9 'Subscript out of range
'we save the pointer to the variable
'so that it can be filled in later
'serving as the pointer to a value
'Tricky!
   StructAddr&(StructIndex%)=addr&
'Save the value and size in bytes
   StructValue&(StructIndex%)=value&
   StructSize&(StructIndex%)=CLNG(size%)
'Point to next item
   StructIndex%=StructIndex%+1
END SUB

SUB LONG (addr&,value&) STATIC
   STORE VARPTR(addr&),value&,4
END SUB
```

```
  SUB STRPTR (addr&,value&) STATIC
    STORE VARPTR(addr&),value&,4
  END SUB

  SUB WORD (addr&,value%) STATIC
    STORE VARPTR(addr&),CLNG(value%),2
  END SUB

  SUB BYTE (addr&,value%) STATIC
    STORE VARPTR(addr&),CLNG(value%),1
  END SUB

  SUB ENDSTRUCT (StructName&,sizeof&) STATIC
  SHARED StructIndex%
  SHARED StructAddr&(),StructValue&(),StructSize&()
  'Only one ENDSTRUCT per customer:
  IF StructName&<>0 THEN ERROR 10 'duplicate definition
  sizeof&=0
  FOR i=1 TO StructIndex%-1
    sizeof&=sizeof&+StructSize&(i)
  NEXT i
  StructName&=AllocMem&(sizeof&,65536&)
  IF StructName&=0 THEN ERROR 7 'not enough memory
  StructAddr&(0)=StructName&
  StructSize&(0)=sizeof&
  count&=0
  FOR i=1 TO StructIndex%-1
    ptrvar&=StructAddr&(i) 'point to variable to be changed
  'sneakily POKE right into the variable
    POKEL ptrvar&,StructName&+count&
    MOVE StructValue&(i),StructName&+count&,StructSize&(i)
    count&=count&+StructSize&(i)
  NEXT i
  END SUB

  SUB MOVE (value&,addr&,sizeof&) STATIC
      IF sizeof&=1 THEN
        POKE addr&,CINT(value&) AND 255
      ELSEIF sizeof&=2 THEN
        POKEW addr&,CINT(value&)
      ELSEIF sizeof&=4 THEN
        POKEL addr&,value&
      ELSE
        ERROR 5 'illegal function
    END IF
  END SUB

  'Deallocate structure memory

  SUB FREESTRUCT (addr&,sizeof&) STATIC
    CALL FreeMem&(addr&,sizeof&)
  END SUB

  'Move null-terminated string at sadr&
  'into string
```

```
SUB MAKESTR(source&,build$) STATIC◄
c=-1:i=0:build$=""◄
WHILE c<>0◄
  c=PEEK(source&+i)◄
  build$=build$+CHR$(c)◄
  i=i+1◄
WEND◄
END SUB◄
```

Incidentally, the "MouseSketch" program in Chapter 10 bypasses the structure calls and uses AllocMem( ) to create a stable sprite image buffer. Examine the RePointer subroutine if you're curious.

Retitling Windows

Another interesting Intuition routine is SetWindowTitles( ), which lets you change the text displayed on a window's title bar without closing and reopening the window. If you try doing this with BASIC's WINDOW command, BASIC always redraws the entire window:

WINDOW 1,"Test",,31

SetWindowTitles( ) also lets you display text on the title bar of a custom screen, something not normally possible in BASIC. This isn't too useful, though, since a window generally covers the screen's title bar.

SetWindowTitles( ) uses the WINDOW(7) function to identify which window should be altered. Follow WINDOW(7) with a pointer to a null terminated string for the window, followed by a pointer to the screen title. If you want to change the window title without affecting the screen title or vice versa, use −1 for the field you'd like to preserve. The following example demonstrates:

Program 9-15. SetWindowTitles

```
◄
 'SetWindowTitles◄
 DEFLNG a-z◄
◄
   CHDIR ":BMAPS"◄
   LIBRARY "intuition.library"◄
◄
 WINDOW 1,"Click to change title",(0,0)-(617,186)◄
 ScreenTitle=-1 'Don't change the screen title◄
 WHILE a$<>"x"◄
  READ a$◄
  IF a$<>"x" THEN◄
    'Wait for click◄
    WHILE MOUSE(0)=0:WEND◄
    WHILE MOUSE(0)<>0:WEND◄
    SetWindowTitles WINDOW(7),SADD(a$+CHR$(0)),-1◄
  END IF◄
 WEND◄
```

```
      ◄
LIBRARY CLOSE◄
END◄
DATA This is a test of SetWindowTitles◄
DATA Edit Mode◄
DATA Display Mode◄
DATA Cursor Enabled◄
DATA Error on Save◄
DATA Finished◄
DATA x◄
```

Another handy call lets you set the mininum and maximum window sizes for a window. Normally, Amiga BASIC lets you specify only two values for window sizing: Windows can either be nonresizable, which limits them to a single, fixed size, or they can have a sizing gadget, which lets the user resize the window to any size or rectangular shape.

You may want to prevent the window from getting larger than a certain size, perhaps to prevent the window from overlapping an adjacent window or to conserve memory. You might also want to set a mininum window size to prevent the user from making a window too small to display certain information.

The Intuition library WindowLimits( ) call does the trick. Program 9-16 opens a window and limits its smallest size to (50,50) and the largest size to (200,100).

Program 9-16. WindowLimits

```
'WindowLimits◄
'Demonstrate WindowLimits◄
◄
   DEFLNG a-Z◄
   CHDIR ":BMAPS"◄
   LIBRARY "intuition.library"◄
◄
WINDOW 1,"Window Limits",(0,0)-(80,80),31◄
MinWidth=50 'mininum width◄
MinHeight=50 'mininum height◄
MaxWidth=200 'maximum height◄
MaxHeight=100 'maximum height◄
◄
CALL WindowLimits(WINDOW(7),MinWidth,MinHeight,MaxWidth,MaxHeigh
t)◄
◄
PRINT "New window limits are established."◄
LIBRARY CLOSE◄
END◄
```

Another BASIC limitation you can overcome with an Intuition routine is the one-way PALETTE statement. Although PALETTE lets you change a color register, there is no complementary function to read the current color values. However, Intuition again comes to the rescue. You can call the ViewPortAddress( )

function to fetch a pointer to the window's ViewPort (for the sake of this discussion, it doesn't matter what a ViewPort is). Within the ViewPort is a pointer to that screen's color table. Program 9-17 displays the RGB and PALETTE settings for the colors allowed in the current screen.

Program 9-17. ReadColors

```
'ReadColors◄
◄
   CHDIR ":BMAPS"◄
   LIBRARY "intuition.library"◄
   DECLARE FUNCTION ViewPortAddress&() LIBRARY◄
◄
 FOR ColorNum=Ø TO WINDOW(6)◄
   vpa&=ViewPortAddress&(WINDOW(7))◄
   ColorTable&=PEEKL(PEEKL(vpa&+4)+4)◄
   r=PEEK(ColorTable&+2*ColorNum)◄
   b.g=PEEK(ColorTable&+2*ColorNum+1)◄
   g=b.g\16◄
   b=b.g MOD 16◄
   COLOR ColorNum,-(ColorNum=Ø)◄
   PRINT◄
   PRINT "Color #";ColorNum;"R=";r;"G=";g;", B=";b◄
   PRINT "PALETTE";ColorNum;",";r/16;",";g/16;",";b/16◄
 NEXT ColorNum◄
 COLOR 1◄
 LIBRARY CLOSE◄
 END◄
```

Table 9-4 is a summary of the Intuition routines.

Table 9-4. Intuition Summary

SetPointer(WINDOW(7),*Sprite.Data,Height,Width,Xoffset,Yoffset*)
SetWindowTitles(WINDOW(7),*WindowTitle,ScreenTitle*)
vpa& = ViewPortAddres(WINDOW(7))
WindowLimits(WINDOW(7),*MinWidth,MinHeight,MaxWidth,MaxHeight*)

If you want to delve more deeply into the operating system, you can find additional structure declarations in the C header files listed in volume 2 of the *Amiga ROM Kernel Manual*. To take full advantage of the operating system, you may want to become at least familiar with C or machine language so that you can translate the techniques to BASIC.

Obviously, we've only sampled a few of the operating system routines in this chapter. It would take another book to explain every routine. But as the saying goes, "Give people a fish and you feed them for a day; teach them to fish and you feed them for life." We hope we've provided the proper tackle and bait, but it's up to you to catch that really big one.

Program 9-18. StructsHeader

```
'Structure Header◄
'STRUCTS.HEAD◄
'DEFLNG a-Z 'optional◄
◄
DECLARE FUNCTION AllocMem&() LIBRARY◄
◄
   CHDIR ":BMAPS"◄
   LIBRARY "exec.library"◄
◄
'This DIM is REQUIRED◄
◄
DIM StructAddr&(32),StructValue&(32),StructSize&(32)◄
```

Program 9-19. StructsTail

```
'STRUCTS.TAIL◄
'Structure simulators:◄
◄
SUB STRUCT (addr&) STATIC◄
SHARED StructIndex%◄
   IF addr&<>Ø THEN ERROR 1Ø 'duplicate definition◄
   StructIndex%=1◄
END SUB◄
◄
'Remembers parameters passed◄
'addr&=pointer to variable (VARPTR)◄
◄
SUB STORE (addr&,value&,size%) STATIC◄
SHARED StructIndex%◄
SHARED StructAddr&(),StructValue&(),StructSize&()◄
   IF addr&+size%=Ø THEN ERROR 5 'Illegal function call◄
   IF StructIndex%=32 THEN ERROR 9 'Subscript out of range◄
'we save the pointer to the variable◄
'so that it can be filled in later◄
'serving as the pointer to a value◄
'Tricky!◄
   StructAddr&(StructIndex%)=addr&◄
'Save the value and size in bytes◄
   StructValue&(StructIndex%)=value&◄
   StructSize&(StructIndex%)=CLNG(size%)◄
'Point to next item◄
   StructIndex%=StructIndex%+1◄
END SUB◄
◄
SUB LONG (addr&,value&) STATIC◄
   STORE VARPTR(addr&),value&,4◄
END SUB◄
◄
SUB STRPTR (addr&,value&) STATIC◄
   STORE VARPTR(addr&),value&,4◄
END SUB◄
◄
SUB WORD (addr&,value%) STATIC◄
```

```
      STORE VARPTR(addr&),CLNG(value%),2
END SUB

SUB BYTE (addr&,value%) STATIC
      STORE VARPTR(addr&),CLNG(value%),1
END SUB

SUB ENDSTRUCT (StructName&,sizeof&) STATIC
SHARED StructIndex%
SHARED StructAddr&(),StructValue&(),StructSize&()
'Only one ENDSTRUCT per customer:
IF StructName&<>0 THEN ERROR 10 'duplicate definition
sizeof&=0
FOR i=1 TO StructIndex%-1
   sizeof&=sizeof&+StructSize&(i)
NEXT i
'Change 65537& to 65539& if you need
'the structure to be in CHIP memory
StructName&=AllocMem&(sizeof&,65537&)
IF StructName&=0 THEN ERROR 7 'not enough memory
StructAddr&(0)=StructName&
StructSize&(0)=sizeof&
count&=0
FOR i=1 TO StructIndex%-1
   ptrvar&=StructAddr&(i) 'point to variable to be changed
'sneakily POKE right into the variable
   POKEL ptrvar&,StructName&+count&
   MOVE StructValue&(i),StructName&+count&,StructSize&(i)
   count&=count&+StructSize&(i)
NEXT i
END SUB

'Primitive for LONG, WORD, BYTE
SUB MOVE (value&,addr&,sizeof&) STATIC
    IF sizeof&=1 THEN
       POKE addr&,CINT(value&) AND 255
    ELSEIF sizeof&=2 THEN
       POKEW addr&,CINT(value&)
    ELSEIF sizeof&=4 THEN
       POKEL addr&,value&
    ELSE
       ERROR 5 'illegal function
    END IF
END SUB

'Deallocate structure memory

SUB FREESTRUCT (addr&,sizeof&) STATIC
   CALL FreeMem&(addr&,sizeof&)
END SUB

'Move null-terminated string at source&
'into string

SUB STRCOPY(source&,build$) STATIC
c=-1:i=0:build$=""
WHILE c<>0
```

```
      c=PEEK(source&+i)
      build$=build$+CHR$(c)
      i=i+1
   WEND
   END SUB
```

Program 9-20. IntuitionMaker

```
'IntuitionMaker
file$=":BMAPS/Intuition.bmap"
READ filesize,checksum
PRINT "Checking DATA statements...":PRINT
FOR i=1 TO filesize
   READ a$:a=VAL("&h"+a$)
   check=check+a
NEXT i
RESTORE IntuitionData
IF check<>checksum THEN PRINT "Checksum mismatch -- error in typ
ing.":END
PRINT "DATA ok, creating the file."
ON ERROR GOTO CreationError
OPEN file$ FOR OUTPUT AS #1
FOR i=1 TO filesize
   READ a$:a=VAL("&h"+a$)
   PRINT#1,CHR$(a);
NEXT i
CLOSE#1
PRINT "Finished."
END
CreationError:
PRINT "ERROR #";ERR:END

DATA 1145,102168
IntuitionData:
DATA 4F,70,65,6E,49,6E,74,75,69,74,69,6F,6E,00,FF,E2
DATA 00,49,6E,74,75,69,74,69,6F,6E,00,FF,DC,09,00,41
DATA 64,64,47,61,64,67,65,74,00,FF,D6,09,0A,01,00,43
DATA 6C,65,61,72,44,4D,52,65,71,75,65,73,74,00,FF,D0
DATA 09,00,43,6C,65,61,72,4D,65,6E,75,53,74,72,69,70
DATA 00,FF,CA,09,00,43,6C,65,61,72,50,6F,69,6E,74,65
DATA 72,00,FF,C4,09,00,43,6C,6F,73,65,53,63,72,65,65
DATA 6E,00,FF,BE,09,00,43,6C,6F,73,65,57,69,6E,64,6F
DATA 77,00,FF,B8,09,00,43,6C,6F,73,65,57,6F,72,6B,42
DATA 65,6E,63,68,00,FF,B2,00,43,75,72,72,65,6E,74,54
DATA 69,6D,65,00,FF,AC,09,0A,00,44,69,73,70,6C,61,79
DATA 41,6C,65,72,74,00,FF,A6,01,09,02,00,44,69,73,70
DATA 6C,61,79,42,65,65,70,00,FF,A0,09,00,44,6F,75,62
DATA 6C,65,43,6C,69,63,6B,00,FF,9A,01,02,03,04,00,44
DATA 72,61,77,42,6F,72,64,65,72,00,FF,94,09,0A,01,02
DATA 00,44,72,61,77,49,6D,61,67,65,00,FF,8E,09,0A,01
DATA 02,00,45,6E,64,52,65,71,75,65,73,74,00,FF,88,09
DATA 0A,00,47,65,74,44,65,66,50,72,65,66,73,00,FF,82
DATA 09,01,00,47,65,74,50,72,65,66,73,00,FF,7C,09,01
DATA 00,49,6E,69,74,52,65,71,75,65,73,74,00,FF
DATA 76,09,00,49,74,65,6D,41,64,64,72,65,73,73,00,FF
```

```
DATA 70,09,01,00,4D,6F,64,69,66,79,49,44,43,4D,50,00◄
DATA FF,6A,09,01,00,4D,6F,64,69,66,79,50,72,6F,70,00◄
DATA FF,64,09,0A,0B,01,02,03,04,05,00,4D,6F,76,65,53◄
DATA 63,72,65,65,6E,00,FF,5E,09,01,02,00,4D,6F,76,65◄
DATA 57,69,6E,64,6F,77,00,FF,58,09,01,02,00,4F,66,66◄
DATA 47,61,64,67,65,74,00,FF,52,09,0A,0B,00,4F,66,66◄
DATA 4D,65,6E,75,00,FF,4C,09,01,00,4F,6E,47,61,64,67◄
DATA 65,74,00,FF,46,09,0A,0B,00,4F,6E,4D,65,6E,75,00◄
DATA FF,40,09,01,00,4F,70,65,6E,53,63,72,65,65,6E,00◄
DATA FF,3A,09,00,4F,70,65,6E,57,69,6E,64,6F,77,00,FF◄
DATA 34,09,00,4F,70,65,6E,57,6F,72,6B,42,65,6E,63,68◄
DATA 00,FF,2E,00,50,72,69,6E,74,49,54,65,78,74,00,FF◄
DATA 28,09,0A,01,02,00,52,65,66,72,65,73,68,47,61,64◄
DATA 67,65,74,73,00,FF,22,09,0A,0B,00,52,65,6D,6F,76◄
DATA 65,47,61,64,67,65,74,00,FF,1C,09,0A,00,52,65,70◄
DATA 6F,72,74,4D,6F,75,73,65,00,FF,16,09,01,00,52,65◄
DATA 71,75,65,73,74,00,FF,10,09,0A,00,53,63,72,65,65◄
DATA 6E,54,6F,42,61,63,6B,00,FF,0A,09,00,53,63,72,65◄
DATA 65,6E,54,6F,46,72,6F,6E,74,00,FF,04,09,00,53,65◄
DATA 74,44,4D,52,65,71,75,65,73,74,00,FE,FE,09,0A,00◄
DATA 53,65,74,4D,65,6E,75,53,74,72,69,70,00,FE,F8,09◄
DATA 0A,00,53,65,74,50,6F,69,6E,74,65,72,00,FE,F2,09◄
DATA 0A,01,02,03,04,00,53,65,74,57,69,6E,64,6F,77,54◄
DATA 69,74,6C,65,73,00,FE,EC,09,0A,0B,00,53,68,6F,77◄
DATA 54,69,74,6C,65,00,FE,E6,09,01,00,53,69,7A,65,57◄
DATA 69,6E,64,6F,77,00,FE,E0,09,01,02,00,56,69,65,77◄
DATA 41,64,64,72,65,73,73,00,FE,DA,00,56,69,65,77,50◄
DATA 6F,72,74,41,64,64,72,65,73,73,00,FE,D4,09,00,57◄
DATA 69,6E,64,6F,77,54,6F,42,61,63,6B,00,FE,CE,09,00◄
DATA 57,69,6E,64,6F,77,54,6F,46,72,6F,6E,74,00,FE,C8◄
DATA 09,00,57,69,6E,64,6F,77,4C,69,6D,69,74,73,00,FE◄
DATA C2,09,01,02,00,53,65,74,50,72,65,66,73,00◄
DATA FE,BC,09,01,02,00,49,6E,74,75,69,54,65,78,74,4C◄
DATA 65,6E,67,74,68,00,FE,B6,09,00,57,42,65,6E,63,68◄
DATA 54,6F,42,61,63,6B,00,FE,B0,00,57,42,65,6E,63,68◄
DATA 54,6F,46,72,6F,6E,74,00,FE,AA,00,41,75,74,6F,52◄
DATA 65,71,75,65,73,74,00,FE,A4,09,0A,0B,0C,01,02,03◄
DATA 04,00,42,65,67,69,6E,52,65,66,72,65,73,68,00,FE◄
DATA 9E,09,00,42,75,69,6C,64,53,79,73,52,65,71,75,65◄
DATA 73,74,00,FE,98,09,0A,0B,0C,01,02,03,00,45,6E,64◄
DATA 52,65,66,72,65,73,68,00,FE,92,09,01,00,46,72,65◄
DATA 65,53,79,73,52,65,71,75,65,73,74,00,FE,8C,09,00◄
DATA 4D,61,6B,65,53,63,72,65,65,6E,00,FE,86,09,00,52◄
DATA 65,6D,61,6B,65,44,69,73,70,6C,61,79,00,FE,80,00◄
DATA 52,65,74,68,69,6E,6B,44,69,73,70,6C,61,79,00,FE◄
DATA 7A,00,41,6C,6C,6F,63,52,65,6D,65,6D,62,65,72,00◄
DATA FE,74,09,01,02,00,41,6C,6F,68,61,57,6F,72,6B,62◄
DATA 65,6E,63,68,00,FE,6E,09,00,46,72,65,65,52,65,6D◄
DATA 65,6D,62,65,72,00,FE,68,09,01,00,4C,6F,63,6B,49◄
DATA 42,61,73,65,00,FE,62,01,00,55,6E,6C,6F,63,6B,49◄
DATA 42,61,73,65,00,FE,5C,09,00◄
```

Program 9-21. ExecMaker

```
'ExecMaker
file$=":BMAPS/Exec.bmap"
READ filesize,checksum
PRINT "Checking DATA statements...":PRINT
FOR i=1 TO filesize
   READ a$:a=VAL("&h"+a$)
   check=check+a
NEXT i
RESTORE ExecData
IF check<>checksum THEN PRINT "Checksum mismatch -- error in typ
ing.":END
PRINT "DATA ok, creating the file."
ON ERROR GOTO CreationError
OPEN file$ FOR OUTPUT AS #1
FOR i=1 TO filesize
   READ a$:a=VAL("&h"+a$)
   PRINT#1,CHR$(a);
NEXT i
CLOSE#1
PRINT "Finished."
END
CreationError:
PRINT "ERROR #";ERR:END

DATA 1202,108180
ExecData:
DATA 53,75,70,65,72,76,69,73,6F,72,00,FF,E2,00,45,78
DATA 69,74,49,6E,74,72,00,FF,DC,00,53,63,68,65,64,75
DATA 6C,65,00,FF,D6,00,52,65,73,63,68,65,64,75,6C,65
DATA 00,FF,D0,00,53,77,69,74,63,68,00,FF,CA,00,44,69
DATA 73,70,61,74,63,68,00,FF,C4,00,45,78,63,65,70,74
DATA 69,6F,6E,00,FF,BE,00,49,6E,69,74,43,6F,64,65,00
DATA FF,B8,01,02,00,49,6E,69,74,53,74,72,75,63,74,00
DATA FF,B2,0A,0B,01,00,4D,61,6B,65,4C,69,62,72,61,72
DATA 79,00,FF,AC,09,0A,0B,01,02,00,4D,61,6B,65,46,75
DATA 6E,63,74,69,6F,6E,73,00,FF,A6,09,0A,0B,00,46,69
DATA 6E,64,52,65,73,69,64,65,6E,74,00,FF,A0,0A,00,49
DATA 6E,69,74,52,65,73,69,64,65,6E,74,00,FF,9A,0A,02
DATA 00,44,65,62,75,67,00,FF,8E,00,44,69,73,61,62,6C
DATA 65,00,FF,88,00,45,6E,61,62,6C,65,00,FF,82,00,46
DATA 6F,72,62,69,64,00,FF,7C,00,50,65,72,6D,69,74,00
DATA FF,76,00,53,65,74,53,52,00,FF,70,01,02,00,53,75
DATA 70,65,72,53,74,61,74,65,00,FF,6A,00,55,73,65,72
DATA 53,74,61,74,65,00,FF,64,01,00,53,65,74,49,6E,74
DATA 56,65,63,74,6F,72,00,FF,5E,01,0A,00,41,64,64,49
DATA 6E,74,53,65,72,76,65,72,00,FF,58,01,0A,00,52,65
DATA 6D,49,6E,74,53,65,72,76,65,72,00,FF,52,01,0A,00
DATA 43,61,75,73,65,00,FF,4C,0A,00,41,6C,6C,6F,63,61
DATA 74,65,00,FF,46,09,01,00,44,65,61,6C,6C,6F,63,61
DATA 74,65,00,FF,40,09,0A,01,00,41,6C,6C,6F,63,4D,65
DATA 6D,00,FF,3A,01,02,00,41,6C,6C,6F,63,41,62,73,00
DATA FF,34,01,0A,00,46,72,65,65,4D,65,6D,00,FF,2E,0A
DATA 01,00,41,76,61,69,6C,4D,65,6D,00,FF,28,02,00,41
DATA 6C,6C,6F,63,45,6E,74,72,79,00,FF,22,09,00,46,72
DATA 65,65,45,6E,74,72,79,00,FF,1C,09,00,49,6E,73,65
```

```
DATA 72,74,00,FF,16,09,0A,0B,00,41,64,64,48,65,61,64←
DATA 00,FF,10,09,0A,00,41,64,64,54,61,69,6C,00,FF,0A←
DATA 09,0A,00,52,65,6D,6F,76,65,00,FF,04,0A,00,52,65←
DATA 6D,48,65,61,64,00,FE,FE,09,00,52,65,6D,54,61,69←
DATA 6C,00,FE,F8,09,00,45,6E,71,75,65,75,65,00,FE,F2←
DATA 09,0A,00,46,69,6E,64,4E,61,6D,65,00,FE,EC,09,0A←
DATA 00,41,64,64,54,61,73,6B,00,FE,E6,0A,0B,0C,00,52←
DATA 65,6D,54,61,73,6B,00,FE,E0,0A,00,46,69,6E,64,54←
DATA 61,73,6B,00,FE,DA,0A,00,53,65,74,54,61,73,6B,50←
DATA 72,69,00,FE,D4,0A,01,00,53,65,74,53,69,67,6E,61←
DATA 6C,00,FE,CE,01,02,00,53,65,74,45,78,63,65,70,74←
DATA 00,FE,C8,01,02,00,57,61,69,74,00,FE,C2,01,00,53←
DATA 69,67,6E,61,6C,00,FE,BC,0A,01,00,41,6C,6C,6F,63←
DATA 53,69,67,6E,61,6C,00,FE,B6,01,00,46,72,65,65,53←
DATA 69,67,6E,61,6C,00,FE,B0,01,00,41,6C,6C,6F,63,54←
DATA 72,61,70,00,FE,AA,01,00,46,72,65,65,54,72,61,70←
DATA 00,FE,A4,01,00,41,64,64,50,6F,72,74,00,FE,9E,0A←
DATA 00,52,65,6D,50,6F,72,74,00,FE,98,0A,00,50,75,74←
DATA 4D,73,67,00,FE,92,09,0A,00,47,65,74,4D,73,67,00←
DATA FE,8C,09,00,52,65,70,6C,79,4D,73,67,00,FE,86,0A←
DATA 00,57,61,69,74,50,6F,72,74,00,FE,80,09,00,46,69←
DATA 6E,64,50,6F,72,74,00,FE,7A,0A,00,41,64,64,4C,69←
DATA 62,72,61,72,79,00,FE,74,0A,00,52,65,6D,4C,69,62←
DATA 72,61,72,79,00,FE,6E,0A,00,4F,6C,64,4F,70,65,6E←
DATA 4C,69,62,72,61,72,79,00,FE,68,0A,00,43,6C,6F,73←
DATA 65,4C,69,62,72,61,72,79,00,FE,62,0A,00,53,65,74←
DATA 46,75,6E,63,74,69,6F,6E,00,FE,5C,0A,09,01,00,53←
DATA 75,6D,4C,69,62,72,61,72,79,00,FE,56,0A,00,41,64←
DATA 64,44,65,76,69,63,65,00,FE,50,0A,00,52,65,6D,44←
DATA 65,76,69,63,65,00,FE,4A,0A,00,4F,70,65,6E,44,65←
DATA 76,69,63,65,00,FE,44,09,01,0A,02,00,43,6C,6F,73←
DATA 65,44,65,76,69,63,65,00,FE,3E,0A,00,44,6F,49,4F←
DATA 00,FE,38,0A,00,53,65,6E,64,49,4F,00,FE,32,0A,00←
DATA 43,68,65,63,6B,49,4F,00,FE,2C,0A,00,57,61,69,74←
DATA 49,4F,00,FE,26,0A,00,41,62,6F,72,74,49,4F,00,FE←
DATA 20,0A,00,41,64,64,52,65,73,6F,75,72,63,65,00,FE←
DATA 1A,0A,00,52,65,6D,52,65,73,6F,75,72,63,65,00,FE←
DATA 14,0A,00,4F,70,65,6E,52,65,73,6F,75,72,63,65,00←
DATA FE,0E,0A,01,00,52,61,77,49,4F,49,6E,69,74,00,FE←
DATA 08,00,52,61,77,4D,61,79,47,65,74,43,68,61,72,00←
DATA FE,02,00,52,61,77,50,75,74,43,68,61,72,00,FD,FC←
DATA 01,00,52,61,77,44,6F,46,6D,74,00,FD,F6,09,0A,0B←
DATA 0C,00,47,65,74,43,43,00,FD,F0,00,54,79,70,65,4F←
DATA 66,4D,65,6D,00,FD,EA,0A,00,50,72,6F,63,75,72,65←
DATA 00,FD,E4,09,0A,00,56,61,63,61,74,65,00,FD,DE,09←
DATA 00,4F,70,65,6E,4C,69,62,72,61,72,79,00,FD,D8,0A←
DATA 01,00←
```

Program 9-22. DiskFontMaker

```
'DiskfontMaker←
file$=":BMAPS/Diskfont.bmap"←
READ filesize,checksum←
PRINT "Checking DATA statements...":PRINT←
FOR i=1 TO filesize←
```

```
   READ a$:a=VAL("&h"+a$)◄
   check=check+a◄
NEXT i◄
RESTORE DiskFontData◄
IF check<>checksum THEN PRINT "Checksum mismatch -- error in typ
ing.":END◄
PRINT "DATA ok, creating the file."◄
ON ERROR GOTO CreationError◄
OPEN file$ FOR OUTPUT AS #1◄
FOR i=1 TO filesize◄
   READ a$:a=VAL("&h"+a$)◄
   PRINT#1,CHR$(a);◄
NEXT i◄
CLOSE#1◄
PRINT "Finished."◄
END◄
CreationError:◄
PRINT "ERROR #";ERR:END◄
◄
DATA 34,3196◄
DiskFontData:◄
DATA 4F,70,65,6E,44,69,73,6B,46,6F,6E,74,00,FF,E2,09◄
DATA 00,41,76,61,69,6C,46,6F,6E,74,73,00,FF,DC,09,01◄
DATA 02,00◄
```

10 Putting It All Together

10 Putting It All Together

If you've survived this far, you should have a well-rounded knowledge of intermediate to advanced Amiga BASIC programming. But you may feel that you've learned many pieces of the puzzle, yet still don't quite know how to fit all the pieces together to form a coherent picture.

One of the best ways to learn programming is to study someone else's programs. "MouseSketch," Program 10-1, is a much-enhanced version of the "TinySketch" program in Chapter 3. It was designed not only to be as powerful as possible, but also to be an invaluable learning tool. It makes extensive use of line labels and structured programming.

MouseSketch is divided into a number of modules. The advantage of modular programming is that you can write your program as if it were an outline. You can get a skeleton program up and running fairly fast, then add one routine at a time until you've developed a program of surprising depth and complexity.

Rather than filling the program with memory-consuming REMarks, we loaded the program into a word processor and inserted external comments throughout the file. Needless to say, you shouldn't type these comments when entering the program. The comments make excellent signposts and also let you chart the flow of MouseSketch without even looking at the actual code.

Using MouseSketch

MouseSketch is a surprisingly powerful drawing program, considering that it is written entirely in BASIC. It would take machine language or at least a compiler to get the same performance on many other machines we've used. Part of this is due to careful programming that minimizes the number of statements being executed at any one time, and part is due to the efficiency of Amiga BASIC coupled with the phenomenal speed of the system's graphics routines.

When you run MouseSketch, be sure that all the .BMAP files are in the BMAPS drawer on the current disk. The screen clears, then turns black. You see the message, *I'll be with you in a moment*. Finally, the screen clears and beeps, indicating that MouseSketch is ready.

Initially, MouseSketch behaves sluggishly, but it speeds up as you go along. The rule is that the first time a function is executed, there can be a significant delay. The next time you execute the same function, there is no delay. This is because some large arrays are moving in memory when new variables in the function routines are declared; see Appendix C, "Memory Management," for an explanation.

You can select a new drawing color by clicking in the color palette window at the top of the screen. The current color appears in the leftmost checkered box. If you click in this box, another window appears, letting you change the colors.

Click on the boxes labeled RED, GREEN, and BLUE to cycle between the 16 luminance values for each color component, and click on Use to keep this color change. If you change your mind, click on Cancel to restore the previous color.

The Picture Menu

There are three pull-down menus in MouseSketch: *Picture, Edit,* and *Tools*. The Picture menu contains the items New, Change Dir, Open, Save, Save As, and Quit. These choices do what you'd think they do—they let you erase the picture, change the current directory, load a previously saved picture, save a picture using the current name, save a picture under a new name, and exit the program. Be aware that opening and saving pictures can be quite slow. (A future revision of Amiga BASIC is expected to add BLOAD and BSAVE commands to help remedy this.) Don't remove the disk until you're sure the program is finished with it.

If you select New, you're given a chance to save your picture if you've made changes since the last time you saved it. Next, you confirm the erasure by selecting OK when asked, "Erase Picture?" If you selected New accidentally, click on Cancel.

You can use the Change Dir command to switch to a different directory. The current directory is the one referenced when you Open a picture and is the destination directory when you Save a picture. By default, MouseSketch uses the root directory. When the Change Directory requester appears, click in the text box to enter a new directory name, then click on either OK to change the directory or Cancel to abort.

When you select Open, an Open requester appears, prompting you to enter a filename in the text box. To proceed with the open, click OK; otherwise, click on Cancel to abort. If you haven't saved the current picture, though, you're first asked if you want to do so before proceeding with Open. It can take several minutes to open a picture, so the message *WORKING...* appears in the window title bar until the picture is loaded.

You can use Save to save the picture under the current filename. When you first run the program, the current filename is UNTITLED, just to remind you that you haven't entered a name. If you haven't entered a new filename, Save falls through to the Save As routine.

With Save As, you first enter a filename in the text box, then click on OK. Again, click on Cancel if you selected Save As by mistake.

When you select Quit, you first get a chance to save your picture, then the Quit requester appears, asking if you really want to exit the program. You can click on NO!, To BASIC, or To System. Use NO! to cancel the Quit. To BASIC exits back to the List window, and To System exits to the Workbench or CLI.

The Edit Menu

MouseSketch's Edit menu contains the entries Undo, Cut, Copy, Clear, Paste, PSET, PRESET, AND, OR, and XOR. This menu lets you cut or copy rectangular images of the screen into a memory clipboard. You can paste this image anywhere on the screen, and you can choose from various pasting styles.

The Undo option restores the last screen. When you draw something with one of the drawing tools, you can undo the last change made. The program makes this possible by saving the entire screen in a memory buffer before any drawing is performed. When you select Undo, the preserved screen is substituted for the current screen.

Use Cut to grab and erase a section of the screen. After selecting Cut, move the pointer to the upper left corner of the area you'd like to cut and hold down the mouse button. Drag the mouse to indicate the lower right corner of the section you want to cut. Then release the button.

You are now in paste mode, and you can move the section around the screen and paste it down by clicking the button. If you hold down the button while dragging the mouse, you can smear the section all over the screen. The previous drawing tool is canceled since you can't use any tools while in paste mode.

The PSET, PRESET, AND, OR, and XOR options let you choose how the section is pasted onto the background image. These directly correspond to the options used with PUT (see Chapter 3). PSET is the default mode, and it stamps down the image as is, replacing everything within its rectangle. PRESET stamps down a reversed-color image of the section. AND stamps down the image only where there are existing pixels. Use OR to blend the image with the background. XOR stamps down the image with "negative ink." The image becomes like a branding iron that determines which areas of the background will be reversed. All modes except PSET cause color distortion to varying degrees.

The Copy command in the Edit menu works like Cut, but doesn't erase the image picked up off the screen. It harmlessly copies the image to the clipboard and goes into paste mode to let you stamp down the image elsewhere.

You can use Clear to erase a section of the screen without affecting the contents of the clipboard. Clear works like Cut, except the image is not copied into the clipboard and paste mode is not activated.

You turn off Paste by selecting any drawing tool. To restore paste mode for the last shape you cut or copied, just select Paste again.

The Tools Menu

MouseSketch's Tools menu lets you select various drawing tools. Sketch connects all movements of the mouse and is ideal for freehand drawing. Hold down the button as you move the mouse to leave behind a trail of the current color.

Line lets you draw lines by clicking once at the starting point and dragging the mouse to the ending point. This tool calls an operating system routine to create the rubber-band effect of a shimmering, animated line (see Chapter 9). When you release the button, the line is stamped down.

Similarly, Oval and Rectangle let you drag out and preview ovals and rectangles.

If you select AutoFill, you toggle the Autofill flag. When AutoFill is off (unchecked), Oval and Rectangle draw hollow figures; otherwise, they draw solid figures.

Analyzing MouseSketch, Program 10-1

```
'MouseSketch ◄
```

• We need to reserve 120K because the arrays used to hold the Undo and Clipboard buffers together use more than 80K, and the program needs about 20K for itself.

```
CLEAR ,25000◄
CLEAR ,120000&◄
```

• Integer variables make a program slightly faster. If an integer BASIC compiler is ever released, we know this program will work with it.

```
DEFINT a-Z◄
```

• Next we open the operating system libraries used by MouseSketch. All the .BMAP files are expected to be in the BMAPS drawer on the current disk. The Graphics library is used to change the drawing mode so that we can rubber-band figures to preview them before they are stamped down; this also permits access to the flexible Flood( ) routine used for flood fills. The Exec library is used by the RePointer subroutine to allocate memory for a new pointer image. The Intuition library is really used only to get access to the window's ViewPort, which contains the definition of the color registers.

```
CHDIR ":BMAPS"◄
LIBRARY "graphics.library"◄
LIBRARY "exec.library"◄
LIBRARY "intuition.library"◄
```

• We now switch to the root directory to prevent inadvertent access to the BMAPS directory. The *dir$* variable is used by the Change Directory menu selection as the default current directory.

```
CHDIR ":":dir$=":"◄
```

• Some library commands are used as functions, so we need to declare them. See Chapter 9.

```
DECLARE FUNCTION AllocMem&() LIBRARY◄
DECLARE FUNCTION ViewPortAddress&() LIBRARY◄
```

• The work%( ) array is used by the Intuits package to flash a requester button (see Chapter 7 for an explanation of the Intuits routines).

```
DIM work%(1000)◄
```

• Similarly, we need to dimension the global arrays used to store the position of Intuits simulated gadgets.

```
'more than 20 gadgets is impractical◄
DIM x1(20),y1(20),x2(20),y2(20)◄
```

• We now define several variables and constants. ScrId (screen-ID) is used by the Intuits package to figure out which screen to use for the windows. Mouse-Sketch uses a custom screen with a screen-ID of 1. The variable *maxlen* holds the maximum length of text fields.

```
ScrId=1 'screen for windows◄
which=0 'which box is selected◄
BoxIndex=1 'How many gadgets◄
maxlen=15 'length of text fields◄
```

• The default filename for the picture.

```
pictname$="untitled"◄
```

• More constants. TRUE and FALSE are handy constants for Boolean tests. The Saved flag detects whether a change has been made to the picture since the last time it was saved. If the picture has changed, we ask whether the user wants to save the picture before erasing it or opening a new picture. CurrColor holds the pen color used by all the drawing commands; it changes when the user selects a new color.

```
TRUE=-1:FALSE=0◄
Saved=TRUE:CurrColor=1◄
```

• If the user has previously cut or copied an image into the clipboard, Pastemode is TRUE (−1), and PasteType specifies which option of PUT to use: PSET, PRESET, AND, OR, or XOR. The default PasteType is 1 for PSET.

```
PasteType=1:PasteMode=0◄
```

• The variables *sx, sy, ex,* and *ey* hold the starting and ending positions of mouse selections.

```
sx=0:sy=0:ex=0:ey=0◄
```

• The current drawing tool is represented by ToolNum and selects which tool (Sketch, Line, Rectangle, etc.) is being used. NumTools holds the total number of these tools. The rest of the variables are initialized to cut down on the delays caused by using the large arrays (see Appendix C).

```
ToolNum=0:NumTools=0:cx=0:cy=0◄
xr=0:yr=0:ratio#=0:MenuItem=0◄
answer=0:x=0:y=0◄
```

• The savscr% array holds the undo buffer.

```
DIM savscr%(20010)◄
```

• Next we open our custom screen and windows, then redefine the arrow pointer.

```
GOSUB Init.Screen◄
GOSUB RePointer◄
```

• Since initialization takes so long, we print a consoling message.

```
PRINT "I'll be with you in a moment..."◄
```

• Set up the menus.

```
GOSUB Define.Menus◄
```

• The CLIP array holds the clipboard. PUT and GET are used to copy screen images between the savscr% and clip% arrays and the screen.

```
DIM clip%(20010)◄
```

• Flood( ) is a Graphics library routine that needs a special memory buffer before it can work (see Chapter 9). The AREA commands are a shortcut to do the trick.

```
'This subterfuge permits flood fills◄
AREA (100,100):AREAFILL◄
```

• These subprograms are convenient ways to toggle between Inverse (COM-
PLEMENT) and Normal (JAM2) drawing modes. For more about SetDrMd( ),
see Chapter 9.

```
SUB Inverse STATIC◄
  CALL SetDrMd&(WINDOW(8),3)◄
END SUB◄
◄
SUB Normal STATIC◄
  CALL SetDrMd&(WINDOW(8),1)◄
END SUB◄
```

• Now that the initialization is finished, we beep to get the user's attention.

```
CLS:BEEP◄
```

• The main loop of MouseSketch is fairly short. First, it loops until a mouse
button has been pressed or a menu item selected. It then processes the button
click or menu item by calling either MouseHandler or MenuHandler. The routine also animates the previously cut or copied image when in PasteMode.
Note that MouseSketch checks for menu selections by polling the MENU(0)
function, not by event trapping. As discussed in Chapters 1 and 7, the BASIC
interrupts activated by event trapping can sometimes drastically slow down the
execution of an intensive program. For maximum speed, therefore,
MouseSketch polls MENU(0) and MOUSE(0) within a WHILE–WEND loop.

```
MainLoop:◄
WINDOW 3:WINDOW OUTPUT 1◄
WHILE TRUE◄
MenuId=0◄
```

• Do we need to animate the image from the clipboard? If so, stamp it down,
so the first PUT within the loop erases this previous image.

```
IF PasteMode THEN PUT (sx,sy),clip%◄
  WHILE MOUSE(0)=0 AND MenuId=0◄
    MenuId=MENU(0)◄
```

• In PasteMode, we use the default XOR option of PUT to animate the image
from the clipboard. We first erase the previous image, then redraw it at a new
position. See Chapter 3 for more information on animation with PUT and GET.

```
    IF PasteMode THEN◄
      PUT (sx,sy),clip%:sx=MOUSE(1):sy=MOUSE(2)◄
      PUT (sx,sy),clip%◄
    END IF◄
  WEND◄
  IF PasteMode THEN PUT (sx,sy),clip%◄
  IF MenuId<>0 THEN GOSUB MenuHandler:GOTO MainLoop◄
  sx=MOUSE(1):sy=MOUSE(2)◄
```

367

• Before changing the screen, save it first in the Undo buffer.

```
GET (0,0)-(319,199),savscr%
```

• The mouse button has been clicked, so decide what to do.

```
GOSUB MouseHandler
WEND
```

• The mouse handler routine first checks to see whether the color palette was selected, then checks whether PasteMode is active. If neither is true, it jumps to the appropriate drawing tool subroutine.

```
MouseHandler:
```

• If the color bar is the active window, we calculate which color is selected until the user releases the mouse button. On the other hand, if the checkered color box is selected, we GOSUB SetPal to change that color's palette setting.

```
IF WINDOW(0)=3 THEN
WINDOW OUTPUT 3
   WHILE ABS(MOUSE(0))=1
      sx=MOUSE(1)
      IF sx>11 THEN
```

• The variable x.*scale#* is the ratio between the window width and the number of colors, defined in the Init.Screen subroutine.

```
         CurrColor=INT((sx-12)/x.scale#)
         LINE (1,1)-(8,7),CurrColor,bf
      ELSEIF sy>1 AND sy<8 THEN
      GOSUB SetPal
      END IF
   WEND
   WINDOW OUTPUT 1
   RETURN
END IF
```

• The PasteMode triggers one of the appropriate PUT actions. The PUT command copies the clipboard image onto the screen.

```
IF PasteMode THEN
   WHILE MOUSE(0)<>0
      ON PasteType GOSUB PPset,PPreset,PAnd,POr,PXor
   WEND
Saved=FALSE
END IF
```

• If ToolNum is nonzero, as it always is except in PasteMode, we choose one of the drawing tools, then clear the Saved flag, so MouseSketch knows the picture needs to be saved.

```
ON ToolNum GOSUB Sketch,Brush,AirBrush,DrwLine,Oval,Rectangle,Do
Paint◄
Saved=FALSE 'picture modified◄
RETURN◄
◄
PPset:◄
  PUT (MOUSE(1),MOUSE(2)),clip%,PSET◄
RETURN◄
PPreset:◄
  PUT (MOUSE(1),MOUSE(2)),clip%,PRESET◄
RETURN◄
PAnd:◄
  PUT (MOUSE(1),MOUSE(2)),clip%,AND◄
RETURN◄
POr:◄
  PUT (MOUSE(1),MOUSE(2)),clip%,OR◄
RETURN◄
PXor:◄
  PUT (MOUSE(1),MOUSE(2)),clip%◄
RETURN◄
```

• Sketch mode simply connects successive mouse positions. The loop is short, so sketching is very fast.

```
Sketch:◄
  PSET(sx,sy),CurrColor◄
  WHILE MOUSE(0)<>0◄
    LINE -(MOUSE(1),MOUSE(2)),CurrColor◄
  WEND◄
RETURN◄
```

• In brush mode, we just draw a solid rectangle at the pointer position as the user moves the mouse.

```
Brush:◄
  WHILE MOUSE(0)<>0◄
    LINE (MOUSE(1),MOUSE(2))-(MOUSE(1)+3,MOUSE(2)+3),CurrColor,bf◄
  WEND◄
RETURN◄
```

• The line mode uses the rubber-band technique to animate the line as it is previewed.

```
DrwLine:◄
```

• During the first pass through the loop, the ending position of the line is the same as the starting position.

```
ex=sx:ey=sy◄
```

- We rubber-band the line as long as the mouse button is held down.

```
WHILE MOUSE(0)<>0◄
```

- Inverse mode causes the line to complement itself against the background, as if it were drawn in negative ink. We use this effect to first erase the previous position of the line.

```
Inverse◄
  LINE (sx,sy)-(ex,ey)◄
```

- Now we draw another line at the new position.

```
cx=MOUSE(1):cy=MOUSE(2)◄
LINE (sx,sy)-(cx,cy)◄
```

- During the next pass through the loop, this line will be erased by the first LINE statement. In inverse mode, each line undoes the previous one.

```
ex=cx:ey=cy◄
WEND◄
```

- Now that the user has released the button, we stamp down the line in normal mode.

```
Normal◄
LINE (sx,sy)-(ex,ey),CurrColor◄
RETURN◄
```

- The airbrush command simply plots pixels at random distances from the pointer position as long as the mouse button is held down. The mouse's rate of movement affects how much paint is sprayed.

```
AirBrush:◄
WHILE MOUSE(0)<>0◄
  PSET (MOUSE(1)+4-9*RND(1),MOUSE(2)+4-9*RND(1)),CurrColor◄
WEND◄
RETURN◄
```

- The Oval routine seems complex, but it's really just like the DrwLine routine except that we're drawing and erasing circles. We just substitute the CALL to the Circloid subprogram for the LINE command. Circloid does the tricky calculations that determine the size and aspect ratio of the oval.

```
Oval:◄
  ex=sx:ey=sy◄
  WHILE MOUSE(0)<>0◄
  Inverse◄
  CALL Circloid(ex,ey)◄
  cx=MOUSE(1):cy=MOUSE(2)◄
  CALL Circloid(cx,cy)◄
```

```
      ex=cx:ey=cy
WEND
   Normal
   CALL Circloid(ex,ey)
```

• We check the AutoFill flag to see whether we should flood fill the circle's interior.

```
      IF AutoFill THEN
         PAINT (sx+xr/2,sy+yr/2),CurrColor
      END IF
   RETURN
```

• Draw a circle centered at *(x,y)*, using *sx, sy, xr,* and *yr* to compute the radius of the circle, which is drawn in the current color, CurrColor.

```
      SUB Circloid(x,y) STATIC
         SHARED sx,sy,CurrColor,xr,yr
         xr=ABS(sx-x)+1:yr=ABS(sy-y)+1:ratio#=yr/xr
         IF xr>yr THEN radius=xr ELSE radius=yr
         CIRCLE (sx+xr/2,sy+yr/2),radius,CurrColor,,,ratio#
      END SUB
```

• Since both the cut/copy functions as well as the Rectangle routine need to rubber-band an expandable box, we'll use the same subroutine for both. It expects that *sx* and *sy* are the beginning point, and it returns *ex* and *ey,* the opposite corner of the rectangle. The RubberBox routine animates the box just like the DrwLine routine animates its line. In fact, the only difference is adding the B option of LINE to draw rectangles instead of lines.

```
      RubberBox:
        ex=sx:ey=sy
        WHILE MOUSE(0)<>0
          Inverse
          LINE (sx,sy)-(ex,ey),,b
          cx=MOUSE(1):cy=MOUSE(2)
          LINE (sx,sy)-(cx,cy),,b
          ex=cx:ey=cy
        WEND
        LINE (sx,sy)-(ex,ey),,b
        Normal
      RETURN
```

• The Rectangle routine calls RubberBox to get the rectangle coordinates, then draws the rectangle. If AutoFill is selected, it draws a solid rectangle.

```
      Rectangle:
        GOSUB RubberBox
          IF AutoFill THEN
            LINE (sx,sy)-(ex,ey),CurrColor,bf
          ELSE
```

```
    LINE (sx,sy)-(ex,ey),CurrColor,b◄
  END IF◄
RETURN◄
```

• Paint mode uses the Graphics library flood fill routine to paint the interior of a closed figure.

```
DoPaint:◄
  COLOR CurrColor◄
  CALL Flood&(WINDOW(8),1,sx,sy)◄
  COLOR 1◄
  WHILE MOUSE(0)<>0:WEND◄
RETURN◄
```

• MenuHandler uses a series of linked ON-GOSUB statements. We first decide which menu to use. Then, within that menu's handler, the appropriate menu item is dispatched. (See the skeleton programs in Chapter 7.)

```
MenuHandler:◄
  MenuItem=MENU(1)◄
  ON MenuId GOSUB Project,Editmenu,Tools,Settings,Special◄
  RETURN◄
```

• The labels clearly identify the names of the menu items, which are self-explanatory, except for CD, which means change directory.

```
Project:◄
ON MenuItem GOSUB NewPict,CD,OpenPict,SavePic,SavePicAs,Quit◄
RETURN◄
```

• Before erasing the picture, we first check to see whether the user wants to save it (if it has been changed since the last Save). Then we doubly verify this by using GetRequest. GetRequest is the requester routine implemented by the Intuits package (see Chapter 7). The Intuits requester subroutine is normally called Request( ), but this conflicts with the Intuition library Request( ) function, so we've renamed the function to prevent any problems.

```
NewPict:◄
  GOSUB CheckSave◄
  CALL GetRequest("Erase Picture?","","NO","Yes",which)◄
  IF which=1 THEN RETURN◄
  WINDOW OUTPUT 1◄
  CLS:Saved=TRUE 'why save nothing?◄
RETURN◄
```

• Before opening a new picture (which destroys the current picture), we give the user a chance to save the masterpiece.

```
OpenPict:◄
   GOSUB CheckSave◄
```

• Another Intuits routine, OpenRequest, handles the entire process of getting a filename from a String requester.

```
CALL OpenRequest(pictname$)◄
```

• If Cancel was pressed or no name was entered, we exit.

```
IF which=3 OR pictname$="untitled" THEN RETURN◄
```

• The variable *filenum* closes the file in case of an error. If there is an error, the user gets a chance to repeat the offending command again (sometimes an error condition can be cleared by inserting a missing disk, defeating write-protection, etc.). If the user selects Cancel, though, the ErrorTrap routine exits to ExitIo.

```
filenum=1◄
ON ERROR GOTO ErrorTrap◄
```

• We call the Intuition library routine SetWindowTitles( ) to display a message in the command line. Since it takes a few minutes to load the picture, we don't want the user to remove the disk inadvertently.

```
CALL SetWindowTitles&(w7&,SADD("WORKING..."+CHR$(0)),-1)◄
```

• The SavePicAs routine has dumped the Undo buffer to disk. We load the array, unpacking the integer strings with CVI, and use PUT to change the screen.

```
OPEN pictname$ FOR INPUT AS #1 LEN=2048◄
FOR i=0 TO 20010◄
   savscr%(i)=CVI(INPUT$(2,1))◄
NEXT◄
CLOSE#1◄
PUT (0,0),savscr%,PSET◄
ExitIo:◄
ON ERROR GOTO 0◄
```

• Now we reset the window title bar.

```
CALL SetWindowTitles&(w7&,SADD("MouseSketch"+CHR$(0)),-1)◄
Saved=TRUE 'new picture doesn't need saving◄
RETURN◄
```

• The SavePic entry falls through to SavePicAs if no filename has been specified.

```
SavePic:◄
   IF pictname$>"" AND pictname$<>"untitled" THEN SkipNameRequest◄
```

• The SaveRequest( ) subprogram gets us the filename. We have to create the file and dump the array to disk, compacting it with MKI$. The OpenPict routine reloads the array and stamps it back on the screen with PUT.

```
SavePicAs:
  CALL SaveRequest(pictname$)
```

• Cancel the save if Cancel was pressed or no filename was entered.

```
    IF which=3 OR pictname$="untitled" THEN RETURN
SkipNameRequest:
  filenum=1
  ON ERROR GOTO ErrorTrap
```

• Display the message *WORKING...* until the save is finished.

```
    CALL SetWindowTitles&(w7&,SADD("WORKING..."+CHR$(0)),-1)
```

• Pick up the screen into the array, then save the array elements.

```
    GET (0,0)-(319,199),savscr%
    OPEN pictname$ FOR OUTPUT AS #1 LEN=2048
      FOR i=0 TO 20010
        PRINT#1,MKI$(savscr%(i));
      NEXT
    CLOSE#1
    Saved=TRUE
    ON ERROR GOTO 0
    CALL SetWindowTitles&(w7&,SADD("MouseSketch"+CHR$(0)),-1)
  RETURN
```

• To change the current directory, we use StringRequest to get the new directory name and assign it with CHDIR.

```
CD:
  CALL StringRequest("Change Directory","Enter new path","OK","Can
  cel",dir$)
  ON ERROR GOTO ErrorTrap
  filenum=0
  CHDIR dir$
  ON ERROR GOTO 0
RETURN
```

• We build a fancy three-button requester to see if the user really wants to quit. If so, we either exit to the Workbench/CLI or back to Amiga BASIC's List window.

```
  Quit:
```

• Has the picture been saved?

```
    GOSUB CheckSave
```

- The statement PEEKW(WINDOW(8)+58) gives us the height of the current font, letting us choose a wider window for the 60-column Topaz 9 font.

```
W=25*(8-2*(PEEKW(WINDOW(8)+58)=9))◄
WINDOW 2,"Quit",(Ø,Ø)-(W,5Ø),Ø,ScrId◄
```

- The next line sets the foreground color to white and fills the background with blue (assuming the default palette).

```
COLOR 1,4:CLS◄
PRINT "    Quit MouseSketch?":PRINT◄
```

- We want the text boxes to be drawn as blue text on a yellow background.

```
COLOR 4,3◄
```

- Display the text boxes for NO!, To System, and To BASIC.

```
BoxIndex=1:PRINT TAB(11);:CALL TxBox("NO!"):PRINT :PRINT◄
LOCATE ,2:CALL TxBox("To System")◄
PRINT TAB(15);:CALL TxBox("To BASIC")◄
```

- Wait for a box to be clicked.

```
CALL WaitBox(which)◄
```

- Flash the box and wait for the mouse button to be released.

```
CALL FlashRelease(which)◄
```

- Reset the normal colors and close the window.

```
COLOR 1,Ø◄
WINDOW CLOSE 2◄
```

- Unless NO! was selected, we reset the menus, close the custom screen, free up the sprite memory, and release the 120K of BASIC memory we requested. If which=1, then NO! was selected; otherwise, it's equal to 2 for To System or 3 for To BASIC.

```
IF which=1 THEN RETURN◄
MENU RESET◄
SCREEN CLOSE 1◄
```

- Free up the memory used by the custom pointer. We don't need to use ClearPointer( ), since SCREEN CLOSE 1 also closes all the windows.

```
CALL FreeMem&(Sprite&,40)◄
```

- Release the memory used by the operating system libraries.

```
LIBRARY CLOSE◄
```

- Be sure you've saved the MouseSketch program before running it and selecting To System.

```
IF which=2 THEN CLEAR ,25000:SYSTEM 'CAREFUL!◂
IF which=3 THEN CLEAR ,25000:LIST:END◂
STOP◂
```

- In the Edit menu, the user can undo the last drawing change, cut or copy a rectangular area of the screen, retrieve the previously copied image with Paste, or change the PasteType to select different pasting options (PSET, PRESET, AND, OR, XOR).

```
Editmenu:◂
  IF MenuItem>5 THEN◂
    MENU 2,5+PasteType,1◂
    PasteType=MenuItem-5◂
    MENU 2,5+PasteType,2◂
  RETURN◂
  END IF◂
  ON MenuItem GOSUB Undo,Cut,Copy,ClrIt,Paste◂
    RETURN◂
```

- Undo slaps the undo buffer back onto the screen.

```
Undo:◂
  PUT (0,0),savscr%,PSET◂
  RETURN◂
```

- Cut just does a copy, then clears the selected area.

```
Cut:◂
  GOSUB Copy:GOSUB ClrBox◂
  RETURN◂
```

- Copy GETs a rectangular section of the screen into the clip%( ) array.

```
Copy:◂
  WHILE MOUSE(0)=0:WEND◂
  sx=MOUSE(1):sy=MOUSE(2)◂
```

- Get the ending position of the box.

```
  GOSUB RubberBox◂
  GET (sx,sy)-(ex,ey),clip%◂
```

- Enter paste mode.

```
  GOSUB Paste◂
  RETURN◂
```

• The Clear option wipes out a rectangular area of the screen. We use RubberBox to get this area, and the BF option of LINE along with the background color to erase it. The lines which do the actual erasing are labeled so they can be reused by Cut.

```
ClrIt:◄
   WHILE MOUSE(Ø)=Ø:WEND◄
   sx=MOUSE(1):sy=MOUSE(2)◄
   GOSUB RubberBox◄
ClrBox:◄
   LINE (sx,sy)-(ex,ey),Ø,bf◄
   RETURN◄
```

• PasteMode is actually implemented by the main loop and MouseHandler. First, the current tool is disabled, since drawing and pasting are mutually exclusive. We only have to set the PasteMode flag to animate the buffer filled by Cut or Copy.

```
Paste:◄
MENU 3,ToolNum,1◄
PasteMode=TRUE:ToolNum=FALSE:RETURN◄
RETURN◄
```

• Unless the last menu item (Autofill) was selected, we use the menu item to change to a new drawing tool; otherwise, we just toggle the AutoFill mode, used by Circle and Rectangle to draw hollow or solid figures.

```
Tools:◄
   IF MenuItem=NumTools THEN◄
      AutoFill=1-AutoFill◄
      MENU 3,NumTools,AutoFill+1◄
   ELSE◄
      PasteMode=FALSE◄
      ToolNum=MenuItem◄
      FOR i=1 TO NumTools-1:MENU 3,i,1:NEXT◄
      MENU 3,ToolNum,2◄
   END IF◄
RETURN◄
```

• Anytime a subroutine threatens to erase the picture, it first calls CheckSave to see whether the picture has already been saved. If not, the user is given a chance to save the picture.

```
CheckSave:◄
   IF NOT Saved THEN◄
      msg1$="Picture is not saved."◄
      msg2$="Save Picture?"◄
      CALL GetRequest(msg1$,msg2$,"YES","NO",which)◄
      IF which=1 THEN GOSUB SavePicAs◄
   END IF◄
RETURN◄
```

• This ErrorTrap routine is a modified version of the ErrorTrap routine explained in Chapter 7.

```
'Custom error trap routine for MouseSketch
'Adapted from ErrorTrap 1.5
ErrorTrap:
 BEEP ' Get user's attention.
 IF ERR=53 THEN
  msg1$="FILE NOT FOUND."
 ELSEIF ERR=61 THEN
  msg1$="DISK FULL."
 ELSEIF ERR=64 THEN
  msg1$="BAD FILENAME."
 ELSEIF ERR=67 THEN
  msg1$="DIRECTORY FULL."
 ELSEIF ERR=68 THEN
  msg1$="DEVICE UNAVAILABLE."
 ELSEIF ERR=70 THEN
  msg1$="DISK WRITE-PROTECTED."
 ELSEIF ERR=74 THEN
  msg1$="UNKNOWN DISK VOLUME."
 ELSE
  msg1$="ERROR NUMBER"+STR$(ERR)
 END IF
 msg2$=" "
```

• Display the requester and get a choice.

```
CALL GetRequest(msg1$,msg2$,"Retry","CANCEL",choice)
IF filenum>0 THEN CLOSE filenum
IF choice=1 THEN RESUME ELSE RESUME ExitIo
STOP
```

• The Init.Screen routine sets up the custom screen, the drawing window, and the color palette window. The last two colors, used to highlight the menus, are changed to a better contrast.

```
Init.Screen:
'Initialize custom screen and
'window
  xsize=320:ysize=200
  SCREEN 1,xsize,ysize,5,1
  WINDOW 1,"MouseSketch",,16,1
  w7&=WINDOW(7) 'save window pointer
  PALETTE 0,0,0,0
  PALETTE 30,0,.5,.5
  PALETTE 31,.5,1,1
  CLS:GET (0,0)-(319,199),savscr%
```

- Draw the color palette window.

```
WINDOW 3,"",(Ø,8)-(311,8),16,1◄
LINE (1,1)-(8,7),CurrColor,bf◄
PATTERN &HAAAA◄
LINE (Ø,Ø)-(9,8),,b◄
PATTERN &HFFFF◄
x.scale#=311/33◄
FOR i=1 TO 32◄
   LINE (i*x.scale#+2,1)-((i+1)*x.scale#,7),i-1,bf◄
NEXT i◄
WINDOW OUTPUT 1◄
RETURN◄
```

- This subroutine is self-explanatory. It just defines all the menus and menu entries (see Chapter 7).

```
Define.Menus:◄
  MENU 1,Ø,1," Picture "◄
    MENU 1,1,1,"New        "◄
    MENU 1,2,1,"Change Dir"◄
    MENU 1,3,1,"Open       "◄
    MENU 1,4,1,"Save       "◄
    MENU 1,5,1,"Save As    "◄
    MENU 1,6,1,"Quit       "◄
  MENU 2,Ø,1," Edit "◄
    MENU 2,1,1,"Undo       "◄
    MENU 2,2,1,"Cut        "◄
    MENU 2,3,1,"Copy       "◄
    MENU 2,4,1,"Clear      "◄
    MENU 2,5,1,"Paste      "◄
    MENU 2,6,1,"      PSET"◄
    MENU 2,7,1,"    PRESET"◄
    MENU 2,8,1,"       AND"◄
    MENU 2,9,1,"        OR"◄
    MENU 2,1Ø,1,"       XOR"◄
    MENU 2,5+PasteType,2◄
  MENU 3,Ø,1," Tools "◄
    MENU 3,1,2,"   Sketch    "◄
    MENU 3,2,1,"   Brush     "◄
    MENU 3,3,1,"   Airbrush "◄
    MENU 3,4,1,"   Line      "◄
    MENU 3,5,1,"   Oval      "◄
    MENU 3,6,1,"   Rectangle"◄
    MENU 3,7,1,"   Paint     "◄
    MENU 3,8,1,"   AutoFill "◄
    ToolNum=1:NumTools=8◄
    MENU 4,Ø,Ø,""◄
  RETURN◄
```

The following routines are part of the Intuits package, covered extensively in Chapter 7. We've customized these routines to use different colors and changed the name of the Request subprogram to GetRequest, since the Intuition library already has reserved the name Request.

- Get a filename to open.

```
SUB OpenRequest(Filename$) STATIC◄
CALL StringRequest("Open Request","Open filename:","Open","Cance
l",Filename$)◄
END SUB◄
```

- Get a filename to save.

```
SUB SaveRequest(Filename$) STATIC◄
CALL StringRequest("Save Request","Save as:","Save","Cancel",Fil
ename$)◄
END SUB◄
```

- Ask for a string.

```
SUB StringRequest(title$,msg$,b1$,b2$,default$) STATIC◄
SHARED maxlen,ScrId,which,BoxIndex◄
BoxIndex=1:height=PEEKW(WINDOW(8)+58)◄
winwidth=maxlen*(8-2*(height=9))+40◄
WINDOW 2,title$,(0,0)-(winwidth,80),0,ScrId◄
COLOR 1,4:CLS◄
PRINT:PRINT "  ";msg$:PRINT◄
COLOR 1,0:LOCATE ,2:CALL TxBox(default$+SPACE$(1+maxlen-LEN(defa
ult$))) 'reserve space◄
Xpos=2:Ypos=CSRLIN 'for GetString◄
COLOR 4,3◄
PRINT :PRINT :LOCATE ,2:CALL TxBox(b1$)◄
PRINT TAB(maxlen+3-LEN(b2$));:CALL TxBox(b2$)◄
COLOR 1,0◄
which=0◄
WHILE which<=1◄
  CALL WaitBox(which) 'Get box #◄
  IF which=1 THEN 'if GetString◄
    CALL GetString(Xpos,Ypos,default$)◄
  END IF◄
WEND 'must be Open or Cancel◄
CALL FlashRelease(which) 'Flash the box◄
WINDOW CLOSE 2◄
IF which=BoxIndex-1 THEN Filename$=""◄
END SUB◄
```

- A custom version of the Request subprogram discussed in Chapter 7.

```
SUB GetRequest(msg1$,msg2$,b1$,b2$,which%) STATIC
SHARED BoxIndex,ScrId
SHARED x1(),y1(),x2(),y2()
BoxIndex=1:height=PEEKW(WINDOW(8)+58)
winwidth=20*(8-2*(height=9))+30
WINDOW 2,"System Request",(0,0)-(winwidth,50),0,ScrId
COLOR 1,4:CLS
PRINT :PRINT TAB(11-LEN(msg1$)/2);msg1$
PRINT TAB(11-LEN(msg2$)/2);msg2$:PRINT
COLOR 4,3
LOCATE ,2:TxBox b1$
PRINT TAB(20-LEN(b2$));:TxBox b2$:which%=0
CALL WaitBox(which%)
CALL FlashRelease(which%)
COLOR 1,0
WINDOW CLOSE 2
END SUB
```

- Flash the selected box and wait for the mouse button to be released.

```
SUB FlashRelease(which%) STATIC
SHARED x1(),y1(),x2(),y2(),work%()
SHARED RelVerify
GET (x1(which%),y1(which%))-(x2(which%),y2(which%)),work%
PUT (x1(which%),y1(which%)),work%,PRESET
ix=MOUSE(1):iy=MOUSE(2):RelVerify=-1
WHILE MOUSE(0)<>0
IF MOUSE(1)<>ix OR MOUSE(2)<>iy THEN RelVerify=0
WEND
PUT (x1(which%),y1(which%)),work%,PSET
END SUB
```

- Display and record a text box.

```
SUB TxBox(msg$) STATIC
SHARED x1(),y1(),x2(),y2()
SHARED BoxIndex
x1=WINDOW(4):y1=WINDOW(5)-10
ty=CSRLIN:tx=POS(0)
PRINT " ";msg$;" ";
x2=WINDOW(4):y2=y1+14
CALL Box(BoxIndex,x1,y1,x2,y2)
BoxIndex=BoxIndex+1
LOCATE ty,tx+1:PRINT msg$;SPC(2);
END SUB
```

- Primitive for TxBox.

```
SUB Box(i%,x1,y1,x2,y2) STATIC
SHARED x1(),y1(),x2(),y2()
IF x2<x1 THEN SWAP x1,x2
LINE (x1,y1)-(x2,y2),1-(WINDOW(6)>1),b
```

```
LINE (x1,y1)-(x2-1,y2-1),3,bf◄
x1(i%)=x1:y1(i%)=y1:x2(i%)=x2:y2(i%)=y2◄
END SUB◄
```

- Turns on or off a box. Not used by MouseSketch.

```
SUB CheckBox(i%,flag) STATIC◄
SHARED x1(),y1(),x2(),y2()◄
x1=x1(i%)+2:y1=y1(i%)+2◄
x2=x2(i%)-2:y2=y2(i%)-2◄
LINE (x1+3,y1+3)-(x2-3,y2-3),WINDOW(6)*-(flag<>Ø),bf◄
END SUB◄
```

- Use WhichBox until a button has been selected.

```
SUB WaitBox(which%) STATIC◄
which%=Ø◄
WHILE which%=Ø◄
   CALL WhichBox(which%)◄
WEND◄
EXIT SUB◄
RETURN◄
END SUB◄
```

- Check to see whether the mouse pointer is within one of the button boxes.

```
SUB WhichBox(which%) STATIC◄
SHARED x1(),y1(),x2(),y2(),BoxIndex◄
IF MOUSE(Ø)=Ø THEN EXIT SUB◄
x=MOUSE(1):y=MOUSE(2):i=1◄
WHILE i<BoxIndex AND NOT (x>x1(i) AND x<x2(i) AND y>y1(i) AND y<
y2(i))◄
   i=i+1◄
WEND◄
which%=i:IF i=BoxIndex THEN which%=Ø◄
END SUB◄
```

- Get an editable line of input, used in conjuction with TxBox in the StringRequest subprogram.

```
SUB GetString(Xpos,Ypos,default$) STATIC◄
SHARED maxlen,which%◄
answer$=default$◄
IF maxlen=Ø THEN maxlen=4Ø◄
'Cursor appears at end of default string◄
csr=LEN(default$)+1◄
k$=""◄
WHILE k$<>CHR$(13)◄
    COLOR 1,Ø:LOCATE Ypos,Xpos+1◄
    PRINT default$;" ";◄
    LOCATE Ypos,Xpos+csr◄
    COLOR Ø,WINDOW(6) 'cursor is max color◄
```

382

```
    PRINT MID$(default$+" ",csr,1)◄
    COLOR 1,0:k$=""◄
  WHILE k$="":k$=INKEY$◄
    CALL WhichBox(i)◄
    IF i>1 AND i<>which% THEN which%=i:k$=CHR$(13)◄
  WEND◄
  LOCATE Ypos,Xpos+1:PRINT default$;" ";◄
  k=ASC(k$)◄
  IF k>=32 AND k<127 THEN◄
    default$=LEFT$(default$,csr-1)+k$+MID$(default$,csr)◄
    default$=LEFT$(default$,maxlen)◄
    csr=csr-(csr<maxlen)◄
  END IF◄
  IF k=31 OR k=8 THEN csr=csr+(csr>1)◄
  IF k=127 OR k=8 THEN◄
    default$=LEFT$(default$,csr-1)+MID$(default$,csr+1)◄
  END IF◄
  IF k=30 THEN csr=csr-(csr<=LEN(default$))◄
WEND◄
END SUB◄
```

• The RePointer routine defines a custom mouse pointer for MouseSketch. For more information on this technique, refer to Chapter 9. Instead of using the overhead of the Structs package, we use AllocMem to reserve a stable chunk of memory to hold the sprite image used for the pointer.

```
RePointer:◄
Sprite&=AllocMem&(40&,65539&)◄
IF Sprite&=0 THEN RETURN◄
RESTORE SpriteData◄
FOR i=0 TO 17◄
  READ a:POKEW Sprite&+i*2,a◄
NEXT◄
```

• This links the sprite into the new pointer definition for this window.

```
CALL SetPointer&(WINDOW(7),Sprite&,7,8,-4,-3)◄
RETURN◄
```

• The first two entries must be zero, followed by the interleaved plane data for each line of the sprite, ending with (0,0).

```
SpriteData:◄
DATA 0,0◄
DATA &h1000,&h2800,&h1000,&h2800◄
DATA &h1000,&h6c00,&hee00,0◄
DATA &h1000,&h6c00,&h1000,&h2800◄
DATA &h1000,&h2800◄
DATA 0,0◄
```

383

• The SetPal subroutine is a tiny substitute for "Palette Panel," the palette editor described in Chapter 7. MouseSketch uses almost all the memory available to the system when running Amiga BASIC, so we just don't have the memory to include the full Palette Panel subprogram here. Even with half a million bytes of RAM, it still pays to conserve memory.

```
SetPal:◄
```

• First, we wait for the button to be released, since the user has clicked on the color selector.

```
WHILE MOUSE(Ø)<>Ø:WEND 'get release◄
```

• We open up our own window for this requester.

```
WINDOW 2,"Set Color",(Ø,Ø)-(16Ø,12Ø),Ø,1◄
```

• BoxIndex is always reset to one before creating your display with TxBox.

```
BoxIndex=1◄
```

• We get the ViewPort address, which lets us find the color table for the current screen. We can then PEEK this table to get the RGB values.

```
vpa&=ViewPortAddress&(WINDOW(7))◄
ColorTable&=PEEKL(PEEKL(vpa&+4)+4)◄
```

• We extract the RGB values and save them in case the user cancels the color change. The blue and green values are part of the same bytes, so we separate them into nybbles.

```
r=PEEK(ColorTable&+2*CurrColor):svr=r◄
b.g=PEEK(ColorTable&+2*CurrColor+1)◄
g=b.g\16:svg=g◄
b=b.g MOD 16:svb=b◄
```

• For each color, we display a label, save the cursor position for when we later increment the color value, and use TxBox to display the current color values and store the boxes in the corner arrays.

```
PRINT :PRINT " RED  : ";:rx=POS(Ø):ry=CSRLIN◄
TxBox RIGHT$("ØØ"+MID$(STR$(r),2),2)◄
PRINT :PRINT :PRINT " GREEN: ";:gx=POS(Ø):gy=CSRLIN◄
TxBox RIGHT$("ØØ"+MID$(STR$(g),2),2)◄
PRINT :PRINT :PRINT " BLUE : ";:bx=POS(Ø):by=CSRLIN◄
TxBox RIGHT$("ØØ"+MID$(STR$(b),2),2)◄
PRINT :PRINT :LOCATE ,2:TxBox "USE":TxBox "Cancel"◄
```

• The current color is displayed as a big fat rectangle.

```
LINE (Ø,8Ø)-(16Ø,12Ø),CurrColor,bf◄
LINE (Ø,8Ø)-(16Ø,12Ø),,b◄
```

- We continually check for buttons until either Use or Cancel is selected.

```
which=0◄
WHILE which<4◄
```

- Convert from RGB values to PALETTE fractional values.

```
    PALETTE CurrColor,r/16,g/16,b/16◄
```

- Wait for a box to be selected.

```
    CALL WaitBox(which)◄
```

- Flash the selected box.

```
    CALL FlashRelease(which)◄
```

- Act on the box.

```
    ON which GOSUB SetRed,SetGreen,SetBlue,Use,Cancel◄
WEND◄
```

- Close window and exit.

```
WINDOW CLOSE 2◄
RETURN◄
```

- SetRed, SetGreen, and SetBlue increment the color component and redisplay it within the box.

```
SetRed:◄
   r=r+1:IF r=16 THEN r=0◄
   LOCATE ry,rx+1:PRINT RIGHT$("00"+MID$(STR$(r),2),2)◄
RETURN◄
SetGreen:◄
   g=g+1:IF g=16 THEN g=0◄
   LOCATE gy,gx+1:PRINT RIGHT$("00"+MID$(STR$(g),2),2)◄
RETURN◄
SetBlue:◄
   b=b+1:IF b=16 THEN b=0◄
   LOCATE by,bx+1:PRINT RIGHT$("00"+MID$(STR$(b),2),2)◄
RETURN◄
```

- Use is a passive choice.

```
Use:◄
RETURN◄
```

- Cancel resets the palette back to the previous setting.

```
Cancel:◄
PALETTE CurrColor,svr/16,svg/16,svb/16◄
RETURN◄
```

Appendices

A Quick BASIC Reference

This appendix is a quick reference guide to the syntax of Amiga BASIC commands. Often, while programming, it's easy to remember what a certain command does, but just as easy to forget the number of parameters it requires, the order in which the parameters must be listed, and the allowable ranges for the parameters. Although the *Amiga BASIC* manual is an excellent source of information, its sheer bulk can make it clumsy to use for quick lookups.

Each entry in this section also refers you to a chapter or appendix that discusses the command, if applicable, and lists some related commands—helpful when you absent-mindedly forget that the opposite of CHR$ is ASC, not STR$, for example.

Another useful reference tool is the complete index found at the end of this book.

All commands in this appendix are listed in a format similar to that used by the *Amiga BASIC* manual:

CAPS   Reserved keywords are in capital letters.
italic   Parameters which you must supply are in italics.
[ ]   Items within square brackets are optional.
...   Ellipses indicate that the preceding item can be repeated any number of times in the parameter list.

ABS(*numeric expression*)

Returns the absolute value of *numeric expression*, converting negative numbers to positive.

Related commands: CDBL, CINT, CLNG, CSNG, DEFDBL, DEFINT, DEFLNG, DEFSNG, DEFSTR, FIX, INT, SGN

AREA [STEP] (*x,y*)

Defines a coordinate point *(x,y)* of a polygon to be drawn with AREAFILL. Ranges for *(x,y)* depend on the screen mode. See Chapter 2.

Related commands: AREAFILL, COLOR, LINE, PATTERN

AREAFILL [*mode*]

Fills a polygon defined by previous AREA statements; *mode* can be either 0 (fill with a pattern determined by PATTERN) or 1 (fill with the complement of the current color. If omitted, *mode* equals 0. See Chapter 2.

Related commands: AREA, COLOR, PATTERN

ASC(*string expression*)

Returns the ASCII code of the first character in *string expression*. See Appendix E, "The Amiga Character Set."

Related command: CHR$

ATN(*radians*)

Returns the arctangent of the numeric expression *radians*. The range for *radians* depends on the size of the circle.

Related commands: CIRCLE, COS, EXP, LOG, SIN, SQR, TAN

BEEP

Sounds a brief beep and flashes the screen. See Chapter 5.

Related commands: SOUND, WAVE

BREAK OFF

Disables event trapping which has been activated by ON BREAK GOSUB and BREAK ON. Allows the user to halt a program by selecting Stop from Amiga BASIC's Run menu or by pressing right Amiga–period, CTRL-C, or CTRL-F3. See Chapters 1 and 7.

Related commands: BREAK ON, BREAK STOP, ON BREAK GOSUB

BREAK ON

Enables event trapping of the user's attempt to halt a program, either by selecting Stop from Amiga BASIC's Run menu or by pressing right Amiga–period, CTRL-C, or CTRL-F3. Requires a previous ON BREAK GOSUB *LineLabel*. See Chapters 1 and 7.

Related commands: BREAK OFF, BREAK STOP, ON BREAK GOSUB

BREAK STOP

Suspends event trapping which has been activated by ON BREAK GOSUB and BREAK ON. The user's attempt to halt the program is still trapped, but ON

BREAK GOSUB is not acted upon until the next BREAK ON. See Chapters 1 and 7.

Related commands: BREAK OFF, BREAK ON, ON BREAK GOSUB

[CALL] *SubroutineName* [(*parameters...*)]

Transfers control to a subprogram set up with SUB, a machine language routine stored at a fixed memory address, or a system library routine. When CALLing a subprogram, *parameters* can be numeric or string constants, or variables which can pass and receive values to and from the subprogram. When CALLing an ML routine, *parameters* must be short or long integers conforming to C conventions. When CALLing library routines, *parameters* must also conform to C conventions. If the optional keyword CALL is omitted, *parameters* need not be enclosed in parentheses. The keyword is required after THEN or ELSE. See Chapters 7 and 9 and Appendix D, "Subprograms."

Related commands: DECLARE FUNCTION LIBRARY, LIBRARY, SADD, SHARED, SUB, VARPTR

CDBL(*numeric expression*)

Converts *numeric expression* to a double-precision number.

Related commands: ABS, CINT, CLNG, CSNG, DEFDBL, DEFINT, DEFLNG, DEFSNG, DEFSTR, FIX, INT

CHAIN [MERGE] *filename*[,*linenumber*][,ALL][,DELETE *LineLabel–LineLabel*]

Allows one program to run another program specified by *filename*. If MERGE is included, the second program is appended to the first program. If the numeric expression *linenumber* is included, execution begins at that line in the second program; otherwise, execution begins at the first line. ALL passes all nonlocal variables to the second program. DELETE removes all lines in the first program defined by *LineLabel–LineLabel*, which can be labels or line numbers.

Related commands: COMMON, MERGE, SHARED

CHDIR *directory name*

Changes the current disk directory to *directory name*. If *directory name* is a literal string, it must be enclosed in quotation marks. CHDIR corresponds to the CD command in AmigaDOS.

Related commands: FILES, KILL, NAME

CHR$(*numeric expression*)

Returns a character string corresponding to the ASCII value of *numeric expression*. See Appendix E, "The Amiga Character Set."

Related command: ASC

CINT(*numeric expression*)
Converts *numeric expression* to an integer by rounding off the fractional portion. The *numeric expression* must be in the range −32786 to 32767.

Related commands: ABS, CDBL, CLNG, CSNG, DEFDBL, DEFINT, DEFLNG, DEFSNG, DEFSTR, FIX, INT

CIRCLE [STEP](*x,y*),*radius*[,*color-ID*][,*start,end*][,*aspect ratio*]
Draws circles and ellipses: (*x,y*) is the centerpoint coordinate, *radius* is the radius in pixels, *color-ID* specifies the color number used to draw the figure, *start,end* are starting and ending angles in radians ranging from −2*pi to 2*pi, and *aspect ratio* is the fractional ratio of the width to the height of a pixel in the current screen mode. If STEP is included, coordinates (*x,y*) are relative offsets from the current pen position. See Chapter 2.

Related commands: ATN, COLOR, COS, LINE, PAINT, PALETTE, SIN

CLEAR [,*BASICdata*][,*stack*]
Initializes BASIC and reallocates memory for BASIC and the system stack. The numeric expression *BASICdata* sets aside memory for the program code, variables, strings, and file buffers. The numeric expression *stack* sets aside memory for the 68000 microprocessor's stack. See Appendix C, "Memory Management."

Related commands: FRE

CLNG(*numeric expression*)
Converts *numeric expression* into a long integer (from −2,147,483,648 to 2,147,483,647) and rounds off any fractional portion.

Related commands: ABS, CDBL, CINT, CSNG, DEFDBL, DEFINT, DEFLNG, DEFSNG, DEFSTR, FIX, INT

CLOSE [#*filenumber*][,#*filenumber*]...
Closes the file specified by #*filenumber* (# is optional). If followed by no filenumbers, CLOSE closes all open files. See Chapter 8.

Related commands: CLEAR, END, OPEN, RESET, STOP, SYSTEM

CLS
Clears the current output window and positions the pen at the upper left corner.

Related commands: WINDOW, WINDOW OUTPUT

COLLISION(*object-ID*)
Returns values stored in the collision queue which can be used to interpret collisions between objects and between objects and the screen borders. *Object-ID* can range from −1 to the highest object-ID number as defined by OBJECT.SHAPE. If *object-ID*=−1, COLLISION returns the window-ID in

which the collision occurred. If *object-ID*=0, COLLISION returns the object-ID of the object which triggered the collision. If *object-ID* is 1 or greater, COLLISION returns the object-ID of the object that collided with *object-ID*. If *object-ID* collided with a screen border, COLLISION returns either −1 (top), −2 (left), −3 (bottom), or −4 (right). All COLLISION calls except COLLISION(0) remove values from the 16-event collision queue. See Chapter 4.

Related commands: COLLISION OFF, COLLISION ON, COLLISION STOP, OBJECT.HIT, ON COLLISION GOSUB

COLLISION OFF
Disables event trapping for object collisions. No collisions are recorded in the collision queue until a subsequent COLLISION ON. See Chapter 4.

Related commands: COLLISION, COLLISION ON, COLLISION STOP, OBJECT.HIT, ON COLLISION GOSUB

COLLISION ON
Enables event trapping for object collisions. Requires a previous ON COLLISION GOSUB statement. See Chapter 4.

Related commands: COLLISION, COLLISION OFF, COLLISION STOP, OBJECT.HIT, ON COLLISION GOSUB

COLLISION STOP
Suspends event trapping for object collisions. Up to the next 16 collisions are recorded in the collision queue, but ON COLLISION GOSUB is not executed until a subsequent COLLISION ON.

Related commands: COLLISION, COLLISION OFF, COLLISION ON, OBJECT.HIT, ON COLLISION GOSUB

COLOR [*foreground*][,*background*]
Sets foreground color to the color-ID specified by *foreground*, and the background color to the color-ID specified by *background*. Both numeric expressions can range from 0 to 31, depending on the screen mode. See Chapter 2.

Related command: PALETTE

COMMON *variable list*
Declares in *variable list* which variables (and their values) should be passed to a CHAINed program. To pass all variables, omit COMMON and use the ALL option of CHAIN. Array variables in *variable list* must be followed by empty parentheses—ARRAY( ).

Related commands: CHAIN, MERGE

CONT
Continues a program that has been stopped by selecting Stop from Amiga BASIC's Run menu, or by pressing right Amiga–period, CTRL-C, or CTRL-F3, or

by executing a STOP statement. Also continues execution after single-stepping from the run menu.

Related command: STOP

COS(*radians*)
Returns the cosine value of the numeric expression *radians*.

Related commands: ATN, CIRCLE, EXP, SIN, SQR, TAN

CSNG(*numeric expression*)
Converts *numeric expression* into a single-precision number.

Related commands: ABS, CDBL, CINT, CLNG, DEFDBL, DEFINT, DEFLNG, DEFSNG, DEFSTR, FIX, INT

CSRLIN
Returns the approximate text line number of the pen as measured from the top of the current output window (always greater than or equal to 1). The calculation is based on the height and width of the character O in the font of the window.

Related commands: LOCATE, POS, PTAB

CVD(*8-byte string*)
Converts *8-byte string* read from a random file into a double-precision number. See Chapter 8.

Related commands: CVI, CVL, CVS, FIELD, LSET, MKD$, MKI$, MKL$, MKS$, RSET

CVI(*2-byte string*)
Converts *2-byte string* read from a random file into a short integer. See Chapter 8.

Related commands: CVD, CVL, CVS, FIELD, LSET, MKD$, MKI$, MKL$, MKS$, RSET

CVL(*4-byte string*)
Converts *4-byte string* read from a random file into a long integer. See Chapter 8.

Related commands: CVD, CVI, CVS, FIELD, LSET, MKD$, MKI$, MKL$, MKS$, RSET

CVS(*4-byte string*)
Converts *4-byte string* read from a random file into a single-precision number. See Chapter 8.

Related commands: CVD, CVI, CVL, FIELD, LSET, MKD$, MKI$, MKL$, MKS$, RSET

DATA *constant list*

Stores numeric and/or string constants accessed by a READ statement. Constants must be separated by commas, and the *constant list* can be as long as permitted by a BASIC line.

Related commands: READ, RESTORE

DATE$

Returns the current system date as a ten-character string in the form *05-09-1986*. Similar to the DATE command in AmigaDOS except that it cannot be used to assign a new date.

Related commands: TIME$, TIMER

DECLARE FUNCTION*id* [(*parameter list*)] LIBRARY

Searches all system library routines opened with LIBRARY for the machine language function specified by *id* in any expression within the program. If the function is found, *parameter list* is passed. See Chapter 9.

Related commands: CALL, LIBRARY.

DEF FN*name*[(*variable,...*)]=*function expression*

Defines a user-definable function. *Name* is any legal variable name (be sure to put no space between DEF FN and *name*). *Variable,...* is a list of variables, separated by commas, that accept the values passed when the function is called (the variable types must match the values). *Function expression* is the expression that performs the function (variable names in *function expression* are local to the function).

Related commands: CHAIN, SUB

DEFDBL *variable range*

Declares all variable names included in *variable range* as double-precision variables (type #). The *variable range* refers to the first letter of the variable names. Use a hyphen for all-inclusive ranges or a comma for exclusive lists (DEFDBL a–f or DEFDBL a,f).

Related commands: CDBL, CINT, CLNG, CSNG, DEFINT, DEFLNG, DEFSNG, DEFSTR, STR$, VAL

DEFINT *variable range*

Declares all variable names included in *variable range* as short integer variables (type %). The *variable range* refers to the first letter of the variable names. Use a hyphen for all-inclusive ranges or a comma for exclusive lists (DEFINT a–z or DEFINT a,z).

Related commands: CDBL, CINT, CLNG, CSNG, DEFDBL, DEFLNG, DEFSNG, DEFSTR, STR$, VAL

DEFLNG *variable range*

Declares all variable names included in *variable range* as long integer variables (type &). The *variable range* refers to the first letter of the variable names. Use a hyphen for all-inclusive ranges or a comma for exclusive lists (DEFLNG a–m or DEFLNG a,m).

Related commands: CDBL, CINT, CLNG, CSNG, DEFDBL, DEFINT, DEFSNG, DEFSTR, STR$, VAL

DEFSNG *variable range*

Declares all variable names included in *variable range* as single-precision variables (type !, the default). The *variable range* refers to the first letter of the variable names. Use a hyphen for all-inclusive ranges or a comma for exclusive lists (DEFSNG a–k or DEFSNG a,k).

Related commands: CDBL, CINT, CLNG, CSNG, DEFDBL, DEFINT, DEFLNG, DEFSTR, STR$, VAL

DEFSTR *variable range*

Declares all variable names included in *variable range* as string variables (type $). The *variable range* refers to the first letter of the variable names. Use a hyphen for all-inclusive ranges or a comma for exclusive lists (DEFSTR a–f or DEFSTR a,f).

Related commands: CDBL, CINT, CLNG, CSNG, DEFDBL, DEFINT, DEFLNG, DEFSNG, STR$, VAL

DELETE [*LineLabel start*]–[*LineLabel end*]

Deletes all program lines in the range specified by *LineLabel start* and *LineLabel end*, which can be alphanumeric labels or line numbers.

Related command: NEW

DIM [SHARED] *variable list*

Sets maximum values for dimensions of arrays in *variable list* and sets all elements to zero. If SHARED is included, the arrays are global to all subprograms as well.

Related commands: ERASE, OPTION BASE, SHARED

END

Stops the program and closes all files. END is optional; programs that are not continuous loops end of their own accord.

Related commands: STOP, SYSTEM

END SUB

Marks the end of a subprogram that was defined with a SUB statement. If END SUB is executed, it branches back to the statement immediately following the

CALL which passed control to the subprogram. See Appendix D, "Subprograms."

Related commands: CALL, DIM SHARED, EXIT SUB, SHARED, SUB

EOF(*filenumber*)
Returns −1 if the end of the sequential file specified by *filenumber* has been reached. When used with a random file specified by *filenumber*, EOF returns −1 if the last GET statement was unable to read an entire record. See Chapter 8.

Related commands: CLOSE, GET, INPUT$, INPUT#, LINE INPUT#, LOC, LOF, OPEN

ERASE *array list*
Erases the arrays specified in *array list*—the opposite of DIM. ERASEd arrays may be reDIMensioned.

Related commands: DIM, SHARED

ERL
Returns the line number on which the last error occurred. If the line which caused the error has no line number, ERL returns the number of the closest preceding numbered line. If ERL returns 65535, the error occurred in immediate mode.

Related commands: ERR, ERROR, ON ERROR GOTO, RESUME

ERR
Returns the Amiga BASIC error code of the last error. See the "ErrorTrap" routine in Chapter 7 and the *Amiga BASIC* manual.

Related commands: ERL, ERROR, ON ERROR GOTO, RESUME

ERROR (*error code*)
Triggers an Amiga BASIC error or defines new error numbers. *Error code* is an integer from 0 to 255; if it coincides with an existing error code, that error is generated when ERROR is executed. See the *Amiga BASIC* manual.

Related commands: ERL, ERR, ON ERROR GOTO, RESUME

EXIT SUB
Branches from a subprogram back to the statement immediately following the CALL which passed control to the subprogram. See Appendix D, "Subprograms."

Related commands: CALL, DIM SHARED, END SUB, SHARED, SUB

EXP(*numeric expression*)
Returns the base of natural logarithms (2.7182818284590) to the power of *numeric expression*, which must be no greater than 88 for single-precision numbers or 709 for double-precision numbers.

Related commands: ATN, COS, SIN, SQR, TAN

FIELD *#filenumber,field length* AS *string variable*...
Makes space for string variables in the random file buffer specified by *#filenumber*. The *field length* is the number of characters allocated for each field defined as *string variable*. Any number of *string variables* is allowed, but the sum of the *field lengths* must not exceed the record length specified in the OPEN statement (default=128). See Chapter 8.

Related commands: GET, LSET, MKD$, MKI$, MKL$, MKS$, OPEN, PUT, RSET

FILES [*directory name*]
Prints a directory listing of all files specified by *directory name*. If *directory name* is a literal string, it must be enclosed in quotation marks. If *directory name* is omitted, FILES defaults to the current directory. Similar to the DIR command in AmigaDOS. See Chapter 8.

Related commands: CHDIR, KILL, NAME

FIX(*numeric expression*)
Returns the truncated integer portion of *numeric expression*. Unlike INT, FIX does not round negative numbers to the next smaller number.

Related commands: ABS, CINT, INT, SGN

FOR *counter variable=start* TO *end* [STEP *stepsize*]
NEXT [*counter variable*][,*counter variable*]...
Performs the number of loops between FOR and NEXT as specified by *start*, *end*, and the optional STEP *stepsize*. Normally, the value of *start* must be less than *end*. If STEP is omitted, *stepsize* defaults to 1. *Stepsize* can be a negative number if the value of *end* is less than *start*. The *counter variable* specified by NEXT defines the end of the FOR loop with the matching *counter variable*. If *counter variable* is omitted from NEXT, the loop circles back to the most recent FOR. Loops can be nested indefinitely if their *counter variables* are different. See Chapter 1.

Related commands: WEND, WHILE

FRE(*area*)
Returns the number of bytes of free memory in the area specified by *area*. If *area* equals −1, FRE returns the amount of free memory in the system. If *area* equals −2, FRE returns the amount of unused stack space. If *area* is any other

number, FRE returns the amount of free memory in Amiga BASIC's data segment. See Appendix C, "Memory Management."

Related commands: CLEAR, ERASE

GET #*filenumber* [,*recordnumber*]

Reads the record specified by *recordnumber* from the random file specified by *filenumber* into a random file buffer. If *recordnumber* is omitted, the record after the last GET is read. *Filenumber* corresponds to the *filenumber* in the OPEN statement; *recordnumber* can range from 1 to 16,777,215. See Chapter 8.

Related commands: EOF, FIELD, GET (see alternative statement below), INPUT#, LINE INPUT#, LOC, LOF, OPEN, PUT

GET (*x1,y1*)–(*x2,y2*),*array%*[(*index*)]...

Copies a rectangular area of screen pixels defined by the coordinates (*x1,y1*)–(*x2,y2*) into *array%*, which can be a multidimensional array as specified by *index*. The minimum size of the integer array must be

$$(6+(y2-y1+1)*2*INT((x2-x1+16)/16)*depth)/2$$

where *depth* equals the screen depth in bit-planes (1 to 5). See Chapter 3.

Related commands: GET (see alternative statement above), DIM, ERASE, PUT

GOSUB *targetline*
RETURN [*returnline*]

GOSUB branches to the alphanumeric line label or line number specified by *targetline*. RETURN jumps back to the line label or line number specified by *returnline*. If *returnline* is omitted, RETURN jumps back to the statement immediately following the GOSUB.

Related commands: ON GOSUB, ON GOTO, SUB

GOTO *targetline*

Branches to the line label or line number specified by *targetline*.

Related commands: GOSUB, ON GOSUB, ON GOTO,

HEX$(*decimal expression*)

Returns the hexadecimal (base 16) equivalent of the base 10 *decimal number*. The *decimal number* is rounded to an integer before the conversion.

Related command: OCT$

IF *expression* GOTO *LineLabel* [ELSE *statement*]
IF *expression* THEN *LineLabel* [ELSE *statement*]
IF *expression* THEN *statement* [ELSE *statement*]
IF *expression* THEN
statement block

[ELSE
    statement block]...
[ELSEIF *expression* THEN
    statement block]...
END IF

Selectively executes certain statements depending on the outcome of *expression*. When *expression* evaluates true, the program branches to the specified *LineLabel* or executes *statement* or *statement block*. If *expression* evaluates false, the program continues to the next line unless ELSE or ELSEIF is included. If ELSE is included, the *statement* or *statement block* following ELSE is executed. If ELSEIF is included, its *expression* is evaluated, and the following *statement block* executed if true. The END IF is required to mark the close of a block IF-THEN. Block IF-THENs can be nested. See Chapter 1.

Related commands: ON GOSUB, ON GOTO

INKEY$
Returns a character corresponding to a keypress, or a null string ("") if no key is pressed. No keypresses are echoed on the screen. See Chapter 8.

Related commands: INPUT, INPUT#, INPUT$, LINE INPUT, LINE INPUT#

INPUT [;][*prompt string*;]*variable*,...
Accepts keyboard input and assigns the characters or values to the specified *variables*. If *prompt string* is included, the prompt is printed before the standard INPUT question mark. If *prompt string* is followed by a comma instead of a semicolon, the question mark does not appear. The keyboard input must match the types of *variables* specified.

Related commands: INKEY$, INPUT#, INPUT$, LINE INPUT, LINE INPUT#

INPUT$(*numchars*[,#*filenumber*])
Returns a string of characters of the length specified by *numchars* from the file specified by *filenumber* (# is optional). If *filenumber* is omitted, characters are read from the keyboard, but not echoed on the screen. See Chapter 8.

Related commands: EOF, GET, INKEY$, INPUT, INPUT#, LINE INPUT, LINE INPUT#, LOF, OPEN, PRINT#, WRITE#

INPUT#*filenumber*,*variable list*
Reads data from a sequential file specified by *filenumber* and assigns it to variables in *variable list*. The variables must match the types of data. Delimiters for numeric data items are spaces, carriage returns, linefeeds, and commas. Delimiters for string data are quotation marks, carriage returns, linefeeds, commas, or the two hundred fifty-fifth character in the string. See Chapter 8.

Related commands: INPUT$, LINE INPUT#, OPEN, PRINT#, WRITE#

INSTR([*start,*]*string$,substring$*)
Searches for the first occurrence of *substring$* within *string$*; if a match is found, INSTR returns the starting character position of *substring$*. If no match is found, or if *string$* is a null string, INSTR returns 0. If the *start* parameter is included, the search starts at that character position within *string$*. If *start* is greater than the number of characters in *string$*, INSTR returns 0. If *substring$* is a null, INSTR returns *start* or 1. See the listing for "Personal Address Book" at the end of Chapter 8.

Related commands: LEFT$, LEN, MID$, RIGHT$, UCASE$

INT(*numeric expression*)
Returns the largest integer less than or equal to *numeric expression*.

Related commands: ABS, CINT, FIX, SGN

KILL *filename*
Deletes a nonOPENed disk file as specified by *filename*. If *filename* is a literal string, it must be enclosed in quotation marks. KILL corresponds to the AmigaDOS DELETE command. See Chapter 8.

Related commands: CHDIR, FILES, NAME

LBOUND(*array*[,*dimension*])
Returns the lower limit (bounds) of *array*. The *dimension* parameter lets you measure a multidimensional array. LBOUND always returns 0 or 1, depending on whether OPTION BASE has been set to 0 or 1.

Related commands: DIM, OPTION BASE, UBOUND

LEFT$(*string$,numchars*)
Returns the leftmost number of characters specified by *numchars* in *string$*. If *numchars* is greater than the length of *string$*, LEFT$ returns the entire string. If *numchars* equals 0, LEFT$ returns a null string.

Related commands: INSTR, LEN, MID$, RIGHT$, UCASE$

LEN(*string$*)
Returns the number of characters in *string$*, including spaces and nonprinting characters.

Related commands: INSTR, LEFT$, MID$, RIGHT$, UCASE$

[LET] *variable = expression*
Assigns the value of *expression* to *variable*; the types must match. As in almost all BASICs, the keyword LET is optional.

LIBRARY *filename*
LIBRARY CLOSE
Opens the library file of machine language routines specified by *filename* and attaches them to BASIC. Up to five library files can be attached at a time. LIBRARY CLOSE closes the file. See Chapter 9.

Related commands: CALL, DECLARE FUNCTION LIBRARY

LINE [STEP] *(x1,y1)*–**[STEP]***(x2,y2)***[,***color-ID***][,b[f]]**
Draws a line from coordinates *(x1,y1)* to *(x2,y2)*. The ranges for these coordinates depend on the screen mode, but out-of-range values are automatically clipped. If the *b* parameter is appended, LINE draws a hollow box with the upper left corner at *(x1,y1)* and the lower right corner at *(x2,y2)*. If *bf* is appended, the box is filled with the drawing color. The drawing color can be specified with *color-ID*, which ranges from 0 to 31 depending on the screen mode. If the first STEP keyword is included, the coordinates in *(x1,y1)* are relative offsets from the current position of the graphics pen. If the second STEP is included, the coordinates in *(x2,y2)* are relative offsets from *(x1,y1)*. See Chapter 2.

Related commands: AREA, AREAFILL, COLOR, PAINT, PATTERN

LINE INPUT [;] ["*prompt string***";]***string variable***
Places an entire line of characters entered from the keyboard into *string variable*. Note that *"prompt string"* must be a literal string, not a string variable. LINE INPUT does not generate a question mark or any other prompt besides that specified in *"prompt string"*. If immediately followed by the semicolon, LINE INPUT does not echo the carriage return when the user presses RETURN.

Related commands: INKEY$, INPUT, INPUT#, INPUT$, LINE INPUT#

LINE INPUT# *filenumber;string variable*
Reads a line of data (as delimited by a carriage return) from the sequential file specified by *filenumber* and puts it in *string variable*. See Chapter 8.

Related commands: EOF, INPUT#, INPUT$, LINE INPUT, LOF, OPEN

LIST [*startline***][–***endline***][,"***filename***"]**
Generates a program listing in the Amiga BASIC List window or any device specified by *"filename"*. The other optional parameters are line labels or line numbers; they let you list a program from *startline* forward, or up to *endline*, or between *startline* and *endline*.

Related command: LLIST

LLIST [*startline***][–***endline***]**
Generates a program listing on the default printer as selected with the Preferences tool. The *startline* and *endline* parameters work the same as with LIST.

Related command: LIST

LOAD [*filename*][*,R*]
Loads the program specified by *filename* into BASIC. If *filename* is omitted, a system requester asks for the filename. The *R* option automatically loads and runs the program, allowing chaining.

Related commands: CHAIN, MERGE, SAVE

LOC(*filenumber*)
Returns I/O information about the random file, sequential file, KYBD: device, or COM1: device specified by *filenumber*. If *filenumber* is a random file, LOC returns the record number of the last record that was read or written. If *filenumber* is a sequential file, LOC returns a number equal to the number of bytes read from or written to the file divided by the record size in bytes. (The default record size is 128 unless otherwise specified in the OPEN statement.) If *filenumber* refers to the KYBD: or COM1: device, LOC returns 1 if any characters are pending to be read, and returns 0 if not. See Chapter 8.

Related commands: EOF, GET, INPUT#, LINE INPUT#, LOF, OPEN, PRINT#, PUT, WRITE#

LOCATE [*textline*][*,textcolumn*]
Places the graphics pen at the vertical and horizontal positions specified by *textline* and *textcolumn*, respectively. If either or both parameters are omitted, LOCATE defaults to the current position. The upper left corner of the screen is position (1,1). The ranges for *textline* and *textcolumn* depend on the size of the font in use. See Chapter 2.

Related commands: CSRLIN, POS, PTAB

LOF(*filenumber*)
Returns the length in bytes of the file specified by *filenumber*. LOF always returns 0 for the KYBD:, LPT1:, and SCRN: devices. See Chapter 8.

Related commands: EOF, INPUT#, INPUT$, LINE INPUT#, LOC, OPEN

LOG(*numeric expression*)
Returns the logarithm of *numeric expression*, which must be greater than zero.

Related commands: COS, EXP, SIN

LPOS(*dummy expression*)
Returns the current position of the printer's printhead as determined by the characters sent to the printer buffer. Since some characters may be nonprinting, LPOS doesn't always indicate the printhead's true position. See Chapter 8.

Related commands: LPRINT, LPRINT USING, PRINT#, WRITE#

LPRINT [*expression list*]
Identical to PRINT except that a file is automatically opened to the LPT1: device and the strings or numeric values in *expression list* are sent to the printer.

If *expression list* is omitted, LPRINT generates a carriage return/linefeed. Note that unlike PRT:, LPRINT does not carry out ISO printer command codes. See Chapter 8 and Appendix B, "ISO Printer Codes."

Related commands: LLIST, LPRINT USING

LPRINT USING *format expression;expression list*
Identical to PRINT USING except that a file is automatically opened to the LPT1: device and the strings or numeric values in *expression list* are sent to the printer. Note that like LPRINT, LPRINT USING does not carry out ISO printer command codes. See Chapter 8 and Appendix B, "ISO Printer Codes."

Related commands: LLIST, LPRINT

LSET *string variable=string expression*
Formats the raw data in *string expression* within *string variable* for random file output. In effect, the data is moved into the random file buffer. If *string expression* is shorter than the room allotted to *string variable* by a previous FIELD statement, LSET appends spaces to left justify the data within *string variable*. Since *string expression* doesn't allow numeric values, they must be converted first with MKI$, MKL$, MKS$, or MKD$. LSET can also left justify *string expression* within *string variable* for other purposes besides random file output. See Chapter 8.

Related commands: FIELD, MKD$, MKI$, MKL$, MKS$, OPEN, PUT, RSET

MENU *menu-ID,item-ID,status[,title string]*
Creates a custom menu on the menu bar or changes the status of an existing custom menu. *Menu-ID* ranges from 1 to 10 and indicates the menu's position starting from the left end of the menu bar. Positions 1–4 replace Amiga BASIC's default menus. *Item-ID* ranges from 0 to 19. If 0, it specifies the entire menu; if 1 to 19, it specifies the selection in the menu starting from the top. *Status* specifies whether a menu or selection is active, ghosted (dimmed), or checked. If *status*=0, the selection (or entire menu, if *item-ID*=0) is ghosted. If *status*=1, the selection (or entire menu, if *item-ID*=0) is active. If *status*=2, the selection is active and preceded by a checkmark. The optional *title string* parameter is a string expression that displays either the name of the menu (if *item-ID*=0) or the name of a selection (if *item-ID*=1 to 19). See Chapters 1 and 7.

Related commands: MENU(0), MENU(1), MENU OFF, MENU ON, MENU RESET, MENU STOP, ON MENU GOSUB, SLEEP

MENU(0)
Returns a number corresponding to a MENU statement's *menu-ID* indicating which custom menu was just selected. If MENU(0)=0, no menu was selected. Reading MENU(0) automatically resets it to 0. See Chapters 1 and 7.

Related commands: MENU, MENU(1), MENU OFF, MENU ON, MENU RESET, MENU STOP, ON MENU GOSUB, SLEEP

MENU(1)
Returns a number corresponding to a MENU statement's *item-ID* indicating which selection on a custom menu was just selected. See Chapters 1 and 7.

Related commands: MENU, MENU(0), MENU OFF, MENU ON, MENU RESET, MENU STOP, ON MENU GOSUB, SLEEP

MENU OFF
Disables event trapping of custom menu selections which have been activated by ON MENU GOSUB and MENU ON. Menu selections are ignored until a subsequent MENU ON. See Chapters 1 and 7.

Related commands: MENU, MENU(0), MENU(1), MENU ON, MENU RESET, MENU STOP, ON MENU GOSUB, SLEEP

MENU ON
Enables event trapping of custom menu selections and allows ON MENU GOSUB to pass control to its specified routine upon a selection. See Chapters 1 and 7.

Related commands: MENU, MENU(0), MENU(1), MENU OFF, MENU RESET, MENU STOP, ON MENU GOSUB, SLEEP

MENU RESET
Cancels the custom menus defined with MENU and restores the menu bar to Amiga BASIC's default menus. See Chapters 1 and 7.

Related commands: MENU, MENU(0), MENU(1), MENU OFF, MENU ON, MENU STOP, SLEEP

MENU STOP
Suspends event trapping of custom menus activated with MENU ON and ON MENU GOSUB. MENU STOP doesn't disable menu trapping like MENU OFF; it temporarily prevents ON MENU GOSUB from acting on a menu selection until the next MENU ON. See Chapters 1 and 7.

Related commands: MENU, MENU(0), MENU(1), MENU OFF, MENU ON, ON MENU GOSUB, MENU RESET, SLEEP

MERGE *filename*
Appends the ASCII disk file specified by *filename* to the BASIC program in memory.

Related commands: LOAD, SAVE

MID$(*string$,start-position*[,*length*])
The MID$ function returns a string within *string$* starting from the character position specified by *start-position*. If *length* is included, it defines the number of characters returned by MID$. If *length* is omitted, or if it is greater than the

number of characters to the right of *start-position*, MID$ returns all characters from *start-position* to the end of the string. MID$ returns a null string if *start-position* is greater than the length of *string*. However, the values for *start-position* and *length* must range from 1 to 32767.

Related commands: INSTR, LEFT$, LEN, MID$ (statement), RIGHT$, UCASE$

MID$(*string1$,start-position[,replace-length]*)=*string2$*
The MID$ statement replaces a part of *string1$* with characters from *string2$*, starting at the character position in *string1$* specified by *start-position*. If *replace-length* is included, it specifies how many characters from *string2$* are used in the replacement. By default, MID$ uses all of *string2$*. The length of *string1$* can never increase, no matter how many characters are replaced.

Related commands: INSTR, LEFT$, LEN, MID$ (function), RIGHT$, UCASE$

MKD$(*double-precision expression*)
Converts *double-precision expression* into an eight-byte string prior to writing the value to a random file. See Chapter 8.

Related commands: CVD, CVI, CVL, CVS, FIELD, LSET, MKI$, MKL$, MKS$, OPEN, PUT, RSET

MKI$(*short-integer expression*)
Converts *short-integer expression* into a two-byte string prior to writing the value to a random file. See Chapter 8.

Related commands: CVD, CVI, CVL, CVS, FIELD, LSET, MKD$, MKL$, MKS$, OPEN, PUT, RSET

MKL$(*long-integer expression*)
Converts *long-integer expression*) into a four-byte string prior to writing the value to a random file. See Chapter 8.

Related commands: CVD, CVI, CVL, CVS, FIELD, LSET, MKD$, MKI$, MKS$, OPEN, PUT, RSET

MKS$(*single-precision expression*)
Converts *single-precision expression* into a four-byte string prior to writing the value to a random file. See Chapter 8.

Related commands: CVD, CVI, CVL, CVS, FIELD, LSET, MKD$, MKI$, MKL$, OPEN, PUT, RSET

MOUSE(*function*)
Returns information about the mouse controller depending on the value of *function*, which can range from 0 to 6. If *function*=0, the values returned indicate the status of the left button:

MOUSE(0)=0	The button is not pressed and has not been pressed since the last time MOUSE(0) was called.
MOUSE(0)=1	The button is not pressed, but has been clicked once since the last time MOUSE(0) was called.
MOUSE(0)=2	The button is not pressed, but has been clicked twice since the last time MOUSE(0) was called.
MOUSE(0)=−1	The button has been clicked once and is still pressed.
MOUSE(0)=−2	The button has been clicked twice and is still pressed.
MOUSE(0)=−3	The button has been clicked three times and is still pressed.
MOUSE(1)	Returns the current horizontal coordinate of the mouse pointer since MOUSE(0) was last called.
MOUSE(2)	Returns the current vertical coordinate of the mouse pointer since MOUSE(0) was last called.
MOUSE(3)	Returns the horizontal coordinate of the mouse pointer when the button was pressed before MOUSE(0) was called.
MOUSE(4)	Returns the vertical coordinate of the mouse pointer when the button was pressed before MOUSE(0) was called.
MOUSE(5)	Returns the horizontal coordinate of the mouse pointer depending on the status of the left button when MOUSE(0) was last called. If the button was pressed, MOUSE(5) returns the horizontal coordinate at the time MOUSE(0) was called. If the button was not pressed, MOUSE(5) returns the horizontal coordinate at the time the button was released.
MOUSE(6)	Returns the vertical coordinate of the mouse pointer depending on the status of the left button when MOUSE(0) was last called. If the button was pressed, MOUSE(6) returns the vertical coordinate at the time MOUSE(0) was called. If the button was not pressed, MOUSE(6) returns the vertical coordinate at the time the button was released.

Related commands: MOUSE OFF, MOUSE ON, MOUSE STOP, ON MOUSE GOSUB, SLEEP

MOUSE OFF

Disables event trapping for presses of the left mouse button which was previously activated by MOUSE ON and ON MOUSE GOSUB. Mouse trapping remains disabled until the next MOUSE ON. All button presses in the meantime are ignored. See Chapter 8.

Related commands: MOUSE, MOUSE ON, MOUSE STOP, ON MOUSE GOSUB, SLEEP

MOUSE ON

Enables event trapping for presses of the left mouse button, allowing ON MOUSE GOSUB to pass control to the subroutine it specifies. See Chapter 8.

Related commands: MOUSE, MOUSE OFF, MOUSE STOP, ON MOUSE GOSUB, SLEEP

MOUSE STOP
Suspends event trapping for presses of the left mouse button. Unlike MOUSE OFF, MOUSE STOP does not disable mouse trapping; it temporarily prevents ON MOUSE GOSUB from branching until the next MOUSE ON. See Chapter 8.

Related commands: MOUSE, MOUSE OFF, MOUSE ON, ON MOUSE GOSUB, SLEEP

NAME *old-filename* AS *new-filename*
Renames the disk file *old-filename* to *new-filename*. Both parameters are string expressions. Similar to the AmigaDOS RENAME command. See Chapter 8.

Related commands: CHDIR, FILES, KILL

NEW
Erases the BASIC program in memory.

Related command: KILL

NEXT [*counter variable*][,*counter variable*]...
See FOR.

OBJECT.AX *object-ID,rate*
Sets the horizontal acceleration of *object-ID* to *rate*, which is expressed in pixels per second per second. Positive values for *rate* specify acceleration toward the right side of the screen; negative values specify acceleration toward the left side of the screen. The sprite or bob must have previously been created with OBJECT.SHAPE. See Chapter 4.

Related commands: OBJECT.AY, OBJECT.VX, OBJECT.VY, OBJECT.X, OBJECT.Y

OBJECT.AY *object-ID,rate*
Sets the vertical acceleration of *object-ID* to *rate*, which is expressed in pixels per second per second. Positive values for *rate* specify acceleration toward the bottom of the screen; negative values specify acceleration toward the top of the screen. The sprite or bob must have previously been created with OBJECT.SHAPE. See Chapter 4.

Related commands: OBJECT.AX, OBJECT.VX, OBJECT.VY, OBJECT.X, OBJECT.Y

OBJECT.CLIP *(x1,y1)–(x2,y2)*
Prevents objects from appearing outside the rectangular screen area defined by *(x1,y1)–(x2,y2)*. OBJECT.CLIP defaults to the border of the current output window. See Chapter 4.

Note: OBJECT.CLIP is not implemented in version 1.0 of Amiga BASIC.

Related commands: OBJECT.OFF, OBJECT.X, OBJECT.Y

OBJECT.CLOSE [*object-ID*][,*object-ID*]...
Deallocates the memory for the objects specified by *object-ID*. OBJECT.CLOSE followed by no *object-IDs* deallocates all objects in the current output window. Objects deallocated with OBJECT.CLOSE cannot be used again unless redefined by another OBJECT.SHAPE. See Chapter 4.

Related commands: OBJECT.OFF, OBJECT.SHAPE

OBJECT.HIT *object-ID*,[*me-mask*][,*hit-mask*]
Defines which objects shall register collisions with the object specified by *object-ID*. The *me-mask* and *hit-mask* parameters are 16-bit masks which are logically ANDed to the me-masks and hit-masks of other objects. *Me-mask* defines the object's class, and *hit-mask* defines which other objects (or screen borders) will be sensitive to collisions with *object-ID*. See Chapter 4 and the "MaskMaker" utility (Program 4-6) for constructing these bit masks.

Related commands: COLLISION, COLLISION OFF, COLLISION ON, COLLISION STOP, ON COLLISION GOSUB

OBJECT.OFF [*object-ID*][,*object-ID*]...
Erases the object(s) specified by *object-ID*. If no parameters are included, all objects in the current output window are rendered invisible. OBJECT.OFF also stops a moving object and prevents it from registering collisions with other objects. See Chapter 4.

Related commands: OBJECT.CLIP, OBJECT.CLOSE, OBJECT.ON, OBJECT.START

OBJECT.ON [*object-ID*][,*object-ID*]...
Turns on the object(s) specified by *object-ID* within the current output window. If no parameters are included, all objects defined within the current output window are made visible. If an object had been set into motion with OBJECT.START, then OBJECT.ON starts it moving again. See Chapter 4.

Related commands: OBJECT.CLIP, OBJECT.CLOSE, OBJECT.OFF, OBJECT.START

OBJECT.PLANES *object-ID*,[*plane-pick*][,*plane-on-off*]
Sets the colors of the bob specified by *object-ID*. (Does not affect sprites.) The *plane-pick* and *plane-on-off* parameters are bit masks that determine the object's colors in relation to each other and to the number of bit-planes in the current screen mode. They can range from 0 to 31, depending on the screen mode. See Chapter 4 and the "PlanePick" utility (Program 4-5) for experimenting with object colors.

Related commands: COLOR, OBJECT.HIT, OBJECT.PRIORITY, PALETTE, SCREEN

OBJECT.PRIORITY *object-ID,rank*
Sets the display priority of the bob specified by *object-ID*. (Does not affect sprites.) The *rank* parameter can range from −32768 to 32767. A bob with a higher numbered *rank* is displayed in front of another bob if they overlap on the screen. The priorities for bobs with equal *ranks* are determined randomly. See Chapter 4.

Related commands: OBJECT.HIT, OBJECT.PLANES

OBJECT.SHAPE *object-ID,string definition*
Creates a new object tagged with the unique identification number *object-ID* using the shape data in *string definition*. Values for *object-ID* can range from 1 to any number, depending on the amount of memory available. The *string definition* can consist of the following expression to read an object file previously created on disk with the Object Editor:

OPEN *"object-file"* **FOR INPUT AS** *filenumber*
OBJECT.SHAPE *object-ID,*INPUT$(LOF(*filenumber*)*,filenumber*)
CLOSE *filenumber*

where *"object-file"* is the filename of the disk file, and *filenumber* is the number of the file to be OPENed. Alternatively, *string definition* can be a string variable filled with shape data previously converted from an object file. See Chapter 4 and the "Object DataMaker" utility (Program 4-4).

Related commands: OBJECT.CLOSE, OBJECT.OFF, OBJECT.ON,
OBJECT.SHAPE (see alternative syntax below)

OBJECT.SHAPE *object-ID1,object-ID2*
Creates a new object tagged with the unique identification number *object-ID1* and defines its shape by copying data from the existing object specified by *object-ID2*. The two objects are completely independent, but use less memory than if defined separately with the alternative syntax of OBJECT.SHAPE above. See Chapter 4.

Related commands: OBJECT.CLOSE, OBJECT.OFF, OBJECT.ON,
OBJECT.SHAPE (see alternative syntax above)

OBJECT.START *[object-ID][,object-ID]*...
Sets the object(s) specified by *object-ID* into motion. If the parameters are omitted, all objects within the current output window are set into motion. Note that each object's position and speed must have been previously defined. See Chapter 4.

Related commands: OBJECT.AX, OBJECT.AY, OBJECT.STOP, OBJECT.VX,
OBJECT.VY, OBJECT.X, OBJECT.Y

OBJECT.STOP *[object-ID][,object-ID]*...
Halts the moving object(s) specified by *object-ID*. If the parameters are omitted, all moving objects within the current output window are stopped.

OBJECT.STOP is executed automatically on an object when it registers a collision. See Chapter 4.

Related commands: OBJECT.AX, OBJECT.AY, OBJECT.START, OBJECT.VX, OBJECT.VY

OBJECT.VX *object-ID,velocity*
Sets the horizontal velocity for the object named by *object-ID*. The *velocity* parameter specifies pixels per second. Positive values move the object across the screen from left to right, and negative values move the object from right to left. The object does not actually start moving until an OBJECT.START. See Chapter 4.

Related commands: OBJECT.AX, OBJECT.AY, OBJECT.START, OBJECT.STOP, OBJECT.VX (see function syntax below), OBJECT.VY, OBJECT.X, OBJECT.Y

OBJECT.VX(*object-ID*)
Returns the current horizontal velocity of the object named by *object-ID*. The velocity is measured in pixels per second. Positive values indicate the object is moving across the screen from left to right, and negative values indicate it is moving from right to left. See Chapter 4.

Related commands: OBJECT.AX, OBJECT.AY, OBJECT.START, OBJECT.STOP, OBJECT.VX (see statement syntax above), OBJECT.VY, OBJECT.X, OBJECT.Y

OBJECT.VY *object-ID,velocity*
Sets the vertical velocity for the object named by *object-ID*. The *velocity* parameter specifies pixels per second. Positive values move the object toward the bottom of the screen, and negative values move the object toward the top of the screen. The object does not actually start moving until an OBJECT.START. See Chapter 4.

Related commands: OBJECT.AX, OBJECT.AY, OBJECT.START, OBJECT.STOP, OBJECT.VX, OBJECT.VY (see function syntax below), OBJECT.X, OBJECT.Y

OBJECT.VY(*object-ID*)
Returns the current vertical velocity of the object named by *object-ID*. The velocity is measured in pixels per second. Positive values indicate the object is moving toward the bottom of the screen, and negative values indicate the object is moving toward the top of the screen. See Chapter 4.

Related commands: OBJECT.AX, OBJECT.AY, OBJECT.START, OBJECT.STOP, OBJECT.VX, OBJECT.VY (see statement syntax above), OBJECT.X, OBJECT.Y

OBJECT.X *object-ID,horizontal coordinate*
Positions the object named by *object-ID* at the horizontal screen coordinate specified by *horizontal coordinate*. Coordinates can be a numeric expression ranging from −32768 to 32767, but only a small number of these coordinates

are actually visible on the screen, depending on the current screen mode and window size. The point of the object that is positioned at *horizontal coordinate* is its upper left corner, as determined by the canvas on which it was created with the Object Editor. The object doesn't actually appear until made visible with OBJECT.ON. See Chapter 4.

Related commands: OBJECT.AX, OBJECT.AY, OBJECT.CLOSE, OBJECT.OFF, OBJECT.ON, OBJECT.VX, OBJECT.VY, OBJECT.X (see function syntax below), OBJECT.Y

OBJECT.X(*object-ID*)

Returns the current horizontal position of the object named by *object-ID*. The point returned is the object's upper left corner, as determined by the canvas on which it was created with the Object Editor. See Chapter 4.

Related commands: OBJECT.AX, OBJECT.AY, OBJECT.CLOSE, OBJECT.OFF, OBJECT.ON, OBJECT.VX, OBJECT.VY, OBJECT.X (see statement syntax above), OBJECT.Y

OBJECT.Y *object-ID,vertical coordinate*

Positions the object named by *object-ID* at the vertical screen coordinate specified by *vertical coordinate*. Coordinates can be a numeric expression ranging from -32768 to 32767, but only a small number of these coordinates are actually visible on the screen, depending on the current screen mode and window size. The point of the object that is positioned at *vertical coordinate* is its upper left corner, as determined by the canvas on which it was created with the Object Editor. The object doesn't actually appear until made visible with OBJECT.ON. See Chapter 4.

Related commands: OBJECT.AX, OBJECT.AY, OBJECT.CLOSE, OBJECT.OFF, OBJECT.ON, OBJECT.VX, OBJECT.VY, OBJECT.X, OBJECT.Y (see function syntax below)

OBJECT.Y(*object-ID*)

Returns the current vertical position of the object named by *object-ID*. The point returned is the object's upper left corner, as determined by the canvas on which it was created with the Object Editor. See Chapter 4.

Related commands: OBJECT.AX, OBJECT.AY, OBJECT.CLOSE, OBJECT.OFF, OBJECT.ON, OBJECT.VX, OBJECT.VY, OBJECT.X, OBJECT.Y (see statement syntax above)

OCT$(*decimal expression*)

Returns the octal (base 8) equivalent of the base 10 *decimal expression*. The decimal value is rounded to an integer before the conversion.

Related command: HEX$

ON BREAK GOSUB *LineLabel*
Specifies that a program should branch to *LineLabel* if break trapping is active and if the user has selected Stop from Amiga BASIC's Run menu, or has pressed right Amiga–Period, CTRL-C, or CTRL-F3. The *LineLabel* is an alphanumeric line label or line number within the program. If *LineLabel* is 0, break trapping is disabled and a new *LineLabel* target can be specified with another ON BREAK GOSUB. Note that event traps for breaks are active only after BREAK ON has been executed. See Chapters 1 and 7.

Related commands: BREAK OFF, BREAK ON, BREAK STOP

ON COLLISION GOSUB *LineLabel*
Specifies that a program should branch to *LineLabel* if collision trapping is active and if one or more objects have registered collisions with each other or the screen borders. The *LineLabel* is an alphanumeric line label or line number within the program. If *LineLabel* is 0, collision trapping is disabled and a new *LineLabel* target can be specified with another ON COLLISION GOSUB. Note that event traps for collisions are active only after COLLISION ON has been executed. See Chapters 1 and 4.

Related commands: COLLISION, COLLISION OFF, COLLISION ON, COLLISION STOP, OBJECT.HIT

ON ERROR GOTO *LineLabel*
Specifies that a program should branch to *LineLabel* if the program is interrupted by an error. The *LineLabel* is an alphanumeric line label or line number within the program. If *LineLabel* is 0, error trapping is disabled and a new *LineLabel* target can be specified with another ON ERROR GOSUB. See Chapter 1 and Program 7-4, the "ErrorTrap" routine in Chapter 7.

Related commands: RESUME, RESUME *LineLabel*, RESUME NEXT

ON *expression* GOSUB *LineLabel-list*
Branches to one of the alphanumeric line labels or line numbers in *LineLabel-list* depending on the outcome of *expression*. If *expression* evaluates to a value which corresponds to the position of a line label or line number in *LineLabel-list*, the program GOSUBs to that line. If *expression* evaluates to zero or a value greater than the number of items in *LineLabel-list*, execution continues at the next statement.

Related commands: GOSUB, GOTO, ON GOTO, RETURN

ON *expression* GOTO *LineLabel-list*
Branches to one of the alphanumeric line labels or line numbers in *LineLabel-list* depending on the outcome of *expression*. This is identical to ON GOSUB above except that the program cannot branch back with RETURN.

Related commands: GOSUB, GOTO, ON GOSUB

413

ON MENU GOSUB *LineLabel*

Branches to *LineLabel* if menu trapping is active and if an item on a custom menu is selected. The MENU(0) and MENU(1) functions are then set to non-zero values to indicate which menu and item was picked. The *LineLabel* is an alphanumeric label or line number. If *LineLabel* is 0, menu trapping is disabled and a new *LineLabel* target can be specified with another ON MENU GOSUB. Note that event traps for menu selections are active only after MENU ON has been executed. See Chapters 1 and 7.

Related commands: MENU, MENU(0), MENU(1), MENU OFF, MENU ON, MENU RESET, MENU STOP

ON MOUSE GOSUB *LineLabel*

Branches to *LineLabel* if mouse trapping is active and if the user presses the left mouse button. The MOUSE function then returns a value indicating which type of button press occurred. The *LineLabel* is an alphanumeric line label or line number. If *LineLabel* is 0, mouse trapping is disabled and a new *LineLabel* target can be specified with another ON MOUSE GOSUB. Note that event traps for button presses are active only after MOUSE ON has been executed. See Chapters 1 and 7.

Related commands: MOUSE, MOUSE OFF, MOUSE ON, MOUSE STOP

ON TIMER(*seconds*) GOSUB *LineLabel*

Branches to *LineLabel* if TIMER trapping is active and if the time interval specified by *seconds* has elapsed. Values for *seconds* can range from 0 to 86400 (that is, up to 24 hours). The *LineLabel* is an alphanumeric line label or line number. If *LineLabel* is 0, TIMER trapping is disabled and a new *LineLabel* target can be specified with another ON TIMER GOSUB. Note that event traps for TIMER values are active only after TIMER ON has been executed. See Chapter 1.

Related commands: TIME$, TIMER, TIMER OFF, TIMER ON, TIMER STOP

OPEN *filename* [FOR *i/o mode*] AS [#]*filenumber* [LEN=*file buffer size*]

Opens a communications channel to the disk file or device named by *filename* for the input/output mode specified by *i/o mode* using the file number specified by *filenumber*. The *filename* can be any device recognized by Amiga BASIC:

DF0:   Internal floppy drive
DF1:   External floppy drive
DH0:   Hard disk drive
RAM: RAM disk
PRT: Printer
LPT1:   Printer
PAR: Parallel port
COM1:   RS-232 serial port
SER: RS-232 serial port
KYBD: Keyboard

SCRN: Screen
CON: Console
RAW: System
NIL: Dummy device

Or it can be a disk filename in the current directory. The *i/o mode* can be OUT-PUT for sequential file output, INPUT for sequential file input, or APPEND for sequential file output onto the end of an existing file. If *i/o mode* is omitted from the OPEN statement, it defaults to random file input/output. The *file buffer size* parameter determines the record length for random files or the size of the memory buffer for sequential files. It can range from 1 to 32767 bytes and defaults to 128 bytes if omitted. The *filenumber* parameter can range from 1 to 255. See Chapter 8.

Related commands: CLOSE, EOF, FIELD, GET, LOC, LOF, OPEN (see alternative syntax below), PRINT#, PRINT# USING, PUT, WRITE#

OPEN *i/o mode*,[#]*filenumber*,*filename*[,*file buffer size*]
Opens a communications channel to the disk file or device named by *filename* for the input/output mode specified by *i/o mode* using the file number specified by *filenumber*. The filename can be any device recognized by Amiga BASIC (see list above) or simply a disk file in the current directory. The *i/o mode* is a string expression whose first character can be

I   Sequential file input
O   Sequential file output
A   Appending onto an existing sequential file
R   Random file input/output

The *filenumber* can range from 1 to 255. The *file buffer size* parameter determines the record length for random files or the size of the memory buffer for sequential files. It can range from 1 to 32767 bytes and defaults to 128 bytes if omitted. See Chapter 8.

Related commands: CLOSE, EOF, FIELD, GET, LOC, LOF, OPEN, PRINT#, PRINT# USING, PUT (see alternative syntax above), WRITE#

OPTION BASE *array-base*
Sets the lowest possible subscript for arrays to *array-base*, which can be either 0 (default) or 1.

Related commands: DIM, LBOUND, UBOUND

PAINT [STEP]*(x,y)*[,*paintcolor-ID*][,*bordercolor-ID*]
Fills the screen area around the pixel coordinates *(x,y)* with the color specified by *paintcolor-ID*. The range of values for *(x,y)* depends on the screen mode and size of the current output window. Normally, *(x,y)* is an absolute pixel position, but if STEP is included, *(x,y)* is a relative offset from the last location of the

graphics pen. The *bordercolor-ID* parameter specifies the color of the pixels which form a border around the area to be filled. If *bordercolor-ID* is omitted, it defaults to the same value as *paintcolor-ID*. If *paintcolor-ID* is omitted, it defaults to the current foreground color. Values for *paintcolor-ID* and *bordercolor-ID* can range from 0 to 31, depending on the screen mode. See Chapter 2.

Note: PAINT works only if the output window was opened with a *type* parameter of 16 through 31.

Related commands: AREA, AREAFILL, COLOR, PALETTE, PATTERN

PALETTE *color-ID,red,green,blue*
Assigns a color composed of *red*, *green*, and *blue* values to the color register specified by *color-ID*. The *color-ID* can range from 0 to 31 depending on the screen mode. (The Workbench screen normally uses color registers 0–3 and colors set with the Preferences tool.) Values for *red*, *green*, and *blue* can range from 0.00 to 1.00. Higher values specify brighter luminances. See Chapter 2 and the "Pick-A-Palette" utility at the end of the chapter; also Program 7-5, the "Palette Panel" subprogram in Chapter 7.

Related commands: COLOR, SCREEN, WINDOW

PATTERN *[line pattern][,area pattern array]*
Defines patterns for printing text, drawing lines, and filling polygons. *Line pattern* defines patterns for line drawing; it is an integer expression that sets up a 16-bit mask. *Area pattern* specifies an integer array that also sets up a bit mask. The mask is 16 bits wide by the number of elements in the array. The number of elements must be a power of two. See Chapter 2.

Related commands: AREA, AREAFILL, COLOR, PALETTE

PEEK(*memory address*)
Returns a one-byte value ranging from 0 to 255 which is stored at *memory address*, a numeric expression which can range from 0 to 16777215.

Related commands: PEEKL, PEEKW, POKE, POKEL, POKEW, SADD, VARPTR

PEEKL(*memory address*)
Returns a four-byte value ranging from −2147483648 to 2147483647 which is stored at *memory address*, an even numeric expression which can range from 0 to 16777215.

Related commands: PEEK, PEEKW, POKE, POKEL, POKEW, SADD, VARPTR

PEEKW(*memory address*)
Returns a two-byte value ranging from −32768 to 32767 which is stored at *memory address*, an even numeric expression which can range from 0 to 16777216.

Related commands: PEEK, PEEKL, POKE, POKEL, POKEW, SADD, VARPTR

POINT*(x,y)*

Reads the color-ID of the pixel *(x,y)* in the current output window. The range of values for *(x,y)* depends on the screen mode and window size. See Chapter 2.

Related commands: COLOR, PALETTE, PRESET, PSET, SCREEN, WINDOW

POKE *memory address,one-byte value*

Stores *one-byte value*, an integer expression ranging from 0 to 255, at *memory address*, an integer expression ranging from 0 to 16777215.

Related commands: PEEK, PEEKL, PEEKW, POKEL, POKEW, SADD, VARPTR

POKEL *memory address,four-byte value*

Stores *four-byte value*, a numeric expression ranging from -2147483648 to 2147483647, at *memory address*, an even integer expression ranging from 0 to 16777216.

Related commands: PEEK, PEEKL, PEEKW, POKE, POKEW, SADD, VARPTR

POKEW *memory address,two-byte value*

Stores *two-byte value*, a numeric expression ranging from 0 to 65535, at *memory address*, an even integer expression ranging from 0 to 16777216. Because of the way the Amiga's number conversion process works, you can also use -32768 to -1 in place of values 32768 to 65535 for the *two-byte value* parameter. The corresponding PEEKW function always returns values in the range -32768 to 32767.

Related commands: PEEK, PEEKL, PEEKW, POKE, POKEL, SADD, VARPTR

POS(*dummy expression*)

Returns the approximate text column number of the graphics pen as measured from the left border of the current output window. The calculation is based on the height and width of the character *O* in the current font.

Related commands: CSRLIN, LOCATE, PTAB

PRESET [STEP]*(x,y)[,color-ID]*

Sets the pixel specified by coordinates *(x,y)* in the current output window. The range for *(x,y)* depends on the screen mode and window size. Normally, *(x,y)* is an absolute pixel location; if STEP is included, *(x,y)* is a relative offset from the last location of the graphics pen. PRESET sets the pixel to the background color unless *color-ID* is included; *color-ID* can range from 0 to 31 depending on the screen mode. See Chapter 2.

Related commands: POINT, PSET

PRINT *expression-list*

Displays the text specified in *expression-list* within the current output window. *Expression-list* can consist of any combination of strings and numeric values. If *expression-list* is not included, PRINT displays a blank line. If an expression is followed by a semicolon, it suppresses the carriage return/linefeed which normally follows PRINT. Commas tab to the next tab stop as set by WIDTH. PRINT can be abbreviated with a question mark.

Related commands: LPRINT, LPRINT USING, PRINT#, PRINT USING, PRINT# USING, WIDTH, WRITE

PRINT USING *format-string;expression-list*

Displays the text specified in *expression-list* within the current output window according to the format defined by *format-string*, a string expression. You can use the following special format characters in *format-string* to display string or numeric expressions (up to 24 digits) in *expression-list*:

Format Character	Result
!	Prints only the first character in the following string.
\ *spaces* \	Prints the number of characters in the following string indicated by the number of spaces between the backslashes, plus two. That is, \\ prints two characters; \ \ prints three characters; and so on.
&	Prints the entire following string, no matter what its length.
#	Specifies how many digits will be printed in the following numeric expression. Use one # symbol for each digit to be printed.
.	Prints a decimal point in the following numeric expression.
+	Prints the sign of the number (+ or −) at the corresponding position in the following numeric expression.
−	Prints a minus sign after negative numbers in the following numeric expression.
**	Prints asterisks in the positions of leading spaces in the following numeric expression.
$$	Prints a dollar sign immediately to the left of a number in the following numeric expression.
**$	Prints asterisks in the positions of leading spaces and a dollar sign immediately to the left of a number in the following numeric expression.
,	Prints a comma every three digits to the left of the decimal point in the following numeric expression.
^^^^	Prints the following numeric expression in exponential format.
_	Prints the following character literally, even if it is a special format character.

Related commands: LPRINT USING, PRINT# USING

PRINT# *filenumber,expression-list*

Stores the numeric and/or string data in *expression-list* in the sequential file specified by *filenumber*. The *filenumber* refers to a file previously OPENed. PRINT# writes the data to the file in the same format as PRINT would display it on the screen. Separate numeric expressions with semicolons as delimiters, for example,

PRINT# 1,A;B;C

Do not use commas, because they write blank spaces in the file. Separate string expressions with semicolons and special delimiters, such as literal commas:

PRINT# 1,A$;",";B$

See Chapter 8 and the discussion of "Personal Address Book."

Related commands: INPUT#, LINE INPUT#, LPRINT, LPRINT USING, PRINT, PRINT# USING, WRITE#

PRINT# *filenumber*,USING *format-string;expression-list*

Stores the numeric and/or string data in *expression-list* in the sequential file specified by *filenumber* using the special formatting defined by *format-string*. This statement is identical to PRINT# except for the *format-string*. The use of *format-string* is identical to that for PRINT USING. See Chapter 8.

Related commands: INPUT#, LINE INPUT#, LPRINT, LPRINT USING, PRINT, PRINT#, PRINT USING, WRITE#

PSET [STEP]*(x,y)*[,*color-ID*]

Sets the pixel specified by coordinates *(x,y)* in the current output window. The range for *(x,y)* depends on the screen mode and window size. Normally, *(x,y)* is an absolute pixel location; if STEP is included, *(x,y)* is a relative offset from the last location of the graphics pen. If *color-ID* is included, the pixel is set using the color from that color register; otherwise, PSET uses the default foreground color. *Color-ID* can range from 0 to 31 depending on the screen mode. See Chapter 2.

Related commands: POINT, PRESET

PTAB(*numeric expression*)

Moves the print position to the horizontal pixel coordinate specified by *numeric expression*. The range for *numeric expression* is 0 to 32767, starting from the left edge of the output window. Allows print positioning by pixel instead of by character, as with TAB.

Related commands: CSRLIN, LOCATE, LPOS, POS, TAB

PUT #*filenumber*[,*recordnumber*]

Moves the record specified by *recordnumber* from the random file buffer into the random disk file named by *filenumber*. The *recordnumber* can range from 1 to 16777215; if omitted, *recordnumber* is set to the next higher number after the last PUT. The *filenumber* can range from 1 to 255 and must have previously been OPENed. See Chapter 8.

Related commands: EOF, FIELD, GET, LOC, LOF, OPEN, PUT (see alternative statement below)

PUT [STEP]*(x,y),array%[(array% index)]...[,putmode]*
Draws a rectangular image of pixels at screen coordinates *(x,y)* using the data found in *array%*, which can be a multidimensional array as specified by *index*. The *(x,y)* coordinates refer to the rectangle's upper left corner, and their range depends on the screen mode and size of the current output window. Normally, *(x,y)* are absolute pixel coordinates; if STEP is included, *(x,y)* refer to a relative offset from the last position of the graphics pen. The *putmode* defines five different ways in which the pixels affect the existing background: PRESET, PSET, AND, OR, and XOR. The default is XOR. See Chapter 3 and the "ShapeIt" utility, Program 3-3, at the end of the chapter.

Related commands: GET, PRESET, PSET, PUT (see alternative statement above)

RANDOMIZE [*integer expression*]
Initializes the random number generator in preparation for returning a new series of random numbers. The *integer expression* can range from −32768 to 32767; if omitted, the program stops and displays a prompt requesting the user to enter an integer in this range. If *integer expression* is replaced with the keyword TIMER, then RANDOMIZE reseeds itself with the current TIMER value. If the random number generator is not initialized with RANDOMIZE, it always returns the same series of random numbers whenever the program is run.

Related commands: RND, TIMER

READ *variable list*
Retrieves numeric and/or string constants from DATA statements and stores them in the numeric and/or string variables in *variable list*. Variable types must agree with the constants. The first READ statement in a program starts with the first DATA statement and proceeds consecutively until otherwise directed with a RESTORE statement.

Related commands: DATA, RESTORE

REM *remark text*
Tells BASIC to ignore anything in *remark text* following REM. (An exception is the DATA statement, which interprets REM as a literal string.) REM allows remarks to be inserted in programs for documentation purposes. REM can be abbreviated with the apostrophe ('). See Chapter 1.

RESTORE [*LineLabel*]
Redirects the next READ statement to the first DATA statement in the program or to the alphanumeric line label or line number specified by *LineLabel*.

Related commands: DATA, READ

RESUME [0]
After an ON ERROR GOTO has been executed, RESUME continues the program at the statement which triggered the error trap. RESUME 0 is synonomous with RESUME. See Chapter 1 and the "ErrorTrap" routine (Program 7-4) in Chapter 7.

Related commands: ERL, ERR, ERROR, ON ERROR GOTO, RESUME *LineLabel*, RESUME NEXT

RESUME *LineLabel*
After an ON ERROR GOTO has been executed, RESUME *LineLabel* branches to the alphanumeric line label or line number specified by *LineLabel*. See Chapter 1 and the "ErrorTrap" routine (Program 7-4) in Chapter 7.

Related commands: ERL, ERR, ERROR, ON ERROR GOTO, RESUME, RESUME NEXT

RESUME NEXT
After an ON ERROR GOTO has been executed, RESUME NEXT continues the program at the statement immediately following the one that triggered the error trap. See Chapter 1 and the "ErrorTrap" routine (Program 7-4) in Chapter 7.

Related commands: ERL, ERR, ERROR, ON ERROR GOTO, RESUME, RESUME *LineLabel*

RETURN [*returnline*]
After a GOSUB has been executed, RETURN branches back to the statement immediately following the GOSUB. If *returnline* is specified, RETURN branches to that alphanumeric line label or line number instead.

Related commands: GOSUB, ON GOSUB

RIGHT$(*string$,numchars*)
Returns the rightmost number of characters specified by *numchars* in *string$*. *Numchars* can range from 0 to 32767. If *numchars* is equal to or greater than the length of *string$*, LEFT$ returns the entire string. If *numchars* equals 0, RIGHT$ returns a null string.

Related commands: INSTR, LEFT$, LEN, MID$, UCASE$

RND[(*numeric expression*)]
Generates a random number between 0 and 1. *Numeric expression* affects the series of random numbers generated. If *numeric expression* is greater than 0 or omitted, RND returns the next random number in the series. If *numeric expression* is 0, RND repeats the last random number. If *numeric expression* is less than 0, RND repeats the entire sequence of random numbers in the current series. RND always returns the same series of random numbers in a program unless a RANDOMIZE statement reseeds the random number generator.

Related commands: RANDOMIZE, TIMER

RSET *string variable=string expression*

Formats the raw data in *string expression* within *string variable* for random file output. In effect, the data is moved into the random file buffer. If *string expression* is shorter than the room allotted to *string variable* by a previous FIELD statement, RSET inserts spaces to right justify the data within *string variable*. Since *string expression* doesn't allow numeric values, they must be converted first with MKI$, MKL$, MKS$, or MKD$. RSET can also right justify *string expression* within *string variable* for other purposes besides random file output. See Chapter 8.

Related commands: FIELD, LSET, MKD$, MKI$, MKL$, MKS$, OPEN, PUT

RUN [*LineLabel*]

Starts execution of the Amiga BASIC program in memory. Normally, execution starts at the first line of the program; *LineLabel* starts execution at the specified alphanumeric line label or line number.

Related command: RUN *filename* (see alternative statement below)

RUN *filename*[,R]

Loads the Amiga BASIC program named by *filename* from disk and immediately starts execution. If the *R* option is appended, any OPENed data files from a previous program remain open.

Related commands: CHAIN, LOAD, MERGE, RUN (see alternative statement above)

SADD(*string expression*)

Returns the memory address of the first character in *string expression*. Because Amiga BASIC dynamically allocates memory for strings, the address returned by SADD is not accurate after another string allocation or manipulation.

Related commands: PEEK, PEEKL, PEEKW, VARPTR

SAVE [*filename*][,A]
SAVE [*filename*][,P]
SAVE [*filename*][,B]

Stores the BASIC program in memory in a disk file named by *filename*. If *filename* is omitted, a requester asks you to enter a filename. Normally, SAVE writes the disk file in a compressed binary format. If *A* is appended, SAVE writes the file in ASCII format. If *P* is appended, SAVE writes the file in a protected format that allows the program to be run but not listed or edited. If *B* is appended, SAVE writes the file in the same compressed binary format that is its default.

Related commands: CHAIN, LOAD, MERGE, RUN

SAY *phoneme-list*[,*mode%*]

Pronounces the phoneme codes in *phoneme-list* using the Amiga's synthesized speech device. For direct English text-to-speech conversion, *phoneme-list* can be returned by the TRANSLATE$ function. *Mode%* is an integer array of at least nine elements that modify various speech parameters. If *mode%* is omitted, the voice uses certain default parameters.

Mode% Element	Parameter	Values
0	Pitch	65–320 Hz (default=110)
1	Inflection	0 or 1; 0=normal inflection (default), 1=monotone
2	Rate	40–400 words per minute (default=150)
3	Gender	0 or 1; 0=male (default), 1=female
4	Tuning	5,000–28,000 Hz (default=22,200)
5	Volume	0–64 (default=64)
6	Channel	0–11. Channels 0 and 3 connect to the left audio output; channels 1 and 2 connect to the right audio output. Values can be 0=channel 0 1=channel 1 2=channel 2 3=channel 3 4=channels 0 and 1 5=channels 0 and 2 6=channels 3 and 1 7=channels 3 and 2 8=either available left channel 9=either available right channel 10=either available left/right pair of channels (default) 11=any available single channel
7	Synch mode	0 or 1; 0=synchronous speech (default), 1=asynchronous speech
8	Asynch mode	0–2; 0=finish first SAY before next SAY (default), 1=cancel next SAY, 2=override first SAY for next SAY

See Chapter 6 and the "Speech Constructor" utility, Program 6-1.

Related command: TRANSLATE$

SCREEN *screen-ID,width,height,depth,mode*

Creates a new custom screen identified by *screen-ID* using the parameters *width, height, depth,* and *mode*. The *screen-ID* can range from 1 to 4. The *width* is expressed in pixels and can range from 1 to 640, though 320 and 640 are the only values commonly used. The *height* is also expressed in pixels and can range from 1 to 400, though 200 and 400 are the only values commonly used. The *depth* specifies the number of bit-planes and therefore the maximum number of simultaneous colors allowed; it can range from 1 to 5:

Depth	Colors	Maximum Color-ID
1	2	1
2	4	3
3	8	7
4	16	15
5	32	31

The *mode* specifies the screen width and number of horizontal scan lines (interlaced mode):

Mode	Width	Interlaced Mode
1	320	200 lines noninterlaced
2	640	200 lines noninterlaced
3	320	400 lines interlaced
4	640	400 lines interlaced

See Chapter 2.

Related commands: SCREEN CLOSE, WINDOW

SCREEN CLOSE *screen-ID*
Closes the custom screen identified by *screen-ID* and frees up its memory. See Chapter 2.

Related commands: SCREEN, WINDOW CLOSE

SCROLL *(x1,y1)–(x2,y2),scroll-x,scroll-y*
Scrolls a rectangular screen area defined by *(x1,y1)–(x2,y2)* within the current output window in the horizontal direction specified by *scroll-x* and/or the vertical direction specified by *scroll-y*. The *scroll-x* and *scroll-y* parameters are expressed in pixels. Positive values scroll to the right or downward, respectively; negative values scroll to the left or upward, respectively. See Chapter 3.

SGN(*numeric expression*)
Indicates whether *numeric expression* is equal to 0, less than 0, or greater than 0. SGN returns a 0 if *numeric expression* equals 0, returns −1 if *numeric expression* is less than 0, and returns 1 if *numeric expression* is greater than 0.

Related commands: ABS, FIX, INT

SHARED *variable-list*
Declares the subprogram variable names in *variable-list* as common variables with the main program. All variable types are allowed in *variable list*; array variable names must be followed by empty parentheses. See Appendix D, "Subprograms."

Related commands: COMMON, DIM SHARED, SUB

SIN(*radians*)
Returns the sine value of the numeric expression *radians*.

Related commands: ATN, CIRCLE, COS, EXP, LOG, SQR, TAN, WAVE

SLEEP
Suspends execution of the program until an event trap is triggered. SLEEP can be used as a do-nothing loop in programs that are completely event-driven. See Chapters 1 and 7.

Related commands: ON BREAK GOSUB, ON COLLISION GOSUB, ON ERROR GOTO, ON MENU GOSUB, ON MOUSE GOSUB, ON TIMER GOSUB

SOUND *frequency,duration*[,*volume*][,*voice*]
Plays a sound at the specified *frequency, duration,* and *volume* using the specified *voice*. The *frequency* is expressed in hertz and can range from 20 to 15,000. The *duration* can range from 0 to 77, where 18.2 equals one second. *Volume* can range from 0 to 255; if omitted, the default is 127. The *voice* parameter specifies whether SOUND uses channel 0, 1, 2, or 3. Channels 0 and 3 are connected to the left audio output, and channels 1 and 2 are connected to the right audio output. The default is channel 0. See Chapter 5.

Related commands: BEEP, SOUND RESUME, SOUND WAIT, WAVE

SOUND WAIT
Holds all subsequent SOUND statements in a queue until the next SOUND RESUME statement. The sounds are not played until SOUND RESUME. See Chapter 5.

Related commands: BEEP, SOUND, SOUND RESUME, WAVE

SOUND RESUME
Plays all the SOUND statements which have accumulated in the sound queue since the last SOUND WAIT. See Chapter 5.

Related commands: BEEP, SOUND, SOUND WAIT, WAVE

SPACE$(*numeric expression*)
Makes a string of blank spaces of the length specified by *numeric expression,* which can range from 0 to 32767.

Related commands: LOCATE, PTAB, SPC, STRING$, TAB

SPC(*numeric expression*)
Inserts the number of spaces specified by *numeric expression* into a PRINT or LPRINT statement. The general form is PRINT SPC(*numeric expression*) *expression-list*. The *numeric expression* can range from 0 to 255.

Related commands: LOCATE, PTAB, SPACE$, STRING$, TAB

SQR(*numeric expression*)

Calculates the square root of *numeric expression*, which must be equal to or greater than zero.

Related commands: ATN, COS, EXP, LOG, SIN

STICK(*n*)

Reads a joystick plugged into either port 1 or port 2. The information returned depends on the value of *n*, which can range from 0 to 3:

STICK(0) Port 1, horizontal direction
STICK(1) Port 1, vertical direction
STICK(2) Port 2, horizontal direction
STICK(3) Port 2, vertical direction

The numbers returned by STICK(*n*) indicate the status of the stick:

STICK(*n*)=1 Stick is deflected downward or to the right
STICK(*n*)=0 Stick is not deflected
STICK(*n*)=−1 Stick is deflected upward or to the left

See Program 4-7, "BattleStation," in Chapter 4.

Related commands: MOUSE, STRIG

STOP

Halts a program without closing any OPENed files, allowing the program to be restarted with CONT.

Related commands: CONT, END, ERROR

STRIG(*n*)

Reads the joystick button from either port 1 or port 2. The information returned depends on the value of *n*, which can range from 0 to 3:

STRIG(0) Returns 1 if joystick button 1 was pressed since the last STRIG(0) call; otherwise returns 0.
STRIG(1) Returns 1 if joystick button 1 is currently pressed; otherwise, returns 0.
STRIG(2) Returns 1 if joystick button 2 was pressed since the last STRIG(0) call; otherwise, returns 0.
STRIG(3) Returns 1 if joystick button 2 is currently pressed; otherwise, returns 0.

See Program 4-7, "BattleStation," in Chapter 4.

Related commands: MOUSE, STICK

STR$(*numeric expression*)

Converts *numeric expression* into a string.

Related commands: ASC, CHR$, MKD$, MKI$, MKL$, MKS$, VAL

STRING$(*string-length,charcode*)
Returns a string of characters corresponding to the ASCII code *charcode* whose length is determined by the numeric expression *string-length*. The *string-length* can range from 0 to 32767; *charcode* must be a valid ASCII character code from 0 to 255. See Appendix E, "The Amiga Character Set."

Related commands: SPACE$, STRING$ (see alternative statement below)

STRING$(*string-length,string-expression*)
Returns a string of characters corresponding to the first character in *string-expression* whose length is determined by the numeric expression *string-length*. The *string-length* can range from 0 to 32767.

Related commands: SPACE$, STRING$ (see alternative statement above)

SUB *subprogram-name*[(*parameter-list*)] STATIC
Defines the start of a subprogram using the label *subprogram-name*, which is a unique title up to 30 characters long. The *parameter-list* is a list of variables, separated by commas, which receive values passed by the main program via the CALL statement. The variable types in *parameter-list* must match the types of values passed by CALL. The variables can be local to the subprogram or global with the main program, as specified by a SHARED statement. *Parameter-list* can be as long as allowed by a BASIC line. See Appendix D, "Subprograms."

Related commands: CALL, DIM SHARED, END SUB, EXIT SUB, SHARED

SWAP *variable1,variable2*
Transfers the value in *variable1* to *variable2* and vice versa. The variables types must match, and the variables must have already been defined.

SYSTEM
Halts the currently running BASIC program (if any), closes all open files, and exits Amiga BASIC to the Workbench or CLI.

Related commands: END, STOP

TAB(*numeric expression*)
Used with a PRINT or LPRINT statement to move the starting print position to the location specified by *numeric expression*. The general form is

PRINT TAB(*numeric expression*) *expression-list*

The *numeric expression* can range from 1 to 155, although the rightmost position is the value of WIDTH$-$1. If the current print position is already past *numeric expression*, TAB moves to the position on the next line.

Related commands: PTAB, SPC

TAN(*radians*)
Returns the tangent of *radians*.

Related commands: ATN, COS, EXP, LOG, SIN, SQR

TIME$
Returns the current time from the system's realtime clock. The eight-character string uses 24-hour time in the format *HH:MM:SS* (hours, minutes, seconds). Similar to the DATE command in AmigaDOS except that TIME$ cannot be used to set a new time.

Related commands: DATE$, TIMER

TIMER
Returns a value which corresponds to the number of seconds past midnight (0–86,400), assuming the system's realtime clock is correctly set. See Chapter 1 and the "Personal Address Book" program at the end of Chapter 8.

Related commands: DATE$, ON TIMER GOSUB, RANDOMIZE, TIME$, TIMER OFF, TIMER ON, TIMER STOP

TIMER OFF
Disables event trapping which has been activated by ON TIMER GOSUB and TIMER ON. Event trapping stops until the next TIMER ON. See Chapter 1.

Related commands: ON TIMER GOSUB, TIMER, TIMER ON, TIMER STOP

TIMER ON
Enables event trapping for TIMER events and allows ON TIMER GOSUB to branch to its specified *LineLabel*. See Chapter 1.

Related commands: ON TIMER GOSUB, TIMER, TIMER OFF, TIMER STOP

TIMER STOP
Suspends event trapping of TIMER events activated by ON TIMER GOSUB and TIMER ON. TIMER STOP doesn't disable event trapping like TIMER OFF; it temporarily prevents ON TIMER GOSUB from branching until the next TIMER ON. See Chapter 1.

Related commands: ON TIMER GOSUB, TIMER, TIMER OFF, TIMER ON

TRANSLATE$(*string expression*)
Converts the English text in *string expression* into phoneme codes which can be pronounced by the SAY statement. Neither *string expression* nor the string of phoneme codes returned by TRANSLATE$ can be longer than 32,767 characters. See Chapter 6.

Related command: SAY

TROFF
Turns off program tracing that was previously enabled with TRON. Can be used in immediate or program mode.

Related command: TRON

TRON
Turns on program tracing. Can be used in immediate or program mode.

Related command: TROFF

UBOUND(*array*[*,dimension*])
Returns the upper limits (bounds) of *array*. The *dimension* parameter lets you measure a multidimensional array.

Related commands: DIM, LBOUND, OPTION BASE

UCASE$(*string expression*)
Returns a copy of *string expression* with all-uppercase letters. See the "Personal Address Book" program at the end of Chapter 8 for an example.

Related commands: INSTR, LEFT$, MID$, RIGHT$, SPACE$, STRING$

VAL(*string expression*)
Converts *string expression* into a numeric value.

Related commands: ASC, CHR$, CVD, CVI, CVL, CVS, STR$

VARPTR(*variable name*)
Returns the memory address of the first byte of *variable name*. The memory address can range from 0 to 16,777,215. Because Amiga BASIC dynamically allocates memory for strings and arrays, the address returned by VARPTR may not be accurate after a new simple variable is assigned.

Related commands: PEEK, PEEKL, PEEKW, SADD

WAVE *voice,wave-array%*
Interprets the data in *wave-array%* as a waveform shape and assigns it to the sound channel specified by *voice*. The *voice* can range from 0 to 3. Channels 0 and 3 are connected to the left audio output, and channels 1 and 2 are connected to the right audio output. The *wave-array%* must be an integer array at least 256 elements long, though only the first 256 elements are significant. Multidimensional arrays are not allowed. *Wave-array%* elements can range from −128 to 127. To restore the default sine waveform, use WAVE *voice*,SIN. See Chapter 5.

Related commands: BEEP, SIN, SOUND

WHILE *expression* [*statements*]:WEND

Executes *statements* as long as *expression* remains a true condition. The *statements* can be one or any number of BASIC statements placed between the WHILE and WEND. If *statements* are omitted, WHILE–WEND acts as a do-nothing loop until *expression* becomes false. WHILE and WEND can be on different lines in the program, and any number of WHILE–WENDs may be nested. When *expression* is no longer true, execution continues at the statement following the associated WEND. See Chapter 1.

Related commands: FOR, NEXT

WIDTH ["*device*",][*numchars*][,*comma-tab*]

Sets the text width of *device* to *numchars* and the tab stops forced by commas in PRINT statements to *comma-tab*. The "*device*" may be "SCRN:", "COM1:", or "LPT1:". If omitted, the default is "SCRN:". The *numchars* parameter specifies the number of characters that will fit on a line using the current text font—the actual number varies when using proportional fonts. Values up to 255 are allowed, but 255 specifies an infinite line width—text never wraps around to the next line. This is the default. The *comma-tab* parameter determines how many spaces a PRINT statement skips if items in its *expression-list* are separated by commas. *Comma-tab* is expressed in spaces using the current text font.

Related commands: LPOS, POS, PRINT, WIDTH (see alternative statement below), WIDTH LPRINT

WIDTH #*filenumber*,[*numchars*][,*comma-tab*]

Sets the text width of the file named by #*filenumber* to *numchars* and the tab stops forced by commas to *comma-tab*. The #*filenumber* is a numeric expression in the range 1–255 which refers to an opened file. *Numchars* can range up to 255 and is expressed as the number of characters which can fit on a line using the file's current text font. The actual number of characters varies when using proportional fonts. *Comma-tab* specifies the number of spaces skipped when items in a PRINT# statement are separated by commas.

Related commands: LPOS, POS, PRINT#, WIDTH (see alternative statement above), WIDTH LPRINT

WIDTH LPRINT [*numchars*][,*comma-tab*]

Sets the text width of the printer to *numchars* and the tab stops forced by commas to *comma-tab*. The printer is the LPT1: device. *Numchars* can range up to 255 and is expressed as the number of characters which can fit on a line using the printer's current text font. The actual number of characters varies when using proportional fonts. *Comma-tab* specifies the number of spaces skipped when items in an LPRINT statement are separated by commas. WIDTH LPRINT *numchars,comma-tab* is the equivalent of WIDTH "LPT1:",*numchars,comma-tab*.

Related commands: LPOS, LPRINT, WIDTH,

WINDOW *window-ID*[*,title*][*,(x1,y1)–(x2,y2)*][*,type*][*,screen-ID*]
Creates an output window, moves it to the front of the screen, and makes it the current output window. The *window-ID* is an identifier that can be 1 or higher; Amiga BASIC already uses WINDOW 1 for its output window, but it can be re-defined by this statement. *Title* is a string expression that displays text on the window's title bar; the maximum length depends on the window's width. The *(x1,y1)–(x2,y2)* parameter is a set of screen coordinates that define the window's size. The range for these coordinates depends on the screen mode on which the window is opened:

Screen Mode	Maximum Window Size
320 × 200	311 × 185
320 × 400	311 × 385
640 × 200	617 × 185
640 × 400	617 × 385

The *type* parameter determines which gadgets the WINDOW has and how it can be manipulated. Add up the following values to get the desired *type*:

Value	Attribute
1	The window has a sizing gadget.
2	The window is movable with the title bar.
4	The window has front and back gadgets.
8	The window has a close gadget.
16	The window's contents are restored after it has been temporarily covered by another window.

The *screen-ID* parameter specifies on which screen the window should appear. The default is −1 for the Workbench screen. For custom screens, *screen-ID* can range from 1 to 4. See Chapters 2 and 7.

Related commands: SCREEN, WINDOW (function), WINDOW CLOSE, WINDOW OUTPUT

WINDOW(*function*)
Returns information about currently opened windows. The *function* parameter can range from 0 to 8 and determines what information is returned:

Function	Information
WINDOW(0)	The *window-ID* of the selected output window.
WINDOW(1)	The *window-ID* of the current output window.
WINDOW(2)	The *width* of the current output window.
WINDOW(3)	The *height* of the current output window.
WINDOW(4)	The horizontal coordinate in the current output window where the next character will be printed.
WINDOW(5)	The vertical coordinate in the current output window where the next character will be printed.
WINDOW(6)	The maximum color number allowed for the screen on which the current output window is placed.

WINDOW(7)   A pointer to the *window structure* for the current output window as maintained by the operating system.

WINDOW(8)   A pointer to the *rastport structure* for the current output window as maintained by the operating system.

See Chapters 2 and 7.

Related commands: SCREEN, WINDOW (statement), WINDOW CLOSE, WINDOW OUTPUT

WINDOW CLOSE *window-ID*

Closes the window named by *window-ID*. If this was the current output window, then the most recent output window that remains open becomes the new current output window. See Chapters 2 and 7.

Related commands: SCREEN, WINDOW (function), WINDOW (statement), WINDOW OUTPUT

WINDOW OUTPUT *window-ID*

Makes the window named by *window-ID* the current output window. All graphics and PRINT statements affect this window. However, the current output window is not necessarily the current *active* window—the one which is at the front of the screen and selected. See Chapters 2 and 7.

Related commands: SCREEN, WINDOW (function), WINDOW (statement), WINDOW CLOSE

WRITE [*expression-list*]

Prints the numeric and/or string expressions in *expression-list* on the screen. If *expression-list* is omitted, WRITE prints a blank line. Items in *expression-list* must be separated by commas. When printed, the text includes the commas, and strings are enclosed by quotation marks. The last item is followed by a carriage return/linefeed. Unlike PRINT, WRITE does not insert a leading space before positive numbers.

Related commands: PRINT, PRINT#, WRITE#

WRITE# *filenumber,expression-list*

Stores the numeric and/or string expressions in *expression-list* in the sequential file identified by *filenumber*. WRITE# is similar to WRITE. Items in *expression-list* must be separated by commas. When stored in the file, the text includes the commas, and strings are enclosed by quotation marks. The last item is followed by a carriage return/linefeed. Unlike PRINT#, WRITE# does not insert a leading space before positive numbers. Since WRITE# inserts its own delimiters in the form of the commas and quotation marks, the data is easier to read from the file. See "Personal Address Book" in Chapter 8 for a discussion of WRITE# versus PRINT#.

Related commands: OPEN, PRINT, PRINT#, WRITE

B ISO Printer Codes

Here is a list of ISO (International Standards Organization) printer control codes recognized by the Amiga's console and printer devices. When these codes are passed by an application program to the console or printer device, the device driver translates them into the escape codes required by the particular printer (or, in the case of the console device, the particular font style required for the screen). These codes make it possible for Amiga application programs to support many different types of printers without printer-specific programming—assuming that the appropriate printer driver has been selected on the Preferences screen. Note that not all printers support all functions, and that only a few of these functions are recognized by the console device. For more information, see Chapter 8, "Programming Peripherals."

Code	Function
CHR$(9)	Moves printhead to next printer tab stop
CHR$(10)	Scrolls paper up one line (linefeed)
CHR$(11)	Negative linefeed; rolls paper back one line
CHR$(12)	Skips to top of next page
CHR$(13)	Moves printhead to column 1
CHR$(14)	Switches to alternate character set, if any
CHR$(15)	Restores normal character set
CHR$(27);"c"	Resets
CHR$(27);"#1"	Initializes
CHR$(27);"D"	Linefeed
CHR$(27);"E"	Carriage return/linefeed
CHR$(27);"M"	Reverse linefeed
CHR$(27);"[0m"	Normal character set
CHR$(27);"[3m"	Italics on
CHR$(27);"[23m"	Italics off
CHR$(27);"[4m"	Underline on
CHR$(27);"[24m"	Underline off
CHR$(27);"[1m"	Boldface on
CHR$(27);"[22m"	Boldface off
CHR$(27);"[0w"	Normal pitch
CHR$(27);"[2w"	Elite on
CHR$(27);"[1w"	Elite off

Code	Function
CHR$(27);"[4w"	Condensed fine on
CHR$(27);"[3w"	Condensed off
CHR$(27);"[6w"	Enlarged on
CHR$(27);"[5w"	Enlarged off
CHR$(27);"[6";CHR$(34);"z"	Shadow print on
CHR$(27);"[5";CHR$(34);"z"	Shadow print off
CHR$(27);"[4";CHR$(34);"z"	Double strike on
CHR$(27);"[3";CHR$(34);"z"	Double strike off
CHR$(27);"[2";CHR$(34);"z"	Near letter quality on
CHR$(27);"[1";CHR$(34);"z"	Near letter quality off
CHR$(27);"[2v"	Superscript on
CHR$(27);"[1v"	Superscript off
CHR$(27);"[4v"	Subscript on
CHR$(27);"[3v"	Subscript off
CHR$(27);"[0v"	Normalize the line
CHR$(27);"L"	Partial line up
CHR$(27);"K"	Partial line down
CHR$(27);"(B"	U.S. character set
CHR$(27);"(R"	French character set
CHR$(27);"(K"	German character set
CHR$(27);"(A"	U.K. character set
CHR$(27);"(E"	Danish I character set
CHR$(27);"(C"	Danish II character set
CHR$(27);"(H"	Swedish character set
CHR$(27);"(Y"	Italian character set
CHR$(27);"(Z"	Spanish character set
CHR$(27);"(J"	Japanese character set
CHR$(27);"(6"	Norwegian character set
CHR$(27);"[2p"	Proportional on
CHR$(27);"[1p"	Proportional off
CHR$(27);"[0p"	Proportional clear
CHR$(27);"[n E"	Set proportional offset
CHR$(27);"[5 F"	Auto left justify
CHR$(27);"[7 F"	Auto right justify
CHR$(27);"[6 F"	Auto full justify
CHR$(27);"[0 F"	Auto justify off
CHR$(27);"[3 F"	Letter space (justify)
CHR$(27);"[1 F"	Word fill (autocentering)
CHR$(27);"[0z"	1/8-inch line spacing
CHR$(27);"[1z"	1/6-inch line spacing
CHR$(27);"[$n$t"	Set form length n
CHR$(27);"[$n$q"	Perforation skip n (n>0)
CHR$(27);"[0q"	Perforation skip off
CHR$(27);"#9"	Set left margin
CHR$(27);"#0"	Set right margin
CHR$(27);"#8"	Set top margin
CHR$(27);"#2"	Set bottom margin

Code	Function
CHR$(27);"[P";top$;";P";bot$;"r"	Top and bottom margins
CHR$(27);"[P";lmar$;";P";rmar$;"s"	Left and right margins
CHR$(27);"#3"	Clear margins
CHR$(27);"H"	Set horizontal tab
CHR$(27);"J"	Set vertical tabs
CHR$(27);"[0g"	Clear horizontal tab
CHR$(27);"[3g"	Clear all horizontal tabs
CHR$(27);"[1g"	Clear vertical tab
CHR$(27);"[4g"	Clear all vertical tabs
CHR$(27);"#4"	Clear all horizontal and vertical tabs
CHR$(27);"#5"	Set default tabs
CHR$(27);"[P";command$;CHR$(34);"x"	Extended commands

C Memory Management

The Amiga can address up to eight megabytes of random access memory, but keeping track of that much memory can be maddening. Fortunately, the operating system takes care of most of this.

However, there are a few things to keep in mind. The most common system crash is caused by an *Out of memory* error, so it's worth your while to conserve memory and allocate it properly.

First, remember that the memory used by screens is not freed up until a SCREEN CLOSE statement. When you're using the system memory allocation routines (demonstrated in Chapter 9), you must be sure to free up memory areas after you no longer need them or when your program ends.

On a 512K RAM Amiga (the most common system configuration when this book was written), Amiga BASIC starts up with 25,000 bytes of memory. Why so little? Since the Amiga is a multitasking computer, no single application—including BASIC—can be allowed to grab all of the memory available in the machine. Otherwise, different applications which may be running in the background would suddenly have the carpet pulled from beneath them, so to speak.

Freeing More Memory

If your BASIC program requires more than 25,000 bytes, Amiga BASIC provides the CLEAR statement for allocating additional memory. For example,

CLEAR *,memsize*

requests *memsize* bytes. This memory is used only for variables and arrays, though. You don't need to declare extra memory to use any of the custom SCREEN modes or to open windows; the system tracks this automatically (just be sure to use SCREEN CLOSE when you're done with a screen). But if you use CLEAR to get extra BASIC memory space, you must also deallocate this memory, or it may never be released to the system.

Before requesting more memory, first ask for the default size of 25000:

CLEAR *,25000*

This has the effect of releasing any bound memory beyond 25000 bytes. You can then ask for more memory—more than 100K if you wish—depending on the amount of free system memory. To find out how much system memory there is, type PRINT FRE(−1). Type PRINT FRE(0) to display the amount of memory free for BASIC.

The CLEAR statement is like a fence that sets the boundary between what belongs to the system and what belongs to BASIC. If you tried to ask for 100,000 bytes without first releasing the previous request, there wouldn't be enough free system memory to give you another 100,000 bytes.

When your program ends, be sure to include a statement such as CLEAR ,25000 to release the extra memory. If you don't do this, subsequent runs of your program quickly use all the memory and crash the system. And even if you don't run the program more than once, the trapped memory may not be released for other applications after you exit BASIC.

Variable Delays

If you write a BASIC program that uses large arrays, a negative side effect is the delays caused by the introduction of new variables. Arrays are stored in memory directly after the last variable encountered. As new variables are declared, they have to be added to the end of the variable list, so the arrays have to be shifted downward in memory to make room. With a large array, or many arrays, this could take awhile. Sooner or later, though, a program has looped through itself often enough to find all the variables, so the delays disappear after every variable has been initialized. You might notice this effect when you run the "MouseSketch" program (Chapter 10).

One way to avoid the delay is to initialize (declare) every variable before dimensioning any arrays. This builds the variable list before the arrays are created. Subsequent references to the variable names reuse the old variables instead of creating new ones, so the arrays aren't shifted in memory.

It may be too much trouble to locate and declare every variable in your program—that takes all the fun out of interactive programming. Also, as in MouseSketch, local variables in subprograms can't be initialized globally before the arrays are defined, so it's not worth the effort to declare all but a few of the most common variables. The initial sluggishness goes away after a few iterations, so it's not overly inconvenient.

Memory Conservation

To make the most memory space available for BASIC, run it from the CLI without loading the Workbench. You can make a CLI boot disk by changing the batch file *startup-sequence* in the *s* subdirectory to delete the *loadwb* and *endcli > nil:* commands.

Another way to free up a few thousand bytes of memory is to unplug any external disk drives connected to the system. Each external drive reserves some memory for its track buffer.

Be aware that memory can quickly evaporate as data is loaded that you're not even aware of. References to devices, such as PRT: or the speech commands load the associated device drivers into memory. You lose memory every time you open a new window, although closing the window frees up the memory. Any other program multitasking in the background may be stealing a lot of memory, even things seemingly as benign as the Clock and Calculator tools.

Inserting a disk uses up memory to hold the disk directory. And an open Workbench window can use a lot of memory to display the icons for a full drawer. It's a good idea to close all unneeded windows to conserve memory as well as to reduce clutter.

Of course, if all else fails, you can always resort to buying more memory. With a megabyte or more, all your memory problems will probably disappear.

D Subprograms

One of the first steps everyone takes on the path toward becoming an advanced programmer is the frequent use of subroutines. GOSUB and RETURN are among the most powerful statements in the BASIC language because they let you build efficient, modular programs with minimal code duplication. The intelligent use of subroutines not only improves performance, conserves memory, and increases readability, but also makes it easier to write future programs. Most programmers gradually build up a collection of commonly used subroutines which they merge into every program they write.

In addition to GOSUB and RETURN, Amiga BASIC has commands that let you create special types of subroutines which bring even more flexibility and power to this style of programming. These special subroutines are known as *subprograms*, and they're very similar to regular subroutines but have several distinct advantages:

- Subprograms are more independent of the main program than subroutines. If a subprogram happens to have variable names which coincide with variables in the main program, Amiga BASIC treats them as completely separate variables. For instance, you can change the value of a subprogram variable named *mousebutton* without affecting the variable *mousebutton* in the main program and vice versa. The subprogram variables are called *local variables*, because their values are local to the subprogram. On the other hand, if you really want a subprogram and main program to share certain variables, you can do that, too. These are called *global variables*. Thanks to local and global variables, you can design subprograms that are as independent of the main program as you wish. If you like to accumulate a library of commonly used subroutines that can be attached to any new program you write, you can take advantage of this feature to make sure your subprograms won't accidentally conflict with the programs they're merged into.
- A main program can pass a number of parameters (values) to a subprogram, and the subprogram can pass values back to the main program. Although you can do this with regular subroutines by setting variables to certain values before a GOSUB, parameter passing is more flexible with subprograms and can be accomplished in a single statement.

- Subprograms can't execute accidentally. Unlike a regular subroutine, which can start executing if the main program inadvertently falls through into the routine, a subprogram executes only when explicitly called. Again, this lets you merge previously written subprograms into a main program without worrying about interference.
- In effect, subprograms let you add your own custom commands to Amiga BASIC. The statement which calls the subprogram can even be made to look like a built-in Amiga BASIC command.

There are a few disadvantages to subprograms, of course. They can't contain error-trapping statements (such as ON ERROR GOTO), user-defined function definitions (DEF FN), or CLEAR and COMMON commands. They can't be nested, and one subprogram can't call another subprogram. And even though subprogram variables are local, *line labels* are not—so you have to watch out for label conflicts with the main program. But these are relatively minor drawbacks that are rarely encountered and detract little from the usefulness of subprograms.

If you've never used a BASIC that supports subprograms, you'll soon wonder how you got along without them.

The SUB Sandwich

Amiga BASIC has six statements dedicated to subprograms: SUB, END SUB, EXIT SUB, CALL, SHARED, and DIM SHARED

The SUB statement defines the beginning of a subprogram, and END SUB defines the end. The subprogram itself consists of any number of BASIC statements sandwiched between SUB and END SUB. The END SUB statement does for a subprogram exactly what RETURN does for a regular subroutine—it returns control back to the main program, continuing execution at the statement following the one which called the subprogram.

The CALL statement, in turn, acts just like GOSUB. CALL tells the main program to branch to the subprogram you specify.

To create a subprogram, then, your first step is to invent a label name for the SUB and CALL statements. This is an alphanumeric label up to 30 characters long, very similar to a standard Amiga BASIC line label. (The only difference is that you can't list the subprogram by typing LIST *sub-label*.) Here's an example of a very simple subprogram:

```
'This is the main program...
CALL HelloPrinter
'Main program continues here...
'
SUB HelloPrinter STATIC
  PRINT "Hello"
END SUB
```

When you run this program, it branches to the subprogram named in the CALL statement. The subprogram prints the message *Hello*, then returns to the main program via the END SUB. The main program continues running at the statement immediately following the CALL. In this simple example, of course, there are no further statements except for the REMark, but you get the idea.

Notice the keyword STATIC in the SUB statement. This means that any variables within the subprogram retain their values between CALLs to that subprogram. In current versions of Amiga BASIC, STATIC isn't an optional part of the SUB statement; it's required.

By the way, this example also demonstrates that subprograms can't execute accidentally. When END SUB branches back to the main program, the main program simply ends. If the subprogram here was replaced by a regular subroutine, the main program would fall through and execute the routine a second time. And the second execution of the subroutine would crash the program with a RETURN without GOSUB error since it wasn't called with a GOSUB.

Local Variables

Now let's see how local variables work. Look at this example:

```
temp=1
PRINT "The main program variable temp equals";temp
CALL YellowSubmarine
PRINT "The main program variable temp still equals";temp
'
SUB YellowSubmarine STATIC
temp=2
PRINT "The subprogram variable temp equals";temp
END SUB
```

When you run this program, you'll see this on the screen:

```
The main program variable temp equals 1
The subprogram variable temp equals 2
The main program variable temp still equals 1
```

Even though both variable names are exactly the same, Amiga BASIC considers them to be completely independent variables. You can manipulate the main program's variable *temp* all you want without the slightest effect on the subprogram's variable *temp*. And, likewise, you can manipulate the subprogram's *temp* without affecting the main program's *temp*. Of course, the same principle holds true for all types of variables: string variables, arrays, and so forth.

There may be times, however, when you *want* the subprogram and main program to share a variable. Perhaps the subprogram is a routine which changes the variable in some way for use in the main program. You can allow for this with the SHARED statement. SHARED declares which variables are global to the main program and subprogram; all other variables used in the subprogram are assumed to be local. Simply insert one or more SHARED statements at the beginning of the subprogram:

```
x=1:y=2:z$="Hello"
PRINT "x equals";x
PRINT "y equals";y
PRINT "z$ equals ";z$
CALL GlobalVillage
PRINT "x now equals";x
PRINT "y now equals";y
PRINT "z$ still equals ";z$
'
SUB GlobalVillage STATIC
SHARED x,y
x=x+10:y=y+10:z$="Goodbye"
END SUB
```

When you run the program, this is the result:

```
x equals 1
y equals 2
z$ equals Hello
x now equals 11
y now equals 12
z$ still equals Hello
```

The SHARED statement here declares that the variables x and y are global variables shared by the main program and this subprogram (but *not* by any other subprogram). When the variables are changed by the subprogram, the changes are reflected in the main program. The main program variable z$, however, remains unaffected by whatever happens to the variable z$ in the subprogram because it wasn't included in the SHARED list.

When you include an array variable in a SHARED statement, you must follow it with empty parentheses to indicate that it's an array variable:

```
SUB GlobalVillage STATIC
SHARED x,y,z$,index( )
```

In addition, there's a special form of the SHARED statement which comes in handy when you want *all* of your subprograms to share certain array variables with the main program. It's called DIM SHARED:

```
DIM SHARED a(20),z$(100)
a(0)=55:z$(0)="Moby"
PRINT "a(0) equals";a(0)
PRINT "z$(0) equals ";z$(0)
CALL MeIshmael
PRINT "a(0) now equals";a(0)
PRINT "z$(0) now equals ";z$(0)
```

```
SUB MeIshmael STATIC
a(0)=86
z$(0)="Ahab"
END SUB
```

When you run this program, the result is

a(0) equals 55
z$(0) equals Moby
a(0) now equals 86
z$(0) now equals Ahab

Notice how the variables $a(\ )$ and $z\$(\ )$ are shared even though the subprogram contains no SHARED statement. If you added any other subprograms to this example, they would automatically share $a(\ )$ and $z\$(\ )$ with the main program, too.

The only problem with DIM SHARED is that it doesn't work with anything but array variables. Ordinary numeric and string variables still must be declared global by a SHARED statement within each subprogram.

Alternative Exits

Just as SHARED has a variation in DIM SHARED, the END SUB statement also comes in a slightly different flavor: EXIT SUB. With EXIT SUB, you can define more than one exit point within a subprogram. Although every subprogram *must* terminate with an END SUB, it may contain several EXIT SUBs.

A good example of EXIT SUB is when you need to branch out of a subprogram at different points depending on a certain condition:

```
SUB TwoExits STATIC
 IF flag=0 THEN
  'Do something here...
 ELSEIF flag=1 THEN
  'Do something else here...
  EXIT SUB 'First exit.
 ELSEIF flag=-1 THEN
  'Do something else here...
 END IF
END SUB 'Second exit.
```

In truth, EXIT SUB isn't all that useful, because you can usually write your subprograms so that execution falls through to the END SUB anyway. In the example above, for instance, the EXIT SUB could be removed with no adverse effects. Furthermore, some programmers believe that to avoid confusion a subroutine or subprogram should have only one exit point. To keep from using EXIT SUB, they jump to a common exit point with GOTO. But, occasionally, a situation comes up when you need to bail out of a subprogram early, and EXIT SUB does the job.

Passing Parameters

Perhaps the most useful feature of subprograms is their ability to accept values passed by the main program and then pass values back again. This is known as *parameter passing*, and it requires only a single statement—a variation of CALL.

To pass parameters to a subprogram, simply enclose them in parentheses after the CALL keyword. The parameters can be constants, variables, arrays, or expressions. Here's an example:

a=1.5:b%=2:c$="Amiga"
CALL ParameterExample (a,b%,c$)

At the other end, the SUB statement must include variables within parentheses to receive the parameters. The variable types in the SUB statement *must match* the types of parameters passed by CALL. *But the variable names themselves don't have to be the same.* For instance, here's an example of a matching SUB for the above CALL:

SUB ParameterExample (x,y%,z$) STATIC

Notice how the variable *names* are different, but their *types* are the same. In other words, the CALL is passing a single-precision numeric variable (Amiga BASIC's default type), an integer variable, and a string variable, in that order. The SUB statement contains matching variable types in the same order: a single-precision variable, an integer variable, and a string variable. If you mixed up this order or left off a type identifier (such as the % or $), the subprogram would crash with a *Type mismatch* error.

When passing numeric constants, keep in mind that Amiga BASIC automatically treats integer constants as integers. If you change the previous example to

CALL ParameterExample (1,b%,c$)
ʼ
SUB ParameterExample (x,y%,z$) STATIC

the result is a *Type mismatch* error, because Amiga BASIC considers the constant 1 to be an integer, and the variable *x* in the SUB statement defaults to single-precision. You'd either have to make *x* an integer variable as in

SUB ParameterExample (x%,y%,z$) STATIC

or force Amiga BASIC to pass the constant as a floating-point number:

CALL ParameterExample (1.0,b%,c$)

The net effect is the same. The subprogram variables in the SUB statement will now contain the values passed to them by the main program variables in the CALL statement. Here's a demonstration:

```
'Define some dummy variables:◄
FOR n=0 TO 3:index%(n)=n:NEXT◄
a=1.5:b%=2:c$="Amiga"◄
'Show initial values:◄
PRINT "The variable a equals";a◄
PRINT "The variable b% equals";b%◄
PRINT "The variable c$ equals ";c$◄
FOR n=0 TO 3◄
 PRINT "The array element index%(";n;") equals";index%(n)◄
NEXT◄
PRINT◄
CALL ParameterExample (a,b%,c$,index%())◄
'◄
SUB ParameterExample (x,y%,z$,array%()) STATIC◄
'Show subprogram values:◄
PRINT "The variable x equals";x◄
PRINT "The variable y% equals";y%◄
PRINT "The variable z$ equals ";z$◄
FOR n=0 TO 3◄
 PRINT "The array element array%(";n;") equals";array%(n)◄
NEXT◄
END SUB◄
```

When you run this program, this is the result:

The variable a equals 1.5
The variable b% equals 2
The variable c$ equals Amiga
The array element index%(0) equals 0
The array element index%(1) equals 1
The array element index%(2) equals 2
The array element index%(3) equals 3

The variable x equals 1.5
The variable y% equals 2
The variable z$ equals Amiga
The array element array%(0) equals 0
The array element array%(1) equals 1
The array element array%(2) equals 2
The array element array%(3) equals 3

As you can see, the main program has passed the values of all the parameters to the subprogram, where they are received by the local variables. (Notice how array variables are passed to a subprogram.)

The advantage of this feature is that if a subprogram needs certain information from the main program to carry out its task, it can receive that information in the form of parameters passed directly by CALL. Although you could do the same thing by using a SHARED statement to declare *a*, *b%*, *c$*, and *index%( )* as global variables, the single CALL is more convenient. And as we'll see in a moment, it lets you simulate the addition of your own custom commands to Amiga BASIC.

Two-Way Passing

Parameter passing isn't a one-way street. The subprogram can pass values back to the main program, too. In fact, this happens automatically unless you deliberately prevent it.

If the local variables which receive the parameters are changed within the subprogram, their counterparts in the CALL statement are changed, too. Look at this variation of the previous example:

```
a=1.5:b%=2:c$="Amiga"◄
PRINT "The variable a equals";a◄
PRINT "The variable b% equals";b%◄
PRINT "The variable c$ equals ";c$◄
CALL ParameterExample (a,b%,c$)◄
PRINT◄
PRINT "The variable a now equals";a◄
PRINT "The variable b% now equals";b%◄
PRINT "The variable c$ now equals ";c$◄
'◄
SUB ParameterExample (x,y%,z$) STATIC◄
x=x*2◄
y%=y%+2◄
z$=z$+" computer."◄
END SUB◄
```

When you run this program, here's the result:

The variable a equals 1.5
The variable b% equals 2
The variable c$ equals Amiga

The variable a now equals 3
The variable b% now equals 4
The variable c$ now equals Amiga computer.

The subprogram has modified its local variables x, $y\%$, and $z\$$, then passed the new values back to the main program using the parameters a, $b\%$, and $c\$$ in the CALL statement.

For a practical application of this powerful feature, look at the subprogram "Requester" at the end of this appendix. (It's also discussed in more detail and listed in Chapter 7.) When added to any Amiga BASIC program, Requester lets you open a requester window with two user-definable prompt lines plus two definable buttons, and gives you the option of highlighting one of the buttons to indicate a preferred selection. All of this is handled by passing parameters to the Requester subprogram via CALL. Then, after the user clicks on either button in the requester window with the mouse, the subprogram passes a parameter back to the main program to indicate which button was clicked. The main program can then respond accordingly. A typical CALL to Requester might look like this:

msg1$ = "Quit program to BASIC?"
msg2$ = "(Current data will be lost.)"
CALL Requester (msg1$,msg2$,"OK","CANCEL",2,answer%)

This tells the Requester subprogram to display two prompt lines inside the requester window—*Quit program to BASIC?* and *(Current data will be lost.)*; then display two buttons labeled OK and CANCEL, highlight the second button (CANCEL), and, finally, receive the result in the variable *answer%*. (Of course, the prompts could be included within the CALL as string constants, or the buttons could be predefined as string variables, and so on; this format just keeps the program line at a manageable length.)

At the other end, Requester's SUB statement looks like this:

SUB Requester (msg1$,msg2$,b1$,b2$,hilite%,answer%) STATIC

If the user clicks on the left button in the requester window (usually the positive-response button), Requester sets *answer%* to a value of 1. If the user clicks on the right button (usually the negative-response button), Requester sets *answer%* to 0. After END SUB branches back to the main program, a simple IF-THEN test of *answer%* reveals which button was clicked. The main program can then respond as required.

This two-way parameter passing happens automatically. But there may be times when you don't want this to happen—you don't want a variable in the CALL statement to be affected when its matching twin in the SUB statement is changed during the course of the subprogram. Solution: Simply enclose one or more CALL parameters you want to preserve inside parentheses:

CALL Requester (msg1$,msg2$,"OK","CANCEL",2,(answer%))

The extra parentheses around *answer%* indicate that whatever value it holds before the CALL will remain there after the CALL—no matter what happens to its corresponding variable in the SUB statement. This turns *answer%* into a one-way parameter; it passes its value to the subprogram, but refuses to take anything back in return.

In this case, of course, it doesn't make sense to protect *answer%*, since Requester uses it to indicate the user's selection. Nevertheless, one-way parameter passing is handy when you want certain variables in a CALL to retain their values.

Adding Commands to BASIC

Considering their abilities to harbor local variables, declare global variables, accept passed parameters, and return parameters back again, subprograms come very close to making Amiga BASIC an *extensible* language. That is, you can think of certain subprograms as more than just fancy subroutines; they are the near equivalent of new high-level BASIC commands. The Requester subprogram, for instance, makes up in part for the missing dialog box commands found in Microsoft BASIC for the Macintosh. The CALL Requester statement, with its list of parameters, even resembles a built-in BASIC command.

If you want to push this resemblance still further, there's an optional format of CALL that makes subprogram references virtually indistinguishable from true BASIC commands. Simply omit the CALL keyword and the parentheses which normally enclose the parameters. Here's what the Requester statement might look like:

Requester "Exit program?","(Attention: Data not saved.)","OK","CANCEL",2,answer%

Amiga BASIC recognizes this as a standard CALL statement. The two prompt lines—*Exit program?* and *(Attention: Data not saved.)*—are passed to the subprogram as usual, as are the other parameters. And the response is returned in the variable *answer%*, just as before. The difference is purely cosmetic, not functional.

To get even fancier, you could capitalize the subprogram name so that it looks like a regular Amiga BASIC keyword:

REQUESTER "Exit program?","(Attention: Data not saved.)","OK","CANCEL",2,answer%

Sometimes, however, this syntax may confuse Amiga BASIC, especially if the subprogram requires no parameters. When Amiga BASIC sees a statement like

REQUESTER: PRINT "Hi, Mom!"

it assumes that REQUESTER: is defining a line label, not CALLing a subprogram. The same thing happens if you put an implied CALL in an IF-THEN or IF-THEN-ELSE statement:

IF a=10 THEN REQUESTER

or

IF a=10 THEN LineLabel ELSE Requester

How is poor BASIC supposed to know that *REQUESTER* or *Requester* is a subprogram, not a line label? Or that *LineLabel* is a line label, not a subprogram? In these cases, you have to include the CALL keyword to keep BASIC happy.

We should also mention that Amiga BASIC isn't the only party which may be confused by transparent CALL statements. There are two points of view regarding this deception. Some programmers think it's fantastic that you can disguise custom-written subprograms as built-in BASIC commands. Others think the practice misleads those who are studying your code and who perhaps aren't familiar enough with Amiga BASIC to figure out what's going on. For maximum clarity, the program listings in this book generally use the standard version of CALL, but as with many other programming techniques, it's really a matter of personal style.

Program D-1. Requester Subprogram

```
SUB Requester (msg1$,msg2$,b1$,b2$,hilite%,answer%) STATIC
' Requester window subprogram
' Prints up to 2 definable prompt lines
' and 2 definable buttons. Can also highlight a button.
' If Preferences is set for 80 columns,
' each prompt line can be up to 39 characters long.
' If Preferences is set for 60 columns,
' each prompt line can be up to 31 characters long.
' If program uses custom screen, must put SCREEN ID
' in global variable scrid before CALL.
' (scrid=1 for custom SCREEN 1, scrid=2 for SCREEN 2, etc.)
' Defaults to Workbench screen (scrid=-1).
' Example of CALL Requester statement:
' msg1$="This is the first prompt line."
' msg2$="This is the second prompt line."
' CALL Requester (msg1$,msg2$,"Button 1","Button 2",1,answer%)
' or alternate syntax:
' Requester msg1$,msg2$,"Button #1","Button #2",1,answer%
' First two arguments are prompt lines for Requester.
' To omit a prompt line, pass null string ("").
' Next two arguments are labels for buttons.
' (Limit 12 characters for each button.)
' Fifth argument allows highlighting of a button.
' 1 = highlight left button, 2 = highlight right button.
' (Any other value highlights neither button.)
' Last argument returns which button pressed:
' answer%=1 for left button (usually positive response),
' answer%=0 for right button (usually negative response).
' Subprogram opens and closes WINDOW 3;
' change to higher number if necessary.
SHARED scrid 'Global variable for SCREEN ID.
IF scrid<1 OR scrid>4 THEN scrid=-1 'Default to Workbench.
WINDOW 3,"Program Request",(0,0)-(311,45),16,scrid
maxwidth=INT(WINDOW(2)/8) 'Truncate prompts if too long...
PRINT LEFT$(msg1$,maxwidth):PRINT LEFT$(msg2$,maxwidth)
b1$=LEFT$(b1$,12):b2$=LEFT$(b2$,12) 'Truncate buttons.
bsize1=(LEN(b1$)+2)*10:bsize2=(LEN(b2$)+2)*10 'Button size.
x1=(312-(bsize1+bsize2))/3  'Calculate button positions...
x2=x1+bsize1:x3=x1+x2:x4=x3+bsize2
'Draw buttons:
LINE (x1,20)-(x2,38),2,b:LINE (x3,20)-(x4,38),2,b
IF hilite%=1 THEN LINE (x1+2,22)-(x2-2,36),3,b
IF hilite%=2 THEN LINE (x3+2,22)-(x4-2,36),3,b
LOCATE 4,1:PRINT PTAB(x1+10);b1$;
PRINT PTAB(x3+10);b2$
Reqloop: 'Loop which acts on mouse clicks...
WHILE MOUSE(0)=0:WEND:m1=MOUSE(1):m2=MOUSE(2)
IF m1>x1 AND m1<x2 AND m2>20 AND m2<38 THEN
  answer%=1 'Left button was selected.
  LINE (x1,20)-(x2,38),1,bf 'Flash left button.
ELSEIF m1>x3 AND m1<x4 AND m2>20 AND m2<38 THEN
```

```
  answer%=0  'Right button was selected.◄
  LINE (x3,20)-(x4,38),1,bf 'Flash right button.◄
  ELSE◄
   GOTO Reqloop 'Neither button selected; repeat loop.◄
  END IF◄
  WHILE MOUSE(0)<>0:WEND:WINDOW CLOSE 3◄
END SUB◄
```

The Amiga Character Set

	Hex	Decimal	Keypress		Hex	Decimal	Keypress
	20	32	space bar	'	2E	46	.
!	21	33	SHIFT-1	/	2F	47	/
"	22	34	SHIFT-'	0	30	48	0
#	23	35	SHIFT-3	1	31	49	1
$	24	36	SHIFT-4	2	32	50	2
%	25	37	SHIFT-5	3	33	51	3
&	26	38	SHIFT-7	4	34	52	4
'	27	39	'	5	35	53	5
(	28	40	SHIFT-9	6	36	54	6
)	29	41	SHIFT-0	7	37	55	7
*	2A	42	SHIFT-8	8	38	56	8
+	2B	43	SHIFT-=	9	39	57	9
,	2C	44	,	:	3A	58	SHIFT-;
-	2D	45	-	;	3B	59	;

	Hex	Decimal	Keypress		Hex	Decimal	Keypress
⟨	3C	60	SHIFT-,	Q	51	81	SHIFT-Q
=	3D	61	=	R	52	82	SHIFT-R
⟩	3E	62	SHIFT-.	S	53	83	SHIFT-S
?	3F	63	SHIFT-/	T	54	84	SHIFT-T
@	40	64	SHIFT-2	U	55	85	SHIFT-U
A	41	65	SHIFT-A	V	56	86	SHIFT-V
B	42	66	SHIFT-B	W	57	87	SHIFT-W
C	43	67	SHIFT-C	X	58	88	SHIFT-X
D	44	68	SHIFT-D	Y	59	89	SHIFT-Y
E	45	69	SHIFT-E	Z	5A	90	SHIFT-Z
F	46	70	SHIFT-F	[	5B	91	[
G	47	71	SHIFT-G	\	5C	92	\
H	48	72	SHIFT-H	]	5D	93	]
I	49	73	SHIFT-I	∧	5E	94	SHIFT-6
J	4A	74	SHIFT-J	–	5F	95	SHIFT-–
K	4B	75	SHIFT-K	'	60	96	'
L	4C	76	SHIFT-L	a	61	97	A
M	4D	77	SHIFT-M	b	62	98	B
N	4E	78	SHIFT-N	c	63	99	C
O	4F	79	SHIFT-O	d	64	100	D
P	50	80	SHIFT-P	e	65	101	E

	Hex	Decimal	Keypress		Hex	Decimal	Keypress
f	66	102	F	{	7B	124	SHIFT-[
g	67	103	G	|	7C	125	SHIFT-\
h	68	104	H	}	7D	126	SHIFT-]
i	69	105	I	~	7E	127	SHIFT-'
j	6A	106	J		A0	160	ALT-space bar
k	6B	107	K	¡	A1	161	ALT-SHIFT-1
l	6C	108	L	¢	A2	162	ALT-SHIFT-'
M	6D	109	M	£	A3	163	ALT-SHIFT-3
n	6E	110	N	¤	A4	164	ALT-SHIFT-4
o	6F	111	O	¥	A5	165	ALT-SHIFT-5
p	70	112	P	¦	A6	166	ALT-SHIFT-7
q	71	113	Q	§	A7	167	ALT-'
r	72	114	R	¨	A8	168	ALT-SHIFT-9
s	73	115	S	©	A9	169	ALT-SHIFT-0
t	74	116	T	ª	AA	170	ALT-SHIFT-8
u	75	117	U	«	AB	171	ALT-SHIFT-=
v	76	118	V	¬	AC	172	ALT-,
w	77	119	W	-	AD	173	ALT--
x	78	120	X	®	AE	174	ALT-.
y	79	121	Y	¯	AF	175	ALT-/
z	7A	123	Z	°	B0	176	ALT-0

	Hex	Decimal	Keypress		Hex	Decimal	Keypress
±	B1	177	ALT-1	Å	C6	198	ALT-SHIFT-F
2	B2	178	ALT-2	Ç	C7	199	ALT-SHIFT-G
3	B3	179	ALT-3	È	C8	200	ALT-SHIFT-H
´	B4	180	ALT-4	É	C9	201	ALT-SHIFT-I
μ	B5	181	ALT-5	Ê	CA	202	ALT-SHIFT-J
¶	B6	182	ALT-6	Ë	CB	203	ALT-SHIFT-K
·	B7	183	ALT-7	Ì	CC	204	ALT-SHIFT-L
¸	B8	184	ALT-8	Í	CD	205	ALT-SHIFT-M
1	B9	185	ALT-9	Î	CE	206	ALT-SHIFT-N
º	BA	186	ALT-SHIFT-;	Ï	CF	207	ALT-SHIFT-O
»	BB	187	ALT-;	Ð	D0	208	ALT-SHIFT-P
¼	BC	188	ALT-SHIFT-,	Ñ	D1	209	ALT-SHIFT-Q
½	BD	189	ALT-=	Ò	D2	210	ALT-SHIFT-R
¾	BE	190	ALT-SHIFT-.	Ó	D3	211	ALT-SHIFT-S
¿	BF	191	ALT-SHIFT-/	Ô	D4	212	ALT-SHIFT-T
À	C0	192	ALT-SHIFT-2	Õ	D5	213	ALT-SHIFT-U
Á	C1	193	ALT-SHIFT-A	Ö	D6	214	ALT-SHIFT-V
Â	C2	194	ALT-SHIFT-B	×	D7	215	ALT-SHIFT-W
Ã	C3	195	ALT-SHIFT-C	Ø	D8	216	ALT-SHIFT-X
Ä	C4	196	ALT-SHIFT-D	Ù	D9	217	ALT-SHIFT-Y
Å	C5	197	ALT-SHIFT-E	Ú	DA	218	ALT-SHIFT-Z

	Hex	Decimal	Keypress		Hex	Decimal	Keypress
Û	DB	219	ALT-[	Ì	EE	238	ALT-N
Ü	DC	220	ALT- \	Ï	EF	239	ALT-O
Ý	DD	221	ALT-]	ð	F0	240	ALT-P
Þ	DE	222	ALT-SHIFT-6	Ñ	F1	241	ALT-Q
ß	DF	223	ALT-SHIFT--	Ò	F2	242	ALT-R
à	E0	224	ALT-'	Ó	F3	243	ALT-S
á	E1	225	ALT-A	Ô	F4	244	ALT-T
â	E2	226	ALT-B	Õ	F5	245	ALT-U
ã	E3	227	ALT-C	ö	F6	246	ALT-V
ä	E4	228	ALT-D		F7	247	ALT-W
å	E5	229	ALT-E	ø	F8	248	ALT-X
æ	E6	230	ALT-F	ù	F9	249	ALT-Y
ç	E7	231	ALT-G	ú	FA	250	ALT-Z
è	E8	232	ALT-H	û	FB	251	ALT-SHIFT-[
é	E9	233	ALT-I	ü	FC	252	ALT-SHIFT- \
ê	EA	234	ALT-J	ý	FD	253	ALT-SHIFT-]
ë	EB	235	ALT-K	þ	FE	254	ALT-SHIFT-'
ì	EC	236	ALT-L	ÿ	FF	255	ALT-- (on numeric keypad)
í	ED	237	ALT-M				

Index

460

To order your copy of *Advanced Amiga BASIC Disk*, call our toll-free US order line: 1-800-346-6767 (in NY 212-887-8525) or send your prepaid order to:

Advanced Amiga BASIC Disk
COMPUTE! Publications
P.O. Box 5038
F.D.R. Station
New York, NY 10150

Send _____ copies of *Advanced Amiga BASIC Disk* at $15.95 per copy.

All orders must be prepaid (check, charge, or money order). NC residents add 4.5% sales tax. NY residents add 8.25% sales tax.

Subtotal $_____

Shipping and Handling: $2.00/disk $_____

Sales tax (if applicable) $_____

Total payment enclosed $_____

☐ Payment enclosed
☐ Charge ☐ Visa ☐ MasterCard ☐ American Express

Acct. No. _____ Exp. Date _____
(Required)

Name _____

Address _____

City _____ State _____ Zip _____

Please allow 4-5 weeks for delivery.

COMPUTE! Books

Ask your retailer for these **COMPUTE! Books** or order directly from **COMPUTE!**.

Call toll free (in US) **1-800-346-6767** (in NY 212-887-8525) or write COMPUTE! Books, P.O. Box 5038, F.D.R. Station, New York, NY 10150.

Quantity	Title	Price*	Total
_____	COMPUTE!'s Beginner's Guide to the Amiga (025-4)	**$16.95**	_____
_____	COMPUTE!'s AmigaDOS Reference Guide (047-5)	**$14.95**	_____
_____	Elementary Amiga BASIC (041-6)	**$14.95**	_____
_____	COMPUTE!'s Amiga Programmer's Guide (028-9)	**$16.95**	_____
_____	COMPUTE!'s Kids and the Amiga (048-3)	**$14.95**	_____
_____	Inside Amiga Graphics (040-8)	**$16.95**	_____
_____	Advanced Amiga BASIC (045-9)	**$16.95**	_____
_____	COMPUTE!'s Amiga Applications (053-X)	**$16.95**	_____

*Add $2.00 per book for shipping and handling.
Outside US add $5.00 air mail or $2.00 surface mail.

NC residents add 4.5% sales tax _____
NY residents add 8.25% sales tax _____
Shipping & handling: $2.00/book _____
Total payment _____

All orders must be prepaid (check, charge, or money order).
All payments must be in US funds.

☐ Payment enclosed.
Charge   ☐ Visa   ☐ MasterCard   ☐ American Express

Acct. No._____ Exp. Date_____

Name_____

Address_____

City_____ State _____ Zip_____

*Allow 4–5 weeks for delivery.
Prices and availability subject to change.
Current catalog available upon request.

If you've enjoyed the articles in this book, you'll find the same style and quality in every monthly issue of **COMPUTE!** Magazine. Use this form to order your subscription to **COMPUTE!**.

For Fastest Service
Call Our **Toll-Free** US Order Line
1-800-247-5470
In IA call 1-800-532-1272

COMPUTE!
P.O. Box 10954
Des Moines, IA 50340

My computer is:
☐ Commodore 64 or 128 ☐ TI-99/4A ☐ IBM PC or PCjr ☐ VIC-20
☐ Apple ☐ Atari ☐ Amiga ☐ Other _____
☐ Don't yet have one...

☐ $24 One Year US Subscription
☐ $45 Two Year US Subscription
☐ $65 Three Year US Subscription
Subscription rates outside the US:
☐ $30 Canada and Foreign Surface Mail
☐ $65 Foreign Air Delivery

Name _____

Address _____

City _____ State _____ Zip _____

Country _____

Payment must be in US funds drawn on a US bank, international money order, or charge card.
☐ Payment Enclosed ☐ Visa
☐ MasterCard   ☐ American Express

Acct. No. _____ Expires ____ / ____
                                      (Required)

Your subscription will begin with the next available issue. Please allow 4–6 weeks for delivery of first issue. Subscription prices subject to change at any time.

COMPUTE! Books

Ask your retailer for these **COMPUTE! Books** or order directly from **COMPUTE!**.

Call toll free (in US) **800-346-6767** (in NY 212-887-8525) or write COMPUTE! Books, P.O. Box 5038, F.D.R. Station, New York, NY 10150

Quantity	Title	Price*	Total
_____	Machine Language for Beginners (11-6)	**$14.95**	_____
_____	The Second Book of Machine Language (53-1)	**$14.95**	_____
_____	COMPUTE!'s Guide to Adventure Games (67-1)	**$12.95**	_____
_____	Computing Together: A Parents & Teachers Guide to Computing with Young Children (51-5)	**$12.95**	_____
_____	COMPUTE!'s Personal Telecomputing (47-7)	**$12.95**	_____
_____	BASIC Programs for Small Computers (38-8)	**$12.95**	_____
_____	Programmer's Reference Guide to the Color Computer (19-1)	**$12.95**	_____
_____	Home Energy Applications (10-8)	**$14.95**	_____
	The Home Computer Wars: An Insider's Account of Commodore and Jack Tramiel		
_____	Hardback (75-2)	**$16.95**	_____
_____	Paperback (78-7)	**$ 9.95**	_____
_____	The Book of BASIC (61-2)	**$12.95**	_____
_____	The Greatest Games: The 93 Best Computer Games of all Time (95-7)	**$ 9.95**	
_____	Investment Management with Your Personal Computer (005)	**$14.95**	_____
_____	40 Great Flight Simulator Adventures (022)	**$ 9.95**	_____
_____	40 More Great Flight Simulator Adventures (043-2)	**$ 9.95**	_____
_____	100 Programs for Business and Professional Use (017-3)	**$24.95**	_____
_____	From BASIC to C (026)	**$16.95**	_____
_____	The Turbo Pascal Handbook (037)	**$14.95**	_____
_____	Electronic Computer Projects (052-1)	**$ 9.95**	_____

* Add $2.00 per book for shipping and handling.
Outside US add $5.00 air mail or $2.00 surface mail.

NC residents add 4.5% sales tax _____
NY residents add 8.25% sales tax _____
Shipping & handling: $2.00/book _____
Total payment _____

All orders must be prepaid (check, charge, or money order).
All payments must be in US funds.
□ Payment enclosed.
Charge   □ Visa   □ MasterCard   □ American Express

Acct. No. _____ Exp. Date _____
                                                                      (Required)
Name _____

Address _____

City _____ State _____ Zip _____

*Allow 4–5 weeks for delivery.
Prices and availability subject to change.
Current catalog available upon request.